CAVALIERS AND PIONEERS

CAVALIERS AND PIONEERS

Abstracts of

Virginia Land Patents and Grants

Edited by

Dennis Ray Hudgins

VOLUME FIVE: 1741-1749

Virginia Genealogical Society

Richmond • 1994

For ordering information contact the

Virginia Genealogical Society
5001 West Broad Street, Suite 115
Richmond, VA 23230

First published serially in the *Magazine of Virginia Genealogy*

This book is printed with soy ink on acid-free paper meeting the requirements of the American National Standard for Permanence of Paper for Printed Library materials.

CONTENTS

INTRODUCTION

This fifth volume of *Cavaliers and Pioneers* abstracts land patents issued by the Virginia Land Office from 1741 through 1749 and recorded in Patent Books 20 through 28. Researchers should carefully read Daphne Gentry's introduction to *Volume IV* of the series because the same laws and regulations applied during the period covered by this volume.

The decade of the 1740s saw the formation of three large frontier Virginia counties within the geographical area encompassed by these patents: Albemarle County, created in 1744 from Goochland County; Augusta County, formed in 1745 from Orange County; and Lunenburg County, formed in 1746 from Brunswick County. The huge land mass contained within the bounds of these new counties graphically demonstrates the extent to which settlement had moved out of the piedmont and beyond the mountains. Not only was the population moving south and west, but the more eastern areas were becoming much more heavily settled — witness the formation of Louisa County in 1742 from Hanover County; and in 1749, of Cumberland County from Goochland County; Southampton County from Isle of Wight County and Chesterfield County from Henrico County.

Expansion also occurred to the northwest, but researchers should remember that the Fairfax Proprietary had its own land office. Northern Neck Land Grants are not included in this volume.

The purchase of unowned land by treasury warrants increased and the number of headright claims continued to decline; therefore, patents during this decade show less direct information about immigration. This loss of information for the researcher is somewhat offset by the rich topographical and geographical detail given. Information about land features, water courses, clues to aboriginal settlements and activities, names of earlier settlers and of adjoining landowners are of great value to the researcher. No less important is the fact that these records enable the researcher to more easily determine the full extent of an individual's holdings of real estate.

It should be remembered that for this decade, as for the entire Colonial period, those documents that were created preliminary to the issuance of land patents are not extant. The warrants and surveys were destroyed annually after the patents were issued. Unless a survey is on record in the county where the land lay (not all counties kept plat books), no plat will be found. Neither were maps created that showed the location of each patent within the county.

Use these records with thoughtful care. While the surface data is obvious, they also contain many historical, geographical and genealogical clues that are not always evident at first glance.

Robert Young Clay

EXPLANATION

Land in the patents was granted at the cost of 10 acres per shilling, or about 50 acres for each head-right transported or imported, or at 2 lbs. of tobacco for every acre. The costs were then rounded off to the nearest 5 shillings; therefore, no pence were charged. For the purpose of this volume, any cost above 20 shillings has been converted to pounds (£); i.e., 20 shillings = £1, 35 shillings = £1.S15.

This volume (Volume V) begins where Volume IV left off. The breakdown of the first three volumes (available from the Library of Virginia) is as follows:

Volume I

PB 1	pp. 1-951	26 Jan 1621/22 to 10 Apr 1644
PB 2	pp. 1-369	24 Feb 1643/44 to 29 Jan 1651/52
PB 3	pp. 1-394	13 Dec 1653 to 6 Oct 1656
PB 4	pp. 1-643	2 Oct 1655 to 3 Oct 1664
PB 5	pp. 1-545 [669]	28 Jan 1662/63 to 7 Sep 1667

Volume II

PB 6	pp. 1-691	22 Oct 1666 to 30 May 1679
PB 7	pp. 1-718	25 Sep 1679 to 25 Apr 1689
PB 8	pp. 1-443	20 Oct 1689 to 21 Apr 1695

Volume III

PB 9	pp. 1-740	25 Oct 1695 to 10 Jun 1706
PB 10	pp. 1-462	12 Dec 1710 to 20 Feb 1719/20
PB 11	pp. 1-346	20 Feb 1719/20 to 8 Jul 1724
PB 12	pp. 1-538	9 Jul 1724 to 7 Jul 1726
PB 13	pp. 1-540	24 Mar 1725/26 to 28 Sep 1730
PB 14	pp. 1-537	28 Sep 1728 to 17 Jan 1732/33

Volume IV and V are currently available from the Virginia Genealogical Society.

Volume IV

PB 15	pp. 1-537	9 Oct 1732 to 19 Jun 1735
PB 16	pp. 1-531	1 Jul 1735 to 10 Jan 1735/36
PB 17	pp. 1-532	10 Jan 1735/36 to 16 Jun 1738
PB 18 (Volume 1 of 2)	pp. 1-566	16 Jun 1738 to 12 Mar 1739/40
PB 19 (Volume 2 of 2)	pp. 567-1140	12 Mar 1739/40 to 12 Oct 1741

Volume V

PB 20 (Volume 1 of 2)	pp. 1-566	15 Oct 1741 to 30 Aug 1743
PB 21 (Volume 2 of 2)	pp. 1-674	30 Jul 1742 to 25 Nov 1743
PB 22 (Volume 1 of 2)	pp. 1-631	1 Mar 1743/44 to 20 Mar 1745/46
PB 23 (Volume 2 of 2)	pp. 567-1147	30 Aug 1743 to 20 Aug 1745
PB 24	pp. 1-631	20 Sep 1745 to 12 Jan 1746/47
PB 25	pp. 1-635	20 Mar 1745/46 to 25 Jun 1747
PB 26	pp. 1-723	25 Jun 1747 to 20 Aug 1748
PB 27	pp. 1-533	1 Dec 1748 to 15 Dec 1749
PB 28	pp. 1-730	12 Jan 1746/47 to 5 Sep 1749 [12 Mar 1749/50]

Volume VI (projected publication is January 1997):

PB 29 pp. 1-532	15 Dec 1749 to 5 Aug 1751
PB 30 pp. 1-531	1 Jun 1750 to 16 Nov 1752
PB 31 pp. 1-750	20 Sep 1751 to 10 Sep 1755
PB 32 pp. 1-716	16 Nov 1752 to 13 Mar 1756
PB 33 pp. 1-1095	8 Jun 1756 to 7 Aug 1761
PB 34 pp. 1-1088	10 Mar 1756 to 24 Feb 1763 (25 Sep 1762)

The final volume, Volume VII, will include:

PB 35 pp. 1-556	25 Sep 1762 to 27 Jun 1764
PB 36 pp. 557-1083	27 Jun 1764 to 12 Aug 1767
PB 37 pp. 1-452	10 Jul 1767 to 20 Sep 1738
PB 38 pp. 453-904	20 Sep 1768 to 12 May 1770
PB 39 pp. 1-454	12 May 1770 to 16 Mar 1771
PB 40 pp. 455-901	16 Mar 1771 to 1 Aug 1772
PB 41 pp. 1-456	1 Aug 1772 to 15 Jun 1773
PB 42 pp. 457-899	15 Jun 1773 to 7 Dec 1774

ABBREVIATIONS

acs. - acres

adj. - adjoining, adjacent, joining, joyning

bef. - before

bet. - between, betwixt

Br., Brs. - Branch, Branches

c. - corner

Chas. City - Charles City [Co.]

ch., chs. - chain, chaines/chains

Cl., Clk. - Clerk

Col. - Collo., Colo., Colonel

Co. - County

Cr. - Creek

Cultiv. - Cultivation

dec'd - deced, deceased

E, Ewd., Ely. - East, Eastward, Easterly

Esq. - Esqr., Esquire

g., gtd. - grant, granted

Genl. - Generll, General

Gent. - Gentleman

Govr. - Governor

Imp. - Importation

Improv. - Improvement

Is. of Wight - Isle/I'le of Wight

K. & Q. - King & Queen [Co.]

King Wm. - King William [Co.]

L. - Land

lb., lbs. - pound, pounds [of tobacco]

Maj. - Majr., Major

Mr - Mister

Mrs - Mistress [not always a married woman]

N, Nwd., Nly. - North, Northward, Northerly

NL - New Land

Norf. - Norfolk [Co.]

OL - Old Land

p. - page

Par. - Parish

pat., ptd. - patent, patented

PB - Patent Book

Pers. - Person, Persons

Pr. Ann or Anne - Princess Ann/Anne

Pr. Geo. - Prince George [Co.]

relinq. - relinquished

Riv. - River

S, Swd., Sly. - South, Southward, Southerly

sd - said, aforesaid

Shill. - Shillings

St. - Saint

Spotsyl. - Spotsylvania [Co.]

Sw. - Swamp

Trans. - Transportation

W, Wwd., Wly. - West, Westward, Westerly

Months are abbreviated: Jan Feb Mar Apr May Jun Jul Aug Sep Oct Nov & Dec.

ff   transcribed as capital *F*.

~   a tilde overscoring any letter is transcribed as a doubled letter, i.e.: Fluvaña = Fluvanna; cro∫ing = crossing

( ) indicates a variant spelling, normally in the PB Index.

/   separates variant spellings within the text.

[ ] brackets surround editor's comments.

?   indicates uncertainty.

--- indicates the absence of a word or letters.

...   replaces extraneous data

PATENT BOOK NO. 20

15 Oct 1741 to 30 Aug 1743

[Volume I of II, PB 23 is Volume II, 30 Aug 1743 to 20 Aug 1745]

JAMES MERIDETH, 400 acs. Hanover Co. on both sides the North fork of Rocky Cr., adj. Joseph Keaton; 15 Oct 1741 *in the 15th Year of our Reign of George the Second, William Gooch Esquire our Lieutenant Governor and Commander in Chief of our Colony and Dominion at Williamsburgh*, p.1. £2.

FOREST GREEN, 284 acs. Hanover Co. on both sides of Foster's Cr., adj. Green & Roger Thomson; 15 Oct 1741, p.2. £1.S10.

THOMAS MASSIE, 68 acs. Goochland Co. among the Brs. of the little Byrd Cr., adj. sd Thomas Massie & Thomas Massie dec'd; 15 Oct 1741, p.3. 10 Shill.

JOHN WRIGHT, 150 acs. Is. of Wight Co. on the N side of Meherin Riv.; by Buckhorn Sw., Farrows Br. & the Windfall Pocoson; 15 Oct 1741, p.5. 15 Shill.

THOMAS SICKS, 42 acs. of Cypress Sw. Land in Norfolk Co., adj. Richard Jolliff; 15 Oct 1741, p.6. 5 Shill.

PATRICK DEMPSIE, 100 acs. Surry Co. on the N side of Nottoway Riv., up Hardwood Run, by the County line [S60°W] & the College line [S40°E], adj. Colonel Cocke; 15 Oct 1741, p.7. 10 Shill.

JOHN MOSS, 400 acs. Goochland Co. among the Brs. of Byrd Cr., adj. Thomas Massie dec'd; 15 Oct 1741, p.9. £2.

1

JOHN WILLIAMSON, 1,165 acs. Goochland Co. on both sides of Meadow Cr. & its brs. on the S side of Rivanna Riv., adj. Thomas Moorman; 15 Oct 1741, p.10. £6.

THOMAS WESTMORELAND, 595 acs. Pr. Geo. Co. crossing Smith's Run & licking Place br.; adj. his own, McKinny, Wall, Brookes, Joseph Wall [the Land he lives on, his 1st Survey], Joseph Westmoreland from Harrison, John High & sd Westmorelands fence; 15 Oct 1741, p.11. £3.

SAMUEL WESTBROOK, 900 acs. Is. of Wight Co. on the N side of Meherin Riv. & down Dunn's br.; adj. his old lines, Thomas Harris & Joshua Cloyd; 15 Oct 1741, p.13. £4.S10.

PHILIP PRYOR, 386 acs. Amelia Co. on the Ridge bet. the Brs. of Great Nottoway & the Brs. of Little Nottoway; adj. Bolling [his Little Survey], Henry Thweat & John Ellis; 15 Oct 1741, p.15. £2.

ROBERT WYNNE, Gentleman, 234 acs. Pr. Geo. Co. on the S side of Stony Cr.; adj. his own line, Capt. Joseph Wynne & Smith; 15 Oct 1741, p.16. £1.S5.

JOHN FITZGERRALD, 630 acs. Amelia Co. on the lower side of the Saylors Cr., Beg. upon the sd Cr. below the Mouth of a Large Br. below the *remarkable good Land*, near a Spring; 15 Oct 1741, p.18. £3.S5. [Included in PB 25 p.171 to John Nash]

ABRAHAM JONES, 103 acs. Pr. Geo. Co. on the upper side of the Great Run, in a Slash; adj. Abraham Jones Jr., Robert Bolling and Evans Alias Ravenscroft's; 15 Oct 1741, p.19. 10 Shill.

WILLIAM BROWN, 400 acs. Amelia Co. on both sides of Morton's Cr. of Bush Riv.; 15 Oct 1741, p.20. £2. [Included in Edward Mackgehee's PB 24 p.594 & PB 26 p.464]

JAMES BANKS, 383 acs. Surry Co. on both sides of Harry's Sw.; adj. James Matthews, Colonel Benjamin Harrison & James Cain; 15 Oct 1741, p.22. £2.

RICHARD SMITH JR. the Younger, 400 acs. Brunswick Co. on S side of Nottoway Riv., over and down the Southerly Br., adj. Reps Jones; 15 Oct 1741, p.23. £2.

WILLIAM CRUTCHFIELD, 596 acs. Caroline Co. in St. Margaret's Par., nigh the Head of a br. of Herring Cr., along the Old lines of Bray & Ingles; 15 Oct 1741, p.25. £3. The same being Surplus Land found within the Bounds of a pat. gtd. David Gray & Mungo Ingles

23 Oct 1703 [David Bray & Mongo Ingles in PB 9 p.564].

THOMAS WOOD, 400 acs. Goochland Co. on both sides of Green Cr. of Appamattox Riv., adj. John Pleasants; 15 Oct 1741, p.26. £2.

FRANCIS WOODHOUSE, 149 acs. Pr. Anne Co. along a Cypress Run in the sd Swamp, adj. to his own Land, near David Scanlen; 15 Oct 1741, p.27. 15 Shill.

JOHN GRAME, Gentleman, 400 acs. in that part of Orange Co. called Augusta, on the W side of the blue ridge of Mountains, Including the fork at the Mouth of Cow Pasture Cr., crossing the Main br. of James Riv. and up the Riv., at the lower end of an Island near the Gap in the North Mountain; 15 Oct 1741, p.29. £2.

FRANCIS HEWLET, 50 acs. of Swamp Land in Norfolk Co. near the head of the New Mill Cr. adj. sd Hewlet's former Survey, at sd Howlet's Line; 15 Oct 1741, p.30. 5 Shill.

JOHN MOSS, 400 acs. Goochland Co. among the Brs. of the Byrd Cr., in Lowgrounds near the E side of a Run, adj. Abraham Venable; 15 Oct 1741, p.31. £2.

THOMAS GIBSON, 400 acs. Henrico Co. on the S side of the North br. of Turkey Br., on the County line [N50°E]; adj. Baugh, Hudson, & Robert Ashurst; 15 Oct 1741, p.33. £2.

WILLIAM PARSONS, 8½ acs. One Island of Marsh Land in Pr. Anne Co.; adj. to New Town, Beg. at the Southernmost side of a Cove near to Nashe's Landing, binding upon the Lots of William Moseley and the sd William Parsons and Major Sayer, to the Southernmost Point of the sd New Town, upon the Eastern Br., upon Colonel Moseley's Cr.; 15 Oct 1741, p.34. 5 Shill.

ROGER QUARLES, 400 acs. Hanover Co. on both sides of Pretty's Cr. beyond the little Mountains, at the heads of 2 bottoms; adj. Haynes, Hickman & Watts; 15 Oct 1741, p.35. £2.

JOHN RAY, 400 acs. Brunswick Co. on the head of Coldwater Run. adj. Adam Sims; 15 Oct 1741, p.37. £2.

JOSEPH WATSON, 400 acs. Henrico Co. on the N side of James Riv., adj. Richard Woodson; 15 Oct 1741, p.38. £2.

JOSEPH WATSON, 400 acs. Henrico Co. on the N side of

James Riv.; 15 Oct 1741, p.40. £2.

JOHN WORSHAM JUNR., 345 acs. Amelia Co. on both sides of Bearbone br. of West's Cr.; adj. William Worsham, Lawrence Brown, Robert Taylor & Feild Jefferson; 15 Oct 1741, p.41. £1.S15.

JOHN INGRUM, 180 acs. Brunswick Co. on the N side of Shining Cr.; adj. his own old line, William Lucas & John Stith; 15 Oct 1741, p.42. £1.

STEPHEN EVANS, 234 acs. Pr. Geo. Co. on the S side of Stony Cr. & on the S side of Morter Br. below the Mill Path; 15 Oct 1741, p.44. £1.S5.

JOHN WINFIELD, 200 acs. Pr. Geo Co. on both sides of the Reedy Br. of Sappone, down the Pocosan Br.; adj. Munford, Lawrence Buckner & his own line; 15 Oct 1741, p.45. £1.

JAMES ROBERTSON, 1,883 acs. Hanover Co. on the Northanna Riv. & Hickory Cr.; adj. Meriwether, Burrus & Davis; 15 Oct 1741, p.46. £7.S10. 400 acs. part formerly gtd. sd James Robertson by Pat. 11 Apr 1732 [PB 14 p.391] and the Residue never before gtd.

TIMOTHY EZELL JUNR., 145 acs. Surry Co. on the N side of Nottoway Riv.; adj. John Weaver, Thomas Atkisson, the Land lately belonging to Colonel Francis Lightfoot Dec'd, & William Bridges; 15 Oct 1741, p.48. 15 Shill.

ROBERT FARRINGTON, 240 acs. Surry Co. on the N side of Nottoway Riv., on the S side of Southwester Sw.; 15 Oct 1741, p.50. £1.S5.

JOHN ALLEN, Gentleman, 350 acs. Is. of Wight Co. on the S side of Nottoway Riv., on the S side of Arthur's Sw., down the Long br., adj. Arthur Whitehead; 11 Dec 1741, p.51. £1.S15.

JOHN JACKSON, 4,440 acs. Pr. Geo. & Amelia Counties on both sides of the Burchen Sw., Beg. at his Old corner in the Co. line on the N side of the open Beaverpond of sd Sw., on the upper side of the Rambling br., down a fork of the Rocky br. and the Main br., along the Co. line [North], by a fork of Batts's Br. of Tommahitton, down the little Burchen and the Main Burchen Sw., up the Buckhorn Br., in the line of his upper Harricane Survey, in the fork & down the Main Harricane Sw.; adj. Joseph Poythress, William Cryer & Thomas Snipe; 15 Oct 1741, p.52. £13.S10. 1,740 acs. part formerly

Gtd. sd John Jackson by Pat. 5 Jun 1736 [PB 17 p.109] & the residue never before Gtd.

FRANCIS LEADBETER, 400 acs. Pr. Geo. Co. on the S side of Brewer's Br., down the on Hog Pen Br.; adj. Hugh Kirkland, Michael Hill, James Pittillo & Francis Haddon; 15 Oct 1741, p.54. £2.

GEORGE WAINRIGHT, 399 acs. Pr. Geo. Co. on the lower side of Tommaheton Sw., by Wolf Pit Br., in a Meadow on the upper side of the Road, on Beaverpond Br.; adj. his old Land purchased of John Yorke, & Thomas Poythress his back line; 15 Oct 1741, p.56. £2. [Included in his 1,000 acs. in PB 27 p.423]

LAWRENCE HOUSE, 350 acs. Brunswick Co. on the S side of Nottoway Riv. & both sides of the Otterdam Sw., over the run of a Br. a little below a Main Road, adj. his own old line & William Whittington; 15 Oct 1741, p.57. £1.S15.

ROBERT MONGERS, 125 acs. Is. of Wight Co. on the N side of Maherin Riv.; 15 Oct 1741, p.59. 15 Shill.

WILLIAM ECHOLS, 152 acs. Brunswick Co. on the N side of Staunton Riv. above the Mouth of a large Cr., beg at the upper end of a small Island; 15 Oct 1741, p.60. 15 Shill.

GEORGE RIVES, 350 acs. Pr. Geo. Co. on the lower side of the Cherry Orchard Br. of Jones Hole Sw., along. the Co. line [E30°N]; adj. his old Lines & Bland; 15 Oct 1741, p.61. £1.S15.

JAMES OWEN, 325 acs. Goochland Co. on both sides of Wildbore Br. of Treasurers Run, near Hanover Co. line; adj. Charles Christian, Stephen Lacy, John Parish & George Hilton; 15 Oct 1741, p.63. £1.S15.

JOSEPH TURNER, 104 acs. Pr. Geo. Co. Adj. his Father, Capt. Joseph Wynne & Capt. Richard Jones; 15 Oct 1741, p.65. 10 Shill.

JOHN WRIGHT, 225 acs. Is. of Wight Co. on the N side of Meherin Riv., up the Wolfpit br. & down Morris's Meadow; adj. Michael Sanders, James Turner & sd Wright's other lines; 15 Oct 1741, p.66. £1.S5.

JOHN BROWDER, 325 acs. Pr. Geo. Co. on the Brs. of Gravilly Run, Beg. on the Flat br. at "A"; adj. James Butler, Munford, Sanders, the sd Browder's Old line, and Joseph & James Crooke; 15 Oct 1741, p.67. £1.S15.

WILLIAM TURNER, 328 acs. Pr. Geo. Co. on the S side of Stony Cr. & both sides of Morter Br., by the great Pond; adj. John Goodwynn, Capt. Richard Jones & William Turner; 15 Oct 1741, p.69. £1.S15.

ARTHUR HOPKINS, 440 acs. Goochland Co. among the Brs. of the Byrd Cr., in a Valley; adj. Ebenezar Adams dec'd & John Cole dec'd; 15 Oct 1741, p.70. £2.S5.

RICHARD ECKHOLES, 1,600 acs. Amelia Co. on the N side of Great Nottoway Riv., Beg. on the Riv. just below the fork, crossing the North fork, adj. Hudson & James Oliver; 15 Oct 1741, p.72. £8. [800 acs. part included in Anthony Griffin's 2,000 acs. in PB 26 p.397]

WILLIAM MOORE, 350 acs. Pr. Geo. Co. on the S side of the Indian Sw., along the Co. line [W30°S] & up Warraocea Br.; 15 Oct 1741, p.73.

EPES MOORE, 350 acs. Pr. Geo. Co. on the S side of Indian Sw. & on Beasley's Br., Adj. his Father William Moore; 15 Oct 1741, p.74. £1.S15.

RICHARD LESTER, 36 acs. of Swamp Land in Pr. Anne Co. Adj. upon a former Survey of the sd Lester & adj. John Lester & Robert Mason's former Survey; 15 Oct 1741, p.76. 5 Shill.

RICHARD TAYLOR, 470 acs. Is. of Wight Co. on the N side of Meherin Riv., by Cock's Sw. & Deep run, adj. his own old line & Robert Rivers; 15 Oct 1741, p.77. £2.S10.

THOMAS BUTTS, HENRY BUTTS & SOLOMON BUTTS, 196 acs. of Swamp Land in Norfolk Co., adj. their own high Land near the great Bridge & adj. Valentine; 15 Oct 1741, p.79. £1.

RICHARD LESTER, 60 acs. Pr. Anne Co. upon the North Riv. near to Oakham's Land, Beg. at a Chincopine Stake against a fork of the sd Riv., near the Percoson, upon a small Cr.; 15 Oct 1741, p.80. 10 Shill.

WILLIAM RIVES, 300 acs. Pr. Geo. Co. on the Upper side of Cherry Orchard Br. of Jones Hole, down Cuthbert Williamson's Branch; adj. his Brother George Rives, Michael Hill & Cuthbert Williamson; 15 Oct 1741, p.82. £1.S10.

JOHN FINLEY, 300 acs. in that part of Orange Co. called Augusta on a Draft of Cathey's Riv. including Plumb tree Bottom, adj.

Alexander Brakenrig; 15 Oct 1741, p.83. £1.S10.

JAMES ALBRATON, HENRY BRINSON, EDWARD ATTWOOD, RICHARD SIMMONS, MOSES ROBERTS & THOMAS AXTEAD, 178 acs. of Swamp & Marsh Land in Pr. Anne Co. by the fresh Pond which makes out of Brinson's Inlet near the Sea Board, upon Kindall's Island, to a small Cr. which makes out of the sd Pond, adj. William Brinson & Robert Man; 15 Oct 1741, p.85. £1.

ELIZABETH ANDERSON, 414 acs. Amelia Co. on both sides of the Beaverpond Br. of Deep Cr., to Andersons Road, down the Dumplin Br.; adj. John Adams, Seth Perkinson, Thomas Bott, Thomas Reames, William Neale & Robert Man; 15 Oct 1741, p.86. £2.S5.

WILLIAM HILL, 721 acs. Brunswick Co. on Brs. of Mitchel's Cr., up the South fork & down the North fork of sd Cr., over and up the long Meadow Br.; 30 Jan 1741/42, p.88. £3.S15.

Colo. WILLIAM MAYO, Gentleman, 200 acs. Goochland Co. adj. to the N side of Fluvanna Riv., against the upper end of Buffalo Island; 30 Jan 1741/42, p.89. £1. [Included in Joseph Mayo's PB 24 p.48]

Colo. WILLIAM MAYO, Gentleman, 300 acs. Goochland Co. adj. to the N side of Fluvanna Riv., against the upper end of Slaughter Island; 30 Jan 1741/42, p.91. £1.S10. [Included in Joseph Mayo's PB 24 p.48]

Colo. WILLIAM MAYO, Gentleman, 290 acs. Goochland Co. on both sides of Soke Arse Run of Willis Riv.; adj. Abraham Bayley, James Daniel & Norvel Burton & sd William Mayo; 30 Jan 1741/42, p.92. £1.S10.

Colo. WILLIAM MAYO, Gentleman, 350 acs. Goochland Co. on both sides of Fluvanna Riv. above Buffalo Island, crossing Stone Wall Cr.; 30 Feb 1741/42, p.94. £1.S15. [Included in Joseph Mayo's PB 24 p.48]

Colo. WILLIAM MAYO, Gent., 350 acs. Goochland Co. on both sides of Fluvanna Riv. including Slaughter Island, crossing Porridge Cr.; 30 Jan 1741/42, p.96. £1.S15. [Included in Joseph Mayo's PB 24 p.48]

HENRY DOULING, 236 acs. Orange Co. on the S side of the South fork of Shanadore Riv. below the mouth of a large Spring; 30 Jan 1741/42, p.96. £1.S5.

WILLIAM DYER, 400 acs. Hanover Co. on the Brs. of Pritty's Cr.; adj. Roger Quarles, John Major & John Dowell; 30 Jan 1741/42, p.98. £2.

LEMUEL LANIER, 200 acs. Surry Co. on the N side of Nottoway Riv. & N side of Cabbin br.; adj. Charles Hay, sd Lanier's Old line, the Land lately belonging to Philip Ludwell Esq. Dec'd, the Nottoway Indians Land & Joel Barker; 30 Jan 1741/42, p.100. £1.

ROBERT GAINES, 400 acs. Spotsyl. Co. among the brs. of Mattapony Riv., on the E side a Glade; on a point, a Level & barren Ground; adj. William Burrus, Mr John Anderson, William Howerton & Charles Oaks/Oakes on a Level; 30 Jan 1741/42, p.101. £2.

JAMES COCKE, Gentleman, 246 acs. Henrico Co. on the Main Run of Chickahominy Sw., through the Islands and Lowgrounds; adj. the Land Purchased by sd Cocke of William & James Watkins, and Edward Curd; 30 Jan 1741/42, p.103. £1.S5.

JAMES TULLEY, 400 acs. Goochland Co. on both sides of Totier Cr., at the North fork of sd Cr., adj. John Lewis; 30 Jan 1741/42, p.105. £2.

JOHN PRICE, 400 acs. Henrico Co. on the N side of James Riv., up the N side of Jordan's Br., adj. John Williamson & Colo. William Byrd; 30 Jan 1741/42, p.106, p.107 & p.108#1. £2.

Colo. GEORGE NEWTON Gent., 1 acre & 131 Square Poles of Low Sunken Land in Norfolk Co. adj. to Norfolk Burrough, Beg. at a Stone on the Westernmost side of the Smith's Shop of the sd Newton, to a Stone near the Publick Land belonging to the sd Burrough, binding upon the sd Riv. upon Reife of Land, bounding on the Lotts of sd Newton, upon a small Point, to a small Wharf near to the Dwelling House of the sd Newton, to a Stone upon the aforesaid Reife of Land at the Easternmost end of the S72°E Line; 30 Jan 1741/42, p.108#1 & p.109#1. 5 Shill.

RICHARD TAYLOR JUNR., 400 acs. Goochland Co. on both sides of the North br. of Slate Riv.; 30 Jan 1741/42, p.109#1, p.108#2 & p.109#2. £2. [Included in his PB 25 p.516]

GEORGE ANDERSON, 330 acs. in that part of Orange County called Augusta on both sides of the South br. of Shanando, Beg. near a Great rock on the S side of sd Riv.; 30 Jan 1741/42, p.109#2 & p.110. £1.S15.

JAMES CHURCHILL, 125 acs. Goochland Co. on a South Run of Deep Cr.; adj. Richard Hubbard, John Ellet, Luke Wile & William Moss; 30 Jan 1741/42, p.111. 15 Shill.

WILLIAM COLLIER, 390 acs. Brunswick Co. on the brs. of Miles Cr., by a Spring, adj. his own lines; 30 Jan 1741/42, p.112. £2.

JOHN ANTHONY, 200 acs. Goochland Co. on both sides of Bisket Run, at a br. of Hardware Riv., by the side of a Mountain, adj. Hugh Dohorty; 30 Jan 1741/42, p.114. £1.

NICHOLAS LANIER, 278 acs. Brunswick Co. on the N side of Shining Cr. & on both sides of the Great Br., adj. Edmunds & Stith; 30 Jan 1741/42, p.115. £1.S10. [Nicholas "the Red Head" Lanier conveyed this 278 acs. to his son Clement Lanier & to his son-in-law Samuel Hudgins, my progenitor. The Great Br. runs into the S side of the Great Cr. of the Meherrin Riv. in NW Brunswick].

JOHN TWITTY, 1,350 acs. Brunswick Co. on both sides Twitty's Cr., on Reess's Br., adj. Talbott & Magehee; 30 Jan 1741/42, p.117. £6.S15.

EDWARD CLANTON, 250 acs. Brunswick Co. on Rattlesnake Cr.; 30 Jan 1741/42, p.119.

WILLIAM ELLIS, 54 acs. Henrico Co. on the N side of James Riv.; adj. John Shoemaker, Richard Randolph & Edward Revis; 30 Jan 1741/42, p.121. 5 Shill.

ABRAHAM ECHOLS, 30 acs. Brunswick Co. on S side of Staunton Riv.; 30 Jan 1741/42, p.122. 5 Shill.

GEORGE HOMES, 400 acs. Goochland Co. on both sides of Slate Riv. & Troublesome Cr.; 30 Jan 1741/42, p.124. £2.

GEORGE TAYLOR, 170 acs. Orange Co. by the SouthWest Mountain Road; adj. Thomas Smith, John Taliaferro, Robert Taliaferro's Orphans & a Pat. of Robert Bickers; 30 Jan 1741/42, p.125. For the Imp. of 4 pers.: *Jeremiah Dare, George Stuart, George Bird & Richard Kemp.*

PLEASANT COCKE, 238 acs. Henrico Co. on the Main Run of Chickahominy Sw., on the Edge of the Lowground, in Reedy Br. parting sd Cocke and Daniel Price; 30 Jan 1741/42, p.127. £1.S5.

RICHARD PARSONS, 80 acs. Goochland Co. on the brs. of the North br. of Muddy Cr. alias Little

Muddy Cr.; adj. Major Bowler Cocke, James Terril & Robert Yancey; 30 Jan 1741/42, p.129. 10 Shill.

JOHN WORLEY, JUNIOR, 250 acs. Goochland Co. on the brs. of Skin Quarter Cr., on Henrico Co. line [N51°E], adj. Thomas Locket; 30 Jan 1741/42, p.130. £1.S5.

ARCHIBALD WOOD, 400 acs. Goochland Co. on the Brs. of Rockfish Riv. adj. Colonel Chiswell; 30 Jan 1741/42, p.132. £2.

Majr: ROBERT WYNNE, Gentleman, 80 acs. Surry Co. on the S side of Nottoway Riv., up a small Slash or br., in a Pond; adj. Matthew Sturdivant, sd Robert Wynne's other Land & Thomas Dinkins; 30 Jan 1741/42, p.134. for 2 lbs. of Tobacco for every Acre. Whereas by Inquisition Indented taken in sd Co. 23 October 1729 by Virtue of a Warrant directed to Henry Harrison Esq. our Escheator for the sd Co. It appears that Joseph Fowler died Seised of 80 acs. of Land which is found to Escheat to us from the sd Joseph Fowler [part of PB 9 p.394 to Robert Hawthorn] And Whereas Robert Wynne Gentleman hath made Humble suit and hath obtained a G. for the same.

JOHN TAYLOR DUKE, 273 acs. Brunswick Co. on both sides of the Old Field Br. on the N side of the Old County line, adj. Sisum & Peter Simmons; 30 Jan 1741/42, p.135. £1.S10. [This sd Old Co. line, N12°E, divided Brunswick from Surry until 1733, and is now near the Brunswick-Greensville Co. line.]

THOMAS PARSONS, 1,375 acs. Surry Co. on the N side of the main Black Water Sw., Beg. at the Mouth of the Great Br. on the SW side of Johnsehawcon Sw., over the Run of the Schoolhouse Br.; adj. Richard Wiggins, Benjamin Rix [Reekes], John Justice, William Cooper, Thomas Washington, Edward Scarborough, Richard Proctor & sd Parson's own old Lines; 30 Jan 1741/42, p.137. £7. Whereas by Pat. 5 Jun 1736 There was gtd. John Parsons now dec'd 1,373 acs. in sd Co. [PB 17 p.111, also see PB 31 p.158] And Whereas the sd John Parsons dec'd and John Parsons his Heir at Law have failed to make Cultiv. and Improv. and Thomas Parsons hath made humble Suit and obtained a G. for the same.

LEMUEL WILES, 112 acs. of Cypress Swamp Land in Norfolk Co. near the Great Bridge; 30 Jan 1741/42, p.140. 15 Shill.

JOHN MARTIN, 403 acs. Brunswick Co. on both sides Wards fork; 30 Jan 1741/42, p.141. £2.

LEMUEL EVEREDGE & WILLIAM EVEREDGE, 84½ acs. of Cypress Swamp Land in Norfolk Co. which makes out from the Great Bridge, adj. Thomas Butts late Survey & sd Everedge's High Land.; 30 Jan 1741/42. p.143. 10 Shill.

DAVID WALKER, Gentleman, 400 acs. Brunswick Co. on the S side of Roanoak Riv., Beg. at his own corner on Grassy Cr.; 30 Jan 1741/42, p.145. 15 Shill. 250 acs. part formerly gtd. sd David Walker 20 Jul 1736 [PB 17 p.121], the Residue never before gtd.

HENRY MARTIN, 400 acs. Goochland Co. on both sides Joshua's Cr. & Slate Riv.; 30 Jan 1741/42, p.146. £2.

JOHN LEWIS, 400 acs. Goochland Co. on the brs. of Totier Cr., adj. William Harris & Major Bolling; 30 Jan 1741/42, p.148. £2.

JOHN LEWIS, 400 acs. Goochland Co. on both sides of Totier Cr., at the Middle fork & the South Br.; 30 Jan 1741/42, p.149. £2.

JOHN DAVIS, 190 acs. Goochland Co. on the N side of Roanoak Riv., Beg. on a point of Rocks; 30 Jan 1741/42, p.151. £2.

MARSHALL SEAT, 70 acs. Surry Co. on the N side of the Cypress Sw., Beg. on the W side of the white Marsh just above the Mouth of Madcaps Br., adj. Capt. Daniel Eelbank & Edward Bailey; 15 Mar 1741/42, p.152. 10 Shill.

JOHN RUFFIN, Gentleman, 190 acs. Is. of Wight Co. on the N side of Meherrin Riv., up and crossing of Halls Br.; adj. Colo. Richard Bland, Edward Lundy, John Johnson, Joseph Tharp & William Wammock; 15 Mar 1741/42, p.154. £2.

JOHN BISHOP, 261 acs. Brunswick Co. on the S side of Halls Br., adj. Robert Clark; 15 Mar 1741/42, p.156. £1.S10.

THOMAS PITTMAN, 375 acs. Is. of Wight Co. on the N side of Meherin, on the S side of Tarraroe Cr., down the Cypress Br.; 15 Mar 1741/42, p.158. £2.

WINTWORTH WEBB, 400 acs. Goochland Co. on both sides of Ned's Cr. a Br. of the Fluvanna Riv., adj. John Goodwin; 15 Mar 1741/42, p.159.

JOHN WOOD, 232 acs. Goochland Co. on the Brs. of Rockfish Riv., adj. Archibald Wood & Colo.

Chiswell; 15 Mar 1741/42, p.161. £1.S5.

WILLIAM WHITESIDES, 400 acs. Goochland Co. on both sides of the South fork Mechums Riv.; 15 Mar 1741/42, p.162. £2.

JOHN STEPHENS, 450 acs. Surry Co. on the S side of Nottoway Riv. & S side of Hunting Quarter Sw.; adj. John King, sd Stephen's other Land & Nicholas Calliham; 15 Mar 1741/42, p.164. £2.S5.

ALLEN HOWARD, Gentleman, 2,053 acs. Goochland Co. on both sides of Nevells's Cr. & on the S side the Fluvanna Riv., running into the Woods; 15 Mar 1741/42, p.165. £6.S5. 800 acs. part formerly gtd. James Holeman in 2 Separate Parcels by Patents 21 Oct 1728 [PB 13 p.330 to James Holman on Nevil's Cr.] & by him Sold & Convey'd to the sd Howard, 120 acs. other part being surplus Land found within the Bounds of sd Patents & the Residue never before Gtd.

PETER HUDSON, 189 acs. Henrico Co. crossing Nut Tree Cr. just below Bowman's Fork, over Sharp Rockey Hills; adj. Leprad, his old Lines, Henry Clay & John Bowman; 15 Mar 1741/42, p.168. £2.

DAVID IRVIN, 100 acs. Brunswick Co. on the S side of Otter Riv. opposite to the Buffelow Lick; 15 Mar 1741/42, p.169. 10 Shill. (Included in his 550 acs. Bedford Co. in PB 34 p.224, 12 May 1759]

HOWELL BRIGGS, Gentleman, 1,380 acs. Surry Co. on the S side Nottoway Riv. & both sides of Thweat's Br.; adj. Richard Woodroofe, Thomas Eldridge & John Hatly; 15 Mar 1741/42, p.171. £7.

ROBERT DAVIS, 196 acs. Amelia Co. on the upper side of the Sweathouse fork of Deep Cr. bet. the Lines of Thomas Booth & William Coleman; 15 Mar 1741/42, p.173. £2.

JOHN JOYNER, 100 acs. Is. of Wight Co. on the N side of Meherin Riv., on the E side of a Swash, near the Nottoway Road, down Jacob's Br., adj. Thomas Williams Junior & his Own Old line; 15 Mar 1741/42, p.174. 10 Shill.

ROBERT HYNDS, 400 acs. Brunswick Co. on the N side of the Stewke Br., by a Pond, adj. Peoples & John Steed; 15 Mar 1741/42, p.176. £2. [Stewke/Stuke Br. may relate to Stuckanocks Indians. Other Sioux references in now Greensville Co.

are Keaway Sw., Occanechy Sw., Sapone old field, Sapone old fort & Toteroe Fort]

HENRY LEE, 100 acs. Surry Co. on the N side of Nottoway Riv., adj. William Bridges, Colo. Benjamin Harrison, John Doby, the sd Henry Lee & Henry Meecham; 15 Mar 1741/42, p.178. 10 Shill.

NICHOLAS CALLAHAM, 250 acs. Brunswick Co. on the N side of Kettle Stick Br.; 15 Mar 1741/42. p.179. £1.S5.

JONATHAN CARTER, 150 acs. Brunswick Co. on the S side of Maherin Riv., on the E side of the Great Sw.; 15 Mar 1741/42, p.181. 15 Shill.

FRANCIS LETT, 380 acs. Brunswick Co. on the S side of Crab Louse Br., adj. John Cock; 15 Mar 1741/42, p.182. £2.

Colo: JOHN ROBINSON, JUNIOR of K. & Q. Co. Gentleman, 5,059 acs. in St. Geo. Par. Spotsyl. Co., on both sides of the North fork of the River Po and on the S side of the South fork of Po; Beg. by some great Stones on a round Hill in Colo. Corbin's line of his 7,100 Tract; on the N side a Meadow - Colo. Corbin's last Survey; adj. the Land called by the Name of *the Alexandria*; adj. Hugh Jones - Mr. Jones on the E side the new markt

Ridge Road; 15 Mar 1741/42, p.184. £25.S10. Whereas by Pat. 2 Dec 1728 Gtd. John Robinson Junior of K. & Q. Co. Gentleman containing 5,059 acs. [PB 13. p.275 dated 2 Sep 1728, a regrant of sd Robinson's Lapsed Land in PB 11 p.198 dated 20 Jun 1723] And Whereas the sd John Robinson hath failed to make Cultiv. and Improv. and *Benjamin Needler* hath made Humble Suit and hath Obtained a G. for the same which he hath Relinquished unto the sd John Robinson.

CHARLES LYNCH, 590 acs. Goochland Co. on the Brs. of the North fork of Hardware Riv., on the side of a Mountain; 15 Mar 1741/42, p.186. £3.

CHARLES MAYBURY, 340 acs. Surry Co. on the S side of Nottoway Riv. & the S side of Raccoon Sw., down the Spring Sw..; adj. Charles Webb & John Battle; 15 Mar 1741/42, p.188. £1.S15.

JACOB MICHEAUX, 120 acs. Goochland Co. on the S side of James Riv. below Solomon's Cr.; adj. George Cox dec'd, Daniel Johnson, John Bolling Gent. & Frederick Cox; 15 Mar 1741/42, p.189. 15 Shill.

CHARLES LYNCH, 400 acs. Goochland Co. on the Brs. of

Stockton's Br. of Mechums Riv., 15 Mar 1741/42, p.191. £2.

JOHN BOWMAN, 255 acs. Henrico Co. crossing Nut Tree Cr. just below the Fork, crossing a Br. of Nut tree at *high round Rounds* known by the Name of *Dumplings*; adj. Andrew Leprade, Peter Hudson, the sd Bowman, Tanner, George Turner & Francis Flournoy; 15 Mar 1741/42, p.193. £1.S10.

DAVIS STOCKTON, 400 acs. Goochland Co. on both sides of Stockton's Br. of Mechum's Riv., adj. Richard Stockton; 15 Mar 1741/42, p.194. £2.

CHARLES LYNCH, 400 acs. Goochland Co. on the Brs. of Stockton's Br. of Mechums Riv., at the Main of Stocktons Run, in stoney Lowgrounds, at the South Fork of Stockton's Br., adj. Lynch; 15 Mar 1741/42, p.196.

WILLIAM PARTIN, 220 acs. Surry Co. on the S side of Nottoway Riv. & S side of Anderson's Br., by the side of a Main Road; 15 Mar 1741/42, p.197. £1.S5.

JAMES BENNITT, 190 acs. Is. of Wight Co. on the S side of Nottaway Riv., on the W side of the South fork of Ridley's Br., adj.

William Turner; 15 Mar 1741/42, p.199. £2.

MARTIN DAWSON, 180 acs. Is. of Wight Co., N side of Meherin Riv., by the side of the round Gut upon the Edge of the Lowgrounds of sd Riv., down the Quarter Br., adj. Thomas Williams Junior; 15 Mar 1741/42, p.200. £2.

WILLIAM CAMP, 185 acs. Is. of Wight Co. on the N side of the Main black Water Sw., by the side of the third Sw.; adj. sd William Camp, Samuel Croft & Colonel Lewis Burwell; 15 Mar 1741/42, p.202. for 2 lbs. of Tobacco for every Acre. Whereas by Inquisition Indented taken in sd Co. 30 Jan 1739/40 by Virtue of a Warrant directed to John Allen Gent. our Escheator for sd Co. It appears that Parnel Atkinson formerly of sd Co. died seised of 185 acs. which is found to Escheat to us from sd Parnel Atkinson And Whereas Mary Atkinson hath made Humble Suit and Obtained a G. for the same which she hath relinquished unto William Camp.

WINTWORTH WEBB, 400 acs. Goochland Co. on both sides of Bear Garden Cr. adj. John Goodwin; 15 Mar 1741/42, p.203. £2.

WILLIAM STURDIVANTE, 327 acs. Pr. Geo. Co. on the S side of

Stoney Cr.; Adj. George Floyd, James Keeth, Thomas Nunnally & Theophilus Feild; 15 Mar 1741/42, p.205. £1.S15. Whereas by Pat. 23 Mar 1733/34 gtd. John Sturdivant [Sturdevant, PB 15 p.175] And Whereas the sd John Sturdivant hath failed to make Cultiv. and Improv. and William Poythress hath made Humble Suit and Obtained a G. for the same Which he hath relinquished unto William Sturdivant.

Capt. JOHN RUFFIN Gentleman, 430 acs. Is. of Wight Co. on the N side of Meherin Riv. on the SW side of the Flatt Sw.; adj. John Scott, Amos Garrass, Henry Harrison, Thomas Smith, Harry Floyd & John Brantly; 15 Mar 1741/42, p.207. £2.S5.

JOHN HALY, 377 acs. Brunswick Co. on the S side of Staunton Riv. on the upper side of Difficult Cr., on the Ridge, adj. Batt: Roberts; 15 Mar 1741/42, p.209. £2.

ROBERT SEAT, 270 ac. Surry Co. on the S side of Nottoway Riv. on the N side of Cock's Br.; 15 Mar 1741/42, p.211. £1.S10. [Included in his PB 25 p.191]

JOHN BROCKWELL, 291 acs. Pr. Geo. Co. on both sides of Picture Br. adj. Mixon, Mayes & Thomas Moore; 15 Mar 1741/42, p.212. £1.S10.

JOHN FARRISH, 400 acs. Goochland Co. on both sides of the North Br. of Slate Riv.; 15 Mar 1741/42, p.213. £2.

CORNELIUS CARGILL, 400 acs. Brunswick Co. on the S side of Staunton Riv. and on both sides of Willey's Cr. & Grassy Cr., Beg. on the Riv. at Cargill's Horse Ford; 15 Mar 1741/42, p.215. £2.

THOMAS APPLEBERRY, 400 acs. Goochland Co. on both sides of Round about Cr. on the N side of the Rivanna, adj. John Marten; 15 Mar 1741/42, p.216. £2.

RICHARD AVERY, 75 acs. Surry Co. on both sides of Nottaway Riv. adj. his own old Lines; 15 Mar 1741/42, p.218. 10 Shill. [Included in his 790 acs. in PB 26 p.266]

HENRY SAWRY, 400 acs. Surry Co. on the S side of the main Black Water Sw. & on both sides of the Tuscarudoe Br.; adj. his own Old lines & Francis Sharp; 15 Mar 1741/42, p.219. £2.

HUGH BOSTON, 550 acs. Brunswick Co. on both sides of Ash Camp Cr., adj. Talbott; 15 Mar 1741/42, p.221. £2.S15.

Majr. PETER BOWDOIN, Gentleman, 50 acs. One Island called Luke's Island in Northampton Co., Beg. at the

South end of a Sand hill near a Salt Water bush at a Stake; 15 Mar 1741/42, p.223. 5 Shill.

JOHN CLANTON, 130 acs. Surry Co. on the S side of Nottoway Riv., adj. Colonel Benjamin Harrison; 15 Mar 1741/42, p.224. 15 Shill.

ALLEN WARREN, JUNIOR, 100 acs. Is. of Wight Co. on the S side the main Blackwater Sw., on the S side of the Lightwood Sw.; adj. Robert Booth & sd Warren's own Old lines; 15 Mar 1741/42, p.226. 10 Shill.

WILLIAM TOWNS, 400 acs. Amelia Co. on both sides of little Saylors Cr.; 15 Mar 1741/42, p.227. £2.

JOHN FARRISH, 400 acs. Goochland Co. on both sides of the North Br. of Slate Riv.; 15 Mar 1741/42, p.229. £2.

WILLIAM HARLOW, 400 acs. Henrico Co. on the Main Run of Chickahomony Sw., Beg. in his line; 15 Mar 1741/42, p.230. £2.

HINSHEAH GUILLUM JUNR., 100 acs. Surry Co. on the S side of the Main black Water Sw., Beg. on the E side of the little Old Town Sw., adj. William Glover & sd Gillium's own old Lines; 15 Mar 1741/42, p.232. 10 Shill. [One

has to wonder if the Surveyor could still see remnants of a Wyanoke Indian Old Town on the sd Sw.]

WINTWORTH WEBB, 345 acs. Goochland Co. on Bear Garden Cr. Beg. in the Lowgrounds of sd Cr.; 15 Mar 1741/42, p.233. £1.S15.

Capt. JOHN RUFFIN, Gent., 95 acs. Is. of Wight Co. on the N side of Meherin Riv., adj. Thomas Smith; 15 Mar 1741/42, p.235. 10 Shill.

JOHN SEAWRIGHT, 400 acs. in that part of Orange County called Augusta on a br. of the North Riv. of Shanando called naked Cr., on a ridge; 26 Apr 1742, p.236. £2.

JOHN SEAWRIGHT, 400 acs. in Orange Co. in that part of sd Co. designed to be called Augusta on a Br. of the North Riv. of Shanando called naked Cr., adj. William King; 26 Apr 1741 [1742], p.238. £2.

WILLIAM BYRD, Esquire, 105,000 acs. Brunswick Co. on both sides Dan Riv. and on both sides of several Brs. of the same Namely Banister Riv., Medway Riv. & Hicomony Riv., at a Great Br. of Sugar Tree Cr., along the County line [West - the Country line] to a white Oak Marked "WB", Beg. at 3 White Hiccory's on the S side of the sd Dan Riv. about a

Quarter of a Mile below the Mouth of the Riv. Hicomony Riv. marked "WB"; 16 Apr 1742, p.239. £525.

REBECCA BUNCH, 400 acs. Goochland Co. on both sides of Ivy Cr. a Br. of the Rivanna, near the North br. of sd Cr., on the County Line [S65°E], in a Swamp, adj. John Williamson & Robert Lewis Gentleman; 15 Mar 1741/42, p.241. £2.

HUGH WILLIAMS, 214 acs. Brunswick Co. on the S side of Nottoway Riv., adj. John Davis; 15 Mar 1741/42, p.243. £1.S5. [This is a duplicate survey of PB 13 p.456 to Thomas House]

JOHN RACHEL, 200 acs. Brunswick Co. on the N side of Bear's Ellement Cr., adj. Mason Bishop; 15 Mar 1741/42, p.244. £1. [Included in Richard Cocke's 503 acs. in PB 28 p.83 dated 25 Jun 1747]

JONATHAN HORSEFORD, 214 acs. Brunswick Co. on the N side of Stanton Riv.; 15 Mar 1741/42, p.245. £1.S5.

JAMES GOSS, 400 acs. Goochland Co. on the Brs. of Randolph's Cr. above Willis's Riv. alias Willis's Cr., adj. Dudley Digges Gent. & Anthony Benning; 15 Mar 1741/42, p.247. £2.

JOHN SMITH, 101 acs. Brunswick Co. on the N side of Fountain's Cr., adj. James Sexton at the Mouth of sd John Smith's Spring Br.; 15 Mar 1741/42, p.248. 10 Shill.

JOHN STEVENS, 260 acs. Brunswick Co. on the little Cr. above the Fort Christiana, adj. Colo. Ravenscroft near the Great Cr. above the Fort; 15 Mar 1741/42, p.250. £1.S10.

JOHN DUNN, 263 acs. Brunswick Co. on the N side of Uriah's br., in a Meadow, adj. Harrison; 20 May 1742, p.251. £1.S10.

GEORGE ROBERTS, 150 acs. Brunswick Co. on the S side of Staunton Riv.; 20 May 1742, p.253. 15 Shill.

JOSEPH WILKINSON, 400 acs. Henrico Co., crossing Sappony Cr.; adj. Philip Worsham, Eppes, Tillotson & sd Wilkinson; 20 May 1742, p.254. £2.

JEREMIAH BULLOCK, 335 acs. Surry Co. on the S side of Nottoway Riv. adj. George Izell [Ezell]; 20 May 1742, p.256. £1.S15.

MICHAEL ROSSER, 170 acs. Pr. Geo. Co. on the N side of Warwick Sw., adj. Edwards, near John

Rosser's Frame; 20 May 1742, p.257. £1.

THOMAS LAWRENCE, 335 acs. Brunswick Co. on the S side of Nottoway Riv. & the E side of Hix's Br., adj. Charles Stewart; 20 May 1742, p.259. £1.S15.

THOMAS BATES, 204 acs. Henrico Co. crossing the Great Br.; adj. John Childers, Abraham Childers, Randolph, & William Gorden; 20 May 1742, p.260. £1.

JAMES DANIEL, 2,032 acs. Brunswick Co. on the Ridge bet. the Heads of the Brs. of Buffeloe Cr. & Elk Cr.; 20 May 1742, p.262. £10.S5.

ROBERT BULLOCK, 285 acs. Surry Co. on the S side of Nottoway Riv. & the N side of Poplar Sw., in a Small Br., by the side of the North fork of the Miery Br., down the sd Br. & the Poplar Sw., adj. Robert Wallace; 20 May 1742, p.263. £1.S10.

SAMUEL STOKES, 250 acs. Surry Co. on the S side of Nottoway Riv. & the N side of Raccoon Sw., adj. his Own Old lines; 20 May 1742, p.265. £1.S5.

THOMAS PENNENTON, 290 acs. Surry Co. on the S side of Nottoway Riv., on the outermost Prong & the innermose Prong of

the double br., up a small br. & down the long br., adj. Captain William Hamlin & sd Pennenton's own Old line; 20 May 1742, p.267. £1.S10. [Included in his (Thomas Pennington's) 730 acs. in PB 28 p.92]

AMOS TIMS, 322 acs. Brunswick Co. on both sides of the Gum Bridge Br., along the Road; adj. Fields, Ravenscroft & Tims's own line; 20 May 1742, p.269. £1.S15.

JOHN THWEAT, 330 acs. Is. of Wight Co. on the N side of Meherrin Riv.; adj. his own Old lines, Joshua Perry, Harman Road's [Read/Reed] & Robert Lundy; 20 May 1742 *in the 15th year of our Reign of George the Second*, p.271. £1. 135 acs. part formerly gtd. sd John Thweat by Pat. 19 Nov 1720 [PB 11 p.49 where the Saponie Indians dwelt] and the Residue never before Gtd.

FRANCIS THORNTON JUNR. & HANCOCK LEE, 400 acs. Orange Co. crossing Garth's run, on a Stoney Ridge, in the Hollow of a Mountain, adj. John Bush; 15 Jun 1742 *in the 16th year of our Reign of George the Second*, p.272. £2. Whereas by Pat. 17 Mar 1736/37 gtd. John Tennent [PB 17 p.235] and Whereas the sd John Tennent hath failed to make Cultiv. and Improv. and Francis Thornton Junr. & Hancock Lee have made

Humble Suit and Obtained a G. for the same.

FRANCIS THORNTON JUNR. and HANCOCK LEE, 1,000 acs. Orange Co. on the S side of the Mountain on the head of the South br. of North Riv., over 2 of the brs. of Cattle Run, adj. George Procter & Edward Price; 15 Jun 1742, p.274. £5. Whereas by Pat. 13 May 1735 gtd. Robert Martin [PB 15 p.486, a regrant of John Mulkey's PB 14 p.106, both then Ptd. as Spotsyl. Co.] and Whereas Robert Martin & John Tennent to whom the sd Robert Martin afterward Sold & Conveyed the sd Land have failed to make Cultiv. & Improv. and Henry Willis Gentleman Dec'd in his life time did make Humble Suit and obtained a G. for the same Land which John Grymes and Francis Willis Dec'd To whom the sd Henry Willis did devise his Land to be Sold for the payment of Debts have relinquished unto Francis Thornton of Spotsyl. Co. and Hancock Lee of King. Geo. Co. Gentlemen.

JOSEPH LEEMAN, 229½ acs. & 20 Perches in Essex Co. by Occupacy Cr., thro' a small Percorson; adj. John Williams & John Cook, William Spicer; 15 Jun 1742, p.276. 10 Shill. 149½ acs. part formerly gtd. John Williams by Pat. 10 Oct 1672 [Rappahannock Co., PB 6 p.436]

and 80 acs. and 20 Perches the Residue being Surplus Land found within bounds of the sd Pat.

WILLIAM RUGLIS, 120 acs. Is. of Wight Co. on the S side of Nottoway Riv. & on the S side of Tarraroe Cr.; adj. by John Lawhon & John Blackburn; 20 May 1742, p.278. 15 Shill.

WILLIAM BROOKS, 190 acs. Is. of Wight Co. on the S side of Nottoway Riv., by the side of a Main Road, adj. William Killygrew & Samuel Lewcy [Samuel Lucy]; 20 May 1742, p.280. £1.

ROBERT SANDYFORD, 440 acs. Surry Co. on the S side of Nottoway Riv., by the side of Coroncesan Pond; adj. Jeremiah Ellis, William Jones, Majr. Benjamin Harrison, William Martin, William Bridges Junr., William Freeman & Colo. Richard Bland; 20 May 1742, p.282. £2.S5.

WILLIAM STONE of Richmond Co., 303 acs. Amelia Co. on the N side of Nottoway Riv., along the Co. line [South]; 20 May 1742, p.284. £1.S10.

HOWELL BRIGGS, Gent., 480 acs. Surry Co. on the S side of the Main black Water Sw., crossing Harrison's br., by his own Old lines; 20 May 1742, p.285. £2.S10.

DAVID JONES, 350 acs. Surry Co. on the S side the Main black Water Sw., by a Slash & a small br., in a Meadowy br.; adj. Thomas Taylor Junr., William Cook, William Cook Junr. & sd David Jones's own Old line; 20 May 1742, p.287. £1.S15.

JONES STOKES, 375 acs. Surry Co. on the S side of Nottoway Riv., adj. Robert Owen & Silvanus Stokes; 20 May 1742, p.289. £2.

JOHN JACKSON JUNR., 200 acs. Brunswick Co. on both sides of the Watry Br.; adj. William Smith, James Cooke & Lanier; 20 May 1742, p.291. £1.

WILLIAM CLIFTON, 200 acs. Surry Co. on the S side of Nottoway Riv., Beg. in the Frying Pan Br.; adj. Henry Sturdivant, William Bridges, Robert Tucker & Mr Howell Briggs; 20 May 1742, p.292. £1.

JOHN BARROW, 200 acs. Is. of Wight Co. on the S side of the three Creeks, by the side of the Angellica Sw., down the run of the flaggey br., adj. Thomas Barrow & William Blake; 20 May 1742, p.294. £1.

THOMAS JACKSON, 400 acs. Brunswick Co. on the S side of the Watry br.; adj. Lanier, Tomlinson,

Chamberlain, Smith, & John Jackson; 20 May 1742, p.296. £2.

THEOPHILUS FIELD of Pr. Geo. Co., Gentleman, 998 acs. Brunswick Co. on the first great Cr. above Christiana Fort, on Genito Cr., adj. Ray, & John Hix; 20 May 1742, p.298. 336 acs. part formerly gtd. Cornelius Cargill by Pat. 28 Sep 1728 [PB 14 p.65] & 662 acs. the Residue likewise gtd. sd Cornelius Cargill by Pat. 25 Aug 1731 [PB 14 p307] & since Conveyed to sd Field by the sd Cargill.

WILLIAM WILKINS, 200 acs. Is. of Wight Co. on the N side of Meherin Riv. & on both sides of the Pine Pole Br., adj. Edward Avery & Thomas Wilkins; 20 May 1742, p.300. £1.

THOMAS PHELPS, 384 acs. Brunswick Co. on the Ridge bet. the Brs. of Buffeloe Cr. & Elk Cr.; 20 May 1742, p.302. £2.

THOMAS OLIVER, 175 acs. Surry Co. on the S side of Nottoway Riv., on the Island Sw. adj. George Pasmore; 20 May 1742, p.303. £1.

THOMAS DUNN, 350 acs. Surry Co. on the S side of Nottoway Riv., on the W side of Guillum's Br.; adj. Richard Felt's, Richard Clanton, John Guillum & sd

Dunn's Own Old lines; 20 May 1742, p.306. £1.S15.

JOHN NANNY, 280 acs. in the Counties of Isle of Wight & Surry on the S side of the three Creeks, in a Meadow & in Hall's br.; adj. Epraim Parham, John Reed, Joseph Tharp, Samuel Alsobrook & William Wammock; 20 May 1742, p.307. £1.S10.

WILLIAM LAND, 200 acs. Surry Co. on the S side of Nottoway Riv., on the W side of Guillum's br.; adj. Thomas Dunn, Richard Felts's, Colo. Benjamin Harrison & Ralph Magee; 20 May 1742, p.309. £1.

WILLIAM SELLARS, 235 acs. Is. of Wight Co. on the S side of Nottoway Riv.; adj. Doctor Samuel Brown, Oliver Woodard & John Braswell; 20 May 1742, p.311. £1.S5.

MAJOR TILLER, 200 acs. Surry Co. on the N side of Meherin Riv., on the S side of the three Creeks & down the great br.; adj. Joseph Tharp, John Nanny, John Reed, Robert Hicks & James Wyche; 20 May 1742, p.312. £1.

WILLIAM ATKIESON, 300 acs. Surry Co. on the S side of Nottoway Riv., on both sides of Spring Sw. & down the Sowerwood br., adj. John Stokes; 20 May

1742, p.314. £1.S10. [Included in Edward Powell's PB 25 p.388]

JAMES CHAPPELL, Gentleman, 270 acs. Surry Co. on the N side of the Atsamoosock Sw. & on the E side of Harrison's br.; adj. Nicholas Jerrett, sd Chappell's own Old lines, William Sawry & Mr Howell Briggs; 20 May 1742, p.316. £1.S10.

BURWELL MACLEMORE, 190 acs. Surry Co. on the S side of Nottoway Riv., by the Poplar Sw. & down the Crooked Pole br., adj. Majr. Samuel Harwood; 20 May 1742, p.318. £1.

JOHN BREWER, 50 acs. Is. of Wight Co. on the S side of the three Creeks, adj. Robert Jones & William Seward; 20 May 1742, p.320. 5 Shill.

THOMAS ATKINSON, 295 acs. Surry Co. on the S side of Nottoway Riv. & down the Spring Sw., adj. his Own Old lines; 20 May 1742, p.321. £1.S10.

NATHANIEL HOOD, 200 acs. Surry Co. on the S side of Nottoway Riv. & in the fork of Hunting Quarter Sw., up the North Prong & down the South Prong of sd Sw., adj. Richard Reeves; 20 May 1742, p.323. £1.

JAMES JOYNER 50 acs. Is. of Wight Co. on the S side of Maherin Riv., adj. Ellis Braddy & Robert Hodge's; 20 May 1742. p.324. 5 Shill.

WILLIAM WOODLAND, 350 acs. Surry Co. on the S side of Nottoway Riv. & up the long Br. of the Poplar Sw; 20 May 1742, p.326. £1.S15.

WILLIAM SMITH, 440 acs. Brunswick Co. on both sides of the Reedy Cr.; adj. Battersby, Gunn & Overbey; 20 May 1742, p.328. £2.S5.

THOMAS JACKSON, 353 acs. Brunswick Co. on the N side of Little Cr. [of the three Creeks]; adj. Raney, his own lines, Hunt & Page; 20 May 1742, p.329. £1.S15.

JOHN WEAVER the son of Henry Weaver, 250 acs. Surry Co. on the S side of Nottoway Riv. & on the S side of Hunting Quarter Sw., at the Mouth of a Small br. above the Mouth of the Myery Br., adj. John Stephens; 20 May 1742, p.331. £1.S5.

SAMUEL BRIGGS, 180 acs. Surry Co. on both sides of Coppohonk Sw., on the S side of the main black water Sw. & down the Reedy Br., adj. Priscilla Thomas; 20 May 1742, p.332. £1.

RICHARD KNIGHT, 200 acs. Surry Co. on the S side of Nottoway Riv. & the E side of the Cypress br., adj. Mr Howell Briggs; 20 May 1742, p.334. £1.

WALTER LASHLEY, 200 acs. Surry Co. on the S side of the main black Water Sw. & the S side of the Old Town Sw., adj. Henry Barker & sd Lashley's Own Old lines; 20 May 1742, p.336. £1.

JOHN ROBERTS, 235 acs. Surry Co. on the S side of Nottoway Riv. & on the E side of the Otter Dam Sw., crossing Lewis' br.; adj. George Hamilton, Capt. Thomas Avent & Richard Moore; 20 May 1742, p.337. £1.S5.

JOHN FORD & THOMAS VANN, 178 acs. Henrico Co. on the N side of James Riv. & on the Northern Brook of Chickahominy; adj. Michael Holland, James Hambleton & John Watson; 20 May 1742, p.339. £1.

RALPH DUNKLEY, 203 acs. Brunswick Co. on the S side of Dearden's br., adj. Vaughan & Fisher; 20 May 1742, p.341. £1.

MATTHEW CABINISS, 390 acs. Amelia Co. on the S side of Little Nottoway Riv., in a Valley of Whetstone Cr., adj. Thomas Yarbrough & Henry Yarbrough; 20 May 1742 *in the 15th year of our*

Reign of George the Second, p.342. £2.

WILLIAM STITH, Clerk, 400 acs. Goochland Co. on the side of a Hill near Goldby's Cr.; adj. John Lewis, Thomas Goldby & Elizabeth Lewis; 30 Jul 1742 *in the 16th year of our Reign of George the Second*, p.344. £2.

HENRY DOWNS, 244 acs. Orange Co. on the E side the Beaver Dam Run, in a Vally, along the Octony line [S71°E], in a Small Poyson Field & on a Ridge; adj. Edward Franklin, Mr Zachariah Taylor & William Bartlett; 30 Jul 1742, p.345. £1.S5.

SAMUEL GENTRY, 700 acs. Hanover Co. on both sides of dirty Sw.; adj. Clark, Henson & Brooks; 30 Jul 1742, p.347. £3. 108 acs. part formerly gtd. Richard Brooks by Pat. 5 Aug 1731 [PB 14 p.219, 400 acs. to Richard Brooks Junr. dated 25 Aug 1731] & by him sold & Conveyed unto the sd Samuel Gentry The Residue never before gtd.

Capt. ALLEN HOWARD Gentleman, 2,380 acs. Goochland Co. on both sides of Rockfish Riv. & on the N side of the Fluvanna Riv., running into the Woods, near a Spring br., Including Howard's Island, adj. William Cabbell; 30 Jul 1742, p.349. 400 acs. part

formerly gtd. unto the sd Allen Howard by Pat. 11 Jan 1730/31 [PB 14 p.56], 250 acs. other part being former gtd. sd Howard by Pat. 12 Mar 1739/40 [PB 18 p.534 a regrant of John Bolling's PB 15 p.29], 500 acs. other Part being part of 1,200 acs. formerly gtd. Samuel Spencer by Pat. 20 Jun 1733 [PB 15 p.64] & by him Sold & Conveyed unto the sd Allen Howard, 400 acs. other part formerly gtd. Allen Howard by Pat. 10 Jan 1735/36 [PB 16 p.439], 34 acs. other Part being an Island in the Fluvanna formerly gtd. the sd Allen Howard by Pat. 22 Sep 1739 [PB 18 p.429] And 796 acs. the Residue never before gtd.

WILLIAM GOSNEY, 400 acs. Orange Co. on the head brs. of Mattopony Riv., on the Lowgrounds; 30 Jul 1742, p.352. £2. Whereas by Pat. 20 Nov 1734 [21 Nov 1734, PB 15 p.373] gtd. Edward Rouse 400 acs. formerly in Spotsyl. Co. but now in Orange and Whereas sd Edward Rouse hath failed to pay Quit Rents and to make Cultiv. & Improv. and Joseph Hawkins hath made Humble suit and hath obtained a G. for the same which he hath Relinquished unto William Gosney.

JOHN CARR, 400 acs. in that part of Orange Co. designed to be called Augusta, on both sides of Cathey's Riv., joining Beverley

Mannor, on a Ridge, near a small Island, adj. James Cathey & James Carr; 30 Jul 1742, p.354. £2.

WILLIAM WALTERS, 400 acs. Brunswick Co. on the S side of Staunton Riv., to a fork of Priff's Cr.; 30 Jul 1742, p.355. £2.

JOHN PHELPS, 140 acs. Brunswick Co. on the S side of Otter Riv.; 30 Jul 1742, p.357. 15 Shill.

EDWARD BROADNAX, 871 acs. Brunswick Co. on both sides of Flatt Rock Cr., on a great br. & near the Falls; 30 Jul 1742, p.356. 570 acs. part formerly gtd. Hannah Rains by Pat. 28 Sep 1732 [Hannah Raines, PB 14 p.509] and 301 acs. the Residue formerly gtd. Samuel Moody by Pat. 10 Jun 1737 [PB 17 p.347] & by them sold and Conveyed unto the sd Broadnax.

HENRY CLAY, 400 acs. Henrico Co. on the S side of James Riv., on the head of br. of Deep Cr., adj. John Pride; 30 Jul 1742, p.360. £2.

BENJAMIN BURTON, 400 acs. Henrico Co. crossing Deep Run, adj. Robert Burton & Mr Joseph Mayo; 30 Jul 1742, p.362. £2.

JOEL TANNER, 200 acs. Amelia Co. on the N side of Winingham's Cr. of Deep Cr. & on Deep Cr.;

adj. Robert Malone, Fitzgerrald & Brown; 30 Jul 1742, p.363. £1. [Included in his 640 acs. in PB 29 p.105]

EDWARD GOODE, 400 acs. Henrico Co. Beg. at his first survey on the W side of the Great Br. of four Mile Cr., up the lower br. of Deep Run, adj. Benjamin Burton & Pleasant; 30 Jul 1742, p.365. £2.

SAMUEL MANNING, 115 acs. Brunswick Co. in the Fork of Avie's Br. & down Parham's Cr.; 30 Jul 1742, p.367. 15 Shill.

RICHARD KNIGHT, 400 acs. Surry Co. on the S side of Nottoway Riv. & on the N side of the Hunting Quarter Sw.; adj. Richard Woodroofe, Howard Briggs & Nicholas Callyham; 30 Jul 1742, p.368. £2.

WILLIAM BRADLY, 100 acs. Surry Co. on the S side of the main black Water Sw.; adj. sd Bradly's own Old lines, Samuel Cornwell, Henry Coker & Robert Atkinson; 30 Jul 1742, p.370. 10 Shill.

THOMAS TANNER, 300 acs. Amelia Co. on both sides of Flatt Cr., to a corner by Flatt Rock [Cr.], adj. Craddock & Mayes; 30 Jul 1742, p.372. £1.S10. [Included in Joseph Motley's 1,383 acs. in PB 28 p.111]

Majr. JOHN BOLLING, Gentleman, 600 acs. Goochland Co. on both sides of Fluvanna Riv. below Buffaloe Lick, on a High Hill, in Lowgrounds; 30 Jul 1742, p.374. £3.

WILLIAM WATSON, 1,600 acs. Amelia Co. on the head brs. of Sandy Riv. & Snales/Snailes Cr., down Bagly's Br., crossing the brs. of Nottoway, crossing a fork of Sandy Riv., by a Spring, adj. William Brown on the Edge of the Lowgrounds; 30 Jul 1742, p.375. £8.

JAMES SINSING, 230 acs. Surry Co. on the S side of Nottoway Riv., Beg. on the E side of the great Plowman's Sw., down Jack's br., adj. Benjamin Adams; 30 Jul 1742, p.378. £1.S5.

THOMAS SPENCER, 250 acs. Brunswick Co. on the W side of the Middle Fork of the three Forks of Licking Hole Cr., adj. Joseph Morton Senior; 30 Jul 1742, p.379. £1.S5. [Included in his 362 acs. in PB 24 p.191 & 821 acs. in PB 26 p.643]

JOHN PHELPS, 226 acs. Brunswick Co. on the N side of Otter Riv.; 30 Jul 1742, p.381. £1.S5.

Majr. JOHN BOLLING, Gentleman, 780 acs. Goochland Co. on both sides of Fluvanna Riv. including Possum Island, by the lower side of Possum Cr., on a Ridge; 30 Jul 1742, p.382. £4.

JOHN PHELPS, 816 acs. Brunswick Co. on the Ridge bet. the heads of the brs. of Buffelo Cr. & Elk Cr.; 30 Jul 1742, p.384. £4.S5.

Capt. THOMAS AVENT, Gentleman, 175 acs. in the Counties of Isle of Wight and Surry on the N side of the Three Creeks, up a small br., down the Poplar br., adj. Christopher Golikely & John Golikely; 30 Jul 1742, p.386. £1.

DRURY STITH, 200 acs. Brunswick Co. on the lower side of Twitty's Cr.; 30 Jul 1742, p.387. £1. [Included in John Sullivant's PB 24 p.399]

RICHARD JONES, 300 acs. Amelia Co. on the S side of Buckskin Cr., in a Meadow, near the head of a br. called Doe head, adj. William Worsham; 30 Jul 1742, p.389. £1.S10.

ROBERT RICKS, 150 acs. Is. of Wight Co. on the N side of Nottoway, on the N side of Coscore Br.; adj. William Scarborough, Colonel John Simmons, & Robert Ricks own Old line; 30 Jul 1742, p.390. 15 Shill.

ROBERT COBBS, 400 acs. Henrico Co. crossing the Second br., on Turk's br.; adj. sd Cobbs Old lines, George Easter, John Purdue, John Belsher, Hatchet, & William More; 30 Jul 1742, p.392. £2.

Colo. RICHARD RANDOLPH, Gent., 10,300 acs. Brunswick Co. (including a small Island in Staunton Riv. commonly known by the name of Fishing Place), on both sides the sd Staunton Riv., on both sides of Licking Hole Cr. & black Walnut Cr., on a High Hill, on the Second forty of licking hole Cr., by a Pond, adj. Jenkins; 30 Jul 1742, p.395. £51.S10.

JAMES YOUNG, 317 acs. Henrico Co. near Mr Young's House on the W side of the Main Road, crossing Mirey br., on the W side & down Brazeels Br.; adj. Thomas Wood, John Gun, Mr John Cole & Colo. Benjamin Harrison; 30 Jul 1742, p.396. £1.S15.

JOHN WHITE, JUNR., 317 acs. Henrico Co. crossing Smith's Road, on the W side & down Brazeel's br.; adj. John Gun, James Young, Nathaniel Vandewall & sd Young's first Survey just above the mouth of Mirey br.; 30 Jul 1742, p.397. £1.S15.

HUBERT FARRELL, 340 acs. Brunswick Co. on Flat Rock Cr.

adj. Lewis Deloney; 30 Jul 1742, p.398. £1.S15.

THOMAS CORE, 290 acs. Nansemond Co. on the N side Summerton Cr., down the Short Sw. & up the Miery br.; adj. Henry Copeland & Abraham Riddick; 30 Jul 1742, p.399. £1.S10.

ROBERT GOOD, 480 acs. Goochland Co. among the S brs. of James Riv. bet. Deep Cr. & Muddy Cr.; adj. Daniel Witmore, William Moss, Bowler Cocke, Robert Speer, Samuel Allen & Nicholas Davis; 30 Jul 1742, p.400. 200 acs. part formerly gtd. John Spear by Pat. 28 Sep 1732 [PB 14 p.462] & 280 acs. the Residue formerly gtd. John Twitty by Pat. 16 Jun 1738 [PB 17 p.523] which sd two Tracts of Land by Mesne Conveyances are become Vested in the sd Good.

JOHN MIRRICK, 648 acs. Brunswick Co. on both sides of Waqua Cr.; 30 Jul 1742, p.402. £2.S10. 204 acs. part formerly gtd. John Simmons Junr. by Pat. 7 Jul 1726 [PB 12 p.510 on Waquayough Cr.] which by Mesny conveyance is become Vested in the sd John Mirrick & the Residue never before gtd.

JOHN DAUGHTRY, 110 acs. in the Upper Par. of Nansemond Co.

near *Wickham*, in or near the reputed Co. line [S49°W]; adj. John Milner, William Baker, Bryant Daughtry Junr. & Joseph Scutchins; 30 Jul 1742, p.403. 15 Shill.

BENJAMIN HARRISON of Brunswick Co., 238 acs. in sd Co. on the head of the Great Br. of the Nap of Reeds Cr., adj. Mason; 23 Nov. 1742, p.405. £1.S5.

LUKE SMITH, 400 acs. Brunswick Co. on the N side of Staunton Riv. & the N side of Turnip Cr., down a Gut, adj. Mays & Kennon; 30 Jul 1742, p.406. £2.

JOHN WILLIAMSON, 310 acs. Henrico Co. on Bridgwaters Lane, on John's Br. & on the S side of Trumpet Br.; adj. Henry Stakes [Stokes], Robert Sharp, John Lankford, John Price, Thomas Williamson & sd Williamson's first survey; 30 Jul 1742, p.408. £1.S15.

JOSEPH MORTON JUNR., 400 acs. Brunswick Co. on the N side of Staunton Riv. & both sides of Wallace's Cr., up a Gut, adj. Randolph; 30 Jul 1742, p.409. £2. [Included in his 704 acs. in PB 25 p.241]

RICHARD WARD, 200 acs. Goochland Co. on Swift Cr. on the

S side of James Riv., in a Meadow; adj. Thomas Watkins, Michael Garthwright & John Maxey; 30 Jul 1742, p.411. £1. Whereas by Pat. 11 Apr. 1732 gtd. Nathaniel Maxey [PB 14 p.394] And Whereas the sd Nathaniel Maxey hath failed to make Cultiv. & Improv. and Richard Ward hath made Humble Suit and obtained a G. for the same. [Included in Thomas Green's PB 27 p.132]

FRANCIS WRAY, 167 acs. Brunswick Co. on the br. of Stoney Cr., on the Path; 30 Jul 1742, p.413.

NICHOLAS HOPSON, 285 acs. Henrico Co. On the N side of the South br. of white Oak Sw.; 30 Jul 1742, p.414. £1.S10. [Included in Robert Jordan's PB 27 p.53]

HENRY FARLY, 902 acs. Amelia Co. on the upper side of flatt Cr. & on both sides of Mayes's Br., by Osbourn's Path, in a Vally; adj. William Jackson, Richard Jones, Philip Jones & William Sizemore; 30 Jul 1742, p.416. 318 acs. part formerly gtd. sd Henry Farly by Pat. 20 Aug 1740 [PB 19 p.733] & 584 acs. the Residue formerly gtd. Samuel Cobbs by Pat. 12 Sep 1738 [PB 18 p.135] & by him Sold & Conveyed to sd Henry Farly.

JOHN WILLINGHAM, 750 acs. Brunswick Co. on the S side of

Staunton Riv.; 20 Dec 1742, p.418. £3.S15.

WILLIAM HEATH, 285 acs. Surry Co. on the S side of main Blackwater Sw. & the E side of the Pedgeon/Pidgeon Sw., adj. his Own Old lines; 30 Jul 1742, p.419. £1.S10.

JOSHUA ROWLAND, 190 acs. Surry Co. on the S side of Nottoway Riv., on the S side of the Great Spring Sw., adj. John Bell & Charles Judkins; 30 Jul 1742, p.421. £1.

WEBSTER GILL, 400 acs. Henrico Co. on the S side of James Riv., in a Sw., adj. Peter Rowlet; 30 Jul 1742, p.423. £2.

WILLIAM THOMPSON, 350 acs. Surry Co. on the S side of Nottoway Riv. & on the N side of the three Creeks, Beg. on the N side of Plowman's Sw., at the head of Jack's br., adj. James Sinsing & Thomas Pate; 30 Jul 1742, p.425. £1.S15.

JOHN HARVEY, 195 acs. Brunswick Co. on both sides of Buffello Cr.; 30 Jul 1742, p.426. £1.

WILLIAM HIX, 175 acs. Hanover Co., joyning to Cecilia Anderson & John Stanly; 30 Jul 1742, p.428. £1.

WILLIAM PEMBERTON & EASTER BELL, 83 acs. Caroline Co.; adj. Mr Secretary Carter, Tinsley & a Pat. gtd. to Katherine and Elenor Proverb; 30 Jul 1742, p.430. 10 Shill.

WILLIAM LEWIS, 400 acs. Henrico Co., in the line formerly Abraham Abney's, adj. John Leason & Joseph Watson; 30 Jul 1742, p.431. £2.

SAMUEL CROFTS, 300 acs. Is. of Wight Co. on the N side of the main Blackwater; adj. William Camp, the sd Crofts own Old lines, Joseph Hallyman, John Hallyman, Arthur Crocher [Crocker], Samuel Taylor, Thomas Moore, Rubin Cook & Solomon Stephenson; 30 Jul 1742, p.433. £1.S10.

JOSEPH MORTON, 589 acs. Brunswick Co. on both sides of the North fork of Lickinghole, Beg. on the Hills; 30 Jul 1742, p.435. £3.

SILVANUS STOKES the younger, 500 acs. Surry Co. on the S side of Nottoway Riv., by a Meadow br.; adj. his own Old lines, William Harris & Robert Owen; 30 Jul 1742, p.437. £2.S10.

WILLIAM GREEN, 2,050 acs. Amelia Co. on the S side of Appamatox Riv. & on the upper side of Winticomaick Cr., on the Edge of the Beaverpond of sd Cr., in a small Spring br., up the long br.; adj. Pattyson, James Tucker, Joseph Pattyson Junr., Powell, Brown, Waller, Bolling & Bell; 30 Jul 1742, p.439. 1,650 acs. part formerly gtd. gtd. sd William Green by Pat. 16 Jun 1738 [PB 18 p.27 which included his 100 acs. in PB 15 p.177 dated 15 Mar 1733/34] & 400 acs. the Residue formerly gtd. Samuel Cobbs by Pat. 12 Sep 1738 [PB 18 p.136] which 400 acs. was Conveyed by sd Cobbs to sd Green.

Feb.17.1742/43 -
Then Settled with Mr. Waller, the Accot. of Right from the former Settlement Feb.13th.1741/42. to this place in this Book and to Wm. Towns Ending page 138. in another Book [PB 21] amounting both to 4805. Rights as Pt Acct. thereof, all which were immediately burnt - John Blair D.Audr.

PHINEAS GLOVER, 400 acs. Goochland Co. on both sides the North & South brs. of Slate Riv., in the Lowgrounds, adj. Samuel Glover; 12 Feb 1742/43, p.442. £2.

RICHARD ROYALL, 322 acs. Amelia Co. on both sides of Beaverbone br. of Wests Cr.; adj. Marshall, Griggs, Moore, John Maye & his own Lines; 12 Feb 1742/43, p.443. £1.S15.

WILLIAM GAY, Gentleman, 475 acs. Goochland Co. on the S side of James Riv., adj. John Sanders; 12 Feb 1742/43, p.445. £1.S15. 350 acs. part formerly gtd. John Bolling Gent. by Pat 10 Jan 1735/36 [PB 16 p.512, a regrant of Richard Dean's 350 acs. Henrico Co. in PB 12 p.339 dated 10 Feb 1725/26] and for want of Cultiv. & Improv. the same became forfeited and Vested again in Us as by the Records of the General Court of our sd Colony Relation being thereunto had may appear & 125 acs. the Residue formerly gtd. John Steavens by Pat. 23 Dec 1714 [PB 10 p.217, Henrico Co.] The Right and Title whereof by mesne Conveyances are become Vested in the sd William Gay.

HENRY CARTER, 183 acs. Spotsyl. Co., S side of the middle Riv. or Riv. Ta, a br. of Mattapony, adj. James or Uriah Garton & a pat. gtd. John Robinson Esq.; 12 Feb 1742/43, p.447. The sd Land being part of 9,400 acs. gtd. Larkin Chew by Pat. 4 Jun 1722 [PB 11 p.91, which included two 400 acre Patents in PB 10 p.58 dated 26 Apr 1712 gtd. Larkin Chew, Richard Buckner, Joseph Chew & John Sutton - no County] and is since by mesne Conveyances become Vested in the sd Henry Carter. [Larkin Chew's 9,400 acs. in PB 11 p.91 also included the land in Joseph Brock's 7,467 acs.

in PB 18 p.140; Rice Curtis Jr. 462 acs. in PB 18 p.149; James Stevens 178 acs. in PB 18 p.151; John Talbert's 36 acs. in PB 18 p.313; William & James Samms 244 acs. in PB 18 p.356; & Bloomfield Long's 331 acs. in PB 23 p.721]

JOHN BUCKHANNAN, 400 acs. Orange Co. on the W side the blue Ridge; 12 Feb 1742/43, p.449. £2.

HENRY HATCHER, 314 acs. Henrico Co. on the Co. line [N52°E], adj. John Burton, through Mr Hatcher's Plantation; 12 Feb 1742/43, p.451. £1.S15.

ROBERT EALOM, 380 acs. Henrico Co. crossing several Slashes; adj. the Honourable William Byrd Esq., the line formerly Soans's, sd Ealom's old line, John Hatcher & John Farmer; 12 Feb 1742, p.453. £2.

RICHARD WARD, 304 acs. Brunswick Co. on the N side of Ward Fork, down sd Cr., adj. Martin; 12 Feb 1742/43, p.454. £1.S10.

JAMES CAMPBELL, 400 acs. Orange Co. on the W side the blue Ridge & the N side the Goose Cr.; 12 Feb 1742/43, p.456. £2.

WILLIAM WATSON, 1,400 acs. Amelia Co. on both sides of Nammisseen Cr., on a br. of the North fork of sd Cr., crossing the Mill Path, along the Co. line [South]; adj. Hamlin, FitzGerrald & Rees; 12 Feb 1742/43, p.458. £7. [Included in his 1,734 acs. in PB 25 p.140]

JOHN INGRAM, 200 acs. Is. of Wight Co. on the N side of Round Hill Sw.; adj. William Holden, the sd Ingrum's own Old lines, John Branch & Joseph Exum; 12 Feb 1742/43, p.461. £1.

RICHARD VICK, 175 acs. Is. of Wight Co. on the S side of Nottoway Riv., up Dick's Sw.; adj. John Vasser, sd Vick's own old line & William Sellers; 12 Feb 1742/43, p.462. £1.

TULLY CHOICE, 1,000 acs. Orange Co. on the brs. of black Walnut Run, on a Levell on the SE side the new Mountain Road; adj. Purvice, Edings & Watts; 12 Feb 1742/43, p.464. Where as Pat. 28 Sep 1728 Gtd. John Sharp & William Sharp [PB 14 p.109] in Spotsyl. Co. now Orange who failed to make cultiv. & improv. & sd Tully Choice made humble Suit & obtained a G. for the same. For the Imp. of 17 pers. to dwell within this our Colony and Dominion of Virginia who names are *John Crawford, James Mills, Thomas Brown, John Newport, Henry Bryne, Francis Bradstreet, John Honey, William Banks, Catherine*

Kelly, William McDaniel, Thomas Parks, Edmund Phillips William Sutherland, Archibald Johnson, John Walker, Ann Bambridge & Elizabeth Hopkins as also for 15 Shill.

JAMES FARLON, 275 acs. Henrico Co. on the S side of James Riv., on the N side of a Fork Nicesams br.; adj. John Burton, Edward Harrison & James Hill; 12 Feb 1742/43, p.467. £1.S10.

JOHN COLLINS, 400 acs. Spotsyl. Co. on the brs. of the River Ta a br. of Mattapony Riv., on the E side of a Glade, on the bluff Sw., on the Lower side of the Bluff run, at the head of a Valley near the new mine bank Road & on the E side of the Old mine road; adj. Mr Griffin Fantleroy, Benjamin Duke, Mr Joseph Brock, George Stubblefield, John Sartin & John Fieldour; 12 Feb 1742/43, p.469. £2.

MARTIN KEY, 50 acs. Louisa Co. on the N side of the North Fork of James Riv., into the Woods, adj. Leonard Terrence Vicus; 30 Mar 1743, p.471. 5 Shill.

HENRY HAYNES, 400 acs. Orange Co. on the Brow of a hill in the head of a small Valley; adj. William Keaton, John Red & Richard Winslow; 30 Mar 1743, p.473. £2.

JOHN PORTLOCK, 70 acs. Norfolk Co. on the Southern Br. of Gillagin Cr. & on Ware Cr., Beg. near the Head of a Cove that makes out of Gillagin Cr.; 21 Apr 1743, p.475. for 2 lbs. of Tobacco for every Acre. Whereas by one Inquisition Indented taken in sd Co. 19 Sep 1718 By Virtue of a Warrant directed to Samuel Boush Gent: our Escheator for sd Co. It appears that Thomas Gillagin late of sd Co. died seised of 70 acs. which is found to Escheat to us from sd Gillagin And Whereas John Portlock hath made Humble Suit and obtained a G. for the same.

ANN MAYO, 787 acs. Amelia Co. on the upper side of Flatt Cr., upon the side of a Beaverpond of Haw Br.; 30 Mar 1743, p.476. 400 acs. part formerly gtd. William Kennon Gent. by Pat. 28 Sep 1730 [PB 14 p.141, Pr. Geo. Co.] & by him Sold & Conveyed unto Richard Kennon Gent. of Charles City Co. & 387 acs. the Residue formerly gtd. sd Richard Kennon by Pat. 17 Mar 1736/37 [PB 17 p.239 to Richard Kennon junr.] & by him both of the sd Tracts were sold & Conveyed unto sd Ann Mayo.

ALEXANDER CUNNINGHAM, 400 acs. Goochland Co. on the S side of James Riv. on the brs. of Little Deep Cr., adj. John Sanders & Peter LeGrand; 30 Mar 1743, p.478. £2. Whereas by Pat. 28

Sep 1732 gtd. Abraham Micheaux [PB 14 p.466] who failed to make cultiv. & improv. and Alexander Cunningham hath made Humble Suit and Obtained a G. for the same.

WILLIAM TRIGG, 157 acs. in the Par. of Saint Margaret, Caroline Co., in a Spring br., up the Edge of the Reedy Sw., adj. William Eubanks; 30 Mar 1743, p.480. £1. the sd 157 acs. being Surplus L. found within the bounds of a Pat. Gtd. John Harris for 162 acs. by Pat. 8 Sep 1730 [28 Sep 1730, PB 13 p.490].

MICHAEL HOLLAND, 300 acs. Amelia Co., on the lower side of the little Saylors Cr. Adj. John Crawford; 30 Mar 1743, p.481. £1.S10. [Included in Ashley Johnson's PB 27 p.401]

WILLIAM MAYO, Gentleman, 530 acs. Goochland Co. on the brs. of Rockfish Riv. near the blue Mountains, adj. John Chiswell Gent.; 30 Mar 1743, p.483. 15 Shill. 400 acs. part formerly gtd. sd William Mayo by Pat. 11 Sep 1738 [12 Sep 1738, PB 18 p.109] & 130 acs. the Residue never before gtd.

BENJAMIN PITMAN, 590 acs. Is. of Wight Co. on the S side of the main black water, by the side of Copohonk br.; adj. Micajah Edwards, James Allen & John Williford; 30 Mar 1743, p.485. £3.

EDWARD HERNDON the Younger, 337 acs. Spotsyl. Co. on the brs. of Mattapony Riv., in a meadow, on a Point on the upper side of Achillis's br., at the head of a small Valley, on the SW side of a Glade, on a Level in Sight of a Pond; adj. Mr Joseph Brock, Mr Booker, Robert Coleman, Hugh Sanders & Iganatius Stureman; 30 Mar 1743, p.487. £1.S15.

THOMAS BARHAM, 190 acs. Is. of Wight Co. on the N side of the three Creeks, up the Flatt br.; adj. Thomas Newsom, Edward Robertson, Henry Manery, Bagley Greve & John Smith; 30 Mar 1743, p.489. £1.

WILLIAM JONES, 260 acs. Is. of Wight Co. on the S side of Roundhill Sw.; adj. John Exum, Joshua Syke, Colo. Benjamin Edwards & sd William Jones's other L.; 30 Mar 1743, p.491. £1.S10.

ABRAHAM VENABLE, 3,300 acs. Amelia Co. on the S side of Appamattox Riv. & on both sides of Harris's Cr., Beg. at his Old Corner on the Riv. near Butterwood Sw., in a Bottom, adj. Randolph; 30 Mar 1743, p.493. £6. 2,100 acs. part formerly gtd.

sd Abraham Venable by Pat. 12 Sep 1738 & 1,200 acs. the Residue never before gtd.

JOHN RUD JUNR., 400 acs. Henrico Co. crossing Middle Sapony Cr. & Several brs. of the lower Sapony Cr.; adj. John Wilkinson, John Rud Senr. & John Worsham; 30 Mar 1743, p.495. £2.

RICHARD CARLILE, 150 acs. Pr. Geo. Co. on the S side of Joseph's Sw.; adj. William Cotton's new Survey, Peoples, his own lines & his Cornfield; 30 Mar 1743, p.497. 15 Shill.

JOHN MAN, 350 acs. Pr. Geo. Co. bet. Jones Hole & the Indian Sw., up the Cabin br.; adj. Samuel Griffin, Thomas Tadlock, his Own line, John Roberts, Peter Harwell & Arthur Reding; 30 Mar 1743, p.499. £1.S15.

HENRY BLOW, 390 acs. Surry Co. on the S side of the main black water Sw., on the E side of the Myery br., adj. Richard Blow; 30 Mar 1743, p.501. £2.

LEWIS SOLOMON the Younger, 250 acs. Surry Co. on the N side of the three Creeks & the E side of Odiam's br., by the Gum br.; adj. Thomas Underwood, Gilbert Hays, John Roberts, George Hamilton &

Richard Hays; 30 Mar 1743, p.502. £1.S5.

THOMAS TAYLOR, 330 acs. Is. of Wight Co. on the E side of Tarraroe Cr. & on the N side of Meherin Riv., down the Beaverdam Sw., adj. Arthur Taylor; 30 Mar 1743, p.504. £1. 130 acs. part thereof being formerly gtd. unto the sd Thomas Taylor by Pat. 17 Sep 1740 [130 acs. gtd. Joseph Lane in PB 12 p.326 dated 21 Sep 1725, not Taylor's 100 acs. in PB 19 p.812] & 200 acs. the Residue never before gtd.

HUGH DANIEL, 392 acs. Brunswick Co. on both sides of Poplar Cr.; 30 Mar 1743, p.506. £2.

DANIEL SINGLETON, 200 acs. Orange Co., among ¥ heads of the brs. of Terry's Run, by the head of a Valley, by Flattground, in a Glade, adj. James Cox; 30 Mar 1743 *in the 16th year of our Reign of George the Second*, p.508-p.506-p.510. £1. [p.509 written as p.506]

RICHARD MALDEN JUNR., 2,000 acs. in that part of Orange designed to be called Augusta, on the S side of the Peaked Mountain near the foot & on the S side of the South Riv. of Shannando; 30 Jun 1743 *in the 17th year of our Reign of George the Second*, p.510. £10.

ROBERT GREEN, 400 acs. Orange Co. in the Goard Vine fork, by a br. of black water run, on a hill Opposite to a round Topped Mountain, adj. Daniel Brown; 30 Jun 1743, p.512. £2.

Capt. JOHN RAVENSCROFT Gent., 450 acs. Brunswick Co. on Jenito Cr. on the S side of Meherin Riv.; adj. Henry Bedingfield, Howard, Smith & George Hix; 30 Jun 1743, p.514. £2.S10.

JOHN BANISTER, Esquire, 1,000 acs. Brunswick Co. on both sides Banister Riv., adj. Byrd & Embry; 30 Jun 1743, p.516. £5.

SETH PETTY POOL, 132 acs. Brunswick Co. on the N side of Fucking Cr., adj. Lanier; 30 Jun 1743, p.518. 15 Shill.

HENRY ROBERSON, Son of Christopher Roberson, 300 acs. Amelia Co. in the fork of the upper fork of Woody Cr., on Stanly's fork, down Roberson's Cr., adj. Henry Roberson, Hudson & Featherstone; 30 Jun 1743, p.520. £1.S10.

MATTHEW GRIFFIN, 200 acs. Is. of Wight Co. on the S side of main black water Sw., Beg. at the mouth of Tarapin Sw. on the E side of Seacock Sw., adj. Thomas Reeves & George Pearce; 30 Jun 1743, p.522. £1. Whereas by Pat.

13 Nov 1713 gtd. John Teasley now Dec'd [John Teasly, PB 10 p.116] and Whereas the sd John Teasley in his life time and Richard Teasley, son and Heir of sd John since his Death have failed to made Cultiv. & Improv. and Matthew Griffin hath made humble Suit and Obtained a g. for the same.

JOHN LYON, 350 acs. Goochland Co. on the brs. of Hardware Riv., adj. Mildred Meriwether; 30 Jun 1743, p.524. £1.S15.

RICHARD WOODSON, 364 acs. Amelia Co. on both sides of Bryer Riv., adj. Joseph Morton; 30 Jun 1743, p.526. £2. [Included in his 1,152 acs. in PB 28 p.432]

JOSEPH EELBECK, 500 acs. Surry Co. on the S side of Nottaway Riv., Beg. in Frying pan br., in Anderson's br.; adj. Mr Howell Briggs, Robert Tucker, William Bridges & John Wynne; 30 Jun 1743, p.528. £2.S10.

WILLIAM THWEAT, 263 acs. Pr. Geo. Co. on the Lower side of Wigg Island br. of white Oak Sw.; bet. the lines of Taylor, Ellis, Mitchel, his own, Peterson alias Thweat's, & Laws; 30 Jun 1743, p.531. £1.S10.

JOHN DOBBINS, 250 acs. Goochland Co. on the brs. of Rock fish Riv., at a fork of Lynch's Cr.

& at the main Cr., adj. Chiswell; 30 Jun 1743, p.533. £1.S5.

JOSEPH WEST, 450 acs. Is. of Wight Co. on the S side of Nottoway Riv. & on both sides of the Doctors br.; adj. his own old line, Colo. John Allen, Doctor Samuel Brown, Oliver Woodard, William Sellers & John Braswell; 30 Jun 1743, p.535. £2.S5.

WILLIAM SMITH, 645 acs. Brunswick Co. on both sides the Otterdams, Beg. on the sd Cr., on Davis's Cart Road, at the main Road; adj. John Davis, Bates, William Hows, Whealband [Wilburn], Laurence Hows, Whittington, Harrison & Brown; 30 Jun 1743, p.537. £3.S5. [220 acs. part Included in Isaac Collier's PB 28 p.354]

ROBERT NICHOLSON, 330 acs. Surry Co. on the S side of the main Black water Sw., Beg. on the S side of the Great Br. of Seacock Sw., by the side of the horse meadow br., adj. James Washington & Thomas Fort; 30 Jun 1743, p.540. £1.S15.

THOMAS MOORE, 300 acs. Surry Co. on the S side of Nottaway Riv.; adj. Silvanus Stokes, William Knight & Abraham Evans; 30 Jun 1743, p.542. £1.S10.

WILLIAM TEMPLE JUNR., 302 acs. Pr. Geo. Co. on the S side of Warwick Sw., Beg. in the old line where it crosses the great br., at the corner of the Cornfield; adj. his old lines, Harrison, & Matthew Lee; 30 Jun 1743, p.545. £1.S10.

JAMES PARHAM, 385 acs. Surry Co. on the N side of Nottaway Riv., Beg. on the W side of the Indian Sw., down the Beaver-pond Sw.; adj. William Petteway, Charles Leeth & William Parham; 30 Jun 1743, p.547. £2.

JAMES BAKER, 320 acs. Is. of Wight Co. on the black water brs.; adj. George Perce's L. now in possession of Philip Wrayford, Matthew Strictland & the Coblers line [by his line NW]; 30 Jun 1743, p.549. £1.S15. Whereas by Pat. 20 Apr 1682 gtd. unto Thomas Mandue [PB 7 p.165, see PB 7 p.20 & p.69-70] and Whereas the sd Mandue in his lifetime and Joseph Godwin, Thomas Jordan and Roger Talton in whom the Right of the sd L. became vested after his Death have failed to make Cultiv. & Improv. & to Pay our Quit Rents and James Baker Hath made humble Suit & obtained a g. for the same.

HENRY LEADBITER, 200 acs. Pr. Geo. Co. bet. Oroccock & Warwick Swamps, Beg. in the line of Francis Leadbiter decd. below the House of sd Henry Leadbiter, Near below the reedy br.; adj. Francis Leadbiter, Skoyles, & John Leonard; 30 Jun 1743, p.552. £1.

EDWARD LUNDY, 240 acs. Is. of Wight Co. on the N side of Maherin Riv., by the side of a meadow; adj. his own old lines, William Lee & John Irby; 30 Jun 1743, p.554. £1.S5.

JAMES PATTON & JOHN LEWIS, Gentlemen., 10,500 acs. Orange Co., Beg. on a Point bet. the great Riv. of the Calf Pasture and the mouth of a Small br. on the N side the sd Riv., to the side of a Steep Rocky Mountain, on a Stony Point, by a Gully, on a poor Point, over a bare barren Hill; 30 Aug 1743, p.556. *for divers good causes and Considerations but more Especially for the Consideration expressed in an order of our Lieutenant Governor and Commander in Chief of our Colony and Dominion of Virginia in Council obtained by James Patton and John Lewis the 27th Day of Apr 1742 to sd Patton & Lewis.*

JAMES PATTON & JOHN LEWIS, 600 acs. in that part of Orange Co. Designed to be called Augusta on Elk Cr. a br. of the Calf Pasture Riv.; 30 Aug 1743, p.558. *for divers good causes and Considerations but more Especially for the Consideration expressed in*

an order of our Lieutenant Governor and Commander in Chief of our Colony and Dominion of Virginia in Council Obtained by James Patton and John Lewis the. 27th Day of Apr 1742 to sd Patton & Lewis.

JOHN LEWIS & JAMES PATTON, 690 acs. Orange Co. on the Calf Pasture Riv., on 2 ridges & by a Gutt; 30 Aug 1743, p.560. *for divers good causes and Considerations but more Especially for the Consideration expressed in an order of our Lieutenant Governor and Commander in Chief of our Colony and Dominion of Virginia in Council Obtained by James Patton and John Lewis the. 27th Day of Apr 1742 to sd Patton & Lewis.*

JAMES TERRY, 354 acs. Brunswick Co. on the S side of Little Roanoke, Beg. at Towns's corner on the sd Cr.; 30 Aug 1743, p.562. £1.S15.

CHARLES WILLIAMSON, 200 acs. Pr. Geo. Co. on both sides of the Rockey run, Beg. on the upper side of the sd Run Opposite to the Mouth of the half Horsepen br., in a meadow; 30 Aug 1743, p.563. £1. [Included in his PB 25 p.194]

DAVID THOMSON, 1,113 acs. Hanover Co. on both sides the East the Middle & the Main forks of the

North fork of North East Cr., Beg. at Captain Clarks Now John Powers's and Richard Estes's corner, by the side of a Stoney Knole, by a Glade; adj. John Estes, Robert Estes & Richard Estes; 30 Aug 1743, p.565-566.   £1.S15. 800 acs. part formerly gtd. sd David Thomson by two separate Patents bearing Date 25 Aug 1731 [David Thompson, PB 14 p.218 & p.228] and 313 acs. the residue never before gtd.

PATENT BOOK NO. 21

30 Jul 1742 to 25 Nov 1743

Rev. JOHN CRAIG, 172 acs. in that part of Orange Co. designed to be called Augusta on the N side a Br. of James Riv. called Craig's Cr., on the side of a Ridge, near the upper end of an Island; 30 Jul 1742 *in the 16th Year of our Reign of George the Second, William Gooch Esquire our Lieutenant Governor and Commander in Chief*, p.1. for the Import. of 4 Pers. to dwell within this our Colony and Dominion of Virginia whose Names are *Alexander McPherson, Susanna McPherson, Joseph Harris and Mark Fink*.

ROBERT SCOTT, 200 acs. in that part of Orange Co. designed to be called Augusta on the N side of the North Riv. of Shanando & on the head of Stoney Lick Br., on a Ridge Side; 30 Jul 1742, p.3. £1.

THOMAS STEVENSON, 241 acs. in that part of Orange Co. designed to be called Augusta on a Br. of Catheys Riv. called Walkers Run; 30 Jul 1742, p.5. for the Import. of 5 Pers.: *John Kaines, Philip Hart, Robert Appleby, Robert McPherson & Margaret McPherson*.

Rev. JOHN CRAIG, 158 acs. in that part of Orange Co. designed to be called Augusta in the Fork of Craig Cr. & Pattersons Br.; 30 Jul 1742, p.7. £1.

ROBERT SCOTT, 350 acs. in that part of Orange Co. designed to be called Augusta on the N side of the North Riv. of Shanando, Beg. on the Top of a High Hill above the Ford, on a Path, down the S side of Stoney Lick Br., adj. James Beard; 30 Jul 1742, p.9. £1.S15.

GEORGE SCOTT, 320 acs. in that part of Orange Co. designed to be called Augusta on the N side of the North Riv. of Shanando, down the S side of Stoney Lick Br., adj. Robert Scott; 30 Jul 1742, p.12. £1.S15.

39

Rev. JOHN CRAIG, 400 acs. in that part of Orange Co. designed to be called Augusta in the Fork made by James Riv. & Craig Cr., at the foot of a Ridge; 30 Jul 1742, p.14. £2.

ALEXANDER THOMPSON, 400 acs. in that part of Orange Co. designed to be called Augusta on both sides of the South Riv. of Shanando above the *Red Banks*; 30 Jul 1742, p.16. £2.

ROBERT LUNEY JUNR., 213 acs. in that part of Orange Co. designed to be called Augusta on a br. James Riv. called Luneys Mill Cr., on the W side of Beaver Dam Sw.; 30 Jul 1742, p.18. 1.S5.

ROBERT LUNEY, 250 acs. in that part of Orange Co. designed to be called Augusta on the W side of the blue Ridge of Mountains & on the Main Br. of James Riv., on a Ridge; 30 Jul 1742, p.19. for the Imp. of 5 Pers.: *James Davis, Mary Davis, Henry Davis, William Davis & Samuel Davis.*

PATRICK CADDAN, 176 acs. in that part of Orange Co. designed to be called Augusta on a Br. of Cathey's Riv. called Walkers Run, on the W side of Benjamin Allens Road; 30 Jul 1742, p.22. for the Imp. of 4 pers.: *Patrick Leonard, Patrick Welsh, Thomas Williams & Nicholas Christopher.*

ROBERT POGE, 306 acs. Orange Co. on the W side the Blue Ridge, adj. Alexander Blair & John Young; 30 Jul 1742, p.24. £1.S15.

STEPHEN GILL, 900 acs. Henrico Co.; adj. Henry Walthal, George Wilson, Henry Wilson, William Brown & Capt. Cobbs; 30 Jul 1742, p.26. £4.S10.

JOHN WILLIAMSON, 340 acs. Henrico Co. on the S side of Trumpet Br., up George's Br.; adj. his own Line, William Patman & Henry Stokes; 30 Jul 1742, p.28. £1.S15.

JOHN BOLLING, Gent., 165 acs. Goochland Co. adj. to the N side of Fluvanna Riv. above Possum Island, above the Mouth of Bollings Cr., on a Ridge; 30 Jul 1742, p.30. £1.

JOHN HILL, 152 acs. Amelia Co. on both side the Great Bent Run; adj. James Hurt, John Bently & Abraham Hurt; 30 Jul 1742, p.32. 15 Shill.

MATTHEW TALBOTT, 241 acs. Brunswick Co. on the S side of Licking Hole opposite to The Fork, Beg. on the North Fork, up Wards Fork; 30 Jul 1742, p.35. £1.S5.

WILLIAM FERRES, 400 acs. Goochland Co. on the Brs. of Snow Quarter Br. of Willis's Riv. alias

Willis's Cr.; adj. Nicholas Davies, Colonel Benjamin Harrison & Benjamin Dumas; 30 Jul 1742, p.37. £2.

MARY RUTLIDGE, 253 acs. Amelia Co. in The Fork bet. Bush Riv. & Sandy Riv. adj. Joseph Molton; 30 Jul 1742, p.39. for 10 Shill. as also for the Imp. of 3 Pers. whose names are *Hugh McDaniel, Honour McDaniel & Mary Rutlidge.*

TIMOTHY JOHNSON, 200 acs. Brunswick Co. on the N side of Otter Riv. above the mouth of Flatt Cr.; 30 Jul 1742, p.41. £1.

THOMAS MERIWETHER, 950 acs. Goochland Co. on both sides of the North Fork of Totier Cr.; adj. Robert Jones, Bolling Clark, Charles Lynch, John Scott & John Lewis; 30 Jul 1742, p.43. £4.S15.

JOHN WATSON, 121 acs. Henrico Co. on the N side of James Riv., adj. John Moseby; 30 Jul 1742, p.47. 15 Shill.

THOMAS JONES, 323 acs. Brunswick Co. on the N side of falling Riv.; 30 Jul 1742, p.49. £1.S15.

BAXTER DAVIS, 232 acs. Pr. Geo. Co. on the S side of Buckskin Cr., in a Slash, adj. Bolling & the sd Baxter Davis; 30 Jul 1742, p.51. £1.S5.

HUGH NICKSON, 404 acs. Amelia Co. on both sides of little Buffillo Riv., by the Path; 30 Jul 1742, p.53. £2.

Maj. JOHN BOLLING, 1,190 acs. Goochland Co. on both sides of Fluvanna Riv. near Buffalo Lick, in Lowgrounds, by the Riv. below a Cliff of Rocks; 30 Jul 1742, p.55. £6.

JOHN MORGAN, 480 acs. Is. of Wight Co. on the S side of Notoway Riv., on the N side of the Great Sw., adj. Thomas Adams & his own old Lines; 30 Jul 1742, p.57. £2.S10.

THOMAS WILLIAMS, 1,200 acs. Pr. Geo. Co. on the S side of Hatchers Run, below the Upper Nottoway Riv. Road; adj. Hawkes, Isham Eppes, Bley, Butler, John Browder, & Hudson; 30 Jul 1742, p.59. £6.

GIDEON SMITH, 333 acs. Brunswick Co. on both sides of Turnip Cr.; 30 Jul 1742, p.61. £1.S15.

EDWARD GOOD, 400 acs. Henrico Co. Beg. in the great Br. of four Mile Cr., on the S side of a Br. of deep Run, on the E side of the lower Br. of deep Run just above the Fork, adj. John Good & Whitloe; 30 Jul 1742, p.63. £2.

ROBERT RICKS, 200 acs. Is. of Wight Co. on the N side of Nottoway Riv., near the Head of Coscore Br., adj. Nicholas Williams & sd Ricks's own old Line; 30 Jul 1742, p.65. £1.

JOHN MARCH, 11 acs. Nansemond Co. on the S side of Sumerton Cr., crossing a Neck of Land; 30 Jul 1742, p.67. 5 Shill.

THOMAS JONES JUNR., 400 acs. Brunswick Co. on the S side of falling Riv.; 30 Jul 1742, p.69. £2.

GEORGE STOVALL, 200 acs. Goochland Co. called *Beech Adventure* adj. to S side of Fluvanna Riv., crossing Stovall's Cr.; 30 Jul 1742, p.70. £1.

WILLIAM POWELL, 322 acs. Amelia Co. on the S side of Harricane Sw., Beg. a little above the Mill Path that crosses the sd Sw. at the Great Falls, to the sd Sw. near below Jehu's Horse Pen; 30 Jul 1742, p.72. £1.S15.

THOMAS CLIFTON, 140 acs. Surry Co. on the S side of the main Black Water Sw., adj. Capt. William Brown; 30 Jul 1742, p.74. 15 Shill.

WILLIAM WEBB, 400 acs. Goochland Co. on the Brs. of Neds Cr. a Br. of the Fluvanna Riv.; 30 Jul 1742, p.76. £2.

INGRAM BLANKS, 316 acs. Brunswick Co. on the S side of Beverpond Cr.; adj. Edloe, & Herbert [her line], to a corner Gum marked [*JB* or *IB*] on the Cr.; 30 Jul 1742, p.78. £1.S15.

EDWARD HARRIS, 283 acs. Surry Co. on the S side of Black Water Sw., adj. William Rogers; 22 Nov 1742, p.80. £1.S10.

JOSEPH EXUM, 50 acs. Is. of Wight Co. on the S side of Seacock Sw.; 30 Jul 1742, p.82. 5 Shill.

JOHN BELSHIRE, 294 acs. Henrico Co. on the main Road, adj. William Pucket & Perdue; 30 Jul 1742, p.84. £1.S10.

REPS JONES, 896 acs. Brunswick Co. on the S side of Nottoway Riv. & on the N side of Green Cr., adj. Dyer; 30 Jul 1742, p.86. £4.S10.

JOHN RAY, 398 acs. Brunswick Co. on the Head of Cold Water [Run], adj. Benjamin Carrel; 30 Jul 1742, p.88. £2.

JAMES JOHNSON, 135 acs. Brunswick Co. on the N side of Otter Riv. adj. his upper c. on the Riv.; 30 Jul 1742, p.90. 15 Shill.

JOSEPH MORTON the Younger, 335 acs. Brunswick Co. on the E side licking hole Cr., adj. Joseph Morton Senr.; 30 Jul 1742, p.92. £1.S15. [Included in his PB 25 p.585 & PB 28 p.667]

THOMAS LOCKETT JUNR., 342 acs. Amelia Co. on the N side on the North Fork of Falling Cr., adj. Randolph; 30 Jul 1742, p.95. £1.S15. [Included in his, Thomas Lockitt Junr., PB 28 p.167]

JOEL MEADOW, 242 acs. Amelia Co. on both sides of Dawson's Cr., adj. Dawson; 30 Jul 1742, p.97. £1.S5.

WILLIAM JOHNSON, 570 acs. Brunswick Co. on both sides Quarrell Sw., adj. George Walton; 30 Jul 1742, p.99. £3.

ABRAHAM JONES, 220 acs. Brunswick Co. on the S side of the North Fork of Green Cr.; 30 Jul 1742, p.102. £1.S5.

JOHN DAVISSON, 400 acs. Amelia Co. on both sides of Mountain Cr., adj. Creed Haskins; 30 Jul 1742, p.104. £2.

JAMES BARNES, 229 acs. Brunswick Co. on both sides of his Horsepen Cr., adj. Martin; 30 Jul 1742, p.106. £1.S5.

WILLIAM SPRAGENS, 273 acs. Henrico Co.; adj. his own Line, Mr Pleasant Cocke & John Robertson; 30 Jul 1742, p.109. £1.S10.

JOHN FARGUSSON, 780 acs. Amelia Co. on the head Brs. of Evans's Cr. of Bush Riv., by a Spring, adj. Randolph; 30 Jul 1742, p.111. £4. [380 acs. part included in Henry Anderson's 1,202 acs. in PB 28 p.160 & 400 acs. other part included in Thomas Watkins Junr. 1,200 acs. in PB 28 p.255]

BENJAMIN WYNSLEY, 400 acs. Brunswick Co. on both sides Bears Element Cr.; 30 Jul 1742, p.114. £2.

ANTHONY WHELER, 400 acs. Brunswick Co. on both sides of Falling Riv.; 30 Jul 1742, p.116. £2.

WILLIAM BRADLEY, 50 acs. Surry Co. on the S side of the main black Water Sw., adj. Robert Atkinson & William Bradley; 30 Jul 1742, p.118. 5 Shill.

WILLIAM FITZGARRALD, 1,053 acs. Amelia Co. on the lower side of the main deep Cr., near a Br. of Wininghams Cr.; adj. Henry Roberson & John Taylor; 30 Jul 1742, p.120. £5.S5.

RICHARD HAGOOD, 350 acs. Brunswick Co. on the W side of Bryery Cr.; 30 Jul 1742, p.122. £1.S15.

MATTHEW TUCKER, 400 acs. Amelia Co. on the lower side of Winticomaick Cr.; adj. William Tesdale, John Parish, Francis Tucker & Thomas Hood; 30 Jul 1742, p.124. £2.

RICHARD CLARK, 754 acs. Amelia Co. on the upper side of Flatt Cr. & on the lower side of Furgussons Horsepen Br.; adj. Furgusson, Nicholas Gillington & William Austin; 30 Jul 1742, p.127. 400 acs. part formerly Gtd. James Clark by Pat. 20 Jun 1733 [Pr. Geo. Co., PB 15 p.61] & 354 acs. formerly Gtd. David Brown by Pat. 17 Mar 1736/37 [David Bourn in PB 17 p.266] the Right whereof is become vested in the sd Richard Clark.

JOSEPH WRIGHT, 187 acs. in Suffolk Par. Nansemond Co. on the S side of Nansemond Riv. & in the Fork of Skinners Cr. near Pigg Point, in a Valley; adj. Thomas Hancock, the Poor's/Poor Land, Bond, Streater, Grimes, Edward Streater Junr., & John Hufler/Husler; 30 Jul 1742, p.129. 15 Shill. 50 acs. part being part of 900 acs. formerly Gtd. John Parrett by Pat. 2 Jul 1650 [John Perrott Gent. of Graungers Point, 900 acs.

Nancemund Co. on Burgage's Cr. in PB 2 p.242; which included 800 acs. to Francis Hough of Up. Co. of New Norf. in PB 1 p.305 dated 12 Nov 1635 & PB 1 p.418 dated 17 May 1637] & by divers mesne Conveyances the Right & Title whereof is become vested in sd Joseph Wright, & 137 acs. the Residue being Surplus L. found within the Bounds of the sd 50 acs.

ABRAHAM COCKE, 2,003 acs. Brunswick Co. on both sides of Hounds Cr., up little Hounds Cr., adj. Walker & William Stroud; 30 Jul 1742, p.131. £10.

WILLIAM FITZGARRALD, 1,817 acs. Amelia Co. on the N side of little Nottoway Riv., up Woody Cr., in the Head of a Br. of Kittle Br., up Charles Irbys Spring Br.; adj. John Burge, John Wallice, the sd Irby, & William Featherstone; 30 Jul 1742, p.134. £9.S5.

WILLIAM TOWNS, 1,595 acs. Amelia Co. on the North Fork & the South Fork of Buckskin Cr. of Wests Cr., adj. his own old Line, Jeremiah Lester, Robert Easly, John Nash & Thomas Jones; 30 Jul 1742, p.136; 1,019 acs. part formerly Gtd. sd William Towns by Pat. 12 Sep 1733 [Pr. Geo. Co., PB 15 p.117], 200 acs. other part formerly Gtd. Samuel Jones by Pat. 9 Mar 1736/37 [17 Mar 1736/37, PB 17 p.246] and 376 acs. the residue formerly Gtd. Thomas Lee Esq. 20 Jul 1738 [PB 18 p.42] the Right of which sd two last mentioned Parcels have been Conveyed to him.

Thus far Settled as Pt rect. in the other Book folo. 441. [PB 20] Feb. 17. 1742 - John Blair D.Audr.

JOHN MCDOWELL, 400 acs. Orange Co. in the Fork of James Riv.; 10 Nov. 1742, p.138. for £1 as also for and in Consideration of the Imp. of 4 Pers. to dwell within this our Colony and Dominion whose Names are *John McDowell, Magdaline McDowell, Samuel McDowell & John Rutter.*

JOHN MCDOWELL, 400 acs. Orange Co. on the S side of James Riv.; 10 Nov. 1742, p.140. £2.

JOHN MCDOWELL, 300 acs. Orange Co. in the Fork of James Riv.; 10 Nov. 1742, p.142. £1.S10.

WILLIAM KENNON JUNR., 400 acs. Amelia Co. on the N side of the North Fork of Buffillo Riv., adj. Randolph & his own old Line; 12 Feb 1742/43, p.143. £2.

GEORGE COOK, 400 acs. Spotsyl. Co. on the W side the New Mine Bank Road, near the Head of a Glade, in the fork of Devils Ditch Sw.; adj. Mr Griffin

Fantleroy, Thomas Shelton, Joseph Roberts, George Musick & Nicholas Randall; 12 Feb 1742/43, p.145. £2.

JAMES CHAMBERLAIN, 400 acs. Orange Co. on the Brs. of James Riv. on the W side the Blue Ridge, adj. Jeremiah Chamberlain; 12 Feb 1742/43, p.147. £2.

the Reverend WILLIAM STITH, Clk., 420 acs. Goochland Co. on both sides of Ballengers Cr.; adj. John Lewis, his own Lines & Thomas Stone; 12 Feb. 1742/43, p.149. £2.S5. [Included in his 2,470 acs. Albemarle Co. in PB 28 p.107]

ROBERT NEWSOM JUNR., 200 acs. Is. of Wight Co. on the S side of Nottoway Riv., on the S side of Toquothunta Sw., down Vicks Br., adj. his own old Lines & George Carter; 12 Feb. 1742/43, p.151. £1.

WILLIAM CROSSWAIT, 400 acs. Orange Co. in the Fork of James Riv.; 12 Feb. 1742/43, p.152. £2.

JEREMIAH CHAMBERLAIN, 400 acs. Orange Co. on the Brs. of James Riv. on the W side the blue Ridge; 12 Feb 1742/43, p.154. £2.

HENRY HUDSON, 358 acs. Henrico Co. in Parish's Br.; adj. his old Line, Francis Farlow &

John Bowman; 12 Feb 1742/43, p.156. £2.

GEORGE GIVINGS, 400 acs. in that part of Orange Co. designed to be called Augusta on the N side of James Riv., Beg. in a Valley, up the Riv. to a Mulberry and a Hoop Wood; 12 Feb 1742/43, p.157. £2.

DAVID DAVIS, 400 acs. in that part of Orange Co. designed to be called Augusta on the head of a Br. of the North Riv. of Shanando called Mossey Cr., in a Hollow; 12 Feb 1742/43, p.159. £2.

JAMES BOYD, 340 acs. Orange Co. Crossing Lunies Mill Cr., Under a steep Hill; 12 Feb 1742/43, p.161. £1.S15.

THOMAS BALDWIN, 400 acs. Amelia Co. on both sides of the main or middle Fork of Spring Cr., adj. Daniel Terry; 12 Feb 1742/43, p.162. £2.

JOHN HARRISON, 366 acs. in that part of Orange Co. designed to be called Augusta on a Br. of James Riv. called Luneys Mill Cr., Beg. on the N side of a Spring Br.; 12 Feb 1742/43, p.164. £2.

ROBERT CAMPBELL, 337 acs. Orange Co., adj. the Line of Beverley Mannor; 12 Feb 1742/43, p.166. £1.S15.

DAVID MITCHEL, 400 acs. in Orange Co. in that part of the Co. designed to be called Augusta on a South Br. of Cataubo Cr.; 12 Feb 1742/43, p.168. £2.

WILLIAM WYNNE, 304 acs. Brunswick Co. on the S side of Banister Riv. adj. Banister; 12 Feb 1742/43, p.169. £1.S10.

WILLIAM SANDERS, 400 acs. Goochland Co. in the Fork of James Riv., crossing a Run of Cooks Cr.; 12 Feb 1742/43, p.171. £2.

GEORGE STEGALL, 400 acs. Amelia Co. on the lower side of Wests Cr. of Deep Cr.; 12 Feb 1742/43, p.173. £2.

JOHN KNIGHT, 383 acs. Brunswick Co. on the S side of Nottoway Riv., up dry Cr., adj. Fisher; 12 Feb 1742/43, p.175. £2.

JOHN PROCTOR, 140 acs. Is. of Wight Co. on the S side of the main black Water Sw.; adj. John Hollyman, Thomas Hollyman, Benjamin Pitman, Joseph Griffin & Robert Mercer; 12 Feb 1742/43, p.176. 15 Shill. [This land is part of William Edwards's 1,450 acs. on Coppohonk Sw. & Little Sw. dated 25 Apr 1701 but no County given in PB 9 p.336. The 1,450 acs. also includes Thomas Pitman junr. 250 acs. in PB 12 p.217,

John Williford's 265 acs. in PB 15 p.192, Benjamin Pitman's 590 acs. in PB 20 p.485, Joseph Griffin's 200 acs. in PB 22 p.589, Anselm Bailey's 320 acs. in PB 33 p.611 and Thomas Pretlow's 170 acs. in PB 33 p.838. This land is apparently now in "Little Surry"]

Mr LEWIS BERKLEY Gent., 762 acs. in Stratton Major Par. K. & Q. Co., up the East Br. of Tassatine [Cr.], near Mr Berkleys Quarter, up Arricaco Sw., near the Road, in the Fork of the Roads, crossing Turemans Spring Br., at the head of a Valley, adj. Tureman & Collins; 12 Feb 1742/43, p.178. £1.S5. 529 acs. part formerly Gtd. Ralph Green by Letters Pat. 10 Feb 1662/63 [PB 4 p.89 (575) PB 4 p.89 (577) 350 acs. on brs. of Assatiam Sw.; plus Green's PB 4 p.89 (577), PB 3 p.340 & PB 3 p.166 on Arsantons Cr. & Aratico Cr.] & 233 acs. the residue being found to be Surplus within the Bounds of sd Pat.

WILLIAM PENNINGTON, 125 acs. Brunswick Co. on the S side of Mohern Riv. on the S side Taylors Cr., adj. William Malone; 12 Feb 1742/43. p.180. 15 Shill.

WILLIAM SMITH, 144 acs. Brunswick Co. on Sandifords /Sandivers Br., adj. Harrison & Sandiford/Sandiver; 12 Feb 1742/43, p.182. 15 Shill.

PETER GRAMMER, 150 acs. Pr. Geo. Co. on the N side of Warwick Sw., up the great Br. of sd Sw.; along the old Line of the L. he purchased of John Gilliam, adj. Michael Rosser & John Rosser; 12 Feb 1742/43, p.184. 15 Shill.

JOHN BURTON, 400 acs. Henrico Co. on the N side of Nisons Br.; adj. Henry Hatcher, James Hill, James Farlow & sd Burton; 12 Feb 1742/43, p.186. £2.

JAMES CHAPPEL, 150 acs. Amelia Co. on the Head Brs. of Stocks Cr. adj. James Hurt; 12 Feb 1742, p.187. 15 Shill.

JOHN BURTON, 133 acs. Henrico Co. on the S side of James Riv., on the County Line [N51°E] adj. Henry Hatcher, Edward Harrison & James Farlow; 12 Feb 1742/43, p.189. 15 Shill.

FRANCIS STEGAR, 400 acs. Goochland Co. at the Head of Muddy Cr., adj. Jacob Winfree, Samuel Allen, William May, John Robinson & Samuel Nuckolls; 12 Feb 1742, p.191. £2. [Regranted Philip Poindexter in PB 26 p.249]

JAMES FREELAND, 100 acs. called *Lousey Camp* in Goochland Co., adj. to the N side of Fluvanna Riv.; 12 Feb 1742/43, p.193. 10 Shill. [The survey contains only one line (S20°W 220 Poles) indicating that this tract is at a (horseshoe) bend in the River. Lousey could refer to Lice, Chiggers, etc.]

RICHARD WARD, 320 acs. Brunswick Co. on the S side of Wards Fork, adj. Martin; 12 Feb 1742/43, p.194. £1.S15.

WILLIAM FOSTER, 400 acs. Amelia Co., on the Heads of Beaverpond Br. of Flatt Cr., Buckskin & Tommahauke Br., in a Meadow & a small Meadow; 12 Feb 1742/43, p.196. £2.

DANIEL JAGGERS, 301 acs. Brunswick Co. on the S side of Staunton Riv. & on both sides of Willey's Cr., Beg. at Cargill's Ford and at his Corner Linn Tree, down Difficult Cr.; 12 Feb 1742/43, p.198. £1.S10.

SIMON BUSBY, 262 acs. Pr. Geo. Co. on the upper side of Wigg Island & [Wigg Island] Br., down the dividing Br., adj. Chichester Sturdivant; 12 Feb 1742/43, p.199. £1.S10.

JAMES BROOKS, 200 acs. Is. of Wight Co. on the N side of Meherin Riv., Beg. in Brooks Br., up the Sweat house Sw.; 12 Feb 1742/43, p.201. £1.

WILLIAM WALLER, 317 acs. Orange Co. on both sides of the Marsh Run, near the Road, by a Vally on flatt Ground & by a small Vally, adj. Mr Hancock Lee & Eusebius Stone; 12 Feb 1742/43, p.203. £1.S10.

JACOB MICHAUX, 1,200 acs. Goochland Co. on both sides of Bad Luck Br. of Appamatox Riv., crossing Long Br., adj. Joseph Woodson; 12 Feb 1742/43, p.205. £6.

JACOB MICHAUX, 800 acs. Goochland Co. on both sides of the West Run of Crooms Quarter Br. of the S side of Willis's Riv.; adj. James Cunningham & James Bolling, William Cox & Robert Bernard; 12 Feb 1742/43, p.206. £2. 400 acs. part formerly Gtd. sd Jacob Michaux by Pat. 30 Oct 1736 [PB 17 p.191] & the Residue never before Gtd.

THOMAS ROSE, 430 acs. Surry Co. on the S side of the main black Water Sw., Beg. on the NW side of the Majors Br.; adj. Howell Briggs, Capt. John Mason, James Jones & Nicholas Jarrett; 30 Mar 1743, p.209. £1.S10. 130 acs. part formerly Gtd. to William Rose by Pat. 9 Jul 1724 [PB 12 p.100] And by the sd William Rose sold and Conveyed to the sd Thomas Rose by Deeds recorded in Surry Co. Court 16 Jun 1731 And the residue never before Gtd.

THOMAS WILLIAMS of Pr. Geo. Co., 350 acs. Pr. Geo. Co. on both sides of Black Water Sw., Beg. in Possum Fork of the long Br. on the N side of sd Sw., down the Fox Br., adj. Butler; 30 Mar 1743, p.211. for 2 lbs. of Tobacco for every Acre of the sd Land. Whereas by Inquisition Indented taken in sd Co. 12 Nov 1734 by Virtue of a Warrant directed to Robert Munford Gent. our Escheator for the sd Co. It appears that John Heath of sd Co. died seised of 350 acs. which is found to Escheat to us from the sd John Heath and Whereas Thomas Williams of sd Co. hath made humble Suit and hath obtained a G. for the same.

BENJAMIN HARRISON, Gent. of Charles City Co., 342 acs. in Brunswick Co. on the S side of the Great Cr., on a Path, adj. his own Line; 30 Mar 1743, p.212. £1.S15.

WILLIAM MAYO, Gent., 800 acs. Goochland Co. on the Brs. of Rock Fish Riv. near the Blue Mountains, adj. Edwin Hickman & James Hendrick; 30 Mar 1743, p.214. £2. 400 acs. part formerly Gtd. sd Mayo by Pat. 11 Sep 1738 [12 Sep 1738, PB 18 p.113], the residue never before Gtd.

MICHAEL HOLLAND, Gent., 400 acs. Hanover Co. on both sides of Cuffy's Cr., on a br. of Bunches Cr., in a Valley, adj. John Dowell; 30 Mar 1743, p.216. £2.

WILLIAM GRAY, Gent., 3,000 acs. Goochland Co. near Appamatox Mountain, crossing several Brs. of Appamatox Riv., adj. sd Gray; 30 Mar 1743, p.218. £15.

JOHN LIDDERDALE, Gent., 864 acs. Brunswick Co. on the N side of Maherrin Riv., down Flatt Rock Cr., up Beaverpond Cr., adj. David Bray & Buller Herbert; 30 Mar 1743, p.221. [David Bray's Corner marked by a large "D" with a "B" inside] The following caveat was included in the Patent indicating that the land was free & surveyed before 1728: *"Whereas our Royal Father of Blessed Memory on the humble Petition of the General Assembly of our Colony and Dominion of Virginia was Graciously Pleased to Grant unto each of our Subjects which should go to settle in the County of Brunswick before the first day of May in the Year of our Lord 1728 the Liberty of taking up any Quantity of Land not exceeding 1,000 Acres free and discharged of the Duty of purchasing Rights for the same"*

JOHN LEONARD, 150 acs. Pr. Geo. Co. on the N side of Mitchel's Br. adj. his old Lines &

Christopher Golightly; 30 Mar 1743, p.222. 15 Shill.

MATTHEW EDMOSTON, 200 acs. in that part of Orange Co. designed to be called Augusta on a Br. of Cathys Riv. called Jennings's Br. & Joyning Thomas Gordons Land, in a Draft; 30 Mar 1743, p.224. £1.

JOSEPH EELBECK, 390 acs. Surry Co. on the S side of Nottoway Riv. & on the N side of Andersons Br., in the Flatt Sw.; adj. Robert Tucker & Richard Jones; 30 Mar 1743, p.226. £2.

SAMUEL GRIFFIN, 100 acs. Pr. Geo. Co. bet. Jones Hole Sw. & the Indian Sw., along the County Line [E30°N], up the Trading Br., adj. Thomas Tadlock, near the Cornfield of sd Griffin; 30 Mar 1743, p.228. 10 Shill.

STEPHEN JOHNSON, 400 acs. Goochland Co. on the S side of Rockfish Riv., by the Mouth of a Gut, into the Woods, crossing a Br. & the South Fork of sd Riv.; 30 Mar 1743, p.230. £2.

JOHN IRBY, 251 acs. Brunswick Co. on the S side of Hounds Cr.; 30 Mar 1743, p.232. £1.S5.

EDWARD FINNEY, 204 acs. Amelia Co.on the S side of Whetstone Cr. in the fork of Nottoway Riv. adj. Edward Thweat; 30 Mar 1743, p.233. £1.

ROBERT WALTON, 400 acs. Goochland Co. on both sides of Rock Fish Cr., adj. Thomas Tindal; 30 Mar 1743, p.235. £2.

ROBERT CHRISTIAN, 1,000 acs. Goochland Co. adj. to N side of Fluvanna Riv. against Rack Island & Piney Island; 30 Mar 1743, p.237. £5.

CHRISTOPHER ROBERTSON, 190 acs. Is. of Wight Co. on the S side of Nottoway Riv. & the S side of the Spring Sw., by the side of a Meadow, adj. Thomas Phillips; 30 Mar 1743, p.239. £1.

JOHN DENSON JUNR., 130 acs. Is. of Wight Co. on the S side of the main black Water Sw., Beg. at the Mouth of Barnes's Br. on the S side of Black Cr., down the Great Br., adj. sd Densons other L.; 30 Mar 1743, p.241. 15 Shill.

ROBERT CHRISTIAN, 200 acs. Goochland Co. on the N side of Fluvanna Riv. including Buffello Island in the sd Riv., in a Bottom; 30 Mar 1743, p.242. £1.

JOHN GRIFFIN, 300 acs. Is. of Wight Co. on the S side of the main Black Water Sw., adj. Mr James Allen & Daniel Harris; 30 Mar 1743, p.244. £1.S10.

EDWARD FINNEY, 189 acs. Amelia Co. on the S side of Whetstone Cr. in the Fork of Nottoway Riv., adj. Bolling & Smart; 30 Mar 1743, p.246. £1.

DANIEL ROBERTS, 140 acs. Surry Co. on the S side of Nottoway Riv., down a br. and up the Poplar Sw., adj. Valentine Williamson & George Ezell; 30 Mar 1743, p.248. 15 Shill.

ANTHONY LAVILLAIN, 400 acs. Goochland Co. among the Brs. of Pidy Rock Run of Willis Riv., adj. William Daniel; 30 Mar 1743, p.249. £2.

DANIEL McENERE, 400 acs. in that part of Orange Co. designed to be called Augusta on a Br. of James Riv. called Burdens Cr., on a Ridge; 30 Mar 1743, p.251. £2.

OBADIAH WOODSON, 400 acs. Amelia Co. on both sides of a Great Br. on lower side of Buffillo Riv.; 30 Mar 1743, p.253. £2. [The survey in this Patent is included in Joseph Morton's 800 acs. in PB 22 p.579 dated 20 Sep 1745 which is a duplicate of sd Woodson's 800 acs. in PB 24 p.460 dated 25 Sep 1746]

OBADIAH WOODSON, 378 acs. Brunswick Co. on both sides Buffillo Cr.; 30 Mar 1743, p.254. £2. [The survey in this Patent is included in sd Woodson's 1,250 acs. in PB 31 p.105 dated 9 Jun 1752]

WILLIAM ANDREWS, 125 acs. Surry Co. on the S side of Nottoway Riv. & on the S side of the Hunting Quarter Sw., adj. Colo. Benjamin Harrison & his own old Lines; 30 Mar 1743, p.256. 15 Shill.

LAWRENCE BARKER, 174 acs. Brunswick Co. on the S side of Staunton Riv. & on both sides of Buffillo Cr.; 30 Mar 1743, p.258. £1.

JOHN SOUTHERN, 250 acs. Goochland Co., on Brs. of Bear Garden Cr. a Br. of the Fluvanna Riv., adj. Wintworth Webb; 30 Mar 1743, p.260. £1.S5.

JOHN BRITTLE, 230 acs. Surry Co. on the S side of the main Black Water Sw. & on the S side of Seacawris Sw., adj. Joseph Richardson & Francis Sharp; 30 Mar 1743, p.261. £1.S5.

THOMAS WIGGINS, 200 acs. Is. of Wight Co. on the S side of Nottoway Riv., on the N side of the Reedy Br., adj. John Pittman; 30 Mar 1743, p.263. £1.

JOHN WIGGINS, 150 acs. Is. of Wight Co. on the S side of Nottoway Riv., on the S side of the

Reedy Br., up Gipps Br.; 30 Mar 1743, p.265. 15 Shill.

WILLIAM JONES, 100 acs. Is. of Wight Co. on the S side of Round Hill Sw., adj. his own old Line & Richard Atkinson; 30 Mar 1743, p.267. 10 Shill.

JOHN HILLS, 375 acs. Surry Co. on the S side of Nottoway Riv., on the S side of the Poplar Sw., in the Mouth of the Crooked Br.; 30 Mar 1743, p.268. £2.

THOMAS DOBBINS, 166 acs. Goochland Co. on the Brs. of Rockfish Riv., adj. Colo. Chiswell; 30 Mar 1743, p.270. £1.

DAVID GRIFFITH, 400 acs. Goochland Co. on both sides of the North Br. of Slate Riv. & Meridith's Cr.; 30 Mar 1743, p.272. £2.

SAMUEL SPENCER, 248 acs. Goochland Co., adj. Capt. Howard; 30 Mar 1743, p.274. £1.S5.

ROBERT HOOK, 400 acs. in that part of Orange Co. designed to be called Augusta on a Br. of the South Riv. of Shanando called Mill Cr., adj. Jacob Stover; 30 Jun 1743 *in the 17th Year of our Reign of George the Second*, p.276. £2.

ROBERT GREEN, 400 acs. Orange Co. in the Goard Vine Fork, Beg. at the foot of a Mountain called Greens and Moores Mountain, on the side of a Mountain by a Br. of Black Water Run, in a Poyson Field, on the falling Ground of a Little Mountain by a large Savannah; 30 Jun 1743, p.278. £2.

ROBERT GREEN, 400 acs. Orange Co. in the Goard Vine Fork, Beg. on the side of a Mountain by a Br. of Black Water Run, in 2 Poyson Fields, adj. Daniel Brown; 30 Jun 1743, p.280. £2.

PATRICK HAYS, 297 acs. Orange Co. on the Brs. of James Riv. on the W side the Blue Ridge, on the E side Luneys Mill Cr., to the top of a naked Ridge; 30 Jun 1743, p.282. £1.S10.

CHRISTOPHER ZIMMERMAN, 400 acs. Orange Co. on the W side of the Blue Ridge, along a Ridge, by a Spring; 30 Jun 1743, p.284. £2.

WILLIAM WILLIAMS, 350 acs. in that part of Orange Co. designed to be called Augusta on a Br. of the South Riv. of Shanando called Mill Cr., adj. Jacob Stover; 30 Jun 1743, p.286. £1.S15.

EDWARD ELLIS the Younger, 145 acs. Surry Co. on the S side of Nottoway Riv. & on the S side of the Poplar Sw.; 30 Jun 1743, p.288. 15 Shill.

JAMES ANDERSON, 350 acs. Amelia Co. on the N or lower side of Mallory's Cr.; 30 Jun 1743, p.290. £1.S15.

JOHN STEVENSON, 367 acs. in the Co. of Orange in that part of the sd Co. designed to be called Augusta on a Br. of Stover's Mill Cr., on the N side of a Glade; 30 Jun 1743, p.292. £2.

RICHARD HARRIS & RICHARD WEATHERFORD, 800 acs. Amelia Co. on both sides of Flatt Cr., down the Great fork, adj. Edward Jones, & Watson; 30 Jun 1743, p.294. £4.

EDWARD DANIEL, 400 acs. Goochland Co. on both sides of Neds Cr. a Br. of the Fluvanna; 30 Jun 1743, p.296. £2.

CHARLES ANDERSON, 400 acs. Goochland Co. on both sides of dry Cr. of Appamattox Riv.; 30 Jun 1743, p.298. £2.

WILLIAM CANNON, 245 acs. Goochland Co. on the Brs. of Willis Riv. alias Willis Cr. near Willis's Mountains; 30 Jun 1743, p.300. £1.S5.

ANDREW BOYDE, 240 acs. Orange Co. on the W side of the blue Ridge, Beg. on the E side a Br. of Stoney Cr., 2 Chains from a White Oak by Mr Burdens Road; 30 Jun 1743, p.302. £1.S5.

JAMES GILL, 186 acs. in that part of Orange Co. designed to be called Augusta on a Br. of the North Riv. of Shanando called Wallings Cr., on the top of a Ridge; 30 Jun 1743, p.304. £1.

WILLIAM INNARWICK, 400 acs. Goochland Co. among the S Brs. of Willis's Riv., crossing Crooms Quarter East Br., crossing Buck Br.; adj. James Knot, Samuel Allen & William Cox; 30 Jun 1743, p.306. £2.

JAMES MATTHEWS, 150 acs. Goochland Co. adj. to the N side of Appamattox Riv.; 30 Jun 1743, p.308. 15 Shill.

JAMES SHEPHARD, 400 acs. Goochland Co. on both sides of Hardware Riv.; 30 Jun 1743, p.310. £2.

JOHN WOODSON, Son of Richard Woodson, 400 acs. Goochland Co. below dry Cr. of Appamattox Riv., adj. Colo. Richard Randolph; 30 Jun 1743, p.312. £2.

JOSEPH GRAY, 387 acs. Amelia Co. on the lower side of

Winninghams Cr. of Deep Cr., Beg. on the Beaverpond of sd Cr.; adj. William Dandy, Henry Thweat, James Anderson & John Winningham; 30 Jun 1743, p.314. £2.

ARTHUR WILLIAMS, 365 acs. Is. of Wight Co. on the N side of Nottoway Riv., in a Meadow, adj. George Williams & Capt. William Crumpler; 30 Jun 1743, p.316. £2.

BENJAMIN VASSER, 100 acs. Is. of Wight Co. on the N side of Nottoway Riv., adj. the Nottoway Indians Lines [SxW & SSW], William Arrington & Arthur Arrington; 30 Jun 1743, p.318. 10 Shill.

WILLIAM HOOF, 120 acs. Is. of Wight Co. on the N side of Maherrin Riv., adj. John Reed & Timothy Thorp; 30 Jun 1743, p.320. 15 Shill.

ABRAHAM WHITWORTH, 496 acs. Goochland Co. on both sides of Rock fish Riv., Beg. at a Beech marked "GC AW" on the S side of Rock fish and running into the Woods, by the Mouth of a Gut in sd Riv.; 30 Jun 1743, p.322. £2.S10.

WILLIAM REED, 162 acs. Brunswick Co. on both sides of Fucking Cr., Beg. near the Head of

sd Cr., down the Spring Br.; 30 Jun 1743, p.324. £1.

EDMUND WOOD, 400 acs. Goochland Co. on the S Brs. of Hatchers Cr.; adj. Edmund Wood, George Holmes & Thomas Christian; 30 Jun 1743, p.326. £2.

ROBERT BRYANT, 175 acs. Is. of Wight Co. on the S side of the main Black Water, by the Co. Line [N60°E], by the Cypress Sw., up the Gallberry Sw., adj. Stephen Darden; 30 Jun 1743, p.328. £1.

JOHN RED, 400 acs. Louisa Co. on both sides naked Cr., adj. John Rogers & Majr. Henry; 30 Jun 1743, p.330. £2.

JOHN PATERSON, 400 acs. Goochland Co. adj. to Appamattox Riv., crossing Broad Br., adj. Joel Chandler & Robert Hancock dec'd.; 30 Jun 1743, p.332. £2.

THOMAS RUTHERFORD, 400 acs. in that part of Orange Co. designed to be called Augusta & on the North Riv. of Shanando above the Great Plane [Plain], Beg. near a Point on the side of a Meadow, near the Mouth of a Gully, on the N side the Riv. a little above a Spring Br.; 30 Jun 1743, p.334. £2.

PETER DUPUY, 575 acs. Amelia Co. on both sides of Flatt Cr.; 30 Jun 1743, p.336. £3.

JOHN HOLT, 86 acs. of Marsh L. in Surry Co. on the N side of Gray's Cr. & joining upon his own L., Beg. at his landing Place on the side of Grays Cr., up the Edge of his high Land, down a Gut which divides him from Richard Andrews; 30 Jun 1743, p.338. 10 Shill.

SAMUEL DAVIS, 195 acs. Goochland Co. on both sides of Patrick's Br. of Bellengers Cr. of the N side of the Rivanna Riv., adj. Thomas Harbour; 30 Jun 1743, p.340. £1.

HENRY DAWSON, Son & heir of John Dawson Gent. dec'd., 300 acs. Amelia Co. on both sides of Sandy Cr., adj. Quarles; 30 Jun 1743, p.342. £1.S10.

JOHN CROWDER, 200 acs. Amelia Co. on the lower side of the Sweat House Cr. of deep Cr.; adj. John Olds, Thomas Booth & Dyson; 30 Jun 1743, p.344. £1.

WILLIAM JONES, Son of Thomas Jones, 393 acs. Amelia Co. in the Fork bet. Nottoway Riv. & the Harricane Sw., up the sd Sw. & Long Br., adj. Jennings & John Jones; 30 Jun 1743, p.346. £2.

MATTHEW CABINIS, 400 acs. Amelia Co. on both sides of the Lazaritta Cr.; 30 Jun 1743, p.348. £2. [Included in his 612 acs. in PB 28 p.437]

MICHAEL MACKEY, 350 acs. Brunswick Co. on the S side of the Nap of Reeds Cr., over & up the Great Br., adj. Irby & Mason; 30 Jun 1743, p.350. £1.S15.

PETER HAWTHORNE, 195 acs. Surry Co. on the N side of Nottoway Riv., by the Co. Line that divides Pr. Geo. Co. from Surry Co. [N60°E], adj. John Doby & Colo. Richard Bland; 30 Jun 1743, p.352. £1.

HENRY CHILES, 265 acs. Goochland Co. on both sides of Holladay Riv.; 30 Jun 1743, p.354. £1.S10.

THOMAS LEE, 400 acs. Goochland Co. on both sides of Fishpond Cr. of Appamattox Riv., in Lowgrounds, adj. Henry Chiles; 30 Jun 1743, p.356. £2.

PETER GREGORY, 71 acs. Hanover Co. bet. the lines of Majr. Barkley & Richard Henderson, crossing the Road; 30 Jun 1743, p.358. 10 Shill.

JACOB SHEPHARD, 211 acs. Goochland Co. on both sides of Hardware Riv., crossing Stevens's

Cr., adj. John Stevens; 30 Jun 1743, p.360. £1.S5.

ARTHUR ARINGTON, 300 acs. Is. of Wight Co. on the S side of the main Black Water Sw., along the Broad Water main Road, adj. his own old Lines; 30 Jun 1743, p.362. £1.S10.

GEORGE HOLMES, 290 acs. Goochland Co. on both sides of little Buffaloe Cr. a Br. of Willis Cr.; adj. Thomas Christian, Grizel Coleman, & Henry Cary Gent.; 30 Jun 1743, p.364. £1.S10.

THOMAS HARDEN, 800 acs. Amelia Co. on both sides of Falling Cr. of Buffillo Riv., adj. Randolph; 30 Jun 1743, p.366. £4.

JOHN GAULING, 400 acs. Amelia Co. on both sides of little Buffillo, by the Path; adj. Joseph Morton, Hugh Nickson & John Mullins; 30 Jun 1743, p.368. £2.

THOMAS LOCKETT, 200 acs. Amelia Co. on the N side of the North Fork of Falling Riv., Beg. on the Fork above his House; 30 Jun 1743, p.370. £1. [Included in his, Thomas Lockitt Junr., PB 28 p.167]
CLEMENT READ, 200 acs. Amelia Co. on the lower side of Knibbs Cr. bet. John Nash, Benjamin Ward & Samuel Jones; 30 Jun 1743, p.372. £1.

EDWARD ROBERSON, 383 acs. Amelia Co. on the N side of the Lazaritta Cr. of little Nottoway Riv., Beg. on the Edge of the Sw. of sd Cr.; 30 Jun 1743, p.374. £2.

JAMES OLIVER, 400 acs. Amelia Co. on the N side of Great Nottoway Riv. & on both sides of Snales Cr., adj. George Bagley; 30 Jun 1743, p.376. £2.

RICHARD HENDERSON, 450 acs. Goochland Co. on both sides of Great Guinea Cr., adj. John Brown & William Cook; 30 Jun 1743, p.378. £2.S5.

JOHN MINTER, 400 acs. Goochland Co. on both sides of Croomes Quarter Br. of Willis's Riv. alias Willis's Cr., adj. Paul Micheaux & Captain Robert Barnard; 30 Jun 1743, p.380. £2.

JOSEPH LEWIS, 400 acs. Goochland Co. on the Brs. of the Bird Cr. on the N side of James Riv., on the Hanover Co. Line [S65°E], adj. Majr. John Henry; 30 Jun 1743, p.382. £2.

OBADIAH WOODSON, 400 acs. Goochland Co. on both sides of the lower Fishpond Cr. of Appamatox Riv.; 30 Jun 1743, p.384. £2.

EDWARD DAVISON, 400 acs. Goochland Co. bet. Angolo Cr. & Green Cr., Beg. at a Corner of other Land of the said Moseby on his old Line, adj. Stephen Stone; 30 Jun 1743, p.386. £2.

CHARLES BLANEY, 391 acs. Goochland Co. on the Brs. of the South Fork of Hardware Riv., on the side of a Mountain; adj. Stephen Heard, John Burns & Mr Abraham Venable; 30 Jun 1743, p.388. £2.

PETER BROOKS, 400 acs. Goochland Co. on both sides of Beaverdam Cr. of Willis's Riv.; 30 Jun 1743, p.390. £2. [Included in his 1,737 acs. in PB 26 p.280]

HUGH MORRIS, 200 acs. Goochland Co. on both sides of Hardware Riv., crossing a Neck of Land and the Riv., adj. John Stevens; 30 Jun 1743, p.392. £1.

JOHN WATKINS, 400 acs. Goochland Co. near the lower side of Green Cr. of Appamattox Riv.; adj. Thomas Tabb, Thomas Walker, Joel Chandler & William Randolph Esq.; 30 Jun 1743, p.394. £2.

JAMES BROWN, 400 acs. Goochland Co. bet. Angolo Cr. & Green Cr., adj. William Randolph Esq. & John Pleasants; 30 Jun 1743, p.396. £2.

PETER BROOKS, 392 acs. Goochland Co. on both sides of a Br. of

Appamattox Riv. above the L. of Richard Randolph Gent.; 30 Jun 1743, p.398. £2. [Included in his 1,737 acs. in PB 26 p.280]

JACOB MORRIS, 437 acs. Goochland Co. adj. Thomas Goldsbie & Revd. William Stith; 30 Jun 1743, p.400. £2.S5.

JOHN CHAFIN, 400 acs. Goochland Co. among the N Brs. of Great Guinea Cr., crossing Bostocks Br. & Allen's Br.; adj. James Allen & William Randolph Esq.; 30 Jun 1743, p.402. £2.

WILLIAM HUDSON, 400 acs. Amelia Co. on the N side of Great Nottoway Riv., Beg. on the Riv. just below the Fork, in the Low Grounds; 30 Jun 1743, p.404. £2.

JOHN ELLIS, 1,066 acs. Amelia Co. on both sides of Flatt Cr., down a Br. & up the North Fork; adj. his own old C., Motley, Tanner, John Crawford & John Mayes; 30 Jun 1743, p.406. £4.S10. 166 acs. part formerly Gtd. sd John Ellis [Jr.] by Pat. 10 Sep 1735 [PB 16 p.218] the residue never before Gtd.

ROBERT COLEMAN, 300 acs. Amelia Co. on the upper side of Winticomaick Cr. adj. William Tesdale; 30 Jun 1743, p.408. £1.S10.

JAMES BRUMFIELD, 380 acs. Amelia Co. bet. the Brs. of Saylors Cr. & Brs. of Dawson's Cr. on both sides the road, adj. Dawson & Meadows; 30 Jun 1743, p.410. £2.

JOHN BAGBY, 643 acs. Amelia Co. on the upper side of Mountain Cr., adj. Randolph & Creed Haskins; 30 Jun 1743, p.412. £3.S5.

GEORGE FORD, 200 acs. Amelia Co. on the N side of Mingo's Horsepen Br. of Tommahitton Sw.; 30 Jun 1743, p.414. £1.

JOHN KIRKLAND, 200 acs. Pr. Geo. Co. on the S side of Warwick Sw., adj. Morris; 30 Jun 1743, p.416. £1.

FRANCIS HADDON, 400 acs. Pr. Geo. Co. on both sides of Rowanty Road bet. Gum Br. & Cunney Br., near the Head of Bobbets Br., adj. Butler & Banks; 30 Jun 1743, p.418. £2.

RICHARD NANCE, 184 acs. Pr. Geo. Co. on the S side of Gravilly Run; adj. his own Line, Francis Eppes, Thomas Gent Junr. & Captain Francis Eppes; 30 Jun 1743, p.420. £1.

JAMES RUD, 400 acs. Henrico Co. on the E side of lower Sapony Cr., crossing the main Sapony Cr., adj. John Worsham; 30 Jun 1743, p.422. £2.

MICHAEL GAWIN, 400 acs. Henrico Co. on a Br. of Farras Br., adj. William Harlows first Survey; 30 Jun 1743, p.424. £2.

THOMAS HARLOW, 327 acs. Henrico Co. on the S side of Chickahominy Sw., in Slashey Ground, near a Slash, on the Co. Line dividing Henrico from Goochland Co. [N20°E]; in or near the Head of sd Sw. where the Countys of Henrico Goochland & Hanover join; adj. William Harlow & Simon Ligon; 30 Jun 1743, p.426. £1.S15.

EDWARD HOWELL, 186 acs. in the upper Par. of Nansemond Co., near John Robins's Tar kiln, adj. John Watson, William Speight Junr. & James Watson; 30 Jun 1743, p.428. £1.

WILLIAM BOYT, 261 acs. Nansemond Co., up Keans Br.; adj. John Keaton, Henry Jernagan, Thomas Boyt & George Jernagan; 30 Jun 1743, p.430. £1.S10.

STEPHEN POWELL, 195 acs. Is. of Wight Co. on the N side of Maherrin Riv., down the Horse Meadow Br., adj. Thomas Porter & William Bittle; 30 Jun 1743, p.432. £1.

EDWARD PETTWAY, 350 acs. Brunswick Co. on the N side of Kettle Stick Br., adj. Callaham; 30 Jun 1743, p.434. £1.S15. [On Kettle Stick Br. of Flatt Rock Cr. in Lunenburg Co., not the Kettle Stick Br. of three Creeks in Greensville Co.]

CLEMENT READ, 500 acs. Brunswick Co. on the N side of Waqua bet. Blaikley/Blaikly & White; 30 Jun 1743, p.436. £2.S10.

WILLIAM DUGLAS, 100 acs. Brunswick Co. on the N side of Fucking Cr.; 30 Jun 1743, p.438. 10 Shill.

WILLIAM BEVERLEY, Gent:, 10,000 acs. Orange Co. on the Great Riv. of the Calf Pasture on W side thereof, on the side of a Mountain, on the Spur of a Mountain, on [3] Ridges, on a Mountain, in the Low Grounds, crossing several Brs. which go into Buffillo Gap; 30 Aug 1743, p.440. *for divers good Causes and Considerations but more especially for the Consideration Expressed in an Order of our Lieutenant Governor and Commander in Chief of our Colony and Dominion of Virginia in Council obtained by James Patton & John Lewis the 27th day of April 1742.*

WILLIAM BEVERLEY, Gent:, 700 acs. in that part of Orange Co. designed to be called Augusta on the head of the Great Riv. of the Calf Pasture, by the side of a Gut, adj. John Preston; 30 Aug 1743, p.443. *for divers good Causes and Considerations but more especially for the Consideration Expressed in an Order of our Lieutenant Governor and Commander in Chief of our Colony and Dominion of Virginia in Council obtained by James Patton & John Lewis the 27th day of April 1742.*

WILLIAM BEVERLEY Gent:, 1,200 acs. Orange Co. on a Br. of the Calf Pasture Riv. called Elk Br., Beg. on the W side of the sd Elk Run, on a Point, by a Path; 30 Aug 1743, p.446. *for divers good Causes and Considerations but more especially for the Consideration Expressed in an Order of our Lieutenant Governor and Commander in Chief of our Colony and Dominion of Virginia in Council obtained by James Patton & John Lewis the 27th day of April 1742.*

JOSEPH BLANKENSHIP, 112 acs. Henrico Co., adj. William Voden & Francis Man; 30 Aug 1743, p.448. 15 Shill.

JAMES CATHIE, 1,350 acs. Orange Co. on the W side the Blue Ridge on Shanandore Riv.; adj.

John Givings, John Ker & sd Cathie; 30 Aug 1743, p.451. £6.S15.

RICHARD ROWELL, 500 acs. Brunswick Co. on the S side of the Rockey Run, down Quarrel Sw. & up Rattle Snake Cr., adj. Walton; 30 Aug 1743, p.453. £2.S10.

GEORGE SIMS, 404 acs. Brunswick Co. on the S side of Cold Water Run, adj. Harrison; 30 Aug 1743, p.456. £2.

ROBERT HOOK, 150 acs. in that part of Orange Co. designed to be called Augusta on a Br. of the South Riv. of Shanando called Mill Cr., adj. Stover; 30 Aug 1743, p.458. 15 Shill.

Capt. WILLIAM ALLEN, Gent., 1,185 acs. Goochland Co. on both sides of the Great Cr. of Slate Riv.; 30 Aug 1743, p.460. £4. 400 acs. part formerly Gtd. sd William Allen by Pat. 13 May 1735 [PB 15 p.490] & 785 acs. the residue never before Gtd.

JOHN BURROUGH, 250 acs. Pr. Geo. Co. on the Head Brs. of Harry's Sw.; adj. Thomas Wilkinson & Joseph Tucker; 30 Aug 1743, p.463. £1.S5.

WILLIAM HATCHER, 1,834 acs. Henrico Co., up Reedy Br., by Grills's Path, in the Head of a Br. of Ligons Br., up Proctor's Cr.; adj. John Farmer, Robert Ealom, Thomas Farmer, Stephen Beasley, Tanner, Worsham, the sd Hatcher, Thomas Frankling, & [the land] formerly Grills alias Eppes; 30 Aug 1743, p.466. £9.S5.

LAWRENCE HOUSE, 195 acs. Brunswick Co. on the E side of Miles Cr.; 30 Aug 1743, p.469. £1.

JOHN SMYTH, 337 acs. Brunswick Co. on the N side of Wards Fork; 30 Aug 1743, p.472. £1.S15.

DAVID HARRIS, 203 acs. Brunswick Co. on the N side of Staunton Riv. opposite the Long Island, adj. Marshall; 30 Aug 1743; p.474. £1.

HENRY REYNOLDS, 300 acs. Brunswick Co. on the N side of Staunton Riv.; 30 Aug 1743, p.476. £1.S10.

WILLIAM LUCAS, 275 acs. Brunswick Co. at the head of a Pine Meadow, adj. William Lucas, John Day & Stith; 30 Aug 1743, p.478. £1.S10.

HUGH REECE, 323 acs. Pr. Geo. Co. on the Lower side of Cooks Br., adj. Mrs Wyatt on Cooks Br. at the Falls thereof & Woodlief; 30 Aug 1743, p.481. £1.S15.

JOHN ROYALL, 1,000 acs. Henrico Co. on a Stoney Hill; adj. William Rowlett, Eppes, sd Royall's other Survey, Anderson & Irby; 30 Aug 1743, p.483. £5.

CHARLES FEATHERSTONE, 247 acs. Henrico Co. on the S side of Middle Creek road; adj. Richard Wood, Joseph Redd, Eppes & Owen; 30 Aug 1743, p.486. £1.S5.

NEWET DREW, 197 acs. Brunswick Co. on the N side of Miles's Cr.; 30 Aug 1743, p.488. £1.

SAMUEL GIVINGS, 311 acs. Orange Co. on the W side the Blue Ridge on Shanandore Riv., adj. John Givings; 30 Aug 1743, p.490. £1.S15.

JAMES GIVINGS, 311 acs. Orange Co. on the W side the Blue Ridge on Shanandore Riv., adj. David Longan; 30 Aug 1743, p.492. £1.S15.

JOHN GIVINGS, 311 acs. Orange Co. on the W side of the Blue Ridge on Shanandore Riv.; 30 Aug 1743, p.494. £1.S15.

WILLIAM GIVINGS & SARAH GIVINGS, 311 acs. Orange Co. on the W side the Blue Ridge on Shanandore Riv., adj. James Givings and Samuel Givings; 30 Aug 1743, p.496. £1.S15.

JOSEPH PHILLIPS, 176 acs. in that part of Orange Co. designed to be called Augusta on the N side of the South Br. of Sharando Riv.; 30 Aug 1743, p.499. £1.

PETER BAUGH, 368½ acs. Henrico Co. down the S side of Deep Cr., adj. John Russel & John Pride; 30 Aug 1743, p.501. £2.

RICHARD STOCKTON, 400 acs. Goochland Co. on both sides Stocktons Cr., adj. Joel [Terril]; 30 Aug 1743, p.503. £2.

DAVID PATERSON, 1,600 acs. Goochland Co. adj. to the N side of Appamattox Riv. on the Head Brs. of Elk Island Cr. & Bridle Cr. of the Fluvanna, crossing Stoney Cr.; 30 Aug 1743, p.506. £8.

JOHN JEFFERIES, 70 acs. Surry Co. on the S side of Black Water Sw., along the Birchen Island Road [N38°E]; adj. his own Line & Richard Fitzpatric; 30 Aug 1743, p.508. 10 Shill.

WILLIAM ROGERS, 400 acs. Surry Co. on the S side of Black Water Sw., on the SE side of the Cappahonk Sw., by the College Lines [S34°E & S55°W], up a br. of Enock Sw., adj. Capt. Henry Browne; 30 Aug 1743, p.510. £1. 220 acs. part formerly Gtd. sd William Rogers [Jr.] by Pat. 16 Jun

1714 [PB 10 p.142] and 180 acs. the residue never before Gtd.

THOMAS DOUGHORTY, 192 acs. Hanover Co. on both sides Moreman's Riv., at Rough Run, adj. Major Henry; 30 Aug 1743, p.513. £1.

HENRY COPLAND, 323 acs. in the upper Par. of Nansemond Co. on the S side of Back Sw.; adj. Thomas Boyts Senr. dec'd., Henry Copland, George Keen & John Ralls; 30 Aug 1743, p.515. £1.S15.

WILLIAM STAYTON, 147 acs. Caroline Co.; adj. Samuel Coleman, Colo. Beverley, Mr Baylor, Mr Buckner & Thomas Samuel; 30 Aug 1743, p.518. 15 Shill.

HENRY BARTLETT, 68 acs. Caroline Co. in the Par. of St. Margaret, on the N side the Road; adj. John Ellis, Martin, Samuel & Bibb; 30 Aug 1743, p.520. 10 Shill.

JOHN JOHNSON JUNR., 230 acs. Surry Co. on the S side of Nottoway Riv., on the E side of a Small Br. of the Otterdam Sw., a little below a main road, adj. Lawrence/Laurence House; 30 Aug 1743, p.522. £1.S5.

ROWLAND WARD, 554 acs. Amelia Co. on both sides of Talley's Horsepen Br.; adj. Thomas Jones, Joseph Wilkinson & Joseph Ward; 30 Aug. 1743, p.524. £2.S15.

RICHARD FLETCHER, 271 acs. Amelia Co. on the lower side of Woody Cr. of Deep Cr. & on both sides the road, Beg. on Woody Cr. below the Bridge; adj. Heath & Gray, John West & John Mayes; 30 Aug 1743, p.527. £1.S10.

ARTHUR WHITEHEAD, 85 acs. Is. of Wight Co. on the N side of Maherrin Riv., on the S side of the little Sw., adj. James Moniham & Matthew Strickling; 30 Aug 1743, p.529. 10 Shill.

HENRY BEST, 150 acs. Is. of Wight Co. on the S side of Nottoway Riv., on the N side of Cyprus Sw.; Arthur Whitehead & William Turner; 30 Aug 1743, p.531. 15 Shill.

JOHN ROBERTSON, 300 acs. Is. of Wight Co. on the S side of Nottoway Riv. & the S side of Spring Sw., by the side of a Slash, adj. Christopher Robertson; 30 Aug 1743, p.533. £1.S10.

ANDREW McCONNALD, 400 acs. in that part of Orange Co. designed to be called Augusta, on a Br. of the South Riv. of Shanando called Mill Cr., near a Spring Br., adj. Robert Hook & William Williams; 30 Aug 1743, p.535. £2.

FRANCIS MACCUNE, 360 acs. in that part of Orange Co. designed to be called Augusta on a Br. of James Riv. called Tees Cr.; 30 Aug 1743, p.537. £2.

FRANCIS MACCUNE, 368 acs. in that part of Orange Co. designed to be called Augusta on a Br. of James Riv. Known by the Name of Tees Cr., adj. Benjamin Burden; 30 Aug 1743, p.539. £2.

WILLIAM SKILLIRN, 343 acs. in that part of Orange Co. designed to be called Augusta on the Head of a Draft of Linwells Cr. & on both sides of the Irish Road, on the E side of Daniel Harrison's Path, on the Top of a Ridge; 30 Aug 1743, p.542. £1.S15.

EDWARD WINDOM, 200 acs. Is. of Wight Co. on the S side of the main Black Water Sw., down the S side of the Lightwood Sw.; 30 Aug 1743, p.544. £1.

ROBERT BRYANT, 100 acs. Is. of Wight Co. on the S side of the main Black Water, by the side of the. Cedar Sw., by the County Line [S60°W]; adj. William Bryant & sd Robert Bryant; 30 Aug 1743,p.546. 10 Shill.

THOMAS CHILDREY, 388 acs. Amelia Co. on both sides of Bryer Riv., beg. on sd Riv. below Morton's marked Path to Williamson's; 30 Aug 1743, p.548. £2.

THOMAS WATKINS JUNR., the younger, 400 acs. Amelia Co. on both sides of Bush Riv.; 30 Aug 1743, p.550. £2. [Included in his 1,200 acs. in PB 28 p.255]

JAMES GIBSON, 40½ acs. Middlesex Co., up the Green Br., on the main Road; adj. Mr Augustine Smith, Colo. Churchill, Mr Christopher Robinson, Gabriel Ray dec'd. & Colo. Grymes; 30 Aug 1743, p.553. 5 Shill.

THOMAS ATKINS, 95 acs. Surry Co. on the S side of the main Black Water Sw., on the SW side of the Reedy Br.; adj. Capt. John Mason, Amos Horton & Jehu Barker; 30 Aug 1743, p.555. 10 Shill.

WILLIAM BAKER, Gent., 314 acs. Nansemond Co. in *Wianoak Neck*, on the N side of Summerton Cr., up the deep Br., through the Horsepen Pocoson, adj. his own L.; 30 Aug 1743, p.557. £1.S15.

JOSEPH GRAY, 220 acs. Is. of Wight Co. on the N side of the Lightwood Sw., down Tarraroe Br., by the Cabin Br. & down Piney Br.; adj. his own old Lines,

William Baley & John Drew; 30 Aug 1743, p.560. £1.S5.

WILLIAM RUSSELL, 468 acs. Pr. Geo. Co. on the N side of the Second Sw. including his old L., up sd Mitchels Br.; adj. Peter Mitchel & Mountcastle; 30 Aug 1745, p.563. £2. 95 acs. part sold & Conveyed unto sd Russell by Peter Mitchel now dec'd. [PB 18 p.51, 150 acs. 20 July 1738] & the residue thereof never before Gtd.

THOMAS RICHARDSON, 354 acs. Henrico Co. on the Beaver Ponds of Swift Cr., adj. Robert Hudson, Ashurst, & Thomas Gilson; 30 Aug 1743, p.565. £1.S15.

STEPHEN DARDEN, 304 acs. Nansemond Co. on the W side of Blackwater Riv. & N side of Cedar Sw., up the Indian Br. & the Fox Trap Br., near the Co. Line; adj. Robert Darden, Jacob Darden, the sd Stephen Darden, James Garner & John Lawrence; 30 Aug 1743, p.568. £1.S10.

NICHOLAS COBB, 500 acs. Is. of Wight Co. on the N side of Nottoway Riv., by the Cedar Sw., down the Gum Pole Br.; adj. William Bryant, James Gardner, Solomon Williams & the sd Cobbs own line; 30 Aug 1743, p.571. £2.S10.

SAMUEL PINCHAM, 900 acs. Amelia Co. on the heads of Knibbs Cr. & the dividing Br.; adj. Anderson, Stoker, Henry Walthall, Roberts & his old L.; 30 Aug 1743, p.574. £2.S10. 400 acs. part formerly Gtd. sd Samuel Pincham by Pat. 28 Sep 1732 [Pr. Geo. Co., PB 14 p.492] & 500 acs. the residue never before Gtd.

LEWIS DELONY the Elder, 7,197 acs. Brunswick Co. on both sides of Flatt Rock Cr. & on the N side of Allens Cr.; adj. Harwell & Stewart; 31 Oct 1743, p.577. £32.S5. 790 acs. part formerly Gtd. Thomas Cock by Pat. 28 Sep 1728 [Thomas Cocke, PB 13 p.347], the residue never before Gtd.

Hon. PHILIP LIGHTFOOT Esq., 6,588 acs. Brunswick Co. on the N side of Meharin Riv., up the Rockey Run, on the Road, adj. Benjamin Harrison; 25 Nov 1743. p.580. £9.S10. 4,245 acs. part formerly Gtd. Nathaniel Harrison Esq. Dec'd. by Pat. 23 Oct 1724 [Surry Co., E of the Sappone Indian Land in PB 12 p.111] and be him devised to his Son Nathaniel Harrison Gent.; 100 acs. other part also Gtd. sd Nathaniel Harrison Esq. dec'd. by Pat. 7 Jul 1726 [PB 12 p.509] & from him the same descended to the sd Nathaniel Harrison as his Heir at Law; 371 acs. other part formerly Gtd.

William Kimball by Pat. 17 Mar 1736/37 [PB 17 p.288] & by him sold & conveyed unto sd Nathaniel Harrison the Son by whom all of the sd 3 last mentioned Tracts were sold & conveyed to the sd Philip Lightfoot & the Residue never before Gtd. [This land extends West of the 4,245 acs. part & includes part of the Fort Christanna Indian Tract].

EDMUND WALLER, 552 acs. Spotsyl. Co. & Parish of St. George, near the Head of a Glade, on a Ridge on the E side of Bushe's Mill Path, on a level; adj. Mr Griffin Fantleroy, George Cook, Joseph Robert & John Chew; 25 Nov 1743, p.584. £2.S15.

WILLIAM PARKER, 150 acs. Goochland Co. adj. to Appamattox Riv. against the Mouth of Rough Cr.; 25 Nov 1743, p.587. 15 Shill.

JOHN WADE, 300 acs. Goochland Co. on the Brs. of Rock Fish Riv., adj. John Read & William Mayo; 25 Nov 1743, p.589. £1.S10.

JOHN FRANCIS, 400 acs. in that part of Orange Co. designed to be called Augusta on a Draft of the North Riv. of Shanando called the long Glade, Beg. at a great Stone; 25 Nov 1743, p.591. £2.

JOHN YOUNGE, 400 acs. in that part of Orange Co. designed to be called Augusta on North Draft of Cathays Riv. below Moffets Bottom; 25 Nov 1743, p.593. £2.

TSCHARNER DEGRAFFEN-REIDT, Son & Heir of Christopher Degraffenreidt Dec'd, 404 acs. Brunswick Co. on the S side of the North fork of Swiss Cr.; 25 Nov 1743, p.596. £2. Whereas by Pat. 13 Oct 1736 Gtd. Richard Leadbetter [PB 17 p.190] And Whereas the sd Leadbetter hath failed to make Cultiv. & Improv. and Christopher Degraffenreidt hath made humble Suit and obtained a G. for the same and is since dead.

JOEL WATKINS, 150 acs. Goochland Co. adj. to Appamattox Riv.; 25 Nov 1743, p.599. 15 Shill.

WILLIAM BELCHER, 336 acs. Henrico Co. on the S side of the Locust Br., up a small Br. parting Dyer & John Gibbs; adj. John Gill, Thomas Man, Frank, & John Bevel; 25 Nov 1743, p.601. £1.S15.

THOMAS RICHARDSON, 60 acs. Goochland Co. above Fine Cr., in a Meadow, adj. John Pleasant; 25 Nov 1743, p.605. 10 Shill.

JAMES ARNOLD, 250 acs. Brunswick Co. on the W side of

Mountain Cr.; 25 Nov 1743, p.609. £1.S5.

GEORGE ANDERSON, 200 acs. in that part of Orange Co. designed to be called Augusta on a Br. of Catheys Riv. called Jennings's Br.; 25 Nov 1743, p.613. £1.

METCALF DICKINSON, 249 acs. Brunswick Co. on the N side of Cedar Cr., Beg. a little below the upper beaver Pond; 25 Nov 1743, p.616. £1.S5.

EDWARD THWEAT, 835 acs. Amelia Co. on the N side of Great Nottoway Riv. & on both sides of the Horsepen Cr.; adj. Richard Nance, Ellis, Munford, Laughlan Flyn & Abraham Cock; 25 Nov 1743, p.619. £4.S5.

EDWARD THWEAT, 1,200 acs. Amelia Co. on both sides of the Falls Br. of Great Nottoway Riv.; adj. Munford, Bolling, Evans & Dewey; 25 Nov 1743, p.624. £6.

WILLIAM WATSON, 1,500 acs. Amelia Co. on both sides of Mallorys Cr., crossing the Brs. of Flatt Cr., adj. James Anderson & Peter Jones; 25 Nov 1743, p.628. £7.S10. [1,150 acs. part included in his 1,500 acs. in PB 28 p.257]

JOHN BIARD, 400 acs. Brunswick Co. on both sides of a Br. of

Falling Riv.; 25 Nov 1743, p.634. £2.

WILLIAM COX, 850 acs. Louisa Co. on both sides Lynches Riv. at the foot of the Great Mountains, along the [Orange] County Line [S65°E], adj. Camm; 25 Nov 1743, p.638. £2.S5. 400 acs. part formerly Gtd. sd William Cox by Pat. 12 Mar 1739/40 [Hanover Co., PB 18 p.542] & 459 acs. the residue never before Gtd.

HENRY BLACKGRAVE, 1,200 acs. Louisa Co. on the Brs. of the North Fork of James Riv. at the foot of the Great Mountains; on the side of a Mountain, the Spur of a Mountain & a Spur of Lick Mountain; adj. Mr James Cox, Thomas Hackett, John Hackett & Thomas Collins; 25 Nov 1743, p.643. £6. [Included in Samuel Garlick's 2,400 acs. in PB 28 p.23]

JOHN LEWIS, 425 acs. Goochland Co., adj. Thomas Stone & Thomas Goldbie; 25 Nov 1743, p.648. £2.S5.

JOHN LEWIS, 380 acs. Goochland Co., in a Glade, adj. John Scott & Micajah Clark; 25 Nov 1743, p.653. £2.

WILLIAM MATLOCK, 400 acs. Goochland Co. on the N side of the Fluvanna Riv., down the S side Hardware Riv.; adj. Thomas

Tindall, William Chamberlayne & Hugh Morris; 25 Nov 1743, p.658. £2.

EDWARD HUGHLAND, 132 acs. Brunswick Co. on both sides of Avents Cr.; 25 Nov 1743, p.664. 15 Shill.

WILLIAM ATKEYSON, 304 acs. Brunswick Co. on both sides of Stoney Cr.; 25 Nov 1743, p.666. £1.S10.

Colo. SAMUEL COBBS Gent., 396 acs. Brunswick Co. on the N side of Wards Fork, adj. John Austine & Hurt; 25 Nov 1743 *In the 17th Year of our Reign of George the Second, William Gooch Esq. our Lieutenant Governor and Commander in Chief of our said Colony and Dominion at Williamsburgh*, p.670-674. £2.

Feb.16.1743
Then Settled with Mr. Waller the Accot. of Rights from page 441 in another Book [PB 20] the former Settlement Feb.17.1742. to page 643. in Same Book Ending with Leander Hughes's patent [PB 23 p.642-643 dated 25 Nov 1743] and from page 138. of this Book to this place, amounting in both to 3246. Rights as Pt Acct. thereof, wch. were immediatly burnt
John Blair D.Audr.

[Due to the lengthy Patents, 2 volumes were needed - PB 20 (p.1-p.566) & PB 23 (p.567-p.1147]

PATENT BOOK NO. 22

Mar 1743/44 to 20 Mar 1745/46

STEPHEN DEWEY Gent., 588 acs. Brunswick Co. on the S side of Nottoway Riv., on Evans's Path, adj. Stokes; 1 Mar 1743/44 *in the 17th year of our Reign of George the Second, by William Gooch Esq. our Lieutenant Governor and Commander in Chief*, p.1. £1.S15. 264 acs. part formerly Gtd. sd Stephen Dewey by Pat. 20 Aug 1740 [PB 19 p.759 a regrant of Henry Morris's PB 14 p.86] & the residue never before gtd.

STEPHEN DEWEY Gent., 704 acs. Brunswick Co. on both sides of Roses Cr., on Maclins Road & up the main Road, adj. Ravenscroft & Harrison; 1 Mar 1743/44, p.2. £3.S10.

GEORGE CARRINGTON, 5,650 acs. Goochland Co. on both sides of Willis's Riv. alias Willis's Cr.; crossing Bostons Br., Snow Quarter Br., Cat Tail Br., Taylors Cr. & Mill Br.; adj. Colo. Benjamin Harrison, Joseph Price, Samuel Glover & William Cannon; 1 Mar 1743/44, p.4. £14. 2,850 acs. part formerly gtd. William Mayo Gent. by Pat. 25 Aug 1731 [PB 14 p.274 on S side of James Riv., by the Long Falls] and since conveyed by sd William Mayo to sd George Carrington & 2,800 acs. the Residue never before Gtd.

JOHN LIDDERDALE, 296 acs. Brunswick Co. on the S side of Crooked Cr.; 1 Mar 1743/44, p.6. £1.S10.

Capt. JAMES NEVIL Gent., 1,850 acs. Goochland Co. on both sides of Watkins's Cr. of Fluvanna Riv. and Hoopers Cr. of James Riv.; adj. Joseph Hooper, Philip Mayo, James Nevil, James Daniel & Richard Taylor; 1 Mar 1743/44, p.8. £9.S5.

WILLIAM COX, 380 acs. Goochland Co. on both sides of Crooms Quarter Br. of Willis's

Riv. alias Willis Cr., adj. James Bolling; 1 Mar 1743/43, p.10. £2.

WILLIAM SHARPE, 372 acs. Henrico Co. by a Br. of deep Cr.; adj. John Russell, John Moore & Thomas Cheatham; 1 Mar 1743/44, p.11. £2.

BOLLING CLARK, 400 acs. Goochland Co. on Totier Brs., adj. Major Bolling & Charles Lynch; 1 Mar 1743/44, p.13. £2.

DAVID LAWSON, 150 acs. Goochland Co. adj. to the W side of little Byrd Cr., adj. Jonas Lawson & John Cole dec'd; 1 Mar 1743/44, p.15. 15 Shill.

PHILIP MAYO, 4,300 acs. Goochland Co. on the S side of James Riv. and upper side of Willis's Riv. alias Willis's Cr., crossing Mill Cr.; adj. James Nevel, Joseph Hooper, George Carrington & James Skelton, Gent.; 1 Mar 1743/44, p.16. £16.S10 600 acs. part formerly gtd. Joseph Mayo Gent. dec'd by Pat. 5 Sep 1723 [300 acs. Henrico Co. in PB 11 p.238 & another 300 acs., same Co. & page]; 400 acs. other part also gtd. sd Joseph Mayo by Pat. 26 Jun 1731 [PB 14 p.175] & the Residue never before Gtd.

WILLIAM TOWNES, 748 acs. Amelia Co. on the S side of Appamatox Riv. & on both sides of

Woods Cr.; adj. Randolph, Osburn & his own old Line; 1 Mar 1743/44, p.19. £2. 348 acs. part formerly Gtd. sd William Townes by Pat. 10 Jan 1735/36 [William Towns, PB 16 p.526] & 400 acs. the Residue never before Gtd.

CHARLES RICHEY, 1,352 acs. Amelia Co. on both sides of the South Fork of Buffilo Riv., Beg. at his first Survey at an old Horse Pen, adj. John Bibb; 1 Mar 1743/44, p.20. £6.S15.

JOHN TULEY, 250 acs. Goochland Co. on both sides of Totier Cr., adj. Edward Scott; 1 Mar 1743/44, p.23. £1.S5.

WILLIAM MATLOCK, 400 acs. Goochland Co. among the Brs. of the Byrd Cr., adj. John Cole dec'd. & Thomas Massie dec'd.; 1 Mar 1743/44, p.25. £2.

JOHN CANNON, 300 acs. Goochland Co. on both sides of Randolphs Cr. of Willis's Riv., adj. Thomas Edwards; 1 Mar 1743/44, p.26. £1.S10.

JAMES McDUELL, 150 acs. Pr. Geo. Co. on the N side of Warwick Sw.; adj. Mitchel, Samuel Temple & Golightley; 1 Mar 1743/44, p.28. 15 Shill.

DAVID WILLIS, 290 acs. Goochland Co. among Brs. of

Tuckahoe Cr., down Broad Br.; adj. John Evans, George Payne, John Woodson, Philip Webber, George Thompson & Stephen Woodson; 1 Mar 1743/44, p.30. £1.S10.

JOHN MORRIS, 200 acs. Amelia Co. on the S side of Appamatox Riv. & on both sides the upper Fork of Cowskin Br. joining Wards and Dawsons Lines; 1 Mar 1743/44, p.31. £1.

CASTLETON HARPER, 254 acs. Goochland Co. on the upper side of Epps's Cr., at the Mouth of Beaverdam Sw., adj. James Lee & Epps; 1 Mar 1743/44, p.33. £1.S5.

SAMUEL HOMES, 101 acs. Brunswick Co. on both sides of Allens Cr.; 1 Mar 1743/44, p.35. 10 Shill.

WILLIAM ALDRIDGE, 400 acs. Pr. Geo. Co. on the N side of Warwick Sw. & on both sides of Peter Leaths Path, Beg. above his clearing thence to a Corner fenced Inwards, adj. Francis Pattyson & Wallice; 1 Mar 1743/44, p.37. £2.

ANDREW MOOREMAN, 190 acs. Brunswick Co. on both sides of Stoney Cr., Beg. on the W side sd Cr. above his Mill Dam, up the great Br., by a Point of Rocks, by a Path; 1 Mar 1743/44, p.39. £1.

JONATHAN WOODSON, 280 acs. Goochland Co., in a Spring thence down the Br. & into the Woods, adj. Capt. Hudson; 1 Mar 1743/44, p.40. £1.S10.

SAMUEL ARNOLD, 200 acs. Goochland Co. on Brs. of Ivy Cr., on the sides of (2) Mountains, adj. Capt. Hudson; 1 Mar 1743/44, p.42. £1.

THOMAS BUTLER, 300 acs. Pr. Geo. Co. on the N side of Rowanty Sw., down the Gum Br.; adj. his Father William Butler & Francis Haddon; 1 Mar 1743/44, p.44. £1.S10.

CHRISTOPHER IRVIN, 223 acs. Brunswick Co. on both sides of flatt Cr. joining James Johnson's upper Line; 1 Mar 1743/44, p.46. £1.S5.

JOHN FOLKS, 314 acs. Henrico Co., down the Horsepen Br., to a Pignut Hiccory Tree, adj. Thomas Cheatham & Curtis Keats; 1 Mar 1743/44, p.48. £1.S15.

BRAZURE COCKE, 400 acs. Goochland Co. on both sides of Green Cr. of Appamatox Riv., on the E side of the Road; adj. William Randolph Esq., John Cook & Joseph Woodson; 1 Mar 1743/44, p.50. £2.

SAMUEL ALLEN, 400 acs. Goochland Co. on the East Br. of Crooms Quarter Br. of Willis Riv., adj. to other Lands of sd Samuel Allen; 11 May 1744 *in 17th year of our Reign of George the Second,* p.52. £2.

NICHOLAS DAVIES, Gent., 154 acs. Goochland Co. on the S side of the Fluvanna, Beg. at his own C. on the River Bank, into the Woods, to Battery Cr.; 16 Jun 1744 *in the 18th year of our Reign of George the Second,* p.53. 15 Shill.

NICHOLAS DAVIES, Gent. 245 acs. Goochland Co. on the S side of the Fluvanna, Beg. on the Riv., to Tuckahoe Cr., at a small Cr. & a Ridge; 16 Jun 1744, p.55. £1.S5.

ABRAHAM VENABLE, 225 acs. Goochland Co. among the brs. of the Byrd Cr., adj. sd Abraham Venable & John Anthony; 16 Jun 1744, p.56. £1.S5.

EDWARD LUNDY, 135 acs. Is. of Wight Co. on the N side of Meherin Riv.; adj. William Lee, Henry Adams & William Beech; 16 Jun 1744, p.58. 15 Shill.

MATTHEW WHISELL, 295 acs. Brunswick Co. on the S side of the South Fork of Allen's Cr., adj.

Thomerson; 16 Jun 1744, p.59. £1.S10.

JOHN PRICE, Son of Daniel, 196 acs. Henrico Co., down a Br. known by the Name of Johns Br., up Jordans Br., to the House Mr Price now lives in; adj. Honorable William Byrd Esq., Obadiah Smith & John Price Senior; 16 Jun 1744, p.61. £1.

JAMES ALLEN, 4,400 acs. Goochland Co. on both sides of Great Guinea Cr. of Appamatox Riv., crossing Bostocks Br. & the Brs. of Lickinghole Run; adj. his former Ptd. L., James Terry; 16 Jun 1744, p.63. £2. 4,000 acs. part formerly Gtd. sd James Allen by Pat. 8 Sep 1736 [PB 17 p.179] & 400 acs. the Residue never before Gtd.

JOSIAH HATCHER, 398 acs. Henrico Co. in the Lowgrounds of Nisons Br.; adj. the upper Survey, John Burton, James Hill & Peter Hudson; 26 Jun 1744, p.65. £2.

DANIEL PRICE JUNR., 174 acs. Henrico Co. on the S side of the main Run of Chicahominy Sw., through the Sunken Grounds, in Reedy Br., adj. Pleasant Cock & Thomas Watkins; 16 Jun 1744, p.67. £1.

JOSHUA PERRY, 200 acs. Is. of Wight Co. on the N side of

Meherin Riv., down the S side of flat Sw.; adj. Jacob Harris, Thomas Smith & Thomas Carter; 16 Jun 1744, p.68. £1.

WILLIAM BLANKENSHIP, 400 acs. Henrico Co. crossing Wintipock Cr.; adj. Thomas Jones, Robert Cole & Jonathan Cheatham; 16 Jun 1744, p.70. £2.

JAMES EDWARDS, 340 acs. Is. of Wight Co. on the N side of Nottoway Riv.; adj. William Pope, Solomon Williams, John Johnson, his own old Line & Richard Williams; 16 Jun 1744, p.72. £1.S15.

WILLIAM BAYLEY, 400 acs. Goochland Co. on both sides of the South Br. of Cary Cr. of the N side of the Rivanna Riv., on a Drain of Crooks Cr.; 16 Jun 1744, p.73. £2.

WILLIAM CROSS, 176 acs. Amelia Co. on the N side of Great Nottoway Riv., up Bear Br., adj. Abraham Cock; 16 Jun 1744, p.75. £1.

JOHN AUSTIN, 203 acs. Brunswick Co. on the N side of Wards Fork, adj. Martin; 16 Jun 1744, p.77. £1.

JOHN HOGSHEAD, 285 acs. in that part Orange Co. designed to be called Augusta on Br. of Catheys Riv. called Moffetts Br., Beg. on a Spur of the Short Mountain; 16 Jun 1744, p.78. £1.S10.

WILLIAM GUNN, 125 acs. Brunswick Co. on the S side of Roanoak Riv.; 16 Jun 1744, p.80. 15 Shill.

JAMES ANDERSON, 120 acs. in that part of Orange Co. designed to be called Augusta on North Br. of the North Riv. of Shanando called Woods Cr.; 16 Jun 1744, p.81. 15 Shill.

WILLIAM GENT, 258 acs. Brunswick Co. on the N side of Dan Riv. on both sides of Horseford Cr.; 16 Jun 1744, p.83. £1.S10.

THOMAS ADKINS, 400 acs. Brunswick Co. on the N side of flatt Rock Cr. below Isaac Masons L.; 16 Jun 1744, p.84. £2.

CORNELIUS MORLEY, 400 acs. in that part of Orange Co. designed to be called Augusta on the North Fork of the North Riv. of Shanando above the Gap in the Mountains, Beg. on the N side of the Road; 16 Jun 1744, p.86. £2.

WILLIAM PARKER, 390 acs. Henrico Co. on the W side of Cornelius's Cr., crossing the Great Br., adj. Mr Peter Randolph; 16 Jun 1744, p.87. £2.

MICAJAH CLARK, 400 acs. Goochland Co. on both sides of Machunk Cr. of the N side of the Rivanna Riv.; adj. the L. lately surveyed for Robert Adams, & Benjamin Wheeler; 16 Jun 1744, p.89. £2.

JOHN SMITH, 190 acs. Brunswick Co. on the N side of Fountains Cr., along the Road & his Line; 16 Jun 1744, p.91. £1.

WILLUTT ROBERTS, 239 acs. Amelia Co. on the upper side of Woody Cr. of Deep Cr.; adj. David Ellington, Benjamin Heath, Richard Fletcher & William Dendy; 16 Jun 1744, p.93. £1.S5.

GOWER PARRUM, 400 acs. Amelia Co. bet. the main deep Cr. & the Sellar Fork thereof, adj. John Wallers and William Edmonds's Surveys; 16 Jun 1744, p.94. £2.

WILLIAM WALL, 223 acs. Brunswick Co. on the S side of Waqua Cr., adj. Semore & Wynfield; 16 Jun 1744, p.96. £1.S5.

HUGH LAWSON, 250 acs. Brunswick Co. on the S side of little Hounds Cr., on a Br. of Great Hounds Cr.; 16 Jun 1744, p.98. £1.S5.

JOHN HENRY, 250 acs. Goochland Co. adj. to the E side of Hardware Riv. near the Mouth of the same, adj. William Cannon; 16 Jun 1744, p.99. £1.S5.

JOHN GRESHAM, 162 acs. Goochland Co. among the N Brs. of Willis Riv., adj. James Robinson & Henry Cary Gent:; 16 Jun 1744, p.101. £1.

WILLIAM POPE, 200 acs. Is. of Wight Co. on the S side of Nottoway Riv., by the Nottoway Indians Line [SE]; 16 Jun 1744, p.102. £1.

ROBERT MORRIS, 112 acs. Henrico Co. in Slashey Ground; adj. Robert Webb, sd Robert Morris & Michael Holland; 16 Jun 1744, p.104. 15 Shill.

JAMES ADAMS, 400 acs. Goochland Co. above Machunk Cr. of the N side of the Rivanna. Riv., adj. Robert Adams; 16 Jun 1744, p.105. £2.

JOHN BRYANT, 115 acs. Is. of Wight Co. on the S side of the main black Water, adj. Bridgman Joiner & sd Bryants own old Line; 16 Jun 1744 p.107. 15 Shill.

ROBERT MONGER, 200 acs. Is. of Wight Co. on the S side of Round Hill Sw.; adj. his own old Line, William Jones & John Dunkley; 16 Jun 1744, p.108. £1.

PETER GUERRANT, 400 acs. Goochland Co. on both sides of Hunts Cr. a Br. of Slate Riv.; 16 Jun 1744, p.110. £2.

BENJAMIN WITT, 200 acs. Goochland Co. on both sides of Hunts Cr. a Br. of Slate Riv., adj. Peter Chastain; 16 Jul 1744, p.111. £1.

VALENTINE WHITE, 155 acs. Is. of Wight Co. on the N side of Maherin Riv., by the flatt Sw., down the Pasture Br., adj. his own old Lines; 16 Jun 1744, p.113. £1.

JOSEPH JACKSON, 400 acs. Goochland Co. on the Brs. of Hardware Riv.; 16 Jun 1744, p.114. £2.

HENRY ADAMS, 375 acs. Is. of Wight Co. on the N side Maherin Riv., by the side of a main Road; adj. Harmon Reed, Edward Lunday, his own old Line & William Beech; 16 Jun 1744, p.115. £2.

LEONARD BALLOWE, 100 acs. Goochland Co. on the S side the Fluvanna, down the Riv., adj. his own Line & Captain Howard; 16 Jun 1744, p.117. 10 Shill.

ROBERT ADAMS, 400 acs. Goochland Co. on both sides of Machunk Cr. of the N side of the Rivanna Riv., adj. his old Line; 16 Jun 1744, p.119. £2.

CHRISTOPHER WADE, 200 acs. Is. of Wight Co. on the S side of black Cr., adj. William Joiner & Eely Eely; 16 Jun 1744, p.120. £1.

WILLIAM MALON, 180 acs. Brunswick Co. on the S side of Maherin Riv.; adj. William Pennington, Edward Ezeld, John Ezeld & Dispane; 16 Jun 1744, p.122. £1.

HENRY POPE, 295 acs. Is. of Wight Co. on the S side of Nottoway Riv. & on the N side of Tockwothunty Sw., by the Nottoway Indians Line [NW]; adj. his own old Lines, Raman Ennis & William Pope; 16 Jun 1744, p.123. £1.S10.

WILLIAM PURDUE, 240 acs. Henrico Co. on the E side of Sappony Cr.; adj. Richard Wood, Walthall, Daniel Brown & Tanner; 16 Jun 1744, p.125. £1.S5.

ANTHONY BENNING, 325 acs. Goochland Co. on the Brs. of Hatchers Cr., adj. Dudley Digges Gent:, Henry Cary Gent: & Edward Kelley; 16 Jun 1744, p.127. £1.S15.

WILLIAM TABOR, 800 acs. Goochland Co. among the Brs. of

Deep Cr., on the W side of a Meadow; adj. William Bradshew, the sd William Tabor, William May, Matthew Herbert & John Robinson; 16 Jun 1744, p.129. £2. 400 acs. part formerly Gtd. sd William Tabor by Pat. 9 Jul 1737 [PB 17 p.368, 369 or 370] & 400 acs. the Residue never before Gtd.

EDWARD COBB, 295 acs. Is. of Wight Co. on the N side of Nottoway Riv., by the Cyprus Sw., adj. John Barnes & John Turner; 16 Jun 1744, p.130. £1.S10.

Colo. RICHARD BLAND Gent., 532 acs. Surry Co. on the N side of the three Creeks, Beg. at the Mouth of the Gum Br., down Odiams Br., adj. George Hamilton & Richard Hay; 30 Aug 1744, p.132. £1. 92 acs. part formerly Gtd. William Moore by Pat. 23 Mar 1715/16 [William More in PB 10 p.277] & 240 acs. other part formerly Gtd. sd Richard Bland by Pat. 17 Sep 1731 [PB 14 p.365] & the Residue never before Gtd. [p.133 numbered as p.132a]

Colo. RICHARD BLAND Gent., 420 acs. Surry & Is. of Wight Countys on the S side of the three Creeks that is to say 130 acs. part thereof in Surry Co. & the Residue in Is. of Wight Co., beg. in a small Br., by the County Line [N60°E], by the Edge of the Low Grounds of the sd Creeks; adj. Samuel

Alsobrook, John Nanny, Edward Lundy & Timothy Tharp; 30 Aug 1744, p.134. £2.S5. [Both of Bland's above Patents included in his PB 28 p.273 & David Mason's PB 34 p.781]

ROBERT ESTES, 1,300 acs. Louisa Co. on both sides Cabin Br., in the Head of a Glade, adj. Richard Estes; 30 Aug 1744, p.136. £5. 300 acs. part formerly Gtd. sd Robert Estes by Pat. 25 Aug 1731 [PB 14 p.229, 400 acs. Hanover Co. on head brs. of North East Cr.] & the Residue never before gtd.

JOHN GRAVES, 400 acs. Spotsyl. Co. at the Head of a Valley near the new Mine bank Road, on a Point, on the lower side a Glade; adj. John Collins, John Fieldour, Mr Griffin Fantleroy, George Musick & Nichols Randall; 30 Aug 1744, p.138. £2.

JOHN HANBERRY, 20 acs. Norfolk Co., adj. Captain Willis Wilsons former Survey; 30 Aug 1744, p.140. 5 Shill.

WILLIAM HUFF, 140 acs. Brunswick Co. on the S side of the Lizard, adj. John Linch & William Moseley; 30 Aug 1744, p.142. 15 Shill.

THOMAS EGLETON, 200 acs. Pr. Geo. Co. on both sides of the

Heads of Warwick Sw., by Rowanty Road Side, adj. Thomas Leath & John Kirkland; 30 Aug 1744, p.143. £1. [Included in his PB 25 p.344]

RICHARD DAMRIL, 200 acs. Goochland Co., Beg. at a White Oak marked *BW* standing on the N side of Hardwar Riv., adj. James Shepard; 30 Aug 1744, p.145. £1. [BW possibly Benjamin Woodson's mark]

ADAM SIMS, 200 acs. Brunswick Co. on the N side of Meherrin Riv., on the new Road; adj. John Ledbetter, Chamberlayne & his own Line; 30 Aug 1744, p.147. £1.

JOSEPH CLARK, 400 acs. Louisa Co. on the Brs. of Fork Cr., adj. Colonel Symes & Francis Clark; 30 Aug 1744, p.149. £2.

JAMES VAULTON, 396 acs. Henrico Co. on the E side a Br. of Tomahauk, on a Stoney Hill, adj. James Hill, in the Line formerly Tullits now Carys; 30 Aug 1744, p.151. £2.

WILLIAM WEST, 50 acs. Is. of Wight Co. on the N side of Seacock Sw.; adj. Benjamin Williamson, Abraham Stephenson & his own old Lines; 30 Aug 1744, p.153. 5 Shill.

HENRY BARLOW, Clerk, 600 acs. of Marsh Land in Pr. Anne Co. bet. the back Bay and Corratuck Bay, Beg. at a Point of Marsh upon the back Bay, by the natural Bounds of a Cr. which divides this Survey from a former Survey of the sd Barlow, to a long Point of Marsh which makes into sd Corratuck Bay, to the Easternmost End of the sd Marsh; 30 Aug 1744, p.155. £3.

JOSEPH WALKER, 487 acs. Hanover Co. on the S side of Owens Cr., on the Goochland Co. Line [S20°W], by the Goochland Road in the Co. Line; adj. Robert Deprest, Thomas Paulet & Mr Webb; 30 Aug 1744, p.156. £2.S10.

CHARLES HOLSWORTH, 308 acs. Henrico Co., up Brs. of Nisons Br.; adj. John Welches Surveys, Friend, Wooldridge & James Hill; 30 Aug 1744, p.158. £1.S15.

ABRAHAM MICHAUX, 400 acs. Brunswick Co. on the N side of Meherrin Riv. & on both sides of Tossekiah; 30 Aug 1744, p.160. £2.

ABRAHAM MICHAUX, 400 acs. Brunswick Co. on the N side of Maherrin Riv. & on both sides of Couches Cr., down the Meadow

Cr., adj. Rivers; 30 Aug 1744, p.162. £2.

JOHN JONES, 190 acs. Surry Co. on the S side of Harrys Sw., on Ducking Fields Br., on the broad Reedy Br., down the Reedy Br., adj. Thomas Jones (of Hardword); 30 Aug 1744, p.163. £1. [Hardword refers to the Hardwood Sw. or Run now in Sussex Co. & Dinwiddie Co.]

JOHN FARMER, 196 acs. Henrico Co.; adj. Robert Ealom, John Hatcher, sd Farmers former Survey & William Adkins; 30 Aug 1744 p.165. £1.

JOSEPH BRADSHEIRE, 80 acs. Is. of Wight Co. on the S side of the main black Water Sw., on the N side of the North Prong of black Cr., in a small Br.; adj. Robert Monger Junr. & Richard Nash; 30 Aug 1744, p.167. 10 Shill.

WILLIAM WATSON, 3,385 acs. Amelia Co. on both sides of the Sweathouse Cr. of Deep Cr., in the Head of a Br. of Nammisseen Cr., on the lower side of the Road, near Dendys Path; adj. Colemans old Line, Abraham Jones & Thomas Booth; 16 Jun 1744, p.169. £15.S15. 235 acs. part formerly Gtd. William Coleman by Pat. 28 Sep 1730 [PB 13 p.530, Pr. Geo. Co. above sd Coleman's Cabin] & the Residue never before Gtd.

PATRICK OBRIAN, 400 acs. Goochland Co. on both sides of Philips Br. of Hatchers Cr., adj. Henry Cary Gent: & Thomas Christian; 30 Aug 1744, p.171. £2.

JOHN BLACKWELL, 297 acs. Brunswick Co. on the S side of Nottoway Riv., at Mouth of the lick Br., down a br. to James Matthews Line where it crosses wild Cat; adj. Brown & James Matthews; 30 Aug 1744, p.173. £1.S10.

JOHN WILLIAMS, 360 acs. Henrico Co. on the S side of the North Br. of White Oak Sw., by a Slash; adj. John Hopson, Edmond Allen & Nicholas Hopson; 30 Aug 1744, p.175. £2.

WILLIAM PARKER, 168 acs. Brunswick Co. on the N side of Maherrin Riv., adj. Munford & John Hix; 30 Aug 1744, p.177. £1.

ROBERT ROSE, Clk., 23,700 acs. Goochland Co. on both sides of Tye Riv. & Piny Riv., in the Low Ground, on the Spur of a Mountain, in an Ivy Thicket; adj. John Carter Esq., Charles Lewis & James Churchil; 30 Aug 1744, p.179. £118.S10.

ROBERT ROSE, Clerk, 9,600 acs. Goochland Co. on both sides little

Pedler alias Harris Cr., on the side of Stoney Ridge & other Ridges, on the Spur of Tobacco Row Mountain, adj. John Rucker; 30 Aug 1744, p.182.

THOMAS TADLOCK, 100 acs. Pr. Geo. Co. on the S side of Jones Hole Sw., up the Trading Br., adj. Tatum, by Samuel Griffins Fence; 30 Aug 1744, p.185. 10 Shill.

WILLIAM TESDALE, 780 acs. Amelia Co. on both sides of Winticomaick Cr.; adj. Parish alias Tallys, Stradford, Fitzgerald, Hamlin, Tally, Perdue & his own old Line; 30 Aug 1744, p.186. £2. 400 acs. part formerly gtd. sd William Tesdale by Pat. 9 Jul 1737 [PB 17 p.371] & the Residue never before Gtd.

WILSON CARY, 1,906 acs. Gloucester Co. on the main Run of the Eastmost Head Br. of Poropotanke Riv., into Purton Road, with the windings of Turks Ferry Road, from the main Road to Turks Ferry, along Pates Sw.; adj. Colo. Grymes, Mr John Royston & Mr James Dudley; 30 Aug 1744, p.188. £4. 1,141 acs. part formerly Gtd. Wingfield Webb and Richard Pate Gent: by Pat. 12 Dec 1650 [PB 2 p.271 on N side of Yorke Riv.] & by divers mesne Conveyances the Right & Title thereof is become vested in the sd Wilson Cary and the Residue never before Gtd..

JOHN WARBERTON, Gent., 275 acs. Surry Co. on the S side black Water Sw., by the Colledge Lines & his own Lines formerly William Andrew's, adj. Benjamin Ellis's; 30 Aug 1744, p.191. £1. 100 acs. part formerly Gtd. William Andrews by Pat. 20 Feb. 1723/24 [PB 11 p.311 on N side of Cappahonk Sw.] & the Residue never before Gtd.

ROBERT MASON & NATHANIEL SENACA, 123 acs. of Swamp Land in Pr. Ann Co. near Nannys Cr.; adj. sd Mason, Richard Lester, William Cornix, sd Senaca & Oakham; 30 Aug 1744, p.193. 15 Shill.

JAMES MOORE, RICHARD BRENSON & WILLIAM CARRILL, 187 acs. of Swamp Land in Pr. Ann Co., adj. Boneys Survey & sd Moore; 30 Aug 1744, p.195. £1.

JOSIAH MORRIS, 300 acs. of Swamp Land in Pr. Ann Co. near Nannys Cr.; adj. Perry, Lester, Oakham, John Berrys Pat. Line & sd Josiah Morris's former Survey; 30 Aug 1744, p.197. £1.S10.

Colo. WILLIAM WOODFORD Gent., 36 acs. Caroline Co., adj.

Abraham Moon, Moss & Wiackley; 30 Aug 1744, p.199. 5 Shill.

THOMAS BAKER, 516 acs. Brunswick Co. on the S side of a Great Br. of Butchers Cr.; 30 Aug 1744, p.200. £2.S15.

CHARLES HEARD, 225 acs. Goochland Co. on the Brs. of Hardware Riv., adj. Mildred Meriwether & Howard Cash; 30 Aug 1744, p.202. £1.S5.

THEOPHILUS FIELD, 120 acs. Brunswick Co. on the S side of Nottoway Riv.; adj. Richard Vaughn, Field, John Wall, Irby & Richard Burch; 30 Aug 1744, p.204. 15 Shill.

Thus far Settled Feb. 12. 1744/45. as in the other Book folo. 795 [PB 23] John Blair, D.Audr.

Capt. WILLIAM RUSSELL, Gent:, 400 acs. Orange Co. in the Fork of James Riv., Beg. on the N side sd Riv. 15 Mar 1744/45, p.206. for 5 Shill. and in consideration of the *Importations* of 7 Persons to dwell within this our Colony and Dominion whose Names are *Thomas Geering, Cavan Dulany, William Smith, Francis Attwood, James Bowie, John Young & Patrick Barclay.*

ROBERT CRAVEN, 400 acs. in that part of Orange Co. designed to be called Augusta on the Head of the dry Fork of Smiths Cr., on the W side of the Irish Road; 15 Mar 1744/45, p.207. £2.

ROBERT CRAVEN, 400 acs. in that part of Orange Co. designed to be called Augusta on a North Br. of the North Riv. of Shanando called Cooks Cr. in the East Fork of the sd Cr.; 15 Mar 1744/45, p.209. £2.

JOHN RODE, 400 acs. in that part of Orange Co. designed to be called Augusta, Beg. in the Fork of Shanadore; 15 Mar 1744/45, p.210. £2.

WILLIAM MOORE, 275 acs. Orange Co. on the Brs. of James Riv. on the W side of the Blue Ridge, adj. John Scott; 15 Mar 1744/45, p.212. £1.S10.

THOMAS HARRISON, 233 acs. in that part of Orange Co. designed to be called Augusta on the East Fork of Cooks Cr., at the upper end of a Meadow, on a Ridge, adj. Thomas Harrison; 15 Mar 1744/45, p.213. £1.S5.

ZACHARY TAYLOR, 1,000 acs. Orange Co. on the N side of the Northanna, on a Ridge, in the Head of a Valley; 15 Mar 1744/45, p.215. £5. Whereas by Pat. 14 Sep 1728 Gtd. Robert Ballard [PB 13 p.338], formerly in Spotsyl. Co.

now Orange, And Whereas the sd Ballard hath failed to make Cultiv. & Improv. and Zachary Taylor hath made humble Suit and obtained a G. for the same.

THOMAS HARRISON, 258 acs. in that part of Orange Co. designed to be called Augusta on the head Spring of the East Fork of Cooks Cr., in a Glade; 15 Mar 1744/45, p.217. £1.S10.

SAMUEL RIDGWAY, 400 acs. Goochland Co. on both sides of Beaver Dam Cr. of Willis's Riv.; 15 Mar 1744/45, p.218. £2.

LEONARD HENLEY, 30 acs. Goochland Co. on Brs. of Tuckahoe Cr., on Henrico Co. Line [N20°E], adj. John Martin & Richard Wade; 15 Mar 1744/45, p.220. 5 Shill.

JOHN RODE, 400 acs. in that part of Orange Co. designed to be called Augusta, Beg. near the Foot of the Piked Mountain in the Fork of Shanadore; 15 Mar 1744/45, p.221. £2.

EDMOND ALLEN, 400 acs. Henrico Co.; adj. Joseph Watson, Valentine Freeman, Woodsons old Survey & sd Allens other Survey; 15 Mar 1744/45, p.223. £2.

JOHN MICHAEL BROCK, 400 acs. in that part of Orange Co.

designed to be called Augusta on the South Fork of the North Riv. of Shanando above the Gap in the Mountain; 15 Mar 1744/45, p.224. £2.

VALENTINE MARTIN, 400 acs. Goochland Co. on both sides of the Cat Tail Br. of Willis's Riv.; adj. Joseph Price, Samuel Glover & John Thompson; 15 Mar 1744/45, p.225. £2.

JOHN SANDERS, 368 acs. Goochland Co. on both sides of Willis Riv. Southward of the Mountain; 15 Mar 1744, p.227. £2.

CHARLES LYNCH, 850 acs. Goochland Co. on both sides the South Fork of Hardware Riv.; 15 Mar 1744/45, p.228. £4.S5.

EDMOND ALLEN, 400 acs. Henrico Co. on both sides of the North Br. of White Oak Sw., near a Slash, down and through a Br. or Great Slash of White Oak Sw.; adj. John Hopson, Joseph Watson & sd Allens former Survey; 15 Mar 1744/45, p.230. £2.

STEPHEN BEDFORD, 329 acs. Brunswick Co. on the upper side of Twittys Cr., adj. his own Lines; 15 Mar 1744/45, p.231. £1.S15.

AARON HASKINS, 342 acs. Henrico Co. on Beaver Pond Br.;

adj. Benjamin Cheatham, James Gates, Moseley, & William Gates; 15 Mar 1744/45, p.233. £1.S15.

LEONARD TERRENCE VICUS, 374 acs. Louisa Co. on the N side of the North Fork of the North Fork of James Riv. & on both sides of Red Bud Br.; adj. Nicholas Meriwether, Captain Clark & Richard Hammock; 15 Mar 1744/45, p.235. £2.

ROBERT GREEN, 400 acs. Orange Co., adj. Francis Thorntons Stirling Tract on Cannons Riv., down the Rush Riv., adj. William Covington & Benjamin Berryman; 15 Mar 1744/45, p.236. Whereas by Pat. 7 Jul 1735 Gtd. Thomas Monroe [PB 16 p.17] And Whereas the sd Monroe hath failed to make Cultiv. and Improv. and Robert Green hath made humble Suit and obtained a G. for the same.

ROBERT GREEN, 1,700 acs. in that part of Orange Co. designed to be called Augusta on the Brs. Muddy Cr. at the Foot of the North Mountain, up the dry Riv., on a Spur of the Mountain; 15 Mar 1744/45, p.239. 400 acs. part formerly gtd. sd Robert Green by Pat. 22 Sep 1739 [PB 18 p.364]; 400 acs. formerly gtd. Charles Robinson 22 Sep 1739 [PB 18 p.381]; 400 acs. formerly gtd. Terence Kelley 22 Sep 1739 [PB 18 p.379], 300 acs. formerly gtd. sd

Robert Green 20 Aug 1740 [PB 19 p.713]; 200 acs. the Residue never before gtd.

JOHN OWEN, 328 acs. Amelia Co. on the lower side of Flatt Cr. bet. lines of Ralph Jackson, John Hill, Edward Hill & John Elam; Beg. at Ralph Jacksons upper C. upon the Cr. opposite to Richard Jones; 15 Mar 1744/45, p.240. £1.S15.

DAVID MITCHEL, 260 acs. in that part of Orange Co. designed to be called Augusta on both sides of Cataubo Cr.; 15 Mar 1744/45, p.241. £1.S10.

DAVID MITCHEL, 220 acs. in that part of Orange Co. designed to be called Augusta on a Br. of James River called Percimon Br., adj. Joseph Lapsley; 15 Mar 1744/45, p.242. £1.S5.

DAVID MITCHEL, 220 acs. in that part of Orange Co. designed to be called Augusta on a Br. of James Riv. known by the Name of Percimmon Br., adj. Joseph Lapsley; 15 Mar 1744/45, p.244. £1.S5.

HUGH MOORE, 400 acs. Goochland Co. on the North Br. of Randolphs Cr. of Willis's Riv., near a small Br.; 15 Mar 1744/45, p.245. £2.

ANDREW REAY, 63 acs. Hanover Co. on both sides of the North Fork of James Riv.; adj. his own Line, John Rogers, Thomas Hatcher, Andrew Reay; 15 Mar 1744/45 *in the 18th Year of our Reign of George the Second*, p.247. 10 Shill.

EDWARD NIX, 2,977 acs. Amelia Co. on the S side of Appamattox Riv., Beg. on the sd Riv. below the Mouth of the Plain Run, up a large Br.; 10 Jul 1745 *in the 19th Year of our Reign of George the Second*, p.248. £15.

WILLIAM ROBERTSON, 613 acs. Henrico Co., crossing a br. of Middle Sappony Cr. & Several Brs. of upper Sappony Cr.; adj. John Rud, Henry Walthall, Daniel Brown & Wilkinson; 10 Jul 1745, p.249a. £1.S5. 400 acs. part formerly Gtd. sd William Robertson by Pat. 17 Mar 1736/37 [William Robinson, PB 17 p.274] & 213 acs. the Residue never before Gtd.

ABRAHAM WOMACK, 403 acs. Amelia Co. on both sides of Saylors Cr., by a Spring, down a fork of sd Cr., adj. Ruffin & Fitzgerald; 10 Jul 1745, p.250-252 [p.251 not used by the Scribe]. £2.

ISHAM EPPES, 1,993 acs. Amelia Co. on the N side of Little Nottoway and on both sides of the Main Seller Fork of Deep Cr., in the Road; adj. Francis Eppes, Thomas Chappel [his new Survey], John Taylor, John Wallice, John Nance & Anderson; along his own old Lines of his Seller Survey; 10 Jul 1745, p.251. £7.S5. 150 acs. part formerly Gtd. the sd Isham Eppes by Pat. 3 Oct 1734 [PB 15 p.345], 400 acs. part formerly Gtd. the sd Isham Eppes by Pat. 21 Nov 1734 [PB 15 p.364] and 1,443 acs. the Residue never before gtd.

FRANCIS BRESSY, 1,087 acs. Pr. Geo. Co. on both sides of the Upper Nottoway Riv. Road bet. Stony Cr. and Gravilly Run and the Heads of the Cattail Run, Beg. at the Main Southern Fork of sd Cattail Run; adj. Captain Francis Eppes and Isham Eppes [their tract of 694 acs.], William Browder [his new and his old Line of his 100 acs.], George Andrew Browder, & Maynard /alias/ Jones Irvins Line; 10 Jul 1745, p.254. £5.S10.

SAMUEL COBBS, Gentleman, 8,038 acs. Amelia Co. on the forks of Buffilo Riv., on the S side of the North fork, along the Lines of the Mountain Survey, below the Mountain, by a Br. of Roanoke, below Bookers Path, down the South Fork, in the Low Grounds; adj. Isham Randolph, Dawson, Cobb, John Bibb & William Kennon; 10 Jul 1745, p.255. £40.S5.

WILLIAM WATSON, 577 acs. Amelia Co. on the lower side of Winticomaick Cr. on both sides of the Road, on Tuckers br. of Nammisseen, by a Spring, above the Bridge; adj. Bolling, Crawley, William Watson, Tucker & Bland; 10 Jul 1745, p.257. £3. [Included in his 619 acs. in PB 28 p.434]

JOHN BIBB, 1,200 acs. Amelia Co. on both sides of the South fork of Buffilo Riv., in a Valley; adj. Kennon now Bakers Line, Samuel Cobb, Woodson, & George Hudson; 10 Jul 1745, p.259. £2. 800 acs. part formerly Gtd. sd John Bibbs by Pat. 12 Sep 1738 [PB 18 p.126] and 400 acs. the Residue never before Gtd.

JOHN KING, 754 acs. Nansemond Co. at a Place called *Kingston*, at the Head of the Meadow br., down the Flatt Sw., up the Run of Summerton Sw., near the main Road, adj. William Coffield; 10 Jul 1745, p.260. £1.S15. 400 acs. being part of a Pat. for 900 acs. formerly gtd. Michael King 24 Feb 1675/76 [PB 6 p.597 in the way to South Key, see PB 25 p.177 to John Folk] the Right and Title of which said 400 acs. by divers Mesne Conveyances is become Vested in the sd John King and 354 acs. the Residue being Surplus L. found within the bounds of the 400 acs. aforesaid.

NATHANIEL WINSTON, 400 acs. Goochland Co. on the Brs. of Totier Cr., adj. Captain Clark and John Scott; 10 Jul 1745, p.261. £2.

SAMUEL RIDGWAY, 1,400 acs. Goochland Co. on both sides of the Mountain Cr. of Willis's Riv. and on Brs. of Barren lick Cr., near the W end of the Rocky Ridge, at the foot of a Hill near a Br. of Great Buffaloe Cr.; adj. Mr Henry Cary, Major John Bolling, Anthony Shereron & John Payn; 10 Jul 1745, p.263. £7.

The Reverend JOHN ORNSBY, Clerk, 384 acs. Pr. Geo. Co. bet. Butterwood and Tommahitton Swamps; adj. William Eaton, Richard Beale & Hugh Kirkland; 10 July 1745, p.264. £2. [Included in his PB 27 p.318]

DANIEL JONES, 231 acs. Pr. Geo. Co. on the N side of Stony Cr., Beg. on the Water Course of the half way Br., near a Pond, on a fork of the flat br.; adj. his old lines, John Avery and Joshua Wynne; 10 Jul 1745, p.265. £1.S5.

JAMES THWEATT, 103 acs. Pr. Geo. Co. on the upper side of Butterwood Sw., near on the lower side of the *Radde*, adj. his own lines and William Coleman; 10 Jul 1745, p.266. 10 Shill.

EDWARD WINFIELD, 220 acs. Pr. Geo. Co. on the N side of Stony Cr., Beg. at the Rooty Miery Br., down Naamans Br.; adj. Thomas Wilkinson, William [Molbek], his own lines, William Malone & Edward Winfield; 10 Jul 1745, p.268. £1.S5.

ANN OVERSTREET, 393 acs. Pr. Geo. Co. on the Brs. of Nammisseen & Mawhipponock Cr.; adj. John Gillum, Hull, & Joseph Glass; 10 Jul 1745, p.269. £2.

LEWIS BURWELL, 4,300 acs. Brunswick Co. on both sides of Butchers Cr. and on the Brs. thereof, up the East fork of Blue Stone Cr., adj. John Ravenscroft & Thomas Ravenscroft; 10 Jul 1745, p.270. £21.S10.

JAMES BROWNE/BROWN, 354 acs. Pr. Geo. Co. on the S side of Moccosneck Cr., in Rives's old Field by the Path; adj. Major James Munford, John Merley & Herbert; 10 Jul 1745, p.271. £1.S15.

FRANCIS MORELAND, 298 acs. Pr. Geo. Co. on both sides of the Reedy Br. and N side of Namans br. of Moccosoneck Cr.; adj. his own Line, James Munford & Edward Winfield; 10 Jul 1745, p.273. £1.S10.

THOMAS BOWS, 600 acs. Goochland Co. adj. to the N side of Appamattox Riv. below Fishpond Cr., adj. John Hodnell; 10 Jul 1745, p.274. £1. 400 acs. part formerly Gtd. sd Thomas Bows by Pat. 11 Sep 1738 [PB 18 p.101] & 200 acs. the Residue never before gtd.

JOSEPH MOTLY, 1,083 acs. Amelia Co. on both sides of Flatt & Little Crs.; adj. Matthew Mayo's old line, Owen, William Mayes, Tanner, John Ellis, William Watson, Matthew Mayes & Clerk; 10 Jul 1745, p.275. £3.S10. 400 acs. part [PB 17 p.33] being part of a Pat. for 1,200 acs. formerly gtd. Matthew Mayes junior by Pat. 15 Mar 1735/36 [PB 17 p.457 dated 2 Jan 1737/38] and by divers Mesne Conveyances is since become Vested in sd Joseph Motly & 683 acs. the Residue never before Gtd. [Included in his, Joseph Motley's, 1,383 acs. in PB 28 p.111]

RICHARD MORTON, 400 acs. Amelia Co. on the lower side of Buffilo Riv. known by the name of *Barren Licks*, by the Path; 10 Jul 1745, p.277. £2.

JOHN MARTIN, 304 acs. Amelia Co. on both sides of Bryer Riv., adj. John Martin; 10 Jul 1745, p.278. £1.S10.

ISAAC MORRIS, 1,254 acs. Amelia Co. on both sides of Neals br. of Flatt Cr., over the Road;

adj. Ruffin, Farley, Hodge, Chappel & William Farly; 10 Jul 1745, p.279. £6.S5.

JOHN SCOTT, 400 acs. Goochland Co. on the Brs. of Totier Cr., Beg. on the S side sd Cr. at a White Oak marked $_s^E$ [for Edward Scott?]; 10 Jul 1745., p.281. £2.

WILLIAM STILL, 430 acs. Goochland Co. on both sides of great Buffilo Cr. a br. of Willis's Riv., adj. Anthony Sherroon & James Terry; 10 Jul 1745, p.282. £2.S5.

JOSEPH WALTON, 400 acs. Goochland Co. on both sides of little Brimmer Cr., crossing both Forks of Brimmer, adj. Benjamin Woodson; 10 Jul 1745, p.283. £2.

MARY WARREN, JANE WARREN, MARTH WARREN & PATIENCE WARREN, 185 acs. Is. of Wight Co. on the S side of the Main Black Water Sw., on the W side of the Horsepen Br.; 10 Jul 1745, p.284. £1. [This land was referred to as Thomas Warren's & Thomas Warren's Orphans' in the adj. Patents]

MICHAEL THOMAS, JUNIOR, 200 acs. Goochland Co. on both sides of Rock fish Riv., Beg. on N side of the sd Riv. bet. the same & a br. Opposite to the lower end of the uppermost of the Swift Island,

running into the Woods, on the S side the Riv. near a great Rock; 10 Jul 1745, p.285. £1.

EBENEZAR ADAMS, Gent., 384 acs. Goochland Co. on the Brs. of the Byrd, crossing Great Cr. of the Byrd; adj. the sd Adams, James Nolin & Arthur Osborne; 10 Jul 1745, p.287. £2.

WILLIAM JONES, 166 acs. Pr. Geo. Co. on the N side of Gravilly Run; adj. his old lines, James Williams, James Jones & Isham Eppes; 10 Jul 1745, p.288. £1.

JOHN BOLLING, Gentleman, 2,980 acs. Albermarle Co. on both sides of the Fluvanna Riv. Including Possum Island Exclusive of the Intermediate Streams of Water therein, Crossing Slipry Gut, on the Riv. Bank below a Cliff of Rocks, at the Mouth of Possum Cr., on a Ridge; 23 Jul 1745, p.289. £1.S5. 600 acs. [PB 21 p.374] 165 acs. [PB 21 p.30] 1,190 acs. [PB 21 p.55] and 780 acs. [PB 20 p.382] part thereof formerly gtd. sd John Bolling by Pat. 30 Jul 1742, and 245 acs. the Residue never before Gtd. [Included in his 3,026½ acs. in PB 26 p.446]

THOMAS NEWSOM, 100 acs. Is. of Wight Co. on the S side of Nottoway Riv., adj. his own old Line; 10 Jul 1745, p.291. 10 Shill.

RICHARD STOCKTON, 400 acs. Goochland Co. on both sides Stocktons Br. of Mechums Riv., adj. Davis Stockton & Charles Lynch; 23 Jul 1745, p.292. £2.

HENRY FREEMAN, 225 acs. Surry Co. on the N side of Nottoway Riv., Beg. at the Mouth of a small Br. on the N side of the Woodyard Sw.; adj. his own old lines, Elizabeth Gawler, William Maloon & Nathaniel Robertson; 10 Jul 1745, p.293. £1.S5.

ARTHUR WILLIAMS, 560 acs. Is. of Wight Co. on the N side of Nottoway Riv., by the Cypress Sw.; adj. Thomas Oberry, Theophilis Joiner, John Barnes & Thomas Drake; 10 Jul 1745, p.295. £3.

JOHN WHEELER, 400 acs. Goochland Co. on the brs. of barren Lick Cr. of Willis's Riv., adj. Henry Cary Gent., John Payne & Samuel Ridgway; 10 Jul 1745, p.296. £2.

JAMES PITTILLO, 600 acs. Pr. Geo. Co. bet. Stony and Moccossneck Creeks below the Main Road, Beg. by small Drain on the lower side of the Main Road, to the Main Road where Kings Path Turns out of the same, by the Ridge Path; adj. Bryan, Herbert, & John Hansel; 10 Jul 1745, p.297. £3.

EDWARD BRITT, 100 acs. Is. of Wight Co. on the S side of the Main black Water Sw., on the S side of Tarapin br.; adj. sd Britt & John Jackson; 10 Jul 1745, p.299. 10 Shill.

THOMAS DELOACH, 250 acs. Is. of Wight Co. on the N side of Nottoway Riv., on the S side of the Lightwood Sw., up the Horsepen br., down Davis's br.; adj. Edward Windham, Robert Booth, the sd Deloach & Leonard Oney; 10 Jul 1745, p.300. £1.S5.

JOHN PERSON, 855 acs. Is. of Wight Co. on the NE side of Maherin Riv., up & crossing the Gum br., in a Pond, up Persons Sw., down the Gum Sw., adj. his own old lines & Allen Howard; 10 Jul 1745, p.301. £2.S15. 76 acs. part formerly gtd. John Person dec'd father of the sd John Person by Pat. 17 Dec 1717 [PB 10 p.343], 132 acs. other Part formerly Gtd. Francis West by Pat. 17 Oct 1717 [PB 10 p.342] and 100 acs. other part being part of a Pat. for 390 acs. formerly gtd. John Gilliam 17 Dec 1717 [John Guillam, PB 10 p.381], the Right and Title of which sd 3 Parcels is become vested in sd John Person, and 547 acs. the Residue never before Gtd. [All 3 sd parcels in PB 10 were part of a tract where the Saponie Indians dwelt before their new Settlement, exchanged for a like quantity at Fort Christanna. The Fort Christanna Tract was a 6-mile square or 23,040 acs. on a N-S axis in Brunswick Co.; while the old Saponie Tract in now Southampton Co. & Greensville Co. was probably on a 45° axis. Both axes were determined by the flow of the Maherin Riv. which ran through each Tract]

HUTCHENS BURTON, 390 acs. Henrico Co., Beg. Standing on the S side of Westham Cr., over Stoney Hill, in the Fork of sd Cr., adj. Mr Randolph; 10 Jul 1745, p.303. £2.

HENRY CRAFFORD, 50 acs. Is. of Wight Co. on the N side of Maherin Riv., in the Country Line, down a small Br. or Swash; 10 Jul 1745, p.304. 5 Shill.

JOHN PHILIPS, 350 acs. Is. of Wight Co. on the S side of Seacock Sw., by the Turraroe Br., in the Wolf Pit Br., over the Run of Blows Br.; adj. sd Philips own old Lines, Thomas Barrow, Henry Coaker, Samuel Cornwall & Richard Blow; 10 Jul 1745, p.305. £1.S15.

JOSEPH PHILIPS, 540 acs. Is. of Wight Co. on the S side of Seacock Sw., on Wolf Pit br., in a Pond; adj. John Gregory, William Cobb, John Philips, Henry Coaker, John Washington & Joseph Philips own

old Lines; 10 Jul 1745, p.307. £2.S15.

JAMES RIDLEY, 820 acs. Is. of Wight Co. on the S side of Nottoway Riv., by Ridleys br., by the West Prong of the fork br., by the North Prong of Ridleys br.; adj. his own old Lines, Timothy Tharp, Edward Harris & Nathaniel Ridley; 10 Jul 1745, p.308. £3. 220 acs. part being part of 815 acs. formerly Gtd. Nathaniel Ridley since dec'd by Pat. 16 Jun 1714 [PB 10 p.152] and by him devised unto sd James Ridley and 600 acs. the Residue never before Gtd.

HENRY TAYLOR, 170 acs. Is. of Wight Co. on the S side of Maherin Riv., adj. Thomas Person & John Hill; 10 Jul 1745, p.310. £1.

JAMES MASSINGALL, 190 acs. Surry Co. on the S side of the main black Water Sw., on the N side of Secawris Sw.; adj. Col. Henry Harrison, the sd Massingall & William Sawry; 10 Jul 1745, p.311. £1.

JOHN RAWLINGS, 170 acs. Surry and Is. of Wight Counties on the N side of the three Creeks, on the S side of the Great Sw., adj. Michael Upchurch, Christopher Golikeley & John Golikeley; 10 Jul 1745, p.312. £1.

THOMAS REECE, 250 acs. Pr. Geo. Co. on the N side of White Oak Sw., by the Road, down the Cabin Br., adj. his own old Lines & his Fathers lines; 10 Jul 1745, p.313. £1.S5.

HUTCHENS BURTON, 191 acs. Henrico Co., crossing Hoggets road, on a br. of Westham; adj. Mr Beverly Randolph, another Survey of sd Burton, William Gordon & the line formerly Jennings's now Randolphs; 10 Jul 1745, p.315. £1.

JOHN ROPER, 1,601 acs. Brunswick Co. on both sides of Bryery Cr.; adj. Richard Hagood, Lanier, Benjamin Williams, Clark, Simmon & Andros; 1 Aug 1745, p.316. £8.

JOSEPH VASSER, 120 acs. Is. of Wight Co. on the N side of Nottoway Riv., adj. Joel Vasser; 1 Aug 1745, p.318. 15 Shill.

ARCHELAUS WEEKS, 450 acs. Is. of Wight Co. on the N side the main Blackwater Sw., on the E side of Kingsale Sw., by the Co. line [S60°W]; adj. Lewis Keel, John Stafford, William Hallowell & William Bryant; 1 Aug 1745, p.319. £2.S5.

EDWARD GREEN, 490 acs. Is. of Wight Co. on the S side of the Main black Water Sw., by the side of the Broad Water Main Road near the head of the Myery Br., adj. Arrington & Edward Green; 1 Aug 1745, p.321. £2.S10.

EDWARD GREEN, 130 acs. Is. of Wight Co. on both sides of Black Cr. on the S side of the Main Black Water Sw., down a small Br., adj. his own old Line; 1 Aug 1745, p.322. 15 Shill.

JOHN GWALTNY, 200 acs. Is. of Wight Co. on the S side of the Flatt Sw. on the S side of Nottoway Riv., in a Meadow; 1 Aug 1745, p.323. £1.

THOMAS NEWSOM, 1,040 acs. Is. of Wight Co. on the S side of Nottoway Riv., on the N side of the three Creeks, up the Hornet Sw., near the Mouth of the Miery Br., over the Run of the Reedy Br.; adj. the sd Newsom, John Holt, William Jelks junior, John Smith, Edward Robertson, Christopher Robertson, William Watkins & the sd Wilkins (sic) line; 1 Aug 1745, p.324. £2. 180 acs. part formerly Gtd. sd Thomas Newsom by Pat. 16 Jun 1714 [PB 10 p.196], 280 acs. other part also formerly Gtd. sd Thomas Newsom by Pat. 28 Sep 1732 [PB 14 p.525], 200 acs. other part formerly Gtd. sd Thomas Newsom by Pat. 16 Sep 1740 [PB 19 p.789] and 380 acs. the residue never before gtd. [plus his 250 acs. in PB 12 p.78]

THOMAS LOYD, JUNIOR, 424 acs. Brunswick Co. on both sides of Butchers Cr., up a great Br.; 1 Aug 1745, p.327. £2.S5.

JOHN MYRICK, 130 acs. Is. of Wight Co. on the S side of Nottoway Riv.; adj. James Sammon, Christopher Foster, Benjamin Cooper & Owin Myrick; 1 Aug 1745, p.328. 15 Shill.

JOSHUA NICHOLSON, 275 acs. Is. of Wight Co. on the S side of the three Creeks, by the North Prong of Ridleys Br.; adj. John Vaughan, James Ridley & James Bennet; 1 Aug 1745, p.329. £1.S10.

JOHN PERSON, 400 acs. Is. of Wight Co. on N side of Maherin Riv., down Powells Br.; adj. Edward Jacquelin, sd Persons own old Lines & Thomas Clark; 1 Aug 1745, p.331. £2.

EDWARD CHITTY, JUNIOR, 295 acs. Is. of Wight Co. on both sides of Rushins Br. on the S side of Nottoway Riv., by the Country Line [West]; 1 Aug 1745, p.333. £1.S10.

JOSEPH JONES, 350 acs. Is. of Wight Co. on the S side of Round Hill Sw., down the Miery Br.; adj.

William Jones, Joseph Bradshaw, William Barrow & Robert Williams; 1 Aug 1745, p.334. £1.S15.

ROBERT HARRIS, 400 acs. Amelia Co. on the S side of the North fork of Falling Cr., adj. Randolph & Harden; 1 Aug 1745, p.335. £2.

JAMES JACKSON, 400 acs. Amelia Co. on N the side of the Hurricane Sw., at the Head of a fork of the upper Rocky Br.; adj. his Father & his Brother William Jackson; 1 Aug 1745, p.337. £2.

WILLIS WILSON, 51 acs. Norfolk Co. in the great dismal Sw. on the S side of the North West Riv. being a Ridge of Land called *Smiths Ridge*; 1 Aug 1745, p.338. 5 Shill.

SAMUEL CARLISLE, 190 acs. Surry Co. on the S side of Nottoway Riv., down Cocke's Br., adj. Gilbert Prince; 1 Aug 1745, p.339. £1.

PETER ROSSER, 100 acs. Pr. Geo. Co. on the N side of Warwick Sw., Beg. at a Ridge bet. his Frame and Gillums Ponds; 1 Aug 1745, p.341. 10 Shill.

JOHN HARDAWAY, 199 acs. Pr. Geo. Co. on the N side of Stoney Cr.; adj. Charles Pistoll, James

Keeth, Hudson, & William Burrows; 1 Aug 1745, p.342. £1.

WILLIAM TUCKER, 300 acs. Amelia Co. on the Lower side of Deep Cr.; adj. William Coleman, Peter Jones, Abraham Jones & Munford; 1 Aug 1745, p.343. £1.S10.

HUGH WILLIAMS, 444 acs. Amelia Co. on the N side of Hurricane Sw., above the Road, adj. Michell; 1 Aug 1745, p.344. £2.S5.

ROBERT HARRIS, 400 acs. Amelia Co. on the S side of Appamattox Riv., adj. Henry Chiles; 1 Aug 1745, p.346. £2.

RICHARD HUBBARD, 400 acs. Amelia Co. on the S side of little Nottoway Riv., down the long Br.; adj. Ellis, George Hubbard, Michel & Binford; 1 Aug 1745, p.347. £2.

WILLIAM WELLS, JUNIOR, 580 acs. Amelia Co. on the N side of Nottoway Riv., adj. Bridgeforth & Burge; 1 Aug 1745, p.349. £3.

THOMAS MARKS, 100 acs. Is. of Wight Co. on the S side of the main Black Water Sw. & the S side of the North Prong of Black Cr., down the Myery Br., adj. John Lucas; 1 Aug 1745, p.350. 10 Shill.

SAMUEL ATKINS, 180 acs. Is. of Wight Co. on the S side of Nottoway Riv. & the E side of the Whitewood Sw., down the Reedy Br., adj. John Rachell; 1 Aug 1745, p.351. £1.

JOHN TOMLINSON, 354 acs. Amelia Co. on the S side of Whetstone Cr. in the fork of Nottoway Riv., down Polecat Br.; adj. Smart, Ellis & Anderson; 1 Aug 1745, p.352. £1.S15.

JACOB MITCHELL, 268 acs. Amelia Co. on the S side of Little Nottoway Riv. bet. Whetstone Cr. and the Long Br., adj. Thomas Anderson & his own old Line; 1 Aug 1745, p.354. £1.S10.

JOHN AVERY, 204 acs. Pr. Geo. Co. on both sides of the heads of the Flat Br. of Stoney Cr., at the Mouth of Averys Br., near a Pond, on a Fork of the Flatt Br., in a Thicket, adj. Joseph Tucker junior; 1 Aug 1745, p.355. £1.

THOMAS SATTERWHITE, 62 acs. Hanover Co. on the Brs. of Chickahominy Sw.; adj. William Hughes, Samuel Morris & John Ellis; 1 Aug 1745, p.356. 10 Shill.

JOHN COSBY, 104 acs. Hanover Co. adj. Francis Smith, Christopher Smith & sd Cosby; 1 Aug 1745, p.357. 10 Shill.

GEORGE HUBARD, 400 acs. Amelia Co. on both sides of Whetstone Cr. in the fork of Nottoway, crossing little Whetstone; adj. Tabb, Michel & Dendy; 1 Aug 1745, p.359. £2.

ANDREW HUNTER, 400 acs. Louisa Co. on both sides of Rocky Cr., near a small Br. of the Byrd Cr.; adj. his own line; 1 Aug 1745, p.360. £2.

ANDREW HUNTER, 400 acs. Louisa Co. on both sides of Fosters Cr. & Forsters Cr.; adj. Captain Hudson & Forest Green; 1 Aug 1745, p.362. £2.

RICHARD BEASLEY/BEASLY, 403 acs. Amelia Co. on the upper or N side of Flatt Cr., by the Path, adj. Watson; 1 Aug 1745, p.363. £2.

PAUL SEARES, 285 acs. Pr. Geo. Co. on N side of Stony Cr. and on the lower side of Flat Br., up the Bryery Br., below Morleys Path; adj. Edward Winfield & sd Paul Seares old Line; 1 Aug 1745, p.365. £1.S10.

GEORGE WYCH, 320 acs. Surry Co. on the N side of Nottoway Riv., to a Bridge on a Br., by the edge & thro' a Cypress Sw., on the upper end of the Horse Island, down Austins Br.; adj. his own lines, Colo. John Allen, Richard

Parker & Richard Griffin; 1 Aug 1745, p.366. £1.S15.

MARY KENNEY, 13 acs. & 8 chains, in the Parish of Blisland in New Kent Co., to the 5 Corner Tree where 5 Persons joyn, in Mrs Kenneys Old field; adj. Eccho, Mrs Kenney & Thomas Crutchfield; 1 Aug 1745, p.368. 5 Shill.

JASON MEADOWS, 327 acs. Amelia Co. on both sides of the South Fork of Sandy Cr., by the Road, adj. Quarles; 1 Aug 1745, p.369. £1.S15.

CHARLES SIMMONS, 216 acs. Amelia Co. on the S side of Appamattox (Riv.), adj. Henry Chiles & Hill; 1 Aug 1745, p.370. £1.S5.

CHARLES HUDSON, 400 acs. Louisa Co. on both sides of Fosters Cr. & Forsters Cr.; adj. Randolph Bobbet, James Merideth & the Secretary's Line; 1 Aug 1745, p.372. £2.

FRANCIS CLARK, 450 acs. Louisa Co. on the brs. of Fork Cr., adj. his own Line; 1 Aug 1745, p.373. £2.S5. [Included in his 2,450 acs. in PB 27 p.144]

ANDREW HUNTER, 400 acs. Louisa Co. on both sides the South fork of Rocky Cr., adj. Charles

Moreman & John Price; 1 Aug 1745, p.374. £2.

JAMES HALL, 400 acs. Amelia Co. on the upper side of the lower Fork of Woody Cr., on Stanleys Fork; adj. John Burge, William Stanley & George Bagley; 1 Aug 1745, p.376. £2.

DANIEL COLEMAN, 196 acs. Amelia Co. on the Ridge bet. Winticomaick Cr. and Sweat House Cr. on both sides the Road; adj. Bevill, Newman, his own lines & Revill (sic); 1 Aug 1745, p.377. £1.

WILLIAM CRENSHAW, 1,243 acs. Amelia Co. on the S side of little Nottoway Riv., up the long Br., down Turkey Pen Br.; 1 Aug 1745, p.379. £3. The sd L. being formerly Gtd. unto Douglass Irby for 648 acs. by Pat. 28 Sep 1728 [Brunswick Co., PB 13 p.361] the Right and Title is since become vested in the sd William Crenshaw and upon a Resurvey is found to contain 1,243 acs.

JOHN ROBERTS, 400 acs. Amelia Co. on the Upper side of Smacks Cr., Beg. near the Head of the main Br. thereof, adj. Richard Walthall & his old L.; 1 Aug 1745, p.380. £2.

JAMES MATTHEWS, 450 acs. Surry Co. on the N side of

Nottoway Riv., on the Reedy Br., adj. James Cain & John Russel; 1 Aug 1745, p.381. £2.S5.

DANIEL COLEMAN, 225 acs. Amelia Co. on the head Brs. of the Great Fork of Flatt Cr., adj. Harris & Watson; 1 Aug 1745, p.383. £1.S5. [Included in William Watson's 5,077 acs. in PB 28 p.615]

ALEXANDER BOLLING, 158 acs. Amelia Co. on Buffalo Cr., adj. his own old Line; 20 Aug 1745, p.384. £1.

MOSES THOMPSON, 100 acs. Orange Co. on the W side of the Blue Ridge & the E side the South Riv. of Shanandore on the *Red Banks*; 20 Aug 1745, p.386. 10 Shill.

WILLIAM RUTLEDGE, 237 acs. in that Part of Orange Co. designed to be called Augusta on a br. of Brocks Cr., on a Ridge; 20 Aug 1745, p.387. £1.S5.

JAMES COCKE, 400 acs. Goochland Co. on the N side of Hardwar Riv., in the Low Grounds of a Br., adj. Richard Damril; 20 Aug 1745, p.388. £2.

JOHN HUGHES, 237 acs. Amelia Co. on both sides of the little Harricane Sw.; adj. Hugh Williams, Mitchel & Jackson; 20

Aug 1745, p.390. for £1 and the Importation of one Person whose Name is *John Hughes*.

JOHN SHARP, 400 acs. Goochland Co. on both sides of a Br. of Slate Riv. known by the Name of the Great Cr.; 20 Aug 1745, p.391. £2.

JAMES HOWERTON, 400 acs. Spotsyl. and Orange Counties, amongst the head Brs. of Mattapony Riv., on Robinson Run; adj. Charles Oaks, Henry Rice & Edward Rouse; 20 Aug 1745, p.392. £2.

JOSIAH MORRIS, 674½ acs. Pr. Ann Co. upon Nanneys Cr., by a Point of Marsh at the fork of sd Cr., by a Fork of the Dams; adj. Richard Lester & Conner; 20 Aug 1745, p.394. 15 Shill. 250 acs. part formerly Gtd. Josiah Morris by Pat. 20 Nov 1683 [Low. Norf. Co. in *Corretuck*, PB 7 p.346], 300 acs. other part being part of 1,517 acs. gtd. John Sandford by Pat. 23 Apr 1688 [by Rattle Snake Ridge, neer *Curratuck* in Low. Norf. Co., PB 7 p.659] the Right and Title of sd 2 Parcels by Divers Mesne Conveyances is become Vested in sd Josiah Morris, and the residue never before Gtd.

ABRAHAM LASSITER, 150 acs. Nansemond Co. near the main Br. of Hawkings's Hole, in Booths Br.; adj. Robert Booth, Joshua Spivie, John Lassiter, Thomas Newby & Joseph Booth; 20 Aug 1745, p.396. 15 Shill.

THEOPHILUS PUGH, 200 acs. of Swamp Land in Nansemond Co. on the S side of Nansemond Riv. in the Main Desart or Sw.; 20 Aug 1745, p.397. £1.

THEOPHILUS PUGH, 400 acs. of Swamp Land in Nansemond Co. on the S side of Nansemond Riv. in the Main Desart or Sw.; adj. his own Line, Daniel Pugh, Richard Parker & John Small; 20 Aug 1745, p.398.

OWIN MYRICK, 375 acs. Is. of Wight Co. on the S side of Nottoway Riv., by the Three Creeks, over the Run of the Poplar Sw., up Wrights Meadow; adj. his own old Lines, Joseph Harrod, Wright Macklemore & John Jones; 20 Aug 1745, p.400. £2.

JAMES SAMMON, 75 acs. Is. of Wight Co. on the S side of Nottoway Riv. & N side of the Three Creeks, adj. his own old Lines & John Holt; 20 Aug 1745, p.402. 10 Shill.

JOHN NUNNALLY, 246 acs. Henrico Co.; adj. William Gates, Thomas Bass & Thomas Rickman; 20 Aug 1745, p.403. £1.S5.

JACOB MACKGEHEE, 904 acs. Brunswick Co. on both sides of the Second Fork of Licking Hole [Cr.], adj. Perrin & Hardin; 20 Aug 1745, p.404. 500 acs. part formerly Gtd. sd Jacob Mackgehee by Pat. 20 Aug 1740 [PB 19 p.730] & 404 acs. the Residue never before gtd.

EDWARD OBSORNE, 400 acs. Henrico Co. crossing Andersons lower Br. & Andersons upper Br., adj. Anderson and Eppes; 20 Aug 1745, p.406. £2.

JOHN MORES, 400 acs. Henrico Co. on the West Br. of Dry Cr.; adj. Edward Hill, William Lockett, the sd Mores upper Survey & Jacob Lester; 20 Aug 1745, p.407. £2.

JOHN NASH, Gentleman, 3,802 acs. Amelia Co. on the S side of Appamattox Riv. and on both sides of Bush, Bryer and Sandy Rivers, in a great Br.; adj. Williamson now Walkers, the Lines of the L. purchased of Randolph, Gross, & Baly; 20 Aug 1745, p.409. £10.S5. 1,782 acs. formerly gtd. Richard Randolph Gent. by Pat. 15 Mar 1735/36 [Brunswick Co. Pr. Geo. Co. in PB 17 p.9], the Right and Title thereof by mesne Conveyances is become vested in the sd John Nash & 2,020 acs. the Residue never before gtd.

JOHN NASH, 1,570 acs. Amelia Co. on both sides of Mountain Cr., crossing the Brs. of Camp Cr., on the Mountain, on the head of a Br. of Meherrin, down the East or lower fork of Mountain Cr. & up Mountain Cr., adj. Randolph & Ligon; 20 Aug 1745, p.411. £8. [Included in his 3,100 acs. in PB 28 p.425]

JOHN NASH, 115 acs. Henrico Co. nigh Swift Cr., on licking Cr., up Alder Br.; adj. Moses Ferguson, Captain Cobb, Thomas Frankling, Thomas Nash, John Grissel & James Ferguson; 20 Aug 1745, p.413. 15 Shill.

HUGH MILLER, 229 acs. Pr. Geo. Co. on both sides of the Butterwood Road, on the upper side the sd Road where it crosses Ledbiters Cr., crossing the main Road, down the Meadow Br.; adj. Laughton Flynn alias Thomas Jordans, Henry Fitz, Isham Eppes, Mixon alias Fitzgeralds, William Andrews, & James Overby alias the sd Andrews's; 20 Aug 1745, p.415. £1.S5.

JOHN GATH [Garth], 400 acs. Louisa Co. on both sides the Southanna Riv., adj. John Ragland; 20 Aug 1745, p.416. £2.

RICHARD BOUSCH, 288 acs. Amelia Co. on both sides of Buffilo Cr. in the fork of Nottoway Riv.;

adj. Bolling, Ellis and Robert Evans; 20 Aug 1745, p.417. £1.S10

JOHN WATKINS, 400 acs. Amelia Co. on the upper side of Saylors Cr.; adj. Benjamin Ruffin, Thomas Osborne, Richard Davis & Randolph; 20 Aug 1745, p.419. £2.

CHARLES POYTHRESS, 300 acs. Pr. Geo. Co. on the lower side of the old field Br. of Butterwood Sw. & the upper side of the Beach Br., adj. Francis Coleman; 20 Aug 1745, p.420. £1.S10.

JOHN FLOYD, 143 acs. Pr. Geo. Co. bet. Jones Holes and the Indian Swamps, next to Reedy Br.; adj. Peter Harrowell/Harwell, Henry Spier, Richard Raynes, Arthur Reding & John Man; 20 Aug 1745, p.422. £15 Shill.

CHARLES FRANCIS, 400 acs. Louisa Co. on both sides the Goochland Road, on the Goochland Co. line [N60°W]; adj. Secretary Carter, James Merideth & Charles Moreman; 20 Aug 1745, p.423. £2.

EDWARD CLARK, 400 acs. Louisa Co., by the Road; adj. John Ragland, Captain Hudson & Francis Whittle; 20 Aug 1745, p.425. £2.

JOHN DURRETT, 400 acs. Spotsyl. Co. on the Brs. of the River Ta a br. of Mattapony Riv., on the upper side of black Rock Sw., near a Glade, on the E side a Glade & on the side of a Ridge, into a Miry br. opposite to the sd Fantleroys Quarter; adj. Mr Joseph Brock, John Durrett/Durret & Mr Griffin Fantleroy; 20 Aug 1745, p.426. £2.

GEORGE HAMM, 274 acs. Amelia Co. on the upper side of Flatt Cr.; adj. Ruffin, Bently and Chappels Surveys; 20 Aug 1745, p.428. £1.S10.

BENJAMIN SEWARD, 95 acs. Is. of Wight Co. on S side of the Three Creeks, adj. his own old Lines; 20 Aug 1745, p.429. 10 Shill.

JOHN MANSON, 200 acs. Pr. Geo. Co. on both sides of the Horsepen Br. of Rockey Run, adj. Bolling; 20 Aug 1745, p.430. £1.

THOMAS ARCHER, 150 acs. Pr. Geo. Co. on the N side of Moccosneck Cr. bet. Lows and Peters Brs., adj. Julian King; 20 Aug 1745, p.432. 15 Shill.

JOSHUA WYNN, 154 acs. Pr. Geo. Co. on the N side of Stony Cr. and on both sides the main Road, in a Thicket, on a Fork of the Flatt Br.; adj. his own, Joshua

Worsham, John Avery and Daniel Jones; 20 Aug 1745, p.433. 15 Shill.

JOSEPH GRAY, Gentleman, 130 acs. Is. of Wight Co. on the S side of the main Black Water Sw. & the E side of Strouds Br.; adj. Brenson, Mr William Gray, William Howel & Thomas Barrow; 20 Aug 1745, p.434. 15 Shill.

BENJAMIN BLICK, 194 acs. Pr. Geo. Co. bet. Peters and Lows Brs. of Moccosneck, adj. Short; 20 Aug 1745, p.436. £1.

ALEXANDER BOLLING, 276 acs. Amelia Co. on the N side of Great Nottoway and on both sides of Little Nottoway Rivers, adj. Abraham Cock on little Nottoway Riv. below the *Stone House*; 20 Aug 1745, p.437. £1.S10,

THOMAS CRENSHAW, 245 acs. Is. of Wight Co. on the S side of Nottoway Riv. & on the N side of Arthurs Sw.; adj. Joseph West, Samuel Bozman, John Bryant & John Brasswell; 20 Aug 1745, p.439. £1.S5.

WILLIAM STONE, 700 acs. Amelia Co. on the N side of the Hurricane Sw.; adj. Henry Green, Powel, Poythress & Wyatt; 20 Aug 1745, p.440. £3.S10.

THOMAS CLARK, 685 acs. Amelia Co. on both sides of Whetstone Cr., down Binfords Br.; adj. Smart, Finney, Bolling, Thweat, Dendy & Hubbard; 20 Aug 1745, p.441. £3.S10.

HENRY TALLY, 265 acs. Amelia Co. on the upper side of Namisseen Cr.; adj. Munford, Perdue & Hamlin; 20 Aug 1745, p.443. £1.S10.

HENRY DANIEL, 294 acs. Pr. Geo. Co. on the S side of Glaneys Quarter br. & on both sides of the main Road; adj. Thomas Harman, Joshua Worsham, James Pittillo, John Hansel, and his Father Roger Daniel; 20 Aug 1745, p.444. £1.S10.

WILLIAM EATON, 1,271 acs. Pr. Geo. Co. on both sides of Butterwood Sw., adj. Rains's alias his own old upper Corner; 20 Aug 1745, p.446. £3.S10. 275 acs. part formerly gtd. Richard Rains by Pat. 2 Jun 1722 [Richard Raynes, 22 Jun 1722, PB 11 p.129 (& PB 11 p.214 on 5 Sep 1723)] The Right and Title by mesne Conveyances is become vested in the sd William Eaton, 303 acs. other part formerly Gtd. the sd William Eaton by Pat. 24 Mar 1725/26 [PB 12 p.374] and 693 acs. the Residue never before Gtd.

WILLIAM ARCHER, 400 acs. Pr. Geo. Co. on both sides of Lows Br. of Moccosoneck Cr., up Peters Br., by the side of Vaughans Road; adj. Benjamin Blick, Jones, Green, Thomas Archer, Julian King, Dearden alias Richard Evans, & Short; 20 Aug 1745, p.448. £2.

JOSEPH MORTON, 1,600 acs. Amelia Co. on both sides of Bryer Riv., to the Corner of the L. purchased of Hamlin; 20 Aug 1745, p.449. 1,200 acs. part formerly Gtd. the sd Joseph Morton by Pat. 26 Mar 1739 [PB 18 p.265] and 400 acs. the Residue formerly Gtd. Daniel Hamlin 22 Nov 1739 [22 Sep 1739, PB 18 p.512] The Right and Title thereof by mesne Conveyeances is become vested in the sd Joseph Morton. [Included in his 2,800 acs. in PB 28 p.359]

STEPHEN EVANS & ROBERT EVANS, 200 acs. Pr. Geo. Co. on the N side of Stony Cr., down the Flatt Br.; adj. their Father John Evans and Paul Seares; 20 Aug 1745, p.451. £1.

RICHARD WOODROOFE, 100 acs. Surry Co. on the S side of Nottoway Riv. and on the N side of Hunting Quarter Sw., adj. sd Woodroofe & Howell Briggs; 20 Aug 1745, p.453. 10 Shill.

ROBERT DEPREST, 352 acs. Hanover Co. in Slashes below Stone Horse Cr.; adj. Lawrence Farginson, Mr Alvis, Gentry, & John Pryer; 20 Aug 1745, p.454. £1.S15.

WILLIAM HARRIS, 350 acs. Hanover Co. on the N side Saxons Sw., near the Rod [Road]; adj. the sd Harris, Davis, Gasse/Gass, Robert Shildrake, Charles Yancey, John Field & John Williams; 20 Aug 1745, p.456. £1. 150 acs. formerly gtd. sd William Harris by Pat. 28 Sep 1730 [PB 13 p.507 in St. Martin's Parish] and 200 acs. the Residue never before Gtd.

JOSEPH TUCKER, JUNIOR, 286 acs. Pr. Geo. Co. on the upper side of the Flatt Br. of Stony Cr., in the Mouth of Avery's Br., near a Pond, down the halfway br.; adj. John Evans, & Stephan and Robert Evans; 20 Aug 1745, p.457. £1.S10.

JACOB COOK, 310 acs. Henrico Co., crossing the main Road, in a Br. of Third Br.; adj. John Red, John Farguson & Moses Farguson; 20 Aug 1745, p.459. £1.S10.

HENRY WYTHE, 1,000 acs. Pr. Geo. Co. on both sides of Chamberlains Bead Run and on the Cadar Island Br., at the upper end of a Valley of Chamberlains Bead Run; adj. Irby Hudson, Winingham alias Whites, Henry Thweat, Thomas and Mosias Jones, John

Thompson and Edward Lewis; 20 Aug 1745, p.460. £5.

WILLIAM GATES, 205 acs. Henrico Co. adj. sd Gates 1st Survey, Richard Sims & Peter Ligon; 20 Aug 1745, p.462. £1.S5.

ABRAHAM CHILDERS, 77 acs. Henrico Co., crossing a thick Slash, under Gravelly Hill, down Spring Br.; adj. Captain John Redford, Francis Redford, Major John Bolling, Hays Whitloe & Joseph Woodson; 20 Aug 1745, p.463. 10 Shill.

CHARLES ALLEN, 19 acs. Louisa Co. on both sides of Goochland Road; adj. Thomas Paulet, Col. Symes, William Walker, Philip Walker & Charles Christian; 20 Aug 1745, p.465. 5 Shill.

WILLIAM DICKENSON, 84 acs. Hanover Co., Beg. on the bank of North Anna, bet. the Lines of John Luck and Captain Isaac Winston; 20 Sep 1745, p.466. 10 Shill.

WILLIAM OWENS, 300 acs. Hanover Co. on both sides a Br. of James Riv., Beg. in the Co. line about a quarter of a mile from the Riv., to Rocky Cr., along the Co. Line [N65°W]; 20 Sep 1745, p.467. £1.S10.

HARDEN BURNLEY, 14 acs. Hanover Co. on the lower side of the South fork of Machumps Cr., adj. Mr John Joyner & Bradley Cock; 20 Sep 1745, p.469. 5 Shill.

LAMBERT ZELL, 250 acs. Surry Co. on the S side of Nottoway Riv., in a Pond, adj. his own old Line & Colonel Philip Lightfoot; 20 Sep 1745, p.470. £1.S5.

JOSEPH PHILLIPS/PHILIPS, 400 acs. Hanover Co. on both sides a Southern Br. of Buck Mountain Cr., on the side of a small Mountain; 20 Sep 1745, p.472. £2.

JAMES SAMMON JUNIOR, 98 acs. Surry Co. on both sides of Nottoway Riv., down the Great Sw.; adj. Martin Johnson, Captain Avent, Colonel Richard Bland, Thomas Underwood, & his Fathers Lines; 20 Sep 1745, p.473. 10 Shill.

JAMES GREENLEE, 250 acs. Orange Co. in the fork of James Riv.; 20 Sep 1745, p.475. £1.S5.

JAMES GREENLEE, 300 acs. Orange Co. on the S side of James Riv., at the Mouth of a Run; 20 Sep 1745, p.476. £1.S10.

WILLIAM GILLS, 152 acs. Hanover Co. on the upper side of

Beverdam Sw.; adj. Abraham Abney, John Oliver & John Custis Esquire; 20 Sep 1745, p.477. for 2 lbs. of Tobacco for every Acre. Whereas by Inquisition Indented taken in sd Co. 5 Mar 1739/40 by Virtue of a Warrant directed to William Byrd Esq. our Escheator for sd Co. It appears that Peter Tickell late of the sd Co. died seised of a Tract supposed to contain only 100 acs. but by a Survey lately made by Ambrose Joshua Smith Gent. Surveyor of the sd Co. is found to contain 152 acs. which is found to Escheat to us from the sd Peter Tickell And whereas Stephen Jones hath made humble Suit and obtained a G. for the same which he hath assigned to William Gills.

JAMES COLEMAN, 300 acs. Louisa Co. on the W side the Little Mountains, on the Top of a Mountain; adj. Timothy Dalton & Holden McGee; 20 Sep 1745., p.479. £1.S10.

JOHN ENNIS, 400 acs. Louisa Co. on the middle fork & the South fork of Rockey Cr., adj. James Meridith; 20 Sep 1745, p.480. £2.

WILLIAM SPILLER, 1,600 acs. Louisa Co. bet. Contrary and Christophers Run; adj. Mr. Chiswell, Colonel Meriweather, Robert Hester, William Taite, Thomas Adams & John Kendrick;

20 Sep 1745, p.482. £2. 400 acs. part formerly Gtd. Samuel White by Pat. 22 Sep 1739 [PB 18 p.508], 800 acs. other part formerly Gtd. John Kembrow by 2 Patents bearing Date 2 Jun 1740 [PB 18 p.627 & p.629] The Right and Title by Mesne Conveyances is become Vested in sd William Spiller and 400 acs. the Residue never before Gtd.

JOSEPH MARTIN, 400 acs. Louisa Co. on the Brs. of Penney run; adj. his own, Henry Bunch & William Keaton; 20 Sep 1745, p.484. £2.

JOSEPH MARTIN, 400 acs. Louisa Co. on both sides of Rockey Cr., adj. Henry Bunch, James Meridith & William Keaton; 20 Sep 1745, p.485. £2.

JAMES HUNT, 104 acs. Surry Co. on the S side of Nottoway Riv.; adj. his own lines, Clements Handcock & Mr Thomas Eldridge; 20 Sep 1745, p.487. 10 Shill.

√ JOHN SMITHING, 1,800 acs. Louisa Co. on both sides the North Br. of the Southanna Riv. and on both sides Mackdonalds Cr., adj. John Ragland & Coleman; 20 Sep 1745, p.488. £2. 400 acs. part formerly Gtd. unto sd John Smithing by Pat. 17 Mar 1736/37 [John Smething, PB 17 p.252], 600 acs. other part also formerly Gtd.

sd John Smithing by Pat. 9 Feb 1737/38 [John Smething, PB 17 p.484], 400 acs. also formerly Gtd. unto sd John Smithing by Pat. 26 Mar 1739/40 [PB 18 p.226] and 400 acs. the Residue never before gtd.

THOMAS HUNT, 385 acs. Pr. Geo. Co. on the S side of Sappona Cr., along the Co. line [E30°N], by the side of a Br. of the Gum Pond, down Harrys Sw.; adj. Goodwyns L. from Butler; 20 Sep 1745, p.490. £2.

JAMES CHRISTIAN, 147 acs. Goochland Co. on both sides of the Mouth of Rack Island Cr. and including Rack Island in the Fluvanna Riv.; 20 Sep 1745, p.491. 15 Shill.

WILLIAM BYRD, 350 acs. Pr. Geo. Co. on the head of the Great Cr. of Nottoway Riv.; adj. Jones, Morris, Mathis, his own old lines, Raney & John May [Mays/Mayes]; 20 Sep 1745, p.492. £1.S15.

JEREMIAH HATCHER, 354 acs. Brunswick Co. on the N side of Staunton Riv., down Falling Riv., adj. Richerson; 20 Sep 1745, p.494. £1.S15.

JAMES KEETH, 389 acs. Pr. Geo. Co. on the S side of Stoney Cr., near the Reedy Br, on the Road,

adj. Avery & Stark; 20 Sep 1745, p.495. £2.

JOHN POYTHRESS, JUNIOR, 844 acs. Pr. Geo. Co. on the N side Tommahitton Sw., up his Spring Br., adj. John Mitchel & Thomas Poythress; 20 Sep 1745, p.496. £3. 250 acs. part formerly Gtd. John Mitchell by Pat. 9 Feb 1737/38 [PB 17 p.469] and 594 acs. the Residue never before Gtd.

JOHN WILLIAMSON, 1,004 acs. Pr. Geo. Co. on the N side of Sappone Cr. and on both sides of the Reedy Br., crossing Pools Mortar br., below the Main Sappone Road, in the lower Corner of Beatons clearing; adj. John Goodwyn, Isaac Tucker & David Williams; 20 Sep 1745, p.498. £5.

WILLIAM PIERCEY, 277 acs. Pr. Geo. Co. on the S side of Butterwood Sw., up Crupper Run; adj. Prichitt, Smart, Raney, Bobbit & Burchitt; 20 Sep 1745, p.500. £1.S10.

EDWARD BURCHITT, 171 acs. Pr. Geo. Co. on the N side of Tommahitton Sw., adj. Richard Beale, Ornsby, Kirkland & Cryer; 20 Sep 1745, p.501. £1.

OBADIAH WOODSON, 800 acs. Goochland Co. on both sides of Dry Cr. of Appomattox Riv., adj.

Colo. Richard Randolph; 20 Sep 1745, p.502. £4.

CHARLES BOSTOCK, 125 acs. Goochland Co. on both sides of great Guinea Cr.; adj. John Bostock, William Hamilton & William Arnold; 20 Sep 1745, p.504. 15 Shill.

ORLANDO HUGHES, 400 acs. Goochland Co. on the N Brs. of the Cat Br. of Willis's Riv., Beg. on the Ridge bet. Randolphs Cr. and the Cat Br.; 20 Sep 1745, p.505. £2. [Included in George Carrington's 2,520 acs. Albemarle Co. in PB 27 p.336]

THOMAS HARBOUR, 400 acs. Goochland Co. on the N Brs. of Horsleys Cr., on the side of a Mountain; 20 Sep 1745, p.506. £2.

WILLIAM BATTERSBY, 112 acs. Goochland Co. bet. the two Manacan Creeks; adj. James Goss, Stephen Chastaine dec'd. & Daniel Guarrand dec'd.; 20 Aug 1745, p.508. 15 Shill.

LEONARD HENLEY, 400 acs. Goochland Co. on both sides and near the Head of a Br. of the Byrd Cr. called Phills Cr., Beg. in a slash; 20 Sep 1745, p.509. £2.

JOSHUA DOSS, 200 acs. Goochland Co. among the Brs. of

Great Guinea Cr., adj. Isaac Allen & Daniel Stoner; 20 Sep 1745, p.510. £1.

HOLMES BOISEAU, 414 acs. Pr. Geo. Co. on the N side of White Oak Sw.; along his old Lines of the L. purchased of Ellis; adj. Thweat, Taylor & Eppes; 20 Sep 1745, p.511. £15 Shill. 260 acs. part formerly Gtd. John Ellis [Junr.] by Pat. 9 Jul 1724 [PB 12 p.63] and 154 acs. the residue never before gtd.

ARTHUR CROCKER, 250 acs. Is. of Wight Co. on the N side of Maherin Riv., by the side of Whitewood Sw., up the Wolf Pitt Br., adj. Charles Porter dec'd.; 20 Sep 1745, p.513. £1.S5.

THOMAS EVANS, 150 acs. Pr. Geo. Co. on the upper side of the Morter Br. of Stony Cr.; adj. his Brother Stephen Evans, Thomas Evans & Jones; 20 Sep 1745, p.514. 15 Shill.

STEPHEN EVANS, 223 acs. Pr. Geo. Co. on both sides the Morter Br.; adj. his own Line & his last Survey, Cornelius Fox [his new Survey & his Creek Survey], the sd Stephen and Thomas Evans; 20 Sep 1745, p.515. £1.S5.

ANTHONY HAYNES & JAMES KEETH, 400 acs. Pr. Geo. Co. on the S side of Stoney Cr.; adj.

Keeth, Lovit & Hankins; 20 Sep 1745, p.517. £2.

ROBERT TUCKER, 250 acs. Pr. Geo. Co. on both sides of the Miery Br. of Bever Pond Cr., adj. his own old Lines & Peter Thomas; 20 Sep 1745, p.518. £1.S5.

JOHN WILLIAMSON, 75 acs. Pr. Geo. Co. on the S side of Stony Cr., along the Co. Line [E30°N], in a Pond; adj. Joseph Tucker [his old Line & his new L. of 150 acs.]; 20 Sep 1745, p.519.   10 Shill.

HUMPHRY MOODY, 100 acs. Pr. Geo. Co. on the Brs. of Gravilly Run; adj. Edmond Browder, his old Line & his new Survey of 100 acs., Maynard alias Irvin, & Joseph Lews (Lewis); 20 Sep 1745, p.521. 10 Shill.

JOHN TUCKER, 252 acs. Pr. Geo. Co. on the lower side of Bever Pond Cr.; adj. Robert Tucker, his Father & Langford; 20 Sep 1745, p.522. £1.S5.

ROBERT WARREN, 200 acs. Pr. Geo. Co. on the S side of Sappony Cr. and on the upper side of the Long Br., adj. Stroud; 20 Sep 1745, p.523. £1.

JACOB JONES, 400 acs. Pr. Geo. Co. on both sides of the Reedy Br. of Stoney Cr., adj. Joseph Tucker

& Stephen Evans; 20 Sep 1745, p.524. £2.

JAMES HARRISON, 300 acs. Pr. Geo. Co. bet. Stoney and Sapponey Creeks, along the Co. line [W30°S], by a Pond, adj. Thomas Wynn & Richard Harrison; 20 Sep 1745, p.525. £1.S10.

EDWARD HAUKINGS JUNR. the Younger, 200 acs. Pr. Geo. Co. on the S side of Stoney Cr., on the Road, adj. Lovit; 20 Sep 1745, p.527. £1.

JOHN HAILES, 74 acs. Pr. Geo. Co. on the Heads of the Brs. of Gravilly Run and Hatchers Run; bet. the Lines of John Browder, William Sanders and Jeffrey/Jeffry Munford; 20 Sep 1745, p.528.   10 Shill.

JOHN LANGFORD, 400 acs. Pr. Geo. Co. on the lower side of Beaver Pond Cr.; adj. Richardson, Joseph Tucker & Whitmore; 20 Sep 1745, p.529. £2.

GEORGE BELCHER, 200 acs. Pr. Geo. Co. on the S side of Sappony Cr., adj. Tabb; 20 Sep 1745, p.531. £1.

HENRY DICKSON, 233 acs. Pr. Geo. Co. on the N side of Sappony Cr.; adj. William Pettepool, Jacob Jones & Robert Warren; 20 Sep 1745, p.532. £1.S5.

PHILIP BURROWS, 304 acs. Pr. Geo. Co. on the Lower side of Harrys Sw.; adj. John Burrow, Joseph Stroud & Thomas Hunt; 20 Sep 1745, p.533. £1.S10.

SAMUEL VAUGHAN, 317 acs. Pr. Geo. Co. on the lower side of George's Br. of Nammiseen Cr.; adj. Eppes, Boiseau, Stell, Mayes, Tatum, Wells, Griffin & Vaughan; 20 Sep 1745, p.534. £1.S15.

ANTHONY HAYNES, 342 acs. Pr. Geo. Co. on the S side Stoney Cr., by the Road; adj. Wagnon, his own, Keeth & Haynes; 20 Sep 1745, p.536. £1.S15.

THOMAS WYNNE, 400 acs. Pr. Geo. Co. on both sides of Sappony Cr., along the Co. Line [W30°S], through the Great Pond, adj. Richardson; 20 Sep 1745, p.537. £2.

JOSEPH TUCKER, JUNIOR, 400 acs. Pr. Geo. Co. bet. Stony & Sappone Creeks, by a Br. of the Reedy Br., on the lower side the great Pond; adj. James Harrison, Richard Harrison, Joseph Tucker, Waren [Warren] alias William Pettepools, Richardson, & Thomas Wynne; 20 Sep 1745, p.538. £2.

WILLIAM HARDING, 240 acs. Henrico Co. crossing the Main Road, in a Slash & a small Br.; adj. John Ealom, Philip Jones, Seth More, Dawson, & James Cashoon; 20 Sep 1745, p.540. £1.S5.

JACOB GILL, 220 acs. Henrico Co. on the S side of Rocky Br., up Stoney Cr.; adj. Benjamin Anders, John William & Royal; 20 Sep 1745, p.541. £1.S5.

JOHN JOHNSON, 400 acs. Henrico Co. on the S side of James Riv.; adj. George Worsham, Henry Dance & Benjamin Andrews; 20 Sep 1745, p.542. £2.

LEONARD HENLEY, 130 acs. Henrico Co. crossing Drinking hole Run, on the N side of Little Drinking Hole, on the Line [@ N17.6°E] dividing this Co. from Goochland, in Slashy Ground; adj. John Martin, Johnson, Shoemaker, Robert Hardwick & the sd Henleys own line; 20 Sep 1745, p.544. 15 Shill.

JOHN SHOEMAKER, 390 acs. Henrico Co. on the falling Grounds of Deep Run, in a Slash, crossing Goochland Road; adj. Thomas Alley, Nicholas Pryor & Thomas Conway; 20 Sep 1745, p.545. £2.

FRANCIS MOSELEY, 396 acs. Henrico Co. on the E side of Tomahauk Br.; adj. the sd Moseleys old Lines, Pollard, Roberts, the Lines of Tullits great Tract, & Giles; 20 Sep 1745, p.546. £2.

THOMAS YARBROUGH, 600 acs. Amelia Co. on both sides of Peters Cr. on the S side of Little Nottoway Riv.; adj. John Nance, Roberson, Yarbrough, Hubbard & Ellis; 20 Sep 1745, p.548. £3.

FRANCIS CHEETHAM, 383 acs. Henrico Co. adj. Thomas Cheetham; 20 Sep 1745, p.549. £2.

WILLIAM WILLIAMS, 256 acs. Henrico Co. adj. John Williams, Lawrence Brown & John Dod; 20 Sep 1745, p.551. £1.S10.

JAMES PITTILLO, 393 acs. Pr. Geo. Co. on the S side of Stoney Cr., down the Reedy Br., adj. Cornelius Fox old Line of the L. whereon he lives; 20 Sep 1745, p.552. £2. which sd L. was gtd. unto Cornelius Fox by Pat. 10 Jun 1740 [PB 19 p.660] and by a Decree of the General Court in Chancery obtained by the sd James Pitillo against the sd Cornelius Fox 29 Apr 1745 is delivered up and cancelled.

WILLIAM MAYO, 1,060 acs. Henrico Co. crossing Almonds Cr., by a small Pond, on the N side of New Kent Road, in a slash near Hell Garden Path, thro' White Oak Sw.; adj. the old Pat. line of a Pat of John & Joseph Pleasant, Burton, that L. Mr Joseph Mayo formerly Purchased of Wale, Robertson &

Abney; 20 Sep 1745, p.553. £4. 286 acs. part formerly Gtd. John Pleasant and Joseph Pleasant by Pat. 20 Oct 1704 [PB 9 p.627] the Right and Title whereof by divers Mesne conveyances is become vested in the sd William Mayo and 774 acs. the Residue never before Gtd.

FRANCIS FLOURNOY, 120 acs. Henrico Co. on the N side of Tomahauk Road; adj. Trabue, John James Flournoy, Lewis Countis & the sd Francis Flournoys old Line; 20 Sep 1745, p.555. 15 Shill.

FRANCIS FLOURNOY, 198 acs. Henrico Co. on the W side of Tomahawk Run; adj. John Welch, Charles Holsworth, the sd Flournoys old Line, & Giles; 20 Sep 1745, p.556. £1.

FRANCIS FLOURNOY, 1,821 acs. Henrico Co. crossing the Butterwood Road, in a Slash & crossing the Otter Br.; adj. Thomas Friend, John Wooldridge, the sd Francis Flournoy, Robert Ashurst, William Bass, Richard Sims, Thomas Rickman & Gilbert Ealom; 20 Sep 1745, p.558. £9.S5.

FRANCIS FLOURNOY, 181 acs. of Swamp & Low Land in Henrico Co. on the E side of Trabues Br., on the S side of great Swamp Road in the edge of Swift Creek Sw., up the stream of the Main Run of

Swift Cr., up Tomahauk Br., adj. Trabue & the high L. of the sd Francis Flournoy; 20 Sep 1745, p.560. £1.

RALPH SHELTON, 400 acs. Amelia Co. on the N side of Great Nottoway Riv., down Buffalo Bed Cr.; adj. James Oliver, Thomas Ellis, Robert Evans & Crenshaw; 20 Sep 1745, p.561. £2.

JOHN JAMES DUPUY, 800 acs. Amelia Co. on both sides of the North or Ellis's fork of Flatt Cr.; adj. Turner, Edward Jones, Childrey; 20 Sep 1745, p.563. £4.

JOHN RAGLAND, 1,289 acs. Hanover Co. on both sides of the Southanna Riv., on the side of a Level, on Rack Punch Spring Br., by the side of a bottom & down Cawthons Run; adj. Mrs Anne Johnson & Richard Welborn /Wellborne; 20 Sep 1745, p.564. £4.S10. 400 acs. part formerly gtd. sd John Ragland by Pat. 9 Feb 1737/38 [PB 17 p.466] and 889 acs. the residue never before gtd.

JOHN RAGLAND, 1,030 acs. Hanover Co. on both sides of North fork of Mechumps Cr., in the head of a Glade, in a slash; adj. John Joiner, George Vaughan, Mary Harris, George Hudson, Benjamin Alsup, Alexander Cock, Thomas Rowland, William Elmore, John Raglands Cornfield, David

Haynes & Thomas Baker; 20 Sep 1745, p.566. £1.S15. 579 acs. part being part of a greater Quantity formerly gtd. James Gibbins by Pat. 7 Nov 1700 [James Gibbons, 1,420 acs. New Kent Co. on the Rangers upper path in PB 9 p.286], Also 100 acs. other part being part of a greater quantity gtd. John Hudson by Pat. 24 Mar 1725/26 [400 acs. in PB 12 p.404], the right and title of which sd two parcels by divers Mesne Conveyances is become vested in sd John Ragland and 351 acs. the residue never before gtd.

JOHN RAGLAND, 400 acs. Hanover Co. on both sides of Great Cawthons Run, crossing both forks of sd Run, adj. his own and Matthew Jouet; 20 Sep 1745, p.568. £2.

EDWARD HARRIS, 400 acs. Amelia Co. on both sides of Harris's Cr., adj. Venable; 20 Sep 1745, p.570. £2.

THOMAS CARTAIN, 204 acs. Amelia Co. on the lower side of Saylor Cr., adj. Hill, Ruffin & Osborn; 20 Sep 1745, p.571. £1.

RICHARD HAYES & STEPHEN BEASLEY, 400 acs. Amelia Co. on the upper side of deep Cr. and both sides of William Motes Path, down Wests Cr.; adj. sd Hayes &

Beasley other Lines, & William McCoon; 20 Sep 1745, p.572. £2.

HENRY GREEN, 300 acs. Amelia Co. on the N side of Hurricane Sw., on the lower side of the Great Br.; 20 Sep 1745, p.574. £1.S10.

MICAJAH EDWARDS, 1,600 acs. Is. of Wight Co. on the S side of Nottoway Riv., by the side of a Pond, by the Nottoway Indians Line [NE], down the Low Grounds, up Tockwothunty Sw., adj. Thomas Jarrel & his own old Lines; 20 Sep 1745, p.575. £1.S10. 540 acs. and 440 acs. part formerly gtd. William Edwards by 2 Patents 16 Jun 1714 [PB 10 p.143 & p.176] and 330 acs. other part also formerly Gtd. sd William Edwards by Pat. 23 Mar 1715/16 [PB 10 p.270] and 290 acs. the residue never before gtd.

THOMAS MERCER, 100 acs. Is. of Wight Co. on the N side of Nottoway Riv., down the Gravelly Run, near the Cyprus Sw.; 20 Sep 1745, p.577. 10 Shill.

HENRY YARBROUGH, 604 acs. Amelia Co. on both sides of little Nottoway Riv., adj. his own Lines, Beasly/Beasley & William Yarbrough; 20 Sep 1745, p.578. £1. 400 acs. part being part of a Pat. for 800 acs. formerly gtd. sd Henry Yarbrough and one Thomas Yarbrough by Pat. 10 Jun 1740 [PB

19 p.657] and 204 acs. the Residue never before Gtd.

JOSEPH MORTON, 800 acs. Amelia Co. on the lower side of Buffelo Riv., on the upper or W side of a Great Br., adj. Bibb; 20 Sep 1745, p.579. £2. 400 acs. part formerly Gtd. Obadiah Woodson by Pat. 30 Mar 1743 [PB 21 p.253] and 400 acs. the Residue never before Gtd. [The 800 acs. survey in this Patent is a duplicate of sd Woodson's PB 24 p.460 dated 25 Sep 1746]

JOSEPH WOMBWELL, 150 acs. Is. of Wight Co. on the N side of Seacock Sw., down the Pasture Neck Br.; adj. Robert Hart, his own old Lines & Arthur Williamson; 20 Sep 1745, p.581. 15 Shill.

JOSEPH JOINER, 190 acs. Is. of Wight Co. on the S side of the main Black Water Sw., on a Pond; adj. Thomas Swan, John Laurance & John Lear; 20 Sep 1745, p.582. £1.

ROBERT MERCER, 240 acs. Is. of Wight Co. on the S side of the main Black Water Sw. & the E side of Tarapin Br.; adj. Thomas Reeves, William Crumpler, George Williamson & his own old Lines; 20 Sep 1745, p.584. £1.S5.

JOSEPH VASSER, 170 acs. Is. of Wight Co. on the N side of Nottoway Riv. & the S side of Suscahannah Br.; adj. John Exum, his own old Line & Joel Vasser; 20 Sep 1745, p.585. £1.

JOHN BARROW, 150 acs. Is. of Wight Co. on the S side of Nottoway Riv., down the Angelica Sw.; adj. his own other Lines, Thomas Wrenn, Thomas Blake & William Blake; 20 Sep 1745, p.586. 15 Shill.

JOHN EDWARDS, 300 acs. Is. of Wight Co. on the N side of Meherin Riv., up Rushins Br.; adj. Oliver Woodward, William Strickland, Arthur Whitehead, George Jackson & Samuel Bridges; 20 Sep 1745, p.588. £1.S10.

JOSEPH GRIFFIN, 200 acs. Is. of Wight Co. on the S side of the Main Black Water Sw., adj. Peter Stephenson & Robert Merser; 20 Sep 1745, p.589. £1.

WILLIAM HOLLYMAN, 200 acs. Is. of Wight Co. on the S side of the Main Black Water Sw., on the E side of Gregory Br. & in Copohonk Pocoson; adj. sd William Hollyman, Thomas Hollyan [Hollyman] & James Allen; 20 Sep 1745, p.591. £1.

REBECCA CHARLES, 285 acs. Is. of Wight Co. on the S side of Black Cr., down the Gravelly Run, adj. Joseph Popes & Matthew Griffin; 20 Sep 1745, p.592. £1.S10.

WILLIAM JELKS JUNR. the younger, 115 acs. Is. of Wight Co. on the N side of the three Creeks, down the Hornet Sw., at the Mouth of the Miery Br., adj. John Smith & William Jelks; 20 Sep 1745, p.593. £15 Shill.

WILLIAM JOYNER, 100 acs. Is. of Wight Co. on the S side of Black Cr., down the small br., adj. his own old Line & Richard Worrell; 20 Sep 1745, p.595. 10 Shill.

PETER RUCKER, 5,850 acs. Goochland Co. bet. Buffalo Riv. and Little Pedlar alias Harris's Cr., at the foot of a mountain, adj. Mr. George Braxton; 12 Mar 1745/46, p.596. £29.S5.

GEORGE DOUGLASS, 100 acs. Accomack Co. near *Jengoteague*; adj. Ralph Corbin, John Taylor & the L. supposed Samuel Burtons; 15 Mar 1745/46, p.598. for 2 lbs. of Tobacco for every Acre. Whereas by Inquisition Indented taken in Accomack Co. 15 Feb 1741/42 by virtue of a Warrant directed to Edmund Bayley Gent. our Escheator of sd Co. It appears that John Glanning late of sd Co. died seised of a certain Tract of L.

containing 100 acs. which is found to Escheat to us from John Glanning And Whereas George Douglas hath made humble Suit and hath obtained a G. for same.

WILLIAM GRAY, Gent., 8,800 acs. Albemarle Co., on a bank; 20 Mar 1745/46, p.599. 5,800 acs. part formerly gtd. sd William Gray by Pat. 29 Jun 1739 [PB 18 p.291, Goochland Co. among the head brs. of Willis Riv.] and 3,000 acs. the Residue also formerly gtd. sd William Gray by Pat. 30 Mar 1743 [PB 21 p.218 near Appamatox Mountain].

WILLIAM GRAY, 200 acs. Goochland Co. among the Brs. of Willis's Riv., adj. John Sanders & the sd Gray; 20 Mar 1745/46, p.601. £1.

WILLIAM GRAY, 400 acs. Goochland Co. on the S Brs. of Randolphs Cr., on a Rockey Ridge, adj. Thomas Edwards; 20 Mar 1745/46, p.602. £2.

CHARLES THOMAS, 400 acs. Goochland Co. on the N Brs. of Willis's Riv. alias Willis's Cr.; adj. William Mayo Gent., Henry Cary Gent. & William Megginis; 20 Mar 1745/46, p.604. £2.

GEORGE CARRINGTON, 3,400 acs. Goochland Co. on both sides of Harris's Cr. of the N side of the Fluvanna Riv., adj. the Reverand Robert Rose; 20 Mar 1745/46, p.605. £17.

RICHARD RANDOLPH, Gentleman, 496 acs. Amelia Co. on both sides of Little Buffalo Riv., on the Hunting Path, along his own Line; 20 Mar 1745/46, p.607. £2.S10.

JOHN BOLLING, 818 acs. Brunswick Co. on the N side of Roanoke Riv., at the Mouth of a Great Br., down Shocko Cr., adj. John Butcher; 20 Mar 1745/46, p.608. £1.S15. 473 acs. part formerly gtd. sd John Bolling by Pat. 1 Dec 1740 [PB 19 p.907 to Maj. John Bolling Gent. & PB 14 p.445 dated 4 May 1732 to John Bolling Junr. Gent.] and 345 acs. the Residue never before Gtd. [Included in his 988 acs. Lunenburg Co., PB 27 p.174 to Colo. John Bolling]

WILLIAM PRIDE, 20½ acs. Henrico Co. on Appomattox Riv., in Low Ground, down the half way Gutt, on the SW point of a Small Island, crossing the narrow stream; 20 Mar 1745/46, p.610. 5 Shill. 19½ acs. Part formerly gtd. Henry Royal and by him Sold and Conveyed unto sd William Pride and one Acre the Residue never before Gtd.

PETER DANIEL, 532 acs. Brunswick Co. on both sides of Crab Louse quarter br., on the S fork of sd br. above the trading Path, up tickle Cunt br., adj. Isaac House; 20 Mar 1745/46, p.612. £2.S15.

RICHARD INKSON, 80 acs. Norfolk Co. in the Western Br. of Elizabeth Riv., adj. the sd Inkson & Capt. John Whiddon; 20 Mar 1745/46, p.613. for 2 lbs. of Tobacco for every Acre. Whereas by Inquisition Indented taken in Norfolk Co. 9 Jan 1743/44 by virtue of a Warrant directed to Samuel Boush Gent. Escheator for sd Co. It appears That John Barney died seised of a certain Tract of L. containing 85 acs. more or less but by Survey lately made by James Nimmo Surveyor of sd Co. is found to contain 80 acs. which is found to Escheat to us from sd John Barney And Whereas Richard Inkson hath made humble Suit and obtained a G. for the same.

RALPH PERKINSON, 198 acs. Amelia Co. on the S side of Appamattox Riv.; adj. Perkinson, Anderson, Bott, & Bevill [her Corner]; 20 Mar 1745/46, p.615. £1.

JOHN NASH, 400 acs. Amelia Co. on both sides of a Great Br. of Appamattox Riv. below Buffilo,

adj. Randolph; 20 Mar 1745/46, p.616. £2.

SAMUEL GLOVER, 300 acs. Goochland Co. on N Brs. of the South Br. of Slate Riv.; 20 Mar 1745/46, p.618. £1.S10.

THOMAS HUGHES, 400 acs. Goochland Co. on both sides of Horn Quarter Run of Willis Riv., adj. William Mayo & Joseph Farrer; 20 Mar 1745/46, p.619. £2.

SAMUEL GLOVER, JUNIOR, 200 acs. Goochland Co. on both sides of Glovers Cr. a Br. of Slate Riv., adj. Samuel Glover Senior; 20 Mar 1745/46, p.621. £1.

DUNCAN GRAHAM, 400 acs. Louisa Co. on both sides of the Mountain Road and Rack Punch Spring Br., near a Br. of Reedy Br., adj. John Ragland; 20 Mar 1745/46, p.622. £2.

DUNCAN GRAHAM, 384 acs. Louisa Co. on both sides of the Mountain Road and Rack Punch Spring Cr.; adj. his own, John Ragland, Mrs Ann Johnson, Major Henry, & Littlepage; 20 Mar 1745/46, p.623. £2.

JOHN PENICK, 382 acs. Amelia Co. on both sides of Sandy Riv., adj. Morton in the Low Grounds thence East crossing the Riv. to

Mortons now Hamlins; 20 Mar 1745/46, p.625. £2.

THOMAS DAWSON, 590 acs. Goochland Co. adj. to the W side of little Deep Cr., adj. Smith, John Pleasants & James Barns; 20 Mar 1745/46, p.626. £1. 400 acs. Part formerly gtd. unto Marmaduke Hix by Pat. 28 Sep 1730 [PB 14 p.134] the Right and Title is since become Vested in sd Thomas Dawson and 290 acs. the residue is found to be Surplus L. within the bounds of the sd former Pat.

WOOD JONES, 400 acs. Amelia Co. on both sides of Tommahitton Sw.; 20 Mar 1745/46, p.628. £2. Whereas by Pat. 22 Sep 1739 gtd. unto Richard Womack [PB 18 p.383] a Tract containing 400 acs. And Whereas the sd Womack hath sold and Conveyed unto Wood Jones who hath failed to pay Quitrents and to make Cultiv. and Improv., and Thomas Jones hath made humble Suit and obtained a G. for the same which he hath assigned to Wood Jones. [see PB 24 p.383]

THOMAS DAWSON, 400 acs. Goochland Co. on the S Brs. of Dittoys Br. of the upper Manacan Cr., near the N side of Dry Br.; adj. Stephen Chastain, John Witt & Thomas Dickins; 20 Mar 1745/46 *in the 19th year of our Reign of George the Second, William Gooch*

Esqr. our Lieutenant Governor and Commander in Chief of our Colony and Dominion at Williamsburgh, p.630-p.631. £2. Whereas by Pat. 20 Jul 1738 there was gtd. unto Daniel Stoner and John James Flournoy since dec'd in joint Tenancy [PB 18 p.64] And Whereas the sd Stoner in whom the Right of the sd L. vested by Survivorship after the Death of the sd John James Flournoy hath failed to pay Quit Rents and to make Cultiv. and Improv. and Thomas Dawson hath made humble Suit and hath obtained a G. for the same.

PATENT BOOK NO. 23

30 August 1743 to 20 August 1745

[Volume II of II, PB 20 was Volume I. The beginning patents in this volume pick up where PB 20 left off; the dates overlap those in PB 21 & PB 22. The formats for these patents are lengthy and not abbreviated; the use of columnar notes to indicate the format, folio or form page number was still discontinued in this volume.]

CHARLES ALLEN, 240 acs. Brunswick Co. on the N side of Staunten Riv., down Sandy Cr.; 30 Aug 1743 *in the 17th year of our Reign of George the Second, William Gooch Esq. our Lieutenant Governor and Commander in Chief at Williamsburgh*, p.567. £1.S5.

DANIEL HAMLIN, 703 acs. Amelia Co. on the head Brs. of the Lower fork of Sandy Riv., on a br. of the Middle or Main fork, over a br. of Nottoway; 30 Aug 1743, p.568. £3.S10.

JOHN STEVENSON, 250 acs. Orange Co. on the W side of the blue Ridge on brs. of Shanando Riv., adj. Christopher Franciskis; 30 Aug 1743, p.570. £1.S5.

JOHN ORNSBY, Clerk, 100 acs. Amelia Co. on Lower side of the lower Seller fork of deep Cr.; adj. Bolling alias Blands, & William Ford; 30 Aug 1743, p.571. 10 Shill. [Included in his PB 26 p.457]

WALTER TRUMBLE, 160 acs. Orange Co. on the W side the blue Ridge, crossing the Plumbtree Bottom br.; 30 Aug 1743, p.573. £1.

JOHN ORNSBY, Clerk, 4,054 acs. Amelia Co. on both sides of Nottoway Road bet. the brs. of Deep Cr. and the brs. of Tommohitton Sw., up the great Br., by Cock's Road, up Mingo's Horsepen br., along the County line [North], crossing Middle Seller Cr. & Butterwood Sw.; adj. Francis Rany, Benjamin Simmons, Arthur Leath, George Ford, William

Thomas, Haynes, Frederick Ford, William Ford, his own lines, Bland, Westbrook & Peter Leath; 30 Aug 1743, p.574. £20.S5. [Included in his PB 26 p.457]

WILLIAM LOVESAY, JUNIOR, Son of John Lovesay, 182 acs. Pr. Geo. Co. on S side of Second Sw.; adj. Joseph Rives, Sturdivant & Lanthrop; 30 Aug 1743, p.577. £1.

WILLIAM BREWER, 250 acs. Brunswick Co., adj. Bedingfield & William Sim; 30 Aug 1743, p.579. £1.S5.

RICHARD ADKINS, 275 acs. Pr. Geo. Co. by the Ponds path; adj. Valentine Williamson, William Heath, Captain Clement & Israel Mark; 30 Aug 1743, p.580. £1.S10.

BENJAMIN RUFFIN, 950 acs. Amelia Co. on both sides of Little Saylors Cr., adj. Osborn; 30 Aug 1743, p.582. £4.S15. Whereas by Pat. 2 Jan 1737/38 gtd. Benjamin Ruffin [PB 17 p.433 which included his 550 acs. in PB 17 p.344 dated 10 Jun 1737] and whereas the sd Benjamin Ruffin hath failed to make cultiv. & improv. and Edmund Ruffin made Humble Suit and obtained a g. for the same which he hath relinquished unto the sd Benjamin Ruffin.

SAMUEL JONES, 135 acs. Amelia Co. on the lower side of Fitzgerralds Fork of Wests Cr. & up West's Cr.;, adj. sd Fitzgerald, Joseph Farley & Joseph Jackson; 30 Aug 1743, p.584. 15 Shill.

ROBERT CARR, JUNIOR, 240 acs. Nansemond Co. on the W side Black water Riv. & S side the Cedar Sw., crossing the Miery Br., in the Cedar Marsh; adj. Jacob Darden, Robert Carr Senr. & Stephen Darden; 30 Aug 1743, p.586. £1.S5.

WILLIAM FAIRCLOTH, 290 acs. Is. of Wight Co. on the S side of Nottoway Riv. & E side of Myery br.; adj. sd Faircloth, Robert Newsom, John Vick & Robert Vick; 30 Aug 1743, p.588. £1.S10.

THOMAS MATTHEWS, 318 acs. Surry Co. on the N side of Nottoway Riv., down Turkey Cock Sw., Colo. Benjamin Harrison, James Matthews, John Russel & Colo. Benjamin Harrison's River Land; 30 Aug 1743, p.590. £1.S15.

JAMES WILLIAMS, 165 acs. Pr. Geo. Co on the N side of Gravilly run, by a pond; adj. his own old line, James Jones, Isham Eppes and William Eppes & Joseph Butler; 30 Aug 1743, p.591. £1.

CALEB ELISTE, 190 acs. Upper Par. of Surry Co. adj. Abraham Evans Patents for 472 acs. [PB 8 p.5] & 300 acs. [PB 7 p.460], Mr John Barker and Thomas Hunt; 30 Aug 1743, p.594. £1. Whereas by Pat. dated 28 Sep 1732 gtd. John Simmons [PB 15 p.149 a regrant of sd Evans' PB 8 p.154 dated 28 Apr 1691] and sd John Simmons failed to make Cultiv. and Improv., and Caleb Eliste hath made Humble suit and obtained a g. for the same.

JOHN WHITMORE, 150 acs. Pr. Geo. Co. on the Upper fork of Beaverpond Cr. of Nottoway Riv.; 30 Aug 1743, p.596. 15 Shill.

WILLIAM GILLUM, 250 acs. Surry Co. on the N side of the SouthWester Sw., adj. George Booth & William Winkfield; 30 Aug 1743, p.597. £1.5.

ARTHUR WHITEHEAD, 430 acs. Is. of Wight Co. on the S side of Nottoway Riv.; adj. William Turner, the sd Whitehead, John Bohoon, Jacob Brake & Thomas Davis; 30 Aug 1743, p.599. £2.S5.

EDWARD ECCLES, 244 acs. Surry Co. on the S side of Nottoway Riv. and E side of Cabbinstick br., in a pond; adj. his Patented Land, John Cox & Hullum Sturdivant; 30 Aug 1743, p.601. 10 Shill. 140 acs. part formerly Gtd. sd Edward Eccles by Pat. 13 Oct 1727 [PB 13 p.249].

JOHN JONES, 1,272 acs. Amelia Co. on the N side of Nottoway Riv., down the long Br. of the Harracane; adj. Ledbiter Jones, William Burges, his own Land Purchased of Jackson, & John Lewis; 30 Aug 1743, p.603. £4.S10. 395 acs. part formerly gtd. John Jackson 20 Jul 1738 [PB 18 p.82] and by Mesne Conveyances the Right and Title is become vested in the sd John Jones, and 877 acs. the residue never before gtd.

ANSELM BAILEY, 380 acs. Surry Co. on the S side of black water Sw.; adj. Edward Pettway, his own line, his own Cornfield, William Pittman & David Sebrel; 30 Aug 1743, p.605. £2.

GEORGE BRAXTON JUNIOR, Gent., 25,000 acs. Goochland Co. on both sides of Buffalo Riv., at Rutlidges Cr., on a Stoney Ridge, by a Spring; adj. the Honourable John Carter and the Reverend Robert Rose, on the Secretary's line [East]; 25 Nov 1743, p.606. £125.

BENJAMIN WALLER, Gentleman, 400 acs. Louisa Co. adj. Giles Rogers & Mr. Martin; 25 Nov 1743, p.609. for £1.S15 as also for the Imp. of one Pers. to dwell within this our Colony and Dominion Whose Name is *Thomas Dickinson*. [This land was regranted to Christopher Curtis, assignee of Thomas Everard, in PB 31 p.304 dated 22 Nov 1752]

JOHN WATSON, 300 acs. Brunswick Co. on both side of Middle fork of Miles's Cr.; 25 Nov 1743, p.610. £1.S10.

JAMES DANIEL, 400 acs. Goochland Co. Near the Head of East br. of Bear Cr. of Willis Riv., near the S side of the Road; adj. William Holladay, Gideon Marr & Norvel Burton; 25 Nov 1743, p.612. £2.

THOMAS JONES, JUNIOR, 404 acs. Brunswick Co. on both sides of Crooked run, down the Mill Pond, adj. his own line; 25 Nov 1743, p.613. £2.

JOHN BOLLING, Gent., 6,300 acs. Goochland Co. on both sides of the Mountain Cr. of Willis's Riv., Beg. on the Rockey Ridge on the E side of the Creek; adj. Richard Guin, John Childers, Alexander Stinson, George Cleinoff & Samuel Ridgway; 25 Nov 1743, p.615. £5. 5,300 acs. part formerly Gtd. the sd John Bolling 1 Dec 1740 [PB 19 p.909] and the residue never before Gtd. [Included in his 6,740 acs. in PB 26 p.450a]

IRBY HUDSON, 481 acs. Pr. Geo. Co. on the N side of Stoney Cr., down Cedar Island br., adj. John Winingham & Jones; 25 Nov 1743, p.617. £2.S15.

RICHARD ROYALL, 400 acs. Amelia Co. on the Lower side of Flatt Cr. bet. the lines of William Mayes, William Craddock, Robert Vaughan, Isham Vaughan, Thomas Tabb and Sherwin, & Matthew Mayes; 25 Nov 1743, p.619. £2.

ELIZABETH LEWIS, 400 acs. Goochland Co. adj. Thomas Stone, the Reverend William Stith & John Lewis; 25 Nov 1743, p.621. £2.

PETER HUBARD, 400 acs. Brunswick Co. on the S side Nottoway Riv., adj. John Evans near the falls, up the Falls Cr.; 25 Nov 1743, p.623. £2.

HENRY BEARD, 370 acs. Goochland Co. on the Brs. of Willis's Riv. alias Willis's Cr. and on the Upper side of sd Riv., adj. Henry Cary, Gent.; 25 Nov 1743, p.626. £2.

HENRY JONES, 404 acs. Brunswick Co. on the S side of Hiccory Run adj. Hicks Jones; 25 Nov 1743, p.628. £2.

JOHN LEDBETTER, 196 acs. Brunswick Co. on the N side of Maherin Riv., Beg. at Ralph

Jackson's a little below the Islands, down the Riv. including all the Islands; 25 Nov 1743, p.629. £1.

JOHN BLACKSTONE, 187 acs. Brunswick Co. on both sides of Stith's Cr., Beg. a little above the Nap of Reeds Opposite to an Island, down a Great Br.; 25 Nov 1743, p.631. £1.

ALEXANDER BOLLING son of Stith Bolling late of Surry Co. dec'd., 897 acs. Pr. Geo. Co. on the Ridge bet. the brs. of Buckskin Cr. and the brs. of Nottoway Riv., next to Smiths run, down along a Meadow of Licking Place br., & by a br. of Ellicks Meadow; adj. James Moody, McKinney, Westmoreland, John Robertson & Captain Walker; 25 Nov 1743, p.633. £4.S10.

FRANCIS WYATT, 377 acs. Pr. Geo. Co. on the Upper side of Butterwood Sw., in a small Meadow below the main Road, by the side of a thickpond near the Church Road; adj. William Westbrooke & Edward Mitchell; 25 Nov 1743, p.635. £2.

HENRY CARY, Gent., 400 acs. Goochland Co. on both sides of Hatchers Cr., a br. of Willis's Cr., adj. his own lines, Edmond Wood & Edward Kelley; 25 Nov 1743, p.636. £2.

WILLIAM CUNNINGHAM, 274 acs. Brunswick Co. on the N side of Turnup Cr., below the Mouth of a great br.; 25 Nov 1743, p.638. £1.S10.

ALEXANDER STINSON, 400 acs. Goochland Co. on the N side of Willis's Riv. alias Willis's Cr. and on both sides of Cat Tail Cr., adj. Henry Cary Gent.; 25 Nov 1743, p.639. £2.

LEANDER HUGHES, 390 acs. Goochland Co. on both sides of Pidy run (Pidy Rock run) of Willis Riv. adj. Henry Cary & Alexander Trent; 25 Nov 1743, p.641. £2.

p.643 - *Thus far settled as Pt rect. in the other Book at the End. Feb.16.1743/44 John Blair D.Audr.*

The Honourable JOHN GRYMES Esq. and Francis Willis Gentl. Executors of the last Will and Testament of Henry Willis Gentl. dec'd., 548 acs. Orange Co. on black Walnut run, Beg. in a Poysoned Field on the W side of sd run; 1 Mar 1743/44, p.643. £1.S10. 280 acs. part formerly Gtd. unto Robert Slaughter by Pat. 30 June 1726 [288 acs. Spotsyl. Co., PB 12 p.491] and by the sd Robert Slaughter sold & Conveyed unto the sd Henry Willis who by his sd Will & Testament devised all his Lands to his Executors to be sold for Payment of his Debts and the residue never before Gtd.

ISHAM EPPES Gent., 1,560 acs. Pr. Geo. Co. bet. Hatchers run and Gravilly run, on Hatchers run near the Mouth of Elbow br., up Gum br., by a Pond; adj. Thomas Nance his 200 acs., Joseph Butler, James Jones, Jeffry Hauk, George Scogin, Sentall, Mayes, Joseph Hauk, & Bley; 1 Mar 1743/44, p.645. £8.

RICHARD KENNON & WILLIAM KENNON, JUNIOR, 31,700 acs. Brunswick Co. on the N side of Stanton Riv. and on both sides of Cubb Cr., on Terrys Run & on the North fork of Louce Cr.; adj. Richard Austin, Ellis, Richard Ward, Joseph Ward, Fuquay, Mays & Anderson; 1 Mar 1743/44, p.647. *for divers good causes and Considerations but more Especially for the Consideration mentioned in an order of our Lieutenant Governor in Council bearing date 3 Nov last passed.*

BENJAMIN WALLER, Gentl., 1,118 acs. Spotsyl. Co. on the W side Raccoon Sw.; adj. Chiles Now Humphry Hill Gentl., Mr George Seaton, Thomas Sartin Now Holladays, Joseph Peterson, William Waller, John Trustee, and the L. Purchased by the sd Benjamin of John Wiglesworth; 1 Mar 1743/44, p.650. 15 Shill. 1,000 acs. formerly part formerly

gtd. unto the sd Benjamin Waller by Pat. 28 Sep 1728 [PB 13 p.296] and 118 acs. the Residue never bef. Gtd.

NICHOLAS DAVIS, Gent., 633 acs. Goochland Co. at the foot of Flemmings Mountain, on the Spur of a Mountain & on Flat Ground; 1 Mar 1743/43, p.652. £3.S5.

NICHOLAS DAVIS, 432 acs. Goochland Co.; 371 acs. part on the S side the Fluvanna & 61 acs. the Residue is contained in an Island in the sd Riv. called Rawleigh's Island and is 310 Poles long, on Rawleigh's Cr., adj. his own line; 1 Mar 1743/44, p.654. £2.S5.

JOHN MILLS, 400 acs. in that part of Orange Co. designed to be called Augusta on a br. of James Riv. called Percimmon Br.; 1 Mar 1743/44, p.655. £2.

JAMES McDOWELL, 400 acs. Orange Co. on the S side of James Riv.; 1 Mar 1743/44, p.657. £2.

ROGER NEALE, 200 acs. Brunswick Co. on the N side of Staunton Riv. and on both sides of Whipping Cr.; 1 Mar 1743/44, p.658. in Consideration of the Imp. of 4 Pers. whose Names are *Roger Neale, Stephen Neale Junr., Nicholas Durnen and John Nevills.*

ROGER NEALE, 104 acs. Brunswick Co. on the N side of Staunton Riv., Beg. on a Point of Rocks on the sd Riv., at the lower end of the Low Grounds; 1 Mar 1743/44, p.660. in Consideration of the Imp. of 2 Pers. whose Names are *Laughland Flyn and Katharine Neale.*

ISAAC BATES, Gent., 3,167 acs. Goochland Co. on both sides of Randolph's Cr. of Willis's Riv.; adj. Thomas Basset, Joseph Dabbs, Thomas Walker, Thomas Edwards & Joseph Price; 1 Mar 1743/44, p.661. £16.

WILLIAM MARSHALL, 481 acs. Brunswick Co. on both sides of Whipping Cr.; 1 Mar 1743/44, p.663. in Consideration of the Sum of £2 as also for the Imp. of 2 Pers. whose Names are *William Marshall and Ann Marshall.*

WILLIAM CANNON, 385 acs. Goochland Co. on both sides of Bear Garden Cr. of the Fluvanna Riv., in the Low Grounds of sd Cr.; adj. Wentworth Webb, John Phelps, John Ripley & John Southern; 1 Mar 1743/44, p.665. £2.

JOSHUA IRBY, 366 acs. Henrico Co., in a Mire br. Near the [sd Irby's] House; adj. Anderson, the sd Irby's upper Survey, Branch, &

the sd Irby's low ground Survey; 1 Mar 1743/44, p.667. £2.

JOSHUA IRBY, 400 acs. Henrico Co. on the Banks of Appomatox Riv. just above the Mouth of a Gut; adj. a C. formerly Grills's, William Branch, the sd Irby's lower Survey, & Womack; 1 Mar 1743/44, p.669. £2.

EDWARD BRISWATE, 1,445 acs. Amelia Co. on both sides of the South fork of falling Cr. of Buffilo Riv., by the Path; adj. Cobb, Randolph & Kennon; 1 Mar 1743/44, p.671. £7.S5.

SAMUEL DAVIS, 200 acs. Is. of Wight Co. on the N side of Meherin Riv., by the side of the Stoney Br. & the little Sw; 1 Mar 1743/44, p.672. £1.

RICHARD GUIN, 400 acs. Goochland Co. on both sides of Great Buffelo Cr. of Willis's Riv. adj. Major John Bolling; 1 Mar 1743/44, p.674. £2.

JONATHAN SYDENHAM, Gent., 317 acs. & 108 Perches of Marsh Land in Essex Co.; Opposite and against Brays Church and the sd Burket, up the Rappahanock Riv., by another small Gut or Cr.; adj. a Pat. gtd. Isaac Flowers; 3 May 1744, p.676. £1.S15. Whereas by Pat. 25 Apr 1716 gtd. unto William Robinson, Nicholas Smith and John

Burket now dec'd. [PB 10 p.288] And Whereas the sd Robinson, Smith and Burket dec'd and their Heirs since their Death have failed to pay Quit Rents and Jonathan Sydenham Gent. hath made humble Suit and hath obtained a G. for the same.

JOHN CARGILL, 400 acs. Brunswick Co. on both sides of Cargills Cr.; 1 May 1744, p.678. £2.

JOHN EPPES, JUNIOR, 260 acs. Amelia Co. on the N side of little Nottoway Riv. and on both sides of the Lazaritta Cr.; 16 Jun 1744 *in the 18th year of our Reign of George the Second*, p.679. £1.S10.

WILLIAM MOTE, SENIOR, 223 acs. Brunswick Co. on the N side of little Beaver Pond Cr.; 16 Jun 1744, p.681. £1.S5.

WILLIAM MOTE, JUNIOR, 54 acs. Brunswick Co. on the N side of Meharin Riv.; 16 Jun 1744, p.682. 5 Shill.

DAVID STEVENSON, 400 acs. in that part of Orange Co. designed to be called Augusta on the N side of Catheys Riv. and on the North br. of the Great meadow, on the E side of Walkers run, Near the Head of the Meadow, adj. Thomas Stevenson; 16 Jun 1744, p.684. £2.

THOMAS KIRKLAND, JUNIOR, 330 acs. Pr. Geo. Co. on the S side of Jones Hole Sw.; adj. John Burge, Titmash, & Pitillo alias Morris's; 16 Jun 1744, p.685. £1.S15.

DRURY STITH, 354 acs. Brunswick Co. on the N side of Mitchel's Cr. & down the Lick Br., adj. William Hill; 16 Jun 1744, p.687. £1.S15.

FRANCIS ELLEDGE, 182 acs. Brunswick Co. on the Rockey br., along the Country line [S87°E], adj. William Moseley & Linch; 16 Jun 1744, p.689. £1.

JAMES WATKINS, 400 acs. Goochland Co. on the S side of Slate Riv. and both sides of Turpins Cr.; 16 Jun 1744, p.691. £2.

W I L L I A M   H A W K I N S /HAWKINGS, 200 acs. Brunswick Co. on both sides of Tossykiah Cr., above Reeds Hunting Path; 16 Jun 1744, p.692. £1.

DAVID SEARES, 280 acs. Pr. Geo. Co. on the S side of Hatchers run, by a Path; adj. the lines of Isham Eppes, William Jones, David McCollo, Herbert, James Williams,

& Hauk; 16 Jun 1744, p.694.
£1.S10.

FRANCIS SHARPE, 270 acs. Is.
of Wight Co. on the N side of
Meherin Riv., up the Flat Sw.; adj.
his own old lines & John Gwaltney;
16 Jun 1744, p.696. £1.S10.

JAMES HUDSON, 400 acs.
Amelia Co. on the upper side of
Stanly's fork of Woody Cr., adj.
FitzGerald and William
Featherstone; 16 Jun 1744, p.698.
£2.

JAMES HILL, 400 acs. Henrico
Co. on both sides of Nisons br.;
adj. Edmond Logwood, John
Welch, James Farlow & John
Burton; 16 Jun 1744, p.700. £2.

JOSEPH REDD, 400 acs. Henrico
Co. on both sides of Sappony Cr.;
adj. the sd Joseph and John Redd,
Henry Walthall, Richard Wood,
Owen, & Benjamin Branch; 16 Jun
1744, p.701. £2.

WILLIAM DUGGER, 328 acs.
Brunswick Co. adj. William
Hagood and Boswell; 16 Jun 1744,
p.703. £1.S15.

JOHN SNEAD, 400 acs. Louisa
Co. on the SW side of Poindexters
Mountain alias Piny Mountain, on
the side of a Ridge, adj.
Poindexter; 16 Jun 1744, p.705.
£2.

THOMAS TABOR, 135 acs. Is. of
Wight Co. on the N side of
Meherin Riv., Down the Miry br.;
adj. John Mundall, the sd Tabor,
Thomas Porter & Stephen Powell;
16 Jun 1744, p.707. 15 Shill.

DANIEL CLAYTON, 200 acs.
Hanover Co. bet. the lines of
Watson and Alves; 16 Jun 1714,
p.709. The sd Tract gtd. unto
Henry Wood Gent. by Pat. 28 Sep
1730 [PB 13 p.502] and by him
sold and Conveied unto the sd
Daniel Clayton by whom the sd
former Pat. is delivered up to be
Cancelled there being an Error in
the bounds of the sd L. mentioned
in the sd Pat.

THOMAS ELDRIDGE, 1,772 acs.
Pr. Geo. Co. on the N side of
Warwick Sw., Crossing Hoggpen
Br., just below Bettis's Path, down
the upper Fork of Units br. & up
the main or lower fork thereof, by
Henry Gee's fence & Gee's Ditch;
adj. his old line, Peter Ive, James
Gee, Haley, Roger Daniel & Henry
Gee; 16 Jun 1744, p.711. £5.S15.
623 acs. part formerly Gtd. unto
William Randolph and Robert
Bolling Gent. by Pat. 20 Nov 1682
[PB 7 p.199, Chas. City Co.] and
by divers Mesne Conveyances is
become Vested in the sd Thomas
Eldridge & the Residue never bef.
Gtd.

SAMUEL LUCK, 140 acs. Hanover Co. adj. Luck, Philips and Brown; 16 Jun 1744, p.714. 15 Shill.

ARTHUR WHITHEAD, 550 acs. Is. of Wight Co. on the N side of Meherin Riv., by the side of the little Sw., by the Country line [West], up the Edge of the Bear Marsh Sw., adj. his old L.; 16 Jun 1744, p.716. £2.S15.

PHILIP THOMAS, 400 acs. Goochland Co. adj. to Appamatox Riv., crossing bad luck br., adj. Richard Randolph & William Randolph Esq.: 16 Jun 1744, p.718. £2.

ABRAHAM COOK, 289 acs. Brunswick Co. on the N side of Roanoak Riv., adj. John Butcher & William Davis; 30 Aug 1744, p.720. £1.S10.

BLOOMFIELD LONG, 331 acs. Spotsyl. Co. adj. Mr Joseph Brock, Mr John Walker & William Branagon; 30 Aug 1744, p.721. which sd L. is part of a Pat. for a larger Quantity Gtd. to Larkin Chew 4 Jun 1722 [9,400 acs. in PB 11 p.91 which included 2 Patents of 400 acs. to Larkin Chew, Richard Buckner, Joseph Chew & John Sutton both in PB 10 p.58 dated 26 Apr 1712] and by divers Mesne conveyances is become Vested in the sd Bloomfield Long. [7,467

acs. to Joseph Brock in PB 18 p.140, 462 acs. to Rice Curtis Jr. in PB 18 p.149, 178 acs. to James Stevens in PB 18 p.151, 36 acs. to John Talbert in PB 18 p.313, 244 acs. to William & James Samms in PB 18 p.356 & 183 acs. to Henry Carter in PB 20 p.447 are all part of the 9,400 acs. gtd. to Larkin Chew in PB 11 p.91]

ROBERT COLEMAN, 400 acs. Spotsyl. Co. in the Parish of St. George, on the S side of the Glady run, on the SW side a Glade; adj. Booker (now Robert Colemans), Hugh Sanders, Mr. Brock & Colonel Corbin; 30 Aug 1744, p.723. £2. Whereas by Pat 28 Sep 1728 Gtd. unto Nathaniel Sanders containing 2,200 acs. [PB 13 p.373 which included 1,200 acs. King William Co. to Nathaniel Sanders in PB 12 p.424], and Whereas the sd Nathaniel Sanders by his last Will and Testament did devise 400 acs. part unto his Son Nathaniel Sanders and Whereas the first Mentioned Nathaniel Sanders is now dead and the sd Nathaniel Sanders the Son hath failed to pay our Quit Rents for the sd 400 acs. and Robert Coleman hath made Humble Suit and obtained a G. for the sd 400 acs.

ASHFORD HUGHES, 350 acs. Goochland Co. on the brs. of Muddy Cr., adj. Thomas Walton, Major Bowler Cocke, William

Walton, Ashford Hughes; 30 Aug 1744, p.726. £1.S15.

JOHN FIELDOUR, 400 acs. Spotsyl. Co.; Beg. on the S side a Hill Near a Glade, on a Steep Point on the SW side a Great Meadow, adj. William Harris; 30 Aug 1744, p.728. £2.

GAFFELL BROWN, 353 acs. Louisa Co. adj. Charles Smith, Francis Smith & Christopher Smith; 30 Aug 1744, p.730. £1.S15.

EDWARD BOOKER, 401 acs. Brunswick Co. on both sides of Couches Cr., down the great br.; adj. Colwell, Briggs & Guilliam; 30 Aug 1744, p.731. £2.

ROBERT PEAKE, 185 acs. Amelia Co. on the S side of Appamattox Riv.; 30 Aug 1744, p.733. £1.

RICHARD BERNARD, 390 acs. Orange Co. on the S side the Goard Vine Riv.; 30 Aug 1744, p.735. for 2 lbs. Tobacco for every Acre. Whereas by Inquisition Indented taken in sd Co. 28 Jul 1738 by Virtue of a Warrant directed to John Robinson Esq. our Escheator for sd Co. Thomas Stonehouse formerly of Westmoreland Co. died Seised of a certain Tract Supposed to contain 507 acs. [Spotsyl. Co., PB 14 p.41 dated 28 Sep 1730] but by Survey lately made by James Wood, Surveyor of sd Co. and returned to our Secretary's Office it is found to contain only 390 acs. which is found to Escheat to us from Thomas Stonehouse and Richard Bernard hath made Humble Suit and obtained a G. for the same.

ARTHUR REDING, 200 acs. Pr. Geo. Co. on the S side of Jones Hole & S side of Tarkill Br.; adj. Thomas Tadlock, Richard Tatum, Lewis, & Richard Raynes; 30 Aug 1744, p.737. £1.

HENRY SPIRES, 100 acs. Pr. Geo. Co. on the N side of the Indian Sw., Beg. on the Reedy br. above the Path from Nathaniel Lees Plantation to the sd Henry Spires; 30 Aug 1744, p.739. 10 Shill.

PETER HARWELL, 198 acs. Pr. Geo. Co. on the N side of the Indian Sw.; adj. Henry Spires, John Roberts, John Man & John Floyd; 30 Aug 1744, p.741. £1.

THOMAS CLARK, 441 acs. Louisa Co. on brs. of Fork Cr., crossing licking Hole br., on the County line the several Courses [N40°W, N52°W, N61°W, N55°W, N45°W, N40°W, N24°W, N38°W & then N31°W]; adj. Major Henry & Francis Clark; 30 Aug 1744, p.743. £2.S5.

SAMUEL BURK, JUNIOR, 200 acs. Goochland Co. Adj. to the S side of Fluvanna Riv. against the Mouth of Tye Riv., Beg. at a Deer's Eye tree against the Upper end of Woods Island, adj. William Cabbel; 30 Aug 1744, p.745. £1.

SAMUEL SCOTT, 400 acs. in that part of Orange designed to be Called Augusta on a br. of the South Riv. of Shanando called Cub Run, on a Stony Hill, on a Spur of the Mountain; 30 Aug 1744, p.746. £2.

JAMES GEMMILL, 6½ acs. York Co. adj. William Wise & Anthony Robinson; 30 Aug 1744, p.748. for the Imp. of one Pers. whose Name is *James Gemmill.*

JOHN DUNKLEY & ROBERT DUNKLEY, 383 acs. Brunswick Co. on the N side of Posshum Quarter br., on a great br. at the falls; 30 Aug 1744, p.750. £2.

THOMAS PAULET, 439 acs. Hanover Co. on the brs. of Owens Cr., on both sides of the Goochland Road, on the Co. line [S20°W & S34°E], near a br. of Wild Boar, adj. Robert Deprest & Col. Syme; 30 Aug 1744, p.752. £2.S5.

LOVE STATHAM, 212 acs. Hanover Co. on the S side the Southanna, Beg. on the River Bank in Colo. Meriwethers line, near the Rowling Road, adj. sd Meriwether & Mr Venable; 30 Aug 1744, p.754. £1.S5.

THOMAS GILLIAM, 577 acs. Brunswick Co. on both sides of the Great Br. of Couche Cr.; 30 Aug 1744, p.756. £3.

WILLIAM MAYO, Gentleman, 1,400 acs. Goochland Co. adj. to the N side of Fluvanna Riv. on both sides of Gilberts Cr., Crossing Swan Cr., adj. William Cabbell; 30 Aug 1744, p.758. £5. 400 acs. part formerly Gtd. unto the sd William Mayo by Pat. 26 Mar 1739 [PB 18 p.214] & 1,000 acs. the Residue never bef. Gtd.

THOMAS CHEATHAM /CHETHAM, 224 acs. Henrico Co. Crossing two brs. of Deep Cr., adj. John Pride, John Russell; 30 Aug 1744, p.760. £1.S5.

WILLIAM BLAKE, 170 acs. Is. of Wight Co. on the W side of Angelica, Beg. by the side of Purcell's Br., down the fork br.; 30 Aug 1744, p.762. £1.

JOHN HOPSON, 354 acs. Henrico Co. up a Small br. of White Oak Sw., down the North br. of sd Sw.; adj. Richard Cocke alias Benjamin Hopson's, & Nicholas Hopson; 30 Aug 1744, p.764. £1.S15.

RICHARD RANDOLPH of Henrico Co., Gentleman, 3,233 acs. Brunswick Co. on the N side of Otter Riv., including the Heads of the brs. of Buffilo Cr. and Elk Cr.; 30 Aug 1744, p.766. £16.S5.

JOHN FORT, 200 acs. Brunswick Co. in the fork of Maharin Riv., adj. Brigs; 30 Aug 1744, p.768. £1. £1.

GEORGE DAMRIL, 400 acs. Goochland Co. on both sides of Hardwar Riv., adj. Benjamin Woodson; 30 Aug 1744, p.770. £2.

THOMAS NOSEE & SOLOMON CREEKMAN, 256 acs. Norfolk Co., binding upon the main Sw., adj. John Creekman & Edward Creekman; 30 Aug 1744, p.772. £1.S10.

WILLIAM MAYO, Gentleman, 100 acs. Goochland Co. on S side of Fluvanna Riv., adj. William Cabbell; 30 Aug 1744, p.774.

ROBERT TUCKER, 176 acs. Amelia Co. in the fork of Tuckers br. of Namazean Cr., down the North Fork of sd br., up the South Fork or the Main br.; adj. Munns, the sd Tuckers own old line, & Bland; 30 Aug 1744, p.775. 5 Shill. 141 acs. part formerly Gtd. unto the sd Robert Tucker by Pat. 15 Jul 1717 [PB 10 p.340 on Namusend Cr. in Pr. Geo. Co.] & the Residue never bef. Gtd.

THOMAS OAKLEY, 532 acs. Henrico Co., Beg. by a Slash Near near Hell Garden Path, on the N side of New Kent Road; adj. Mayo, Robertson & Abny; 30 Aug 1744, p.777. 20 Shill. 370 acs. part being part of 570 acs. formerly Gtd. Dennet Abny and Abraham Abny by Pat. 20 Jun 1733 [Dennit & Abraham Abney in PB 15 p.71] and the Residue never bef. gtd.

ROBERT BOLLING, Gentleman, 1,660 acs. Pr. Geo. Co. adj. and Including his old Squerril Leavil Tract, down a br. Rohowick Sw., in a Slash by a Pond, on the lower side of the Upper Fork of the Great Run, on the lower side of a Pond of second Sw., on Mocossoneck main Road, on the lower & upper side of Moccossoneck Road, Near the Head of Wildcat fall Down; adj. Henry Wall alias Eatons, Wood alias Jones, John Ravenscroft, Fitzgerald, Sears, Green and Jones; 30 Aug 1744, p.780. £6.S15. 323 acs. part formerly Gtd. unto Nicholas Overby by Pat. 21 Apr 1690 [Chas. City Co. to Nicholas Overbee the younger in PB 8 p.77] and by divers Mesne Conveyances the Right and title thereof is become Vested in the sd Robert Bolling and the Residue never bef. Gtd.

ROBERT BOLLING, Gentleman, 2,750 acs. Pr. Geo. Co. upon the Head brs. of Sappone Cr. and Rocky run and on both sides the Upper Nottoway Riv. Road, Beg. at his old upper c. upon Sappone Cr. below the mouth of the long br., by the side of the Road from Stony Cr. to Sappone Chappel, in a Meadow at the Head of Wills run, upon rocky run below where the Chappel Road Crosses the same, up the first Great br. above Roger Rany's, at the Upper fork of sd br., Crossing Turkey Egg Road, Down the Dividing br.; adj. John Stith & John Tabb; 30 Aug 1744, p.783. £10.S15. 613 acs. part being part of a Pat. for 2,604 acs. formerly Gtd. unto the sd Robert Bolling by Pat. dated 4 Aug 1721 [PB 11 p.64], & the residue never bef. Gtd. [892 acs. part of Bolling's 2,604 acs. in PB 11 p.64 was included in 3,596 acs. to Drury Stith Junr. in PB 13 p.192]

RALPH PHLIPPING, 400 acs. Goochland Co. on both sides of Rocky run of Willis Riv., adj. John Martin; 30 Aug 1744, p.785. £2.

SIMON EVERITT, JUNIOR, 308 acs. Nansemond Co. on the S side of Nottoway Riv., Crossing Davis's br., Down Lewis's br.; adj. his own & Lazarus Whitehead; 30 Aug 1744, p.787. for £1.S10 as also for the Imp. of one Pers. whose Name is *Thomas Williams*.

JOHN HARE, 275 acs. Nansemond Co. on the S side the back Sw.; adj. Henry Copeland, John Ralls, Thomas Boyt, William Boyt & James Ralls; 30 Aug 1744, p.790. £1.S10.

HENRY DOWNS, 160 acs. Orange Co., on the side of a Mountain, on an Ivey point; adj. Samuel Taliaferro, David Jones & Henry Downs; 30 Aug 1744, p.792. £1.

WILLIAM BLAKE, 275 acs. Is. of Wight Co. on the S side of Nottoway Riv., over the run of Angelica Sw., down Purcells br., adj. his own old lines & John Barrow; 30 Aug 1744, p.793. £1.S10.

p.795. Feby. 12th. 1744/45 Then Settled to this Place & to page 205 [PB 22] of the other Book & burnt 2280 Rights Due Since the last Settlem't. page 643. of this Book. John Blair D.Audr.

ALEXANDER SPALDING & JOHN LIDDERDALE, 16,993 acs. Brunswick Co. on both sides of Little Roanoake and Wards Fork, down Donefants fork, down Pictures br., up Little Roanoake Riv., on the Ridge bet. Brunswick Co. and Amelia; adj. Richard Ward, Dawson, Thomas Williams & John Austin; 18 Feb 1744/45, p.796. £85.

STEPHEN DEWEY, Gent., 304 acs. Brunswick Co. on the lower side of Twittys Cr., adj. Twitty & McGehe; 15 Mar 1744/45, p.799. £1.S10.

The Reverand JAMES MARYE, Clerk, 400 acs. Spotsyl. Co., Beg. on a Hill side on the lower side the Bluff Run, on the S side of a Hill near a Glade, on the SW side of a great Meadow, adj. John Sartin; 15 Mar 1744/45, p.801. £2.

CORNELIUS ROBINSON, 400 acs. in that part of Orange Co. designed to be called Augusta on the N side of the North Riv. of Shanando on both sides of Fort run; 15 Mar 1744/45, p.803. £2.

MATTHEW MILLS, 400 acs. Goochland Co. on the brs. of Mechums Riv., on the Spire of a Mountain, adj. his own line & Michael Wood; 15 Mar 1744/45, p.804. £2. [Included in his PB 27 p.316]

GEORGE STUBBLEFIELD, 502 acs. Spotsyl. Co. on the brs. of Cat Tail Sw. a br. of Mattapony, on a Knole, on a Ridge in Poyson fields, near a Glade, on a Levell, on the S side of the Cattail Lick Sw.; adj. Mr Zachary Lewis, a Pat. Gtd. to Larkin Chew Gent. dec'd., John Sertain & Edward Herndon Junior; 15 Mar 1744/45, p.806. 10 Shill. 400 acs. part formerly Gtd. unto

Edward Herndon by Pat. 16 Jun 1727 [Edward Hernton of K. & Q. Co. in PB 13 p.91] and by divers Mesne Conveyances is become Vested in sd George Stubblefield and 102 acs. the Residue never bef. Gtd.

DANIEL BROWN, 400 acs. Amelia Co. on the brs. of Sandy Riv. on the lower side thereof, on the S side of the Road, adj. Joseph Ligon & Charles Burkes; 15 Mar 1744/45, p.809. £2.

JOHN HALL, 1,800 acs. Brunswick Co. on the N side of Maherin Riv. and on both sides of Briary Cr., along the Indian line [North & N1°W] to the Road, adj. Cocke & his own line; 15 Mar 1744/45, p.811. £6.S15. 318 acs. part formerly Gtd. George Walton by Pat. 7 Jul 1726 [PB 12 p,511]; 137 acs. other part formerly Gtd. Daniel Hix by Pat. 7 Jul 1726 Which by divers Mesne Conveyances are become Vested in the sd John Hall and the residue never bef. Gtd. [Daniel Hix's 137 acs. Brunswick Co. in PB 12 p.516 dated 7 Jul 1726 was surveyed by Robert Bolling as Pr. Geo. Co. on 23 Oct 1723 for Daniel Hix, opposite to his brother George Hix. Both Hix tracts were adj. to the Fort Christanna tract.]

MATTHEW MILLS, 400 acs. Goochland Co. on Brs. of

Mechems Riv., and adj. his own and Michael Wood; 15 Mar 1744/45, p.813. £2. [Included in his PB 27 p.316]

CHARLES ROBINSON, 400 acs. in that part of Orange Co. designed to be called Augusta on a br. of the North Riv. of Shanando called fort run; 15 Mar 1744/45, p.815. £2.

MATTHEW MILLS, 327 acs. Goochland Co. on the brs. of Mechums Riv., in a Bottom, adj. his own lines & Michael Wood; 15 Mar 1744/45, p.817. £1.S15. [Included in his PB 27 p.316]

CHARLES MILLS, 1,800 acs. Goochland Co. on the brs. of Licking hole Sw. and Beverdam Sw., by Woods Road, on the North fork of Beverdam, adj. Charles Moreman; 15 Mar 1744/45, p.819. £9.

VALENTINE FREEMAN, 400 acs. Henrico Co., through a Miary Slash, on the N side of the New Kent Road; adj. Joseph Watson, Richard Woodson, Martin Martin & Woodsons old Survey; 15 Mar 1744/45, p.821. £2.

ANDREW LEPRADE, 381 acs. Henrico Co. on the N side Buckingham Road & Crossing the Road; adj. Tanner and Farmer, Colo. William Byrd & the sd Leprade formerly Lewis Countis's; 15 Mar 1744/45, p.823. £2.

FARQUHARD GRANT, 400 acs. Pr. Geo. Co. on the Upper side of old field br. of Butterwood Sw., in a Valley; adj. Francis Coleman, Wyat, & Mrs Woodlief; 15 Mar 1744/45, p.825. £2. [Included in Robert Ferguson's 840 acs. in PB 28 p.168]

THOMAS OWEN, 496 acs. Henrico Co.; adj. John Shepperd, Robert Webb, Robert Morris, Wheeler, Holland and Royall; 15 Mar 1744/45, p.827. £2.S10.

WILLIAM WALTHALL, 346 acs. Henrico Co. on the S side of the Main run of the Ashen Sw., in the old field, up the Appomatock Riv. to a c. Opposite to a point of High Hills, up Rooty run; adj. John Baugh, Richard Walthall, Francis Walthall & William Pride; 15 Mar 1744/45, p.829. £1.S15.

JOHN NASH, 1,098 acs. Amelia Co. on the Upper side of Namisseen Cr., on the North fork of sd Cr.; adj. Hamlin, Stradford, Thomas Hood, & Bolling; 15 Mar 1744/45, p.831. £5.S10.

SAMUEL SABRILL, 350 acs. Is. of Wight Co. on the N side of Nottoway Riv., in a Pocoson, in the Lightwood Sw.; adj. Thomas Davis, Thomas Williams & James

Washington; 15 Mar 1744/45, p.833. £1.S15.

ANDREW LEPRADE, 103 acs. Henrico Co. on the N side of Buckingham Road; adj. the sd Leprade, Parker & Lewis Countis; 15 Mar 1744/45, p.835. 10 Shill.

RICHARD TALIAFERRO, 1,387 acs. Brunswick Co. on both sides of the great br. of Waquay, Near the head of the pine br.; adj. Peter Jones, & Irby; 15 Mar 1744/45, p.837. £2.S10. 922 acs. part formerly Gtd. Benjamin Simmons by Pat. 28 Sep 1728 [PB 14 p.71] and 465 acs. the Residue never bef. Gtd.

BENJAMIN COCKE/COCK, 370 acs. Goochland Co. on both sides of Buffalo br. of Beverdam Cr., to an Heap of stones on the S side of a Road; adj. James Nowland, Ebenezar Adams dec'd., Ralph Fuqua, Francis Sampson, Richard Cocke, Richard Pleasants & Thomas Pleasants; 15 Mar 1744/45, p.840. £2. [this land includes the 282 acs. Henrico Co. in PB 11 p.45 to James Nowellin /Nowland and part of the 500 acs. in PB 10 p.132 to William Lead/Lad]

ROBERT CARTER, 400 acs. Goochland Co. on the N side of Willis's Riv. alias Willis's Cr.; adj. Philip Mayo, Colo. Benjamin

Harrison & James Skelton Gent.; 15 Mar 1744/45, p.842. £2.

THOMAS CLAPTON, 237 acs. Brunswick Co. on the N side of Barrs Ellement Cr.; 15 Mar 1744/45, p.844. £1.S5.

MICHAEL HOLLAND, Gent., 4,753 acs. Goochland Co. adj. Terrill, Lewis, Thomas Moreman & James Fiddler; 15 Mar 1744/45, p.846. £2. 4,365 acs. part formerly [gtd.] sd Michael Holland by Pat. 10 Sep 1735 [PB 16 p.242 on Ivy Cr., S side of Rivanna Riv.] & 388 acs. the residue never bef. gtd.

JAMES BRIDGWATER, 400 acs. Goochland Co. both sides of Snow Quarter, Potatoe Quarter and Turkey Cock brs. of Willis's Riv., adj. Merry Webb, Jonathan Cunningham & Benjamin Dumas; 15 Mar 1744/45, p.849. £2.

JOHN MITCHELL, 400 acs. in that part of Orange Co. designed to be called Augusta on br. of James Riv. called broad Spring br., adj. Benjamin Burden; 15 Mar 1744/45, p.851. £2.

JOSHUA CLARK, 420 acs. Brunswick Co. on the S side of Meherin Riv., & the S side of the Cane Br., adj. James Parham; 15 Mar 1744/45, p.853. £2.S5.

THOMAS HARRISON, 250 acs. in that part of Orange Co. designed to be called Augusta on the East br. of Cooks Cr., Near the Head of a Meadow; 15 Mar 1744/45, p.854. £1.S5.

HUMPHREY BELL, 2,825 acs. Spotsyl. Co. by his [Robert Coleman's] New Plantation Fence, on a Levell, on the Upper side of Poppoy run, on a Ridge, near the Head of a br. of Robinsons Sw. & near the Head of a br. of Warrins Sw., up the Upper side of Warrins Sw., near the Head of a Glade; Beg. in Colo. Robinson "*Cleasby* Patent line"; adj. Robert Coleman, Colo. Waller, George Carter, Benjamin Matthews, Robert Goodloe, & Warrin; 15 Mar 1744/45, p.856. £5. 1,850 acs. part formerly Gtd. unto John Robinson Esq. by Pat. 25 Jul 1722 [PB 11 p.152 on S side the River Tae] and by him sold and conveyed unto sd Humphrey Bell and 975 acs. the Residue is Surplus L. found within the bounds of the sd former Pat. [Colo. Robinson's "*Cleasby* Patent line" refers to John Robinson's 2,200 acs. King Wm. Co. in PB 10 p.373 dated 23 Apr 1718 where it was called "*Chesby*"]

WILLIAM RANDOLPH & GEORGE CARRINGTON, Church Wardens of the Parish of Southam in the County of Goochland for a Glebe, 340 acs. Goochland Co. on the S side of James Riv.; adj. William Mayo, William Randolph Esq., Thomas Williamson, Richard Williamson & George Hudspeath; 3 Jun 1745, p.859. £1.S15. "unto the said William Randolph & George Carrington and to their Successors the Church Wardens of the said parish of Southam for the time being forever to be set apart for a Glebe To the only Use and behoof of the Minister of the said parish of Southam and his Successors forever ... Yielding and paying unto us our Heirs and Successors forever 50 Acres of Land and so proportionably for a lesser or greater Quantity than 50 Acres the Fee Rent of one shilling yearly to be paid upon the Feast of Saint Michael the Arch angel and also Cultivating and Improving 3 Acres part of every 50 of the Tract abovementioned within 3 Years after the Date of these presents" [Included in PB 24 p.460 to Nicholas Davies & Thomas Turpin]

WOOD JONES, 98 acs. Amelia Co. on the upper side of the Sweathouse Cr. of Deep Cr., adj. Munford; 3 Jun 1745, p.861. 10 Shill.

BENJAMIN HOOMES, 300 acs. Pr. Geo. Co. on white oak Sw. including the fork thereof, on the upper side of the South fork & down the North fork of sd Sw., adj. Charles Williams; 3 Jun 1745, p.863. £1.S10.

ROBERT ROWLAND, 400 acs. Amelia Co. on both sides of the Lazaritta Cr., on the long br., adj. Edward Robertson & Christopher Robertson; 3 Jun 1745, p.864. £2.

DANIEL JONES, 400 acs. Albemarle Co. on both sides of Biskit run, adj. Patrick Nowland; 3 Jun 1745, p.867. £2.

THOMAS BALDWIN, 400 acs. Amelia Co. on the S side of Appamattox Riv., adj. Venable; 3 Jun 1745, p.869. £2.

JOHN HOOD, 202 acs. Amelia Co. on both sides of the great br. of Winticomaick Cr., adj. Bolling & his [Hood's] fathers line; 3 Jun 1745, p.870. £1.

WILLIAM CRENSHAW, JUNIOR, 128 acs. Amelia Co. bet. the Lower fork of Woody Cr. and the upper fork of the Seller Cr.; adj. Isham Eppes, John Wallice, Francis Eppes & John Nance Senior; 3 Jun 1745 *in the 18th year of our Reign George the Second*, p.872. 15 Shill.

GEORGE GIBSON, 404 acs. Amelia Co. on the N or Lower side of Mallory's Cr., adj. Yarbrough; 10 Jul 1745 *in the 19th year of our*

Reign of George the Second, p.874. £2.

SAMUEL CHAMBERLIN, 1,335 acs. Brunswick Co. on the N side of Meherin Riv., Down the Rockey run; adj. Allin, Simes [her line], Smith, Thomas Jackson, his own line, John Tomlinson, Ralph Jackson & John Jackson; 10 Jul 1745, p.876. £5.S15. 220 acs. part formerly Gtd. unto Richard Ledbeter by Pat. 22 Feb 1724/25 [Richard Ledbetter, 220 acs. Surry Co. in PB 12 p.160] the Right and Title of which by divers Mesne Conveyances is become Vested in the sd Samuel Chamberlin and 1,115 acs. the Residue never bef. Gtd. [This Rockey run is now called Greensville Cr.]

ELIZABETH PINCHBACK, 500 acs. Goochland Co. on the Brs. of the Little Byrd; adj. Mary Massie, William Massie, John Moss & Charles Massie; 10 Jul 1745, p.879. £2.S10.

CHARLES SPRADLING, 400 acs. Amelia Co. in the fork of Saylor Cr.; adj. Elam, Towns, Osbourn & Richee; 10 Jul 1745, p.880. £2.

BURNELL CLAIBORNE, 150 acs. Pr. Geo. Co. on both sides the S side of white Oak Sw., Beg. on the Lower side the sd fork, by the side of Fitzgerralds Mill Path; adj. Captain Francis Poythress, &

Stewart; 10 Jul 1745, p.882. 15 Shill.

WILLIAM DAVIS, 285 acs. Amelia Co. on the S side of Winninghams Cr. of Deep Cr., bet. Stark and Sherwin; 10 Jul 1745, p.883. £1.S10.

WOOD JONES, 343 acs. Amelia Co. in the main fork of the Burchen Sw., up the Little Burchen & Down the Main Burchen Sw.; adj. Cryer, & Bryan Fennin; 10 Jul 1745, p.885. £1.S15.

JOHN BENTLY, 200 acs. Amelia Co. on the Heads of Pruits Cr. bet. the lines of William Gates, William Evans, William Hendricks and William Hurt; 10 Jul 1745, p.887. £1.

BARNABY WELLS, 200 acs. Amelia Co. on the S side of Flatt Cr., adj. William Watson & John Mayes; 10 Jul 1745, p.888. £1. [Included in William Watson's 5,077 acs. in PB 28 p.615]

RICHARD WITT, 400 acs. Goochland Co. bet. Angolo Cr. & Green Cr., adj. Joel Chandler; 10 Jul 1745, p.890. £2.

RICHARD CLERKE, 269 acs. Amelia Co. on the N side of Great Nottoway Riv.; adj. Stephen Dewey, Thweat & Munford; 10 Jul 1745, p.891. £1.S10.

EDWARD HASKINS, 535 acs. Amelia Co. on both sides of Sandy Riv., in the Low Grounds of the Haw Br.; adj. William Ligon, Walker, the L. purchased of Hudson, Rutledge, and Morton now Nashes line; 10 Jul 1745, p.892. £1.S5. 288 acs. part formerly Gtd. unto Samuel Hudson by Pat. 12 Mar 1739/40 [PB 19 p.568] and by Mesne Conveyances is become Vested in the sd Edward Haskins and the residue never bef. Gtd.

CHARLES WILLIAMSON, 228 acs. Amelia Co. on the lower side of the forked Br. of Little Nottoway Riv., down the fork and the Main Brs. of sd Br., adj. Abraham Cocke; 10 Jul 1745, p.894. £1.S5.

JOHN DAVIS, 200 acs. in that part of Orange Co. designed to be called Augusta on a Br. of the North Riv. of Shanando called Smiths Cr., Beg. on a hill on the N side of a Spring Br.; 10 Jul 1745, p.896. £1.

ANN DUFFEE, 200 acs. Pr. Geo. Co. on the N side of Josephs Sw., in a Bottom of sd Sw., Down the Reedy Br., adj. Harrison and Jacob Dunheart; 10 Jul 1745, p.897. £1.

JOHN HANSELL, 204 acs. Pr. Geo. Co. on the S side of Moccossneck Cr., adj. Herbert; 10 Jul 1745, p.899. £1.

JOHN MAY, 102 acs. Pr. Geo. Co. on the E or Lower side of Bever pond Cr., adj. Joseph Tucker; 10 Jul 1745, p.900. £10 Shill.

THOMAS BAUGH, 404 acs. Pr. Geo. Co. on the Lower side of the Flat Br. of Stoney Cr., on the Briery Br., up the Miery Br.; adj. Paul Seares, John Morley, & Herbert; 10 Jul 1745, p.901. £2.

SAMUEL ATKINSON, 400 acs. Goochland Co. at the Head of the East Br. of Bear Cr. of Willis Riv., near the S side of the Road; adj. William Kent, Stephen Cox & Gideon Marr; 10 Jul 1745, p.903. £2.

JOHN KIRBY, 196 acs. Pr. Geo. Co. on then N side of Moccossneck Cr. and on the upper side of White Oak Sw., in a Thicket; adj. Irby, James Pittillo/Pittello & his own old lines; 10 Jul 1745, p.905. £1.

JAMES MACKANE, 170 acs. Goochland Co. among Brs. of Rock Fish Riv. Near the blue Mountains, Beg. on the S side of Rock Fish Riv. West Br.; adj. Edwin Malloy, Edwin Hickman, James Hendrick & Josias Clapham; 10 Jul 1745, p.906. £1.

STEPHEN SANDERS, 430 acs. Goochland Co. on both sides of Willis Riv., Beg. in a slash, adj.

William Grey; 10 Jul 1745, p.907. £2.S5.

BENJAMIN MIMS, 200 acs. Goochland Co. adj. to the S side of Fluvanna Riv., on Top of a Cliff by the Riv., adj. William Cabbell; 10 Jul 1745, p.909. £1.

EBENEZAR ADAMS, 400 acs. Goochland Co. adj. to the E side of the Byrd, near the Fork of Elk run Thence down Elk run and up the Byrd; 10 Jul 1745, p.910. £2.

JOHN HARRIS, 75 acs. Goochland Co. on the N side of Fluvanna Riv.; l0 Jul 1745, p.911. 10 Shill.

JAMES WILKINS, 400 acs. Goochland Co. on both sides of the Barren Lick Cr. a Br. of Willis's Riv., adj. John Phelps & John Payne; 10 Jul 1745, p.913. £2.

WILLIAM WALTON, 400 acs. Goochland Co. on both sides of the North Br. of Waltons Fork of Slate Riv.; 10 Jul 1745, p.914. £2.

WILLIAM MASSIE, 390 acs. Goochland Co. Down the W side of the Little Byrd Cr., adj. John Cole dec'd; 10 Jul 1745, p.915. £2.

THOMAS BALLOW, 300 acs. Goochland Co. on both sides of Slate Riv.; 10 Jul 1745, p.917. £1.S10.

DANIEL SCOTT, 400 acs. Goochland Co. on the Brs. of Hatchers Cr., adj. George Holmes; 10 Jul 1745, p.918. £2.

JOHN HEARD, 218 acs. Goochland Co. on the Brs. of Rock fish Riv., adj. John Read & William Mayo; 10 Jul 1745, p.919. £1.S5.

ROBERT TUCKER, Gent., 3 acs. & 60 Square poles of Sunken Land and Water, in the Burrough of Norfolk in the Co. of Norfolk adj. to a Lott where he now liveth, Beg. at a corner Stone 2 Poles from his Westernmost corner stone upon the main Street, by the publick Land. into the Riv. to Low water marke, to the Publick Wharff, into the riv. facing his sd Lott, by a Cove Binding upon his sd Lott to his Wharf, to a pine Stump near the sd Riv. that parts the Lotts of Mr Smith and sd Tucker; 10 Jul 1745, p.921. 5 Shill.

PHILIP MORGAN, 120 acs. Brunswick Co. on both sides of Stiths Cr. adj. Drury Stith; 10 Jul 1745, p.922. 15 Shill.

WILLIAM HOWELL, 286 acs. Nansemond Co. on the N side the Back Sw.; adj. John Watson, Joseph Rogers Junior & Doctor Henry Jenkings dec'd.; 10 Jul 1745, p.924. £1.S10.

WILLIAM MASSIE, Gentleman, 1,500 acs. Goochland Co. on the Brs. of the Little Byrd, near Straw Br.; adj. Cole, John Moss & Edmond Lilly; 10 Jul 1745, p.925. £7.S10.

WILLIAM WALTON, 220 acs. Goochland Co. on both sides of Slate Riv.; 10 Jul 1745, p.926. £1.S5.

BENJAMIN HAWKINS, 404 acs. Brunswick Co. on the S side of Nottoway Riv. adj. Timothy Murrill & Stockes [Stokes]; 10 Jul 1745, p.928. £2.

RICHARD YOURK, 204 acs. Brunswick Co. both sides of Butchers Cr., adj. Cook; 10 Jul 1745, p.929. £1.

JAMES SEXTON, 190 acs. Brunswick Co. on the S side of Fountains Cr.; 10 Jul 1745, p.931. £1.

GEORGE KLEINHOFF, 400 acs. Goochland Co. on the N Brs. of Willis's Riv. near Willis's Mountains, adj. Henry Cary Gent.; 10 Jul 1745, p.932. £2.

WILLIAM JOHNSON, 150 acs. Spotsyl. Co. above the Little Mountains, at the foot of a Piney Mountain; adj. William Bartlett, John Taylor, & Felpes line; 10 Jul 1745, p.933. 15 Shill.

WILLIAM REID, 300 acs. in that part of Orange Co. designed to be Called Augusta, Beg. by a Valley corner to a Survey made for James Bartone in the fork of Shannandore and Nigh the foot of the Piked Mountain; 10 Jul 1745, p.935. for the Imp. of 6 Pers. to Dwell within this our Colony and Dominion of Virginia whose Names are *William Reid, George Gray, John Jackson, John Jones, David Morrison and Richard Stacey.*

GEORGE MUSICK & JOHN GRAVES, 520 acs. Spotsyl. Co., Beg. in the fork of the Devils Ditch Sw., in a Glade, on a Barren Levell, in a Valley; adj. Joseph Roberts, Coneas Wyatt, a Tract of L. formerly Surveyed for the sd George Musick, John Sartin, William Harris, and along the sd Harris's, John Fieldour, Thomas Sheltons and George Cooks line; 10 Jul 1745, p.936. £2.S15.

GILES KELLEY, 301 acs. Brunswick Co. on the S side of Waqua, Down the Great Br., along the Road, adj. John Scoggins, & Tabb; 10 Jul 1745, p.938. £1.S10. Whereas by Pat. 26 Mar 1739 Gtd. James Hudson [PB 18 p.233] who hath failed to make Cultiv. and Improv. and Pay Quit Rents and James Pittillo hath made humble Suit and Obtained a G. for the same which he hat assigned to Giles Kelley.

THOMAS TATOM, 430 acs. Brunswick Co. on the N side of Fountains Cr., up the Pine Br.; adj. William Weaver, Avent, Scott & his own line; 10 Jul 1745, p.940. £1.S10. 145 acs. part formerly Gtd. unto John Scott by Pat. 18 Feb 1722/23 [PB 11 p.170, a little above Beech Island in Is. of Wight Co.] and by divers Mesne Conveyances is since become Vested in the sd Thomas Tatom and 285 acs. the Residue never bef. Gtd.

JOHN HAMBLETON, 370 acs. Brunswick Co. on Nippers Cr., adj. William Tucker & Thomas Eldridge; 10 Jul 1745, p.942. £2.

WILLIAM MORRIS, 180 acs. Brunswick Co. on the N side of the three Creeks, by the dividing Br., adj. John Davis; 10 Jul 1745, p.943. £1.

ALEXANDER MCDOWELL, 350 acs. in that part of Orange Co. to be called Augusta on a Br. of James Riv. called the Mary, on the W side of Evans Run; 10 Jul 1745, p.946. £1.S15.

JAMES BENNETT, 382 acs. Brunswick Co. on both sides of Graveley Run, up the Rocky Run, adj. Edward Jackson; 10 Jul 1745, p.946. £2.

JOANNAH GILBERT, 400 acs. Brunswick Co. on the S side of Totero Cr., adj. Thomas Austin, & Hagood; 10 Jul 1745, p.948. £2.

ROBERT HESTER, JUNIOR, 300 acs. Brunswick Co. on the S side of Butchers Cr.; 10 Jul 1745, p.949. £1.S10.

WILLIAM BROADNAX, 521 acs. Brunswick Co. on the Brs. of the Reedy Cr.; 10 Jul 1745, p.951. 315 acs. part formerly Gtd. William Smith by Pat. 18 Feb 1722/23 [PB 11 p.185, on the S side of the Cattail Meadow in Surry Co.] and 206 acs. the residue being part of a Pat. of 300 acs. Gtd. Thomas Wilson by Pat. 28 Sep 1730 [PB 14 p.118, Surry Co.] the Right and Title of which sd 2 Parcels by divers mesne Conveyances is become Vested in the sd William Broadnax.

JOSEPH BLOODWORTH, 300 acs. in that part of Orange Co. designed to be called Augusta on both sides of the South Riv. of Shanando below William Russells Land; 1 Aug 1745, p.952. £1.S10.

ROBERT KING, 91 acs. Orange Co. on the W side of the blue Ridge, Beg. on a Point by the falling Spring run; 1 Aug 1745, p.954. 10 Shill.

BENJAMIN DAVIS, 100 acs. in that part of Orange Co. designed to be Called Augusta on the S side of James Riv., on a Ridge, adj. Robert Luney; 1 Aug 1745, p.956. 10 Shill.

MICHAEL UTZ, 291 acs. Orange Co. on the N side of Robinsin Riv.; 1 Aug 1745, p.958. for 2 lbs. of Tobacco for every acre of the sd Land for our Use already Paid to our Receiver General of our Revenues. Whereas by Inquisition Indented taken in sd Co. 27 Mar 1741 by Virtue of a Warrant directed to William Robinson, Deputy Escheator for the sd Co. It appears that John Michael Stolts of sd Co. died Seised of a certain Tract [PB 14 p.438, Spotsyl. Co. dated 11 Apr 1732] which is found to Escheat to us from the sd Stolts and Whereas William Fowler hath made humble Suit to the Honourable James Blair, Clerk late President of our Council and Commander in Chief of our sd Colony and Dominion of Virginia and Obtained a G. for the same which he hath sold unto Michael Utz.

JOHN MICHAUX, 303 acs. Brunswick Co. on the N side of Rattle Snake Cr., down the Rockey run, adj. William Ledbetter; 1 Aug 1745, p.959. £1.S10.

HENRY BAILEY, 274 acs. Brunswick Co. on the N side of Sturgeon run, adj. Sparrow & Robinson; 1 Aug 1745, p.961. £1.S10.

JOHN BRITTLE, 221 acs. Brunswick Co. on the S side of the great Cr. adj. Jones; 1 Aug 1745, p.962. £1.S5.

JOSIAS BAKER, 153 acs. Brunswick Co. on both sides of Butchers Cr.; 1 Aug 1745, p.964. 15 Shill.

THOMAS JONES, 391 acs. Brunswick Co. on the N side of Crooked run adj. his old line; 1 Aug 1745, p.965. £2.

WILLIAM HARLOW, 400 acs. Brunswick Co. on both sides of Hounds Cr., up Huckleberry br.; 1 Aug 1745, p.967. £2.

THOMAS WILLIAMS, 1,300 acs. Brunswick Co. on both sides of Turnup Cr.; 1 Aug 1745, p.969. £6.S10.

RICHARD DAVIS, 386 acs. Brunswick Co. on the N side of Wards Fork, adj. Hurt, Austin & Cobb; 1 Aug 1745, p.971. £2.

ROBERT RIVERS, 216 acs. Brunswick Co. on both sides of the North Fork of Meherin Riv.; 1 Aug 1745, p.972. £1.S5.

JOSEPH RIGHT, 238 acs. Brunswick Co. on the S side of the Reedy Br., adj. John Jeff [PB 18 p.553 to John Jefferson/Jeffries]; 17 Aug 1745, p.974. £1.S5. [This land is now in Greensville County, S of Fountains Cr. on the Reedy Br. of Beaverpond Cr. near the head of Cattail Cr.; also adj. John Parson/Person's PB 12 p.513, Joseph Sturdurt's PB 33 p.962, William Batts' PB 38 p.564 & John Spraberry's PB 38 p.824]

JOHN ELLIS, 193 acs. Brunswick Co. on the S side of Nottoway Riv., down the falls Cr.; adj. Stephen Dewey, John Evans & William Evans; 1 Aug 1745, p.975. £1.

THOMAS WORD, 400 acs. Brunswick Co. on both sides of Cub Cr., down Turkey Cock Br.; 1 Aug 1745, p.977. £2.

JOSHUA CLARK, 339 acs. Brunswick Co. on the S side of Fountains Cr.; adj. Peter Vinsson, John Brewer, Blunt, Bradford, & John Peopels; 1 Aug 1745, p.979. £1.S15.

JOHN BORROUGH, 400 acs. Brunswick Co. on Laniers Br., adj. Lanier & Gee; 1 Aug 1745, p.981. £2.

THOMAS TOMLINSON, JUNIOR, 400 acs. Brunswick Co.

adj. Thomas Tomlinson Senior & William Cook; 1 Aug 1745, p.983. £2.

HENRY CHILDS, 104 acs. Brunswick Co. on the S side of Staunton Riv.; 1 Aug 1745, p.984. 10 Shill.

WILLIAM BARROW/BURROW, 375 acs. Pr. Geo. Co. on the S side of the Main Cattail Run; adj. Captain Francis Eppes, Edward Smith, Charles Pistoll, Hudson, & Maynard alias Jones Irvins; 1 Aug 1745, p.986. £2.

JOHN BIRD, 213 acs. upper Parish of Nansemond Co. on the S side of the Knuckle Sw.; adj. John Cole Junior, John Cole Senior, Joseph Horton & Joseph Rogers; 1 Aug 1745, p.988. £1.S5.

JOHN COLE, JUNIOR, 125 acs. Nansemond Co. on the S side of the Knuckle Sw.; adj. Andrew Ross, John Cole, William Fryer & Edward Roberts; 1 Aug 1745, p.990. 15 Shill.

THOMAS HOWARD, JUNIOR, 403 acs. in the upper Parish of Nansemond Co. near a place called *Wickham*, adj. Ann Ballard & Mrs Mary Baker; 1 Aug 1745, p.992. £2. Whereas by Pat. 13 Nov 1723 Gtd. unto Christopher Jackson [PB 11 p. 293] who failed to Cultiv. & Improv. and Thomas Hobgood hath

made humble Suit and obtained a G. for the same which he hath assigned unto Thomas Howard Junior.

HENRY JONES, 404 acs. in the upper Parish of Nansemond Co. up a br. issuing out of the Cabin Sw.; adj. Michael Archer, William Maclenney, Edward Boite, James Bird & Robert Sanders; 1 Aug 1745, p.994. £2. Whereas by Pat. 13 Nov 1723 gtd. unto Christopher Jackson [PB 11 p.293] who failed to make Cultiv. & Improv. and Thomas Hobgood hath made humble Suit and hath obtained a G. for the same which he hath assigned unto Henry Jones.

WILLIAM WINN, 470 acs. Surry Co. on the N side of Nottoway Riv. & on Each side of the South Wester Sw., adj. Peter Green & Nathaniel Robinson; 1 Aug 1745, p.997. £1.S10.

RICHARD PEPPER, 332 acs. Surry Co. on the S side of Harrys Sw., the E side of Duckingfields Br. & both sides of Reedy Br.; adj. Peter Randall, John Mitchell, Stephen Cauldler & Hugh Davis; 1 Aug 1745, p.999. £1.S15.

WILLIAM JOHNSON, 121 acs. Surry Co. on the N side of the Black Sw., adj. his own line & John Tomlinson; 1 Aug 1745, p.1001. 15 Shill.

MOSES JOHNSON, 168 acs. Surry Co. on the S side of Nottoway Riv., up the run of Hunting Quarter Sw., to Colo. Benjamin Harrisons Mill Dam, by the edge of sd Harrison's Mill Pond, up the run of the Mirey Br.; adj. Colo. Allen, his own line & William Edmunds; 1 Aug 1745, p.1003. £1.

DAVID BELL, 730 acs. Goochland Co. bet. Great Guine and Angolo Creeks; adj. Daniel Stoner, Joseph Eckolls & John Francis; 1 Aug 1745, p.1005. £1.S15. 400 acs. part formerly Gtd. unto the sd David Bell by Pat. 8 Sep 1736 [PB 17 p.170] and 330 acs. the Residue never bef. Gtd.

THOMAS HENDERSON, 400 acs. Goochland Co. on Brs. of Randolphs Cr.; adj. Wentworth Webb, Stephen Hughes & John Alexander; 1 Aug 1745, p.1008. £2.

JOSEPH SCOTT, 2,200 acs. Goochland Co. on the Brs. of Angolo Cr. and great Guinea Cr. of Appamatox Riv.; adj. Daniel Stoner, John Chafin, John Pleasants, John Brown, Edward Mackgeehee, Jacob Mackgeehee & James Allen; 1 Aug 1745, p.1010. £1.S5. 1,950 acs. part formerly Gtd. the sd Joseph Scott by Pat. 10 Jun 1740 [Joseph Scot, PB 19 p.688 which included his 1,700 acs. in PB 17 p.381] and 250 acs. the Residue never bef. Gtd.

ANTHONY HOGATT, 3,200 acs. Goochland Co. near Appamatox Mountain adj. to Appamatox Riv., adj. William Grey & Henry Chiles; 1 Aug 1745, p.1012. £16.

STEPHEN SANDERS, 300 acs. Goochland Co. on both sides of Willis's Riv., adj. William Gray; 1 Aug 1745, p.1014. £1.S10.

JOHN CHILDERS, 400 acs. Goochland Co. on both sides of a br. of Willis's Riv. alias Willis's Cr. that heads above Willis's Mountain; 1 Aug 1745, p.1016. £2.

SAMUEL GLOVER, 200 acs. Goochland Co. on both sides of Slate Riv. including the fork known by the Name of Waltons Fork, Beg. on a Hill side the N side of the North Br. of Slate Riv., at the first Point of Hills below the Fork; 1 Aug 1745, p.1018. £1.

HUGH MOORE, 300 acs. Goochland Co. on the N side of Slate Riv.; 1 Aug 1745, p.1020. £1.S10.

JOHN HARDIMAN, 380 acs. Goochland Co. on the upper side of the Barren Lick Br. of Willis's Riv., adj. Henry Cary, Gent.; 1 Aug 1745, p.1022. £2.

THOMAS WILLIAMSON, 400 acs. Goochland Co. on both side of the North Br. of Ivy Cr., on the County line [S65°E], adj. Robert Lewis Gentleman; 1 Aug 1745, p.1023. £2.

JAMES GATES, 382 acs. Henrico Co. on the E side of Skinquarter Cr., in a Slash of Horsepen Br., adj. Thomas Bass; 1 Aug 1745, p.1025. £2.

ROBERT JONES, 200 acs. Goochland Co. on both sides of Totier Cr.; 1 Aug 1745, p.1027. £1.

SAMUEL GLOVER, 200 acs. Goochland Co. on both sides of Slate Riv.; 1 Aug 1745, p.1029. £1.

WILLIAM GATES, 400 acs. Henrico Co. adj. James Gates & Thomas Bass; 1 Aug 1745, p.1031. £2.

JOHN ROBERTS & STEP ROBERTS, 298 acs. Henrico Co., Crossing Buckengaim Road; adj. Morris Roberts, John Bramall, Wooldridge, & Step Roberts; 1 Aug 1745, p.1033. £1.S10.

WILLIAM JONES, 195 acs. Pr. Geo. Co. on the S side of the Reedy Br. of Arthurs Sw.; adj. Francis Evans, William Vaughan & David McCollo, by Richard

Archers Field; 1 Aug 1745, p.1035. £1.

SAMUEL BUGG, 400 acs. Henrico Co., in a thick place of Smiths Br.; adj. Smith, Joshua Irby & John Bugg; 1 Aug 1745, p.1037. £2.

JOHN BUGG, 390 acs. Henrico Co. adj. Joshua Irby & Joseph Wilkinson; 10 Aug 1745, p.1039. £2.

DAVID MAN, 302 acs. Henrico Co. on Winterpock Road & Neals Br.; adj. Thomas Man, Robert Man, Mark Mor & Francis Man; 1 Aug 1745, p.1041. £1.S10.

MORRIS ROBERTS, STEP ROBERTS, JOHN ROBERTS & JOSHUA ROBERTS, 400 acs. Henrico Co. on the S side of James Riv., adj. John Tillot & Hannah Tillot; 1 Aug 1745, p.1043. £2.

THOMAS MAN, 386 acs. Henrico Co. on the S side of Swift Cr. and on both sides the Rockey Br.; adj. Robert Man, William Voden, John Andrews & Mark Mor; 1 Aug 1745, p.1046. £2

GEORGE CARRINGTON, 1,950 acs. Goochland Co. on both sides of Bear Garden Cr. of the Fluvanna Riv. and Randolphs Cr. of Willis's Riv., adj. Dudley Digges Gent.; 20 Aug 1745, p.1048. £9.S15.

[Included in his 2,520 acs. Albemarle Co. in PB 27 p.336]

RICHARD RANDOLPH, Gentleman, 350 acs. Goochland Co. on both sides of Solomons Cr. of the S side of James Riv.; adj. Daniel Johnson, George Cox dec'd., John Woodson Gent., & John Hide Sanders; 10 Aug 1745, p.1050. £1.S15.

JOHN HARRIS, 114 acs. Goochland Co. adj. to the S side of James Riv., on the S side of the Road; adj. Stephen Chastain dec'd, Anthony Rapin dec'd & Nicholas Soullie dec'd; 20 Aug 1745, p.1053. for 2 lbs. of Tobacco for every Acre of sd L. already paid to our Receiver General of our Revenues. Whereas by Inquisition Indented taken in sd Co. 18 Feb 1729/30 by Virtue of a Warrant directed to William Byrd Esq., our Escheator for sd Co. It appears that Jacob Maton late of sd Co. died Seised of a Tract of L. Supposed to contain 165 acs. [Anthony Mattoone's 107 acs. & 58 acs. in PB 10 p.285 & p.298, then part of the 1st 5,000 acs. surveyed for the *French Refugees* then in Henrico Co.] but by a Survey lately made by William Mayo Gent. Surveyor of sd Co. is found to contain only 114 acs. which is found to Escheat to us from the sd Jacob Maton and whereas Susanna Carnor hath made

humble Suit and obtained a G. for the same which she hath relinquished unto John Harris. [Also see Gideon Chamboon's 59 acs., also a resurvey of the 165 acs. in PB 14 p.446]

LEMUEL BUTT, 235½ acs. of Swamp Land known by the Name of *Wild Horse Ridge* in Norfolk Co., by the Cypress Sw., binding upon the Green Sea to a Juniper Sw.; 20 Aug 1745 p.1055. £1.S5.

PETER GUERRANT, 400 acs. Goochland Co. on both sides of Joshua's Cr. a br. of Slate Riv.; 20 Aug 1745, p.1057. £2.

EDMUND LILLY, 400 acs. Goochland Co. adj. to the E side of the Byrd Cr., adj. Ebenezar Adams dec'd.; 20 Aug 1745, p.1059. £2.

CHRISTOPHER IRVINE, 100 acs. Goochland Co. on both sides of Davids Cr. of the Fluvanna Riv.; 20 Aug 1745, p.1061. 10 Shill.

ANTHONY BENNING, 400 acs. Goochland Co. on both sides of Turpins Cr. a Br. of Slate Riv., adj. Thomas Turpin Gent.; 20 Aug 1745, p.1063. £2.

DAVID LESUEUR, 400 acs. Goochland Co. on both sides of Hunts Cr. a br. of Slate Riv.; 20 Aug 1745, p.1065. £2.

SAMUEL GLOVER, 2,915 acs. Goochland Co. on both sides of Slate Riv., Crossing Glovers Cr. & the North Br. of sd Riv.; adj. Samuel Glover Junior, John Jones & Phineas Glover; 20 Aug 1745, p.1067. £7.S10. 1,440 acs. part formerly Gtd. unto the sd Samuel Glover by 2 Patents bearing Date respectively 15 Mar 1735 [241 acs. & 1,200 acs. in PB 17 p.24 & p.40], the Residue never bef. Gtd.

CHARLES ANDERSON, 400 acs. Goochland Co. near the Head of Green Cr. of Appamatox Riv.; adj. Obadiah Woodson, the sd Charles Anderson, Joseph Woodson & Jacob Micheaux; 20 Aug 1745, p.1070. £2.

RICHARD TAYLOR, 1,200 acs. Goochland Co. on the Mill Br. of Willis's Riv. & the Head of Watkins's Cr. of the Fluvanna Riv.; adj. William Cannon, James Daniel & George Carrington; 20 Aug 1745, p.1072. £6.

THOMAS MANKSFIELD, 25 acs. Goochland Co. adj. to the N side of fine Cr., adj. John Pleasants & Nathaniel Bassett dec'd; 20 Aug 1745, p.1075. 5 Shill.

CHARLES ANDERSON, 130 acs. Goochland Co. on both sides of Dry Cr. of Appamattox Riv., adj. Obediah Woodson & the sd Charles

Anderson; 20 Aug 1745, p.1076. 15 Shill.

CHARLES ANDERSON, 400 acs. Goochland Co. on both sides of Little Guinea Cr. adj. William Hamilton; 20 Aug 1745, p.1078. £2.

RICHARD TAYLOR, 400 acs. Goochland Co. on the W side of the North Br. of Slate Riv., adj. John Farrish & Richard Taylor; 20 Aug 1745, p.1081. £2. [Included in his PB 25 p.516]

RICHARD TRUEMAN, 400 acs. Goochland Co. on Brs. of great Buffaloe Cr. and the Barren Lick Cr.; adj. Samuel Ridgway, John Payn, William Still & Thomas Edwards; 20 Aug 1745, p.1083. £2.

ABRAHAM SAY, 386 acs. Goochland Co. in the fork of James Riv. on both sides of Crooks Cr.; 20 Aug 1745, p.1085. £2.

BENJAMIN BORDEN, 312 acs. Orange Co. on the Brs. of James Riv. on the W side the Blue Ridge, adj. James McUtchin; 20 Aug 1745, p.1087. £1.S5.

BENJAMIN BORDEN, 182 acs. Orange Co. the Brs. of James Riv. on the W side the blue Ridge, Beg. on the W side the South Br. of the Cotabo, by the Cedar Spring Br., adj. the sd Benjamin Borden; 20 Aug 1745, p.1089. £1.

BENJAMIN BORDEN, 400 acs. Orange Co. on the Brs. of James Riv. on the W side the blue Ridge, on a Ridge, adj. John Hayes; 20 Aug 1745, p.1091. £2.

JAMES CUNNINGHAM, 400 acs. in that part of Orange Co. designed to be Called Augusta on a Br. of James Riv. called Tees Cr., in a Hollow, on a Piney Ridge & at the foot of a Ridge; 20 Aug 1745, p.1093. £2.

ROBERT FOSTER, 85 acs. K. & Q. Co. adj. Ambrose Vaun, Mr Beveley Whiting, & Turner; 20 Aug 1745, p.1095. in Consideration of 170 lbs. of Tobacco for our use paid to our Receiver General of our Revenues ... 85 acs. part of the sd 250 acs. Whereas by Inquisition Indented taken in sd Co. 25 Jan 1741/42 by Virtue of a Warrant directed to John Robinson Esq. Escheator for the sd Co. It appears that Robert Tunwell late of the sd Co. died Seised of 250 acs. of L. lying and being in the sd Co. which is found to Escheat to us from the sd Robert Tunwell and whereas Robert Foster hath made humble Suit & hath obtained a G. for same.

ROBERT FOSTER, 140 acs. K. & Q. Co. on a hill by Broadass, on

Levell Ground, adj. Mr Beverly Whiting & Colo. Digges; 20 Aug 1745, p.1098. for 280 lbs. of Tobacco ... 140 acs. part of the sd 250 acs. Whereas by Inquisition Indented taken in sd Co. 25 Jan 1741/42 by Virtue of a Warrant directed to John Robinson Esq. our Escheator for the sd Co. It appears that Robert Tunwell late of the sd Co. died Seised of 250 acs. of L. lying and being in the sd Co. which is found to Escheat to us from the sd Robert Tunwell and whereas Robert Foster hath made humble suit & hath obtained a G. for the same.

HENRY PURKEY, 110 acs. in that part of Orange Co. designed to be called Augusta on the S side of the South Riv. of Shanando, on the Top of a steep Hill, adj. George Boon & James Barton; 10 Aug 1745, p.1100. 15 Shill.

JAMES COLEMAN, 400 acs. Brunswick Co. on the N side of Roanoke Riv., down a Gut, adj. Colo. John Allen & David Allen; 20 Aug 1745, p.1102. for 2 lbs. of Tobacco for every acre of sd L. Whereas by Inquisition Indented taken in sd Co. 1 Aug 1734 by Virtue of a Warrant directed to Robert Munford Gentleman our Escheator for the sd Co. It appears that Miles Royley late of the sd Co. died Seised of 400 acs. in sd Co. [part of the 499 acs. in PB 14 p.510 dated 28 Sep 1732, at the Occanechy Company's lower corner on the Riv.] which is found to Escheat to us from the sd Miles Royley and whereas James Coleman hath made humble Suit & hath obtained a G. for the same. [The adj. land to the West, referred to as the Occanechy Company's, was Ptd. by John Allen of Surry Co. [the Surveyor of Is. of Wight & Surry Counties) in PB 14 p.302, 1,780 acs. Brunswick Co. dated 25 August 1731. The Company could have been Virginia Militia posted near the Occanechy-Sioux or a Trading Company formed to trade with the sd Indians]

EDWARD PARKER, 145 acs. Brunswick Co. on the S side of Staunton Riv., adj. Batt Roberts; 20 Aug 1745, p.1104. 15 Shill.

THOMAS JORDON, 200 acs. Brunswick Co. adj. his own line, Donaldson., Lucas, Dupree & Taylor; 20 Aug 1745, p.1106. £1.

RICHARD WITTON, 373 acs. Brunswick Co. on both sides of the North Fork of Twittys Cr., on the Main Cr., adj. Fitz & Williams; 20 Aug 1745, p.1108. £2.

DAVID GWINN/GWIN, 700 acs. Brunswick Co. in the Fork of Little Roanoke Riv., at the Mouth of Wards fork, adj. John Turner; 20 Aug 1745, p.1110. £3.S10.

PETER KING, 100 acs. Brunswick Co. on both sides of Buffelo Cr., adj. Magahee; 20 Aug 1745, p.1112. 10 Shill.

ELIZABETH MEREDITH, 314 acs. Brunswick Co. on the S side of Nottoway Riv.; adj. Hinchea Mabry, Samuel Russell, William Smith, & Meredith [his line]; 20 Aug 1745, p.1114. £1.S15.

SAMUEL COBBS, Gentleman, 200 acs. Amelia Co. on both sides of the North fork of Sandy Riv., adj. John Hudson; 20 Aug 1745, p.1116. £1.

JAMES LOVE, 154 acs. Brunswick Co. on the N side Waqua Cr., adj. Charles Golston & Richard Taliaferro; 20 Aug 1745, p.1118. 15 Shill.

WILLIAM LAWSON, 143 acs. Brunswick Co. on the N side of Falling Riv.; 20 Aug 1745, p.1120. 15 Shill.

EDWARD HUGHES, 347 acs. Brunswick Co. on both sides of Allens Cr., adj. Dunkley; 20 Aug 1745, p.1123. £1.S15. [This patent & survey is a duplicate of PB 24 p.274 to Richard Wood]

WILLIAM ECKHOLES, 102 acs. Brunswick Co. on the N side of Staunton Riv., adj. the sd William

Eckholes; 20 Aug 1745, p.1125. 10 Shill.

WILLIAM MACLIN, 350 acs. Brunswick Co. on the N side of Miles Cr.; 20 Aug 1745, p.1127. £1.S15.

WILLIAM EDWARDS, 372 acs. Brunswick Co. on both sides of Allens Cr.; 20 Aug 1745, p.1129. £2.

JOHN TURNER, 113 acs. Brunswick Co. on the N side of Wards fork, adj. Talbot; 20 Aug 1745, p.1131. 15 Shill.

JOHN JONES, Gentleman, 342 acs. Brunswick Co. on a Br. of Poplar Cr., adj. Carrol; 20 Aug 1745, p.1133. £1.S15.

MARY DEANE, 80 acs. Brunswick Co. on the N side of Fountains Cr.; 20 Aug 1745, p.1135. 10 Shill.

WILLIAM LINSEY, 174 acs. Brunswick Co. on the South [sic] side of Maherin Riv.; adj. John Rane, Jackson, Ralph Jackson, John Walker & James Lee; 20 Aug 1745, p.1137. £1. [This land is on the S side of the three Creeks on the N side of Maherin Riv.]

WILLIAM FOX, 151 acs. Brunswick Co. on the Mirey Br.,

adj. Clark; 20 Aug 1745, p.1139. 15 Shill.

THOMAS JONES, 840 acs. Brunswick Co. on the E side of Little Roanoake Riv. & on both sides of Ash Camp Cr.; 20 Aug 1745, p.1140. £1.S10. 550 acs. part thereof formerly Gtd. to Hugh Boston by Pat. 15 Mar 1741/42 [PB 20 p.221] and 290 acs. the Residue never bef. gtd.

JOSIAH FLOID, 398 acs. Brunswick Co. bet. the lines of George Hix & Eldridge/Eldrige, adj. John Johnson; 20 Aug 1745, p.1143. £2.

WILLIAM BRIGGS, 418 acs. Brunswick Co. on both sides of Sturgeon Run; 20 Aug 1745, p.1145-1147. £1.S5. 165 acs. part formerly Gtd. unto Henry Briggs by Pat. 13 Oct 1727 [PB 13 p.176] and 253 acs. the Residue never bef Gtd.

PATENT BOOK NO. 24

20 Sep 1745 to 12 Jan 1746/47

TULLY ROBINSON, 31 acs. of Marsh Land in Pr. Anne Co. called & known by the Name of the *sheep Island*, near long Island and the Marsh of the sd Robinson, Surrounded with a Cr.; 20 Sep 1745 *in the 19th year of our Reign of George the Second by William Gooch Esq. our Lieutenant Governor and Commander in Chief at Williamsburgh*, p.1. 5 Shill.

DAVID LOGAN, 192 acs. Orange Co. on Shanadore Riv. and down Cathies Riv., adj. William Thompson & Samuel Giving; 20 Sep 1745, p.4. £1.

JOHN NEALANDS, 330 acs. that part of Orange Co. designed to be called Augusta, on the S side of a Br. of Goose Cr.; 20 Sep 1745, p.4. £1.S15.

JAMES STONE, 178 acs. Orange Co. on the brs. of James Riv. on the W side the Blue Ridge, on a br.

of Lunies Mill Run, on a Ridge; 20 Sep 1745, p.6. £1.

MORGAN BRYAN, 400 acs. Orange Co. on the S side of Linwell's Cr. Joining to a Tract of Land Surveyed for Jost Hyte, on the N side of a Ridge; 20 Sep 1745, p.8. £2.

JOHN BALFOUGHT, 400 acs. in that part of Orange Co. designed to be called Augusta on a N Draft of the North Riv. of Shanando bet. Stover's Mill Cr. and the Naked Cr., on a Ridge, on the N side of a Glade; 20 Sep 1745, p.9. £2.

ROBERT MARTIN, 400 acs. in that part of Orange Co. designed to be called Augusta, on Gilgo run, Crossing a Br. of the Hawksbill; 20 Sep 1745, p.11. £2.

JAMES BEARD, 400 acs. in that part of Orange Co. designed to be called Augusta on the North Riv. of the Shanando above the fork of the

147

sd Riv., adj. William Thomson the Younger & Alexander Thomson; 20 Sep 1745, p.13. £2.

GEORGE ROBINSON, 191 acs. Orange Co. on the W side of the blue Ridge, adj. John Buchanan; 20 Sep 1745, p.15. £1.

JAMES COLE, 400 acs. Orange Co. on the W side of the Blue Ridge, adj. Mark Cole; 20 Sep 1745, p.17. £2.

THOMAS WALKER, 340 acs. Orange Co. adj. John Powell; 20 Sep 1745, p.19. £1.S15.

JOHN ANTHONY, 109 acs. Goochland Co. on both sides of Hardware Riv., adj. his own line & Hugh Morris; 20 Sep 1745, p.21. 15 Shill.

JULIUS ALLEN, 400 acs. Goochland Co.on the N Brs. of Little Guinea Cr., Near the S side of the road; adj. John Watson, Richard Hubbard, Stephen Mallet & William Tabor; 20 Sep 1745, p.23. £2.

PHILIP WEBBER, 2,590 acs. Goochland Co. on both sides of Flemings Park Cr. of the N side of James Riv. lying all round 200 acs. of Land Ptd. to Robert Napier Junior (& externally bounded), near the N side of a run of Treasurers Run; adj. David Mims, Daniel Johnson, Henry Webb, Thomas Ballow, Thomas Carter, Isham Randolph Gent., John Bolling Gent., Tarlton Fleming, Bowler Cocke Gent, Ashford & Stephen Hughes, Thomas Massie dec'd, Leonard & Thomas Ballow, & William Cabbel Gent.; 20 Sep 1745, p.25. £13. Whereas by Pat. 12 March 1739/40 Gtd. unto John Woodson [PB 17 p.550] and whereas the sd John Woodson hath failed to make Cultiv. and Improv. and Stephen Dabbs hath made humbly Suit and hath obtained a G. for the same Land which he has Assigned unto Philip Webber. [2,320 acs. of this 2,590 acs. was included in Arthur Hopkins's PB 31 p.353]

DOUGLAS BAKER, 400 acs. Goochland Co. on both sides of the Main Br. of Willis Riv., by the edge of the Low Grounds; 20 Sep 1745, p.28. £2.

JOHN ANTHONY, 400 acs. Goochland Co. on both sides of Hudsons Cr., adj. Micajah Clark; 20 Sep 1745, p.31. £2.

WILLIAM BRADSHEW, 800 acs. Goochland Co. on both sides of Deep Cr.; adj. William Tabor, the sd Bradshew & Samuel Nuchols; 20 Sep 1745, p.32. £4.

JAMES ANDERSON, 400 acs. Goochland Co. among the Brs. of

Little Guinea Cr. and Tearwallet Run; adj. Stephen Cox, Samuel Atkinson, Thomas Anderson, Paul Pigg & John Williams; 20 Sep 1745, p.34. £2.

JOHN REYNOLDS, 400 acs. Goochland Co. on both sides of the Byrd Cr., adj. Abraham Venable & Thomas Kent; 20 Sep 1745, p.36. £2.

JAMES RENTFROE, 148 acs. Orange Co. on the West side of the Blue Ridge, near the Buffillo Cr.; 20 Sep 1745, p.38. 15 Shill.

FRANCIS CALLAWAY, 400 acs. Goochland Co. on both sides of Tommahawk Sw., on the Edge of a Meadow; 20 Sep 1745, p.40. £2.

JOEL WATKINS, 150 acs. Goochland Co. adjacent to Appamatox Riv. & Richard Parker; 20 Sep 1745. p.42. 15 Shill.

JOHN HUNTER, 200 acs. Goochland Co. on both sides of Crooked Cr. of Slate Riv.; 20 Sep 1745, p.44. £1.

JOSEPH MAYO, 100 acs. Goochland Co. on the S side of Fluvanna Riv. adj. William Mayo Gent.; 20 Sep 1745, p.46. 10 Shill.

JOSEPH MAYO, 1,450 acs. Goochland Co. on both sides of

Fluvanna Riv. above Buffelo Island, crossing Porridge Cr., to the upper end of Slaughter alias Chace Island, crossing Stone Wall Cr.; 20 Sep 1745, p.48. £1.S5. 1,200 acs. part formerly Gtd. unto William Mayo dec'd by 4 several Patents bearing Date Respectively 30 January 1741/42 [PB 20 p.89, p.91, p.94 & p.96 to Colo. William Mayo, Gent.] and by him devised by his last Will and Testament to the sd Joseph Mayo 1,200 acs. and 250 acs. the residue never before Gtd.

MICHAEL DUNALOW, 288 acs. Brunswick Co. on both sides of Stony Hill Run; adj. Isaac Hous, Tilman, Dunnavant & Hows; 20 Sep 1745, p.50. £1.S10.

SAMUEL BRIDGWATER 400 acs. Goochland Co. on S Brs. of Randolphs Cr.; adj. Stephen Hughes, Isaac Bates, Thomas Edwards & Joseph Dabbs; 20 Sep 1745, p.52. £2.

BENJAMIN BORDEN, 800 acs. Orange Co. on the North Br. of Sherando Riv., *near the Gap Where the River runs thro the Mountains*, near a Point of Rocks, on a Stony Point, *to the Chimney Rock*; 20 Sep 1745, p.54. £4.

WILLIAM PETTEPOOLE, 380 acs. Pr. Geo. Co. on the N side of Sappone Cr., near his old Barn, in a small Slash or Drain, adj. his 49 acs. from Westmoreland & Robert Warren; 20 Sep 1745, p.56. £2.

RICHARD CARTER, 400 acs. Pr. Geo. Co. on the S side of Sapone Cr., on both sides of the Miry Br. adj. John Goodwyn; 20 Sep 1745, p.58. £2.

JAMES RICHARDSON, 390 acs. Pr. Geo. Co. on both sides of Sappone Cr., at a large Rock below the Governors Road; 20 Sep 1745, p.60. £2.

GEORGE BOOTH, JUNIOR, 400 acs. Pr. Geo. Co. on the Lower side of Turkey Egg Cr., adj. his own lines & Matthis; 20 Sep 1745, p.62. £2. [Included in his 1,854 acs. in PB 28 p.351]

WILLIAM PETTEPOOLE, 300 acs. Pr. Geo. Co. on the N side of Sappone Cr., in a Slash, adj. the L. he Purchased of Joseph Stroud; 20 Sep 1745, p.63. £1.S10.

JOHN MAY, JUNIOR, 800 acs. Pr. Geo. Co. on the head Brs. of Great Cr., on a fork of the Rockey Run; adj. Blackstone now Williamson's, Richard White, Jones, Raney & Walker; 20 Sep 1745, p.66. £4.

JOSEPH CARTER, 400 acs. Pr. Geo. Co. on the S side of Sappone Cr., at the Miry Br.; adj. his

Brother Richard Carter, Thomas Wynn, Thomas Hunt & John Goodwynn; 20 Sep 1745, p.68. £2.

RICHARD DENNIS, 740 acs. Amelia Co. on the Lower side of the Middle Seller Cr. of Deep Cr.; adj. Peter Leath, Bolling [her line] & Vaughan; 20 Sep 1745, p.69. £2. 340 acs. part thereof formerly Gtd. unto the sd Richard Dennis by Letters Pat. 13 Oct 1736 & 400 acs. the Residue never before Gtd.

JOHN VAWTER, 70 acs. Essex Co. in the Parish of Saint Annes, along a run called Popoman; adj. Colo. William Robinson, Mr William Gray, Gains, Daniel Noel, Boleware, & Thomas Ramsey; 20 Sep 1745, p.71. for the Imp. of 2 Pers. whose Names are *John Glen and Patrick Donohoe.*

JOHN PEEBLES, 143 acs. Brunswick Co. in the Fork of the Cane Br., down Fountains Cr., adj. James Parham & John Tuke; 20 Sep 1745, p.73. 15 Shill.

CARY WILLS DANIEL, 400 acs. Brunswick Co. on both sides of Cedar Cr.; 20 Sep 1745, p.75. £2.

JOHN PEOPLES, 286 acs. Brunswick Co. on both sides of Fountains Cr. adj. Peter Vinttant; 20 Sep 1745, p.76. £1.S10.

HUGH WILLIAMS, 168 acs. Brunswick Co. on the S side of Cedar Cr., a Little below the Fork; 20 Sep 1745, p.79. £1.

EDWARD BOOKER, 694 acs. Brunswick Co. on the N side of Stanton Riv., adj. Mattox May & West Crook [Westbrook]; 20 Sep 1745, p.88. £2.S10. 200 acs. part formerly gtd. John Ellis Junior by Pat. 13 Oct. 1736 the Right & Title whereof is become vested in the sd Edward Booker & 494 acs. the Residue never before Gtd.

CHARLES ROSS, 450 acs. Brunswick Co. on both sides of the three Creeks, adj. Harwell; 20 Sep 1745, p.82. £1.S15. 100 acs. part formerly Gtd. John Harwell by Pat. 7 Jul 1726 & 350 acs. the residue never before gtd.

JAMES JUDKINS, 394 acs. Brunswick Co. on the N side of Fountains Cr. adj. Cook, Peoples & Scot; 20 Sep 1745, p.84. £1.S15. 50 acs. part formerly Gtd. William Rainey by Pat. 5 Sep 1723 & 344 acs. the residue never before Gtd.

GEORGE PHILLIPS, 400 acs. Brunswick Co. on the S side of Nottoway Riv., Beg. at Thomas Jones corner on the sd Riv. Opposite to the Fork; 20 Sep 1745, p.87. £2.

JAMES COLEMAN, 274 acs. Brunswick Co. on both sides of the South fork of Allens Cr.; 20 Sep 1745, p.88. £1.S10.

PETER WYTCH, 1,165 acs. Brunswick Co. on the N side of Fountains Cr. & up the Sw.; adj. his own, Joshua Clark, Cook, Robert Clark, Bishop, Thomas Scott, Peterson & Ezell.; 20 Sep 1745, p.90. £3.S15. 115 acs. part formerly Gtd. George Wytch by Pat. 5 Sep 1723 [George Wyche, Is. of Wight Co. in PB 11 p.263], 150 acs. other part formerly Gtd. sd George Wytch by Pat. 7 July 1726 [George Wyche in PB 12 p.519] the Right and Title of which sd 2 parcels of Land by divers Mesne Conveyeances is become Vested in the sd Peter Wytch, also 150 acs. other part of the above Tract formerly Gtd. unto the sd Peter Wytch by Pat. 5 June 1736 [Peter Wych in PB 17 p.86] and 750 acs. the residue never before Gtd.

JAMES BARNES, 400 acs. Brunswick Co. on both sides of the Second Fork of the Horse pen Cr., adj. Robert Williams; 20 Sep 1745, p.93. £2.

WILLIAM MALONE, 234 acs. Brunswick Co. on the S side of Taylors Cr. & both sides of the Wolfpit Br., adj. his own & Bennit; 20 Sep 1745, p.94. £1.S5.

DAVID LILES, 304 acs. Brunswick Co. on Couches Cr.; adj. his own line, Gillam & Callwell; 20 Sep 1745, p.96. £1.S10.

WILLIAM GARRIOT, 165 acs. Brunswick Co. on the S side of Staunton Riv. and both sides of Childreys Cr., adj. Mattox Mayes; 20 Sep 1745, p.98. £1.

JOHN SIMS, 235 acs. Brunswick Co. on the N side of Rattle Snake, adj his own line; 20 Sep 1745, p.100. £1.S5.

NICHOLAS EDMONDS, 201 acs. Brunswick Co. on the E side of the Little Cr., adj. Edmonds & Riggby; 20 Sep 1745, p.101. £1.

NICHOLAS EDMONDS, 174 acs. Brunswick Co. on the S side of the great Cr., in the Head of the great Br.; adj. his own line, Lanier, Stith, Lucas & Harroson; 20 Sep 1745, p.103. £1.

JAMES FARGUSON, 270 acs. Brunswick Co. on both sides of Meherin Riv; 20 Sep 1745, p.105. for the Imp. of 6 pers. whose names are *Matthew Crawley, Edward Kent, Robert Pinnel, James Creighton, Matthew Ward & John Martin.*

ROBERT SANDFORD, 380 acs. Brunswick Co. on the S side of

flatt Rock Cr., adj. Edloe; 20 Sep 1745, p.107. £2.

JOHN INGRAM, 2,476 acs. Brunswick Co. on the E side of Williams's Cr.; 20 Sep 1745, p.108. £12.S10. [Included in Thomas Williams's 4,380 Lunenburg Co. in PB 27 p.209]

ALLEN HOWARD, 40 acs. Goochland Co. on the Upper side of Sycamore Island Cr., up the Fluvanna, adj. Samuel Spencer; 20 Sep 1745, p.111. 5 Shill.

JOHN BICKERTON, 200 acs. Goochland Co. among the brs. of the Byrd Cr.; adj. John Anthony, Edmund Lilly, Benjamin Johnson & Abraham Venable; 20 Sep 1745, p.112. £1.

JOHN PHELPS, 54 acs. Goochland Co. among the brs. of Deep Cr. of the S side of James Riv.; adj. his old line, William Randolph, John Hudspeath dec'd. & Thomas Cardwell; 20 Sep 1745, p.113. 5 Shill.

JAMES ANDERSON, 400 acs. Goochland Co. Near Appamatox Riv. above dry cr., adj Colo. Richard Randolph; 20 Sep 1745, p.115. £2.

JAMES CHRISTIAN, 540 acs. Goochland Co. on the S side of the Fluvanna Riv. Opposite to the

Buffaloe Island, Beg. against the upper end of sd Island; 20 Sep 1745, p.117. £1.S5.

JAMES CHRISTIAN, 70 acs. Goochland Co. on the S side of the Fluvanna Riv.; 20 Sep 1745, p.118. 10 Shill.

JOHN DARRICOTT Gent., 500 acs. Goochland Co. on the Brs. of the Little Byrd; adj. Thomas Massie, Mary Massie, Charles Massie & Mrs. Pinchback; 20 Sep 1745, p.120. £2.S10.

SAMUEL BAILEY, 400 acs. Gooch-land Co. on the head of Turpins Cr. of Slate Riv.; 20 Sep 1745, p.121. £2.

JOHN FLOYD, 170 acs. Gooch-land Co. on the Brs. of Randolphs Cr.; adj. Isaac Bates, Thomas Edwards & Hugh Moor; 20 Sep 1745, p.123. £1. [Included in George Carrington's 2,520 acs. Albemarle Co. in PB 27 p.336]

JAMES FENLY, 400 acs. Goochland Co. on the N side of Slate River Mountain on both sides of a Br. of Davids Cr.; 20 Sep 1745, p.124. £2.

JOHN MOSS, 475 acs. Goochland Co. on the S side of the Little Byrd; adj. Marble Mosely, Thomas Massie, Cole, & Charles Massie; 20 Sep 1745, p.125. £2.S10.

THOMAS MASSIE, 500 acs. Goochland Co. on Brs. of the Little Byrd, adj. Cole, Mary Massie & Thomas Massie; 20 Sep 1745, p.127. £2.S10.

JOHN DOUGLAS, 400 acs. Goochland Co. on the Western Brs. of Bear Garden Cr. of the Fluvanna Riv., adj. Dudley Digges Gent.; 20 Sep 1745, p.129. £2.

GEORGE HOLMES GWIN, 350 acs. Goochland Co. on both sides of the Slate Riv., crossing Great Cr., adj. James Watkins; 20 Sep 1745, p.130. £1.S15.

JOHN WATSON, 425 acs. Goochland Co. among the Brs. of Little Guinea Cr., near the N side of the Road; adj. John Ellett, John Jones, William Hamilton, the sd John Watson & Richard Hubbard; 20 Sep 1745, p.132. £2.S5.

JAMES GATES, 370 acs. Gooch-land Co. on both sides of Slate Riv., Crossing Flatt/Flat Cr.; 20 Sep 1745, p.133. £2.

ARTHUR HOPKINS, 400 acs. Goochland among the Brs. of Treasurers Run; adj. Charles Tony, John Lane & Christopher Cawthon; 20 Sep 1745, p.135. £2.

ARTHUR HOPKINS, 275 acs. Goochland Co. among Brs. of Treasurers Run; adj. Charles Tony,

Christopher Cawthon, John Man & Philip Ryen; 20 Sep 1745, p.136. £1.S10.

JOHN BOLLING, Gent., 425 acs. Goochland Co. on the S side of the Fluvanna Riv. including Anthonys Island and Chain Island, crossing black Water Cr.; 20 Sep 1745, p.138. £2.S5.

JOHN BOLLING, Gent. 165 acs. Goochland Co. on the N side of the Fluvanna Riv. at the Mouth of Harris's Cr. and Including Jacks Island and Sams Island; 20 Sep 1745, p.139. £1.

THOMAS STOCKTON, 400 acs. Goochland Co. on both sides of the South Fork of Mechums Riv., adj. Davis Stockton; 20 Sep 1745, p.141. £2.

JOHN THRASHER, 388 acs. Goochland Co. on both sides of Buffelo Riv., near Davis's Path, at twenty five Puppies Cr., by a Rock a Little below the Mouth of Puppies Cr. on the S side of Buffelo, adj. the sd Thrasher; 20 Sep 1745, p.143. £2.

JOHN SMITH, 500 acs. Goochland Co. on the Brs. of the Little Byrd; adj. Capt. John Darricott, Thomas Massie, Valentine Amos & John Moss; 20 Sep 1745, p.144. £2.S10.

JAMES LEE, 270 acs. Goochland Co. on both sides the South Fork of Hardware Riv., on the Secretarys line [S59°E], up Eppes's Cr., into the Woods; 20 Sep 1745, p.147. £1.S10.

ROBERT WALTON, 400 acs. Goochland Co. on both sides of a Br. of Slate Riv. near Slate River Mountain; 20 Sep 1745, p.147. £2.

GIDEON PATERSON, 350 acs. Goochland Co. on both sides of the Main Br. of Willis Riv., by the Edge of the Low Grounds, crossing Beverdam Cr., adj. Land Surveyed for Douglas Baker; 20 Sep 1745, p.148. £1.S15.

THOMAS WILLIAMS, 400 acs. Goochland Co. at the head of Badluck Br. of Appamattox Riv.; adj. Obadiah Woodson, Jacob Micheaux & Sanbourn Woodson; 20 Sep 1745, p.150. £2.

SANBURN WOODSON, 400 acs. Goochland Co. near Appamattox Riv., above Dry Cr., adj. Colo. Richard Randolph; 20 Sep 1745, p.151. £2.

JAMES SANDERS, 400 acs. Goochland Co. on both sides of Willis Riv.; 20 Sep 1745, p.153. £2.

JAMES TERRY, 930 acs. Goochland Co. among the N Brs. of Great Guinea Cr., in a Valley; adj. William Womack, James Allen, John Chafin, John Bostock, William Arnold, Paul Pigg, Daniel Terry, John Williams & Robert Peak; 20 Sep 1745, p.154. 15 Shill. 400 acs. part formerly Gtd. sd James Terry by Pat. 17 March 1736/37, 400 acs. other part formerly Gtd. sd James Terry 25 July 1741 & 130 acs. the residue never before Gtd.

WILLIAM ALLEN, 300 acs. Goochland Co. on the N side of the Fluvanna Riv. above Fishing Cr., in a Bottom; 20 Sep 1745, p.156. £1.S10. Whereas by Pat. 22 Sep 1739 Gtd. William Cabbell [PB 18 p.434] and Whereas the sd William Cabbell hath failed to make Cultiv. and Improv. and William Allen hath made humble Suit and hath obtained a G. for the same.

THOMAS DAWSON, 400 acs. Goochland Co. on both sides of Pole Cat Br. of the Lower Manacan Cr.; adj. Daniel Guarrand dec'd, Thomas Dickens & Stephen Chastain; 20 Sep 1745, p.158. £2. Whereas by Pat. 16 Jun 1738 Gtd. Daniel Stoner Gent. and John James Flournoy Gent. since dec'd. in Jointenancy and Whereas Daniel Stoner in whom the Right of sd Land Vested by Survivorship after the Death of the sd John James Flournoy hath failed to pay Quit Rents and to make Cultiv. and Improv. and Thomas Dawson hath made humble Suit and hath obtained a G. for the same.

WILLIAM ALLEN, 140 acs. Goochland Co. on both sides of Fishing Cr. adj. to the N side of the Fluvanna Riv. including 2 islands called Elk Islands in the sd Riv., in a Bottom; 20 Sep 1745, p.159. 15 Shill. Whereas by Pat. 22 Sep 1739 Gtd. unto William Cabbell [PB 18 p.431] and Whereas the sd William Cabbell hath failed to made Cultiv. and Improv. and William Allen hath made humble Suit and hath obtained a G. for the same Land.

WILLIAM BALCHER, 88 acs. Amelia Co. on Lower side of Smacks Cr.; adj. Wilson, Belcher, Brookes/Brooks & Towns; 20 Sep 1745, p.161. 10 Shill.

JOHN PETERSON, 204 acs. Amelia Co. on both sides of the Head of the Dry or Lower Fork of Winticomaick Cr.; adj. Thomas Hood, Matthew Tucker, & Tesdale; 20 Sep 1745, p.162. £1.

JOHN NASH, 400 acs. Amelia Co. on the S side of Appamattox Riv., adj. William Randolph Esq. & his own lines; 20 Sep 1745, p.164. for 15 Shill. as also for the Imp. of 5 pers. whose names are *David*

Burn, Michael McDearma Row, John Hays, Joseph Steatherd and Katharine Hays.

ISAAC ROBERTSON, 400 acs. Amelia Co. on the Upper side of Buffelo Riv., Beg. at a Pile of Rocks by a Br., adj. Randolph; 20 Sep 1745, p.165. £2.

JOSHUA FRY, Gent., 290 acs. Albemarle Co., up Eppes's Spring Br. & crossing Eppes's Cr., adj. Eppes, a little above Hudson & White; 3 Feb 1745/46, p.167. £1.S10.

STEPHEN COLLINS, 2,400 acs. Amelia Co. on both sides of the North Fork of Spring Cr. of Buffillo Riv., adj. Cobbs; 18 Feb 1745/46, p.168. £12.

WILLIAM BEVERLEY, Gent., 70 acs. Caroline Co. on Puamanzeno Sw., adj. John Carter Esq. dec'd, Capt. Richard Taliaferro & sd William Beverley; 5 Mar 1745/46, p.160. for Imp. of 2 pers. whose names are *James Newman and Richard Pringle.*

RICHARD BLAND, 135 acs. Surry Co. on the S side of Nottoway River, on the E side of Lewis Br., adj. sd Hamiltons other Land; 5 Mar 1745/46, p.171. 15 Shill. Whereas by Pat. 9 July 1724 Gtd. George Hamilton since dec'd. [PB 12 p.106] and Whereas the sd

George Hamilton in his lifetime and Marmaduke Hamilton in whom the Right of the sd Land after the Death of the sd George Hamilton [became] Vested, have failed to made Cultiv. and Improv., and Richard Bland hath made humble Suit and hath obtained a G. for the same Land. [Included in Bland's 1,167 acs. in PB 28 p.273 & David Mason's PB 34 p.781]

JOHN GRILLS, 390 acs. Albemarle Co. on the brs. of Moores Cr., on a Ridge, adj. Joel Terril & David Lewis; 20 Mar 1745/46, p.172. £2.

RICHARD TUNSTALL, Gent., 1,120 acs. Amelia Co. on both sides of little Flatt Cr., in a Valley; adj. the Land. Purchased of Mayes, Thomas Jones now John Ellis's line, Clark, Fitzgerrald now John Gillums line, Royall & Watson; 20 Mar 1745/46, p.174. £1. 953 acs. part formerly Gtd. John Mayes by Pat. 9 Feb 1737/38 and by him sold and Conveyed to the sd Richard Tunstall.

HENRY JARRARD, 650 acs. Surry Co. near Majors Br., up Parkers Br.; adj. Thomas Wallace and Sarah his wife, Thomas Jarrard, John Thomason and Jane his wife, & his own Land; 20 Mar 1745/46, p.176. £3.S5. [This land is part of Nathaniel Harrison's 1,720 acs. on the S side of

Blackwater Sw. in PB 10 p.176 dated 16 Jun 1714]

WILLIAM BRITTLE, 380 acs. Surry Co. on the S side of black Water Sw., at the head of Snake Br., down the Broad Meadow Br., adj. William Smith & John Megarrity; 20 Mar 1745/46, p.177. £1. 215 acs. part formerly Gtd. sd William Brittle by Pat. 9 Jul 1724 [PB 12 p.103] & 165 acs. the residue never before Gtd.

THOMAS MARTIN, 205 acs. New Kent Co. down the Chickahominy Sw.; adj. sd Thomas Martin and Morgan, Major Pate & Samuel Meridith; 20 Mar 1745/46, p.178. 15 Shill. 130 acs. part thereof being Surplus Land found within the bounds of 75 acs. devised to the sd Thomas Martin by the last Will and Testament of Martin Martin dec'd.

HENRY HATCHER, 400 acs. Goochland Co. on the N Brs. of Swift Cr.; adj. Henry Hudson, Benjamin Harris & James Smith; 20 Mar 1745/46, p.180. £2. Whereas by Pat. 16 Jun 1738 Gtd. Daniel Stoner and John James Flourncy since dec'd in Joint Tenancy [PB 18 p.7] and Whereas the sd Daniel Stoner in whom the right of the sd Land Vested by Survivorship after the Death of the sd John James Flourncy hath failed to pay Quit Rents and to make Cultiv. and Improv. and Henry Hatcher hath made humble Suit and hath obtained a G. for the same.

WILLIAM DENDY, 595 acs. Amelia Co. on the S side of Whetstone Cr. in the fork of Nottoway; adj. Thweat, Ellis & Finny; 20 Mar 1745/46, p.181. £2. 195 acs. part formerly Gtd. William Dendy by Pat. 2 Jan 1737/38 [PB 17 p.432] and 400 acs. the residue never before Gtd.

THOMAS WOOLDRIDGE, 300 acs. Goochland Co. adj. to the N side of Swift Cr., Thomas Watkins, Benjamin Harris & Henry Hudson; 20 Mar 1745/46, p.183. £1.S10. Whereas by Pat. 16 Jun 1738 Gtd. Daniel Stoner and John James Flourncy since dec'd., in Joint Tenancy [PB 18 p.5] and Whereas the sd Daniel Stoner in Whom the right of the sd Land Vested by Survivorship after the death of the sd John James Flourncy hath failed to pay Quit Rents and to make Cultiv. and Improv. and Henry Hatcher hath made humble Suit and hath obtained a G. for the same which he hath Assigned unto Thomas Wooldridge.

JOSEPH MARTIN, 1,420 acs. Louisa Co. on the N side the North Br. of the North Fork of James Riv., and on both sides Pritties Cr., on the main fork of sd Cr., crossing the first fork of sd Cr.;

Beg. at the Mouth of a Gutt; adj. Ambrose Joshua Smith, Thomas Collins, Timothy Dalton, William Cradock, his other line & William Carr; 20 Mar 1745/46, p.184. £2. 626 acs. part of 1,200 acs. formerly Gtd. Thomas Carr by 3 Patents respectively dated 6 Jun 1734 [PB 13 p.447-448, 400 acs. other part formerly Gtd. Michael Holland by Pat. 22 Apr 1736 [1 Dec 1740 in PB 19 p.841] the Right and Title of which sd 626 acs. and 400 acs. by divers Mesne Conveyance is since become Vested in the sd Joseph Martin and 394 acs. the residue never before Gtd. [see William Carr's PB 17 p.415 & PB 18 p.326].

EDWARD GOODE, 1,125 acs. Henrico Co. in the great Br. of four Mile Cr., on the S side of a Br. of Deep run, along or near a Path known by the Name of Daniels Path; adj. John Good, Whitlow, & Benjamin Burton; 20 Mar 1745/46, p.186. 800 acs. part formerly Gtd. sd Edward Goode by 2 several Patents for 400 acs. each bearing Date respectively 30 Jul 1742 and 325 acs. the residue being Purchased by the sd Edward Goode of Thomas Pleasant and Joseph Pleasant as by Deeds Recorded in Henrico Co. Court may appear.

WILLIAM MEGGINSON, 580 acs. Goochland Co. on the S side of Fluvanna Riv.; 20 Mar 1745/46, p.188. 400 acs. part formerly Gtd. William Cabbel by Pat. 22 Sep 1739 [PB 18 p.519] , 180 acs. other part also formerly Gtd. sd William Cabbel by Pat. 29 Jun 1739 [PB 18 p.348] the Right and Title of which sd 2 parcels is since become Vested in the sd William Megginson.

HENRY DICKSON, 931 acs. Pr. Geo. Co. on the S side of Sappone Cr.; at the Mirey Br., down the long Br.; adj. James Richardson, Joseph Carter, his Brother Richard Carter, & Goodwynn; 20 Mar 1745/46, p.189. £4.S10. 75 acs. part formerly Gtd. by Pat. and Sold and Conveyed to Henry Dickson by John Stroud & Joshua Stroud, and 856 acs. the residue never before Gtd.

THOMAS SPENCER, 362 acs. Brunswick Co. on both sides of the Middle Fork of the 3 forks of Licking hole, adj. Joseph Morton; 20 Mar 1745/46, p.191. 15 Shill. 250 acs. part formerly Gtd. the sd Thomas Spencer by Pat. 30 Jul 1742 [PB 20 p.379] and 112 acs. the residue never before Gtd. [Included in his 821 acs. in PB 26 p.643]

RICHARD JONES, 617 acs. Amelia Co. on the S side of Bush Riv., up Jones's Br; adj. Bobbit now Walker's, & Randolph; 20 Mar 1745/46, p.192. £1.S10. 337

acs. part formerly Gtd. Richard Jones by Pat. 28 Sep 1728 [Richard Jones Junr. of Pr. Geo. Co., PB 14 p.89, Brunswick Co.], 280 acs. the residue never before Gtd.

WILLIAM MAY, 517 acs. Amelia Co. on the N side of little Nottoway Riv.; adj. William Batts, Cox, Peter Wynn & Arthur Leath; 20 Mar 1745/46, p.194. £2.S15.

WILLIAM MACKEWIN, 794 acs. Amelia Co. between Deep Cr. and West's Cr., on Deep Cr. just below the bridge; adj. William Hayes & John Gillum; 20 Mar 1745/46, p.195. £1.S10. 122 acs. part formerly Gtd. Thomas Satterwhite by Pat. 24 Mar 1725/26 [Thomas Suttowhite, Pr. Go. Co. in PB 12 p.372] the Right & Title is since become vested in sd William Mackewin, 400 acs. other part formerly gtd. sd William Mackewen by Pat. 10 Sep 1735 [William McCoon in PB 16 p.233] and 272 acs. the residue never before Gtd.

FRANCIS MERRIMOON, 400 acs. Pr. Geo. Co. on the on Lower side of Nammiseen Cr.; adj. Featherstone, Bolling & Taylor; 20 Mar 1745/46, p.197. £2.

JOHN HARRIS, 243 acs. Amelia Co. on the Head of Neales Br. of Flatt Cr., adj. Morris & Turner; 20 Mar 1745/46, p.198. £1.S5.

WILLIAM SADLER, 250 acs. Amelia Co. on S side of Appamattox Riv.; adj. Nash & Foster; 20 Mar 1745/46, p.199. £1.S5.

WILLIAM MAYES, JUNIOR, 400 acs. Amelia Co. on the N side of Ellis's fork of Flatt Cr.; adj. Hurt, Crawford & Ellis; 20 Mar 1745/46, p.200. £2.

JACOB SEAY, 150 acs. Amelia Co. on the Brs. of the Great Bent Run Adj. the upper end of his 400 acs. [PB 17 p.157]; 20 Mar 1745/46, p.202. 15 Shill.

RICHARD TAYLOR, 393 acs. Amelia Co. in the fork bet. the Main Harricane Sw. and the long Br., Beg. on the Harricane below the Horsepen, adj. William Powell & John Leveritt; 20 Mar 1745/46, p.203. £2.

JOSEPH MOTLEY, 390 acs. Amelia Co. on the N side of Ellis's fork of Flatt Cr. on both sides of the Road, Beg. at the Hunting Path; adj. Richard Ward, William Eckholes, Hurt, & William Mayes; 20 Mar 1745/46, p.204. £2.

WILLIAM STONE, 400 acs. Amelia Co. on the N side of Nottoway Riv., along the Co. line [South], down the Burchen Sw.; adj. his own old lines, Jones, Parr; 20 Mar 1745/46, p.205. £2.

WILLIAM WALLICE, SENIOR, 400 acs. Amelia Co. on the S side of Harricane Sw., crossing the Road, adj. Furguson; 20 Mar 1745/46, p.207. £2.

JOHN GRANT, 200 acs. Amelia Co. on both sides of the Lazaritta Cr., adj. Christopher Roberson; 20 Mar 1745/46, p.208. £1.

ROBERT BUMPAS, 391 acs. Amelia Co. in the fork of Little Nottoway Riv., Beg. on the South fork at the Mouth of a small Spring Br., down the North fork or main Riv.; 20 Mar 1745/46, p.209. £2.

LODWICK ELAM, 400 acs. Amelia Co. on the Head Brs. of the North fork of falling Cr., in a Br. of Vaughans Cr.; 20 Mar 1745/46, 210. £2.

JAMES ATWOOD, 400 acs. Amelia Co. on both sides of little Bryer Riv.; 20 Mar 1745/46, p.211. £2.

JAMES RICHEE, 400 acs. Amelia Co. in the fork of Saylors Cr., adj. Musick alias Norris's in Hill's line, & Cartain [Sartain]; 20 Mar 1745/46, p.213. £2.

JAMES RICHEE, 400 acs. Amelia Co. on the upper side of Saylor Cr.; adj. Goodlow & Morris; 20 Mar 1745/46, p.214. £2.

WILLIAM BROWN, 400 acs. Amelia Co. in the Main fork of Sandy Riv.; 20 Mar 1745/46, p.215. £2.

EDWARD SELBEY, 154 acs. Amelia Co. on both sides of Little Saylor Cr.; adj. Elam, Crawford & Towns; 20 Mar 1745/46, p.216. 15 Shill.

WILLIAM THORNTON SMITH, 400 acs. Amelia Co. on the lower side of Sandy Riv., adj. Joseph Ligon, & Womack; 20 Mar 1745/46, p.217. £2

Settled thus far June.7.1746 & to the 46. page of the other Book.
John Blair D.Audr.

BATTE JONES, 400 acs. Amelia Co. on the S side of Little Nottoway Riv., down the South fork, adj. his Brother Peter Jones; 5 Jun 1746, p.219. £2.

NATHANIEL MALONE, 178 acs. Surry Co. on the S side of Sappony Cr., up the Miery Br., adj. his own line & John Gillison; 5 Jun 1746, p.220. £1.

JOHN EMMERY, 54 acs. Surry Co. on the N side of black Water Sw., on Cotton Reeds Br., adj. John Smith; 5 Jun 1746, p.221. 5 Shill.

WILLIAM SMITH, 95 acs. Surry Co. on the N side of Nottoway Riv., adj. Colo. Benjamin Harrison; 5 Jun 1746, p.223. 10 Shill.

JOHN WATKINS, 83 acs. Louisa Co. adj. Thomas Rice, Colo. David Meriwether & William Brown; 5 Jun 1746, p.224. 10 Shill.

JOHN HARRIS, 400 acs. Louisa Co. on the Brs. of Contrary Riv., adj. Mrs. Thompson; 5 Jun 1746, p.225. £2.

WILLIAM RICE, 400 acs. Louisa Co. on the Brs. of Dyles Riv., on the Goochland Co. line [S65°E], adj. David Mills; 5 Jun 1746, p.226. £2.

STEPHEN TERREY, JUNR. 149 acs. Hanover Co. in the second Fork of Pamunkey Riv.; adj. John Williams, William Winston, Major Blair & Captain Keeling; 5 Jun 1746, p.228. 15 Shill.

ARTHUR LEATH, 303 acs. Amelia Co. on both sides of the Middle Seller fork of Deep Cr., adj. Rany; 5 Jun 1746, p.229. £1.S10.

ANTHONY HONLY, 168 acs. Amelia Co. on the S side of Ellis's fork of flat Cr.; adj. John Ellis, John Mayes, Dyer & Hurt; 5 Jun 1746, p.230. £1.

JOHN JONES, 27 acs. Amelia Co. on both sides of Smacks Cr.; adj. George Robertson, Lodwick Tanner, Thomas Robert & George Wilson; 5 Jun 1746, p.232. 5 Shill.

JOHN PERDUE, 400 acs. Amelia Co. on both sides of the Head of Winticomaick Cr., adj. Tesdale, Coleman & Munford; 5 Jun 1746, p.233. £2.

JOHN WALLICE, 194 acs. Amelia Co. bet. the Seller Cr. and the Harricane Sw., adj. Isham Eppes & Freeman; 5 Jun 1746, p.234. £1.

HENRY NELSON, 400 acs. Amelia Co. on the Head Brs. of the North fork of Sandy Cr., adj. Dawson & Lovitt; 5 Jun 1746, p.236. £2.

WILLIAM FARLEY, SENIOR, 487 acs. Amelia Co. on the upper side of flatt Cr.; adj. Powell, Turner, Cobb, Henry Farley, Isaac Morris & Harris; 5 Jun 1746, p.237. £2.S10.

CHARLES LEWIS, 204 acs. Amelia Co. on the S side of the South fork of little Nottoway Riv., adj. Lewellin Jones; 5 Jun 1746, p.238. £1.

JACOB GARRATT, 400 acs. Amelia Co. on the N side of Flatt

Cr.; adj. Beasley, Dyer, Hurt & Childrey; 5 Jun 1746, p.239. £2.

WILLIAM THOMAS, 400 acs. Amelia Co. on the N side of Mingo's Horsepen Br. of Tommahitton Sw., adj. Anthony Haynes & George Foard; 5 Jun 1746, p.241. £2.

WILLIAM FORD, 342 acs. Amelia Co. on the lower side of the lower Seller fork of Deep Cr., near Nottoway Road, adj. Fredrick Ford & Bolling [her line]; 5 Jun 1746, p.242. £1.S15.

EDWARD JONES, 654 acs. Amelia Co. on both sides of Flatt Cr.; 5 Jun 1746, p.243. £3.S5.

GEORGE BAGLEY, 400 acs. Amelia Co. on the N side of Mallorys Cr., on the long Br.; adj. Nathaniel Roberson, Pressley & Edward Roberson; 5 Jun 1746, p.245. £2.

LEWELLIN JONES, JUNIOR, 400 acs. Amelia Co. on the S side of the South fork of little Nottoway; 5 Jun 1746, p.246. £2.

JAMES BARROW, 181 acs. Pr. Geo. Co. on the upper side of the lower Rockey Run, adj. Walker; 5 Jun 1746, p.248. £1.

ABRAHAM SALLE, 400 acs. Goochland Co. on the S side of

James Riv., on little Deep Cr. & Main Deep Cr., adj. Samuel Arrington; 5 Jun 1746, p.249. £2.

JOHN MORSOM, 300 acs. Goochland Co. among the S Brs. of Willis Riv., in a valley, adj. William Gray & Stephen Sanders; 5 Jun 1746, p.251. £1.S10. [Included in his (John Mossom's) 600 acs. Albemarle Co. in PB 29 p.421]

RICHARD AVERY, 100 acs. Pr. Geo. Co. on the Head of the Reedy Br. of Sappony, on both sides the Road, adj. Haukings; 5 Jun 1746, p.252. 10 Shill. [Included in his PB 26 p.443]

THOMAS MOSLEY, 404 acs. Brunswick Co. on both sides of Peahill Cr., on a Ridge, adj. Jones; 5 Jun 1746, p.253. £2.

CHARLES JENNINGS, 518 acs. Brunswick Co. on the S side of Nottoway Riv., Beg. at the Mouth of the Southerly Br., down Hounds Cr.; adj. Cox, & Reps Jones; 5 Jun 1746, p.254. £2.S15.

THOMAS WILLIAMS, 154 acs. Brunswick Co. on the N side of Butchers Cr.; 5 Jun 1746, p.256. 15 Shill.

CHARLES STEWART, 300 acs. Brunswick Co. on both sides of

Allens Cr., on the Reedy Br.; 5 Jun 1746, p.257. £1.S10.

JOHN PARKER, 327 acs. Brunswick Co., on the N side of Dry Cr. Joining Stephen Evans's upper line; 5 Jun 1746, p.259. £1.S15. [Included in Joseph Minor's 1,325 acs. Lunenburgh Co. in PB 27 p.248]

JOHN INGRAM, 250 acs. Brunswick Co. on the lower side of Ledbetters Cr.; 5 Jun 1746, p.260. £1.S5.

JOHN MORGAN, 130 acs. Brunswick Co. on the N side of Beaver Pond Cr., adj. his own line, Jones & Howell Briggs; 5 Jun 1746, p.261. 15 Shill.

RICHARD KENNON, 379 acs. Brunswick Co. on both sides of the Mill Cr.; 5 Jun 1746, p.263. £2.

THOMAS WYSE, 200 acs. Brunswick Co. on the Cattail Cr., on the Gum Br.; adj. Thomas Tomlinson, his own line & Scott; 5 Jun 1746, p.264. £1.

SILVANUS STOKES, 390 acs. Surry Co. on the S side of Nottoway Riv.; adj. Jones Stokes, Thomas Davis & Abraham Browne & his own lines; 5 Jun 1746, p.266. £2.

LEONARD DOZER, 404 acs. Brunswick Co. on the lower side of Tosekiah Cr. & up the fork; 5 Jun 1746, p.267. £2.

WILLIAM CRAGG, 340 acs. Surry Co. on the S side of Nottoway Riv., up the Sowerwood Br., down the long Br., adj. William Woodland & Richard Rose; 5 Jun 1746, p.269. £1.S15

CHARLES STEWART, 323 acs. Brunswick Co. on the S side of Allens Cr., Beg. at the mouth of the Mine Br., adj. his old line; 5 Jun 1746, p.271. £1.S15.

HENRY BATES, 328 acs. Brunswick Co. on both sides of Taylors Cr.; 5 Jun 1746, p.272. £1.S15.

RICHARD WOOD, 347 acs. Brunswick Co. on both sides of Allens Cr., adj. Dunkley; 5 Jun 1746, p.274. £1.S15. [This patent & survey is a duplicate of PB 23 p.1123 to Edward Hughes]

JOHN WYNNE, 230 acs. Brunswick Co. on the S side of Fucking Cr.; adj. Young Stokes & Thomas Wynne; 5 Jun 1746, p.275. £1.S5.

RICHARD MAULDIN, 230 acs. Augusta Co., down [the E side of] Shanadore Riv.; 5 Jun 1746, p.276. £1.S5.

WILLIAM ROGERS, 387 acs. Brunswick Co. on both sides of Spur Cr.; 5 Jun 1746, p.278. £2.

CHARLES PARISH, 215 acs. Brunswick Co. on the S side of Crooked Run, adj. Thomas Jones; 5 Jun 1746, p.279. £1.S5.

THOMAS JONES, 364 acs. Brunswick Co. on the S side of Nottoway Riv., Beg. at the mouth of Cedar Cr., adj. his own line & Hugh Williams; 5 Jun 1746, p.280. £2.

THOMAS JONES, 202 acs. Brunswick Co. on the S side of Crooked Run, adj. his own line; 5 Jun 1746, p.282. £1.

GEORGE ROBINSON, 400 acs. Augusta Co. on the W side the Blue Ridge, Beg. by a Spring of Buffalo Cr.; 25 Jul 1746, p.283. £2.

BENJAMIN HOOMES, 200 acs. Pr. Geo. Co. on the N side of White Oak Sw., adj. Thomas Rees & Fitzgerrald; 25 Jul 1746, p.285. £1.

HENRY CHILES, 250 acs. Brunswick Co. on the N side of Stanton Riv.; 25 Jul 1746, p.286. £1.S5.

HENRY CHILES, 300 acs. Brunswick Co. on the N side of

Stanton Riv.; 25 Jul 1746, p.288. £1.S10.

WILLIAM WISE, JUNIOR, 120 acs. Brunswick Co. on Cattail Cr., adj. William Wise; 25 Jul 1746, p.289. 15 Shill.

JOSEPH TERRY, 400 acs. Goochland Co. on the Head of the East Br. of Bear Cr. of Willis Riv.; adj. William Holladay, James Daniel, Samuel Atkinson & Adolphus Hendrick; 25 Jul 1746, p.290. £2.

JOSEPH LONG, 400 acs. Augusta Co. on a Br. of James Riv. called Buffalo Cr. on the N side of the Short Mountain; 25 Jul 1746, p.292. £2.

PETER RANEY, 250 acs. Pr. Geo. Co. on both sides of Rockey Run, adj. Pennistone; 25 Jul 1746, p.293. £1.S5.

RICHARD SMITH, JUNIOR, 150 acs. Brunswick Co. on the N side of Banister Riv.; 25 Jul 1746, p.295. 15 Shill.

JOHN PETER SALLING, 400 acs. Augusta Co. on the E side of the North Br. of James Riv.; 25 Jul 1746, p.296. £2.

ROBERT ROWLINS, 369 acs. Augusta Co. on the Head Brs. of

Luney's Mill Cr.; 25 Jul 1746, p.298. £2.

SAMUEL LONG, 400 acs. Augusta Co. on a br. of James Riv. called Buffalo Cr. on the N side of the Short Mountain, near a Point of Rocks on the Cr.; 25 Jul 1746, p.299. £2.

JOHN ORNSBY, 200 acs. Pr. Geo. Co. on the N side of Tommahitton Sw., on the Co. line [South], adj. Cryer; 25 Jul 1746, p.301. £1. [Included in his PB 27 p.318]

ROBERT HARRIS, JUNIOR, 150 acs. Is. of Wight Co. on the S side of the Main Blackwater Sw. & both sides of the North fork of black Cr., in a Pocoson, adj. Robert Monger Junior; 25 Jul 1746, p.302. 15 Shill.

MOSIAS JONES, 200 acs. Pr. Geo. Co. on the N side of Stoney Cr., Beg. at the Bent of sd Cr. above Cedar Island, down Chamberlayns Bed; 25 Jul 1746, p.304. £1.

THOMAS KIRKE, 150 acs. Pr. Geo. Co. on the lower side of Georges Br., adj. Ravenscroft & Griffin; 25 Jul 1746, p.305. 15 Shill.

AMBROSE JOSHUA SMITH, 50 acs. Goochland Co. on the N side

of Fluvanna Riv., adj. Edward Scott dec'd; 25 Jul 1746, p.306. 5 Shill.

ERWIN PATTERSON, 400 acs. Augusta Co. on the W side of the blue Ridge, on the S side a br. of Lunies Mill Cr.; 25 Jul 1746, p.308. £2.

JOHN WALL, 41 acs. Brunswick Co. on the S side of Nottoway Riv. bet. the lines of Samuel Harwell & John Cook; 25 Jul 1746, p.309. 5 Shill.

THOMAS EDWARDS, 400 acs. Goochland Co. on the Upper side of Willis's Cr. on the Brs. of Barren Lick Cr., adj. John Payne; 25 Jul 1746, p.311. £2.

NATHANIEL MASON, 277 acs. Pr. Geo. Co. bet. the Burchen Sw. and the Rambling Br., adj. William Harper & John Jackson; 25 Jul 1746, p.312. £1.S10.

THOMAS EDWARDS, 400 acs. Goochland Co. on both sides of the Cattail Cr. of Willis's Riv. near Willis's Mountain; 25 Jul 1746, p.314. £2.

JOHN MORRIS, 193 acs. Pr. Geo. Co. on both sides of the Reedy Cr., adj. Jones, Thrower, & Lucy Mathis [her lines]; 25 Jul 1746, p.315. £1.

THOMAS HARRIS, 200 acs. Pr. Geo. Co. on the N side of White Oak Sw. & the W side of Chits Br., adj. Taylor; 25 Jul 1746, p.317. £1.

AUSTIN HIGHTOWER, 400 acs. Brunswick Co. on the S side of Cedar Cr., down the Mountain Br., adj Mary Brown; 25 Jul 1746, p.318. £2.

JOHN ROBINSON, 400 acs. Augusta Co. on the South fork of Goose Cr.; 25 Jul 1746, p.320. £2.

ROGER DOUGLAS, 400 acs. Augusta Co. on the N side of James Riv., above mouth of Craig Cr., on side of a Mountain; 25 Jul 1746, p.321. £2.

GOING JOHNSON, 300 acs. Pr. Geo. Co. bet. Butterwood and Tommahitton Swamps; adj Wright, Fisher, Poythress & Glover; 25 Jul 1746, p.323. £1.S10.

JOHN PATTERSON, 300 acs. Goochland Co. on both sides of Stony Cr. of Appamattox Riv., crossing the Drains of Bridle Cr., adj. John Phelps; 25 Jul 1746, p.324. £1.S10.

WILLIAM FARLEY, JUNIOR, 200 acs. Amelia Co. bet. the Brs. of Flatt Cr. and Sandy Cr., adj. Hans Hendrick & Craddock; 25 Jul 1746, p.326. £1.

WILLIAM FAIN, 400 acs. Amelia Co. on the S side of Appamattox Riv., below the mouth of the Great Br., adj. Thomas Baldwin; 25 Jul 1746, p.327. £2.

WILLIAM CARRAVIN, 150 acs. Augusta Co. on a Br. of Smiths Cr.; 25 Jul 1746, p.329. 15 Shill.

ABRAHAM CHILDERS, 350 acs. Goochland Co. on both sides of a Br. of Willis's Riv. alias Willis's Cr. that heads among the Mountains of Willis's Riv; 25 Jul 1746, p.330. £1.S15.

JOHN HARRIS, 200 acs. Goochland Co. on both sides of Great Buffalo Cr. of Willis Riv., adj. Anthony Shereron; 25 Jul 1746, p.332. £1.

JOHN SIMKINS, 200 acs. Brunswick Co. on the upper side of Falling Riv. on the N side of Stanton Riv., adj. Hughes & Hosford; 25 Jul 1746, p.333. £1.

THOMAS RAVENSCROFT, 1,050 acs. Brunswick Co. on both sides of Butchers Cr.; 25 Jul 1746, p.334. £5.S5. [Regranted to William Starke, Gent. in PB 31 p.324]

JOHN PORTIS, 25 acs. Is. of Wight Co. on the N side of the long Br.; adj. James Barnes,

Joyner, & Randall Revell; 25 Jul 1746, p.336. 5 Shill.

DAVID BURN, 120 acs. Is. of Wight Co. on the N side of Nottoway Riv., up the Cypress Sw. & down the Rooty Br., adj. Thomas Oberry; 25 Jul 1746, p.337. 15 Shill.

JOSEPH DELK, 390 acs. Is. of Wight Co. on the N side of Meherin Riv., on a Prong of the Cabbin Br., in the Great Pocoson; 25 Jul 1746, p.338. £2.

JAMES CHAPPEL, 68 acs. Surry Co. on the W side of Assamuseck Sw., on Main run of sd Sw., adj. his own lines, Mrs Cargill & Robert Jones; 25 Jul 1746, p.340. 10 Shill.

WILLIAM BARNES, 170 acs. Is. of Wight Co. on the S side of Nottoway Riv., on the SW of Blunts Sw., by the Nottoway Indians line [NW]; 25 Jul 1746, p.341. £1.

ISAAC CLOUD, 304 acs. Brunswick Co. on both sides of Banister Riv.; 25 Jul 1746, p.342. £1.S10.

ALEXANDER FRASER, 400 acs. Amelia Co. on the Upper side of Sandy Riv., near Randolphs line; 25 Jul 1746, p.343. £2.

WILLIAM FEATHERSTONE, JUNIOR, 100 acs. Pr. Geo. Co. on both sides of Georges Br. of Nammisseen Cr., adj. his father; 25 Jul 1746, p.345. 10 Shill.

CHARLES HUBARD, 400 acs. Brunswick Co. on both sides of falls Cr., joining Peter Hubard; 25 Jul 1746, p.346. £2.

DANIEL FARLY, 400 acs. Amelia Co. on the upper side of Saylor Cr. adj. Gustavas now Womacks, Morris & Richee; 25 Jul 1746, p.347. £2.

HUMPHREY FOY TABB, 190 acs. Gloucester Co., adj. Mr Burgess & Baylor; 25 Jul 1746, p.348. for 2 lbs. of Tobacco for every Acre of sd Land. Whereas by Inquisition Indented and taken in sd Co. 29 May 1741 by Virtue of a Warrant directed to John Robinson Esq. our Escheator for the sd Co. It Appears that Sarah Allaman died Seised of 190 acs. which is found to Escheat to us from the sd Sarah Allaman and Whereas Humphrey Toy Tabb hath made humble Suit and hath obtained a G. for the same.

HUMPHREY TOY TAB, 928 acs. Gloucester Co. on Peanckatanck Riv. & Queen's Cr., on Cartwheel Br. parting this land from Mrs Armistead, to Burtons Point, adj. Mrs Armistead & Allaman; 25 Jul

1746, p.350. for 2 lbs. of Tobacco for every Acre of sd Land. Whereas by Inquisition Indented and taken in sd Co. 29 May 1741 by Virtue of a Warrant directed to John Robinson Esq. our Escheator for sd Co. It appears that Sarah Allaman died Seised of certain Land Supposed to contain 713 acs. but upon a Survey lately made by John French, Surveyor of sd Co. is found to contain 928 acs. which is found to Escheat to us from the sd Sarah Allaman. Whereas Humphrey Toy Tab hath made humble Suit and hath obtained a G. for the same.

STERLING CLACK, 250 acs. Brunswick Co. on both sides of the Church Road, on Ralphs long br.; adj. Henry Jackson, Munford, Tatum, & Henry Jackson; 28 Aug 1746, p.352. £1.S5. [Ralphs long br. refers to Ralph Jackson, an early settler of Greensville Co. & Brunswick Co.]

PETER JOHNSON, 154 acs. Surry Co. on the N side of black Water Sw., up the Run and Drain of the Meadow Br., down Barkers Sw.; adj. Richard Johnson & Colo. Willis; 28 Aug 1746, p.353. 15 Shill.

JOHN MARSHALL, 110 acs. Brunswick Co. on the S side of the Rocky run, up Roses Cr.; 28 Aug 1746, p.354. 15 Shill.

JARVIS WINKFIELD, 263 acs. Surry Co. on the N side of Stony Cr.; adj. George Booth, William Gillum & William Winkfield; 28 Aug 1746, p.355. £1.S10.

JAMES PARRISH, 208 acs. Lunenburgh Co. on the S side of Dan Riv., including Wolf Island; 28 Aug 1746, p.357. £1.S5.

JOSEPH SHELTON, 400 acs. Amelia Co. on the N side of Bryer Riv., adj. Joseph Morton; 28 Aug 1746, p.358. £2.

ABNER GRIGG, 300 acs. Pr. Geo. Co. on the Lower side of the old field Br. of Butterwood Sw.; adj. Poythress, Coleman, John Bain & FitzGerrald; 28 Aug 1746, p.359. £1.S10.

RICHARD BEALE, 404 acs. Pr. Geo. Co. on the N side of Tommahitton Sw., adj. Mitchell; 28 Aug 1746, p.360. £1. 204 acs. part formerly Gtd. John Hill by pat. 20 Jun 1733 [PB 15 p.12] the Right and Title of which sd 204 acs. is since become Vested in the sd Richard Beale and 200 acs. the residue never before Gtd.

ALEXANDER CUNNINGHAM, 348 acs. Amelia Co. on both sides of Little Mountain Cr. on the Lower side of Bush Riv., in the Lowgrounds of the Riv., adj.

Randolph, & George Walker; 28 Aug 1746, p.362. £1.S15.

WOOD JONES, 600 acs. Amelia Co. on both sides of Tommahitton Sw., adj. Ornsby; 28 Aug 1746, p.363. £1. 400 acs. part formerly Gtd. Richard Womack by Pat. 22 Sep 1739 [PB 18 p.383 and regranted to Wood Jones (assignee of Thomas Jones) in PB 22 p.628 dated 20 Mar 1745/46] the right and title of which is since become Vested in sd Wood Jones and 200 acs. the residue never before Gtd.

JOHN RUD JUNR., 400 acs. Amelia Co. on both sides of the Great Br. on the N side of Bush Riv.; 28 Aug 1746, p.364. £2.

PAUL WHITLEY, 400 acs. Augusta Co. on the W side of the blue Ridge on a Br. of James Riv., on the N side of a Br. of Buffelo Cr.; 28 Aug 1746, p.365. £2.

JOSEPH MASON, 243 acs. Brunswick Co. on the N side of Bears Element Cr.; 28 Aug 1746, p.367. £1.S5.

AMOS TIMMS SHELLEY, 326 acs. Brunswick Co. on the N side of Flat Cr.; 28 Aug 1746, p.368. £1.S15.

JOHN MORE, 170 acs. Brunswick Co. on both sides of Long Br., adj.

William Kimball & Munford; 28 Aug 1746, p.369. £1.

JOHN THORNTON, 400 acs. Goochland Co. on the S side of Rockfish Riv., on the side of a Valley, on a ridge; 28 Aug 1746, p.370. £2.

THOMAS PHELPS, 300 acs. Goochland Co. on both sides of Bridle Cr.; 28 Aug 1746, p.371. £1.S10.

THOMAS MERIWETHER, 300 acs. Goochland Co. on the brs. of Rockfish Riv.; adj. his own, Clapham, Colo. Chiswell & Alexander Henderson; 28 Aug 1746, p.372. £1.S10

THOMAS THORNWELL, 140 acs. Goochland Co. on the S side of the Fluvanna Riv., Beg. a little below Phelps's Falls, on a high Hill; 28 Aug 1746, p.373. 15 Shill.

HUGH DOBBINS, JUNIOR, 390 acs. Goochland Co. in the North Garden; adj. Robert Lewis, Dobbins's Cornfield & William Taylor; 28 Aug 1746, p.375. £2.

JOHN GREER, 250 acs. Goochland Co. on the Top of Grannies Hill, adj. William Shaw; 28 Aug 1746, p.376. £1.S5.

JOHN BLANKENSHIP, 227 acs. Henrico Co. adj. Thomas More & Gilbert Ealom; 28 Aug 1746, p.377. £2.S5.

JOHN CRAWFORD, 300 acs. Hanover Co. on both sides the Goochland Road and the Timber'd Fork of the Byrd, along the County Line [N68°W]; 28 Aug 1746, p.378. £1.S10.

JOHN LEWIS, 6 acs. K. & Q. Co. by the Dragon Sw. & the Axell Sw. it being an Island in the Mouth of Axell Sw.; 28 Aug 1746, p.379. 5 Shill.

HENRY KINDALL, 400 acs. Orange Co. on the S side of the Southernmost Br. of the Rappidann joining on a tract of Land Surveyed for James Dyer, up the Riv. to the fork & up the South fork; 28 Aug 1746, p.380. £2.

GEORGE WOOD, 150 acs. Is. of Wight Co. on the N side of Nottoway Riv.; adj. the sd Woods old Lines, Benjamin Clifton & Benjamin Edwards; 28 Aug 1746, p.382. 15 Shill.

EDWARD SHELTON, 125 acs. Surry Co. on the S side of Nottoway Riv., down the Gaul leaf Meadow to its Mouth in the Spring Sw.; adj. Robert Wallace, Gregory Rawlins & his own Lines; 28 Aug 1746, p.383. 15 Shill.

JOHN STOKES, 184 acs. Surry Co. on the S side of Nottoway Riv., on the edge of the Miery br.; adj. Silvanus Stokes, Abram [Abraham] Brown, Samuel Stokes & Thomas Pennington; 28 Aug 1746, p.384. £1.

JAMES SANDERS, 200 acs. Pr. Geo. Co. on the S side of the Mortar Br. of Stoney Cr.; adj. Jacob Jones, John Row & Stephen Evans; 28 Aug 1746, p.385. £1.

JAMES OVERBY, 300 acs. Pr. Geo. Co. on the lower side of Georges Br. of Nammisseen Cr., adj. Vaughan; 28 Aug 1746, p.386. £1.S10.

WILLIAM SCOTT, 400 acs. Amelia Co. on the head Brs. of Spring Cr.; 28 Aug 1746, p.387. £2.

WILLIAM WATSON & WILLIAM CRAWLEY, 377 acs. Amelia Co. on the upper side of West Cr.; adj. Neale, Rowlitt, William Marshall, Clarke, Roberson, Peter Farly & Joseph Farly; 28 Aug 1746, p.389. for £1 and also for the Imp. of 4 pers. to dwell within this our sd Colony & Dominion of Virginia whose names are *Thomas Thorpe John Abbet Thomas Brown and Joseph Darby*.

JOHN SMITH, 400 acs. Amelia Co. on the lower side of Saylor

Cr., adj. Goodlow & FitzGerrald; 28 Aug 1746, p.390. £2.

EVAN JONES, 400 acs. Amelia Co. on both sides of a great Br. on the lower side of Vaughans Cr., adj. Hudson; 28 Aug 1746, p.391. £2.

SAMUEL YOUNG, 77 acs. Amelia Co. on the S side of Wests Cr., adj. Beasley & Hayes; 28 Aug 1746, p.392. 10 Shill.

SILVANUS WALKER, 993 acs. Brunswick Co. on the S side of Nottoway Riv. & on both sides of Fucking Cr.; adj. Munford, John Wynne & Evans; 28 Aug 1746, p.393. £5.

JOHN MACLIN, 995 acs. Brunswick Co. on the S side of Mitchells Cr.; 28 Aug 1746; p.394. £5.

JOHN MASON, SENR., 530 acs. Brunswick Co. on the N side of Waqua Cr.; adj. Thomas Seemore, John Wall, Richard Vaughan & Richard Burch; 28 Aug 1746, p.396. £1.S10. 242 acs. part being part of 342 acs. formerly Gtd. Richard Vaughan by Pat. 7 July 1726 [PB 12 p.528] the right and title of which sd 242 acs. by Mesne Conveyeances is become Vested in sd John Mason & 288 acs. the Residue never before Gtd.

JAMES JUDKINS, 393 acs. Brunswick Co. on the N side of Stuke Br., adj. Peoples; 28 Aug 1746, p.397. £2. [The Stuke or Stewke Branch feeds into Fountains Creek in Greensville County and may refer to the Stuckanocks Indians. Other Sioux Indian references in southern Greensville County include the old Sappone Fort, the Keaway Sw. & the Occoneechy Sw.]

JOHN NANCE, 400 acs. Brunswick Co. on both sides of Meherrin Riv., up Owls Cr.; 28 Aug 1746, p.398.

JOHN SULLIVANT, 400 acs. Brunswick Co. on the S side of Twittys Cr.; 28 Aug 1746, 399. £1. 200 acs. part formerly Gtd. Drury Stith by Pat. 30 Jul 1742 [PB 20 p.387] the Right and Title whereof is since become vested in sd John Sullivant & 200 acs. the Residue never before Gtd.

EDWARD HAMILTON, 200 acs. Goochland Co. on the Brs. of Randolphs Cr. & on the Head of the Cattail Br. of Willis Riv., adj. Joseph Price; 28 Aug 1746, p.401. 20 Shill.

THOMAS PHELPS, JUNIOR, 280 acs. Goochland Co., on both sides of Bridle Cr., 28 Aug 1746, p.402. £1.S10.

WILLIAM WILLIS, 250 acs. Goochland Co., on the brs. of Snow Quarter br. & Turkey Cock Cr., adj. Thomas Carter & John Blevin; 28 Aug 1746, p.403. £1.S5.

JAMES MATTHEWS, 250 acs. Goochland Co. at the Point of a great Rock by the Appamattox Riv., on a ridge above Wolf Cr. & at a Point of Rocks by the Riv.; 28 Aug 1746, p.404. £1.S5.

WILLIAM SHAW, 304 acs. Goochland Co. on the brs. of Ivey Cr., adj. Robert Lewis & Charles Hudson, running on Newen lines; 28 Aug 1746, p.405. £1.S10.

MILDRED MERIWETHER, Daughter of Nicholas Meriwether Junior Dec'd, 1,600 acs. Goochland Co. in the South Garden on both sides of the South Br. of Hardware Riv., adj. Abraham Venables & Robert Davis; 28 Aug 1746, p.406. £8.

JAMES WOOD, 400 acs. Goochland Co. on the brs. of Rockfish Riv., on the side of a Mountain, adj. Hickman, & William Miller; 28 Aug 1746, p.407. £2.

THOMAS SATTERWHITE, 121 acs. Hanover Co. on the S side of the Main Run of Chickahominy Sw., on the edge of the Lowgrounds, along the main Road; adj. Thomas Smith, William Baughan & James Pyrant; 28 Aug 1746, p.408. 10 Shill. 50 acs. part being part of a Greater Quantity formerly Gtd. Richard Littlepage by Pat. 21 Oct 1684 [871 acs. New Kent Co. in PB 7 p.400 on N side Chickahominy Sw. & S side of York Riv.] the Right & Title by divers Mesne Conveyances is become Vested in sd Thomas Satterwhite & 71 acs. the residue never before Gtd. [277 acs. of Littlepage's 871 acs. was included in John Ellis's 380 acs. Hanover Co. in PB 33 p.259 on N side of Chickohomony Sw.]

WILLIAM CHETHAM, 191 acs. Henrico Co. on a br. of Dry Cr. parting Thomas Chetham, Jacob Lester & Benjamin Farmer, in the old Field; adj. Thomas Chetham, Curtis Real/Reats, Grills, Turpin & sd Chethams old line; 28 Aug 1746, p.409. £1.

GEORGE BOOTH, 1,140 acs. Surry Co. on the side of Stoney Cr. & Sapponey Cr., down the run of the Great Br.; adj. John Thrower, Jarvis Winkfield, William Winkfield, John Bonner, Nathaniel Malone, Thomas Mullen & Thomas Thrower; 28 Aug 1746, p.410. £1.S10. 850 acs. part formerly Gtd. sd George Booth by Pat. 8 Sep 1730 [PB 13 p.523 which included part of Nathaniel Maloon's

PB 10 p.265, John Rayburn's PB 10 p.269 & sd Booth's PB 11 p.280] & 290 acs. the residue never before Gtd.

JOSEPH CROOKE & JAMES CROOKE, 179 acs. Pr. Geo. Co. upon the Brs. of Gravelly Run, down the Flatt br. & the Horse br., adj. Solomon Crooke & John Browder; 28 Aug 1746, p.412. £1.

THOMAS MAN, 400 acs. Goochland Co. on the Brs. of Rockfish Riv., on the side of a Mountain, adj. Col. Chiswell & James Wood; 28 Aug 1746, p.413. £2.

JOHN ORNSBY, Clerk, 125 acs. Pr. Geo. Co. on the N side of Tommahitton Sw., along the Co. Line [South], adj. Kirkland, his own line & Goodwin; 28 Aug 1746, p.414. 15 Shill.

JOHN HARRISON JUNR., 175 acs. Augusta Co. on Smith Cr.; 25 Sep 1746, p.415. £1.

JOHN HARRISON, JUNIOR, 350 acs. Augusta Co. on the S side of Woods Riv., on the N side of the North fork of Neck Cr. ; 25 Sep 1746, p.41. £1S.15.

JOHN HARRISON JUNR., 400 acs. Augusta Co. on Smiths Cr., crossing Lick Run; 25 Sep 1746, p.417. £2.

JOHN HARRISON, JUNIOR, 400 acs. Augusta Co. on a Br. of Woods Riv. called Meadow Cr., near a Glassy Glade, on the Meadow Br., crossing a Meadow; 25 Sep 1746, p.418. £2.

JOHN HARRISON, JUNIOR, 241 acs. Augusta Co. on a br. of James Riv. at the East end of the Short Hill; 25 Sep 1746, p.419. £1.S5.

SAMUEL HARRISON, 200 acs. Augusta Co. on a br. of Cooks Cr., crossing a Spring br.; 25 Sep 1746, p.421. £1.

DANIEL HARRISON, 387 acs. Augusta Co. on the E side of Muddy Cr., near a point of Rocks on the N side of the North riv. below the Mouth of sd Cr.; 25 Sep 1746, p.422. £2.

DANIEL HARRISON, 400 acs. Augusta Co. on a br. of Muddy Cr., adj. Jacob Dye; 25 Sep 1746, p.423. £2.

DANIEL HARRISON, 215 acs. Augusta Co. on the West fork of Naked Cr.; 25 Sep 1746, p.424. £1.S5.

DANIEL HARRISON, 400 acs. Augusta Co. on the Head Linwells Mill Cr., in a Hollow, adj. Jost Hyte; 25 Sep 1746, p.425. £2.

HUGH CAMPBELL, 400 acs. Augusta Co. on a Br. of the North Riv. of Shanando called Naked Cr., adj. Jacob Stover; 25 Sep 1746, p.426. £2.

HUGH CAMPBELL, 400 acs. Augusta Co. on the Waters of a Br. of Shanando called naked Cr., on a Ridge, adj. Michael Dickey; 25 Sep 1746, p.427. £2.

FINLA MCLURE, 400 acs. Augusta Co. on the W side the Blue Ridge, Beg. above the Mouth of a Large Run on the N side of Goose Cr., adj. George Home; 25 Sep 1746, p.428. £2.

MICHAEL DICKEY, 170 acs. Augusta Co. on the Waters of a Br. of Shanando called naked Cr., adj. sd Dickeys former Survey; 25 Sep 1746, p.429. £1.

MICHAEL DICKEY, 350 acs. Augusta Co. on a Br. of Naked Cr.; 25 Sep 1746, p.430. £1.S15.

WILLIAM FRAZER, 157 acs. Augusta Co. on the S side of Shanando Riv., Beg. on a Stoney Hill bet. the Riv. and the blue Ridge, to a small Rockey Island in Stovers line, down the Riv. to the Mouth of the two Mile Run at a Clay Bank; 25 Sep 1746, p.431. £1.

WILLIAM FRAZER, 243 acs. Augusta Co. on the S side of Shanando Riv. opposite to Stovers 5,000 Acre Tract, Beg. in a Savanna bet. the Riv. and the Blue Ridge, on the Riv. side above Frazers House, at the Mouth of a Gut or small run; 25 Sep 1746, p.433. £1.S5.

DANIEL DAVISON, 46 acs. Augusta Co. on a Br. of Shanando called Daniel Jones's Br.; 25 Sep 1746, p.434. 5 Shill.

DANIEL DAVISON, 156 acs. Augusta Co. on a Br. of Shanando called Smiths Cr., adj. Stephen Howarth; 25 Sep 1746, p.435. £1.

JOHN BUMGARDNER, 400 acs. Augusta Co. on the Head Spring of Stoney Lick Br., on the side of a Ridge, adj. Andrew McConnald; 25 Sep 1746, p.436. £2.

SAMUEL BROWN, 348 acs. Augusta Co. on the Waters of a Br. of Shanando called Naked Cr., adj. Michael Dickey & James Trotter; 25 Sep 1746, p.437. £1.S15.

CHRISTIAN CLAYMAN, 80 acs. Augusta Co. on the SE side of the South Riv. of Shanando above Henry Dooleys Land; 25 Sep 1746, p.438. 10 Shill.

WILLIAM MITCHELL, 200 acs. Augusta Co. on a Br. of James

Riv. called the Mary; 25 Sep 1746, p.439. £1.

ALEXANDER MCKAGE, 400 Acs. Augusta Co. on the S side of James Riv. below the wild ford, Beg. on the Riv. opposite to a small Island, at the side of a Hollow; 25 Sep 1746, p.440. £2.

JOHN TREMBLE, 300 acs. Augusta Co. on both sides of Cathys Riv., Beg. on a Ridge on the S side of the Riv. opposite to the Mouth of Buffaloe Lick br.; 25 Sep 1746, p.441. £1.S10.

ROBERT BOLLING, 130 acs. Pr. Geo. Co. on the S side of Stoney Cr.; adj. Cornelius Fox, his old & new Lines, and Evans; 25 Sep 1746, p.443. 15 Shill.

WILLIAM ELDER, 400 acs. Pr. Geo. Co. on both sides of the Reedy Br. of Butterwood Sw., adj. William Poythress; 25 Sep 1746, p.444. £2.

WILLIAM BARTLETT, son of Samuel Bartlett dec'd, 200 acs. Pr. Geo. Co. on both sides of Turkey Egg Cr., adj. George Booths upper Line; 25 Sep 1746. p.445. £1.

WILLIAM CLEYTON, 200 acs. Pr. Geo. Co. on the upper part of the Beaver pond Br. of Nottoway Riv., adj. John Whitmore; 25 Sep 1746, p.446. £1.

THOMAS DARBY, 268 acs. Pr. Geo. Co. on the Brs. of Chamberlaynes Bed Run; adj. Thomas Lewis, Joseph Lewis & Henry Thweatt; 25 Sep 1746, p.447. £1.S10.

JOHN WAGNON, 576 acs. Pr. Geo. Co. on the S side of Stoney Cr., by the side of the Nottoway River Road and sd Wagnons fence; Beg. at his old Corner in Bollings Line, to the Land purchased of William Poythress; 25 Sep 1746, p.448. £1. 400 acs. part formerly Gtd. William Poythress by Pat. 24 Mar. 1734/35 [PB 15 p.461] the Right and Title of which sd 400 acs. by Mesne Conveyances is since become Vested in the sd John Wagnon and 176 acs. the residue never before Gtd.

JOHN EVANS, JUNR., 656 acs. Pr. Geo. Co. on the S side of Sappone Cr.; adj. William Starks old and new lines & sd Evans's old Lines, by the side of a small Meadow in Munfords Alias Williams Line, near the Widow William's Fence; 25 Sep 1746, p.450. £1.S15. 350 acs. part thereof formerly Gtd. sd John Evans by Pat. 30 Nov 1721 and 306 acs. the residue never before Granted.

JOHN TAPLEY, 400 acs. Pr. Geo. Co. on both sides the Mealy Br. of Sapponey Cr.; adj. Captain Starks,

Richard Stokes's, James Keith, and Capt. David Walker & John Bolling [their Lines]; 25 Sep 1746, p.452. £2.

JOHN ROWLAND, 284 acs. Amelia Co. on the S side of Lazaritta Cr., on the edge of the Bever Pond of the sd Cr., adj. Henry Robertson & Edward Robertson; 25 Sep 1746, p.453. £1.S10.

PHILEMON CRANE, 200 acs. Amelia Co. on both sides of Winninghams Cr. of Deep Cr., adj. William Stark; 25 Sep 1746, p.454. £1.

PATRICK MULLEN, 390 acs. Amelia Co. on Bearbone Br. of West Cr., by the Church Road; adj. William Worsham, William Watson, Richard Jones Junior, Osbourn, Benson, Hall, & Robert Taylor; 25 Sep 1746, p.455. £2. Whereas by Pat. 10 Jun 1740 gtd. unto Feild Jefferson And whereas the sd Field Jefferson hath failed to make Cultiv. & Improv. and John FitzGerrald hath made humble Suit and hath Obtained a g. for the same which he hath Assigned unto Patrick Mullen.

WILLIAM LIGON, 400 acs. Amelia Co. on the Lower side of Sandy Riv., adj. his own lines & Henry Ligon; 25 Sep 1746, p.457. £2.

JOHN MARTIN, 350 acs. Amelia Co. on both sides of Bryer Riv.; adj. his old Line & Samuel Morton; 25 Sep 1746, p.458. £1.S15.

OBADIAH WOODSON, 800 acs. Amelia Co. on the Lower side of Buffilo Riv., on the upper or W side of a Great Br., adj. Bibb; 25 Sep 1746, p.460. £2. 400 acs. part formerly gtd. sd Obadiah Woodson by Pat. 30 Mar 1743/44 [PB 21 p.253] and 400 acs. the Residue never before Gtd. [The survey in this Patent is a duplicate of Joseph Morton's 800 acs. in PB 22 p.579 which is included in Joseph Morton's 2,800 acs. in PB 28 p.359]

WILLIAM BROWN, 400 acs. Amelia Co. on both sides of Mortons Cr. on the N side of Bush Riv., adj. Randolph & Macgehee; 25 Sep 1746, p.461. £2.

HUGH NIXON, 193 acs. Amelia Co. on the Lower side of Buffillo Riv.; adj. Rice, Bibb & Woodson; 25 Sep 1746, p.463. £1.

THOMAS TURPIN, 400 acs. Amelia Co. on both sides of the Great Br. of Sandy Riv.; 25 Sep 1746, p.464. £2.

JOHN MAXEY, 400 acs. Goochland Co. on both sides of Troublesome Cr. of Slate Riv., adj.

Sacheveral Whitebread; 25 Sep 1746, p.466. £2.

JOHN MAXEY, 400 acs. Goochland Co. on both sides of Great Cr. of Slate Riv., adj. George Holmes Guin; 25 Sep 1746, p.467. £2.

WILLIAM MAXEY, 400 acs. Goochland Co. on both sides of Great Cr. of Slate Riv.; 25 Sep 1746, p.468. £2.

CHARLES BOND, 150 acs. Goochland Co. on both sides of Shepherds Cr., adj. James Shepherd; 25 Sep 1746, p.470. 15 Shill.

THOMAS BASSETT, 385 acs. Goochland Co. between Great Guinea & Angola Creeks, on the N side of a Run; adj. his old line, John Francis & Joseph Echolls; 25 Sep 1746, p.471. £2.

HENRY BELL, 400 acs. Goochland Co. among the S Brs. of Willis Riv.; adj. Joseph Dabbs & Henry Cary; 25 Sep 1746, p.473. £2.

ADRIAN ANGLIN, 200 acs. Goochland Co. on both sides of Slate Riv. and Rockey Cr.; 25 Sep 1746, p.474. £1.

JOHN COBBS, 400 acs. Goochland Co. on both sides of the South Br.

of Cooks Cr. in the fork of James Riv., adj. Dudley Diggs Gent. & George Payne Junr. ; 25 Sep 1746, p.475. £2.

WILLIAM CABBELL, 50 acs. Goochland Co. on the S side of the Fluvanna Riv., adj. John Lad; 25 Sep 1746, p.477. 5 Shill.

WILLIAM CABBELL, 200 acs. Goochland Co. on the S side of Tye Riv.; 25 Sep 1746, p.478. £1.

WILLIAM CABBELL, 400 acs. Goochland Co. on the S side of Tye Riv.; adj. John Mackenny, John Peartree Burk & Mr. Ross; 25 Sep 1746, p.480. £2.

JOHN PAYNE, 400 acs. Goochland Co. on the Brs. of Bremor and Raccoon Creeks, in a Slash of Bremor Cr., adj. the Land lately Surveyed for John Bybe; 25 Sep 1746, p.481. £2.

SAMPSON FLEMING, 75 acs. Goochland Co. near the Head of Muddy Cr.; adj. Jacob Winfree, Samuel Allen, James Knot & Richard Taylor; .25 Sep 1746, p.482. 10 Shill.

ROBERT HUDGENS, 400 acs. Goochland Co. among the S Brs. of Willis Riv., crossing the East Br. of Bear Cr.; adj. William Holladay, Samuel Allen, Abraham

Bayley, John Allen & Robert Hughes; 25 Sep 1746, p.484. £2.

JAMES NIX, 400 acs. Goochland Co. Adj. to the N side of Appamattox Riv. & John Phelps; 25 Sep 1746, p.485. £2.

THOMAS UPTON, 400 acs. Goochland Co. on both sides of Bryerry Br. of Rockfish Riv.; 25 Sep 1746, p.487. £2.

JOHN MOSELEY, 225 acs. Goochland Co. on both sides of a Br. of the Bryd Cr. called Phills Cr.; adj. Robert Kent, Ebenezar Adams dec'd, Arthur Hopkins & Philip Thurmond; 25 Sep 1746, p.488. £1.S5.

ALEXANDER PATTON, 400 acs. Goochland Co. on the Brs. of Stocktons Br. of Mechams Riv. and on the brs. of Rockfish Riv., at a br. of Stocktons run, adj. Richard Stockton & Charles Lynch; 25 Sep 1746, p.490. £2.

WILLIAM LITTLE, 200 acs. Goochland Co. on both sides of Stocktons Br. of Mechums Riv., adj. John Wood & William Whiteside; 25 Sep 1746, p.491. £1.

HENRY EVANS, 280 acs. Goochland Co. at the Head of Little Guinea Cr., near the S side of the Road, adj. James Daniel & Samuel Atkinson; 25 Sep 1746, p.493. £1.S10.

THOMAS HODGES, 400 acs. Goochland Co. among the S Brs. of Willis Riv., adj. Henry Cary; 25 Sep 1746, p.494. £2.

ARTHUR HOPKINS, 400 acs. Goochland Co. among the brs. of the Byrd Cr., crossing the South Br. of Elk run, adj. Ebenezar Adams dec'd & John Cole dec'd; 25 Sep 1746, p.495. £2.

MATTHEW JORDAN, 400 acs. Goochland Co. on the N side of the Fluvanna Riv., adj. his own Lines & Thomas Golsbie; 25 Sep 1746, p.497. £2.

JAMES HOLEMAN/HOLMAN, 22 acs. Goochland Co. on the brs. of Tuckahoe Cr.; adj. his own, Stephen Sampson, Richard Crouch & Henry Graves; 25 Sep 1746, p.498. 5 Shill.

JOHN PEARTREE BURK, 400 acs. Goochland Co. on the brs. of Tye Riv., adj. John Mackenny /Mckenny; 25 Sep 1746, p.500. £2.

JAMES NEVELL, 400 acs. Goochland Co. on the N side of Tye Riv., on Ruckers Run, adj. William Matthews; 25 Sep 1746, p.501. £2.

WILLIAM FLOYD, 400 acs. Goochland Co. on the S side of Pedlar Riv., into the Woods, on Maple Run; 25 Sep 1746, p.503. £2.

ROBERT CROCKET, 350 acs. Augusta Co. on the W side of the blue ridge, Beg. at the foot of a Hill on the S side Lunies Mill Cr.; 25 Sep 1746, p.504. £1.S15.

WALTER LEEK, 150 acs. Albemarle Co. on the brs. of Hardway Riv., adj. Thomas Fitzpatrick & Mildred Meriwether; 25 Sep 1746, p.506. 15 Shill.

GEORGE BRIGGS, 330 acs. Is. of Wight Co. on the N side of Nottoway Riv.; adj. William Hickman, Benjamin Johnson, Stephen Darden & Thomas Sharp; 25 Sep 1746, p.507. £1.S10. [p.507 was followed by p.508, the Scribe skipped p.508]

JOSEPH JOINER, 140 acs. Is. of Wight Co. on the S side of the main black Water Sw., by the side of Black Cr., on Sandy Bridge Br., crossing the Cattail Br.; adj. Thomas Brewer, Matthew Griffin & William Joiner; 25 Sep 1746, p.510. 15 Shill.

AMOS GARRESS, 20 acs. Is. of Wight Co. on the N side of Meherin Riv.; adj. Hugh Norvell, the sd Garress's other Line & John Scott; 25 Sep 1746, p.512. 5 Shill.

JAMES TURNER, 50 acs. Is. of Wight Co. on the S side of Meherrin Riv.; Beg. on the bank of Maherin Riv., by the Country Line [S87½E°], adj. William Deloach & Joseph Wall; 25 Sep 1746, p.513. 5 Shill.

ARTHUR WHITEHEAD JUNR., 320 acs. Is. of Wight Co. on the N side of Meherrin Riv., down the Whitewood Sw.; adj. Howell Edmonds, Samuel Atkinson & John Morgan Hunsden; 25 Sep 1746, p.514. £1.S15.

RICHARD BLOW JUNR., 290 acs. Is. of Wight Co. on the S side of Nottoway Riv., by the side of Dicks Sw.; adj. Richard Vick, the sd Blows old lines, William Register, Joseph Register & Nicholas Gurley; 25 Sep 1746, p.516. £1.S10. [Note the unique version of the name Rochester]

JOHN WICKENS, 61 acs. of Swamp Land in Pr. Ann Co. in Black Water; adj. sd Wickens formerly bought of Solomon Oliver, Lawrence Dolley & Colo. Swann, near Corprews &tc. former Survey; 25 Sep 1746, p.518. 10 Shill.

JAMES NEVIL, 2,550 acs. Goochland Co. on the S side of the

Fluvanna Riv., Beg. at a Gut above a parcel of Rocks, crossing Hoopers Cr., crossing Watkins's Cr.; adj. the sd Nevil's line, Philip Mayo, Joseph Hooper, Richard Taylor & James Daniel Gentl.; 25 Sep 1746, p.520. 700 acs. part formerly Gtd. sd James Nevil by Pat. 28 Sep 1732 [James Nevel in PB 14 p.463] and 1,850 acs. the residue also form Gtd. sd James Nevil by Pat. 1 March 1743/44.

CHARLES PORTLOCK, 280 acs. Is. of Wight Co. on the W side of Pagan Cr., on the Eastermost Point of Bennets Park, down the back Cr., up the Old James Sw., down the Cold Spring br.; adj. the Late Thomas Walton dec'd, Thomas Cassey, William Hodsden & John Clark; 25 Sep 1746, p.522. for 2 lbs. of Tobacco for every Acres of sd Land. Whereas by Inquisition Indented and taken in sd 30 Nov 1742 by Virtue of a Warrant directed to Thomas Cocke our Escheator for the sd Co. It appears that Thomas Walton died Seised of Certain Land supposed to contain 200 acs. but upon a Survey lately made by James Baker, Surveyor of sd Co. is found to contain 280 acs. which is found to Escheat to us from the sd Thomas Walton And Whereas Charles Portlock hath made humble Suit and hath obtain'd a G. for the Same.

ABRAHAM BAKER, 400 acs. Amelia Co. on the S side of the South fork of Buffillo Riv., down a small br. & up a great Br. of the sd Fork; 25 Sep 1746, p.524. £2.

JOHN ROGERS, JUNIOR, 400 acs. Louisa Co. on both sides the main fork of Pritties Cr., along the Co. Line [S65°E], at Haynes's Fork; adj. Bartholomew Durat, David Watts, Churchill & Mrs. Rippon [N37°E]; 25 Sep 1746, p.525. £2.

JOHN ORNSBY, Clerk, 239 acs. Brunswick Co. on Both sides of Staunton Riv., Beg. at the Mouth of a great Br. in Thomasons Lowgrounds, adj. Ravenscroft; 25 Sep 1746, p.527. £1.S5.

WILLIAM HARPER, 80 acs. Surry Co. on the W side of Sappony Cr., on Gillions Br., adj. Isaac Robertson, his own Line; 25 Sep 1746, p.528. 10 Shill.

HENRY MAY, 328 acs. Lunenburg Co. on both sides of the first fork of Little Roanoak, adj. Richard Randolph; 25 Sep 1746, p.529. £1.S15.

JOSEPH SCOUTS, 200 acs. Surry Co. on both sides of Harrys Sw.; adj. Thomas Wilkerson, John Woodard, John Davis & James Matthews; 25 Sep 1746, p.531. £1.

GEORGE LONG, 275 acs. Surry Co. on the S side of Nottoway Riv., Beg. in the Lowgrounds of the spring Sw.; adj. his own lines, Benjamin Cooper & Gregory Rawlins; 25 Sep 1746, p.532. £1.S10.

THOMAS PATE, 490 acs. Surry Co. on the S side of Nottoway Riv., beg. on the NE side of the great Plowman Sw., down the Reedy Br., adj. William Thompson & Edward Harris; 25 Sep 1746, p.534. £2.S10.

EDWARD POTTER, 127 acs. York Co., on (Mr or Mrs?) Colliers Ditch, up York main Road bearing near Westerly to the fork of white Marsh Road, along the white Marsh Road bearing SW to where the Line crosses the sd Road, to a hole in a pond; 12 Jan 1746/47, p.535. for 2 lbs. of Tobacco for every Acre. Whereas by Inquisition Indented and taken in York Co. 4 Jun 1742 by Virtue of a Warrant directed to William Bird Esqr. Escheator for sd Co. It appears that Mary Jefferson died Seised of certain Land supposed to contain 100 acs. more or Less and by a Survey thereof lately made by James Shields Surveyor of sd Co. is found to contain 127 acs. which is found to Escheat to us from the sd Mary Jefferson And whereas Edward Potter hath made humble Suit and hath obtained a g. for the same.

RICHARD DRUMMOND, 250 acs. Accomack Co. on the Head of a Br. Issuing into Hunting Cr.; adj. William Chance, Henry Custis & Francis Heirs; 12 Jan 1746/47, p.537. for 2 lbs. of Tobacco for every Acre of sd Land. Whereas by Inquisition Indented and taken in Accomack Co. 26 Jan 1739/40 by Virtue of a Warrant directed to Edmund Bayley Gent. our Escheator for sd Co. It Appears That John Thompson died seised of 250 acs. which is found to Escheat to us from sd John Thompson And whereas Richard Drummond hath made Humble Suit and hath obtained a g. for the same.

JAMES WOOD, 400 acs. Augusta Co. on the Brs. of Muddy Cr., near the North Mountain; 12 Jan 1746/47, p.538. £2.

JAMES WOOD, 176 acs. Augusta Co. on a Br. of James Riv. called Looneys Mill Cr., adj. Robert Looney; 12 Jan 1746/47, p.539. £1.

JAMES WOOD, 400 acs. Augusta Co. on a Br. of the South Riv. of Shanando called Cub Run, on a Spur of the Peaked Mountain; 12 Jan 1746/47, p.541. £2.

JAMES WOOD, 268 acs. Augusta Co. on the Waters of a Br. of Shanando called naked Cr., adj. Michael Dickey; 12 Jan 1746/47, p.542. £1.S10.

JAMES WOOD, 400 acs. Augusta Co. including the great plane [plain] on the North Riv. of Shanando, Beg. on a Hill above the great spring; 12 Jan 1746/47, p.544. £2.

JAMES WOOD, 350 acs. Augusta Co. on Muddy Cr. including a Meadow on the sd Cr., to a rock near the Head of a Grassye glade; 12 Jan 1746/47, p.545. £1.S15.

AUGUSTINE CLAIBORNE, 656 acs. formerly in Brunswick Co. now Lunenburg on the N side of Maherrin Riv., beg. on a little Cr.; 12 Jan 1746/47, p.547. [The following Caveat explains why there was no charge for this patent and also indicates this patent was from an old survey] *Whereas our Royal Father of Blessed memory on the humble petition of the General Assembly of our Colony and Dominion of Virginia was Graciously pleased to grant unto each of our Subjects which should go to settle in the County of Brunswick before the 1st day of May in the year of our Lord 1728 the Liberty of taking up any Quantity of Land not exceeding 1,000 Acres free and discharged of the duty of purchasing Rights for the Same.*

JAMES WOOD, 245 acs. Augusta Co. on Goose Cr., adj. Francis Betty; 12 Jan 1746/47, p.548. £1.S5.

JAMES WOOD, 287 acs. Augusta Co. on the Head of the Middle br. of Catawbo Cr.; 12 Jan 1746/47, p.550. £1.S10.

JAMES WOOD, 370 acs. Augusta Co. on both sides of Smiths Cr., Beg. on the S side of the sd Cr. a little below a fall in the sd Cr., on the S side of the Waggon Road; 12 Jan 1746/47, p.551. £2.

JAMES WOOD, 400 acs. Augusta Co. on the N side of Looneys Mill Cr. including a Beaver Dam Sw.; 12 Jan 1746/47, p.553. £2.

JAMES WOOD, 400 acs. Augusta Co. on the W side of the blue Ridge of Mountains on both sides of Buffoloe Cr. it being a br. of the North fork of James Riv.; 12 Jan 1746/47, p.554. £2.

JAMES WOOD, 300 acs. Augusta Co. on a br. of Muddy Cr., at the foot of the North Mountain, adj. Jacob Dye; 12 Jan 1746/47, p.556. £1.S10.

THOMAS WATERSON, 300 acs. Augusta Co. on a br. of Naked

Cr., on a ridge, adj. James Wood; 12 Jan 1746/47, p.557. £1.S10.

THOMAS WATERSON, 120 acs. Augusta Co. on the N side the North Riv. of Shanadore, crossing Cooks Cr., in a Valley; 12 Jan 1746/47, p.559. 15 Shill.

THOMAS WATERSON, 185 acs. Augusta Co., Beg. on a piney hill, on a ridge; 12 Jan 1746/47, p.560. £2.

JAMES LEEPER, 116 acs. Augusta Co. on a br. of Shanando called naked Cr., Beg. on the Top of a Hill on the N side the Cr., on a ridge; 12 Jan 1746/47, p.562. 15 Shill.

JAMES BELL, 400 acs. Augusta Co. on a br. of Catheys Riv. called Jennings's br., Beg. on the N side of a Spring br.; 12 Jan 1746/47, p.563. £2.

SILAS HART, 400 acs. Augusta Co. on the W side of the blue Ridge and on both sides the North br. of James Riv., Beg. at 2 Hoopwoods & a Hiccory on the E side of the sd Riv. Opposite to an Island; 12 Jan 1746/47, p.564. £2.

GEORGE FORBUSH, 400 acs. Augusta Co. on the North br. of Shanando in the Gap of the Mountain, on the E side of Beaver Dam Run, crossing the Riv. to

Barnard McHenrys Line; 12 Jan 1746/47, p.566. £2.

ROBERT FOWLER, 400 acs. Augusta Co. on the S side the North Riv. of Shanando, near a Gully on the Riv., adj. Alexander Thomson; 12 Jan 1746/47, p.567. £2.

EPHRAIM VOSE, 200 acs. Augusta Co., Beg. on the N side of Goose Cr., crossing a Large Run, on the lower side the Mouth of a gut against some Rocks in the sd Cr., adj. Finla McLure; 12 Jan 1746/47, p.569. £1.

JOHN DOGE, 400 acs. Augusta Co. on James Riv. on the W side the blue Ridge; 12 Jan 1746/47, p.570. £2.

CHRISTOPHER FRANCISKI, 150 acs. Augusta Co. on the W side the blue ridge, adj. a pat. formerly gtd. to Jacob Stover; 12 Jan 1746/47, p.571. 15 Shill.

JACOB MACKGEHEE, 727 acs. Amelia Co. on both sides of Sandy Riv., on the upper great Br. & the lower great Br., Beg. at his own old Corner of the Land purchased of Morton, adj. William Ligon & Joseph Ligon; 12 Jan 1746/47, p.573. £1.S15. 400 acs. part being part of a pat. for 1,072 acs. formerly gtd. unto Joseph Morton by Pat. 9 Feb 1737/38 [Joseph

Moreton in PB 17 p.478] the Right and Title of which sd 400 acs. is since become Vested in the sd Jacob Mackgehee and 327 acs. the residue never before gtd.

WILLIAM SEARCEY, 400 acs. Amelia Co. on the Lower side of Lower fork of Sandy Riv., adj. Daniel Hamlin & John Morton; 12 Jan 1746/47, p.575. £2.

JAMES HUDSON, 400 acs. Amelia Co. on the head Brs. of ʼuffillo Bed Cr. in the fork of Nottoway; adj. Daniel Jones, Thomas Ellis & Robert Tucker; 12 Jan 1746/47, p.576. £2.

WILLIAM CANNON, 70 acs. Amelia Co. on the Lower side of Flatt Cr., adj. Elam, & Robert Vaughan; 12 Jan 1746/47, p.578. 10 Shill.

DAVID ELLINGTON, 325 acs. Amelia Co. bet. the Brs. of Snales Cr. and Little Nottoway, on Baglys Br., up the South fork of Little Nottoway Riv. to the Head thereof; adj. Dejarnet, Peter Jones, Batte Jones, Charles Lewis, Lewellin Jones, Daniel Jones & George Bagly; 12 Jan 1746/47, p.579. £1.S15.

DAVID ELLINGTON, 400 acs. Amelia Co. on the lower side of Snales Cr., adj. George

Bagley/Bagly & Daniel Jones; 12 Jan 1746/47, p.581. £2.

BARTHOLOMEW STOVALL, 400 acs. Amelia Co. on the S side of Appamattox Riv. and on both sides of Vaughans Cr., adj. Franklin & Senter; 12 Jan 1746/47, p.583. £2.

ABRAHAM VAUGHAN, 525 acs. Amelia Co. on the Lower side of Saylors Cr., on a great Br.; adj. Hill, Richee, Spradling, Elam, Crawford, his own Lines & Wilcock; 12 Jan 1746/47, p.584. £2.S15.

THOMAS JONES, JUNR., 510 acs. Amelia Co. on both sides of the North fork of Nammisseen Cr., adj. Munford & Watson; 12 Jan 1746/47, p.586. £2.S15.

GEORGE FOSTER, 163 acs. Amelia Co. on the S side of Appamattox Riv. and on the upper side of Sailors Cr., bet. the Lines of William Towns, Richard Booker & Thomas Osbourn; 12 Jan 1746/47, p.587. £1.

GEORGE FOSTER, 200 acs. Amelia Co. on the S side of Appamattox Riv.; adj. Joseph Ward, Matthew Harris, Osborn, Towns, & Richard Booker; 12 Jan 1746/47, p.589. £1.

NATHANIEL ROBERSON, 298 acs. Amelia Co. on the N side of the Lazaritta Cr., in the head of a Valley; adj. Edward Roberson, Stark & Reeves; 12 Jan 1746/47, p.590. £1.S10.

ROBERT ROWLAND, 200 acs. Amelia Co. on the S side of the Lazaritta Cr., up the Long Br., adj. his own lines; 12 Jan 1746/47, p.592 [incorrectly written as p.492]. £1.

EDWARD MACKGEHEE, 2,830 acs. Amelia Co. bet. Bush and Bryer Rivers, on the N side of Mortons Cr.; adj. Randolph in the Lowgrounds of Bush Riv., adj. Woodson & Morton in the Lowgrounds of Bryer Riv., along the old lines of the Land Purchased of Brown; 12 Jan 1746/47, p.594. £12.S5. 400 acs. part formerly gtd. William Brown by Pat. 15 Oct 1741 [PB 20 p.20] the Right and Title of which is since become Vested in sd Edward Mackgehee and 2,430 acs. the Residue never before gtd. [Included in his 5,798 acs. in PB 26 p.464]

SAMUEL COBBS, Gentleman, 638 acs. Amelia Co. on the Road bet. the brs. of flatt Cr. and Stocks Cr.; adj. Harris, Morris's now Whitworth's line, Dawson, Hurt, Wood & Wingo; 12 Jan 1746/47, p.596. £3.S5.

SAMUEL EWING, 395 acs. Amelia Co. on both sides of the North fork of Fort Cr., by the Path; adj. Briswate, Cobb, Harden & Wallace; 12 Jan 1746/47, p.597. £2.

ISAAC DUFFO, 375 acs. Amelia Co. on the Lower side of Flatt Cr., at the head of the Lazaritta; adj. Hugh Leaden, Watson, Weatherford & Coleman; 12 Jan 1746/47, p.599. £2.

ROBERT DOWNING, 104 acs. Amelia Co. on the N side of the Lazaritta Cr.; adj. Rives & Eppes [their lines]; 12 Jan 1746/47, p.600. 10 Shill.

JAMES RUTLIDGE, 100 acs. Amelia Co. on the N side of the North fork of Sandy Riv.; 12 Jan 1746/47, p.602. 10 Shill.

EDWARD BOOKER, 71 acs. Amelia Co. on the N side of the Beaver pond br. of Deep Cr.; adj. Robert Thompson, Thomas Bottom, Thomas Bott, Anderson & Burton; 12 Jan 1746/47, p.603. 10 Shill.

JOSEPH RICE, 400 acs. Amelia Co. on the Lower side of Sandy Riv.; adj. Atwood, Jos. Ligon, Morris, & Henry Ligon; 12 Jan 1746/47, p.605. £2.

WILLIAM CLEMMONS, 518 acs. Amelia Co. on the N side of Little

Cr. of Deep Cr., Beg. at his own old lower Corner at the sd Cr. at the dry Beaver ponds; adj. Jones, Bolling & Hudson; 12 Jan 1746/47, p.606. 15 Shill. 400 acs. part formerly gtd. sd William Clemmens by Pat. 9 August 1735 [William Clemment in PB 16 p.130] and 118 acs. the residue never before gtd.

WILLIAM BROWNING, 400 acs. Amelia Co. on the upper side of Buffilo Riv., at the head of a Bottom, adj. Hatcher; 12 Jan 1746/47, p.608. £2.

NICHOLAS WILLIAMS, JUNR., 440 acs. Is. of Wight Co. on the N side of Nottoway Riv., by the side of the North prong of the Cabbin br., at the head of a Meadow, in a pocoson; adj. Richard Drake, Nicholas Williams Senr., Richard Drake junr., Lazarus Joyner, Arthur Williams & George Williams; 12 Jan 1746/47, p.609. £2.S5.

JOHN UPCHURCH, 100 acs. Is. of Wight Co. on the SW side of the great Sw., adj. William Heath; 12 Jan 1746/47, p.611. 10 Shill.

RICHARD VICK, 250 acs. Is. of Wight Co. on the N side of Nottoway Riv., by the side of Bardens br.; adj. Ann Thornton, John Jent & Richard Brasswell; 12 Jan 1746/47, p.612. £1.S5.

RICHARD WORRELL, 270 acs. Is. of Wight Co. on the S side of black Cr., on the W side of the Gravelly run, adj. Francis Little; 12 Jan 1746/47, p.614. £1.S10.

WILLIAM WATKINS, 200 acs. Is. of Wight Co. on the S side of Nottoway Riv., in the head of the Cabbin/Cabin br.; adj. Thomas Phillips, Christopher Robertson & the sd Watkins's other Land; 12 Jan 1746/47, p.615. £1.

DAVID ADAMS, 75 acs. Is. of Wight Co. on the N side of Meherin Riv., by the side of the three Creeks, by the side of the great Br.; adj. Henry Adams, Henry Ivey, William Maberry & the sd David Adams's other Land; 12 Jan 1746/47, p.617. 10 Shill.

JOHN FORT, 200 acs. Is. of Wight Co. on the S side of Nottoway Riv., on the N side of the three Creeks, adj. the sd Forts other Land by the edge of the Lowgrounds of the sd Creeks; 12 Jan 1746/47, p.618. £1.

JAMES BROOKS, JUNIOR, 200 acs. Is. of Wight Co. on the N side of Meherin Riv., by the side of the pine pole Br., crossing the Deep run; adj. William Wilkins, William Finney, Richard Taylor & John Clement; 12 Jan 1746/47, p.620. £1.

HENRY IVY, 150 acs. Is. of Wight Co. on the S side of Nottoway Riv., by the side of the Flatt Sw., by the side of the South West prong of Herberts br.; adj. Valentine White, Nathaniel Morrell, James Bass & the sd Ivys old Lines; 12 Jan 1746/47, p.621. 15 Shill.

THOMAS TAYLOR, 40 acs. Is. of Wight Co. on the N side of Meherin Riv., by the County line [West - the Country line], down the Beaver Dam Sw., down Tarraro Cr. & up the Mirey Gut; 12 Jan 1746/47, p.623. 5 Shill.

EDWARD CALDWELL /CALWELL, 2,740 acs. Brunswick Co. on both sides of Couches Cr., up a fork; adj. Thomas Briggs /Brig's & Embry; 12 Jan 1746/47, p.624. £13.S15.

HENRY TRENT, 400 acs. Goochland Co. on both sides of Rock Fish Cr., crossing Wolf trap Sw., adj. Majr. Henry; 12 Jan 1746/47, p.626. £2.

WILLIAM BRANHAM, 176 acs. 176 acs. Goochland Co. on the North Garden, adj. Thomas Evans & Robert Lewis; 12 Jan 1746/47, p.628. £1.

Augt.20.1747. Settled all in this Book & to pag. 84 [PB 26] & 117.

[PB 28] in New Books. John B Blair. D.Audr.

WILLIAM SANDIDGE, 1,416 acs. Spotsylvania Co. in the fork of the Devils Ditch Sw., on a Stoney Ridge & a Stoney Hill side, Beg. in a Line of a Pat. Gtd. to James Taylor dec'd below a br. called Bare Garden Br., along the line that divides this L. and the L. that the sd Taylor sold to Wyatt; adj. Mr Baylor, William Lee, Thomas White by his new cleared ground, a Pat. gtd. John Chew Gent., George Musick and John Graves; 12 Jan 1746/47 by William Gooch Esq. our Lieutenant Governor and Commander in Chief at Williamsburg under the Seal of our sd Colony *in the 20th year of our Reign of George the Second*, p.629-631. £4.S10. 300 acs. part being part of a Pat. for 8,500 acs. formerly gtd. unto James Taylor by Pat. 21 Jul 1721 [PB 11 p.149], 212 acs. other part being also part of a Pat. for 1,000 acs. formerly gtd. to Joseph Roberts by Pat. 28 Sep 1728 [PB 14 p.111] the Right and Title of which 2 parcels is since by divers mesne Conveyances become vested in the sd William Sandidge and 904 acs. the residue found to be within the bounds of the aforesaid Pat. gtd. to the sd Joseph Roberts was by our General Court adjudged to be forfeited and vested again in us and by Order of our Council bearing date 12 Jun

1745 Ordered to be gtd. to the sd
William Sandidge.

PATENT BOOK NO. 25

20 Mar 1745/46 to 25 Jun 1747

ROBERT COOK, 296 acs. Brunswick Co. on both sides of Cooks Cr., by the Road; adj. Munford, Cargill & Naper; *20 Mar 1745/46 in the 19th year of our Reign of George the Second by William Gooch Esqr. our Lieutenant Governor and Commander in Chief*, p.1. £1.S10.

JOSEPH DICKESON, 187 acs. Brunswick Co. on both sides of the North Fork of Howns Cr. [Hounds Cr.], adj. Crenshaw; 20 Mar 1745/46, p.2. £1.

DAVID WILLIAMS, 100 acs. Pr. Geo. Co. on the N side of Sappone Cr., Beg. at 4 Poles below the Mouth of the Reedy Br. of sd Cr., to a Corner of Bentings clearing [Beatons clearing?]; 20 Mar 1745/46, p.3. 10 Shill.

RICHARD ACOCK, 195 acs. Pr. Geo. Co. adj. Samuel Lees line on the N side of Warwick Sw., in a

thickett; 20 Mar 1745/46, p.4. £1. £1.

BENJAMIN WHITE, 100 acs. Goochland Co. on the S side of Hardware Riv., on the Riv. thence into the Woods, adj. Captain Hudson; 20 Mar 1745/46, p.5. 10 Shill.

THOMAS ADKINS, 81 acs. Brunswick Co. on the N side of Meherin Riv., on the lower bent; 20 Mar 1745/46, p.6. 10 Shill.

WILLIAM WEIGHLY, 414 acs. Brunswick Co. on both sides of Crooked Run; adj. Reps Jones, Liverit & Floyd; 20 Mar 1745/46, p.7. £2.S5.

JOHN INGRAM, 338 acs. Brunswick Co. on the N side of Shining Cr., on the Road; adj. his own, Lucas, William Andrews & Brewer; 20 Mar 1745/46, p.8. £1.S15.

189

EDWARD CURD, 294 acs. Henrico Co. on the S side of the main run of Chickahomony Sw., through the Sw. and the Low Grounds, in the edge of the miery Ground, under the hills of the main high Land, in Slashy Ground, standing on a hill side just above the holly br. which now divides Edward Curd and Obediah Smith, through very miery Ground, adj. Captain James Cocke, Henry Wyatt dec'd; 20 Mar 1745/46, p.10. £1.S10.

DAVID LEE, 1,800 acs. Brunswick Co. on the W side of Wards fork, adj. John Martin & Kennon; 20 Mar 1745/46, p.11. £9.

JOHN JONES, 104 acs. Brunswick Co. on the N side of Stanton Riv., adj. Cargill; 20 Mar 1745/46, p.12. 10 Shill.

RICHARD DICKESON, 200 acs. Brunswick Co. on the N side of Howns Cr., adj. Michaux & Chrenshaw; 20 Mar 1745/46, p.13. £1.

THOMAS SCOTT, 770 acs. Pr. Geo. Co. on both sides of Stoney cr., down the Licking Br., crossing White Oak Sw., down Butterwood Sw.; adj. George White, Hall, his own old Lines, Haynes, Pritchit, Burchit & Smart; 20 Mar 1745/46, p.14. £4.

THOMAS WESTMORLAND, 200 acs. Pr. Geo. Co. on the Licking Place Br., 20 Mar 1745/46, p.15. £1.

JETHRO BARKER, 104 acs. Surry Co. on the N side of Black Water Sw., up the Middle Br., adj. his own Line; 20 Mar 1745/46, p.16. 10 Shill.

LAWRENCE DOLLEY, 77½ acs. Pr. Ann Co. in black Water, adj. his own and Thomas Owld; 20 Mar 1745/46, p.18. 10 Shill.

FRANCIS FLOURNOY, 400 acs. Henrico Co. adj. Edward Hill, the sd Flournoy, John Mores Survey, John Russel & William Sharp; 20 Mar 1745/46, p.19. £2.

SAMUEL CORNWELL, 130 acs. Surry Co. on the S side of the main Blackwater Sw., on the S side of Seacock Sw., adj. Richard Blunt; 20 Mar 1745/46, p.20. 15 Shill.

FRANCIS BEATY/BEATEY, 112 acs. Orange Co. on the W side of the blue Ridge, on the S side of Goos Cr.; 20 Mar 1745/46, p.21. 15 Shill.

WILLIAM PHELPS, 400 acs. Goochland Co. on the East Br. of Bear Garden Cr. of the Fluvanna Riv., adj. John Southern; 20 Mar 1745/46, p.22. £2.

THOMAS WHITMORE, 150 acs. Surry Co. on the N side of Black Water Sw., down the Reedy Br., adj. John Averis & Edward Ezell; 20 Mar 1745/46, p.23. 15 Shill.

GILES ALEGREE, 250 acs. Goochland Co. on the South br. of Buck Island Cr. of the S side of the Rivanna Riv., in a bottom, adj. Henry Wood; 20 Mar 1745/46, p.24. £1.S5.

GEORGE BARKER, 95 acs. Surry Co. on N side of Blackwater Sw., down the middle Br., in the Round about Br. adj. his own Line & John Smith; 20 Mar 1745/46, p.25. 10 Shill.

JOHN MOSSUM, 200 acs. Goochland Co. among the head Brs. of Willis Riv., to naked Land; 20 Mar 1745/46, p.26. £1.

JOHN MOSSUM, 250 acs. Goochland Co. among the S Brs. of Willis Riv.; adj. Stephen Sanders, James Sanders & Henry Chiles; 20 Mar 1745/46, p.27. £1.S5.

ROBERT ADAMS, 400 acs. Goochland Co. on the N side of James Riv., near the head of a Br. of the Broad Br. of Tuckahoe Cr., near the head of Stoney Cr.; adj. Col. Thomas Randolphs Land bought of Robert Woodson, & Henry Holman; 20 Mar 1745/46, p.28. £2.

JOHN HENRY, 300 acs. Goochland Co. at Rock Fish Cr.; adj. James Christian, William Walton & Thomas Tindal; 20 Mar 1745/46, p.30. £1.S10.

CHARLES MASSIE, 350 acs. Goochland Co. adj. to the W side of the little Byrd Cr., in the Fork of sd Cr.; adj. Thomas Massie dec'd & John Cole dec'd; 20 Mar 1745/46, p.31. £1.S15.

VINCENT LACY, 400 acs. Goochland Co. on the Brs. of Dry Cr. of Appamattox Riv., adj. Joseph Dabbs; 20 Mar 1745/46, p.32. £2.

HUGH DENNUM, 150 acs. Goochland Co. on both sides of Owens Cr.; 20 Mar 1745/46, p.33. 15 Shill.

WATSON BROMFIELD, 400 acs. Goochland Co. among the Brs. of dry Cr. of Appamatox Riv., in a bottom, adj. Obadiah/Obediah Woodson & Richard Randolph Gentlemen; 20 Mar 1745/46, p.34. £2.

MATTHEW WOMACK, 400 acs. Amelia Co. on the Brs. of Sandy Riv. on the lower side thereof, adj. Daniel Brown & Charles Burks; 20 Mar 1745/46, p.36. £2.

JAMES ANDERSON, 404 acs. Amelia Co. on the N side of

Mallorys Cr., adj. his own old Lines, Bagley, & Edward Roberson; 20 Mar 1745/46, p.36. £2.

JAMES ARCHTACON, 400 acs. Amelia Co. on the S side of the South Fork of Buffilo Riv., adj. Richey; 20 Mar 1745/46, p.37. £2.

JOSEPH MORTON, 353 acs. Amelia Co. on both sides of Sandy Riv., adj. his own Old Lines & Daniel Hamlin; 20 Mar 1745/46, p.38. £1.S15.

RICHARD BEASLEY, 400 acs. Amelia Co. on both sides of little Nottoway Riv., on the S fork of the sd Riv., adj. Bumpas/Bumpass; 20 Mar 1745/46, p.40. £2.

THOMAS SPENCER, 400 acs. Amelia Co. on the Head Brs. of Bryer Riv., crossing the Riv., over the Road; 20 Mar 1745/46, p.41. £2.

WILLIAM CLARKE, 400 acs. Amelia Co. on the N side of Great Nottoway Riv., adj. Lewellin Jones & Bagley; 20 Mar 1745/46, p.42. £2.

ISHAM EPPES, 403 acs. Amelia Co. on the lower side of the lower fork of Woody Cr. bet. the Lines of John Wallice, Francis Eppes, Matthew Cabinis, John Ragsdell &

James Grigg; 20 Mar 1745/46, p.43. £2.

DANIEL JONES, 400 acs. Amelia Co. on both sides of little Nottoway Riv., adj. Jones & Hamlin; 20 Mar 1745/46, p.44. £2.

ABRAHAM BAKER, 344 acs. Amelia Co. on both sides of the Horsepen Br. of Bryer Riv., adj. Martin; 20 Mar 1745/46, p.45. £1.S15.

Settled thus far & to pag. 219 in tother book [PB 24] Jun 7. 1746
John Blair D.Audr.

WILLIAM WATSON, 4,623 acs. Amelia Co. on both sides of Flatt Cr. and on the Head brs. of Deep Cr., Beg. at his old Corner on the lower side of Flatt Cr. above the Hunting Path, up Little Cr., Down Deep Cr., Down the Great Fork to Flatt Cr., to the old Corner Haybury [Hagberry tree?] on Flatt Cr.; adj. Ellis, Tunstall, More/Moor, Hudson, Coleman, Weatherford, Harper & Beasley; 5 Jun 1746, p.47. £3.S10. 3,952 acs. part formerly gtd. sd William Watson by Pat. dated 12 Sep 1738 [PB 18 p.131 which included his 2,000 acs. in PB 17 p.343 dated 10 Jun 1737] and 671 acs. the Residue never before Gtd. [4,423 acs. part included in his 5,077 acs. in PB 28 p.615]

THOMAS BALDWIN, 731 acs. Amelia Co. between Appamattox and Buffilo Rivers; adj. Randolph, his own Line & Hugh Nickson; 5 Jun 1746, p.48. £3.S15.

'RICHARD WINSTON, 1,000 acs. Orange Co. on both sides of the North fork of the Northanna, adj. Robert Martin; 5 Jun 1746, p.50. Whereas by Pat. 16 Jun 1727 gtd. Theodosius Staige, Clerk formerly in Orange Co. formerly Spotsyl. [PB 13 p.92] who hath failed to pay Quit Rents and Richard Winston hath made humble Suit and hath obtained a G. for the same.

LAWRENCE BROWN, 644 acs. Amelia Co. on both sides of the South fork of Deep Cr.; adj. Hall Hudson, Rowland, Matthew Cabinis, Hudson, & Robert Moody; 5 Jun 1746, p.51. £3.S5.

JONAS JORDAN, 653 acs. Amelia Co. on the N side of Sandy Cr.; adj. Quarles, Dawson, Joel Meadows & Arnold; 5 Jun 1746, p.52. £3.S5.

JOHN DYER, 390 acs. Amelia Co. on the N side of Flatt Cr.; adj. Mayes, Hurt, Beasley & Watson; 5 Jun 1746, p.53. £2. [2 acs. part included in William Watson's 5,077 acs. in PB 28 p.615]

SAMUEL, WILLIAM, HEZEKIAH & MOSES YARBROUGH, 1,372 acs. Amelia Co. on both sides of little Nottoway Riv. and Mallorys Cr.; adj. their Fathers Lines, Henry Yarbrough, Beasly, Bumpas, Watson, Edward Robinson & Presley; 5 Jun 1746, p.54. £7.

JOHN HOARD, 100 acs. Essex Co. in the Par. of Saint Ann, in the *Indian Line*, at the Road by *Sandy Valley*, adj. Scott; 5 Jun 1746, p.56. for 2 lbs. of Tobacco for every Acre of the sd L. Whereas by Inquisition Indented taken in the sd Co. on 19 May 1742 by Virtue of a Warrant directed to John Robinson Esq. our Escheator for the sd C. It appears that James Thelwell died siesed of a certain Tract of L. which is found to Escheated to us And whereas Thomas Hoard hath made humble Suit and hath obtained a G. for the same which he hath assigned unto John Hoard. [The Indian Line could refer to the Rappahannock Indians and/or to the 150 acs. in Rappahannock Co. Patented by Nedd Gunstocker, Indian, in PB 5 p.536 dated 14 Oct 1665]

WILLIAM MAYO, 1,800 acs. Goochland Co. on both sides of Angola Cr. & Great Guinea Cr. of Appamatox Riv., crossing a Run of Green Cr., crossing the main Road, Crossing Bear Br. of Willis Riv.;

adj. John Brown, John Pleasants, Abraham Cook, Richard Woodson, Joseph Dabbs & Richard Henderson; 5 Jun 1746, p.57. £9.

JEDEDIAH BRISTOW, 400 acs. Goochland Co. on the S brs. of Fluvanna Riv., adj. William Cannon; 5 Jun 1746, p.58. £2. Whereas by Pat. 12 March 1739/40 gtd. John Thompson [PB 18 p.559] And Whereas the sd John Thompson hath failed to make Cultiv. & Improv. and Jedediah Bristow hath made humble Suit and hath obtained a G. for the same.

JOHN ORANGE, 210 acs. Henrico Co. crossing the main Road, on the S side of a Br. of Beechey Br., in a Piney Slash; adj. William Ford, James Hamilton, John Watson, Stokes, Watkins, John Law & John Cornet; 5 Jun 1746, p.60. £1.S5.

JOHN ELLIS, 2,284 acs. Amelia Co. on the N side of Great Nottoway Riv., crossing Buffilo Cr., by a Path, on the edge of Whetstone Cr.; adj. Thomas Hardiway, Robert Evans, Bolling, Edward Finney & John Evans; 5 Jun 1746, p.61. £9.S10. 400 acs. part formerly gtd. sd John Ellis by Pat. dated 16 Sep 1740 [PB 19 p.809], 1,884 acs. the residue never before gtd.

NICHOLAS DAVIES, 4,284 acs. Goochland Co. on both sides of

Muddy Cr., crossing the West Br. of Muddy Cr., down Buck Br. to Muddy Cr.; adj. Richard Parson, Benjamin Dumas, James Terrel, Ashford Hughes, Benjamin Harrison, Thomas Dillon, Thomas Carter, Robert Carter, Isaac Hughes, Robert Hughes, Isham Randolph, Jacob Micheaux, Daniel Witmore, John Twitty, Samuel Allen & Bowler Cocke; 5 Jul 1646, p.62. 420 acs. part of the above Tract being part of 1,200 acs. formerly Gtd. Robert Hughes by Pat. 27 Sept 1729 [PB 14 p.179 dated 26 Jun 1731, which included his 400 acs. Henrico Co. in PB 12 p.285 dated 17 Aug 1725 & his 400 acs. Henrico Co. in PB 13 p.417 dated 27 Sep 1729], 164 acs. other part being part of 400 acs. formerly Gtd. George Briggs by Pat. 20 Jun 1733 [PB 15 p.29] the Right and Title of which sd 420 acs. and 164 acs. by Mesne Conveyances is become vested in the sd Nicholas Davis, also 1,680 acs. other part of the above mentioned tract being formerly Gtd. sd Nicholas Davies [Nicholas Davis, PB 18 p.393] by Pat. 22 Sep 1739 and 2,020 acs. the Residue also formerly Gtd. sd Nicholas Davies [Nicholas Davis, PB 19 p.957] by Pat. 1 Jun 1741.

WILLIAM TURNER, 400 acs. Henrico Co. Crossing Hungary Br., on the E side of Pigg Pen Br.; adj. William Ford, John Watson,

Obadiah Smith & Wheeler; 5 Jun 1746, p.64. £2.

JOHN TILLOTSON, 400 acs. Henrico Co. crossing several Brs. of Lower Sappony Cr., crossing the Beaver Pond br. of Wintopock twice; adj. John Worsham, Thomas Knibb, Francis Eppes, the sd Tillotson & John Rud Senr.; 5 Jun 1746, p.65. £2.

THOMAS MOORE, 400 acs. Henrico Co. crossing Middle Cr.; adj. John Robertson, Thomas Tanner, William Mosley, John Skelton & William Perdue; 5 Jun 1746, p.66. £2.

JOHN WYNNE, 280 acs. Brunswick Co. on the E side of Fucking Cr., up the Piney br.; adj. his own Line, Timothy Murrill & Richard Stokes; 5 Jun 1746, p.67. £1.S10.

WILLIAM LOFFTES, 150 acs. Henrico Co. on both the N & S sides of the second br., adj. Henry Wilson, Thomas Tolly & Henry Vadin; 5 Jun 1746, p.69. 15 Shill.

SAMUEL WORTHAM, 193 acs. Henrico Co. crossing Robertsons Br.; adj. John Hales, William Warburton, Colo. Benjamin Harrison & the sd Wortham; 5 Jun 1746, p.70. £1. The same being

Surplus L. found within the bounds of a Pat. Gtd. Thomas Cock dec'd in the year MDXCIX [1699]. [Probably part of 1,983 acs. 3 roods then in Chas. City Co. Ptd. by Thos. Cock in PB 6 p.563 dated 4 Oct 1675; then 943 acs. part Gtd. to his son Capt. Thomas Cock in PB 9 p.198 dated 6 Jun 1699, known by the names of *Mongyes* on the N side of James Riv. nigh deep runne and crossing bridge road]

THOMAS WOMACK, 72 acs. Henrico Co. in the low Ground of Appamattox Riv., on Sappone Cr.; adj. Richard Wood, the sd Womack, Joseph Wilkinson & Benjamin Branch; 5 Jun 1746, p.71. 10 Shill.

JOHN PURDUE/PERDUE, 400 acs. Henrico Co. on the S side of the Sappony Road; adj. Thomas Pucket, Belsher, & Moses Ferguson; 5 Jun 1746, p.72. £2.

JOHN ROBERTSON, 400 acs. Henrico Co. adj. William Clay, William Perdue, Thomas Tanner, Charles Fetherston & Richard Wood; 5 Jun 1746, p.73. £2.

JAMES BAINS, 375 acs. Surry Co. on the S side of Black Water Sw., over Birchen Island Road, adj. James Massingall & Joseph Hix; 5 Jun 1746, p.74. £2.

WILLSON SHEHORN, 287 acs. Brunswick Co. adj. Cook, Thomas Tomlinson, Avent, Wyse & Massey; 5 Jun 1746, p.75. £1.S10.

PETER LOUIS SOBLET, 385 acs. Henrico Co. on the French Line [NW], on the County Line [S50°W], on Meacheaux or the French Line [S8°W]; adj. Micheaux, Tullit, Wooldridge, Easly & Gee; 5 Jun 1746, p.76. £2.

ISHAM EPPES, 365 acs. Pr. Geo. Co. on the N side of the Picture Br. and on both sides of the upper Nottoway River Road; adj. Henry Fitz, Mr James Boisseau, the sd Eppes Old Lines, William Wells & Mixon; 5 Jun 1746, p.77. £2.

THOMAS NEAL, 156 acs. Henrico Co. down a Spring Br. & Nooning Cr., up Poplar Br.; adj. Fowler, David Man, other L. of sd Thomas Neal, & Mark Moore; 5 Jun 1746, p.78. £1.

SAMUEL COBBS & WILLIAM WATSON, 1,850 acs. Amelia Co. on the lower side of Buffilo Riv.; adj. Baldwin, Hudson, Hugh Nickson, Gauling, Richard Morton & Hatcher; 5 Jun 1746, p.79. £9.S5.

WILLIAM TOTTY, 408 acs. Henrico Co. on Appamattox Riv.

on the S side of Reedy Br., adj. George Worsham & Colo. Francis Eppes; 5 Jun 1746, p.88. £2.S5.

THOMAS CALDWELL, 334 acs. Brunswick Co. on the S side of Bannister Riv., 5 Jun 1746, p.81. £1.S15.

JOHN NASH, 400 acs. Amelia Co. on both sides of Bryer Riv.; 5 Jun 1746, p.82. £2. [Included in his 1,334 acs. in PB 28 p.427]

LISWELL SEXTON, 200 acs. Brunswick Co. on both sides of Rockey Run on the S side of Meherin Riv.; 5 Jun 1746, p.83. £1.

ALEXANDER TRENT, 1,500 acs. Goochland Co. on both sides of Willis Riv., up the Barren lick Br., adj. John Phelps & Henry Cary; 5 Jun 1746, p.84. £3.S10. 800 acs. part thereof being part of 17,000 acs. formerly Gtd. Henry Cary, Gentleman by Pat. 20 Jul 1738 [PB 18 p.90 which included his 3,492 acs. in PB 13 p.423 at a place Called *Buckingham*] and by Mesne Conveyances the Right and Title of the sd 800 acs. is become Vested in the sd Alexander Trent and 700 acs. the Residue never before Gtd. [see Trent's PB 28 p.164]

ROBERT HUGHES, 400 acs. Goochland Co. on both sides of a Br. of Soke Arse Run of Willis

Riv., adj. Nowel Burton & William Mayo; 5 Jun 1746, p.85. £2.

JAMES MILLS, 200 acs. Pr. Geo. Co. on the licking hole Br. of Butterwood Sw.; adj. Woodleif, & Robert West; 5 Jun 1746, p.86. £1.

MARTIN KEY, 241 acs. Goochland Co. on both sides of Keys Mill Sw.; adj. John Key, the Heirs of Jonathan Clark, Major Carr & Thomas Smith; 5 Jun 1746, p.87. £1.S5.

JOSEPH ROBERTS, 204 acs. Goochland Co. on both sides Keys Mill Sw., on the Louisa Co. Line [S65°E]; adj. Thomas Smith, John Key, Richard Hammock, Captain Clark & Major Carr; 5 Jun 1746, p.88. £1.

FRANCIS MORELAND, 200 acs. Pr. Geo. Co. on the S side of the Mortar/Morter Br., adj. John Goodwin & Stephen Evans; 5 Jun 1746. p.89. £1.

PETER BROOKS, 400 acs. Goochland Co. on both sides of Malorys Br. of Appamattox Riv.; adj. sd Brooks other L. & Thomas Bows; 5 Jun 1746, p.90. £2. [Included in his 1,737 acs. in PB 26 p.280]

JOHN WINFIELD, 250 acs. Pr. Geo. Co. on the S side of Sappony

Cr., below the Road, adj. Munford & Dickson; 5 Jun 1746, p.91. £1.S5.

RICHARD LEDBITER, 296 acs. Pr. Geo. Co. on the N side of the little Rockey Run & down Rockey Run; adj. his own old Line & Rany; 5 Jun 1746, p.92. £1.S10.

WILLIAM CROSS, 300 acs. Pr. Geo. Co. on the upper side of Stells br. of Bear Sw.; adj. George Stell, John Bradshaw & Christopher Rowland; 5 Jun 1746, p.93. £1.S10.

JOHN PHELPS of Deep Creek, 267 acs. Goochland Co. on the brs. of Flemings Cr.; adj. Thomas Edwards, the sd Phelps, Henry Cary Gent. & William Still; 5 Jun 1746, p.94. £1.S10.

JOHN PHELPS of Deep Creek, 400 acs. Goochland Co. on the Brs. of Flemings Cr.; adj. John Payn /Payne, James Wilkins, Thomas Edwards & sd John Phelps; 5 Jun 1746, p.95. £2.

RICHARD KENNON, 303 acs. Brunswick Co. on the S side of Bannister Riv., adj. Isaac Cloud; 5 Jun 1746, p.96. £1.S10.

THOMAS PUCKET, WILLIAM PUCKET & DOUGLAS PUCKET, 486 acs. Henrico Co., on the N side of the third Br., down the

South Br.; adj. John Perdue, Peter Baugh, John Ferguson, John Hatchet & Belsher; 5 Jun 1746, p.97. £2.S10.

JOHN WINFIELD, 140 acs. Pr. Geo. Co. on the S side of Sappone Cr. & on both sides of the Reedy Br., Beg. upon the Pocoson Br., in a small Spring Br., in a Thicket of Saplins on the lower side the Road, near a Meadow; adj. his own and Munfords Lines; 5 Jun 1746, p.98. 15 Shill.

WILLIAM PETTY POOL, 676 acs. Brunswick Co. on the E side of Fucking Cr., along his own Line; 5 Jun 1746, p.99. £2. 276 acs. part formerly Gtd. sd William Petty Pool by Pat. 28 Sep 1732 [PB 14 p.510] and 400 acs. the residue never before Gtd. [Included in his 877 acs. Lunenburg Co. in PB 25 p.507]

JOHN INGRAM, 394 acs. Brunswick Co. on both sides of Ledbetters Cr., opposite to his Lower Corner on the Cr., adj. DeGraffenreidt; 5 Jun 1746, p.100. £2.

WILLIAM CALDWELL, 404 acs. Brunswick Co. on the N side of Banister Riv. Opposite to the Fork, up Whit thorne Cr.; 5 Jun 1746, p.101. £2.

SAMUEL BURK, 400 acs. Goochland Co. adj. to the N side of the Rivanna Riv., crossing a Neck; adj. William Randolph, Samuel Burk, William Moor & William Witt; 5 Jun 1746, p.102. £2.

CHRISTOPHER MARTIN, 516 acs. Henrico Co. crossing Frank's Br., up Hawk Br., on the S side the Road, by Youls Br.; adj. John Gill, Joseph Gill, Richard Anders, John Anders & Timothy Harris; 5 Jun 1746, p.104. £2.S15.

WILLIAM FOSTER, 753 acs. Amelia Co. on the heads of the Bever Pond Br. of Flatt Cr., Buckskin and Tommahawk, in a Meadow; adj. Easley, his own old Line, the L. purchased of Irby Hudson, John Elam, Langford Owen & Edward Hill; 5 Jun 1746, p.105. 400 acs. part thereof formerly gtd. sd William Foster by Pat. 12 Feb 1742/43 [PB 21 p.196], 353 acs. the residue also formerly gtd. unto Irby Hudson by Pat. 22 Sep 1739 [PB 18 p.426] the Right and title whereof is since become vested in the sd William Foster.

WILLIAM PEOPLES, 597 acs. Pr. Geo. Co. on the S side of Josephs Sw., down the Mirey Meadow, along the County Line [E30°N], on the side of a bottom; adj. Richard Carlisle, the sd Peoples, William

Cotton, Tatum, Green alias his own Line from Green, & Doby; 5 Jun 1746, p.106. £2.S10. 99 acs. part thereof being part of a Pat. formerly Gtd. unto Richard Carlile 22 Jun 1722 [177 acs. in PB 11 p.124] the Right and Title of which by Mesne Conveyances is become Vested in the sd William Peoples, 498 acs. the Residue never before Gtd.

JOHN HATCHET, JUNIOR, 796 acs. Henrico Co. on the S side of Sappony Road, crossing Worsham's Br.; adj. John Perdue, Moses Ferguson, Pucket, John Worsham, Colonel Samuel Cobbs, Brown, Wilson, George Hastings & Robert Cobbs; 5 Jun 1746, p.107. £4.

ROBERT COOK, 42 acs. Henrico Co. crossing Mudy Spring Br.; adj. Step, Colo. Benjamin Harrison, the Honourable William Byrd Esquire, & Thomas Wood; 5 Jun 1746, p.108. 5 Shill.

JOHN THARP, 1,295 acs. Is. of Wight Co. on the S side of Nottoway Riv. and on the S side of Three Creeks, up Robins Br. & the Schoolhouse Br., down the side of the Great Meadow & up Georges Br., down the Whitewood Br.; adj. his own old Lines, Charles Bass, Henry Rose & Lewis Harris; 5 Jun 1746, p.109. £3.S15. 450 acs. part formerly Gtd. sd John Tharp by Pat. 24 Mar 1725/26 [PB 12

p.443], 95 acs. other part formerly Gtd. Joseph Seward by Pat. 15 Jun 1714 [PB 10 p.145] & 750 acs. the Residue never before Gtd.

JOHN HAMMON, 206 acs. Amelia Co. on the N side of Appamattox Riv.; adj. Eglestone, Tally, Broadway, Clay, Pettypool now Wilsons Line, & Cogan; 5 Jun 1746, p.111. 15 Shill. 93 acs. part thereof being part of 878 acs. formerly gtd. John Tally by Pat. 5 Nov 1724 [Pr. Geo. Co., PB 12 p.119 which included Tally's 300 acs. in PB 10 p.340 dated 15 Jul 1717 on Namusend/Nummiseen Cr.] and 113 acs. the Residue never before Gtd.

HALL HUDSON, 930 acs. Amelia Co. on the Head Brs. of Winninghams Cr. and Hixes Cr., in the Head of a Valley; adj. Crane, Starke, Christopher Robinson, Edward Roberson, Rowland, & Isham Vaughan; 5 Jun 1746, p.112. £4.S15.

RICHARD JONES, Gentl., 1,706 acs. Amelia Co. on the Lower side of Deep Cr., by Spinners Br., by a Meadow, on the Seller fork of the sd Cr. Thence down the same and the main Cr.; adj. his own old Lines, Clay, Haukes, Chiswell & Short; 5 Jun 1746, p.113. £2.S5. 1,287 acs. part thereof formerly Gtd. sd Richard Jones by Pat. 9 Aug 1735 [PB 16 p.137 which included his (Richard Jones Junr.) 452 acs., Pr. Geo. Co. below Whoods ford, in PB 13 p.535 dated 28 Sep 1730] and 419 acs. the Residue never before Gtd.

YOUNG STOKES, 2,000 acs. Brunswick Co. on both sides of Fucking Cr., up Douglas's Br.; adj. Couch, John Wynn, Richard Stokes, Seth Petty Pool, & Douglass; 5 Jun 1746, p.115. £10.

JAMES CHEATAM, 550 acs. Amelia Co. on the North fork of Buckskin Cr. and the Bever Pond br. of Flatt Cr., near the Mouth of a small Spring Br.; adj. Thomas Coveington, Joseph Wilkinson, Towns, Thomas Spencer & John Hill; 5 Jun 1746, p.116. 200 acs. part thereof formerly gtd. Lewis Tanner by Pat. 20 May 1735 [Pr. Geo. Co., PB 15 p.515], 350 acs. the residue also formerly Gtd. sd Lewis Tanner by Pat. 15 Aug 1737 [PB 17 p.398] the Right and Title of which sd 2 Parcels is since become vested in the sd James Cheatam.

RICHARD RANDOLPH, Gentleman, 1,673 acs. Henrico Co. on Tuckahoe Cr.; 25 Jul 1746 *in the 20th year of our Reign of George the Second*, p.118. £1.S15. 945 acs. part formerly gtd. Allison Clark and Charles Russel by Pat. 2 May 1705 [Allenson Clark & Charles Russell

in PB 9 p.673 named *"Windsor Forrest"*] the Right and Title whereby by divers mesne Conveyances is since become Vested in the sd Richard Randolph, 400 acs. other part formerly Gtd. sd Richard Randolph by Pat. 23 Mar 1733/34 [PB 15 p.185] also 2 acs. Part being part of a Pat. formerly gtd. John Ellis [400 acs. on Peter's Br. in PB 12 p.410] and 326 acs. the residue being surplus L. found within the bounds of the sd Patents.

JAMES NEALY, 280 acs. Augusta Co. on W side of the Blue Ridge of Mountains and on N side of Goose Cr.; 25 Jul 1746, p.119. £1.S10.

PETER JEFFERSON, 322 acs. Goochland Co. on the S side of James Riv., up Matthew Agees br., adj. Peter Ford, & Agee; 25 Jul 1746, p.120. The sd 322 acs. having been formerly gtd. unto the sd Peter Jefferson by Pat. 28 Sep 1730 [PB 13 p.495, Vacated by order of the General Court, 23 Apr 1746] "and by the sd Peter Jefferson lately in our General Court in Chancery the said Letters Patent several material Mistakes being therein were delivered up and Ordered to be cancelled and a new Patent Granted him"

HANS HENDRICK, JUNR., 200 acs. Amelia Co. on the heads of the brs. of Sandy Cr., Beg. on the

Ridge; 25 Jul 1746, p.121. 20 Shill.

ANN WRENN, 316 acs. Essex Co. down a br. of Prices Run, to Gouges Path; adj. John Williamson & Booth; 30 Jul 1746, p.122. for 2 lbs of Tobacco for every Acre of the sd L. Whereas by Inquisition Indented and taken in sd Co. 19 Mar 1740/41 by Virtue of a Warrant directed to Henry Robinson Deputy Escheator for sd Co. It appears that David Catlett & John Catlett died seised of a certain Tract or Parcel supposed to contain 248 acs. but upon a Survey lately made by Robert Brooke Surveyor of sd Co. is found to contain 316 acs. which is found to Escheat to us from sd David Catlett & John Catlett And Whereas Ann Wrenn hath made humble Suit and hath obtained a G. for the same. [Gouges Path probably Gonges Path, See John Smith's 634 acs. Rappahannock Co. in PB 7 p.612 & PB 4 p.107 (604) on S side of Rappahannock Riv. adj. James Merriot/Merritt]

HANS HENDRICK, SENIOR, 304 acs. Amelia Co. bet. the Brs. of Sandy Cr. and Flatt Cr.; adj. his son Hans Hendrick, William Farly, Henry Isbell & Morris; 25 Jul 1746, p.123. £1.S10.

HANS HENDRICK, SENIOR, 200 acs. Amelia Co. on both sides of a Br. of Mayes's Br. of Flatt Cr.; adj. Smith, Sizemore, his own Line, Turner & Powell; 25 Jul 1746, p.124. £1.

JAMES RANEY/RANY, 250 acs. Pr. Geo. Co. on both sides of Rockey Run; adj. Parsons, Penniston, Williamson & Rany; 25 Jul 1746, p.125. £1.S5.

HENRY ROBERTSON, JUNIOR, 100 acs. Pr. Geo. Co. on the N side of White Oak Sw., up Chits br.; adj. Sturdivant, Robert West, Harris & Featherstone; 25 Jul 1746, p.126. 10 Shill.

WILLIAM WALTERS, 400 acs. Brunswick Co. on the S side of Staunton Riv., adj. John Nash; 25 Jul 1746, p.127. £2.

HUGH BOSTON, 411 acs. Brunswick Co. on both sides of Twittys Cr. joyning Davis's upper Line; 25 Jul 1746, p.128.

EDWARD THOMAS, 168 acs. Pr. Geo. Co. bet. Butterwood and Tommahitton Swamps; adj. Eaton, Ornsby, Beal, Poythress & Fisher; 25 Jul 1746, p.129. £1.

RICHARD DRAKE, JUNIOR, 320 acs. Is. of Wight Co. on the N side of Nottoway Riv. & down the Village Br.; adj. William Hern, Captain William Brown, Captain William Crumpler & George

Williams; 25 Jul 1746, p.130.
£1.S15.

CHARLES BARHAM, 180 acs. Is.
of Wight Co. on the S side of
Nottoway Riv. & up the Run of the
Cabbin Br.; adj. William Watkins,
Thomas Philips, John Tann [John
Kiquotan?], Arthur Foster, his own
old Line, Christopher Foster junr.
& Christopher Foster Senr.; 25 Jul
1746, p.131. £1.

THOMAS EASTLAND, 238 acs.
Brunswick Co. on both sides of
Mitchells cr., along his own old
Line; 25 Jul 1746, p.132. £1.S5.

BENJAMIN JOHNSON, 150 acs.
Is. of Wight Co. on the N side of
Nottoway Riv.; 25 Jul 1746, p.133.
15 Shill.

ROBERT CHILDERS, 111 acs.
Henrico Co. on the S side of James
Riv.; adj. John Read, Owen Evans,
William Harding, Colo. Eppes &
Good; 25 Jul 1746, p.134. 15
Shill.

JOHN WILLIS, 204 acs. Bruns-
wick Co. on Uriahs Br., crossing a
Pond & the Joyners Br., in a
Meadow; adj. Davis, Harrison &
along his [Harrisons] Line formerly
Benfords; 25 Jul 1746, p.135. £1.

JOHN CHAFIN, 300 acs.
Goochland Co. between Great
Guinea Cr. and Willis Riv.; adj.

James Allen, William Mills, John
Martin, Beverley Randolph Esq.,
the sd Chafin, & James Allen; 25
Jul 1746, p.136. £1.S10.

HENRY LIGON, 400 acs. Amelia
Co. on the Lower side of Sandy
Riv., down the Great Br.; adj.
William Ligon, Morris, & Joseph
Ligon; 25 Jul 1746, p.137. £2.

JOSEPH LIGON, 183 acs. Henrico
Co. down a br. known by the name
of good Luck spring & down
Boxdale Sw., adj. the sd Ligon &
Edward Folks; 25 Jul 1746, p.138.
for 2 lbs. of Tobacco for every
Acre. Whereas by Inquisition
Indented and taken in sd Co. 1 Sep
1741 by Virtue of a Warrant
directed to William Byrd Esq. our
Escheator for sd Co. It appears that
Robert Hancock died seised of 625
acs. but upon a Survey thereof
lately made by Sackvile Brewer,
Surveyor of sd Co. is found to
contain but 623 acs. [Probably his
500 acs. in PB 10 p.255, N of
Appamatuc Riv. on Skin Quarter
Cr.] which is found to Escheat to
us from the sd Robert Hancock
And Whereas Margaret Hancock
hath made humble Suit and
obtained a g. for the same, 183
acs. part thereof she hath assigned
to Joseph Ligon.

JOSEPH GODWIN, 565 acs. Is. of
Wight Co. on the S side of the long
Br., a little above the mouth of the

Poley br., adj. Barnaby Mackquinny; 25 Jul 1746, p.139. £3.

WILLIAM WATSON, 1,734 acs. Amelia Co. on both sides of Nammisseen Cr., on a fork of the North fork of sd Cr., along the County Line [South]; adj. Hamlin, FitzGerrald, Rees, FitzGerralds now Claiborne's, Trent, Hinton, Thomas Jones & his own old line; 25 Jul 1746, p.140. £1.S15. 1,400 acs. part being formerly Gtd. sd William Watson by Pat. 12 Feb 1742/43 [PB 20 p.458] & 334 acs. the Residue never before Gtd.

WILLIAM LAFOON, 628 acs. Henrico Co. on a Br. of Farrars Br., in a Slash; adj. Nicholas Cox now Simon Ligons, Evan Shoemaker & William Harlow; 25 Jul 1746, p.142. £3.S5.

MARGARET HANCOCK, 440 acs. Henrico Co. crossing the Red Water to the Glebe Line, in the head of a Valley near the Main Road; adj. Gilbert Ealom & Edwards; 25 Jul 1746, p.143. for 880 lbs. of Tobacco for our Use already paid to our Receiver General of our Revenues. Whereas by Inquisition Indented and taken in sd Co. 1 Sep 1741 by Virtue of a Warrant directed to William Byrd Esquire our Escheator of sd Co. It appears that Robert Hancock died seised of 625 acs. but upon a Survey thereof lately made by Sackvile Brewer, Surveyor of sd Co. is found to contain but 623 acs. [see PB 25 p.138] which is found to Escheat to us from sd Robert Hancock And Whereas Margaret Hancock hath made Humble Suit and hath obtained a G. for the same

JOHN SANDERS, 400 acs. Pr. Geo. Co. bet. the Brs. of Butterwood Sw. and Turkey Egg Cr.; adj. William Poythress, Bartlet, Peter Thomas & William Elder; 25 Jul 1746, p.144. £2.

HOWEL EDMONDS, 330 acs. Is. of Wight Co. on the N side of Meherin Riv., up the Run of Tockwothunty Sw., adj. William Pope & his own old Line; 25 Jul 1746, p.145. £1.S15.

CHARLES BARHAM, 320 acs. Is. of Wight Co. on the S side of Nottoway Riv., up the Raccoon Sw.; adj. Christopher Foster the Younger, the sd Barhams own old Line, John Fort & Thomas Holt; 25 Jul 1746, p.146. £1.S15.

JOHN ASKEW, 400 acs. Orange Co. on the N side of a Br. of Pritty's Cr., on falling Ground, in a Valley, on a level & on level Ground; adj. Benj. Henslee, William Howard & Ripon; 25 Jul 1746, p.147. £2.

MATTHIAS AYERS, 12½ acs. Henrico Co., Beg. on the Top of a bank of Four Mile Cr., up the Edge of Pleasants Mill Pond; adj. Robert Blau dec'd, to the head of the Pond or the uppermost flowing of the Water thence up the Main Stream of Four Mile Cr., up the bank through thick Ivey Bushes; 25 Jul 1746, p.148. 5 Shill.

WRIGHT MACKLEMORE, 200 acs. Is. of Wight Co. on the S side of Nottoway Riv.; adj. John Pitman, Owen Myrick, his own old Lines, David Wiggins & Thomas Wiggins; 25 Jul 1746, p.149. £1.

JOHN PHILIPS, 330 acs. Is. of Wight Co. on the N side of Round Hill Sw., on the S side of the Reedy Br., adj. Capt. Benjamin Edwards & the sd Edmonds [sic]; 25 Jul 1746, p.150. £1.S15.

ANTHONY MATTHEWS, 66 acs. of Swamp, Islands and Low Land in Henrico Co., on the main Chicahominy Sw., through Low Grounds and Slash; adj. Woodsons Pat. dividing the sd Matthews and Charles Winfrey, under the Hills dividing this from the Highland of the sd Anthony, adj. Edmond Allen; 25 Jul 1746, p.151. 10 Shill.

MATTHEW SMART, 129 acs. Pr. Geo. Co. on the N side of Rockey Run; adj. Hill, Pritchet, Roger Rany & his own old line; 25 Jul 1746, p.152. 15 Shill.

RICHARD HAYNES, 804 acs. Pr. Geo. Co. on the S side of White Oak Sw.; adj. Gregory, Pritchet, Westbrook & his own old Line of the L. purchased of Moody; 25 Jul 1746, p.153. £2.S15. 151 acs. part formerly Gtd. Robert Moody by Pat. 22 Jun 1722 [PB 11 p.115] and 103 acs. other part being also formerly Gtd. Christopher Roberson by Pat. 18 Feb 1722/23 [PB 11 p.179] The Right and Title by Mesne Conveyances is become Vested in the sd Richard Haynes and 550 acs. the residue never before Gtd.

JOHN ROBINSON, 400 acs. Augusta Co. on the South fork of Goose Cr.; near a large Fall, in an Island; 25 Jul 1746, p.154. £2.

RICHARD HOWELL, 337 acs. Pr. Geo. Co. on the upper side of Butterwood Sw., down the edge of the Beaver Pond & sd Sw.; adj. Joshua Pritchet, Westbrook, Wyatt, Anderson & his own old line; 25 Jul 1746, p.155. 15 Shill. 184 acs. part formerly Gtd. Robert Enon dec'd by Pat. 28 Sep 1720 [PB 14 p.16] the right and title by divers Mesne Conveyances is become Vested in the sd Richard Howell and 153 acs. the residue never before Gtd.

WILLIAM WALTHALL, 138 acs. of Marsh, Swamp and Sunken L. in Henrico Co. by the side of the Swift Creek Marsh, to the Mouth of Reed Gut just under the N side of a high Point of L., down a Run to a small thoroughfare, down Stuarts Cr., down the Main Cr. taking in the round Marsh; adj. Richard Walthall, sd William Walthalls high L., & Henry Randolph; 25 Jul 1746, p.156. 15 Shill.

THOMAS HARDAWAY Sr., 800 acs. Pr. Geo. Co. on the N side of Rockey Run; adj. his old Lines, Coleman, Eppes & Parsons; 25 Jul 1746, p.157. £2. 400 acs. part formerly gtd. the sd Thomas Hardaway by Pat. 5 Sep 1723 [Thomas Hardyway in PB 11 p.207] and 400 acs. the Residue never before gtd.

WILLIAM MACLIN, 104 acs. Brunswick Co. on the S side of Stanton Riv., adj. George Roberts & Bowling; 25 Jul 1746, p.159. 10 Shill.

MATTHEW WHITTELL, 400 acs. Hanover Co. on both sides of the South fork of the North Fork of James Riv., along the Co. Line [S65°E] crossing the Riv., adj. James Warren; 25 Jul 1746, p.159. £2.

GEORGE STELL, 400 acs. Pr. Geo. Co. on the N side of Bear Sw., adj. Staples's alias his own old line; 25 Jul 1746, p.160. 100 acs. part formerly gtd. sd George Stell by Pat. 2 Jan 1737/38 [PB 17 p.428] and 300 acs. the Residue never before Gtd. [Staples's = Thompson Stapley's PB 10 p.337, above the Occonunche Path]

EDWARD ROBERSON, 400 acs. Amelia Co. on both sides of Malorys Cr., adj. Pressly; 25 Jul 1746, p.161. £2.

WILLIAM JOHNSON, 380 acs. Orange Co. below the Blue Ridge, on Billies Mountain, adj. Lawrence Franklin & William Lucas/Lucus; 25 Jul 1746, p.162. £2.

HOLLADAY FORT, 385 acs. Is. of Wight Co. on the S side of Nottoway Riv., up the Hornet Sw., by the Co. Line [N60°E]; adj. his own old Line, Thomas Grantham, Henry Mannery, Charles Barham & Bagley Greeves; 25 Jul 1746 p.163. £1. 185 acs. part formerly gtd. Thomas Johnson by Pat. 18 Feb 1722/23 [PB 11 p.173] & by sd Thomas Johnson sold & Conveyed to the sd Holladay Fort and 200 acs. the Residue never before Gtd.

FREDERICK JONES, 768 acs. Pr. Geo. Co. on the Lower side of Great Cr. & on both sides of Walls Run; adj. his old Lines of the L.

purchased of Collwell, Crawley, Thomas Jones, Holloway, Edward Davis & William Jones; 25 Jul 1746, p.165. £2. 375 acs. part formerly Gtd. Edward Collwell by Pat. 17 Aug 1725 [PB 12 p.279] the Right and Title whereof is since become Vested in sd Frederick Jones and 393 acs. the residue never before Gtd.

WILLIAM MACLIN, 404 acs. Brunswick Co. on the N side of Shining Cr., on both sides of Moses's Cr.; adj. his own Line, Moses Johnson, Spell & Taylor; 25 Jul 1746, p.166. £2.

WOOD JONES, 543 acs. Amelia Co. on both sides of the Burchen Sw., down the Little Burchen & the Main Burchen, up Jacksons Br., adj. Jackson & Fannin; 25 Jul 1746, p.167. £1. 343 acs. part formerly Gtd. sd Wood Jones by Pat. 10 Jul 1745 [PB 23 p.885] and 200 acs. the Residue never before Gtd.

RICHARD DRAKE, JUNR., 290 acs. Is. of Wight Co. on the N side of Nottoway Riv., in a Meadow; adj. Captain Nicholas Williams & Robert Reeks; 25 Jul 1746, p.168. £1.S10.

HENRY LIGON, 772 acs. Amelia Co. on both sides of Mountain Cr., over the North fork, at a Gully; adj. his own old Lines, John Nash,

John Davidson & Collins; 25 Jul 1746, p.169. 15 Shill. 618 acs. part formerly Gtd. sd Henry Ligon by Pat. 9 Feb 1737/38 [PB 17 p.504] and 154 acs. the residue never before Gtd.

THOMAS TABB, 400 acs. Amelia Co. on both sides of Tommahitton Sw.; adj. Haynes, Womack, Robert Cryer & William Cryer; 25 Jul 1746, p.170. £2.

JOHN NASH, 784 acs. Amelia Co. on both sides of Saylors Cr.; adj. the L. purchased of John Fitzgerrald, Richey, Farly & Womack; 25 Jul 1746, p.171. 15 Shill. 630 acs. part formerly Gtd. John Fitzgerrald by Pat. 15 Oct 1741 [PB 20 p.18] the Right and Title whereof is since become Vested in the sd John Nash and 154 acs. the residue never before Gtd.

JOHN HARRISON, 80 acs. in the Upper Parish of Nansemond Co., near the Holly Pocoson; adj. Robert Yeats, John Porter, John Ballard, Oliver Worrell/Worrel & William Harrison; 25 Jul 1746, p.173. 10 Shill.

THOMAS DEVONPORT /DAVENPORT, 1,650 acs. Goochland Co. on both sides of Little Guinea Cr. and Tear Wallet Run, in a Slash; adj. William Arnold, Paul Pigg, Thomas Anderson, William Hamilton, John

Jones, Francis Allen, Lewis Jenkins & John Law; 25 Jul 1746, p.174. £4. 200 acs. part formerly Gtd. Daniel Terry by Pat. 17 Mar 1736/37, 400 acs. other part also formerly Gtd. sd Daniel Terry by Pat. 17 Mar 1736/37 [PB 17 p.244 and p.265] the Right and Title by Mesne Conveyances is become Vested in sd Thomas Devonport, 250 other part formerly Gtd. sd Thomas Devonport by Pat. 1 Dec 1740 [PB 19 p.895] and 800 acs. the residue never before Gtd.

NATHANIEL RIDLEY, 340 acs. Is. of Wight Co. on the E side of Angelica Sw., by the side of the Boushy Pond, by the Nottoway Indians Line [SE]; adj. William Pope, Simons Turner & Hugh Matthews; 25 Jul 1746, p.175. £1.S15.

THOMAS DANCE JUNR., 350 acs. Henrico Co. on the S side of James Riv., at a fork of Peters Br.; adj. Peter Rowler, Peter Gill & William Totty; 25 Jul 1746, p.176. £1.S15.

JOHN FOLK, 754 acs. in the Upper Parish of Nansemond Co. at a Place called *Kingston*, on the N side of Summerton Sw.; adj. John King & William Coffield; 25 Jul 1746, p.177. £1.S15. 400 acs. part being part of 900 acs. formerly Gtd. Michael King by Pat. 24 Feb 1675/76 [PB 6 p.597, see PB 22

p.260 to John King] the Right and Title of which sd 400 acs. by divers Mesne Conveyances is become Vested in sd John Folk, 354 acs. the residue being Surplus L. found within the bounds of the sd Pat.

ISRAEL PETERSON, 335 acs. Brunswick Co. on the head Brs. of the North fork of Hounds Cr.; 28 Aug 1746, p.178. £1.S15.

MICHAEL PEARSON, 300 acs. Orange Co. on a Stoney Knole, a Knowle, a Levell, a Stoney Hill & by a Mountain; adj. George Head, Mr Zachariah Taylor, John Bryson, James Cox & Edward Franklin; 28 Aug 1746, p.179. £1.S10.

NATHANIEL FELTS, 300 acs. Surry Co. on the N side of the Poplar Sw., on the drain of the br. which divides his L. from his brother Thomas Felts; adj. Matthew Wilkinson & Thomas Felts; 28 Aug 1746, p.181. 25 Shill. 85 acs. part being part of a Pat. for 285 acs. formerly Gtd. Thomas Felts by Pat. 28 Sep 1732 [PB 14 p.495] the right & title of sd 85 acs. is now become vested in the sd Nathaniel Felts and 215 acs. the residue never before Gtd. [see Thomas Felts 1,070 acs. in PB 28 p.170]

SAMUEL JORDAN, 270 acs. Henrico Co. Crossing the Horsepen

Br., near the Head of a Bottom; adj. Roberts & John James Flournoy; 28 Aug 1746, p.182. £1.S10.

WILLIAM ELDER JUNR., 280 acs. Pr. Geo. Co. on the S side of Butterwood Sw.; adj. Peter Wynne, Samuel Moore & Robert Poythress; 28 Aug 1746, p.183. £1.S10.

JAMES CUNNINGHAM, 285 acs. Goochland Co. among the S Brs. of Willis Riv., crossing Buck Br., crossing Turkey Cocke Run; adj. William Innarwick, William Cox, James Bolling, Christopher Bolling, Thomas Carter & Silvanus Witt; 28 Aug 1746, p.184. £1.S10.

WILLIAM PETTYPOOLE, JUNIOR, 400 acs. Pr. Geo. Co. on the S side of Sappony Cr., adj. John Winfield; 28 Aug 1746, p.186. £2.

WILLIAM STARKE, 5,290 acs. Pr. Geo. Co. on both sides of Sappone Cr., up the dividing branch, in the main Road, near Hawkins's Run, crossing the Church Road and Meale Br.; adj. John Stith, Pegram, Keith, his old Line from Drury Stith, John Evans, Stunkes, Baxter Davis, Tabb, Belcher & the sd Starks old Line; 28 Aug 1746, p.186. £8.S10. 3,596 acs. part formerly Gtd. Drury Stith [Junr.] by Pat. 13 Oct 1727 [PB 13 p.192 which included 892 acs. of Robert Bolling's 2,604 acs. in PB 11 p.64] and by him sold to the sd Starke and 1,694 acs. the residue never before Gtd. [see Robert Bolling's 2,750 acs. in PB 23 p.783]

WILLIAM READ & HUBARD QUALLS, 536 acs. Brunswick Co. on both sides of Red Oak Run; adj. John Edmonds, Thomas House & John Davis; 28 Aug 1746, p.188. £2.S15.

WILLIAM REDMON, 400 acs. Brunswick Co. on lower side of Walls Cr., adj. Woodson; 28 Aug 1746, p.189. £2. [Walls Cr. also as Wallace's Cr. & Wallis's Cr., on the N side of Staunton Riv.]

STEPHEN WATKINS, 200 acs. Goochland Co. on both sides of the Lower Manacan Cr.; adj. Thomas Dickins, William Sallee & Edward Harrison; 28 Aug 1746, p.190. £1. Whereas by Pat. dated 20 Jul 1738 gtd. Daniel Stoner & John James Flournoy since dec'd in Joint Tenancy [PB 18 p.38] And Whereas the sd Daniel Stoner (in whom the right of the sd L. vested by Survivorship after the Death of the sd John James Flournoy) hath failed to make Cultivat. & Improv. and George Renyer Turner hath made Humble Suit and hath obtained a G. for the same which he hath assigned unto Stephen Watkins.

ROBERT SEAT, 433 acs, Surry Co. on the S side of Nottoway Riv. and on both sides of Cocks Br., adj. his old Lines; 28 Aug 1746, p.191. £1. 270 acs. part formerly Gtd. sd Robert Seat by Pat. 15 Mar 1741/42 [PB 20 p.211] and 153 acs. the residue never before Gtd.

WILLIAM PASLAY, 319 acs. Hanover Co. on the S side of the South Anna, down the Cattail Br.; adj. sd Paslay, George Mitchel, William Gouch, James Massie, Mrs Ann Aylett & Merriwether; 28 Aug 1746, p.192. £1.S15.

WILLIAM HAPPER, 168 acs. Norfolk Co. on the Western Br. of Elizabeth Riv., by the head of a branch that makes out of the sd Western Br. near the Road; 28 Aug 1746, p.193. for 2 lbs. of Tobacco for every Acre of sd L. Whereas by Inquisition Indented taken in Norfolk Co. 6 Sep 1742 by virtue of a Warrant directed to Samuel Boush our Escheator for the sd Co. It appears that Roger Howson died seised of certain L. supposed to contain 100 acs. but upon a survey lately made by James Nimmo, surveyor of sd Co. is found to Contain 168 acs. which is found to Escheat to us from Roger Howson [PB 9 p.134] And Whereas William Happer hath made humble Suit and hath obtained a G. for same.

CHARLES WILLIAMSON, 1,850 acs. Pr. Geo. Co. on both sides of Rockey Run; adj. Smart, Rany, Bolling, Manson, Tabb, William White, along the old Lines of the 200 Acre Tract & the Lines of the L. purchased of John Hill; 28 Aug 1746, p.194. £5.S5. 364 acs. Part formerly Gtd. John Hill & Cuthburt Williamson by Pat. 28 Sep 1728 [PB 14 p.21] and 232 acs. other Part formerly gtd. John Hill by Pat. 20 Jul 1738 [PB 18 p.84] and also 200 acs. other Part formerly gtd. sd Williamson by Pat. 30 Aug 1743 [PB 20 p.563] the right and title of sd 364 acs. and 232 acs. by mesne Conveyances is since become vested in the sd [Charles] Williamson and 1,054 acs. the residue never before Gtd.

ROBERT ROWLAND, 400 acs. Amelia Co. on lower side of lower fork of Sandy Riv.; adj. Peter Jones, Searcey, John Morton & Hamlin; 28 Aug 1746, p.196. £2.

JOHN ROBERTS, 200 acs. Pr. Geo. Co. on the N side of the Indian Sw., down Cabin Br., adj. the sd Roberts & Peter Harwell; 28 Aug 1746, p.197. £1.

THOMAS GODWIN JUNR., 100 acs. Is. of Wight Co. by the Island Pond side, by a path; bet. the Lines of Andrew Munrow/Monrow, John Rutter, Barnaby Kerny/Kerney & James Webb; 28 Aug 1746, p.198.

10 Shill. Whereas by Pat. 3 Mar 1715/16 gtd. William Wilkason [PB 10 p.259] And the sd Whereas William Wilkason hath failed to make Cultiv. and Improv. and Thomas Godwin Junr. hath made humble Suit and obtained a Grant for the same.

THOMAS DICKSON. 982 acs. Pr. Geo. Co. on the S side of Sappone Cr., on the Pocoson Br. of the Reedy Br. of Sappone Cr. in the same County; adj. John Winfield, Munford, William Pettepool Junior, Henry Dickson & his old Line; 28 Aug 1746, p.200. £3. 400 acs. part formerly gtd. sd Thomas Dickson by Pat. 12 Sep 1733 [PB 15 p.117] and 582 acs. never before gtd.

MORRIS ROBERTS & JOHN ROBERTS, 311 acs. Henrico Co. in a br. of Falling Cr., on the S side of a Br. called the Horsepen, on the Top of a Hill & on a Stoney Hill, adj. William Woolridge; 28 Aug 1746, p.201. £1.S15.

WILLIAM HILL, 362 acs. Brunswick Co. on the W side of Butchers Cr., adj. Josiah Baker; 28 Aug 1746, p.202. £2.

SACHEVERAL WHITEBREAD, 400 acs. Goochland Co. on both sides of Troublesome Cr. of Slate Riv.; 28 Aug 1746, p.203. £2.

JOSEPH ANTHONY, 2,042 acs. Goochland Co. on both sides of Bisket Run; adj. Charles Hudson, Daniel Jones & Patrick Noland; 28 Aug 1746, p.204. £10.S5.

WILLIAM KNIGHT, 630 acs. Surry Co. on the S side of Nottoway Riv. and on the N side of Cocks br., in the Hornet Sw.; adj. Mr Henry Tyler & his old Lines; 28 Aug 1736, p.205. £2. 230 acs. part formerly Gtd. Thomas Cocke Gent. by Pat. 27 Sep 1729 [PB 13 p.417, which included 100 acs. of 445 acs. Is. of Wight Co. to Samuel Harwood Junr. in PB 10 p.143] the Right and Title is since become vested in the sd William Knight and 400 acs. the Residue never before Gtd.

TARLTON FLEMING, 800 acs. Goochland Co. on the N side of James Riv. on the back of Mr Flemings Rock Castle Tract, Beg. near the Path below Flemings Park Cr., adj. Fleming; 28 Aug 1746, p.207. £4. Whereas by Pat. 6 May 1727 Gtd. John Bolling Gent. [PB 13 p.73], 800 acs. Goochland Co. formerly Henrico And Whereas the sd John Bolling hath failed to pay Quitrents and to make Cultiv. and Improv. and Tarlton Fleming hath made humble Suit and obtained a G. for the same.

THOMAS MINSKIP & GEORGE STILES, 400 acs. Henrico Co.

down a Br. of Peters Br., crossing the Road, adj. Catherine Male & John Gibbs; 28 Aug 1746, p.208. £2.

WILLIAM COLLICOAT, 800 acs. Amelia Co. on both sides the Road bet. the brs. of Flatt and Saylor Creeks, crossing little Saylor Cr.; adj. William Eckholes, Smith, Dupuy, Childers, Hurts & Motley; 28 Aug 1746, p.209. £4.

JOHN PHILIPS, 320 acs. Is. of Wight Co. on the S side of the main Black Water, on the S side of Lightwood Sw.; adj. Etheldred Taylor & John Branch; 28 Aug 1746, p.210. £1.S15. ·

THOMAS PHILIPS, 300 acs. Is. of Wight Co. on the S side of Nottoway Riv., down the Spring Sw. & the Raccoon Sw.; adj. John Kiquotan & the sd Philips's other L.; 28 Aug 1746, p.211. £1.S10.

CHARLES BARHAM, 250 acs. Is. of Wight Co. on the S side Nottoway Riv. & down the Raccoon Sw., adj. Joseph Holt; 28 Aug 1746, p.212. £1.S5.

JOHN ORNSBY, Clerk, 1,703 acs. Pr. Geo. Co. on both sides of Butterwood Sw. and [Butterwood] Road, along the Co. Line [South]; adj. Goodwin, Eaton, Poythress, Ellington, Reece, Claiborne,

Watson, Trent & his own old Line; 28 Aug 1746, p.213. £8.S10.

PARMENAS PALMER, 176 acs. Pr. Geo. Co. on the N side of White Oak Sw., up Bear Sw.; adj. Henry Robertson, John Stell, Stanly, Griggs & Westbrooke; 28 Aug 1746, p.215. £1.

WILLIAM HARRIS, 400 acs. Goochland Co. on both sides of Green Cr., at the South fork of sd Cr., on a Ridge; 28 Aug 1746, p.216. £2.

RICHARD WARD, 400 acs. Amelia Co. on the S side of Appamattox Riv.; adj. his own & Osbornes/Osbourns Lines; 28 Aug 1746, p.217. £2. Whereas by Pat. 20 Jul 1738 Gtd. John Dawson since dec'd [PB 18 p.81] And Whereas Henry Dawson, Son and heir of the sd John Dawson, hath failed to make Cultiv. and Improv. and Richard Ward having made humble Suit and hath obtained a G. for the same.

DAVID GWIN, 700 acs. Lunenburgh Co. on the S side of Little Roanoke and Wards fork, adj. John Towns; 28 Aug 1746, p.218. £3.S10.

SAMUEL WHITWORTH, 325 acs. Amelia Co. on both sides of Stocks Cr., in the head of a Slash, adj.

David Crawford; 28 Aug 1746, p.219. £1.S15.

PETER GILL, 317 acs. Henrico Co. crossing Jones's Road, in a Br. of Reedy Br., by the main Road, crossing Stoney Cr.; adj. sd Gills former Survey, Totty, an old obscure Line of Kennons, Williams, Dod & Anders; 28 Aug 1746, p.220. £1.S15.

CATHERINE MALE, 220 acs. Henrico Co. on the N side of Locust Br., down Males br.; adj. Perkinson & John Gibbs; 28 Aug 1746, p.222. £1.S5.

ROGER RANY, 444 acs. Pr. Geo. Co. on Rockey Run, on a drain of the first Great Br. of the Lower Rockey Run above the sd Roger Rany's Plantation, by the Church Road, adj. William Bobbit, John Hill, Robert Bolling; 28 Aug 1746, p.223. £1.S5. 200 acs. part formerly gtd. sd Roger Rany by Pat. dated 28 Sep 1730 [PB 13 p.524] and 244 acs. the Residue never before Gtd.

JOHN MALONE, 185 acs. Pr. Geo. Co. on lower side of Turkey Egg Cr.; adj. William Tucker, George Booth, Lucy Mathis, Morris, his own old Line & Walker; 28 Aug 1746, p.224. £1.

JOHN RACHELL, 250 acs. Is. of Wight Co. on the S side of Nottoway Riv. & on the E side of the Whitewood Sw., down Browns Br.; adj. Arthur Crocker, sd Rachells other L. & James Braswell; 28 Aug 1746, p.225. £1.S5.

WILLIAM HARPER, 500 acs. Surry Co. on the N side of Nottoway Riv. & on the N side of Southwester Sw.; adj. Peter Green, John Jones, Isaac Robertson & Thomas Wade; 28 Aug 1746, p.226. £2.S10.

SIMON MURPHEY/MURFEY, 203 acs. Surry Co. on both sides of Assamuseck Sw., Beg. in the Low ground of sd Sw. near the High land, on the W side of the main run of sd Sw.; adj. his Patented Land, Mr James Chappel & William Hines; 27 Aug 1746, p.227. 10 Shill. 140 acs. part formerly Gtd. Simon Murfey by Pat. 2 Sep 1732 [Simon Murphey, PB 14 p.499 on Atsamoosock Sw.] and 63 acs. the Residue never before Gtd.

WILLIAM JACKSON, 744 acs. Amelia Co. on the S side of Burchen Sw., down fork of the upper Rockey Br.; adj. William Stone, Richard Parr, Hammack, James Jackson and his Father; 28 Aug 1746, p.229. £3.S15. [his Father (William and/or James Jackson's Father) refers to John Jackson's 4,440 acs. in Pr. Geo. Co. & Amelia Co. in PB 20 p.52

dated 15 Oct 1741. For James Jackson's land, see his 400 acs. Amelia Co. in PB 22 p.337 dated 1 Aug 1745]

WILLIAM MILLS, Son of William Mills of *Aberdeen*, 380 acs. Goochland Co. on both sides of Pidy Rocky Run of Willis Riv.; adj. Ralph Hipping, Anthony Levellain, William Daniel & William Easley; 28 Aug 1746, p.230. £2.

JOHN MERRIT, 218 acs. Pr. Geo. Co. on the N side of Nottoway Riv., crossing Walls Run; adj. his own L. purchased of Mitchell, & Josa. Wall; 28 Aug 1746, p.231. 142 acs. part formerly gtd. Peter Mitchell by Pat. 14 Jul 1718 [PB 10 p.403] the right & title is since vested in the sd John Merrit and 76 acs. never before gtd. [The 142 acs. in PB 10 p.403 was also included in the 342 acs. patented by of sd Peter Michall Junr. in PB 13 p.125]

AMOS TIMMS, 464 acs. Brunswick Co. in the fork of Roses Cr., up Rowlins br., down the middle Cr., adj. the sd Timms line; 12 Jan 1746/47, p.232. £2. 100 acs. part being part of a pat. for 541 acs. formerly Gtd. John Humphris by Pat. 28 Sep 1728 [PB 13 p.391] the right & Title of sd 100 acs. is now become Vested in the sd Amos Timms and 364 acs.

the residue never before Gtd. [305 acs. part of Humphris' 541 acs. was included in Richard Witton's 638 acs. in PB 28 p.67 also dated 12 Jan 1746/47]

SAMUEL GOODE, 302 acs. Brunswick Co. on the Heads of the Brs. of Blewstone Cr. and Possom Quarter; adj. William Hayward, Ravenscroft, Edmonds & Cargill; 12 Jan 1746/47, p.234. £1.S10.

DRURY MELONE, 200 acs. Brunswick Co. on both sides of beech Lick br.; 12 Jan 1746/47, p.235. £1.

RICHARD WOODSON, 400 acs. Brunswick Co. on both sides of Wallis's Cr., adj. Joseph Morton; 12 Jan 1746/47, p.236. £2.

JOHN MIDDLETON, 400 acs. Brunswick Co. on both sides of Wallis's Cr., adj. Kennon; 12 Jan 1746/47, p.238. £2.

WILLIAM NANCE, 318 acs. Brunswick Co. on the S side of Jeneto cr.; adj. Josiah Floyd, Eldridge, Melone & Johnson; 12 Jan 1746/47, p.239. £1.S15.

JOSEPH MORTON JUNR., 704 acs. Brunswick Co. on the N side of Stanton Riv. and both sides of Wallis's cr.; adj. Randolph & Richard Woodson; 12 Jan 1746/47, p.241. £1.S10. 400 acs. part formerly gtd. sd Joseph Morton by Pat. 30 Jul 1742 [PB 20 p.409] and 304 acs. the Residue never before gtd.

NATHANIEL CARTER, 67 acs. Brunswick Co. on a br. of Cattail Cr.; 12 Jan 1746/47, p.243. 10 Shill.

NICHOLAS CHRISTOPHER, 388 acs. Brunswick Co. on both sides of Dry Cr.; 12 Jan 1746/47, p.244. £2.

JOHN HAILEY, 150 acs. Louisa Co. on the upper side of a small Br. of Roundabout Cr., on the Co. Line [S67°E], adj. Thomas Clark & Major John Henry; 12 Jan 1746/47, p.245. 15 Shill.

RICHARD PHILIPS, 56 acs. Louisa Co. adj. Fleming, Hughes, Colo. William Merriwether, Colo. David Meriwether & Mr Coles; 12 Jan 1746/47, p.247. 10 Shill.

RICHARD BENNET, 400 acs. Louisa Co. on the Brs. of Beverdam Sw., on the side of a Mountain, adj. David Mills & Mr Webb; 12 Jan 1746/47, p.248. £2.

JOSEPH FARLEY, 44 acs. Henrico Co. on the S side of Proctors Cr., adj. John Farley, the sd Joseph's old Line & John Nunnally; 12 Jan 1746/47, p.249. 5 Shill.

WILLIAM LOCKET, 395 acs. Henrico Co. down a br. of Deep Cr.; adj. John Pride, Gilbert Ealom & Francis Chetham; 12 Jan 1746, p.250. £2.

DAVID MAN, 216 acs. Henrico Co. crossing the main Road, adj. Mark More, Godfry Fowler; 12 Jan 1746/47, p.252. £1.S5.

JOHN CAMMEL, 150 acs. Henrico Co. on both the S & N sides of Skinquarter Road; adj. John Skelton, William Gates, Peter Liggon & Mosley; 12 Jan 1746/47, p.253. 15 Shill.

ROBERT ALLISON, 285 acs. Augusta Co. on the SW side of the North Br. of James Riv. opposite to a place called *the Narrows*; 12 Jan 1746/47, p.254. £1.S10.

EDMOND SCARBURGH, JUNIOR, 200 acs. Accomack Co. on the head of br. issuing into Matchapongo Cr.; adj. William Niblit, Jacob Fox, Edmund Pelson, Thomas and Joseph Aimes & Henry Clark; 12 Jan 1746/47, p.255. £1.

HUGH CORROTHERS, 300 acs. Augusta Co. on a br. of Luneys Mill Cr., on a Ridge; 12 Jan 1746/47, p.257. £1.S10.

CHARLES CAMPBELL, 50 acs. Augusta Co. adj. Robert Brown & William McGill; 12 Jan 1746/47, p.258. 5 Shill.

WILLIAM ALLEN, 333 acs. Augusta Co. on a br. of Catheys Riv. called Linwells Run, on the River side in *Beverley Mannor* Line

[North], on a Ridge, adj. John Moffet & James Allen; 12 Jan 1746/47, p.260. £1.S15.

JOHN COLLIAR, 400 acs. Augusta Co. on the W side of the Blue Ridge and on a Br. of the north Br. of James Riv. known by the name of Buffoloe Cr., on N side of the north most br. of the sd Cr. near the *ship Rock* at the mouth of the dry Draft, in a Bottom, on a point of a Ridge near a great Spring; 12 Jan 1746/47, p.261. £2.

JAMES COLLIAR, 400 acs. Augusta Co. on W side of the Blue Ridge and on a Br. of the North Br. of James Riv. known by the name of Buffoloe Cr., on the point of a Ridge near a great spring; 12 Jan 1746/47, p.263. £2.

ROBERT GREEN, 2,464 acs. Augusta Co. on Middle Br. of the south Br. of Potomack Riv., Beg. at the foot of a Hill on the E side of the Riv., on a Ridge, on the E side of the Riv. above the Gap in the Mountain; 12 Jan 1746/47, p.264. £12.S10.

ROBERT GREEN, 2,643 acs. Augusta Co. on southernmost Br. of the south Br. of Potomack Riv., Beg. near a *square Rock* on the side of a Ridge and on the W side of the sd Riv.; 12 Jan 1746/47, p.266. £13.S5.

ROBERT GREEN, 1,120 acs. Augusta Co. on the south Br. of Potomack Riv., on S side the north

Fork of the sd Br.; 12 Jan 1746/47, p.267. £5.S15.

ROBERT GREEN, 370 acs. Augusta Co. on the south Br. of Potomack Riv., Beg. on the N side of the north Fork of the south Br. by a ford and against a small piece of Lowgrounds, by a large Rock and by where the Mountains comes close to the sd Br.; 12 Jan 1746/47, p.269. £2.

ROBERT GREEN, 800 acs. Augusta Co. on S Brs. of Potomack Riv., Beg. on N side of the North fork of the sd Br. by a Hill; 12 Jan 1746/47, p.270. £4.

ROBERT GREEN, 350 acs. Augusta Co. on south Br. of Potomack Riv., Beg. under a Hill in a Bottom on the N side of the north fork of the sd Br., by a Br. in a steep Gully, on a steep Clift of the Br.; 12 Jan 1746/47, p.272. £1.S15.

WILLIAM TUCKER, 400 acs. Amelia Co. both sides of Kitts Horse Pen Br. of the lower fork of the Seller Cr.; adj. Christopher Hinton, Munford, Baldwin & Bland; 12 Jan 1746/47, p.273. £2.

JAMES TRIMBLE, 250 acs. Augusta Co. on a Br. of James Riv. called Buffoloe Cr., on one side of the north Br. of sd Riv.; adj. another Tract belonging to Silas Hart; 12 Jan 1746/47, p.275. £1.S5.

JOHN DAVISON, 350 acs. Augusta Co. on both sides of the

north Br. of James Riv., Beg. on the N side the sd Riv. above the mouth of Buffoloe Cr.; 12 Jan 1746/47, p.276. £1.S15.

VALENTINE SEVEAR, 400 acs. Augusta Co. on both sides of Smith's Cr., Beg. on the SW side of Daniel James his Branch, adj. Absalom Hayworth; 12 Jan 1746/47, p.278. £2. for 10 Shill. And also for and in Consideration of the Imp. of 6 persons to Dwell within this our sd Colony and Dominion of Virginia whose Names are *John Morgan, Mary Morgan, John Coleman, Margaret Coleman, Richard Scales & John Wheeler.*

ROBERT DAVIS, 300 acs. Augusta Co. on the W side the Blue Ridge, in a Valley, with the Line of *Beverley Mannor* [S73°W]; adj. James Cathey; 12 Jan 1746/47, p.279. £1.S10.

WILLIAM WALLING, 100 acs. Augusta Co. on the north Riv. of Shannando above the Gap in the Mountain, Beg. in an island, down the Riv. to the Point of the Island; 12 Jan 1746/47, p.280. 10 Shill.

JOHN HOPES, 200 acs. Augusta Co. on a small Br. of naked Cr.; adj. Jost Hite, Robert McCoy, William Duff & Robert Green [the Lines of sd Hites etc. Land]; 12 Jan 1746/47, p.282. £1.

JOHN RISKE, 138 acs. Augusta Co. on the W side the Blue Ridge, adj. Robert Campbell; 12 Jan 1746/47, p.283. 15 Shill.

WILLIAM McMACHON, 400 acs. Augusta Co. on a Br. of the South Riv. of Shanando on the W side of the Peaked mountain called Cub Run; 12 Jan 1746/47, p.284. £2.

HUGH DIVERT, 400 acs. Augusta Co. on south fork of the north Riv. of Shannando below John Smiths Land, Beg. in the lower End of a Meadow, crossing the Riv. at an Island, adj. John Smith; 12 Jan 1746/47, p.286. £2.

JOHN CAMPBELL, 400 acs. Augusta Co. on the N side of Cathey's Riv. on the Sinking Spring Br. at the head of Littles Run; 12 Jan 1746/47, p.287. £2.

JAMES BAGG, 220 acs. Augusta Co. on N side of *Third Hill* on a Br. of the north Riv. of Shannando; 12 Jan 1746/47, p.288. £1.S5.

WILLIAM McMACHON, 400 acs. Augusta Co. on the head of a North Br. of Buffoloe Cr., adj. Benjamin Borden; 12 Jan 1746/47, p.290. £2.

WILLIAM McMACHON, 400 acs. Augusta Co. on the N side of the north Riv. of Shanando on the next Spring Br. below the mouth of Cook's Cr.; 12 Jan 1746/47, p.291. £2.

PATRICK SHIRKEY, 400 acs. Augusta Co. on S side of James Riv. including the *Locust Bottom*, at the point of an Island; 12 Jan 1746/47, p.292. £2.

JOHN MITCHELL, 400 acs. Augusta Co. on the W side the Blue Ridge on a Br. of the north br. of James Riv. called Buffoloe Cr., Beg. at the point of the first fork of sd Cr.; 12 Jan 1746/47, p.293. £2.

JOHN HODGE, 200 acs. Augusta Co. on a Br. of the north Riv. of Shannando called Smith's Cr., Beg. in a Hollow on the E side of Smiths Cr., on the E side of Daniel James his Br.; 12 Jan 1746/47, p.295. £1.

JOHN HAMILTON, 200 acs. Augusta Co. Beg. on the N side of the north fork of James Riv. bet. a steep hill and the sd Riv.; 12 Jan 1746/47, p.296. £1.

RICHARD TICKTON, 160 acs. Augusta Co. on the north br. of Shanando beyond the Gap in the Mountain, on the side of a Ridge near the *Clover Lick*; 12 Jan 1746/47, p.297. for the Imp. of 4 persons whose Names are *Patrick McNiel, William Crawford, Elizabeth Chambers & William Edgear.*

WALTER LEEK, JUNR., 226 acs. Albemarle Co. on the brs. of Hardway Riv., adj. Thomas Fitzpatrick & William Fitzpatrick; 12 Jan 1746/47, p.298. £1.S5.

CHARLES LAVENDER, 200 acs. Albemarle Co. on the Brs. of Tye Riv., adj. John Peartree Burk; 12 Jan 1746/47, p.300. £1.

WILLIAM MATTHEWS, 150 acs. Albemarle Co. on N side of Tye Riv., Beg. at Capt. Cabells Corner on Tye Riv. above the Mouth of Joes Cr.; 12 Jan 1746/47, p.301. 15 Shill.

GIDEON MARR, 200 acs. Albemarle Co. on both sides of Rocky Cr. of Slate Riv., Beg. near Rocky Ridge the E side of the Cr.; 12 Jan 1746/47, p.303. £1.

WALTER LEEK, JUNR., 194 acs. Albemarle Co. on the Brs. of Mechums Riv., Beg. on the side of a Mountain; 12 Jan 1746/47, p.304. £1. [Regranted to Walter Leek Senr. in PB 34 p.407]

RICHARD TAYLOR JUNR., 200 acs. Albemarle Co. on both sides of Greens Cr. of Slate Riv.; 12 Jan 1746/47, p.305. £1.

THOMAS LANE, 100 acs. Albemarle Co. on the N side of Tye Riv.; 12 Jan 1746/47, p.307. 10 Shill.

ARTHUR DONALLEY, 300 acs. Albemarle Co. on both sides the south Fork of Totier Cr., adj. Bolling Clark & Mr Stith; 12 Jan 1746/47, p.308. £1.S10.

ROBERT BABER JUNR., 300 acs. Albemarle Co. both sides of Bear Garden Cr., adj. William Cannon & Wentworth Webb; 12 Jan 1746/47, p.310. £1.S10.

ANTHONY BENOINE, 400 acs. Albemarle Co. both sides of Slate Riv., adj. Samuel Glover & Philip Thomas; 12 Jan 1746/47, p.312.

ARTHUR DONALLEY, 150 acs. Albemarle Co. on the Brs. of Totier, in a Glade, adj. Bolling Clark & Thomas Meriwether; 12 Jan 1746/47, p.313. 15 Shill.

JOHN PLEASANTS, 400 acs. Albemarle Co. on both sides of a Run of Elk Cr. of the Fluvanna Riv., near the W side of the sd run; 12 Jan 1746/47, p.315. £2.

PETER LEATH, 719 acs. Pr. Geo. Co. both sides of Warwick Sw., up the Reedy Br., above Burges Path, down Jacobs Br. & Butlers Br.; adj. Wallice & Weekes; 12 Jan 1746/47, p.316. 112 acs. part formerly gtd. sd Peter Leath by Pat. 1 Apr 1717 [Peter Lee (sic) in PB 10 p.319] and 131 acs. other part formerly gtd. sd Leath by Pat. 20 Feb 1723/24 [PB 11 p.334] and 476 acs. the residue never before gtd.

NICHOLAS OVERBY, 128 acs. Pr. Geo. Co. on the upper side of Ledbetters Cr., adj. his own Line & Jordan; 12 Jan 1746/47, p.318. 15 Shill.

JAMES OVERBY, 300 acs. Pr. Geo. Co. on lower side of Georges Br. of Nammisseen Cr., adj. Vaughan; 12 Jan 1746/47, p.320. £1.S10.

THOMAS LEATH, 222 acs. Pr. Geo. Co. on the N side of Warwick Sw. bet. the Lines of John Thomas, Michael Rosser & Howard Owen; adj. John Edwards, Thomas Rosser & John Rosser; 12 Jan 1746/47, p.321. £1.S5.

JAMES PITTILLO, 1,605 acs. Pr. Geo. Co. on N side of Moccosoneck Cr., on the upper side of the main Road near Enix's Shop, along Rowanty Road, crossing Jemmy's br., up White Oak Sw., in a Thicket; adj. Tucker, his old Line, King als. Beckwiths, Furgusson, John Simmon's alias Keith's, Morris, Irby, John Kirby & Richard Crook; 12 Jan 1746/47, p.323. £4. 844 acs. part formerly gtd. sd Pittillo by Pat. 25 May 1734 [PB 15 p.226] and 761 acs. the residue never before gtd.

MILES THWEAT, 900 acs. Pr. Geo. Co. bet. Butterwood & White Oak; adj. Fitzgerrald, Bains, Griggs, Colemans, James Thweat, Nunnally, Wyatt, Michel & Crossland; 12 Jan 1746/47, p.326. £4.S10.

ISAAC TUCKER, 562 acs. Pr. Geo. Co. on the N side of the Reedy Br. of Sapponey Cr., by Flatt Rock br.; adj. John Jones als. John Williams's and John Williamsons Lines, his own old Lines, and Walker & Bolling als. John Williams's new line; 12 Jan 1746/47, p.327. £1. 400 acs. part formerly gtd. sd Isaac Tucker by Pat. 10 June 1740 [PB 19 p.695] and 162 acs. the Residue never before gtd.

RICHARD WITTON, 184 acs. Pr. Geo. Co. on both sides of the Jones Hole and Moccosoneck Roads, by the side of a pond; adj. Ferguson, John Kerby, Chamnis, Keith, Thomas Leath, and Simmons alias

Keiths Line; 12 Jan 1746/47, p.329. £1.

JOSEPH WORSHAM, 233 acs. Pr. Geo. Co. on the N side of Stoney Cr., on both side the main road, in a drain, on the main road at Kings Path; adj. his old Lines, John Avery, Thomas Harman & James Pittillo; 12 Jan 1746/47, p.331. £1.S5.

PETER WOODLIEF/WOODLEIF, 450 acs. Pr. Geo. Co. on the N side of Butterwood Sw. bet. the lower Line of his dec'd Father John Woodleif and the upper Line of Henry Wyatt dec'd and Mary Wyatt the Relict of the sd Henry on the lower sd of Cooks Br., in a Valley; 12 Jan 1746/47, p.333. £2.S5.

THOMAS FITZPATRICK, 497 acs. Albemarle Co. on the Brs. of Hardway; 12 Jan 1746/47, p.334. £2.S10.

JOHN WILLIAMS, 247 acs. Pr. Geo. Co. on both sides the Reedy Br. of Sapponey Cr. adj. Walker and Bolling, John Tapley, James Keith, Isaac Tucker & his own Lines; 12 Jan 1746/47, p.336. £1.S5.

JONES WILLIAMS, 200 acs. Pr. Geo. Co. on the N side of Buckskin Cr., adj. Davis; 12 Jan 1746/47, p.338. £1.

ANN STEWART, 100 acs. Pr. Geo. Co. on the S side of White Oak Sw., adj. FitzGerrald; 12 Jan 1746/47, p.339. 10 Shill.

SAMUEL RATHER, 303 acs. Pr. Geo. Co. on the S side of Stoney Cr. and both sides of Rocky Run, in the road; adj. Bobbit, Burchet, Scot, Smart, & Richard Ledbetter; 12 Jan 1746/47, p.340. £1.S10.

JOHN WALKER, 82 acs. Pr. Geo. Co. on both sides of Beaver Pond Cr.; adj. Butler now Worshams, Robert Wynn, Jos. Harper, William Jones, John Jones & Robert Wynn; 12 Jan 1746/47, p.342. 10 Shill.

THOMAS EGLETON, 441 acs. Pr. Geo. Co. on both sides of the Moccosoneck Road, on the N side of Warwick Sw., by Rowanty Road; adj. Thomas Leath, Ferguson, James Pittillo, his old Land & John Kirkland; 12 Jan 1746/47, p.344. £1.S5. 200 acs. formerly gtd. sd Thomas Egleton by pat. 30 Aug 1744 [PB 22 p.143] and the Residue never before gtd.

ABNER GRIGG, 200 acs. Pr. Geo. Co. on the S side of White Oak Sw., adj. Capt John FitzGerrald; 12 Jan 1746/47, p.346. £1.

EDWARD HOLLOWAY, 254 acs. Pr. Geo. Co. on the Head Brs. of Walls Run; adj. his own, Jones, Bolling & Moody; 12 Jan 1746/47, p.347. £1.S5.

JOHN ELLINGTON JUNR., 242 acs. Pr. Geo. Co. on the S side of White Oak Sw.; adj. Stewart, & Joseph Noble; 12 Jan 1746/47, p.349. £1.S5.

THOMAS JONES, 400 acs. Pr. Geo. Co. on Walls Run; adj.

Merrit, Joseph Wall, & Crawley; 12 Jan 1746/47, p.350. £2.

THOMAS JONES, 170 acs. Pr. Geo. Co. on the upper side of Turkey Egg Cr.; adj. Peter Thomas, George Booth, Philip Jones, Wynn, & Robert Tucker; 12 Jan 1746/47, p.352. £1.

JOHN EDWARDS, 140 acs. Pr. Geo. Co. on the S side of Sappone Cr., adj. George Belcher & Capt. William Starke; 12 Jan 1746/47, p.354. 15 Shill.

WILLIAM LEE, 245 acs. Albemarle Co. on the Brs. of Hardway Riv., adj. Mildred Meriwether & Thomas Fitzpatrick; 12 Jan 1746/47, p.355. £1.S5.

JOHN TAPLEY, 354 acs. Pr. Geo. Co. on the N side of Sappone Cr. and upper side of the Mealy Br.; adj. Capt. Stark, John Evans & Munfords called *Gamlins*; 12 Jan 1746, p.357. £1.S15.

JOHN GOODWYNN, 1,503 acs. Pr. Geo. Co. on both sides Sappone Cr. and the Morter Br. of Stoney Cr., by the side of Pettipooles fork of the Morter Br., by the side of the Middle Morter Br., by the flat Rock Br., crossing the Road, just below the mouth of the Pigg Pen Br., by the side of a Highland Pond; adj. his own Line, Isaac Tucker, Richard Jones & William Pettipooles new line; 12 Jan 1746/47, p.359. £3.S15. 780 acs. part thereof formerly gtd. sd John Goodwyn by Pat. 10 June

1740 [PB 19 p.692] and 723 acs. the residue never before gtd.

WILLIAM EPPES, 400 acs. Pr. Geo. Co. on both sides the Road on the lower side of Nammiseen Cr.; adj. Fitz, Bolling, Merrimoon, William Featherstone & Thomas Rees; 12 Jan 1746/47, p.362. £2.

EDWARD LEWIS, 376 acs. Pr. Geo. Co. upon the Head and in the upper Fork of Walls Run and on both sides of the Upper Nottoway Road, on Buckskin Cr., adj. Mr William Jones & Edward Holloway; 12 Jan 1746/47, p.364. £2.

RICHARD HARRISON, 400 acs. Pr. Geo. Co. between Stoney Cr. and Sappone Cr. and on lower side of the Reedy Br., along the Co. Line [E30°N]; adj. Joseph Tucker his 150 acs. & John Williamson; 12 Jan 1746/47, p.366. £1. 200 acs. part formerly gtd. sd Richard Harrison by Pat. 10 June 1740 [PB 19 p.676 on Tarrapin Br. and Curtis's Path] and 200 acs. the Residue never before gtd.

RICHARD CROSS, 335 acs. Pr. Geo. Co. between Butterwood Sw. & White Oak Sw.; adj. Woodleif, Hugh Rees, Taylor, Robert West & James Mills; 12 Jan 1746/47, p.367. £1.S15.

JOHN HARDAWAY, 170 acs. Pr. Geo. Co. on the S side of Butterwood Sw.; adj. Nunnally, Pritchet, Addison & Hardaway; 12 Jan 1746/47, p.369. £1.

JAMES BASS, 325 acs. Is. of Wight Co. on the N side of Meherrin Riv., Beg. by the SW Prong of Herberts Br., by the Green Pond Br.; adj. Nathaniel Morrel, Henry Ivy, sd Basses other old Line & Joshua Claud; 12 Jan 1746/47, p.370. £1.S15.

GEORGE CORNETT, 170 acs. Is. of Wight Co. on the S side of Nottoway Riv., crossing the Hornett Sw., by the Co. Line [N60°E]; adj. sd Cornetts old Land, Charles Maberry & Joseph Harrod [Harwood]; 12 Jan 1746/47. p.372. £1.

JAMES ATKINSON, 225 acs. Is. of Wight Co. on the N side of Meherrin Riv., up the Run of the three Creeks; adj. John Irby, William Lee, Edward Lundy, Amy Gulledge, David Adams & William Maberry; 12 Jan 1746/47, p.374. £1.S5.

ABRAM MARTIN, 989 acs. Lunenburg Co. on both sides of the Horsepen Cr.; 12 Jan 1746/47, p.376. £5.

ROBERT HART, 70 acs. Is. of Wight Co. on the N side of Seacock Sw. Beg. by the side of Barbacue Br. at the Mouth of a small Br.; adj. Arthur Williamson & Joseph Wombwell; 12 Jan 1746/47, p.377. 10 Shill.

JOSEPH DOLES, 170 acs. Is. of Wight Co. on the S side of the Main Black Water Sw., by the side of the Tarrapin Sw. at the Mouth of the Long Br.; adj. Thomas

Joiner, Thomas Stephenson, Abraham/Abr a m Stephenson & Gwin Summerrell; 12 Jan 1746/47, p.379. £1.

JOHN DAWSON, 210 acs. Is. of Wight Co. on the N side of the Nottoway Riv., by the side of Nottoway Sw., down the Great Br.; adj. Joseph Denson, Bridgman Joyner & Joseph Vick; 12 Jan 1746/47, p.380. £1.S5.

JOSEPH GARNER, 270 acs. Is. of Wight Co. on the N side Maherrin Riv., up the Long Br.; adj. Walter Bryant, his own old Line, William Outland [William Oudelant], Edward Johnson & Simon Everitt; 12 Jan 1746/47, p.382. £1.S10.

SAMPSON NEWSOM, 165 acs. Is. of Wight Co. on the S side Nottoway Riv., up the North Prong of the Hornet Sw., by the Co. Line [S60°W], down the Rattle Snake Br.; 12 Jan 1746/47, p.383. £1.

THOMAS NEWSOM, 170 acs. Is. of Wight Co. on the S side of Nottoway Riv.; adj. William Watkins, his own old Lines & Moses Newsom; 12 Jan 1746/47, p.384. £1..

ROBERT BOOTH, 320 acs. Is. of Wight Co. on the S side of the Lightwood Sw.; adj. Edward Windham, Thomas Deloch, Allens Warren & sd Robert Booths own old Lines; 12 Jan 1746/47, p.386. £1.S15.

EDWARD POWELL, 730 acs. Surry Co. on the S side of

Nottoway Riv., down the Sowerwood Br., crossing the Spring Sw.; adj. John Stokes, Richard Rose & Thomas Weathers; 12 Jan 1746/47, p.388. £2.S5. 300 acs. part formerly granted William Atkieson by Pat. 20 May 1742 [PB 20 p.314] the Right and Title of which is now become vested in the sd Powell and 430 acs. the Residue never before gtd.

HENRY JOHNSON, 100 acs. Surry Co. on Clays Br., adj. Mr Newsom; 12 Jan 1746/47, p.390. 10 Shill.

FRANCIS HUTCHINS, 70 acs. Surry Co. on the S side of Nottoway Riv. & on the N side of Raccoon Sw., in the Edge of the Lowgrounds, adj. Robert Webb junior; 12 Jan 1746/47, p.391. 10 Shill.

JAMES DAVIS, JUNIOR, 170 acs. Surry Co. adj. William Baldwin & Major Benjamin Harrison; 12 Jan 1746/47, p.393. £1.

THOMAS WADE, 350 acs. Surry Co. on the N side of Nottoway Riv., up the Run of Southwester Sw., adj. John Gillion & John Freeman; 12 Jan 1746/47, p.394. £1.S15.

THOMAS HUNT, 270 acs. Surry Co. on the W side of Sapponey Cr., on the Tanyard Br., on the Co. Line [S60°W], crossing the Buckhorn Br., down the Crow Br., adj. his own Lines; 12 Jan 1746/47, p.396. £1.S10.

JOHN FERRINGTON, 270 acs. Surry Co. on the SW side of the Southwester Sw., up the Hogpen Br.; 12 Jan 1746/47, p.397. £1.S10.

JAMES CAIN, 270 acs. Surry Co. on the SW side of Southwester Sw., down the Run of the Hogpen Br., near a Meadow Br.; adj. William Rainey, Hinshea Mabery & his own old Lines; 12 Jan 1746/47, p.399. £1.S10.

FRANCIS FELTS, 180 acs. Surry Co. on the S side of Nottaway Riv., down Cockes's Br.; 12 Jan 1746/47, p.401. £1.

ROBERT FERRINGTON, 154 acs. Surry Co. on the SW side of Southwester Sw., adj. William Rainey by sd Raineys Mill Path & his own Lines; 12 Jan 1746/47, p.402. 15 Shill.

JAMES MASSINGALL, 254 acs. Surry Co. on the S side of Black Water Sw., over Birchin Island Road, adj. his own Lines & James Bains; 12 Jan 1746/47, p.404. £1.S5.

WILLIAM RICHARDSON, 54 acs. Surry Co. on the N side of Southwester Sw., near a Pond, adj. William Wynne & Thomas Wade; 12 Jan 1746/47, p.405. 5 Shill.

THOMAS PEEPLE, 115 acs. Surry Co. on the S side of the Black Sw. adj. William Saunders & William Peeple; 12 Jan 1746/47, p.407. 15 Shill.

CURTIS LAND, 65 acs. Surry Co. on the S side of Nottoway Riv., up a Br. which divides this L. from Abrãm Evans, in Prickly Ash Br., adj. William Longbottom; 12 Jan 1746/47, p.409. 10 Shill.

THOMAS NEWSUM, 154 acs. Surry Co. on the S side of Nottoway Riv., near the edge of the Low Grounds of Spring Sw.; adj. his own Line, John Battle & Gregory Rawlins; 12 Jan 1746/47, p.410. 15 Shill.

RICHARD NORTHCROSS, 338 acs. Surry Co. on the S side of Nottoway Riv., adj. William Atkeison; 12 Jan 1746/47, p.412. £1.S15.

ELIAS MILLER, 200 acs. Surry Co. near the Head of Upper Chipoaks Cr., down the Wolf Pit Br. & the Reedy Br., adj. his own Lines & John Averis; 12 Jan 1746/47, p.413. £1.

WILLIAM RAINEY, 145 acs. Surry Co. on the SW side of Southwester Sw., down the Hogpen Br., near an old Horsepen, on his own Mill Path; adj. John Ferrington, his own Line & Hinshea Mabery; 12 Jan 1746/47, p.415. 15 Shill.

NATHANIEL CHAMBLIS, 400 acs. Surry Co. on the N side of Nottoway Riv.; adj. his own Line, John Davis Junior, Mr Pepper & Ralph Rachel; 12 Jan 1746/47, p.417. £2.

EDWARD BUCKNER, 250 acs. Surry Co. on the W side of Harrys Sw., by the Co. Line [N60°E], adj. Mr Richard Pepper & James Porch; 12 Jan 1746/47, p.419. £1.S5.

JOHN BAINS, 150 acs. Surry Co. on the S side of Black Water Sw.; adj. Edward Ellis, his own Line & Mr Edmund Ruffin; 12 Jan 1746/47, p.420. 15 Shill.

GREGORY RAWLINGS, JUNIOR, 195 acs. Surry Co. on the S side of Nottoway Riv. and on both sides of the Hornet Sw.; adj. Thomas Newsum, & his father Gregory Rawlings; 12 Jan 1746/47, p.422. £1.

GRIFFIN EVANS, 157 acs. Goochland Co. on the N side of James Riv. on Brs. of Tuckahoe, on the N side the Main Road; adj. Daniel Hix dec'd, Colonel William Randolph, John Martin dec'd, Richard Crouch & Evans; 12 May 1747, p.424. £1.

JOHN CURTIS, 90 acs. Surry Co. on the W side of Stoney Cr., down the Run of the Great Pond, by the Co. Line [N60°E], adj. his own Line; 12 Jan 1746/47, p.425. 10 Shill.

RICHARD CARTER, 564 acs. Surry Co. on the N side of Nottoway Riv., by the Pr. Geo. Co. Line [N60°E], Beg. in the Rockey Run above the Mouth of the Straw Meadow Br.; adj. Ralph Rachel, Thomas Hunt & Richard Hewson [Huson]; 12 Jan 1746/47, p.427. £3.

SAMUEL SPENCER, 400 acs. Goochland Co. on both Forks of Swans Cr., adj. William Mays; 12 Jan 1746/47, p.429. £2.

WILLIAM SALLEE, 1,200 acs. Goochland Co. on both sides of Joshua's Cr. of Slate Riv., near the Head of a Br. of Hatchers Cr., adj. Benjamin Witt; 12 Jan 1746/47, p.431-432. £6.

ROBERT HARDY, 400 acs. Goochland Co. on both sides of Bold Br. of Berringers Cr., on the N side of the Rivanna, adj. John Robinson; 12 Jan 1746/47, p.433. £2.

ALEXANDER PATTON, 172 acs. Goochland Co. on both sides of Taylors Cr., on the Spurr of a Mountain, adj. Archibald Wood; 12 Jan 1746/47, p.434. £1.

JOSEPH TERRY, 800 acs. Goochland Co. on both sides the Road between Willis Riv. and Appamattox Riv., adj. William Wamack & David Harris; 12 Jan 1746/47, p.436-437. £4.

JOSEPH PRICE, 260 acs. Goochland Co. on both sides of Willis's Riv. alias Willis's Cr.; adj. Benjamin Dumas, Absolom Jordan, Samuel Bridgwater, Merry Webb, the same Price, & George Carrington; 12 Jan 1746/47, p.438. £1.S10.

MERADITH MANNING, 150 acs. Goochland Co. on the N side of

Slate Riv.; 12 Jan 1746/47, p.439. 15 Shill.

JOHN JOHNSON, 200 acs. Goochland Co. on the S Brs. of Willis's Riv.; adj. John Cunningham dec'd., Thomas Carter, James Bolling & James Cunningham; 12 Jan 1746/47, p.441. £1.

ARTHUR HOPKINS, 52 acs. Goochland Co. among the W Brs. of Treasurers Run; adj. William Swift dec'd., Arthur Hopkins, John Johnson & George Sutherland; 12 Jan 1746/47, p.442. 5 Shill.

THOMAS TURPIN, 350 acs. Goochland Co. on Brs. of Randolphs Cr.; adj. Anthony Benoine, Dudly Digges & Edward Kelly; 12 Jan 1746/47, p.444. 35 Shill.

ALEXANDER TRENT, 410 acs. Goochland Co. on Brs. of Great Buffolo Cr. & Little Buffolo Cr.; adj. Anthony Sharroon/Sherroon, Susannah Carnor, William Rice, Grisel Coleman & William Still; 12 Jan 1746/47, p.446. £2.S5.

JOHN DAVIS, 400 acs. Goochland Co. on both sides the Wilderness Run, adj. Robert Davis junr.; 12 Jan 1746/47, p.447. £2.

JOHN ROBINSON, Joiner, 400 acs. Goochland Co. on both sides Phills Cr. on the N side the Rivanna, Beg. on the S side the Cr. near the Horspen, on the Draughts of Barringers Cr.; 12 Jan 1746/47, p.449. £2.

JOHN ROBINSON, Joiner, 20 acs. Goochland Co. on both sides of Johns Cr. of the S side James Riv.; adj. Mary Reynolds, Stephen Hughs, John Fleming & Joseph Johns; 12 Jan 1746/47, p.451. 5 Shill.

DAVID KINKEAD, 400 acs. Goochland Co. on the Brs. of RockFish Riv., on the End of a Mountain, adj. Colo. John Chiswell; 12 Jan 1746/47, p.453. £2.

WILLIAM CABELL, 100 acs. Albemarle Co. on the N side of Tye Riv., Beg. on the Riv. Bank opposite to the Middle of an Ivy Island, on the Cedar Cliffs of Tye Riv.; 12 Jan 1746/47, p.455. 10 Shill.

HUMPHRY PARISH, 90 acs. Goochland Co. on the N side of James Riv. among the Brs. of the Byrd & Fork Cr. and on both sides of the Three Notched Mountain Road, on the Co. Line that divides Louisa & Goochland Countys [[N58½°W, N47°W & N31°W], by a Pond; adj. Thomas Watson, Joseph Lewis & Charles Massie; 12 Jan 1746/47, p.456. 10 Shill.

HUMPHRY PARISH, 183 acs. Goochland Co. on the N side of James Riv. among the Brs. of the Byrd, adj. John Moss & Joseph Lewis; 12 Jan 1746/47, p.458. £1.

THOMAS OGILSBY, 200 acs. Goochland Co. on the S side of Hardway Riv., adj. George Damrill

& Hugh Morris; 12 Jan 1746/47, p.460. £2.

THOMAS OGILSBY, 200 acs. Goochland Co. on the North Fork of Totier Cr. [also as Toteir Cr.], adj. Arthur Donalley & Ambrose Joshua Smith; 12 Jan 1746/47, p.462. £1.

JOHN BULLOCK, 400 acs. Goochland Co. on the Brs. of Rockey Run of Willis's Riv.; adj. Thomas Johns, Beverley Randolph Esq., John Martin & Ralph Flipping; 12 Jan 1746/47, p.464. £2.

THOMAS FITZPATRICK, 335 acs. Goochland Co. on both sides the North Fork of Hardware Riv.; adj. Mildred Meriwether, Robert Lewis & Howard Cash; 12 Jan 1746/47, p.465. £1.S15.

JOSEPH FITZPATRICK, 400 acs. Goochland Co. on both sides of the South Br. of the North fork of Hardwar Riv., on the top of a hill, in a Bottom, adj. Mildred Meriwether & Robert Lewis; 12 Jan 1746/47, p.467. £2.

BENJAMIN DUMAS, 1,000 acs. Goochland Co. on both sides of Snow Quarter br. of Willis's cr.; adj. Samuel Bridgwater, Jonathan Cunningham, Joseph Price, Absalom Jordan, William Ferres, John Bleven & Jonathan Cunningham; 12 Jan 1746/47, p.469. £2. 400 acs. part formerly gtd. sd Benjamin Dumas by pat. 10 Jun 1737 [PB 17 p.332] and 200 acs. other part formerly gtd. sd

Benjamin Dumas by pat. 22 Sep 1739 [PB 18 p.432] and 400 acs. the Residue never before gtd.

ARCHIBALD CARY, 440 acs. Goochland Co. on the N Brs. of Willis's Riv.; adj. John Wheeler, Henry Cary Gent. & Henry Beard; 12 Jan 1746/47, p.471. £2.S5.

JOHN MAYO, 200 acs. Goochland Co. among the Brs. of Willis's Riv., crossing Bear Cr.; adj. Richard Woodson, Vincent Lacy, Joseph Dabbs & William Mayo; 12 Jan 1746/47, p.473. £1.

ROBERT BARNETT, 211 acs. Goochland Co. on the Brs. of Rockfish Riv., adj. William Mayo & Hickman; 12 Jan 1746/47, p.475. £1.S5.

CHARLES BURK, 275 acs. Goochland Co. on both sides of Frisbys Cr., adj. William Jones & the sd Charles Burk; 12 Jan 1746/47, p.477. £1.S10.

DRURY TUCKER, 400 acs. Goochland Co. on the N side of the Fluvanna Riv. against the seven Island, adj. William Cannon & Amos Lad; 12 Jan 1746/47, p.479. £2.

JOHN BONDURANT, 400 acs. Goochland Co. on both sides of Flatt Cr. a Br. of the Slate Riv., Beg. in Flatt Cr. Lowgrounds, adj. James Gates; 12 Jan 1746/47, p.480. £2.

THOMAS STILL, 200 acs. Goochland Co. on both sides of

Great Buffalo Cr.; adj. James Terry, William Still & Henry Cary Gent.; 12 Jan 1746/47, p.482. £1.

SAMUEL STEVENS, 400 acs. Goochland Co. on both sides of Mill Cr. of Slate Riv.; 12 Jan 1746/47, p.484. £2.

JAMES NEVELL, 3,226 acs. Goochland Co. on both sides of South Fork of Rockfish Riv., on a Stoney ridge, adj. Stephen Johnson & John Johns; 12 Jan 1746/47, p.486. £11. 1,050 acs. part formerly gtd. David Paterson by three several patents for 350 acs. one bearing date 1 Jun 1741 [David Patterson, PB 19 p.970] & the other two bearing Date respectively 6 Jul 1741 [PB 19 p.1003 & p.1015] & by him sold and conveyed unto the sd James Nevells, and 2,176 acs. the Residue never before gtd.

AMBROSE HUDGENS, 400 acs. Goochland Co. among the S Brs. of Willis's Riv.; adj. William Holladay, James Daniel, Noel Burton & Robert Hughes; 12 Jan 1746/47, p.488. £2.

RICHARD HUBBARD, 400 acs. Goochland Co. among the N Brs. of Little Guinea Cr., adj. William Hamilton & John Watson; 12 Jan 1746/47, p.490. £2.

WINTWORTH WEBB, 725 acs. Goochland Co. on the Brs. of Bear Garden Cr.; adj. John Southern, William Phelps, George Carrington, John Floyd, Hugh Moor, Joseph Dabbs & William

Webb; 12 Jan 1746/47, p.492. £3.S15.

ROGER WILLIAMS, JUNIOR, 350 acs. Goochland Co. among the Brs. of Appamattox Riv. above Dry Cr., adj. Colo. Richard Randolph; 12 Jan 1746/47, p.494. £1.S15.

JOHN WOODSON, Son of Richard Woodson, 800 acs. Goochland Co. on both sides of Little Dry Cr. of Appamattox Riv., adj. Colo. Richard Randolph; 12 Jan 1746/47, p.496. £4.

ABSALOM JORDAN, 275 acs. Goochland Co. on both sides of Snow Quarter Cr. of Willis's Riv. alias Willis's Cr., crossing Snow Quarter Br.; adj. Colo. Benjamin Harrison, Benjamin Dumas & George Carrington; 12 Jan 1746/47, p.498. £1.S10.

JOHN BOWLS, 300 acs. Goochland Co. at the Head of Stinking Water Run of Appamattox Riv., in the Fork of sd Run; adj. John Law, Thomas Davenport, William Arnold, Charles Bostick & William Hamilton; 12 Jan 1746/47, p.500. £1.S10.

HUGH GREEN, 230 acs. Goochland Co. on both sides Slate Riv., Beg. at the Mouth of Greens Cr.; 12 Jan 1746/47, p.502. £1.S5.

JOHN WATKINS, 425 acs. Goochland Co. adj. to Appamattox Riv. and on both sides of Mallory's Br., adj. Richard Randolph Gent.

& Thomas Bows; 12 Jan 1746/47, p.503. £2.S5.

THOMAS JONES, 400 acs. Goochland Co. on the N Brs. of Slate Riv.; adj. William Jones, Samuel Glover & Charles Burk; 12 Jan 1746/47, p.506. £2.

WILLIAM PETTY POOL, SENIOR, 877 acs. Lunenburg Co. on the E side of Fucking Cr.; 12 Jan 1746/47, p.507. £1. 676 acs. part formerly gtd. sd William Petty Pool by pat. 1 Jun 1746 [PB 25 p.99 Brunswick Co. which included his 276 acs. in PB 14 p.510] and 201 acs. the Residue never before gtd.

JOHN JOHNS, 300 acs. Goochland Co. on both sides the South fork of Rockfish Riv., on a Stoney Ridge, at Bear Br., by the side of a Valley; 12 Jan 1746/47, p.509. £1.S10. [regranted to John Leek as Albemarle Co. in PB 34 p.407 dated 10 Aug 1759]

PHILIP THOMAS, 400 acs. Goochland Co. on both sides of Troublesome Cr. of Slate Riv., adj. Anthony Benoine; 12 Jan 1746/47, p.511. £2.

PETER KING, 340 acs. Brunswick Co. on the S side of Staunton Riv.; 12 Jan 1746/47, p.512. £1.S15.

WILLIAM CHULMLEY, 400 acs. Goochland Co. on the Ridge bet. Appamattox & Willis's Rivers, crossing the Main Road; adj. John Twitty, Thomas Johns, Beverley Randolph Esq., John Chaffin,

James Terry, David Harris & Joseph Terry; 12 Jan 1746/47, p.514. £2.

RICHARD TAYLOR, JUNIOR, 1,073 acs. Goochland Co. on both sides of the north Br. of Slate Riv.; adj. John Farrish, Phineas Glover & Samuel Glover; 12 Jan 1746/47, p.516. £1.S10. 400 acs. part formerly gtd. sd Richard Taylor by pat. 30 Jan 1741/42 [PB 20 p.109#1, 400 acs. part formerly gtd. sd Richard Taylor by pat. 20 Aug 1745 [PB 23 p.1081] and 273 acs. the Residue never before gtd.

RICHARD TAYLOR, JUNR., 185 acs. Goochland Co. on both sides of Rack Island Cr.; 12 Jan 1746/47, p.518. £1.

RICHARD TAYLOR, JUNIOR, 85 acs. Goochland Co. on both sides of Wrack Island Cr.; 12 Jan 1746/47, p.520. 10 Shill.

RICHARD TALIAFERRO, 400 acs. Goochland Co. on both sides of Puppies Cr., on the Spur of a Mountain & on the Spur of Taliaferro's Mountain, adj. John Thrasher; 12 Jan 1746/47, p.522. £2.

RICHARD TALIAFERRO, 400 acs. Goochland Co. on the head Brs. of Joes Cr., Beg. near the Head of a Br. of the south Fork of Rockfish, by a Br. of Findleys Cr., adj. James Nevill; 12 Jan 1746/47, p.524. £2.

RICHARD TALIAFERRO, 380 acs. Goochland Co. on both sides of Puppies Cr., adj. Charles Taliaferro; 12 Jan 1746/47, p.526. £2.

PETER HAIRSTONE, 250 acs. Goochland Co. in the *North Garden*, adj. Robert Lewis; 12 Jan 1746/47, p.528. £1.S5.

JAMES WOOD, 190 acs. Goochland Co. on the Head Brs. of Ivy Cr.; adj. Machael/Michael Wood, Robert Lewis & Hugh Dobbins; 12 Jan 1746/47, p.530. £1.

JAMES CHRISTIAN, 100 acs. Goochland Co. on both sides of Wrack Island Cr., adj. the sd Christians Line; 12 Jan 1746/47, p.532. 10 Shill.

ORLANDO HUGHS, 160 acs. Goochland Co. on the Brs. of Muddy Cr.; adj. Benjamin Dumas, Ashford Hughes, Bowler Cocke Gent. & Matthew Watson; 12 Jan 1746/47, p.534. £1.

TIMOTHY MURRELL/MURREL, 195 acs. Brunswick Co. on the S side of Hounds Cr.; 12 Jan 1746/47, p.535. £1.

PHILEMON BOWERS, 250 acs. Brunswick Co. on the N side of the Great Cr.; 12 Jan 1746/47, p.537. £1.S5.

NICHOLAS EDMUNDS, 167 acs. Brunswick Co. on the N side of Great cr., up Evans's Cr.; 12 Jan 1746/47, p.539. £1.

HENRY CHILES, 204 acs. Brunswick Co. on the S side of Staunton Riv. opposite the mouth of Otter; 12 Jan 1746/47, p.541. £1.

JOSEPH ECKHOLS/ECKOLS, 103 acs. Brunswick Co. joining Richard Bookers Survey at the Mouth of Falling Riv.; 12 Jan 1746/47, p.542. 10 Shill.

JOHN EZEL, 279 acs. Brunswick Co. on the S side of Meherren Riv., up Taylors Cr.; 12 Jan 1746/47, p.544. £1.S10.

LEWIS DUPRA, JUNIOR, 315 acs. Brunswick Co. joining the lines of James Turner, David Comins, Simon Turner, John Dupra, John Lucas & Lewis Dupra Senr.; 12 Jan 1746/47, p.546. £1.S15.

SILVESTER JUNIOR, 400 acs. Brunswick Co. on the N side of Dan Riv., up White Walnut Cr.; 12 Jan 1746/47, p.549. £2.

JOHN CATO, 354 acs. Brunswick Co. on the S side of Fountains Cr.; adj. his own old Line, John Parson & John Jeffers; 12 Jan 1746/47, p.551. £1.S15.

JOHN BRADFORD, 340 acs. Brunswick Co. on the S side of Fountain Cr., adj. John Lynch; 12 Jan 1746/47, p.553. £1.S15.

THOMAS WORTHEY, 324 acs. Brunswick Co. on the N side of Stanton Riv., adj. Randolph & John Nash; 12 Jan 1746/47, p.554. £1.S15.

DRURY RAGSDALE, 370 acs. Brunswick Co. on the S side the South fork of the Falls Cr. & the on N side of Little Hounds Cr.; 12 Jan 1746/47, p.556. £2.

JOHN PARRISH/PARISH, 394 acs. Brunswick Co. on both sides of Medway Riv. joining Birds Line; 12 Jan 1746/47, p.558. £2.

NINION MITCHEL, 346 acs. Brunswick Co. on both sides of Cattail Cr., Beg. a little below Nathaniel Perry's lower Line; 12 Jan 1746/47, p.560. £1.S15.

THOMAS WORTHEY, 494 acs. Brunswick Co. on the N side of Stanton Riv., adj. Joseph Morton junior his lower line; 12 Jan 1746/47, p.562. £2.S10.

HENRY MORRIS, 1,842 acs. Brunswick Co. on both sides of Loyds Run, on the Road, adj. Pettillo; 12 Jan 1746/47, p.564. £7. 438 acs. part formerly gtd. sd Henry Morris by pat. 28 Sep 1728 [PB 14 p.81] and 1,404 acs. the Residue never before gtd.

JOHN DUPREY, 503 acs. Brunswick Co.; adj. Simon Turner, Lewis Duprey, his own Line, Thomas Parsons, John Fenill, Mary Haley, & Parker; 12 Jan 1746/47, p.567. £2.S10.

DANIEL NANCE, 244 acs. Brunswick Co., down Avents Cr.; 12 Jan 1746/47, p.569. £1.S5.

JOHN PARRISH, 254 acs. Brunswick Co. on the N side of Dan Riv. adj. Robert Humphrys upper Line; 12 Jan 1746/47, p.571. £1.S5.

THOMAS MUCKLEHUNNY, 330 acs. Brunswick Co. on the N side of Flat Rock Cr., adj. Adkins; 12 Jan 1746/47, p.572. £1.S15.

CATLET MANN, 400 acs. Brunswick Co. on both sides of Meherrin Riv., on the Harracane Cr., adj. Abraham Mishaux; 12 Jan 1746/47, p.574. £2.

HUGH MOOR, 253 acs. Brunswick Co. on both sides of Mirey Cr., on Byrds Line; 12 Jan 1746/47, p.576. £1.S5.

JOHN PARKER, 278 acs. Brunswick Co. on both sides of the Little Cr.; adj. James Maclin, MacDaniel & William Maclin; 12 Jan 1746/47, p.578. £1.S10.

JOHN PARRISH, 204 acs. Brunswick Co. on the S side of Dan Riv., Beg. on the Riv. bet. the sd Parrish & Lewis Green; 12 Jan 1746/47, p.579. £1.

JAMES PARISH, 240 acs. Brunswick Co. on the N side of Dan Riv. opposite to the Wolf Island; 12 Jan 1746/47, p.582.

PATRICK MOOR, 354 acs. Brunswick Co. on both sides of Mirey Cr., up the Fork, adj. Hugh Moor; 12 Jan 1746/47, p.583. £1.S15.

JOSEPH MORTON, JUNIOR, 600 acs. Brunswick Co. on both sides of Licking Hole cr., on Mortons Cr., down the Beaver Pound Cr., adj. Joseph Morton Senr.; 12 Jan 1746/47, p.585. £1.S10. 335 acs. part formerly gtd. sd Joseph Morton by pat. 30 Jul 1742 [Joseph Morton the Younger in PB 21 p.92] and 265 acs. the residue never before gtd. [Included in his 1,437 acs. Lunenburgh Co. in PB 28 p.667]

JOHN TWITTY, 1,000 acs. Brunswick Co. on both sides of Meherrin Riv., Beg. at the Mouth of Blackstones Cr., on the Robersons Fork, adj. John Cox & Henry Roberson; 12 Jan 1746/47, p.587. £5.

JOHN CARGILL, 210 acs. Brunswick Co. on the N side of Dan Riv., joining Hogen's upper Line; 12 Jan 1746/47, p.589. £1.S5.

FRANCIS HAYWARD, 175 acs. Brunswick Co. on the S side of Roanoak Riv. and including the Island opposite to the sd Tract; 12 Jan 1746/47, p.591. £1.

HENRY MORRIS, 404 acs. Brunswick Co. on the S side of Loyds Run, adj. his own Line; 12 Jan 1746/47, p.593. £2.

HENRY MORRIS, 83 acs. Brunswick Co. on the N side of Dan Riv. on Byrds Line; 12 Jan 1746/47, p.594. 10 Shill.

THOMAS JONES of Slate River, 86 acs. Brunswick Co. on both sides of Falling Riv., adj. his own old Line; 12 Jan 1746/47, p.596. 10 Shill.

[Beginning with the next Patent, William Gooch Esqr., our Lieutenant Governor and Commander in Chief, was upgraded to Sir William Gooch Bart.]

ROBERT HARRIS, 200 acs. Is. of Wight Co. on the N side of Black Cr., by the side of Franks Br., in Black Creek Pocoson; adj. Thomas Marks, George Harris & his own old Lines; 12 May 1747, p.597. £1. [Franks Br. relates to *Indian Frank's Quarter* in Barneby MackQuinny's 3,435 acs. in PB 10 p.222 dated 23 Dec 1714. Indian Frank also had a part of the Nottoway Indian 6-mile Circle Tract.]

GEORGE BRANCH, 50 acs. Is. of Wight Co. on the N side of Lightwood Sw., adj. his own old Lines & Joseph Gray; 25 Jun 1747 *in the 21st year of our Reign of George the Second*, p.599. 5 Shill.

ROBERT GREEN, 1,470 acs. Augusta Co. on South br. of Potomack Riv., Beg. on the lower side the Mouth of a small Run and on the N side of the South Fork of the South Br. under a piney Hill, at the Foot of a Hill on the Lowground, at the back of the Bank Lick; 25 Jun 1747, p.601. £7.S10.

THOMAS SMITH, Gent., 225 acs. Is. of Wight Co. on the N side of the Cypress Sw., adj. the late James Everat dec'd & Thomas Uzzell; 25 Jun 1747, p.603. for 2 lbs. Tobacco for every of sd L. Whereas by inquisition Indented taken in sd Co. 23 Sep 1742 by Virtue of Warrant directed to Thomas Cocke, Escheator for the sd Co. it appears that James Everat died seised of 200 acs. more or less but by a Survey lately made by James Baker, Surveyor of the sd Co. is found to contain 225 acs. which is found to escheat to us from the sd James Everat, And Whereas Joseph Wright hath made humble Suit and hath obtained a G. for the same which he hath assigned to Thomas Smith, Gent.

ROBERT GREEN, 1,080 acs. Augusta Co. on the south Br. of Potomack Riv., Beg. at the foot of a Hill on the N side the north Fork of Mill Cr., by Muddy Lick, on Stoney Point at the Foot of a Hill; 25 Jun 1747, p.605. £5.S10.

WILLIAM GRAY, 400 acs. Goochland Co. on the Brs.. of the Cat Br. of Willis's Riv. alias Willis's Cr.; adj. Joseph Dabbs, Job Thomas, William Meginis & Orlando Hughes; 25 Jun 1747, p.607. £2.

JOHN PLEASANTS, 400 acs. Albemarle Co. on both sides of the south Br. of Rack Island Cr.; 25 Jun 1747, p.609. £2.

JOHN PLEASANTS, 400 acs. Albemarle Co. on both sides of a

Run of Elk Cr. of the Fluvanna Riv., on the Ridge betwixt the Fluvanna & Stanton Riv.; 25 Jun 1747, p.610. £2.

JOHN PALMER, 150 acs. Goochland Co. on both sides of the Cat-Br. of Willis's Riv.; adj. Henry Cary Gent., Job Thomas, Orlando Hughes & Edmund Gray; 25 Jun 1747, p.612. 15 Shill.

JOHN PIERCE, 500 acs. Goochland Co. on the Brs. of the Little Bird, near Straw Br., adj. Mr Massie & Cole; 25 Jun 1747, p.613. £2.S10.

NATHANIEL WINSTON, 400 acs. Goochland Co. amongst the East Brs. of Machunk Cr.; 25 Jun 1747, p.615. £2.

HUGH MORRIS, 400 acs. Goochland Co. on the Brs. of Totier, in a Glade, adj. Matthew Harris & John Lewis; 25 Jun 1747, p.617. £2.

HUGH RICE MORRIS, 200 acs. Goochland Co. on brs. of Totier, adj. Hugh Morris & Matthew Harris; 25 Jun 1747, p.618. £1.

JOHN MOOR, 200 acs. Goochland Co. on the Brs. of Bear Cr. of Willis's Riv., at Moors Br., by Buckingham Road, adj. Thomas Tilman & Thomas Harvey; 25 Jun 1747, p.620. £1.

ROBERT ADAMS, 400 acs. Goochland Co. among the Brs. of Bird Cr., adj. Land lately survey'd

for Anthony Pouncey; 25 Jun 1747, p.622. £2.

JOHN HUGHES, 248 acs. Goochland Co. on the S Brs. of Deep Cr.; adj. William Tabor, Richard Hubbard & William Bradshew; 25 Jun 1747, p.624. £1.S5.

JOHN HARRISON, 234 acs. Augusta Co. on the Draughts of Smiths Cr., on the NE side of the Big Spring Br.; 25 Jun 1747, p.625. £1.S5.

JOHN HARRISON, 166 acs. Augusta Co. on both sides of Smiths Cr.; 25 Jun 1747, p.627. £1.

CHARLES HUNGATE, 150 acs. Augusta Co. on the S side of Goose Cr. opposite to Charles Campbell; 25 Jun 1747, p.629. 15 Shill.

JAMES HOGSHEAD, 400 acs. Augusta Co. on a br. of Catheys Riv. called Moffet Br., on a Ridge; 25 June 1747, p.630. for the Imp. of 8 pers.: *John Smith & Margaret his wife, Abraham Smith, Henry Smith, Daniel Smith, John Smith junr., Joseph Smith & Robert McDowell.*

JAMES HUMPHRIES, 400 acs. Augusta Co., on a Br. of the north Fork of Shanando called *Free Masons Br.*, in a Draft, on the Top of *Castle Hill* on the S side the north Riv., adj. David Davis; 25 Jun 1747, p.632. for the imp. of 8 pers.: *George Hutchinson & Eleanor his wife, Jennet*

Hutchinson, Francis Hutchinson, John Hutchinson, William Hutchinson, Jennet Hutchinson & Jacob Carr.

JAMES ALLEN, 264 acs. Augusta Co. on a Br. of Catheys Riv. called Allens Run, in a Hollow; adj. Thomas Stevenson & John Moffet; 25 Jun 1747, p.633-p.635. £1.10.

Augt. 20th. 1747
Settled all in this Book & to pag. 84. in one New Book [PB 26] & to 117 [PB 28] in tother
                    John Blair D.Audr.

PATENT BOOK NO. 26

25 Jun 1747 to 20 Aug 1748

JOHN LACKEY, 74 acs. Albemarle Co. on the Brs. of Rockfish Riv., adj. Colo. Chiswell; 25 Jun 1747 *in the 21st year of our Reign of George the Second, Witness our trusty and welbeloved Sir William Gooch Bart. and Lieutenant Governor and Commander in Chief*, p.1. 10 Shill.

JAMES BARNET, 136 acs. Albemarle Co. on the Brs. of Rockfish Riv., on Corbies Cr., adj. Colo. Chiswell; 25 Jun 1747, p.2. 15 Shill.

ROBERT MACKNEELY, 200 acs. Albemarle Co. on both sides of Mechums Riv., on both the N & S sides of Beaver Cr., adj. Michael Wood; 25 Jun 1747, p.3. £1.

ALEXANDER MOUNTGOMARY, 450 acs. Albemarle Co. on both sides of Buck Cr., on the side of a spring, adj. Colo. Chiswell; 25 Jun 1747, p.5. £2.S5.

JOHN DICKEY, 200 acs. Albemarle Co. on the Brs. of Mechums Riv., adj. Robert Lewis

& Archibald Wood; 25 Jun 1747, p.6. £1.

JOSEPH FITZPATRICK, 180 acs. Albemarle Co. on Brs. of Hardway Riv.; adj. his own, Robert Lewis, Thomas Fitzpatrick & William Fitzpatrick; 25 Jun 1747, p.7. £1.

SAMUEL BURK, JUNIOR, 350 acs. Albemarle Co. on both side of Tye Riv., opposite to the upper end of a small Ivy Island; 25 Jun 1747, p.9. £1.S15.

THOMAS FITZPATRICK, 276 acs. Albemarle Co. on the Brs. of Hardway Riv., on the side of a Stoney Hill & at the south fork of Hardway, adj. Charles Lynch; 25 Jun 1747, p.10. £1.S10.

SAMUEL JEMMERSON, 300 acs. Albemarle Co. on the Brs. of Spring Cr., adj. Charles Mills; 25 Jun 1747, p.12. £1.S10.

CHARLES LYNCH, 400 acs. Albemarle Co. on the N side the Rivanna and on both sides of the three chopt mountain Road, on the heads of the Brs. of Barringers, Mychunk and Camp Creek Brs.,

Beg. on the Draughts of Camp Cr., on Martin Kings Road, on the Draughts of Mychunk, at the Three Notch'd Road; 25 Jun 1747, p.13. £2.

HENRY MARR, 150 acs. Albemarle Co. on both sides of Lickinghole Cr.; 25 Jun 1747, p.14. 15 Shill.

CHARLES LYNCH, 400 acs. Albemarle Co. on the Brs. of Mechums Riv., by a Spring; adj. William Whiteside, Colo. John Chiswell & Henry Terril; 25 Jun 1747, p.15. £2.

ROBERT GREEN, 660 acs. Augusta Co. on the south Br. of Potomack Riv., on the S side the north fork of sd Br. of Potomack, at the foot & the side of a Piney Hill; 25 Jun 1747, p.17. £3.S10.

RICHARD TICKTOM, 100 acs. Augusta Co. on the north Riv. of Shanando above the Gap in the Mountain, to the Mouth of Beaver Run, near a large Spring, adj. Bernard McHenry; 25 Jun 1747, p.19. for the Imp. of 2 Pers. whose names are *Valentine Sevier and Margaret Gibson*.

JAMES LEEPER, 66 acs. Augusta Co. on a Br. of Naked Cr., adj. a Tract of L. belonging to the sd James Leeper; 25 Jun 1747, p.20. 10 Shill.

HUGH DOUGLAS/DUGLAS, 130 acs. Augusta Co. on a Br. of Stovers Mill Cr., on the side of a

meadow, adj. John Stephenson; 25 Jun 1747, p.21. 15 Shill.

THOMAS STEVENSON, 232 acs. Augusta Co. on a Br. of Cooks Cr., on the Path side; 25 Jun 1747, p.22. £1.S5.

JACOB DYE, 377 acs. Augusta Co. on the head Draughts of Muddy Cr., at the Foot of the Mountain, adj. Daniel Harrison; 25 Jun 1747, p.23. £2.

JOHN ARCHER, 225 acs. Augusta Co. on a Br. of Catheys Riv. called Buffalo Lick Br., adj. Robert Rennick; 25 Jun 1747, p.25. £1.S5.

JOHN GRAVES, 400 acs. Louisa Co. on both sides of the Beaver Dam Fork of Mechunks Cr., at the north Fork of sd Cr., on the S side of the south fork on the Bank; 25 Jun 1747, p.26. £2.

JOHN EVANS, JUNR., 261 acs. Pr. Geo. Co. on the N side of Sappone Cr.; adj. his own old Line, Capt. Stark, John Tapley, & Munford alias *Gamlins* Lines; 25 Jun 1747, p.28. £1.S10.

DAVID REES, 400 acs. Albemarle Co. on the S side the Rivanna on the Brs. of Moores Cr., on the E side of Piney Mountain, adj. George Bell; 25 Jun 1747, p.29. £2.

JOHN JONES, 211 acs. Pr. Geo. Co. on the upper side of Wallaces/Wallices Cr. and on both sides of the Long Br., adj.

Nicholas Overby [along the sd Overbys Chains Breadth] & Captain William Hamlin; 25 Jun 1747, p.30. £1.S5.

JOHN PALMER, 400 acs. Goochland Co. on both sides of the Cat Br. of Willis's Riv.; adj. Henry Cary Gent., Edmund Gray & William Maginnis; 25 Jun 1747, p.32. £2.

ALEXANDER GRANT, 370 acs. Goochland Co. on both sides of Elk Licking Br. a Run of Lickinghole, adj. Henry Chiles; 25 Jun 1747, p.33. £2.

DAVID MERIWETHER, 400 acs. Louisa Co. on the S side of Negro Cr., adj. Capt. John Aylet & Thomas Walker; 25 Jun 1747, p.34. £2.

NATHAN WOOD, 370 acs. Albemarle Co. on the N side of Moremans Riv., on the side of a Mountain, to a Br. of Rockey Cr., on the Louisa Co. Line [S65°E], up & across Mechums Riv., by a great Rock on the N side of the sd Riv., adj. John Jemmerson & Thomas Moreman; 25 Jun 1747, p.35. £2.

JOHN McDOWELL, 400 acs. Augusta Co. in the Fork of James Riv. on the Brs. of Cedar Cr., in a Valley; 25 June 1747, p.37. £2.

WILLIAM WYNNE, 340 acs. Brunswick Co. on the S side of Dan Riv., on a Great Br., adj. James Parish; 25 June 1747, p.38. £1.S15.

THOMAS HOWELL, 400 acs. Pr. Geo. Co. on the S side of Stoney Cr.; adj. Keith, Haynes & Wagnon; 25 Jun 1747, p.39. £2.

THOMAS TILMAN, 400 acs. Goochland Co. on Bear Cr. of Willis's Riv., on Moores Br., by the Road; adj. William Holliday, Hendricks & Lavilian; 25 Jun 1747, p.41. £2.

JOHN SMITH, 400 acs. Augusta Co. on the south Fork of the North Riv. of Shanando, at the lower end of a Meadow, adj. James Wood; 25 Jun 1747, p.42. for the Imp. of 8 Pers. whose names are *James Leeper, Margaret Leeper, Nicholas Leeper, Sarah Leeper, James Leeper, Andrew Leeper, James Leeper & Guine Leeper.*

SAMUEL MURRILL, 350 acs. Albemarle Co. on both sides of Rockfish Riv., by a Gulley; adj. Colo. Chiswell, Clapham, Edward Malloy & James Wood; 25 Jun 1747, 43. £1.S15.

THOMAS WYNNE, 425 acs. Brunswick Co. on a Great Br.; adj. his own Line, William Pool, Stone & Young Stokes; 25 Jun 1747, p.45. £2.S5.

JAMES PARRISH, 385 acs. Brunswick Co. on the W side of Butchers Cr.; adj. William Thomerson, John New, Thomas Baker & Abraham Cook; 25 June 1747, p.46. £2.

JOHN RAGSDELL, 600 acs. Amelia Co. on both sides of the Little Harricane & on the head Brs.

of Burchin Swamps, by a Path, by a Br. of the Burchen; adj. Hugh Williams, John Hughs, Jackson & Bryan Fannan; 25 Jun 1747, p.48. £3.

JOHN BLACKSTONE, 254 acs. Brunswick Co. down the Reedy Cr. & up the Reedy Br.; adj. his own Line, Lazarus Williams, Embry & Hawkins; 25 Jun 1747, p.49. £1.S5.

GEORGE SANDERSON, 1,100 acs. Brunswick Co. on the Heads of the Brs. of Williams's Cr., adj. John Lidderdale; 25 Jun 1747, p.51. £5.S10.

WILLIAM HAWKINS, 400 acs. Brunswick Co. adj. the Land he now Lives on; 25 Jun 1747, p.52. £2.

HENRY FREEMAN, 396 acs. Brunswick Co. on the N side of Flat Rock Cr., up the great Br., on Kettle Stick Br., adj. Blanks & Petway; 25 Jun 1747, p.54. £2.

THOMAS CHAPPELL, 350 acs. Is. of Wight Co. on the N side of Nottoway Riv., up the Cosunkorow /Cosonkorow Sw., by the Nottoway Indians Lines [SSW, SWxS & SW], adj. Arthur Arrington & Henry Briggs; 25 Jun 1747, p.55. £1.S15. Whereas by Pat. 28 Sep 1730 gtd. James Chappell [PB 13 p.499] And Whereas James Chappell, Thomas Day & Jane his Wife, Thomas Beddingfield & Mary his Wife, William Arrington, William Barton & Anna his Wife, William Barker & Priscilla his Wife, and Robert Hill & Hannah his Wife, Heirs of Henry Briggs dec'd., who purchased the sd L. of the aforesaid James Chappell, have failed to pay Quitrents and to make Cultiv. and Improv. and Thomas Chappell hath made humble Suit and hath obtained a G. for the same. [This land adjoined the Nottoway-Iroquois Indian 6-mile circle Tract which consisted of 32 straight lines of 188 Poles, with an area of 17,942.68 acs. versus the 18095.616 acs. in a true 6-mile circle. The Nottoway Indians also had a 6-mile square Tract of 23,040 acs., SW of the Nottoway Riv.]

WILLIAM MOSS, 24 acs. 4 chains, York Co. on the S side the Road (then) running North; 25 Jun 1747, p.57. for 2 lbs. of Tobacco for every Acre. Whereas by Inquisition indented taken in sd Co. 17 Apr 1741 by Virtue of a Warrant directed to William Byrd Esq. our Escheator for sd Co. It appears that David Petty John died seized of 25 acs. more or less but by a Survey lately made by James Shields Surveyor of the sd [Co.] is found to contain but 24 acs. and 4 Chains, which is found to escheat to us from sd David Petty John and Whereas William Moss hath made humble Suit and hath obtained a G. for the same.

JOHN HARRIS, 273 acs. Albemarle Co. on the S side the Rivanna on both sides Moores Cr., on a Ridge, adj. Charles Caffrey & David Rees; 25 Jun 1747, p.58. £1.S10.

GEORGE RENYER TURNER, 400 acs. Goochland Co. on both sides of the lower Manakin Cr.; adj. William Sallee, William Battersby, Daniel Guarrand dec'd & Thomas Dickins; 25 Jun 1747, p.60. £2. Whereas by Pat. 16 Jun 1738 gtd. Daniel Stoner & John James Flournoy since dec'd in joint Tenancy [PB 18 p.6] And Whereas the sd Daniel Stoner (in whom the Right of the sd Land vested by Survivorship after the death of the sd John James Flourney) hath failed to make Cultiv. and Improv. and George Renyer Turner hath made humble Suit and hath obtained a g. for the same.

GEORGE DAVISON, 250 acs. Albemarle Co. on Grannies Hill, on the side of Mountscrutiny; adj. John Greer, Charles Hudson & Davis Stockton; 25 Jun 1747, p.61. £1.S5.

LE ROY GRIFFIN, 1,292 acs. Brunswick Co. on both sides of Sturgeon Run; adj. Fisher, Stroud, Massy (her Line), Henry Bailey & Joseph Boswell; 25 Jun 1747, p.63. £4. 521 acs. part formerly gtd. Thomas Williams by Pat. 8 May 1738 [PB 17 p.520 a regrant of Joseph Boswell's PB 13 p.540 dated 28 Sep 1728/30] and by him sold & conveyed unto the sd Le Roy Griffin & 771 acs. the Residue never before gtd.

HENRY DOWNS, 800 acs. Augusta Co. on the south Riv. of Shannando, adj. another Tract of sd [Jacob] Stoner containing 5,000

acs.; 25 Jun 1747, p.64. £4. Whereas by Pat. 13 Dec 1738 [PB 18 p.148] there was gtd. unto Jacob Stover since dec'd, 800 acs. Orange Co. now Augusta, And Whereas Jacob Stover, Son and Heir of the sd Jacob Stover dec'd, hath failed to pay Quit Rents and to make Cultiv. & Improv. and Henry Downs hath made humble Suit and hath obtained a G. for the same.

LUKE RALLS, 200 acs. Nansemond Co. on the SE side of Back Sw.; adj. John Bryans Pat., William Ralls, John Yeats & Elias Ballard; 25 Jun 1747, p.66. £1.

Reverend JOHN ORNSBY, 1,816 acs. Amelia Co. on both sides of the main north Fork of Buffalo Riv., below the Mountain, adj. Cobbs; 25 Jun 1747, p.68. £9.S5.

EDWARD BRISWATE, 400 acs. Amelia Co. on the upper side of Buffalo Riv.; adj. Hudson, Wallace & Baker; 25 Jun 1747, p.69. £2.

WILLIAM HAILEY, 200 acs. Louisa Co. near the head of Cross Cr.; adj. Francis Clark, Hughs & William Hooper; 25 Jun 1747, p.70. £1.

MARY BREWER, 46 acs. Nansemond Co. on the S side of Nansemond Riv., in the main Desert; adj. Thomas Duke, John Duke & Paul Brewer dec'd; 25 Jun 1747, p.72. 5 Shill.

JOHN HARRISON, 147 acs. Nansemond Co. running through some Part of Butlers Pocoson, by the Snake Pond; adj. William Butler, William Yeats, John Butler, Thomas Pierce & John King; 25 Jun 1747, p.73. 15 Shill.

RICHARD WELBORN, 210 acs. Louisa Co. adj. James Churchill, John Ragland, Majr. Henry, Mrs Anne Johnson & Thomas Johnson; 25 Jun 1747, p.75. £1.S5.

JOHN JAMES DUPUY, 400 acs. Amelia Co. on both sides of Flatt Cr., adj. Edward Jones; 25 Jun 1747, p.76. £2.

GEORGE EWINGS, 287 acs. Amelia Co. on the upper side of Buffolo Riv.; adj. Baker, Briswate, Wallace & Glasby; 25 Jun 1747, p.77. £1.S10.

JOHN VILLAN, 400 acs. Amelia Co. on the head of Flat Cr., adj. Dupuy; 25 Jun 1747, p.78. £2.

CHARLES ANDERSON, 3,122 acs. Amelia Co. on the Brs. of Buffalo and Bryer Rivers, in a Valley; adj. George Hudson, Bibbs, Joseph Morton, Shelton, Gauling & Nickson; 25 Jun 1747, p.80. £15.S15.

AMBROSE CRANE, 204 acs. Amelia Co. on the N side of Winninghams Cr.; adj. Philemon Crane, Thomas Tanner & Joel Tanner; 25 Jun 1747, p.82. £1.

THOMAS MORTON, 400 acs. Amelia Co. on the lower side of Bryer Riv., adj. Joseph Morton & Mackgehee; 25 Jun 1747, p.83. £2.

Augt. 20. 1747.
Settled for Y Rights thus far in this Book & to pag. 117 in the other Book [PB 28]. John Blair D.Audr.

ROBERT JENINGS, 400 acs. Amelia Co. on both sides of Vaughans Cr., at the Head of the Mill Fork, adj. his own Line; 20 Aug 1747, p.84. £2.

JOHN COX, 404 acs. Brunswick Co. on both sides of Blackstones Cr., adj. John Twitty; 20 Aug 1747, p.86. £2.

WILLIAM BANKS, 223 acs. Goochland Co. on the N side of James Riv. among the Brs. of the Byrd; adj. his own Line, Thomas Emeson, Henry Parish, Peter Massie & John Kerby; 20 Aug 1747, p.87. £1.S5.

[pages 88 & 89 were skipped by the Scribe].

MOSES REAVES, 233 acs. Brunswick Co. on both sides of the Fox Br., adj. Simon Turner; 20 Aug 1747, p.90. £1.S5.

NICHOLAS DAVIS, 75 acs. Albemarle Co. on the S side of the Fluvanna Riv. on both sides of Second Cr.; 20 Aug 1747, p.92. 10 Shill.

FRANCIS CALLAWAY, 244 acs. Brunswick Co. on the lower side of Buffaloe Cr.; 20 Aug 1747, p.93. £1.S5.

EDWARD THOMAS, 140 acs. Albemarle Co. on the lower

Millstone Br. of Rock Island Cr.;
20 Aug 1747, p.94. 15 Shill.

JOHN BROWN, 150 acs.
Goochland Co. bet. Angolo &
Green Creeks of Appamattox Riv.;
adj. John Watkins, Richard Witt,
James Brown & Beverly Randolph
Esq.; 20 Aug 1747, p.96. 15 Shill.

GILES ALLEGRE, 362 acs.
Albemarle Co. on both sides
Horsleys Cr. on the N side the
Rivanna, at Horsepen Br., adj.
Robert Bruse; 20 Aug 1747, p.97.
£2.

GEORGE MOORE, 400 acs.
Amelia Co. on the upper side of
Flat Cr.; adj. Crawford, Holland,
Henry Isbell & Hendricks; 20 Aug
1747, p.98. £2.

JOHN WHATLEY, 400 acs.
Hanover Co. on both sides the
south Fork of Buckmountain Cr.,
adj. Robert Thompson & John
Hacket; 20 Aug 1747, p.99. £2.

RICHARD CALLAWAY, 244 acs.
Brunswick Co. on the lower side of
Buffalo Cr., by the side of a Mill
Pond & just below the Mill; 20
Aug 1747, p.101. £1.S5.

Colo. WILLIAM BEVERLY,
GENT., 141 acs. Augusta Co. on a
Br. of the Little Riv. of the Calf
Pasture called Halls Br., on a Pine
Hill & on the side of a Stoney Hill
near the Gap of the Mountain, adj.
the Land George Hall lives on; 1
Oct 1747, p.102. 15 Shill.

Colo. WILLIAM BEVERLY,
GENT., 400 acs. Augusta Co. on a
Br. of the Little Riv. of the Calf
Pasture called Smiths Cr., at the
Foot of the Brown Hill, adj.
William McCutching; 1 Oct 1747,
p.104. for the Imp. of 8 Pers.:
Richard Pringle, William Wood,
William Heming, James Newman,
William Philips Clark, James
Miles, Sybella Wood & Benjamin
Hubbard.

Colo. WILLIAM BEVERLY, 361
acs. , in Augusta Co. on a Br. of
the Little Riv. of the Calf Pasture
called Halls Br., on the side of the
Black Oak Hill & on the side of a
Mountain, adj. Colo. Beverlys pat.
L.; 1 Oct 1747, p.105. for £1.S10
as also for the Imp. of 2 Pers.:
Thomas Miller & Jane Shaw.

MARQUIS CALMEES, 400 acs.
Augusta Co. on the E side of
Woods Riv. below the mouth of
Little Riv.; 1 Oct 1747, p.106. £2.

MARQUIS CALMEES, 100 acs.
Augusta Co. on the W side of
Woods Riv., at a Mountain Foot;
1 Oct 1747, p.107. 10 Shill.

MARQUIS CALMEES, 400 acs.
Augusta Co. on a W Br. of Woods
Riv. called Happy Cr. near the
Peak Mountain, Beg. in the Fork of
the sd Cr. against a Point of Rocks
and Yew Trees, on a Clift near the
Cr. & on a Mountain side; 1 Oct
1747, p.108. £2.

Capt. HENRY DOWNES, 400 acs.
Augusta Co. on the W side of the
Peeked Mountain and on a Br. of

the South Riv. of Shanando called Cubb Run, on a Ridge, in a Glade of Smiths Cr.; 1 Oct 1747, p.110. £2.

HENRY DOWNES, 388 acs. Augusta Co. on a Br. of the North Riv. of Shanando at the End of Buck Hill, on a Ridge; 1 Oct 1747, p.111. £2.

ROBERT HOOK, 200 acs. Augusta Co. on the S side the Land the sd Hook now lives on, by a small Draft; 1 Oct 1747, p.112. £1.

FRANCIS BEATY, 359 acs. Augusta Co. on the W side of the Blue Ridge on a Br. of Roanoak called Mudlick Run, near *an Iron Mine*; 1 Oct 1747, p.114. £2.

WILLIAM SAYORS, 290 acs. Augusta Co. on the W side the Blue Ridge, Beg. amongst a parcel of Stones by a Spring of Buffalo Cr.; 1 Oct 1747, p.115. £1.S10.

JOHN WOOLDRIDGE, 314 acs. Henrico Co. on the S side of James Riv., on the N side of Falling Cr., on the line of the *French Parish*, on the *French Road*; adj. John Tillot, the sd Wooldridges old Line, John Roberts & Richard Dean; 1 Oct 1747, p.116. £1.S15.

JOHN SNYDOR, JUNIOR, 200 acs. Albemarle Co. on both sides of Bear Br. of Rockfish Riv., at the Head of a Valley; 1 Oct 1747, p.117. £1.

DRURY TUCKER, 400 acs. Albemarle Co. on the Brs. of Hardware; 1 Oct 1747, p.119. £2.

SAMUEL BAILEY/BAYLEY, 100 acs. Albemarle Co. on the S side of James Riv. on Glovers Cr. of Slate Riv.; 1 Oct 1747, p.120. 10 Shill.

JOHN BLACKBURN, 395 acs. Albemarle Co. on S side of James Riv. on a north fork of Willis's Cr. above Saunders's Survey; 1 Oct 1747, p.121. £2.

DANIEL SCOTT, 380 acs. Albemarle Co. on Totier; adj. John Lewis, John Tuly, the sd Daniel Scott & Arthur Hopkins; 1 Oct 1747, p.122. £2.

EDMUND WOOD, 350 acs. Albemarle Co. on Brs. of Hatchers Cr., adj. William Cannon & Scott; 1 Oct 1747, p.124.

WILLIAM ALLEN, 394 acs. Albemarle Co. on both sides of Slate Riv., crossing the great Cr.; 1 Nov 1747, p.125. £2.

WILLIAM ALLEN, 100 acs. Albemarle Co. on the Brs. of the Great Cr. on the S side of Slate Riv., by the sd Allens own Line, near his new House; 1 Oct. 1747, p.126. 10 Shill.

WILLIAM ALLEN, 400 acs. Albemarle Co. on the Brs. of Hatchers Cr., crossing Glovers Road & crossing Horn Quarter Road, adj. Mr Thomas Turpin; 1 Oct 1747, p.127. £2.

JAMES HOGGARD, 220 acs. Goochland Co. on the Brs. of Horseleys Cr. on the N side of the Rivanna; adj. Robert Bruce, John Cannaday & John Martin; 1 Oct 1747, p.128. £1.S5.

PHILIP HUDGINS, 400 acs. Goochland Co. on the lower side of Willis's Cr. on its Brs.; adj. by William Chumley, Joseph Terry, Mr Henry Cary & Archer; 1 Oct 1747, p.129. £2.

THOMAS HARVEY, 400 acs. Goochland Co. on the Brs. of Pidey Rock of Willis's Riv., adj. Thomas Harvey, Mr Henry Cary & Levillian; 1 Oct 1747, p.130. £2.

JOHN DAVIS, 122 acs. Albemarle Co. on the S side the Rivanna on a small Br. of Biskett Run, adj. Joseph Anthony & Hugh Dohorty; 1 Oct 1747, p.132. 15 Shill.

JOHN HUGHES, 400 acs. Albemarle Co. on a Br. of the Mountain Cr. of Willis's, crossing Glovers Road; 1 Oct 1747, p.133. £2.

JOSEPH RETTEFORD, 260 acs. Albemarle Co. on the S side James Riv. of the lower side of Willis's Riv., on the upper side of the Muster Field Br., adj. Joseph Terry & Mr Cary; 1 Oct 1747, p.134. £1.S10.

JOSEPH BENOINE, 400 acs. Albemarle Co. on both side of Crooked Cr. a Br. of Slate Riv.; 1 Oct 1747, p.136. £2.

JAMES DAVIS, 312 acs. Albemarle Co. on the S side of the Rivanna on the Brs. of Bisket Run, by the E side of one of the Ragged Mountains, adj. Joseph Anthony; 1 Oct 1747, p.137. £1.S15.

ABRAHAM BEGUIN/BEGNIN, 400 acs. Albemarle Co. on both sides of Great Cr. of Slate Riv.; 1 Oct 1747, p.138. £2.

ELIAS JONES, 200 acs. Albemarle Co. on Powers's Cr. a Br. of Randolphs Cr., adj. Dudley Digges Gent. & James Goss; 1 Oct 1747, p.140. £1.

GEORGE HOMES GWIN, 347 acs. Albemarle Co. on the Wolf Trap Br. of Mountain Cr.; adj. Strange, Bolling, Edmund Wood & Christian; 1 Oct 1747, p.141. £1.S15.

JOHN MARTIN, 3,811 acs. Amelia Co. on both sides of Bryer Riv., crossing Mundingo Br., crossing Little Bryer; adj. his own, Morton, Brown, Baker, Samuel Morton, Mackgehee, & Jos. Morton; 1 Oct 1747, p.142. £9.S5. 933 acs. part formerly gtd. sd John Martin by pat. 20 Aug 1740 [PB 19 p.754 which included his 612 acs. in PB 17 p.482], 304 acs. other part also formerly gtd. sd John Martin by pat. 10 July 1745 [PB 22 p.278], 350 acs. other part formerly gtd. sd John Martin by pat. 25 Sep 1746 [PB 24 p.458] and 400 acs. other part formerly gtd. Thomas Morton by pat. 25 Jun 1747 [PB 26 p.83] and by him sold & conveied unto the sd John Martin and 1,824 acs. the Residue never before gtd.

WILLIAM RICHLEY/RICKLEY, 285 acs. Albemarle Co. on both sides of Slate Riv., adj. Goss & Hunter; 1 Oct 1747, p.145. £1.S10.

THOMAS LOVET, 21 acs. Pr. Ann Co. binding upon a Cypress Sw. and the L. of the sd Lovet; 12 Jan 1747/48, p.146. 5 Shill.

WILLIAM ECKHOLES, 104 acs. Amelia Co. on the Head Brs. of Stocks Cr., adj. Wood, Dawson & Crawford; 12 Jan 1747/48, p.147. for the Imp. of 2 pers.: *Dennis MacCoy & Catherine his Wife.*

FRANCIS ALLEN, 340 acs. Goochland Co. among the Brs. of Burtons Cr. of Appomattox Riv.; adj. George Freeman, the sd Francis Allen, Hutchins Burton & John Owen; 12 Jan 1747/48, p.149. £1.S15.

WILLIAM RAY, 133 acs. Amelia Co. on the S side of Appamattox Riv.; adj. Brumfield, Dawson, Harris, & Thomas Osborne now Alexander Spiers's; 12 Jan 1747/48, p.150. 15 Shill.

JAMES PATTON, 70 acs. Augusta Co. on the Brs. of James Riv. on the W side of the Blue Ridge, Beg. on the W side of the south Br. of sd Riv., on Purgatory Br.; 12 Jan 1747/48, p.152. 10 Shill.

JAMES CRAIG, 150 acs. Augusta Co. on a Draft of the north Riv. of

Shanando, near the old Line, on the N side of a large Draft, on a Dry Br., adj. William Thompson; 12 Jan 1747/48, p.153. 15 Shill.

THOMAS LANIER, 380 acs. Brunswick Co. on both sides of Mitchels Cr., adj. Shepard Lanier, his own & William Hill; 12 Jan 1747/48, p.155. £2.

THOMAS JACKSON, JUNR., 217 acs. Brunswick Co. in the Fork of Bearskin Cr.; 12 Jan 1747, p.156. £1.S5.

ROBERT WYNNE, 200 acs. Brunswick Co. on the upper side of Difficult Cr., at the lower end of the Great Meadow; 12 Jan 1747/48, p.158. £1.

JOHN BLACKWILDER, 290 acs. Lunenburg Co. on both sides of the Horsepen Br. of Allen Cr.; 12 Jan 1747/48, p.159. £1.S10

MANASSES MCBRIDE, 300 acs. Amelia Co. on both sides of Falling Cr., adj. King, Culwell & Martin; 12 Jan 1747/48, p.160. £1.S10.

HENRY PERKY, 95 acs. Augusta Co. on Lick Run bet. Shanando and the Peeked Mountain, crossing the sd Run above a Lick; 12 Jan 1747/48, p.162. 10 Shill.

JOAB MITCHELL, 240 acs. Brunswick Co. on the N side of Beaver Pond Cr., along the Country line [East], down the sd Beaver Cr.; 12 Jan 1747/48, p.163. £1.S5.

JOSEPH HEATHCOCK, 254 acs. Brunswick Co. on the N side of Fountains Cr., on the Road, adj. his own old Line; 12 Jan 1747/48, p.165. £1.S5.

HUGH MILLER, 222 acs. Brunswick Co. on both sides of the south Fork of Polcat Cr., adj. Hugh Moor; 12 Jan 1747/48, p.166. £1.S5.

JOSEPH WESTMORLAND, 6 acs. Pr. Geo. Co. on the N side of Nottoway Riv., adj. his own Lines & Jos. Wall; 12 Jan 1747/48, p.168. 5 Shill.

JOHN HILL, 150 acs. Amelia Co. on the Head Brs. of the Great Bent Run, adj. Jacob Seay & Gillington; 12 Jan 1747/48, p.169. 15 Shill.

JOHN KING, 200 acs. Amelia Co. on both sides of Falling Cr., adj. Culwell; 12 Jan 1747/48, p.171. £1.

ANDREW MCCOMB /MCCOMBE, 173 acs. Augusta Co. adj. Thomas Waterson; 12 Jan 1747/48, p.172. £1.

JOHN WILLIAMSON, 200 acs. Pr. Geo. Co. on the lower side of Turkey Egg Cr., adj. George Booth & Bartlott; 12 Jan 1747/48, p.174. £1.

BAXTER DAVIS, 243 acs. Pr. Geo. Co. on the N side of Buckskin Cr.; adj. Jones Williams, Stark & Tabb; 12 Jan 1747/48, p.176. £1.S5.

ROBERT MARTIN, 400 acs. Amelia Co. at the Head of Falling Cr., by a Spring; 12 Jan 1747/48, p.177. £2.

SAMPSON ARCHER, 380 acs. Augusta Co. on Andersons Br. at the Elk Meadow; 5 Mar 1747/48, p.179. £2.

ARCHIBALD HAMILTON, 110 acs. Augusta Co. on the Head of a Draught running into the L. of one Givens, on the W side of a Road; 5 Mar 1747/48, p.180. 15 Shill.

ROBERT POAGE, 263 acs. Augusta Co. on Catapa Cr. at the End of the Cross Mountain at a Place called the *Fork Bottom*, in the Mouth of a Hollow; 5 Mar 1747/48, p.181. £1.S10.

ROBERT POAGE, 350 acs. Augusta Co. on a Br. of James Riv. called Catapa in a Place called *the Indian Camp*, Beg. on the SE side of the sd Catapa Cr. opposite to the mouth of Holstons Br.; 5 Mar 1747/48, p.183. £1.S15.

MATTHEW THOMPSON & MATTHEW THOMPSON JUNR., 316 acs. Augusta Co. on Stoney Lick Br., on a naked Hill, near the L. of William Lamb, on a Ridge; 5 Mar 1747/48, p.185. £1.S15.

NICHOLAS DAVIES, 167 acs. Albemarle Co. on the N side the Fluvanna, at Wilderness Run; 5 Mar 1747/48, p.186. £1. [p.188-p.189 skipped by the Scribe].

NICHOLAS DAVIES, 1,755 acs. Albemarle Co. on the Brs. of Ivey Cr. of the Fluvanna Riv.; 5 Mar 1747/48, p.190. £9.

NICHOLAS DAVIES, 100 acs. Albemarle Co. on both sides of Licking Hole Br. being a south fork of Porrige Cr., bet. Braxtons & Bollings Grants; 5 Mar 1747/48, p.192. 10 Shill.

NICHOLAS DAVIES, 203 acs. Albemarle Co. on the S side of the Fluvanna; 5 Mar 1747/48, p.193. £1.

NICHOLAS DAVIES, 235 acs. Albemarle Co. on the N side of the Fluvanna, Beg. below Hollowing point on the N side the Riv.; 5 Mar 1747/48, p.195. £1.S5.

WILLIAM STITH, 1,172 acs. Albemarle Co. on the Brs. of Ivey Cr. of the Fluvanna; 5 Mar 1747/48, p.197. £6.

WILLIAM STITH, 555 acs. Albemarle Co. on both sides of Judiths Cr. and on the S side of Fluvanna; 5 Mar 1747/48, p.199. £3.

WILLIAM STITH, 939 acs. Albemarle Co. on both sides of Tomahauk Sw., at the south fork of sd Sw.; 5 Mar 1747/48, p.201. £4.S15.

JOHN DAVIS, 350 acs. Augusta Co. on Mossey Cr. & on both sides of the north Riv. of Shanando, on a Bank opposite to an Island thence down the Island crossing the Riv.,

on the Riv. opposite to the round Hill, adj. Hugh Diver; 5 Mar 1747/48, p.203. £1.S15.

WILLIAM ANDERSON, 400 acs. Augusta Co. on the S side of the Middle Riv. of Shanando called Catheys Cr., adj. another Tract of L. belonging to the sd Anderson; 5 Mar 1747/48, p.205. £2.

WILLIAM DOWNES, 200 acs. Augusta Co. on the N side of Shanando Riv., crossing Stovers Mill Cr., near the L. of William Lamb; 5 Mar 1747/48, p.206. for 5 Shillings also for and in Consideration of the Imp. of 3 pers. whose Names are *John Blower, Mary Blower & Jane Blower.*

ANDREW EREWIN, 94 acs. Augusta Co. on a Br. of the North Riv. of Shanando called Long Glade Cr., adj. William Magill & the L. sd Erewin now lives on; 5 Mar 1747/48, p.208. 10 Shill.

FRANCIS PINCHER, 236 acs. Augusta Co. on Muddy Cr., Beg. on a Br. above a field, in a Hollow; 5 Mar 1747/48, p.210. £1.S5.

EDWARD ERVIN, 220 acs. Augusta Co. adj. William Brown & John Anderson; 5 Mar 1747/48, p.212. £1.S5.

THOMAS WALKER, 108 acs. Orange Co. below the Blue Ridge of Mountains, Beg. on the point of a Mountain, on the side of a

Mountain by a spring Br.; 5 Mar 1747/48, p.213. 15 Shill.

CHARLES CAMPBELL, 100 acs. Augusta Co. on the S side of Beverly Mannor on Hammocks Br. on the S side of the L. the sd Charles Campbell now lives on, Beg. on the Mannor L., near a small Meadow, adj. Francis Beaty; 5 Mar 1747/48, p.215. 10 shill.

MORISH OFREEL, 188 acs. Augusta Co. on a Br. of Catheys Riv. called McClures Run; adj. the said Morish OFreel, Samuel Wallace & James Bell; 5 Mar 1747/48, p.216. £1.

THOMAS FOSH, 269 acs. Augusta Co. on the W side the Blue Ridge, up Goose Cr., on an Ivy point; 5 Mar 1747/48, p.218. £1.S10.

THOMAS CLANTON, Son and Heir of Edward Clanton dec'd, 1,710 acs. Brunswick Co. on the N side of Pea Hill Cr.; 5 Mar 1747/48, p.220. £8.S15. 760 acs. part formerly gtd. Henry Beddingfield junr. by Pat. 16 Jun 1727 [PB 13 p.113] and by a Judgement of our General Court bearing date 30 Oct 1736 the sd L. for want of Cultiv. and Improv. according to Law and the condition of the sd former pat. is adjudged to be forfeited and vested again in us.

WILLIAM SNODGRAS, 400 acs. Augusta Co. on a sinking spring Br. of Cataubo Cr.; 5 Mar 1747/48, p.222. £2.

ROBERT SCOTT, 157 acs. Augusta Co. on stoney Lick Br. below the L. of Jacob Thomas, to the Head of a Briery Hollow; 5 Mar 1747/48, p.223. £1.

ABRAHAM BAILEY, 450 acs. Henrico Co. along Almonds Creek; adj. Herbert, Cocke, Colonel Randolph, Henry Cox, Mayo & Alday; 5 Mar 1747/48, p.225. £2.S5.

JOHN WILKINS MARSHALL, 186 acs. Lunenburg Co. on both sides of Cubb Creek, down a Fork; 5 Mar 1747/48, p.227. £1.

NATHANIEL BARLOW, 350 acs. Surry Co. on the N side of the three Creeks, down the Great Plowman Sw., adj. James Bass; 5 Mar 1747/48, p.229. £1.S15.

THOMAS LEE, 300 acs. Amelia Co. on both sides of Natts Br. on the N side of Vaughans Cr.; 5 Mar 1747/48, p.231. £1.S10.

JOHN NEVILL, 403 acs. Amelia Co. on the S side of Mallorys Cr.; adj. Watson, Yarbrough & Edward Roberson; 5 Mar 1747/48, p.232. £2.

ABRAHAM BAILEY, 21 acs. Henrico Co. crossing the Mirey Run; adj. his old Line & Charles Ballow; 5 Mar 1747/48, p.234. 5 Shill.

JOHN ALLDAY, 400 acs. Henrico Co. along Tom Fields Cr., to Arthurs Run; adj. Cock, Herbert & Mayo; 5 Mar 1747/48, p.236.

JOSHUA PERRY, 115 acs., Is. of Wight Co. on the N side of Meherrin Riv.; adj. Henry Harris, Jacob Harris, the sd Joshua Perrys other L., William Wiggs & Simon Turner; 5 Mar 1747/48, p.237. £15.

THOMAS CRENSHAW, 100 acs. Is. of Wight Co. on the S side of Nottoway Riv., down the Run of Arthurs Sw., adj. Samuel Boazman; 5 Mar 1747/48, p.239. 10 Shill.

MARY BOYKIN, 50 acs. Is. of Wight Co. on the N side of Meherin Riv., adj. James Turner & sd Boykins (her) own old line; 5 Mar 1747/48, p.241. 5 Shill.

WILLIAM BOWER, 160 acs. Is. of Wight Co. on the N side of the Flatt Sw., by the side of a small Marsh, adj. James Ramsey & John Clements; 5 Mar 1747/48, p.243. £1.

RICHARD AVERY, 135 acs. Surry Co. on the N side of Meherin Riv.; 5 Mar 1747/48, p.245. 15 Shill. Whereas by pat. 22 Feb 1724/25 gtd. William Wyche since dec'd [PB 12 p.154] And Whereas William Edmunds and Judith his Wife, Daughter and Heir of the sd William Wyche have failed to make Cultiv. and improv.; and Richard Avery hath made humble Suit and hath obtained a G. for the same. [This L. was in Brunswick Co., now Greensville Co.]

JAMES MITCHELL, 200 acs. Amelia Co. on the lower side of Flatt Cr. and on both sides of Tomahawke Br. opposite to Philip Jones's L., adj. Robert Vaughan; 5 Mar 1747/48, p.247. £1. Whereas by pat. 10 Jan 1735/36 gtd. John Elam [PB 16 p.473] And Whereas the sd John Elam hath failed to make Cultiv. & Improv. and John Leonard hath made humble Suit and hath obtained a G. the same which he hath assigned unto James Mitchell.

PHILIP POINDEXTER, 400 acs. Goochland Co. at the Head of Muddy Cr.; adj. Jacob Winfrey, Samuel Allen, William May, John Robinson & Samuel Nuckolls; 5 Mar 1747/48, p.249. Which sd L. was formerly gtd. Francis Stegar by pat. 12 Feb 1742/43 [PB 21 p.191] and on the petition of the sd Francis Stegar to our Lieutenant Governor and Council the 4th day of May 1745 a new pat. for the sd L. was ordered to be gtd. the sd Francis Stegar who hath assigned all his Right and Title to the same to Foliet Power and the sd Power hath assigned the same unto the sd Philip Poindexter.

WILLIAM KILLEBREW, 95 acs. Is. of Wight Co. on the S side of Cocks Sw., by the side of Black Point Br., adj. the sd Killebrews other L. & Samuel Lucy; 5 Mar 1747/48, p.250. 10 Shill.

WILLIAM WOMMACK, 105 acs. Is. of Wight Co. on the N side of Meherin Riv., by the Co. Line bet. Is. of Wight and Surry [N60°E];

adj. Edward Lund, William Wommack Senior, John Nanny & Colo. Richard Bland; 5 Mar 1747/48, p.252. 15 Shill.

ROBERT BREAKINRIDGE, 200 acs. Brunswick Co. on both sides of the south Fork of Meherin Riv.; 5 Mar 1747/48, p.255. £1.

BENJAMIN HARRIS, 699 acs. Louisa Co. on both sides of Hickory Cr., Beg. at Dumas & Browns former C., on the Orphans Line [Orphans of Hugh Owen], adj. Benjamin Brown; 5 Mar 1747/48, p.256. £1.S10. The sd L. being formerly gtd. Jeremiah Dumas by pat. 28 Sep 1728 [PB 13 p.468] for 400 acs. but upon a Survey lately made by Robert Harris Surveyor of sd Co. is found to contain 699 acs. the Right & Title of which is since become vested in the sd Benjamin Harris.

ROBERT BREAKINRIDGE, 187 acs. Brunswick Co. on the N side of the south fork of Meherin Riv.; 5 Mar 1747/48, p.259. £1.

JOSEPH COLLINS, 250 acs. Brunswick Co. on both sides of the north fork of Panter Cr.; 5 Mar 1747/48, p.260. £1.S5.

JOSEPH COLLINS, 72 acs. Brunswick Co. on the S side of Staunton Riv. opposite to the Long Island on both sides of the Mouth of Straitstone Cr.; 5 Mar 1747/48, p.262. 10 Shill.

DAVID KINKEAD, 400 acs. Albemarle Co. on the Brs. of

Stocktons Br. of Mechums Riv., adj. David Stockton & Charles Lynch; 5 Mar 1747/48, p.264. £2.

RICHARD AVERY, 790 acs. Surry Co. on the S side of Nottoway Riv., up the Indian Br., crossing the Great Br., by the side of a Pond; adj. his own former Survey, Thomas Briggs, his old L. ptd. by William Lee, Capt. Henry Harrison, his new Survey & William Andrew; 5 Mar 1747/48, p.266. £2.S5. 300 acs. part formerly gtd. William Lee by pat. 9 Jul 1724 [PB 12 p.103] since become vested in the sd Avery, 75 acs. other part formerly gtd. the sd Avery by pat. 15 Mar 1741/42 [PB 20 p.218] and 415 acs. the Residue never bef. gtd. [Included in Cereal Avery's 1,234½ acs. Sussex Co. in Grant Book V p.542 dated 2 Dec 1785]

DANIEL MAUPIN, 400 acs. Albemarle Co. on both sides Moremans Riv., adj. Charles Moreman; 5 Apr 1748, p.269. £2.

GEORGE BRAXTON, 41 acs. Parish of [St.] Stephen, K. & Q. Co. adj. Thomas Watts, Mr Birds, the sd Braxton, Morgan Cormer /Conner, & Bushel; 5 Apr 1748, p.270. 5 Shill.

LAZARUS DAMREL, 212 acs. Albemarle Co. on the N side of the Fluvanna Riv.; adj. his line; 5 Apr 1748, p.271. £1.S5.

JAMES FREELAND, 200 acs. Albemarle Co. on the N side of

James Riv. on both sides of Elk Island Cr.; 5 Apr 1748, p.273. £1.

EDWARD LOVELY, 210 acs. Albemarle Co. on the south Br. of Moors Cr. called the Plumb Orchard, cross the Plumb Orchard Br.; adj. Joseph Anthony, Daniel Jones, John Carter Esqr. dec'd & Patrick Nowlin; 5 Apr 1748, p.274. £1.S5.

THOMAS WATTS, 400 acs. Albemarle Co. on the Brs. of Pedlar Riv., in a Valley; 5 Apr 1748, p.276. £2.

JOSEPH CHILDRES, 200 acs. Albemarle Co. on the N side of the Fluvanna, up Rockhouse Cr., crossing the main Road, adj. Major Allen Howard; 5 Apr 1748, p.277. £1.

PETER BROOKS, 400 acs. Albemarle Co. on the Brs. of Appomattox Riv.; adj. the sd Brooks Line, Joseph Dabbs & Obediah Woodson; 5 Apr 1748, p.279. £2.

PETER BROOKS, 1,737 acs. Albemarle Co. on the Brs. of Appamattox Riv., crossing Mallorys Br.; adj. Anderson, Dabbs, John Hodnet, Thomas Bows, Elkanah Anderson & Charles Anderson; 5 Apr 1748, p.280. £2.S15. 392 acs. formerly gtd. the sd Peter Brooks by pat. 30 Jun 1743 [PB 21 p.398], 400 acs. other part also gtd. unto the sd Brooks by pat. bearing the same day [PB 21 p.390] and 400 acs. other part being also gtd. unto the

sd Brooks by pat. 5 Jun 1746 [PB 25 p.90] and 545 acs. the residue never bef. gtd.

FREDERICK BLAKE, 400 acs. Amelia Co. on the upper side of Sandy Riv., adj. Hudson & Harrison; 5 Apr 1748, p.282. £2.

BARTHOLOMEW ZACHARY, 800 acs. Amelia Co. on both sides of the Mill Fork of Vaughans Cr., adj. Charles Hudson; 5 Apr 1748, p.284. £4.

THOMAS FLEAKE, 120 acs. Amelia Co. on the upper side of the Great Br. of the Middle Seller Cr., adj. Arthur Leath & Rany; 5 Apr 1748, p.285. 15 Shill.

JOHN WATKINS, 400 acs. Amelia Co. on the S side Appomattox Riv.; adj. Sadler, Foster, Ruffin & Nash; 5 Apr 1748, p.287. £2.

THOMAS JONES, 203 acs. Amelia Co. on the N side of Sandy Cr.; adj. Abraham Hurt, Quarles & Crawford; 5 Apr 1748, p.289. £1.

ARTHUR LEATH, 336 acs. Amelia Co. on the S side of the long Br. of Harricane Sw., up the forked Br.; adj. Charles Williamson, Ledbiter Jones & Bridgeforth; 5 Apr 1748, p.290. £1.S15.

JAMES CAMPBELL, 267 acs. Augusta Co. on the W side of Roanoak above a place on sd Riv. called *Arthurs Bottom*, by a Gully, by a Meadow at the foot of a

Stoney Hill; 5 Apr 1748, p.292. £1.S10.

WILLIAM CARVINE, 174 acs. Augusta Co. on the Waters of Roanoak; 5 Apr 1748, p.293. £1.

WILLIAM CARVINE, 252 acs. Augusta Co. on the Waters of Roanoak; 5 Apr 1748, p.295. £1.S5.

FRANCIS REILEY, 334 acs. Augusta Co. on the E side of Woods Riv. below the Mouth of the Little Riv. and joining on Marquis Calmees; 5 Apr 1748, p.296. £1.S15.

FRANCIS REILEY, 100 acs. Augusta Co. on a Br. of Woods Riv. called the Little Riv., at the foot of a Ridge; 5 Apr 1748, p.298. 10 Shill.

EPHRAIM VAUSE/VANSE, 243 acs. Augusta Co. on the south Br. of Roanoak; 5 Apr 1748, p.299. £1.S5.

JOHN MILLS, 300 acs. Augusta Co. on Buffalo Cr. on the W side the Blue Ridge, to 3 Locust Trees standing in *Little Hell*; 5 Apr 1748, p.301. £1.S10.

JOHN STEPHENSON, 262 acs. Augusta Co., Beg. in a Bottom by a Br. of Buffalo; 5 Apr 1748, p.302. £1.S10.

SAMUEL PORTER, 300 acs. Augusta Co. below the Fork of Buffalo Cr.; 5 Apr 1748, p.304. £1.S10.

ERWIN PATTERSON, 381 acs. Augusta Co. on a Br. of Mill Cr., Beg. on a Ridge bet. Mill Cr. and Ann Salleys Hill, in a Hollow, near a Meadow; 5 Apr 1748, p.305. £2.

JAMES MOOR, 325 acs. Augusta Co. on the NE side of the north Br. of James Riv. below the Mouth of the south Riv., on the side of a piney Hill, below the End of an Island, adj. Bordens great Tract; 5 Apr 1748, p.307. £1.S15.

ROBERT POAGE, 380 acs. Augusta Co. on the W side of the Blue Ridge and on a Br. of James Riv. called Catapa above a tract of L. surveyed for Stephen Holston, at the Mouth of a Hollow on the E side of the Cr. and along the Mountains foot; 5 Apr 1748, p.309. £2.

JOSHUA HICKMAN, 100 acs. Augusta Co. on the S side of the north Riv. of Shanando below the Fork; 5 Apr 1748, p.310. 10 Shill.

JOHN WATSON, 330 acs. Amelia Co. on the lower side of Buffalo /Buffilo Riv.; adj. Joseph Morton, his own Lines & Randolph; 5 Apr 1748, p.311a. £1.S15.

ROBERT FRAZIER, 228 acs. Augusta Co. crossing Collins Br., in a Hollow, adj. Beard; 5 Apr 1748, p.312. £1.S5.

EDWARD ERVIN, 350 acs. Augusta Co. adj. the widow Patterson; 5 Apr 1748, p.315. £1.S15.

JOHN FRANCIS, 217 acs. Augusta Co. on a Br. of Catheys Riv. called Andersons Br., adj. William Anderson; 5 Apr 1748, p.317. £1.S5.

JAMES BENNIT, 404 acs. Brunswick Co. on both sides of Rocky Run; 5 Apr 1748, p.318. £2.

EADE SMITH, 300 acs. Brunswick Co. on the S side of Meherrin Riv., up the Occonechy Sw., up the Wolf Pitt Br.; adj. Mason, Wallis, his own Line, Williams Batts & Stroud; 5 Apr. 1748, p.320. 10 Shill. 140 acs. part formerly gtd. Roger Smith by pat. 7 Jul 1726 [PB 12 p.536], 100 acs. other part formerly gtd. William Stroud by pat. 13 Nov 1721 [Surry Co., PB 11 p.71] the Right & Title of which sd 2 parcels of L. is since become vested in the sd Eade Smith and 60 acs. the Residue never bef. gtd. [Roger Smith's 140 acs. was on the old Co. Line between Surry Co. & Is. of Wight Co., later to be the Co. Line between Brunswick Co. & Is. of Wight Co.]

JOHN ROBERSON JUNR., 190 acs. Brunswick Co. on the N side of Roan Oak Riv., adj. Matthew Roberson & John Eastland; 5 Apr 1748, p.322. £1.

JOHN DENNEY, 191 acs. Brunswick Co. on the N side Staunton Riv.; 5 Apr 1748, p.324. £1.

JOHN DENNEY, 150 acs. Brunswick Co. on the S side of Staunton Riv., down the sd Riv. & including Mush Island; 5 Apr 1748, p.325.

JOHN OBGUN, 104 acs. Brunswick Co. on the Brs. of Shining Cr.; adj. John Stith, Lemuel Lancer/Lanier, Jones & Ingram; 5 Apr 1748, p.327. 10 Shill.

JOHN DUGER, 337 acs. Brunswick Co. on the N side of the Great Cr., up Gravely Run, adj. Capt. John Brown & Abraham Brown (Abr a m Brown); 5 Apr 1748, p.329. £1.S15.

THOMAS DICKSON, 104 acs. Lunenburg Co. on the [N] side of Little Roanoak Riv., adj. Joseph Ward & his own Line; 5 Apr 1748, p.330. 10 Shill.

RICHARD PARR, 400 acs. Brunswick Co. on the N side of Waqua Cr., on the Rocky Run, on the Road; adj. White, Matthews, John Birch, Mirrick & Gillam; 4 Apr 1748, p.332. £2.

THOMAS POWELL, JUNIOR, 204 acs. Brunswick Co. on the S side of BedingFields Cr., adj. Henry Bedingfield; 5 Apr 1748, p.334. £1.

RICHARD WOMACK, 283 acs. Brunswick Co. on the Brs. of the middle Fork of Little Roan Oak Riv.; 5 Apr 1748, p.336. £1.S10.

JOHN OGBUN, 427 acs. Brunswick Co. on the S side of the Great Cr., in Spell's Mill Pond on the sd Cr., adj. James Jones & John Spell; 5 Apr 1748, p.337. £2.S5.

JOHN DAVIS, 104 acs. Augusta Co. on both sides of Mossey Cr.; 5 Apr 1748, p.339. 10 Shill.

JOHN CUNNINGHAM, 400 acs. Augusta Co. on a Br. of the North Riv. of Shanando called Thorney Br., Beg. on a Hill by second Fork, crossing several Drafts of sd Br. to a stone Ridge, adj. Abraham Smith; 5 Apr 1748, p.340. £2.

JOHN BUCHANAN, 360 acs. Augusta Co. on a Br. of Woods Riv. called Stroubles Br.; 5 Apr 1748, p.342. £2.

JOHN BUCHANAN, 100 acs. Augusta Co. on the N side of Woods Riv., Beg. at the foot of a Ridge; 5 Apr 1748, p.343. 10 Shill.

JOHN BOYD, 150 acs. Brunswick Co. on the S side of Dan Riv., adj. William Wynne; 5 Apr 1748, p.345. 15 Shill.

ABRAHAM BAKER, 180 acs. Lunenburg Co. in the Fork of Banister Riv., Beg. at the Mouth of Bearskin Cr., adj. Moses Echoles; 5 Apr 1748, p.347. £1.

ABRAHAM BAKER, 316 acs. Brunswick Co. on both sides of Banister Riv., adj. Ralph Elkins; 5 Apr 1748, p.348. £1.S15.

JACOB MCGEHEE, 400 acs. Amelia Co. on the N side of Bush Riv.; adj. Randolph, John Morton & Davis; 5 Apr 1748, p.350. £2.

ALEXANDER MCCONNELL, 268 acs. Lunenburg Co. on both sides Turnip Cr., adj. William Law & Cunningham; 5 Apr 1748, p.352. £1.S10.

JEREMIAH HATCHER, 177 acs. Lunenburg Co. on both sides of the south Fork of Meherrin/Maherrin Riv. 5 Apr 1748, p.353. £1.

SAMUEL HARRIS, 234 acs. Lunenburg Co. on the S side of Staunton Riv., adj. Cargil; 5 Apr 1748, p.355. £1.S5.

SAMUEL HARRIS, 252 acs. Lunenburg Co. on the N side of Stanton Riv. adj. his own Lines; 5 Apr 1748, p.357. £1.S5.

SAMUEL HARRIS, 353 acs. Lunenburg Co. on the N side of Stanton Riv., on Hogons Cr., adj. Byrds upper line & Munford; 5 Apr 1748, p.358. £1.S15.

SAMUEL HARRIS, 404 acs. Lunenburg Co. on the N side Stanton Riv., on Hogons's Cr., adj. Byrd & his own Lines; 5 Apr 1748, p.360. £2.

WILLIAM HARRIS, 70 acs. Lunenburg Co. in Stanton Riv. bet. Byrds Island & Cargils Island. 5 Apr 1748, p.363. 10 Shill. [This land is obviously another Island because there were no metes & bounds in the Pat.]

WILLIAM HOGON, 294 acs. Lunenburg Co. on the N side of Dan Riv.; 5 Apr 1748, p.364. £1.S10.

HENRY EMBRY, 237 acs. Lunenburg Co. on the N side of Couches Cr., adj. his own old Line; 5 Apr 1748; p.365. £1.S5.

CHARLES TALBOTT, 190 acs. Lunenburg Co. on both sides of Twittys Cr.; 5 Apr 1748, p.367. £1.

WILLIAM RANDOLPH, Gentleman, 202 acs. Lunenburg Co. on the N side of Stanton Riv., at the Mouth of Senaca Cr. thence down sd Riv. including 2 small Islands at the upper End of the Long Island. 5 Apr 1748, p.368. £1.

WILLIAM RANDOLPH, Gentleman, 378 acs. Lunenburg Co. on the N side of Stanton Riv., adj. Hills upper Line & his own Line; 5 Apr 1748, p.370. £2.

WILLIAM MOSS, 400 acs. Goochland Co. on both sides of Bear Garden Cr. of the Fluvanna Riv.; 5 Apr 1748, p.372. £2.

EDMUND BUTLER, 400 acs. Goochland Co. bet. Green Cr. and Badluck Br. of Appomattox Riv.; adj. Jacob Micheaux, Joseph Woodson, William Paterson, William Randolph Esqr. dec'd. & Philip Thomas; 5 Apr 1748, p.373. £2.

BENNET GOODE, 369 acs. Goochland Co. on the S side of James Riv., crossing the main Road, in the Head of a Br. of the upper Manikin Cr.; adj. his [Bennet Goode's], John Pleasant, Peter Chastain dec'd & James Holeman; 5 Apr 1748, p.375. £2.

JOSIAS CHAMBERS, 400 acs. Goochland Co. among the Brs. of Appomattox Riv., crossing Long Br.; adj. Sanbourn Woodson, Col. Richard Randolph & Jacob Micheaux; 5 Apr 1748, p.377. £2.

JOSEPH COLLINS, 142 acs. Brunswick Co. on the S side of Staunton Riv., Beg. on the Riv. opposite to an Island, adj. Abraham Echolds; 5 Apr 1748, p.379. 15 Shill.

THOMAS CUNNINGHAM, 295 acs. Lunenburg Co. on the N side of Childreys Cr., adj. William Cunningham; 5 Apr 1748, p.380. £1.S10.

WILLIAM CUNNINGHAM, 335 acs. Lunenburg Co. on the N side of Childreys Cr.; 5 Apr 1748, p.382. £1.S15.

WILLIAM CALDWELL, 280 acs. Lunenburg Co. on both sides of a Br. of Louse Cr.; 5 Apr 1748, p.383. £1.S10.

EDWARD ECHOLES, 548 acs. Amelia Co. on the Heads of Little Harricane and Burchen Swamps; adj. Ragsdell, Hugh Williams & his own Line; 5 Apr 1748, p.385. £2.S15.

ABRAHAM ECHOLES, 182 acs. Lunenburg Co. on both sides of Childreys Cr.; 5 Apr 1748, p.387-p.388-p.389. £1. [Double folio]

ROBERT WATHAN & ROBERT JENNINGS, 3,820 acs. Lunenburg Co. on both sides of Mortons Fork of Falling Riv., near the Petole Mountain [Pilot Mountain?], on Otter River Road, down Mortons Cr., adj. Bolling & Ornsby; 5 Apr 1748, p.389-p.388a-p.389a. £19.S5. [Double folio].

BENJAMIN LANIER, 368 acs. Brunswick Co. on both sides of Allens Cr., up the great Br.; 5 Apr 1748, p.389a-390. £2.

EDWARD JORDAN, 654 acs. Brunswick Co. on both sides of Couches Cr., down the great Br.; adj. Edward Calwell, Abraham Micheaux & Henry Embry; 5 Apr 1748, p.391. £3.S5.

FRANCIS GRYMES, 992 acs. Brunswick Co. on both sides of Cubb Cr., up Rough Cr., down Turkey Cocke/Cock Br.; adj. Terry, Wood Jones & Thomas Word; 5 Apr 1748, p.393. £5.

SARAH JONES, 404 acs. Brunswick Co. on the S side of the Great Cr.; adj. Edmunds, James Jones & John Brittle; 5 Apr 1748, p.395. £2.

ANTHONY GRIFFIN, 2,000 acs. Amelia Co. on the N side of Great Nottoway Riv., and on both sides the north fork thereof; adj. Collins, Carroll, Sil Johnson, his own old Line & Hudson; 5 Apr 1748, p.397. £6. 800 acs. part being part of a pat. for 1,600 acs. formerly gtd. Richard Echoles 15 Oct 1741 [PB 20 p.72], the Right & Title of which sd 800 acs. is since become vested in sd Anthony Griffin & 1,200 acs. the Residue never bef. gtd.

SIL JOHNSON, 934 acs. Amelia Co. on both sides of Snales Cr.; adj. Watson, Echoles & Griffin; 5 Apr 1748, p.399.

JOHN TRENT, 221 acs. Amelia Co. on the Head Brs. of Nammiseen Cr.; adj. Watson, Ornsby, Frederick Ford & Hinton; 5 Apr 1748, p.401. £1.S5.

HENRY LEE, 195 acs. Surry Co. on the S side of Nottoway Riv. and in the Fork of the great Ploughman Sw., Beg. at the Mouth of the western Br. of the sd Ploughman Sw. called Huckleberry Br., down the Run of the eastern Br. of the sd Plowman Sw., adj. Benjamin Adams; 5 Apr 1748, p.402. £1.

THOMAS WILKERSON JUNR., 365 acs. Surry Co. on the E side of Harrys Sw.; adj. Joseph Scouls, his own line, James Banks & James Cain; 5 Apr 1748, p.404. £2.

MATTHEW STURDIVANT, 330 acs. Surry Co. on the S side of Nottoway Riv., Beg. in the Cypress Sw., near the Edge of Cabbin Stick Sw., adj. John Williamson & Charles Partin; 5 Apr 1748, p.406. £1.S15.

JEREMIAH BULLOCK, 230 acs. Surry Co. on the S side of Nottoway Riv., down the Huckleberry Br.; adj. Edmund Pate, his own Lines, John Ellis & William Hix; 5 Apr 1748, p.407. £1.S5.

HENRY BARNES/BARNS, 350 acs. Surry Co. on the N side of Black Water, down the Drain of the Horse Meadow Br.; adj. William Andrews, Stephen Granthom & William Jordan; 5 Apr 1748, p.409. £1.S15.

WILLIAM BROWN, 795 acs. Surry Co. on the S side of Nottoway Riv., on the S side of the Spring Sw., down the Little Spring Sw.; adj. the sd Browns other L.; 5 Apr 1748, p.411. £2.S10. 295 acs. part of a pat. for 516 acs. formerly gtd. Francis Clements by Pat. 16 Jun 1714 [PB 10 p.184] and 500 acs. the residue never bef. gtd.

THOMAS COCKE, Gent., 300 acs. Surry Co. bet. Black Water and the Otterdam Swamps, on lower Wintecoc Br.; adj. his Otterdam Land, his *Wintecoc Land* & James Anderson; 5 Apr 1748, p.412. £1.S10.

WILLIAM EZELL, 215 acs. Surry Co. on N side of Nottoway Riv., Beg. in the Double Br., up Parkers Br., down the Long Br., by his own Lines; 5 Apr 1748, p.414. £1.S5 Shill.

THOMAS RAY, 497 acs. Spotsyl. Co. among the Brs. of Mattapony

Riv., on a Point, on the NE side of Robinson Run; adj. Obediah Howerton, Mr John Anderson, William Howerton, Henry Rice, Thomas Foster & Taliaferro Craigg; 5 Apr 1748, p.415. £2.S10. Whereas by pat. 20 July 1738 gtd. unto Thomas Wisdom [PB 18 p.70] And Whereas the sd Wisdom hath failed to make Cultiv. & improv. and Thomas Ray having made humble Suit & hath obtained a G. for the same.

ALEXANDER BOLLING, 1,972 acs. Pr. Geo. Co. on both sides of Buckskin Cr., down Highs Br.; adj. David Walker, John Roberson, Harwell, Abernathy & the old line of Stith Bolling dec'd; 5 Apr 1748, p.417. £3.S5. 1,340 acs. part formerly gtd. unto Stith Bolling dec'd. Father of the sd Alexander Bolling by pat. 22 June 1722 [PB 11 p.123] which is now become vested in sd Alexander as son and Heir of sd Stith Bolling and 632 acs. the Residue never bef. gtd.

ROBERT WHITEHALL, 18½ acs. Pr. Geo. Co. on the N side of Buckskin Cr.; adj. Tabb, Davis & Stark; 5 Apr 1748, p.420. 5 Shill.

WILLIAM PARRUM, 216 acs. Pr. Geo. Co. on both sides of the Reedy Br. of Sappone; adj. John Williams, Avery, Haukins, Thompson, & Isaac Tucker; 5 Apr 1748, p.421. £1.S5.

JOHN HAWKINS/HAUKINS, 300 acs. Pr. Geo. Co. on both sides of the Lower Rocky Run; adj. James Burrows, Fields, Edward Haukins

& Keith; 5 Apr 1748, p.423.
£1.S10

GABRIEL HARRISON, 143 acs.
Pr. Geo. Co. on the N side of
Nottoway Riv.; adj. his own line,
John High & Hardaway;
5 Apr 1748, p.425.

JOSEPH TUCKER, 138 acs. Pr.
Geo. Co. at the head of the Mirey
Br. of Beaver Pond Cr.; adj. Peter
Thomas, Tucker, Gerrald &
Jackson; 5 Apr 1748, p.427. 15
Shill.

ABRAHAM COCKE & CHARLES
JENNINGS, 354 acs. Pr. Geo. Co.
on the lower side of Georges Br. of
Nammiseen Cr., Beg. on the
Horsepen Br.; adj. William
Featherstone junr., William
Featherstone Senr., Richard
Taylor, Eppes, John Eppes &
Henry Cabbinis; 5 Apr 1748,
p.428. £1.S15.

BENJAMIN PORTER, 400 acs.
Orange Co. on the S Brs. of the
south fork of Rappidan Riv., Beg.
on the W side of a Br. about 60
poles above a great Stone marked
$^+_8$, on the Mountain side, adj. Mr
Anthony Thornton; 5 Apr 1748,
p.429. for 10 Shill. also for the
Imp. of 6 pers. whose Names are
*Humphrey Wallace, John Lynch,
William Gibbins, Thomas Piner,
Thomas Howson & William Kelly.*
[Note the reference to the *Octonia
Stone*. This land was referred to as
John Christopher's in James
Wood's 200 acs. in PB 18 p.363
dated 22 Sep 1739]

JOHN DAVIS JUNR., 215 acs.
Surry Co. on the N side of
Nottoway Riv.; adj. Ralph Rachel,
Richard Pepper, himself, his
fathers Line, John Woodard &
Nathaniel Chamblis; 5 Apr 1748,
p.431. £1.S5.

[There is a very large blot in the
following document. The inferred
text is indicated by brackets]

HENRY ROBINSON, 1,000 acs.
King William Co., on the S side of
Mattopony/Mattapony Riv., in the
Lowgrounds of Herring Cr.; adj.
Major Barclay, Colo. Grymes &
Mr Bell; 5 Apr 1748, p.433. for 2
lbs. of Tobacco for every Acre of
the sd L. Whereas by Inqui[sition
indented taken in the Co. of] King
William 28 Mar [17]45 by Virtue
of a Warrant directed to John
Robin[son Escheator] of sd Co. It
appears that Elizabeth Beverley
died [seised of a certain] parcel of
L. containing 1,061 acs. [more or
less but a] Survey thereof lately
made by Benjamin Winslow
Surveyor [for the] sd [Cou]nty is
found to contain but 1,000 acs.
which is found to escheat to [us]
from the sd Elizabeth Beverley And
whereas Henry Robinson hath made
humble Suit and obtained a G. for
the Same. [This Land was
probably part of Edmund Jenings'
patents]

ADAM OVERBY, 127 acs. Pr.
Geo. Co. on the N side of White
Oak Sw.; adj. Harris, Taylor &
Merrimoon; 5 Apr 1748, p.434.
15 Shill.

WILLIAM TURNER, 225 acs. Pr. Geo. Co. on S side of Stoney Cr.; adj. Robert Wynn, Smith, Thompson, his own old Line, Robert Jones & Thomas Wynn; 5 Apr 1748, p.436. £1.S5.

JOHN HIGH JUNR., 36 acs. Pr. Geo. Co. on the Licking Place Br. on the N side of Nottoway Riv.; adj. his father, Roberson, Richard Wall & Westmoreland; 5 Apr 1748, p.438. 5 Shill.

STEPHEN DEWEY, 408 acs. Pr. Geo. Co. on the N side of White Oak Sw., by the Road; adj. Jordan, his own old Line, James Hall, Stell, & Roger Moor; 5 Apr 1748, p.439. £2.S5. 108 acs. part formerly gtd. Robert Davis by pat. 13 Nov 1721 [PB 11 p.78] which for want of Cultiv. and Improv. on the petition of sd Stephen Dewey was by Judgment of the General Court 21 Apr 1744 adjudged to be forfeited and vested again in us.

THEOPHILUS FIELD, 780 acs. Pr. Geo. Co. on the upper side of Stoney Cr., adj. Edward Hawkins, his own old Line of the L. purchased of Lovit, James Burrows, Walker & Keith; 5 Apr 1748, p.441. £3. 200 acs. part formerly gtd. John Lovit by pat. 17 Aug 1733 [PB 15 p.103] the Right & Title of which is since become vested in the sd Field and 580 acs. the residue never bef. gtd.

RICHARD AVERY, 154 acs. Pr. Geo. Co. on the Lower side of the lower Rocky Run, in the Head of the Reedy Br.; adj. Thompson,

Hawkins & Keeth; 5 Apr 1748, p.443. 5 Shill. 100 acs. formerly gtd. unto the sd Richard Avery by pat. 5 Jun 1746 [PB 24 p.252] & 54 acs. the Residue never bef. gtd.

WILLIAM EDWARDS, 100 acs. Is. of Wight Co. on the S side of Nottoway Riv., adj. his [John Vick's] old Land; 5 Apr 1748, p.445. 10 Shill. Whereas by pat. 22 Feb 1724/25 [PB 12 p.215] gtd. John Vick since dec'd And whereas John Vick (in whom the Right of the sd L. became vested as Son and Heir at Law of the sd John Vick dec'd) hath failed to make Cultiv. & Improv. and William Edwards having petitioned the Lieutenant Governor and Commander in Chief of the sd Colony & Dominion and hath obtained a G. for the same.

JOHN BOLLING, Gent., 3,026½ acs. Albemarle Co. crossing the Fluvanna Riv. & crossing Slippery Gutt, on the River Bank below a Clift of Rocks, crossing Possom Cr., on the Ridge; 20 Jul 1748, p.446. 5 Shill. 2,980 acs. part formerly gtd. unto the sd John Bolling by pat. 23 Jul 1745 [PB 22 p.289] and 46½ acs. the Residue never bef. gtd.

JOHN BOLLING, Gent., 6,740 acs. Albemarle Co. on the Brs. of Willis's Cr., Beg. in a Meadow, crossing the Mountain Cr.; adj. Ridgway, Anthony Sheroon, on Susanna Carner, Richard Gwin, Alexander Stinson & George Kleinhooff; 20 Jul 11748, p.449.-p.450-p.450a. £2.S15. (6,300 acs. part formerly gtd. unto sd John

Bolling by pat. 5 Nov 1743 [PB 23 p.615] and 400 acs. the Residue never bef. gtd.)

JOHN HARRISON, 178 acs. Nansemond Co. near Butlers Pocoson; adj. his own Line, William Butler & John King; 20 Jul 1748, p.450a-p.452-p.453. £1. [no p.451]

PETER HUDSON, 366 acs. Henrico Co. adj. Francis Farley, Laprad, Henry Hudson, John Bowman, Abraham Bowman, Tanner & Countis; 20 Jul 1748, p.453-p.452a. £2.

JAMES ATWOOD, 1,765 acs. Amelia Co. on both sides of Little Bryer Riv.; adj. Martin, Elisha Eastis, Davis, Cobb, Watson & his own old Line; 20 Jul 1748, p.453a-p.454-p.455. £7. (400 acs. part formerly gtd. unto the sd James Atwood by pat. 20 Mar 1745/46 [PB 24 p.211] and 1,365 acs. the residue never bef. gtd.

JOHN PLEASANTS, 1,200 acs. Goochland Co. on Angola Cr. of Appomattox Riv., Beg. near the N side of a Br. of Green Cr., adj. William Randolph Esqr.; 20 Jul 1748, p.455. £3.S10. the sd L. having been formerly gtd. unto the sd John Pleasants by pat. 15 Aug 1737 [PB 17 p.405] and 700 acs. Part thereof upon the petition of Richard Ward for want of Cultiv. and Improv. by Judgment of the General Court bearing date 18 Oct 1746 was adjudged to be forfeited and vested again in us and for reasons mentioned in an Order of

our Lieutenant Governor and Council bearing date 20 Oct 1747 a new pat. for the sd 1,200 aces was ordered to be gtd. to the sd John Pleasants.

JOHN ORNSBY, Clk., 4,154 acs. Amelia Co. on both sides of Nottoway Road bet. the Brs. of Deep Cr. and the Brs. of Tommahitton Sw., up the Great Br., by Cocks road, up Mingos Horsepen Br., along the County Line [North], crossing Butterwood Sw., up the Middle Seller Cr.; adj. Francis Raney, Benjamin Simmons, Fleak, Arthur Leeth, George Ford, William Thomas, Haynes, Frederick Ford, William Ford, Bland, & Chisolm/Chisolin; 20 Jul 1748, p.457. 4,054 part acs. formerly gtd. the sd John Ornsby by pat. 20 Aug 1743 [30 Aug 1743, PB 23 p.574] and 100 acs. the Residue also formerly gtd. the sd John Ornsby by pat. 30 Aug 1743 [PB 23 p.571].

NICHOLAS DAVIES & THOMAS TURPIN, Church Wardens of the Parish of Southam in Goochland Co. for a Glebe, 340 acs. in sd Co. on the S side of James Riv.; adj. William Mayo, William Randolph Esq., Thomas Williamson, Richard Williamson & George Hudspeath; 10 Jul 1748, p.460. the sd L. was gtd. unto William Randolph & George Carrington former Church Wardens of sd Parish of Southam by pat. 3 Jun 1745 [PB 23 p.859] and by order of our Lieutenant Governor and Council dated 17 Apr 1748 a new pat. was ordered to be gtd. to the sd Nicholas Davies and

Thomas Turpin. To have hold ... unto the sd Nicholas Davies and Thomas Turpin and to their Successors, the Church Wardens of the sd par. of Southam for the Time being, forever to be set apart for a Glebe to the only use and Behoof of the Minister of the sd par. and his Successors forever.

STEPHEN DEWEY, Gent., 400 acs. Amelia Co. on the N side of great Nottoway Riv., Beg. on the Riv. below the Falls, adj. Evans; 20 Jul 1748, p.462. £2.

EDWARD MACKGEHEE, 5,798 acs. Amelia Co. bet. Bush & Bryer Rivers, on the N side of Mortons Cr.; adj. Randolph, Cottrell, Woodson, Morton, Rud, Dickens & Brown; 20 Jul 1748, p.464. £15. 2,830 acs. part formerly gtd. unto the sd Edward Mackgehee by pat. 15 Oct 1741 [PB 24 p.594] and 2,968 acs. the Residue never bef. gtd.

JOHN WATSON, 404 acs. Amelia Co. on the lower side of Little Buffalo; adj. his own, Walthall, Mullins, Randolph & Gross; 20 Jul 1748, p.466. £2.

WILLIAM RAINS, 400 acs. Amelia Co. on the lower side of the Seller Cr., by the Road; adj. Williams, Moor, Leath, Ornsby, Isham Eppes & Francis Eppes; 20 Jul 1748, p.468. £2.

CALEB BAKER, 304 acs. Amelia Co. on the S side of the South fork of Buffalo Riv., adj. Gillespie &

Bartlet Anderson; 20 Jul 1748, p.470. £1.S10.

JAMES DYER, 200 acs. Amelia Co. on the lower side of the Lower Fork of Sandy Riv., adj. Daniel Hamlin; 10 Jul 1748, p.471. £1.

JOHN MORRISON, 203 acs. Amelia Co. in the Fork of Spring Cr.; adj. Thomas Baldwin, Douglas Baker & Collins; 20 Jul 1748, p.473. £1.

JAMES HUDSON, 403 acs. Amelia Co. on the S side of Little Nottoway Riv., by a Pond; adj. Johnson, Yarbrough, Jones, Ellis, Major Waller & Cabinis; 20 Jul 1748, p.474. £2.

PETER GUERRANT, 400 acs. Amelia Co. on the lower side of Mountain Cr.; adj. Smith, Collins & Davison; 20 Jul 1748, p.476. £2.

JOHN MAY, 304 acs. Amelia Co. on the S side of Appomattox Riv.; adj. Baldwin, Randolph & Venable; 20 Jul 1748, p.478. £1.S10.

ELISHA EASTIS, 400 acs. Amelia Co. bet. Bush & Bryer Rivers; adj. Rud, his own Line, Atwood, Davis & Macgehee; 20 Jul 1748, p.479. £2.

PATRICK GILLESPIE, 400 acs. Amelia Co. on both sides of the Great Br. on the S side of the South Fork of Buffalo Riv., adj. Richey & Anderson; 20 Jul 1748, p.481. £2.

CHARLES LEWIS, 400 acs. Amelia Co. on the Head Brs. of Yarbroughs Run in the fork of Nottoway Riv.; adj. Johnson, Ellis, Evans & Bumpas; 20 Jul 1748, p.483. £2.

BRYAN FANNING, 280 acs. Amelia Co. on the Head of the Burchen Sw.; adj. Robert Cryer, his own old line, Tabb, Stanly & Ragsdell; 20 Jul 1748, p.484. £1.S10.

JOHN RAGSDELL, JUNIOR, 180 acs. Amelia Co. on the Head Brs. of Burchen Sw. & Tommahitton Sw.; adj. Grigg, Stanly & John Ragsdell; 20 July 1748, p.486. £1.

JOHN ROGERS, 400 acs. Louisa Co. on both sides of Naked Cr.; adj. Andrew Reay, Major Henry & Thomas Hacket; 20 Jul 1748, p.487. £2.

HENRY WALTHALL, 435 acs. Amelia Co. on the Lower side of Buffalo Riv.; adj. John Woodson, Morton, Cobb, Watson & Hatcher; 20 Jul 1748, p.489. £2.S5.

JOHN ROGERS, 400 acs. Louisa Co. on the S side of the Rappidane, on the Brs. of Pritteys Cr., on the Orange Co. Line [N65°W]; adj. Henry Haynes, Roger Quarles, Richard Durrat & Bartholomew Durrat; 20 Jul 1748, p.491. £2. Whereas by pat. 23 Jul 1722 there was gtd. unto Edward Ripping, Richard Hickman & Ralph Gough [PB 11 p.151] one certain Tract or parcel of L. containing 10,000 acs. then in the Spotsyl. Co. And

whereas the sd Edward Ripping, Richard Hickman and Ralph Gough have failed to make Cultiv. and Improv. and Samuel Cobbs hath made humble Suit and hath obtained a G. for the same And hath relinquished all his Right and Interest in 400 acs. part unto John Rogers.

JOHN BROWDER JUNR., 303 acs. Amelia Co. on the S side of Mingos Horsepen Br. of Tomahitton Sw.; adj. Ornsby, Womack, Tabb & Haynes; 20 Jul 1748, p.493. £1.S10 Whereas by pat. 20 Aug 1741 there was gtd. unto Joseph Pattison junior And Whereas the sd Joseph Pattison junr. [Joseph Pattyson junr., PB 19 p.1110] hath failed to pay Quit Rents and to make Cult. & Improv. and John Browder junr. hath made humble Suit and obtained a g. for the same.

ISAAC DUFFO, 318 acs. Amelia Co. bet. the Brs. of Knibs Cr. and the Brs. of Smacks Cr.; adj. Bradby, Edward Booker, George Booker, Walthall, Roberts & Pincham; 20 Jul 1748, p.495. £1.S15. Whereas by pat. 22 Sep 1739 gtd. unto Ralph Blankenship [PB 18 p.463] And whereas Ralph Blankenship hath failed to make Cultiv. & Improvement And whereas James Thompson hath made humble Suit and obtained a g. for the same which he hath assigned to Isaac Duffo.

GEORGE ROGERS, 400 acs. Louisa Co. on both sides Piney Run; adj. Mr John Rogers, John

Red, Joseph Martin & William Keaton; 20 Jul 1748, p.497. £2.

JOHN ROGERS, 400 acs. Louisa Co. on the Brs. of Buck Mountain Cr.; adj. John Red, David Mills & William Keaton; 20 Jul 1748, p.499. £2.

THOMAS WILLIAMSON, 400 acs. Fredericksville Par., Louisa Co., on the Albemarle Co. Line [N65°W], adj. Nathaniel Winston; 20 Jul 1748, p.500. £2.

HENRY TOMLINSON, 200 acs. Amelia Co. on the lower side of Seller Cr.; adj. Moor, Gamlin, Rany & Leath; 20 Jul 1748, p.502. £1.

DAVID MILLS, 6,196 acs. Louisa Co. on both sides of Henrys Cr., Naked Cr. and Buck Mountain Cr.; on the south Fork of Jacobs Run, on the north Fork of Henrys Cr. & on the main fork of Buck Mountain Cr.; on the side of a small Mountain; adj. John Henry, William Carr, Mr Webb, William Bunch & David Mills; 20 Jul 1748, p.503. £31. Whereas by pat. 26 Mar 1739 there was gtd. unto William Robertson Esqr. since dec'd. [PB 18 p.218] 6,196 acs. in Hanover Co. now Louisa And whereas John Lidderdale and Elizabeth his wife Daughter and Heir at Law of the sd William Robertson dec'd have failed to pay Quit Rents and David Mills hath made humble suit and obtained a g. for the same.

CHARLES BOSTICK, 380 acs. Albemarle Co. on the S side of James Riv. & on the Brs. of Willis's Cr., crossing Bairds Road; 20 Jul 1748, p.506. £2.

THOMAS TURPIN, 222 acs. Albemarle Co. on both sides of Slate Riv., adj. Patrick Obrian & Thomas Jones; 20 Jul 1748, p.508. £1.S5.

PETER SALLE, 400 acs. Albemarle Co. on the S side of James Riv., on the S Brs. of Slate Riv. & on the W side of Troublesome Cr.; 20 Jul 1748, p.509. £2.

JAMES GRAY, 340 acs. Albemarle Co. on the S side of James Riv., on the N side of Willis's Cr., adj. Samuel Sanders; 20 Jul 1748, p.510. £1.S15.

JOHN GOODWIN, 400 acs. Albemarle Co. on the S side James Riv. on the N Brs. of Slate Riv., adj. William Nowlin; 20 Jul 1748, p.512. £2.

ARTHUR HOPKINS, 2,288 acs. Albemarle Co. on the Brs. of Totier Cr., crossing the north Fork of the Cr.; adj. James Tully, John Lewis, Matthew Harris, Charles Lynch, Merriwether/Meriwether, Scott & Clark; 20 Jul 1748, p.513. £11.S10.

SACHEVEREL WHITEBREAD, 400 acs. Albemarle Co. on the S side of James Riv. on a North Br. of Willis's Cr. called and known by the Name of Tongue Quarter; 20 Jul 1748, p.515. £2.

JOHN HOY, 400 acs. Albemarle Co. on both side of the North Br. of Slate Riv.; 20 Jul 1748, p.516. £2. Whereas by pat. 15 Mar 1741/42 gtd. John Farish [John Farrish, PB 20 p.213 or p.229] in Goochland Co. now Albemarle And Whereas the sd John Farish hath failed to make Cultiv. and Improv. And Whereas John Martin hath made humble suit and obtained a g. for the same which he assigned to John Hoy.

WILLIAM MORRISON, 2,460 acs. Albemarle Co. on the Brs. of Rockfish Riv. near the Blue Mountains; 20 Jul 1748, p.518. the sd L. having been formerly gtd. John Chiswell, Gent. by pat. 26 Mar 1739 [PB 18 p.209], and there being several material Mistakes in the same on the petition of the sd John Chiswell 4 Jun 1745 a new pat. was ordered to be gtd. the sd John Chiswell who hath assigned all the Right & Title thereto to the sd William Morrison.

JOHN WOODSON JUNR., 400 acs. Albemarle Co. on both sides of the Great Cr. of Slate Riv.; 20 Jul 1748, p.520. £2.

JOHN HOY, 400 acs. Albemarle Co. on both sides of the North Br. of Slate Riv.; 20 Jul 1748, p.521. 40 Shill. Whereas by pat. 15 Mar 1741/42 gtd. John Farish [John Farrish, PB 20 p.213 or p.229] in Goochland Co. now Albemarle And Whereas the sd John Farish hath

failed to make Cultiv. and Improv. and John Martin hath made humble Suit and hath obtained a g. for the same which he hath assigned to John Hoy.

ROBERT GOODWIN, 325 acs. Albemarle Co. on the S side James Riv. lying on the N Brs. of Slate Riv., Beg. in a piece of flat Ground near a Br., crossing Muddy Cr.; 20 July 1748, p.523. £1.S15.

OBEDIAH WOODSON, 285 acs. Albemarle Co. on [the N side of] Appomattox Riv.; adj. John Hodnet, John Peak & Obediah Woodson; 20 Jul 1748, p.524. £1.S10.

THOMAS SANDERS, son of John Sanders, 400 acs. Albemarle Co. on the S side of James Riv., on N side of Willis's Cr., adj. John Sanders; 20 Jul 1748, p.526. £2.

ADRIAN ANGLIN/ANGLAN, 165 acs. Albemarle Co. on the S side of James Riv. on both sides of Slate Riv., adj. his own old Line & Hugh Green; 20 Jul 1748, p.527. £1.

ALEXANDER STINSON, 395 acs. Albemarle Co. on the S side of James Riv. on a Br. of Willis's Cr. known by the Name of Cattail, crossing the Cattail Cr., adj. Thomas Edwards; 20 Jul 1748, p.529. £2.

ALEXANDER STINSON, 385 acs. Albemarle Co. on the S side of James Riv. on the N side of Willis's Cr.; adj. Alexander Trent,

Thomas Edwards, Colo. John Bolling & Alexander Stinson; 20 Jul 1748, p.530. £2.

R O B E R T   T H O M P S O N /THOMSON, 1,140 acs. Albemarle Co. on the S side of James Riv. on the S Brs. of Slate Riv., crossing Troublesome Cr. & Glovers Cr.; adj. Peter Salley, Sacheverel Whitebread & John Glover; 20 Jul 1748, p.532. £5.S15.

SAMUEL MARTIN, 150 acs. Augusta Co. on the W side the blue Ridge in the North Fork of James Riv., Beg. where John Heart crosses the north Riv. of James Riv., into the Fork of James Riv.; 20 Aug 1748, p.533. 15 Shill.

DANIEL LUNEY, 180 acs. Augusta Co. on a Br. of James Riv. called Long Run, adj. Robert Luney Senr.; 20 Aug 1748, p.535. £1.

HUGH MILLER, 370 acs. Lunenburg Co. on the N side of Difficult Cr., down a Piney Br.; 20 Aug 1748, p.537. £2.

STERLING CLACK, 120 acs. Brunswick Co. near the Road; adj. James Clack, Peter Tatum & Peter Jackson; 20 Aug 1748, p.538. 15 Shill.

WILLIAM CAMP, 14 acs. and 30 poles, Gloucester Co. being two Islands in York Riv., one containing 11 acs. and 30 poles, the other 3 acs.; 20 Aug 1748, p.540. 5 Shill.

ARTHUR HOPKINS, 180 acs. Goochland Co. on the S side of the Fluvanna Riv. about 4 miles above the Mouth of Tye Riv.; 20 Aug 1748, p.541. £1. Whereas by pat. 29 Jun 1739 gtd. William Cabbell [PB 18 p.348] And Whereas the sd Cabbell sold and conveied the same unto William Megginson who hath failed to make Cultiv. & Improv. and Arthur Hopkins hath made humble Suit and obtained a G. for the same.

JOHN JONES, 438 acs. Lunenburg Co. on the N side of Difficult Cr., up the North Fork of sd Cr.; adj. Roberts, John Russell, Hudson & Captain Robert Wynn; 20 Aug 1748, p.543. £1.S5.

JOHN JONES, 1,736 acs. Lunenburg Co. on the N side of the north fork of Difficult Cr., on a Ridge, adj. Roberts & Russell; 20 Aug 1748, p.545. £18.S15.

WILLIAM JONES, 665 acs. Lunenburg Co. on the W side of Butchers Cr., adj. Ravenscroft & Burwell; 20 Aug 1748, p.547. £3.S10.

DENNETT ABNEY, 290 acs. Hanover Co. on the N side of Chickahominy Sw., up the main Run; 20 Aug 1748, p.549. £1.S10.

JOHN HATCHET, 390 acs. Henrico Co. on the S side of James Riv., by the third Br.; adj. William Puckett, John Belshire & Lewis Tanner; 20 Aug 1748, p.550. £2.

JAMES COX, 370 acs. Orange Co.; adj. James Cox, Mrs Fleet, Captain Queen & Andrew Harrison; 20 Aug 1748, p.552. £2.

JAMES CARTER, 83 acs. Lunenburg Co. on both sides of Allens Cr., on the fork of sd Cr., adj. Holmes; 20 Aug 1748, p.554. 10 Shill.

JAMES HEARN, 254 acs. Surry Co. on the S side of Nottoway Riv.; adj. Thomas Dun, Richard Clanton & William Felt's; 20 Aug 1748, p.555. £1.S5.

ANTHONY POUNCY, 400 acs. Albemarle Co. on the N side of the Rivanna Riv. on the Mountain Falls Cr.; adj. Charles Lynch, William Randolph Gent. & Charles Moreman; 20 Aug 1748, p.557. £2.

WILLIAM FRAME, 300 acs. Augusta Co. on the South Br. of the north Riv. of Shanando called the naked Cr., Beg. on the N side of a Draft of the South Br. of sd Cr., on a ridge, at the Head of a Hollow of the Middle Riv. & near the head of a Hollow of the long Glade; 20 Aug 1748, p.559. £1.S10.

PETER TATUM, 389 acs. Brunswick Co. on the N side of the Reedy Cr., adj. Thomas Jackson Junior & John Jackson; 20 Aug 1748, p.560. £2.

PETER TATUM, 611 acs. Brunswick Co. on the S side of the

Reedy Cr., on a Path; adj. Thomas Jackson, James Clack, his own old Line & Edward Tatum; 20 Aug 1748, p.562. £2. (227 acs. part formerly gtd. unto the sd Peter Tatum by Pat. 28 Sep 1728 [455 acs. in PB 14 p.76] and 384 acs. the Residue never bef. gtd.)

WILLIAM THOMPSON, 139 acs. Augusta Co. on the W side the blue Ridge, Beg. by a Path on the W side the south Riv. of Shanando; 20 Aug 1748, p.563. 15 Shill.

HENRY RICE, 230 acs. Orange Co. on Brs. of the Pamunkey Riv., on the Road Side; adj. John Clerk, Edward Broadus, George Hardin & John Smith; 20 Aug 1748, p.565. for the Imp. of 5 Pers. whose Names are *William Buntine, John Page, Edward Jennings, John Forrester & Abel Gibson.*

THOMAS BEAL, 400 acs. Augusta Co. on a Br. of Broad run, Beg. near a large Rock, on a Draft of Brocks Cr.; 20 Aug 1748, p.567. £2.

CHARLES COTTREL, 123 acs. Goochland Co. on both sides of bad luck Run on the N side of Appamattox Riv.; adj. Edmond Butler, Philip Thomas & Michaux; 20 Aug 1748, p.568. 15 Shill.

ABEL THAXTON, 220 acs. Goochland Co. on the N side James Riv. on the Brs. of the Bird, on a Br. of Phill's Cr.; adj. David Parish, Robert Rent [Robert Kent] & Philip Thurmond; 20 Aug 1748, p.570. £1.S5.

JOSEPH WOODSON, 63 acs. Goochland Co. on Green Cr.; adj. Abraham Cook, Joseph Woodson, William Pattison & John Cook; 20 Aug 1748, p.571. 10 Shill.

JOSIAH BURTON, 400 acs. Goochland Co. on the Heads of the Brs. of Soakarse and little Guinea and on both sides of Buckingham Road, crossing the Heads of several Brs. of Little Guinea; adj. Julias Allen, William Patman, Adolphus Hendrick, Matthew Marks, James Daniel & Burton; 20 Aug 1748, p.573. £2.

DAVID DAVIS, 177 acs. Goochland Co. on the lower Brs. of the little Byrd on the N side of James Riv., down deep Cr.; adj. Michael Holland, Thomas Sanders, John Godbee, Silvester Prophet, John Johnson & the sd David Davis; 20 Aug 1748, p.575. £1.

HENRY DAWSON, 400 acs. Is. of Wight Co. on the N side of Meherrin Riv., in Buckhorn Sw., down the black Gut & a small Gut, at the Head of a small Gut; adj. the sd Dawsons own old Lines, Thomas Williams & Martin Dawson; 20 Aug 1748, p.576. £2.

NATHANIEL RIDLEY, 215 acs. Is. of Wight Co. on the S side of Nottoway Riv., up the Reedy Br., adj. John Wiggin's & James Jones; 20 Aug 1748, p.578. £1.S5.

THOMAS ATKINSON, 350 acs. Is. of Wight Co. on the S side of the main Blackwater Sw., down the Run of the Meadow Br.; adj.

William Kinchen, James Atkinson, Robert Harris & John Jackson; 20 Aug 1748, p.570. £1.S15.

JOHN THARP, 171 acs. Surry & Is. of Wight Countys, on the S side of Blackwater Sw., up the Run of the Lightwood Sw.; adj. William Hix, Joseph Lane, Benjamin Kitchin/Kitching, Samuel Sebrel, James Davis & Walter Bayly/Baily; 20 Aug 1748, p.581. £1.

THOMAS CLARY, 430 acs. Surry Co. on the S side of Blackwater Sw., on the W side of Chincopin Sw., down Savages Br., adj. his old Survey; 20 Aug 1748, p.583. £1.S5.

ROBERT LAND, 225 acs. Surry Co. on the S side of Nottoway Riv.; adj. William Loftin, Robert Webb & William Longbottom; 20 Aug 1748, p.585. £1.S5.

WILLIAM HIX, 280 acs. Surry Co. on the S side of Nottoway Riv. & on the S side of the Great Ploughman Sw., on the Side of the Woolf pit Meadow, near the Head of Huccleberry Br. which is the western prong of the Ploughman Sw., adj. James Evan's & Robert Sanderfer; 20 Aug 1748, p.586. £1.S10.

WILLIAM THOMPSON, JUNIOR, 2,000 acs. Pr. Geo. Co. on both sides of Burnt Quarter Run, crossing Chamberlayne Bed, by the road; adj. Bressy, Baugh, Charles Thompson, Wyth, Thomas Scott, James Hall & Stephen Dewey; 20 Aug 1748, p.588. £10.

RICHARD SMITH, JUNIOR, 100 acs. Pr. Geo. Co. on the S side of Stoney Cr., by a pond; adj. his own Line, Turner & Wynn; 20 Aug 1748, p.590. 10 Shill.

ISHAM EPES, 353 acs. Pr. Geo. Co. on the S side of Hatcher's Run; adj. his own Lines, Browder, Munford & Peterson; 20 Aug 1748, p.591. £1.S15.

JOSEPH DICKASON, 84 acs. Pr. Geo. Co. on both sides of the Nammisseen Road and above the long Br. of Wallice's Cr.; adj. Overby, Wynn & Herbert; 20 Aug 1748, p.593. 10 Shill.

NATHANIEL LEE, 150 acs. Pr. Geo. Co. on the N side of Indian Sw., in the Head of a Valley, down the Reedy Br., adj. William Harwell; 20 Aug 1748, p.594. 15 Shill.

WILLIAM EPES, 1,013 acs. Pr. Geo. Co. on the S side of Josephs Sw., near along the Side of the main Road; adj. Lines of his own old 172 acs., Whitmore, Hill alias Bigings's, Michael Hill, Richard Carlisle, Abbitt & Davis; 20 Aug 1748, p.595. £4.S5. 172 acs. part formerly gtd. unto the sd William Epes by Pat. 13 Oct 1727 [PB 13 p.279] and 841 acs. the Residue never bef. gtd.

THOMAS HARDAWAY, JUNIOR, 895 acs. Pr. Geo. Co. on the N side of Nottoway Riv.; adj. his old Lines, High, Roberson, Bolling & Harwell; 20 Aug 1748, p.597. £1. 695 acs. part formerly gtd. John Rayborn by Pat. 13 Oct 1727 [John Raybourn in PB 13 p.272, which included sd Raybourn's 300 acs. in PB 11 p.179 dated 18 Feb 1722/23] the right and Title os which sd L. is since become vested in the sd Thomas Hardaway and 200 acs. the Residue never bef. gtd.

GEORGE THWEAT, 200 acs. Pr. Geo. Co. on the Great Br. of Chamberlaynes Bed, adj. his Brother Henry Thweat; 20 Aug 1748, p.599. £1.

CHARLES LYNCH, Gent., 245 acs. Albemarle Co. on the S side the Rivanna; adj. Carr, Lynch & Williamson; 20 Aug 1748, p.600. £1.S5.

ELIAS CLARKE, 195 acs. Pr. Geo. Co. on the S side of Hatchers Run, crossing the Road; adj. Thomas Williams, Lewis, Richards, Munford & his own old C.; 20 Aug 1748, p.602. £1.

GEORGE LOVIN, 125 acs. Brunswick Co., down Cub Cr., adj. Allen, & Christopher Parson; 20 Aug 1748, p.603. 15 Shill.

HENRY PARISH, 330 acs. Brunswick Co., up Morris's Cr., adj. Morris, Spill [Spell], & James Parish; 20 Aug 1748, p.605. £1.S15.

SAMUEL DASPINS, 200 acs. Brunswick Co. on the S side Meherrin Riv.; adj. William Maclin, Pennington & John Ezeld; 20 Aug 1748, p.607. £1.

HENRY COOKE, 1,760 acs. Brunswick Co. on the S side of the Great Sw., up cane Br.; adj. Robert Clark & George Wych; 20 Aug 1748, p.608. £4.S15. 500 acs. part formerly gtd. sd Henry Cooke by Pat. 7 Jul 1726 [PB 12 p.526] and 310 acs. other part also formerly gtd. sd Henry Cooke by Pat. 31 Oct 1726 [Henry Cook, PB 13 p.56] and 950 acs. the Residue never bef. gtd.

JOHN QUARLES, 157 acs. Brunswick Co. on Reaves's Path; adj. Swanson, Edmonds & Chamberlain; 20 Aug 1748, p.610. £1.

JOHN DOUGLASS, 351 acs. Brunswick Co. on the S side of Meherrin Riv., in Turkey Island, adj. his own Lines; 20 Aug 1748, p.612. £1.S5.

THOMAS BASSETT, 300 acs. Goochland Co. among the S Brs. of Willis's Riv.; adj. Paul Micheaux, John Minter, Robert Bernard dec'd. & William Mayo; 20 Aug 1748, p.614. 30 Shill.

THOMAS BASSETT, 500 acs. Goochland Co. on Angolo Cr.; adj. David Bell, Daniel Stoner, Stephen Stone, Richard Ward & John Francis; 20 Aug 1748, p.615. £2.S10.

HUGH LAMBRETH, 400 acs. Brunswick Co. on the W side of the Rocky run, down the great Br.; 20 Aug 1748, p.617. £2.

THOMAS WILLIAMS, 1,510 acs. Pr. Geo. Co. on the Head of the rocky run; adj. Hardaway, Cleaton, Poythress, Jackson, Bartlot, Williamson, Booth, Maidlen, Bird, Rany & Peniston; 20 Aug 1748, p.618. £7.S15.

THOMAS WILLIAMS, 3,815 acs. Pr. Geo. Co. on both sides of Hatchers Run, crossing the South fork of sd Run, by the Road; adj. Murril, Drury Oliver, May's, the Line of the L. purchased of Cross, Baugh, Thweat, Darby, Lewis, Elias Clarke & Peirce; 20 Aug 1748, p.620. 200 acs. formerly gtd. William Cross by Pat. 22 Sep 1739 [PB 18 p.465] since vested in the sd Thomas Williams and 3,615 acs. the Residue never bef. gtd.

THOMAS BASSETT, 400 acs. Goochland Co. among the S Brs. of Willis Riv., adj. Paul Micheaux & William Mayo; 20 Aug 1748, p.622. £2.

OWIN MYRICK, JUNIOR, 340 acs. Is. of Wight Co. on the S side of Nottoway Riv., down the run of the Hornet Sw.; adj. Robert Owin, Joseph Harrod, George Cornett & Charles Maberry; 20 Aug 1748, p.624. £1.S15.

OWIN MYRICK, JUNIOR, 200 acs. Is. of Wight Co. on the S side of Nottaway Riv., adj. Owin Myrick; 20 Aug 1748, p.625. £1.

OWIN MYRICK, 470 acs. Lunenburgh Co. bet. Flatt Cr. and Parhams Cr., adj. Cole; 20 Aug 1748, p.627. £2.S10.

ABRAHAM ECHOLDS, 334 acs. Lunenburgh Co. on both sides of Childers Cr., adj. Hodges lower Line & his own Line; 20 Aug 1748, p.629. £1.S15.

RICHARD ECHOLS, 532 acs. Lunenburgh Co. on both sides of Bannister Riv. and on the lower side of Bearskin Cr., adj. Burton; 20 Aug 1748, p.630. £2.S15.

JAMES McDAVID, 291 acs. Lunenburgh Co. on both sides of little Falling Riv.; 20 Aug 1748, p.632. £1.S10.

JAMES McDAVID, 250 acs. Lunenburgh Co. on both sides of little Falling Riv.; 20 Aug 1748, p.634. £1.S5.

HENRY GREEN, 381 acs. Lunenburgh Co. on both sides of Buffilo Cr., adj. his own upper line; 20 Aug 1748, p.635. £2.

HENRY GREEN, 404 acs. Lunenburgh Co. on both sides of Buffilo Cr.; 20 Aug 1748, p.637. £2.

THOMAS HILTON, 270 acs. Lunenburgh Co. on both sides of Terrible Cr., adj. Parish; 20 Aug 1748, p.638. £1.S10.

WILLIAM IRBY, 200 acs. Lunenburgh Co. on the N side of Difficult Cr., adj. Wynn; 20 Aug 1748, p.640. £1.

ABRAHAM ECHOLDS, 418 acs. Lunenburgh Co. on both sides of Childers Cr., adj. William

Cunningham; 20 Aug 1748, p.641. £2.S15.

THOMAS SPENCER, 821 acs. Lunenburgh Co. on both sides of the Middle Fork of the Three Forks of Licking Hole; adj. Joseph Morton Junior; 20 Aug 1748, p.643. £3. 250 acs part formerly gtd. unto the sd Thomas Spencer by Pat. 13 Jul 1742 [PB 20 p.379 Brunswick Co. which was also included in his 362 acs. in PB 24 p.191] PB and 571 acs. [sic] the Residue never bef. gtd.

THOMAS BASSETT, 1,000 acs. Goochland Co. bet. Great Guinea and Angolo Creeks, adj. Andrew Crew, the sd Thomas Bassett, Joseph Eckolls, David Bell, Daniel Stoner & Isaac Allen; 20 Aug 1748, p.645. £5.

RICHARD BROWN, 274 acs. Lunenburgh Co. on S side of the north fork of Difficult Cr., adj. Russells upper Line; 20 Aug 1748, p.647. £1.S10.

ISRAEL BROWN, 323 acs. Lunenburgh Co. adj. Rachel & Edloe; 20 Aug 1748, p.649. £1.S15.

JOSEPH ROYALL, 365 acs. Lunenburgh Co. on both sides of Butchers Cr.; 20 Aug 1748, p.650. £2.

WILLIAM WYNNE, Gent., 400 acs. Lunenburgh Co. on N side of Bannister Riv., crossing the Brs. of Joshua's Cr., down Wood's Cr.

adj. Colonel Embrey & Wood; 20 Aug 1748, p.652. £2.

WILLIAM WYNNE, 400 acs. Lunenburgh Co. crossing Wolf Trap Cr., adj. his own old Line & Bannister; 20 Aug 1748, p.654. £2.

JOHN KING, 238 acs. Lunenburgh Co. on both sides of Grassy Cr., down and crossing Buckhorn Br.; 20 Aug 1748, p.655. £1.S5.

PETER WILSON, 240 acs. Lunenburgh Co. on the N side of Dann Riv., up white Walnut Cr.; 20 Aug 1748, p.657. £1.S5.

PETER OVERBY, 222 acs. Lunenburgh Co. on the S side of Dann Riv. on both sides of the north Fork of Tewayhomoney Cr., near the Mouth of the reedy Br.; 20 Aug 1748, p.658. £1.S5.

NATHANIEL COOK, 400 acs. Lunenburgh Co. on both sides of Crabb Tree Br.; 20 Aug 1748, p.660. £2.

THOMAS ANDERSON, 400 acs. Albemarle Co. on S side of James Riv., on Brs. of Appomattox Riv., adj. Elkanah Anderson [him], Joseph Dabbs & Charles Anderson; 20 Aug 1748. p.661. £2.

JOHN LEAKS, 123 acs. Albemarle Co. adj. Christopher Armstrong; 20 Aug 1748, p.663. 15 Shill.

PATRICK NAPIER, 400 acs. Albemarle Co. on the Head Brs. of Cunningham Cr., on the S side of

Court house Road, crossing the Road; 20 Aug 1748, p.664. £2.

DAVID GRIFFITH, 200 acs. Albemarle Co. on both sides of Griffiths Cr. of Slate Riv., on a Ridge, in Low Grounds, adj. John Henson; 20 Aug 1748. p.666. £1.

JOHN PAYNE, 138 acs. Albemarle Co. in the Fork of James Riv. on both sides of Bremore Cr.; 20 Aug 1748, p.667. 15 Shill.

JOHN DOUGLASS/DOUGLAS, 175 acs. Albemarle Co. in the Fork of James Riv. on both sides of Rock Fish Cr., adj. Robert Walton; 20 Aug 1748, p.669. £1.

JOHN ROBERTSON, Joiner, 250 acs. Albemarle Co. on the N side the Rivanna Riv., to the upper end of a small Island, adj. Samuel Burk & John Robinson; 20 Aug 1748, p.671. £2.S5.

GEORGE BROCK, 95 acs. Albemarle Co. on both sides of Bremore Cr. near the Head, adj. John Payne & Joseph Walton; 20 Aug 1748, p.673. 10 Shill.

SAMUEL DAVIS, 100 acs. Albemarle Co. on Bryery Br. of Green Cr., adj. William Harris; 20 Aug 1748, p.674. 10 Shill.

JOHN COBBS, 400 acs. Albemarle Co. on both sides of Crook's Cr., adj. George Payne; 20 Aug 1748, p.676. £2.

HENRY THOMAS, 172 acs. Albemarle Co. on Rock Island Cr. S of the Fluvanna, adj. Edward Thomas; 20 Aug 1748, p.678. £1.

FRANCIS MOSELEY, 400 acs. Albemarle Co. on the S of James Riv. on the Brs. of Willis's Cr., crossing Hodnetts Br.; 20 Aug 1748, p.679. £2.

MARY PATTERSON, 200 acs. Albemarle Co. on the S side of James Riv. & crossing Arthur's Cr. of Slate Riv.; 20 Aug 1748, p.681. £1.

JOSHUA FRY, 400 acs. Albemarle Co. on Glover's Road, adj. Thomas Harvey; 20 Aug 1748, p.682. £2.

ALLEN HOWARD, 183 acs. Albemarle Co. S of the Fluvanna on Rock Island Cr.; 20 Aug 1748, p.684. £1.

SAMUEL STEPHENS, 225 acs. Albemarle Co. on the S side of James Riv. on both sides of middle Slate Riv.; 20 Aug 1748, p.685. £1.S5.

LEONARD BALLOW, JUNIOR, 119 acs. Albemarle Co. on the N side of the Fluvanna; adj. John Lewis, Matthew Jordan & Thomas Gooldsby; 20 Aug 1748, p.687. 15 Shill.

JAMES IRELAND, 147 acs. Albemarle Co. on the north fork of Green Cr., adj. Christopher Armstrong; 20 Aug 1748, p.689. 15 Shill.

SAMUEL BURNETT, 400 acs. Lunenburgh Co. on the S side of the middle fork of Meherrin Riv., adj. Henry Robertson, Twitty & John Doak; 20 Aug 1748, p.690.

GEORGE WILSON, 250 acs. Chesterfield Co., Beg. on the S side Swift Cr. at a great Rock; adj. James Robinson, William Worsham & P. Rowlett; 20 Aug 1748, p.692. which sd 250 acs. was formerly gtd. unto John Wilson.

CHARLES CARD, 178 acs. Albemarle Co. on the Brs. of Rockfish Cr. of the Fluvanna; adj. Drury Tucker, Robert Walton & Henry Trent; 20 Aug 1748, p.693. £1.

THOMAS PHELPS, 9 acs. Albemarle Co., one certain Island in the Fluvanna Riv. near the north channel opposite the Plantacon of the sd Phelps; 20 Aug 1748, p.695. 5 Shill.

MATTHEW JORDAN, 200 acs. Albemarle Co. joining the N side of the Fluvanna, up rockhouse Br., adj. John Childers & the sd Jordan; 20 Aug 1748, p.696. £1.

JAMES IRELAND, 296 acs. Albemarle Co. on the north fork of Green Cr.; 20 Aug 1748, p.698. £1.S10.

JOHN DOKE, 354 acs. Lunenburgh Co. on both sides of the middle Fork of Maherrin Riv., adj. Henry Roberson; 20 Aug 1748, p.700. £1.S15.

VALENTINE BROWN, 392 acs. Lunenburgh Co. on the N side of the middle Fork of Maherrin Riv.; 20 Aug 1748, p.701. £2.

RICHARD GREEN, 400 acs. Brunswick Co. on the S side of Nottoway Riv., down Cedar Cr., at the Mouth of the Lick Br.; 20 Aug 1748, p.703. £2.

THEOPHILUS FIELD, 365 acs. Brunswick Co. on the N side of the Great Cr., along the Road; adj. Ravenscroft, Harrison, Brown & Edloe; 20 Aug 1748, p.705. £2. Whereas by pat. 20 Aug 1740 gtd. William Gunn [PB 19 p.705] and Whereas the sd William Gunn hath failed to pay Quitrents and Theophilus Field hath made humble Suit and obtained a g. for the same.

THEOPHILUS FIELD, 292 acs. Brunswick Co. on the Pigeon Roost Cr.; 20 Aug 1748, p.707. £1.S10. Whereas by pat. 3 Oct 1734 gtd. William Roberts [PB 15 p.347] and Whereas William Gunn in whom the sd L. is since become vested hath failed to pay Quitrents and Theophilus Field hath made humble suit and obtained a G. for the same.

AMBROSE BENSON, 132 acs. Accomack Co. 20 Aug 1748, p.708. for 2 lbs. of Tobacco for every Acre of sd L. Whereas by Inquisition indented and taken in sd Co. 18 Jun 1724 by Virtue of a Warrant directed to Hancock Custis Escheator for the sd Co. it appears Bartholomew Asgood died seised of 132 acs. which is found to Escheat to us from the sd Asgood and Whereas Ambrose Benson hath made humble Suit and obtained a G. for the same.

JOHN MANN & ESSEX WORSHAM, 254 acs. Brunswick Co. on both sides of Louce Cr., adj. Kennon; 20 Aug 1748, p.710. £1.S5.

GEORGE MOSELEY, 226 acs. Brunswick Co. on the N side of Fountains Cr., adj. Chapman; 20 Aug 1748, p.712. £1.S5.

JOSEPH DANIEL, 367 acs. Brunswick Co. on both sides of Waqua Cr.; 20 Aug 1748, p.713. £2.

GEORGE CLATON, 202 acs. Brunswick Co. adj. Benjamin Harrison, Thomas James & Richard Bryan; 20 Aug 1748, p.715. £1.

LANIER BREWER, 300 acs. Brunswick Co. on the S side of Beaver Pond Cr., adj. Witche & Brewer; 20 Aug 1748, p.717. £1.S10.

JOHN PETERSON, 128 acs. Brunswick Co. on both sides of Halls Br., adj. Bishop & his own Line; 20 Aug 1748, p.719. 15 Shill.

JOHN VICK, 394 acs. Brunswick Co. on the N side of the Beaver Pond Br., up Beaver Pond Cr. aforesaid; 20 Aug 1748, p.720. £2.

NICHOLAS BREWER, 254 acs.
Brunswick Co. on the N side of the
Beaver Pond Cr., along the
Country Line [East], adj. Richard
Carter & George Wytches; 20 Aug
1748, p.722-723. £1.S5.

*Feb. 8. 1749/50 Then Settled &
burnt the Rights to the finishing this
Book. John Blair.*

PATENT BOOK NO. 27

1 Dec 1748 to 15 Dec 1749

EDWARD MOODY, 250 acs. Albemarle Co. on both sides of Cunninghams Cr. of the S side of the Rivanna Riv.; 1 Dec 1748 *in the 22nd year of our Reign of George the second, Sir William Gooch Baronet our Lieutenant Governor and Commander in Chief*, p.1. £1.S5.

JAMES FENDLY, 400 acs. Albemarle Co. on both sides of David's Cr.; 1 Dec 1748, p.2. £2.

WILLIAM FLOWERS, 215 acs. Albemarle Co. on S side James Riv. on both sides of middle Slate Riv., adj. William Jones; 1 Dec 1748, p.3. £1.S5.

JOHN WARD, 300 acs. Albemarle Co. on S side James Riv. & on both sides Hollyday Riv., adj. Henry Chiles; 1 Dec 1748, p.5. £1.S10.

CONSTANT PERKINS, 50 acs. Albemarle Co. on S side of the Fluvanna, adj. Constant Perkins [his Line]; 1 Dec 1748, p.6. 5 Shill.

CONSTANT PERKINS, 100 acs. Albemarle Co. on the S side of the Fluvanna, adj. the sd Perkins; 1 Dec 1748, p.8. 10 Shill.

GEORGE HILTON, JUNIOR, 200 acs. Albemarle Co. on both sides of Cunningham Cr. of the Rivanna; 1 Dec 1748, p.9. £1.

JOHN COBBS, 115 acs. Albemarle Co. on both sides of Cary Cr. of the Rivanna, adj. Benjamin Woodson; 1 Dec 1748, p.11. 15 Shill.

JOHN GRAVES, 400 acs. Albemarle Co. on Huffs Cr., adj. Benjamin Stennet; 1 Dec 1748, p.12. £2.

GILES ALLEGREE, 390 acs. Albemarle Co. on the N side the Rivanna on the Brs. of Horsleys Cr., adj. the sd Allegree & John Cannady; 1 Dec 1748, p.14. £1.S10.

GILES ALLEGREE, 63 acs. Albemarle Co. on the W side of a Mountain, on Hanover Co. Line [N65°W], adj. Thomas Ker; 1 Dec 1748, p.15. 10 Shill.

ROBERT BABER, 200 acs. Albemarle Co. on both sides Bear Garden Cr. of Fluvanna; adj. Mr

275

Richard Cocke near the Mill, Baber, Phelps, & Wentworth Webb; 1 Dec 1748, p.17. £1.

GILES ALLEGREE, 178 acs. Albemarle Co. on the Brs. of Biskett Run of Moore's Cr.; 1 Dec 1748, p.18. £1.

HENRY TRENT, 175 acs. Albemarle Co. on the S side of the Fluvanna Riv., Beg. at a Hornbeam Tree standing on the River Bank at the upper End of a Peice of narrow low Grounds; 1 Dec 1748, p.20. £1.

DANIEL REYNOLDS, 100 acs. Albemarle Co., S of the Fluvanna, adj. Michael Thomas; 1 Dec 1748. p21. 10 Shill.

BOOTH NAPIER, 400 acs. Albemarle Co. on both sides of Island Cr. of the N side of the Rivanna Riv., crossing a Br. of Phill's Cr., adj. the L. lately surveyed for Philip Thurmond; 1 Dec 1748, p.23. £2.

MICHAEL THOMAS, JUNIOR, 400 acs. Albemarle Co. on the N side of Rockfish Riv. on Hogg Cr., to a Point of Rocks on the Riv.; 1 Dec 1748, p.24. £2.

THOMAS GRIGG YARBROUGH, 100 acs. Albemarle Co. on the north Fork or Br. of Cunningham, adj. Martin Duncan; 1 Dec 1748, p.25. 10 Shill.

THOMAS JARROLD, 400 acs. Albemarle Co. on the S side James Riv. on the N Brs. of Slate Riv.,

adj. Samuel Stepens; 1 Dec 1748, p.28.

THOMAS SAUNDERS, 500 acs. Goochland Co. on the head Brs. of the little Byrd and Lickinghole Cr., adj. Michael Holland; 1 Dec 1748, p.28. £2.S10.

THOMAS MCDANIEL, 350 acs. Goochland Co. on both sides of Ballingers Cr., adj. Eppes; 1 Dec 1748, p.30. £1.S15.

JAMES TULEY, 200 acs. Goochland Co. on the Brs. of Totier Cr., at the South Fork of Totier; 1 Dec 1748, p.31. £1.

EDWARD BABER, 325 acs. Albemarle Co. on the Brs. of Bear Garden Cr. of the Fluvanna; adj. Thomas Phelps, Ripley & William Cannon; 1 Dec 1748, p.33. £1.S15.

JAMES DANIEL, 7 acs. Albemarle Co., one certain Island in the Fluvanna Riv. near the North Channel opposite to the L. of William Walton; 1 Dec 1748, p.35. 5 Shill.

JAMES DANIEL, 150 acs. Albemarle Co. on the S side of the Fluvanna Riv. including Part of the seven Islands exclusive of the intermediate Streams of the Riv.; Beg. on the S side the Riv. over against Tindals Island, to the W end of Ridge Island, down the N side the Riv. to the E End of Burnt Island; 1 Dec 1748, p.36. 15 Shill. Whereas by Pat. 20 June 1733 gtd. unto George Abbot [George Abbat,

PB 15 p.11], 150 acs. formerly in Goochland Co. now Albemarle and whereas the sd George Abbot hath failed to pay Quitrents and whereas Edmund Gray hath made humble Suit and hath obtained a G. for the same which he hath assigned to James Daniel. [The survey appears to include Ridge Island & Burnt Island, both to the E of Tindals Island]

GEORGE DAMERIL, 147 acs. Albemarle Co. on the S side of the Fluvanna, adj. Michael Thomas & Major Howard; 1 Dec 1748, p.38. 15 Shill.

JOHN DAMERON, 200 acs. Albemarle Co. on both sides of Woodson's Cr. of Hardware Riv., adj. Benjamin Woodson & Richard Dameron; 1 Dec 1748, p.40. £1.

WILLIAM HARRIS, 400 acs. Albemarle Co. on the Head of the Beaver Dam Fork of Epes's Cr., on the Mountain Side adj. Thomas Sorvel; 1 Dec 1748, p.41. £2.

JOHN PEAK, 200 acs. Albemarle Co. adj. to Appomattox Riv. and on both sides of the Great Cr., in Lowgrounds, adj. Lands Surveyed for Thomas Anderson; 1 Dec 1748, p.43. £1.

JOHN CHILDRES, JUNIOR, 225 acs. Albemarle Co. on the N side of the Fluvanna Riv. on the Brs. of Mullenasse/Mullinasse Cr., adj. Major Allen Howard; 1 Dec 1748, p.45. £1.S5.

JOSEPH HART, 204 acs. Surry Co. on the S side of black Water Sw., in a small Br. of the Lightwood Sw., in Tuskaruro Br.; adj. Henry Blow, his own Lines & George Brigg's; 1 Dec 1748, p.47. £1.

THOMAS DENTON, 266 acs. Goochland Co. on the N side the Rivanna on the Head of Martins Br.; 1 Dec 1748, p.48. £1.S10.

THOMAS WHITESIDES, 400 acs. Goochland Co. on both sides of Stocktons Br. of Mechums Riv.; 1 Dec 1748, p.50. £2.

ISHAM ANDREWS, 231 acs. Henrico Co. on the N side of Appamattox Riv., adj. his own Line & John Bott; 1 Dec 1748, p.52. £1.S5.

ROBERT JORDAN, 285 acs. Henrico Co. on the N side of the South Br. of white Oak Sw.; 1 Dec 1748, p.53. £1.S10. whereas by pat. 30 Jul 1742 gtd. unto Nicholas Hopson [PB 20 p.414] and whereas the sd Nicholas Hopson hath failed to pay Quitrents and to make Cultiv. & Improv. and Robert Jordan hath made humble Suit & hath obtained a G. for the same.

JOHN BLANKINSHIP, 372 acs. Henrico Co. on both the S & N sides of the Run of deep Cr.; adj. Gilbert Elam, Clary, Belcher, Gates & Nunnery; 1 Dec 1748, p.55. £2.

RICHARD DEAN, 224 acs. Henrico Co., adj. Furkrun, John

Robert, Wooldridge & Martin; 1 Dec 1748, p.58. £1.S5.

DANIEL SMITH, 198 acs. Brunswick Co. on both sides of Panther Cr.; 1 Dec 1748, p.59. £1.

JOHN BONEY & RICHARD DYAR, 119½ acs. Pr. Anne Co., adj. the sd Boney's Pat. & a former Survey made for James Moore; 1 Dec 1748, p.61. 15 Shill.

HARTWELL MARRABLE, 100 acs. Surry Co. on the S side of Nottoway Riv.; adj. Robert Sandefur, Colo. Benjamin Harrison, Thomas Renn, William Bishop & William Dansy; 1 Dec 1748, p.63. 10 Shil.

JOSEPH HIX, 128 acs. Surry Co. on the S side of black Water Sw. on the miery Br.; adj. Joseph Richardson, James Bains & his own lines; 1 Dec 1748, p.65. 15 Shill.

WILLIAM FELTS, 160 acs. Surry Co. on the S side of Nottoway Riv., adj. Richard Felts & Colo. Benjamin Harrison; 1 Dec 1748, p.67. £1.

NICHOLAS JONES, 86 acs. Surry Co. on the S side of blackwater Sw. on Jeremy's Br., down the Run of Jeremy's Sw., adj. his own Line; 1 Dec 1748, p.68. 10 Shill.

TIMOTHY EZELL, JUNIOR, 365 acs. Surry Co. on the S side Nottoway Riv. & the S side of the North Prong of the Poplar Sw.; 1 Dec 1748, p.70. £2.

HUMPRY BAYLIS, 440 acs. Surry Co. on the College Line [N85°E], adj. Samuel Maget; 1 Dec 1748, p.71. £2.S5.

ROBERT NICHOLSON, 240 acs. Surry Co. on the S side of black Water Sw., up the Run of the Snake Br.; adj. William Brown, William Davidson & Richard Andrew Junr.; 1 Dec 1748, p.73. £1.S5.

ROBERT NICHOLSON, 178 acs. Surry Co. on the S side of blackwater Sw., Beg. at a Paupau on the long Br., crossing the Wildcat Br.; adj. Charles White, his own Line, John Handcock, Edward Harris & Thomas Clary; 1 Dec 1748, p.75. £1.

JAMES JOLET, 61½ acs. Spotsyl. Co. & Par. of Saint George, in a Glade and on a ridge; adj. Mr John Allan, John Robinson Junr. Esq. & Thomas Salmon; 1 Dec 1748, p.77. 10 Shill.

JOHN HINES, 150 acs. Nansemond Co. on the S side of Jornagan's Bridge Run, at the Mouth of the deep Br., adj. Richard Hines & John Hines Son of William Hines dec'd; 1 Dec 1748, p.79. 5 Shill. 100 acs. Part being Part of a Pat. for 400 acs. formerly gtd. Richard Hines by Pat. 12 Apr 1653 [Richard Haines in PB 3 p.33 neer the head of the Southerne br. of Nanzemond Riv.] the Right & Title of sd 100 acs. by diverse mesne Conveyances is since become vested in the sd John Hines & 51 acs. the Residue being found to be surplus L. within the Bounds aforesd.

JOHN GOODWIN, 1,190 acs. Surry Co. on both sides of the main Road leading from Cooks Bridge to Nottoway Riv., crossing Cooks Road, on both sides of Warwick Sw., down the Drain of the black Sw., in the Drain of Tarkiln Br., up the Run of Pidgeon Sw., down the Run of Cottens Br.; adj. James Jones, David Jones, Richard Tomlinson, Francis Reading, Thomas Peeples, William Saunders, Colo. Benja. Harrison, William Shands, his old Patent Lines, John Mason, James Gee & Robert Hunnycut; 1 Dec 1748, p.81. £4. 425 acs. part formerly gtd. unto Thomas Goodwin [Thomas Goodwyn, PB 10 p.350] by Pat. 22 Jan 1717/18 the Right & Title whereof is since become vested in the sd John Goodwin and 765 acs. the Residue never bef. gtd.

WILLIAM HEALEY, 400 acs. Louisa Co. on the Brs. of Fork Cr., on the N side of Elkhorn Br.; adj. Joseph Clark, Syms, & Francis Clark; 10 Feb 1748/49, p.84. £2.

ALEXANDER GLASBEY, 390 acs. Louisa Co. on both sides a S Br. of Rockey Cr.; adj. Andrew Hunter, the sd Glasbey, & James Buckhannan; 10 Feb 1748/49, p.85. £2.

JOHN SIMS, 632 acs. Louisa Co. on the Brs. of Locust & Hinsons Creeks; adj. Matthew Sims dec'd, William Gooch, Chamberlayne, Pouncey Anderson & Jno. Walton; 10 Feb 1748/49, p.87. £1. 432 acs. part formerly gtd. William Chambers by Pat. 12 Sep 1733 [Hanover Co., PB 15 p.118] the Right & Title is since become vested in the sd John Sims and 200 acs. the Residue never bef. gtd.

HENRY ROSE, 740 acs. Is. of Wight Co. on the S side of Nottoway Riv., Beg. at the Head of Georges Br. near the wolf Pond, down the Fork Br., up the great Meadow, adj. Joshua Nicholson; 10 Feb 1748/49, p.89. £3.S15.

Col. JOHN SIMMONS, Gent., 725 acs. Is. of Wight Co. on the N side of Nottoway Riv., down the Cabbin Br. & down the Island Br., adj. his own old Lines; 10 Feb 1748/49. p.91. £3.S15.

JOHN EMBRE, 400 acs. Orange Co. on Brs. of Pamunkey, adj. the sd John Embres nigh the beaverdam Run; 10 Feb 1748/49, p.93. £2.

DAVID WALKER, 200 acs. Lunenburg Co. on the N side of Smiths Cr., down Smiths reedy Br.; adj. William King, his own old Lines & Fox; 10 Feb 1748/49, p.94. £1.

ROBERT BICKERS, 100 acs. Orange Co. on the Brs. of Pamunkey, adj. another Tract of the sd Bickers's; 10 Feb 1748/49, p.96. for the Imp. of 2 Pers. whose Names are *Edward Green & James Hopkins*.

PETER MARSHALL, 150 acs. Accomack Co. on the Sea Side, Beg. at the Sound Side, adj. Marshall & Walburn; 10 Feb 1748/49, p.97. for 2 lbs. Tobacco for every Acre of sd L. Whereas by Inquisition indented & taken in sd Co. 3 Aug 1741 by Virtue of a Warrant directed to Edmund Bayley Gent. Escheator for sd Co., It appears that Love, late the Wife of George Corbin, died siesed of one undivided Moity or half Part of a Parcel of certain L. containing 300 acs. which is found to Escheat to us from the sd Love Corbin and whereas Peter Marshall hath made humble Suit and obtained a G. for the same.

ELISHA FOWLER, 165 acs. Augusta Co. on the S side of the North Br. of Shanandore Riv. against the Mouth of Fort Run; 10 Feb 1748/49, p.99. £1.

JOHN WINDLEKITE, 316 acs. Augusta Co. on the N side Shanando Riv.; 10 Feb 1748/49, p.101. £1.S15.

WILLIAM MARSHALL, 484 acs. Brunswick Co. on the N side of Stanton Riv. opposite to the Long Island, Beg. on the River near the Falls; 10 Feb 1748/49, p.102. £2.S10.

JOHN FOWLER, 200 acs. Augusta Co. on both sides of naked Cr. a Br. of Shanando Riv., adj. Hites

&c Line; 10 Feb 1748/49, p.104. £1.

WILLIAM BERD, 220 acs. Augusta Co. on the Island Draft of the North Riv. Shanando, Beg. near a Road; 10 Feb 1748/49, p.106. £1.S5.

THOMAS BARID, 183 acs. Augusta Co. on a Br. of Cathay's Riv., called Jennings Br., adj. Daniel Mcenere; 10 Feb 1748/49, p.107. £1.

JEREMIAH HARRISON, 370 acs. Augusta Co. on the Drafts of Cooks & & Linwells Creeks, on a stoney Ridge, on the side of a Gully; 10 Feb 1748/49, p.108. £2.

JOHN HARRISON, JUNR., 200 acs. Augusta Co. on the Drafts of Smiths Cr., Beg. on a Ridge near a Road; 10 Feb 1748/49, p.110. £1.

SAMUEL DAVIS, 296 acs. Albemarle Co. on Green Cr., adj. Leonard Phillps; 10 Feb 1748, p.112. £1.S10.

JOHN SMITH, 100 acs. Augusta Co. on a Br. of Catheys Riv. called Moffets Br.; 10 Feb 1748/49, p.113. 10 Shill.

ROBERT CRAVEN, 200 acs. Augusta Co. on both sides of Cooks Cr. including Dyes meadow; 10 Feb 1748/49, p.115. £1.

ROBERT CRAVEN, 136 acs. Augusta Co. on the Drafts of the South Br. of Linwells Mill Cr., adj. Samuel Harrison; 10 Feb 1748/49, p.116. 15 Shill.

ROBERT CRAVEN, 123 acs. Augusta Co. on the Head of Cooks Cr., crossing McCurttes/McCurtles Br.; 10 Feb 1748/49, p.118. 15 Shill.

ROBERT CRAVEN, 169 acs. Augusta Co. on both sides of Cooks Cr., crossing the Cr. on the N side of a Field, in a Glade, adj. a Survey of James Fisher & a Tract belonging to the sd Craven; 10 Feb 1748/49, p.120. £1.

WILLIAM KING, 400 acs. Augusta Co. on a Br. of Catheys Riv. called Moffets br., Beg. on the E side of Ralstons Path; 10 Feb 1748/49, p.121. £2.

ZEBULON HARRISON, 165 acs. Augusta Co. on Smiths Cr.; 10 Feb 1748/49, p.123. £1.

JOHN HARRISON, 400 acs. Augusta Co. on the dry Fork of a Br. of Smiths Cr.; 10 Feb 1748/49, p.125. £2.

REUBEN HARRISON, 233 acs. Augusta Co. on the dry Fork of Smith, on a Stony Hill, adj. John Harrisons Survey; 10 Feb 1748/49, p.126. £1.S5.

JOHN CALWELL, 1,085 acs. Brunswick Co. on both sides of Cubb Cr., Beg. near the Mouth of Louce; 10 Feb 1748/49, p.128. £5.S10.

CHARLES CURTIS, 1,300 acs. Orange Co. on the Brs. of Pamunkey Riv.; adj. Theodosius Stage, Robert Holdiness, Larkin Chew & Charles Stevens; 10 Feb 1748/49, p.130. for £2.S5 & also for the Imp. of one Pers. whose name is *Joseph Sews [Serus?]*. 400 acs. Part formerly gtd. sd Charles Curtis by Pat. 20 Jun 1733 [PB 15 p.51, on the North Fork of the Northanna in Spotsyl. Co.] & 400 acs. other part also formerly gtd. sd Curtis by Pat. 10 Jan 1735/36 [PB 16 p.434] & 500 acs. the Residue never before gtd.

THOMAS GREEN, 200 acs. Goochland Co. on both sides of Swift Cr. on the S side of James Riv., in a Meadow; adj. Thomas Watkins, Michael Gartharight & John Maxey; 10 Feb 1748/49, p.132. £1. Whereas by Pat. 30 Jul 1742 gtd. Richard Ward [PB 20 p.411 which included Nathaniel Maxey's PB 14 p.394] and whereas the sd Ward hath failed to pay Quitrents and to make cultiv. & improv. and Thomas Green hath made humble Suit and obtained a G. for the same.

WILLIAM LONGBOTTOME /LONGBOTTOM, 335 acs. Surry Co. on the S side of Nottoway Riv., adj. Robert Webb Junr.; 10 Feb 1748/49, p.134. £1.S15.

GEORGE PAYNE, 400 acs. Goochland Co. on both sides of the middle Br. of Cunningham Cr. & crossing the North Br. of Cunninghams Cr.; adj. Michael

Holland; 10 Feb 1748/49, p.136. £2.

GEORGE PAYNE, JUNR., 400 acs. Goochland Co. on both sides of the North Br. of Crooks Cr.; 10 Feb 1748/49, p.138. £2.

WILLIAM VAUGHAN, 400 acs. Pr. Geo. Co. on the S side of Nammiseen Cr.; adj. Henry Fitz, Claiborne/Claibourn, & Williams; 10 Feb 1748/49, p.139. £2.

JOHN WHITMORE, 300 acs. Pr. Geo. Co. on the lower side of Beaver Pond Cr., over the Mirey Br.; adj. Whitmore, Cleaton, Tucker & Langford; 10 Feb 1748/49, p.141. £1.S10.

WALTER LEONARD, 1,200 acs. Orange Co. on the Brs. of the Rappidan Riv.; adj. Anthony Thornton, William Neal, Isaac Tinsley & another pat. gtd. to the aforesd. Anthony Thornton; 10 Feb 1748/49, p.142. £6.

FRANCIS CLARK, 2,450 acs. Louisa Co. on both sides of Fork Cr., crossing the Road, near the Head of the south Fork of cross Cr., on the Brow of the Creeke Hill, by a Spring Br., along the Goochland Co. Line [N44°W]; adj. Syme, Love Statham, John Healey, Hughes & Colo. David Meriwether; 10 Feb 1748/49, p.144. £2. 400 acs. Part being Part of 5,820 acs. formerly gtd. John Syme Gent. by Pat. 28 Sep 1730 [Hanover Co., PB 13 p.487], 1,200 acs. other Part formerly gtd. sd Francis Clark by Pat. 17 Mar

1736/37 [1,600 acs., PB 17 p.304], 450 acs. other Part also formerly gtd. unto the sd Francis Clark by Pat. 1 Aug 1745 [PB 22 p.373] and 400 acs. the Residue never bef. Gtd.

JOHN LIDDERDALE, 1,196 acs. Louisa Co., in the Par. of Fredericksville on both sides of Buck Mountain Cr. and the Brs. thereof; 10 Feb 1748/49, p.147. £6.

ROBERT HOLT, 415 acs. Goochland Co. on the Brs. of Great Buffalo Cr. and little Buffalo Cr.; adj. Henry Cary Gent., Thomas Still, James Terry, Grizel Coleman & James Robinson; 20 May 1749, p.149. £2.S5.

BENJAMIN WOODSON, 394 acs. Goochland Co., among the Brs. of Cary Cr. of the S side of the Rivanna Riv., on the N side of the Horsepen Br. of Cary Cr., adj. the sd Benjamin Woodson; 20 May 1749, p.150. £2.

JOSEPH HOOPER, 390 acs. Albemarle Co. on the S side of James Riv. on both sides of a large Br. of Willis's Riv., adj. Gideon Patterson & Charles Lee; 20 May 1749, p.152. £2.

JOSEPH PRICE, 400 acs. Goochland Co. on the N Brs. of Willis's Riv., on the S side of Catail Br.; adj. Thomas Basset, Merry Webb, Samuel Glover, Stephen Hughes & John Alexander; 20 May 1749, p.154. Whereas by pat. 22 Sep 1739 gtd. Joseph Price

[PB 18 p.492] and whereas the sd Joseph Price hath failed to make cultiv. & improv. and whereas Edmund Gray hath made humble Suit and hath obtained a G. for the same which he assigned to the sd Joseph Price.

JOHN JAMES DUPUY, 400 acs. Goochland Co. on the S side of James Riv. on the W side of the lower Manakan Cr., down the Manakan Cr.; 20 May 1749, p.156. £2. Whereas by Pat. 28 Sep 1730 gtd. Peter Dep [PB 13 p.507] And Whereas the Right & Title of the sd Peter Dep is since become vested in William Gray and Elizabeth his Wife who have failed to pay Quit Rents and John James Dupuy hath made humble Suit and hath obtained a G. for the same.

WILLIAM CHAMBERS, 300 acs. Albemarle Co., bet. Holliday Riv. and Fish Pond Cr., adj. his own Line & Henry Chiles; 20 May 1749, p.157. £1.S10.

JOHN RIPLEY, 250 acs. Goochland Co. on both sides of the North Br. of Waltons Fork of Slate Riv., Beg. in the Lowgrounds, crossing Ripleys Cr.; 20 May 1749, p.159. £1.S5.

ROBERT DAVIS, 400 acs. Goochland Co. on the S side of Pedlar Riv., adj. William Floyd; 20 May 1749, p.161. £2.

RICHARD WITTON, 178 acs. Lunenburg Co. on both sides of Seneca Cr., on the Cr. opposite to

the fork thence up the last Fork; 20 May 1749, p.162. £1.

ROBERT DAVIS, JUNIOR, 400 acs. Goochland Co. on both sides the Wilderness Run; 20 May 1749, p.164. £2.

BENJAMIN PORTER, 380 acs. Orange Co. on the S side of Rappidan Riv., adj. Anthony Thornton & Christopher; 20 May 1749, p.165. £2.

SAMUEL HOMES, 348 acs. Lunenburg Co. on the S side of Allens Cr., adj. Byrd Lanier; 20 May 1749; p.167. £1.S15.

PETER HUDSON, 403 acs. Lunenburg Co. on the N side of Stanton/Staunton Riv. & both sides of Buffalo Cr., near Horsefords Path; 20 May 1749, p.169. £2.

JOHN BIARD, 53 acs. Lunenburg Co. on the N side of Stanton Riv.; 20 May 1749, p.171. £5 Shill.

JOHN CANNON, 1,214 acs. Lunenburg Co. on great Polecat and its Brs., adj. Thomas Rowel & Redmon Fallow; 20 May 1749, p.172. £6.S5.

Colo. JOHN BOLLING, Gent., 988 acs. Lunenburg Co. on the N side Roanoak Riv. joyning the Mouth of Butchers Br., down Mitchels Cr.; adj. Butcher, James Davis & Glass; 20 May 1749, p.174. £1. 818 acs. part formerly gtd. sd John Bolling by Pat. 20 Mar 1745/46 [Brunswick Co. PB 22 p.608 which included his 473 acs. in PB 19 p.907 dated 1 Dec 1740 & PB 14 p.445 dated 13 May 1732] and 170 acs. the Residue never bef gtd.

JOHN BOLLING, 440 acs. Goochland Co. on the Brs. of great Buffalo Cr., in a Meadow; adj. the sd Bolling, Richard Guin, Susannah Carnor, Anthony Sherroon & Samuel Ridgway; 20 May 1749, p.176. £2.S5. [This L. is within the bounds of Bollings 6,740 acs. in PB 26 p.449]

HENRY BROWN/BROWNE, 790 acs. Surry Co. on the S side Nottoway Riv. and on the Brs. of Spring Sw. and Poplar Sw., Beg. on the N side of the little Spring Sw., down the Run of Cocke's Br.; adj. Charles Judkins, Samuel Norrington, Thomas Felts, Robert Seat & William Browne; 20 May 1749, p.178. £4.

ROBERT PARKER, 81 acs. Nansemond Co., by the Main Run of the Nuckles Sw.; adj. his own, William Rogers, Thomas Boyt & John Ralls; 20 May 1749, p.180. 10 Shill.

RICHARD PARKER, 82 acs. Nansemond Co., through Summerton Sw.; adj. Thomas Boyt, Robert Parker & William Rogers; 20 May 1749, p.181. 10 Shill.

HENRY COPELAND, 733 acs. the upper Par. of Nansemond Co. on the E side the Back Sw.; adj. Sampson Meredith's Pat. & Thomas Jornagans Pat.; 20 May

1749, p.183. £1.S10. 440 acs. Part formerly gtd. Sampson Meredith by Pat. 21 Oct 1687 [Sampson Meridith, PB 7 p.608] the Right & Title whereof is since become vested in the sd Henry Copeland and 293 acs. the Residue being surplus L. within the Bounds of the sd Pat.

JACOB DARDEN, 202 acs. Nansemond Co. on the W side of black Water Riv. and on both sides Cypress Sw., on the NE side mirery Br., on the Cedar Marsh, near the main Road, adj. Robert Carr & Daniel Batten; 20 May 1749, p.185. £1.

DANIEL BATTEN, 53 acs. Nansemond Co. on the N side Nottoway Riv., adj. Christopher Reynolds & Thomas Edwards; 20 May 1749, p.187. 5 Shill.

MICHAEL BRINKLEY, 237 acs. Nansemond Co., in the main Desart; adj. John Cleve, the sd Michael Brinkley, & Humprey Griffin; 20 May 1749, p.189. £1.S5.

ALEXANDER WAUGH, 100 acs. Orange Co., adj. Taliaferro, & Francis Conway; 20 May 1749, p.191. in consideration of the Importation of 2 Pers. whose Names are *William Hughes & Roaston Holland.*

ALEXANDER WAUGH, 300 acs. Orange Co. crossing Conways Br., in a Poison Field, on Adams Lick Br., adj. Francis Conway; 20 May 1749, p.193. in consideration of the Imp. of 6 Pers. whose Names are *John Gorden, Erasmus Johns, John Anderson, James Malcolm, James Wright & William White.*

BENJAMIN HAWKINS, 2,480 acs. Lunenburg Co. on both sides of the North Fork of Meherrin Riv. and both sides Owl Cr., in a Fork of sd Cr., adj. John Nance & Richard Nance; 20 May 1749, p.194. £12.S5.

JOHN TWITTY, 247 acs. Lunenburg Co. on both sides of the South Fork of Meherrin Riv., opposite to the Mouth of Meadow Br., adj. William Hawkins; 20 May 1749, p.196. £1.S5.

MATTHEW WILLS, 400 acs. Pr. Geo. Co. lying bet. the Brs. of Bear Sw. and Hatchers Run, in a slash, adj. John Mays & Stell; 20 May 1749, p.198. £2.

BENJAMIN WOODSON, 394 acs. Goochland Co., among the Brs. of Cary Cr. of the S side of the Rivanna Riv., on the N side of Horsepen Br. of Cary Cr., adj. the sd Benjamin Woodson; 20 May 1749, p.200. £2.

HUGH MILLER, 400 acs. Lunenburg Co. on both sides of Bannister Riv.; 20 May 1749, p.201. £2.

HUGH MILLER, 400 acs. Lunenburg Co. on both sides of Bannister Riv.; 20 May 1749, p.203. £2.

THOMAS WILLIAMS, 2,395 acs. Lunenburgh Co. on both sides Twitty's Cr.; adj. his own, Bentley, Perrin & Bedford; 20 May 1749, p.205. £12.

THOMAS WILLIAMS, 435 acs. Lunenburg Co. on both sides of blue Stone Cr., adj. Stith; 20 May 1749, p.207. £2.S5.

THOMAS WILLIAMS, 4,380 acs. Lunenburg Co. on both sides Williams's Cr., down Maple Sw.; adj. Lidderdale, Sanderson, Christopher Parson, Roberson & Thomas Word; 20 May 1749, p.209. £9.S10. 2,476 acs. part formerly gtd. John Ingram by Pat. 20 Sep 1745 [Brunswick Co., PB 24 p.108] and by the sd Ingram sold & conveyed unto the sd Thomas Williams and 1,904 acs. the Residue never bef gtd.

SAMUEL ARBUCKLE, 800 acs. Amelia Co. on the S side of the South Fork of Buffalo Riv.; adj. Baker, Archtacon, Richey & Anderson; 25 Jul 1749 *in the 23rd year of our Reign of George the second*, p.212. £4. *[Memorandm. Rts. & Fee recd. by T.D.]*

GEORGE DAVIS, 400 acs. Amelia Co. on the S side of the South Fork of Buffalo Riv.; adj. Richey & Archtacon; 25 Jul 1749, p.214. £2. *[Memorandum Rts. & Fee recd. by T.D.]*

JOHN BIGGER, 400 acs. Amelia Co. on the S side of the S Fork of Buffalo Riv., adj. Woodson; 25 Jul

1749, p.216. £2. [*Memorandm. Rts. & Fee recd. by T.D.*]

JOHN BRADSHAW, 766 acs. Pr. Geo. Co. on both sides of Bowens Br. of Nammisseen Cr., Beg. at the L. now in the Tenure and Occupation of Thomas Kirk, adj. the sd Kirk, Ravencroft, Gilliam (now Harrisons), Brathwate (now Richard Georges) & Broadway now Richard Glascocks; 25 Jul 1749, p.217. 380 acs. part formerly gtd. to the sd John Bradshaw by Pat. 12 Mar 1739/40 [PB 18 p.545] and 386 acs. the Residue formerly gtd. William Hamlin by Pat. 26 Mar 1739 [PB 18 p.290] which sd L. the sd Hamlin hath sold & conveyed unto the sd John Bradshaw.

MATTHEW TALBOT, 400 acs. Lunenburg Co. on both sides Twitty's Cr., adj. Charles Talbot & Hugh Boston; 25 Jul 1749, p.220. £2.

JOSEPH JACKSON, 400 acs. Amelia Co. on the N side of Bryer Riv., adj. Gauling, Mullins & Franklin; 25 Jul 1749, p.222. £2.

JAMES THACKSTON, 1,020 acs. Amelia Co. on the S side of the South Fork of Buffalo Riv., in the Road, in a Br. of Codees Cr.; adj. Baker now Andersons, Bartelot Anderson & Arbuckle; 25 Jul 1749, p.223. £5.S5.

MICHAEL McDERMOT ROW, 200 acs. Amelia Co., in the main Fork of sandy Riv.; adj. Alexander Womack & his own old Line; 25 Jul 1749, p.225. £1.

WILLIAM WINKFELD, 450 acs. Surry Co. on the N side of Nottoway Riv. and on the N side of Southwester Sw., up the Great Br. & the eastermost Prong of the same, adj. William Wynne & his ptd. L.; 25 Jul 1749, p.227. 15 Shill. (300 acs. part formerly gtd. to the sd William Winkfield by Pat. 12 Sep 1733 [PB 15 p.120] and 150 acs. the Residue never bef gtd.) [This pat. was apparently amended in PB 27 p.446]

JAMES BARNES, 29 acs. Hanover Co., adj. Peter Claybrook & Winston; 25 Jul 1749, p.229. 5 Shill.

LENIRE BREWER, 150 acs. Brunswick Co. on the Beaver Pond Cr., at a Pond, & the Country Line [East], adj. John Poythress; 25 Jul 1749, p.231. 15 Shill.

JOHN DUGGER, 400 acs. Brunswick Co. on both sides of the Rockey Run, along Tatums Road; 25 Jul 1749, p.232. £2.

WILLIAM COVINTON, 400 acs. Lunenburg Co. on both sides of the Harricane Br. of Meherrin Riv., crossing the North Fork & the South fork of the Br.; 25 Jul 1749, p.234. £2.

JAMES TERRY, 400 acs. Goochland Co. on both sides of Bostocks Br. of Great Guinea Cr.; 25 Jul 1749, p.236. £2.

THOMAS MOSELEY, 460 acs. Lunenburgh Co. on the N side of Otter Riv. including some of the Head Brs. of Elk Cr., adj. William Stith; 25 Jul 1749, p.237. £2.S10.

JOHN PHELPS, 444 acs. Lunenburg Co., including some of the Brs. of the South Fork of little Otter Riv., adj. Aaron Burleson; 25 Jul 1749, p.239. £2.S5.

PHILIP PLEDGER, 480 acs. Lunenburg Co. on the S side of Nottoway Riv. on both sides of the Rocky Br.; adj. Fisher, Joseph Minor & Barnes; 25 Jul 1749, p.240. £2.S10.

JOHN MITCHEL, 400 acs. Lunenburgh Co. on the S side of Nottoway Riv., in a Meadow, adj. Nicholas Hudson; 25 Jul 1749, p.242. £2.

SYLVANUS JOHNSON, 400 acs. Lunenburgh Co. on the lower side of Ledbetters Cr.; adj. Ingram & James Oliver; 25 Jul 1749, p.243. £2.

ADAM COHOON, 800 acs. Lunenburgh Co. on the Brs. of the middle and Horsepen Forks of Cub Cr.; adj. Thomas Duggins & Joseph Morton; 25 Jul 1749, p.245. £4.

JOHN NANCE, 385 acs. Lunenburg Co. on both sides the North Fork of dry Cr.; adj. Wynn, Dunkin Blue & Nicholas Christopher; 25 Jul 1749, p.247. £2.

JOSEPH MINOR, 1,325 acs. Lunenburgh Co. on both sides of dry Cr., crossing the Rocky Br.; adj. John Knight, Richard Wynn, Crew & Fisher; 25 Jul 1749, p.248. £5. (327 acs. Part formerly gtd. John Parker by Pat. 5 Jun 1746 [Brunswick Co., PB 24 p.259], the Right whereof is since become vested in the sd Joseph Minor and 998 acs. the Residue never bef. gtd.)

ROBERT MOOR, 284 acs. Lunenburgh Co. on both sides of Mirery Cr., adj. Patrick Moor at the Fork; 25 Jul 1749, p.250. £1.S10.

PERRIN ALLDAY, 725 acs. Lunenburg Co. on the upper side of Wards Fork, adj. Richard Austin & his own Line; 25 Jul 1749, p.252. £3.S15.

THOMAS STAPLES, 400 acs. Lunenburg Co. on both sides Swish Cr.; adj. Degraffenreidt & Ingram; 25 Jul 1749, p.254. £2.

OWEN FRANKLIN, 400 acs. Lunenburg Co. on the S side of Nottoway Riv. including both sides of dry Cr., adj. Nicholas Christopher; 25 Jul 1749, p.255. £2.

OBEDIAH PERRY, 150 acs. Lunenburg Co. on the N side of Otter Riv., including both sides of the Lick Run, adj. John Phelps; 25 Jul 1749, p.257. 15 Shill.

THOMAS BALDEN, 445 acs. Lunenburgh Co. on the Head of the

Horsepen Fork of Cubb Cr.; adj. Thomas Duggins & Morton; 25 Jul 1749, p.258. £2.S5.

WILLIAM LOVE, 433 acs. Lunenburg Co. on both sides Meherrin Riv., Beg. on a small Island in the sd Riv., down Polecat Br., adj. Robert Scott; 25 Jul 1749, p.261.

JOHN DAVID, 400 acs. Lunenburg Co. on the E side of Wards Fork including both sides of Wild Cat Br.; 25 Jul 1749, p.262. £2.

BENJAMIN HAWKINS, 350 acs. Brunswick Co. on the S side Owls Cr. and on both sides of the Mouth of little Owls Cr.; 25 Jul 1749, p.263. £1.S15.

ROBERT JENINGS, 300 acs. Lunenburgh Co. on both sides of Cub Cr. including the Mouth of long Cr.; 25 Jul 1749, p.265. £1.S10.

ROBERT WATHEN, 340 acs. Lunenburg Co., including both sides of the middle Fork of falling Riv., adj. his old Survey; 25 Jul 1749, p.266. £1.S15.

ROBERT WATHEN, 250 acs. Lunenburg Co. including both sides of Cubb Cr.; 25 Jul 1749, p.268. £1.S5.

ROBERT WATHEN & ROBERT JENINGS, 340 acs. Lunenburgh Co. including both sides of the Middle Fork of falling Riv.; 25 Jul 1749, p.269. £1.S15.

JAMES OLIVER & JAMES OLIVER JUNR., 625 acs. Lunenburg Co. on both sides both Forks of Ledbetters Cr., Beg. on the W side of the East Fork of the same, adj. Degraffenreidt; 25 Jul 1749, p.271. £3.S5.

WILLIAM HILL, 400 acs. Lunenburg Co. on the Ridge bet the Brs. of Butchers Cr. and Allins Cr., adj. Ravenscroft; 25 Jul 1749, p.273. £2.

RICHARD WYNN, 425 acs. Lunenburgh Co. on both sides of dry Cr., down the North Fork of sd Cr.; adj. Crew [their Lines] & Nicholas Christopher; 25 Jul 1749, p.274. £2.S5.

JAMES BARON, 1,200 acs. Lunenburgh Co. on both sides Stoney Cr., adj. Garrat & Adkins; 25 Jul 1749, p.276. £6.

EDWARD PARKER, 450 acs. Lunenburg Co. on the Ridge bet. the Brs. of Difficult Cr. and the Brs. of Clover Cr., adj. Anthony Pouncey; 25 Jul 1749, p.277. £2.S5.

RICHARD DENNIS, 361 acs. Amelia Co. on the upper side of the main Seller Cr. of Deep Cr.; adj. West, John Mays & the L. purchased of West; 25 Jul 1749, p.279. 15 Shill. 235 acs. Part formerly gtd. to Francis West by Pat. 17 Sep 1731 [on the Hunting Path in Pr. Geo. Co., PB 14 p.357] the Right & Title is since become vested in the sd Richard Dennis;

and 126 acs. the Residue never bef. gtd.

JOHN BUTLER, 346 acs. Pr. Geo. Co. on the S side James Riv.; adj. Joseph Meatchump, Mr Wallis & Edward Hollaway; 25 Jul 1749, p.280. £1.S15. Whereas by Pat. 21 Apr 1695 gtd. John Bonner [PB 8 p.440 in Weynoake Par.] in Charles City Co. now Pr. Geo. and whereas the sd John Bonner hath failed to pay Quitrents and to make Cultiv. and Improv. and John Butler hath made humble suit and hath obtained a G. for the same.

JOHN BURN, 180 acs. Lunenburgh Co. including both sides of the middle Fork of Cubb Cr., adj. William Watson & Thomas Harvy; 25 Jul 1749, p.282. £1.

JOHN MOOR, 243 acs. Brunswick Co. on both sides the North Fork of mirey Cr.; 25 Jul 1749, p.284. £1.S5.

JOSEPH BENNET, 285 acs. Lunenburg Co. on both sides of Parhams Cr., on a Ridge; adj. Amos Timms, Adam Tapley & his own Line; 25 Jul 1749, p.285. £1.S10.

JOSEPH BENNETT, 298 acs. Lunenburgh Co. on both sides of Parhams Cr.; adj. Tanner & Adam Tapley; 25 Jul 1749, p.287. £1.S10.

ROBERT WATHEN, 210 acs. Lunenburg Co. on the upper side of

falling Riv., by his own old Line; 25 Jul 1749, p.288. £1.S5.

WILLIAM McGINNIS, 231 acs. Lunenburg Co. on both sides of the lower Fork of difficult Cr.; 25 Jul 1749, p.290. £1.S5.

RICHARD CREW & JOHN CREW, 480 acs. Lunenburgh Co. on the lower side of dry Cr., adj. John Roe & Nicholas Christopher; 25 Jul 1749, p.291. £2.S10.

MARY ENGLISH, 100 acs. Louisa Co. on both sides Camp Cr.; adj. George Thompson, Adduston Rogers & Forrest Green; 25 Jul 1749, p.293, *Witness our trusty and welbeloved Sir William Gooch Baronet our Lieutenant Governor and Commander in chief of our sd Colony and Dominion at Williamsburg under the [Great] Seal of our sd Colony.* 10 Shill.

JOHN DORCH, JUNIOR, 384 acs. Lunenburgh Co., in the Fork of Miles Cr.; adj. Dennis Lark; 5 Sep 1749, p.294, *Witness our trusty and welbeloved Thomas Lee Esqr. President of our Council and Commander in chief of our sd Colony and Dominion at Williamsburg.* £2.

Listed Exd.
Feb 8. 1749/50. Settled the Rights thus far in this Book & burnt them this day. John Blair

ABRAHAM VAUGHAN, 400 acs. Lunenburg Co., down a Br. of the second Fork of Lickinghole, adj.

John Twitty; 5 Sep 1749, p.295. £2.

BARTELOT ANDERSON of Hanover Co., 953 acs. in the Counties of Amelia & Lunenburgh on the Heads of the Brs. of the South Fork of Buffalo and little Roanoak, Beg. on a great Br. of Buffalo; adj. Abraham Baker now Charles Andersons, Lidderdale & his own old Line; 5 Sep 1749, p.297. £4.S15.

DAVID CALDWELL, 400 acs. Lunenburgh Co. on both sides Snow Cr., crossing Crabtree Cr., adj. William Caldwell; 5 Sep 1749, p.298. £2.

JOHN NICHOLDS, 4,450 acs. Lunenburgh Co. on the head Brs. of black Walnut, Clover and Difficult Creeks; adj. Colo. Richard Randolph, John Jones, Peter Hudson, Edward Parker & John Owen; 5 Sep 1749, p.300. £22.S5.

JOHN VAUGHAN, 37 acs. Pr. Geo. Co. on both sides of Rockey Br. on the lower side of Mawhipponock Cr., Beg. on the Great Br. on the Road; adj. Tucker, Henry Mayes, Matthew Mayes & Henry Crowder; 5 Sep 1749, p.302. 5 Shill.

JOHN WELLS, 354 acs. Amelia Co. on the S side of the Lazaritta Cr., down the long Br.; adj. Rowland, Cabinis, Bruce, James Anderson, Bagly & Nathaniel Roberson; 5 Sep 1749, p.304. £1.S15.

JOHN ROBERTS, 400 acs. Amelia Co. on the head Brs. of Mountain Cr., up a Fork of the sd Cr., by the Road; adj. Collins, Nash & Ligon; 5 Sep 1749, p.305. £2.

TRAVIS GRIFFIS, 295 acs. Surry Co. on the N side of black Water Sw., by the Co. Line [N49½°E & N47°E]]; adj. his own, Mr Richard Jones, Thomas Griffis & William Short; 5 Sep 1749., p.306. £1.S10.

HENRY STURDIVANT, 236 acs. Surry Co. on the S side of Nottoway Riv., on the Cabbin Stick Sw. & the Woodyard Sw., just over a Pond; adj. Edward Acolls, John Rottenberry, his own Line, Robert Green & Hollum Sturdivant; 5 Sep 1749, p.308. £1.S5.

JOSHUA FRY, 400 acs. Albemarle Co. on the N side of the Buffalo Ridge, adj. John Harvie; 5 Sep 1749, p.309. £2.

ELIAS CLARKE, 400 acs. Pr. Geo. Co., bet the Brs. of Bear Sw. and Hatchers Run; adj. Matthew Wills, Stall & Thompson; 5 Sep 1749, p.311. £2.

JOHN THREEWITS, 214 acs. Surry Co. on the North (sic) side of Nottoway Riv., Beg. in the Westernmost Br. of the Cabbinstick Sw.; adj. Matthew Whitehead, Colo. Robert Bolling & his own Lines; 5 Sep 1749, p.312. £1.S5. [This L. is South of the Nottoway Riv., now in SW Sussex Co.]

CHARLES LEWIS, 400 acs. Albemarle Co. on both sides of Hiccory Cr., at the South Fork, adj. Thomas Henderson; 5 Sep 1749, p.313. £2.

JOHN OWEN, 2,235 acs. Amelia Co. on both sides of Mountain Cr., Beg. on the upper or W side of the lower Fork of the sd Cr., up the upper Fork of sd Cr., on the Ridge, adj. Ligon & Akin; 5 Sep 1749, p.315. £11.S5.

MATTHEW MILLS, 1,527 acs. Albemarle Co. on the Brs. of Mechums Riv., in a Bottom, adj. Michael Wood; 5 Sep 1749, p.316. 400 acs. part formerly gtd. unto the sd Matthew Mills by Pat. 15 Aug 1737 [Goochland Co., PB 17 p.387], and three other Tracts or Parcels two for 400 acs. Each & the other for 327 acs. were also formerly gtd. to the sd Matthew Mills by Pat. 15 Mar 1744/45 [Goochland Co., PB 23 p.804, p.813 & p.817].

the Reverend JOHN ORNSBY, 584 acs. Pr. Geo. Co., bet. Butterwood and Tommahitton Swamps, along the Co. Line [North]; adj. William Eaton, Richard Beale, the 200 acs. purchased of Hugh Kirkland, & Cryer; 5 Sep 1749, p.318. 384 acs. Part formerly gtd. unto the sd John Ornsby by Pat. 10 Jul 1745 [PB 22 p.264] and 200 acs. other Part also formerly gtd. unto the sd John Ornsby by Pat. 25 Jul 1746 [PB 24 p.301].

JOHN LABAREAR, 175 acs. Henrico Co., crossing the hundred Road; adj. Farmer, Lepraid, Newby, Jenkins & Adkins; 5 Sep 1749, p.319. £1.

JOSHUA FRY, 400 acs. Albemarle Co. on both sides of the Road on the N side of the Buffalo Ridge, adj. John Harvie; 5 Sep 1749, p.321. £2.

JOSHUA FRY, 400 acs. Albemarle Co. on a Br. of Porridge Cr. on the N side, adj. Mr James Christian; 5 Sep 1749, p.322. £2.

JOSHUA FRY, 293 acs. Albemarle Co. on both sides of Porridge Cr., Beg. at the lower End of a Piece of Lowgrounds, adj. Robert Johns; 5 Sep 1749, p.323. £1.S10.

DANIEL HARRISON, JUNIOR, 262 acs. Augusta Co. on a Br. of Muddy Cr., adj. Daniel Harrison Senr.; 5 Sep 1749, p.325. £1.S10.

THOMAS MILLSAP, 400 acs. Augusta Co. on a Br. of Smith Cr., Beg. in a Lined of the L. of Benjamin Borden, with the dividing Line bet. Us and Lord Fairfax [N46°W]; 5 Sep 1749, p.326. £2.

THOMAS ARMSTRONG, 120 acs. Augusta Co. on a Br. of Catheys Riv. called Jennings Br.; 5 Sep 1749, p.327. 15 Shill.

JOHN KEER, 180 acs. Augusta Co. on both sides of the middle Riv. of Shanando, Beg. on the Point of a Hill bet. Christians Cr. and the long Meadow Run Corner to Beverly Mannor; 5 Sep 1749, p.328. £1.

BENJAMIN HIGGENBOTHAM, 300 acs. Albemarle Co. on Both Sides of Buffalo Riv., adj. Aaron Higgenbotham; 5 Sep 1749, p.329. £1.S10

ELLIOT ROBERTS, 225 acs. Albemarle Co. on the N side of Rockfish Riv.; 5 Sep 1749, p.331. £1.S5.

JOHN HOPES, 200 acs. Augusta Co. on Cooks Cr.; 5 Sep 1749, p.332. £1.

HENRY SWICHARD, 168 acs. Augusta Co. on the Waters of James Riv., adj. Bordens Pat. L. on the N side of Cotapa Cr., by the Side of a Brook; 5 Sep 1749, p.333. £1.

THOMAS NUSUM, 400 acs. Surry Co. on the S side of Spring Sw., down the Run of the Hornet Sw.; adj. George Cornet, Henry Manwaring & Henry Tyler; 5 Sep 1749, p.334. £2.

GEORGE CARRINGTON, 2,520 acs. Albemarle Co. on both sides of Randolph Cr. and bear Garden Cr.; adj. Dudley Digges Gent., John Palmer, Charles Lee, Joseph Dabbs, John Cannon, Isaac Bates Gent., Hugh Moor, William Webb, William Moss & John Douglas; 5 Sep 1749, p.336. 1,950 acs. Part formerly gtd. unto the sd George Carrington by Pat. 20 Aug 1745 [PB 23 p.1048]; 400 acs. other Part also formerly gtd. unto Orlando Hughes by Pat. 20 Sep 1745 [PB 22 p.505] and 170 acs. the Residue also formerly gtd. to John Floyd by

Pat. 20 Sep 1745 [PB 24 p.123] the Right and Title of which sd two last mentioned Tracts is since become vested in the sd George Carrington.

ROBERT PETTWAY, 125 acs. Surry Co. on the S side of Nottoway Riv., Beg. near the Mouth of Raineys Br.; adj. Matthew Sturdivant, Majr. Robert Wynne, Colo. Richard Bland & Benjamin Weathers; 5 Sep 1749, p.337. 15 Shill.

JOHN THREEWITS, 325 acs. Surry Co. on the S side of Nottoway Riv. and on the W side of Cabbinstick Sw., Beg. at the Mouth of the great Slash; adj. Henry Sturdivant, his own Lines & CoLo: Robert Bolling; 5 Sep 1749, p.339. £1.S15.

WILLIAM SPENCE, 335 acs. Is. of Wight Co. on the N side of Meherrin Riv.; adj. John Brantley, Hugh Norvell, John Ward & Harry Floyd; 5 Sep 1749, p.340. £1.S15.

ETHELDRED TAYLOR, 335 acs. Is. of Wight Co. on the S side of Lightwood Sw.; adj. Robert Cobb, Thomas Deloach, his own old Lines & Thomas Kitchen; 5 Sep 1749, p.342. £1.S15.

JOHN ELDER, 200 acs. Pr. Geo. Co. on the S side of Butterwood Sw.; adj. William Poythress, Thomas Elder, Whitmore, his own old line, Moore & Charles Poythress; 5 Sep 1749, p.343. £1.

JOHN ROBERTS, 400 acs. Amelia Co., bet the Brs. of Bush and

Meherrin Rivers, by the Road; adj. Collins, Davisson, Nash & Degraffenreidt; 5 Sep 1749, p.345. £2.

EDWARD GRESHAM, 380 acs. Amelia Co. on the upper side of Harris's Cr.; adj. Venable, Holland, Williamson, Lockit & Harris; 5 Sep 1749, p.346. £2.

BUFFINGTON JOSEPH DARVILL, 1,090 acs. Pr. Geo. Co., bet. the Head Brs. of Beverpond Cr. and Butterwood Sw. on both sides the Road; adj. Johnson, Glover, John Poythress, Wainwright, Cleaton, Whitmore & Elder; 5 Sep 1749, p.347. £5.S10.

THOMAS WHITWORTH, 230 acs. Amelia Co. bet. the Brs. of flatt and Stocks Creeks on both sides the Road; adj. Wingo, Hurt, Chapple, Morris & his own lines; 5 Sep 1749, p.349. £1.S5.

JOHN ROBERTS, 200 acs. Amelia Co. on the Heads of the Brs. of sandy Riv. and flatt Cr.; adj. Searcey, Lester, Villan, Dupuy & Rowland; 5 Sep 1749, p.350. £1.

ROBERT JENNINGS, 400 acs. Amelia Co. on both sides of the North Fork of Sawneys Cr., in the Lowgrounds, adj. William Hill; 5 Sep 1749, p.351. £2.

JOHN DAVIS, 166 acs. Augusta Co. on a Br. of Smiths Cr. called Yayers Br., on the W side a Meadow Br., adj. Adam Yayer; 5 Sep 1749, p.353. £1.

ANDREW BURD, 190 acs. Augusta Co. on Smiths Cr.; adj. Benjamin Borden, and Thomas & Robert Millsap; 5 Sep 1749, p.354. £1.

DANIEL LOVE, 250 acs. Augusta Co. on the Drafts of Cooks Cr., Beg. on the NW Side of a sinking Spring Br., on a stony Ridge; 5 Sep 1749, p.355. £1.S5.

DANIEL HARRISON, 200 acs. Augusta Co. on a Br. of Muddy Cr., adj. Daniel Harrison; 5 Sep 1749, p.356. £1.

WILLIAM KEER, 250 acs. Augusta Co., at a Place called *Flagspring* on the SE side of the middle Riv.; 5 Sep 1749, p.358. £1.S5.

EPHRAIM LOVE & WILLIAM HOPKINS, 204 acs. Augusta Co. on the Head Brs. of muddy Cr. bet. the L. Jacob Dye lives on and the Mountain, Beg. at the foot of the sd Mountain, on a Ridge, on the SW side of Aspe Bottom Br.; 5 Sep 1749, p.359. £1.

REPENTANCE TOWNSEND, 277 acs. Augusta Co. on a Br. of the North Riv. of Shanando called the second Fork of Thorney Br., on a stony Point, adj. Smith; 5 Sep 1749, p.360. £1.S10.

JOHN MATHEWS, 296 acs. Augusta Co. on the NW side of the North Br. of James Riv. opposite to Philip Weavers Bottom, Beg. on the Riv. at a Fall, on the side of a stoney Hill, crossing McDowals

Meadow Cr., adj. McDowal; 5 Sep 1749, p.361. £1.S10.

ANDREW FOSTER, 300 acs. Augusta Co. on a Br. of Cathey's Riv. called McClurs Run near the North Mountain on the W Side of the L. James Bell lives on, near the Foot of the Mountain, adj. Morish Offreel; 4 Sep 1749, p.363. £1.S10.

JOHN DAVIS, 159 acs. Augusta Co. on a Br. of Smiths Cr. called Yayers Br., on the W side of a Meadow; 5 Sep 1749, p.364. £1.

ANDREW KEER, 230 acs. Augusta Co. on both sides of the middle Riv. of Shanando Riv., adj. John Carr; 5 Sep 1749, p.365. £1.S5.

SWAN RAMBO, 400 acs. Augusta Co. on Smith Cr., adj. Andrew Burd & John Philip; 4 Sep 1749, p.367. £2.

DANIEL GIBBSON, 79½ acs. Augusta Co. on Moffets Cr. a Br. of Catheys Riv., adj. John Davison; 5 Sep 1749, p.368. 10 Shill.

MARGARET & ANDREW CROCKET, 48 acs. Augusta Co., in the Calf Pasture known by the Name of *David Mill Place* on Mill Cr., Beg. at the Foot of a Mountain; 5 Sep 1749, p.369. 5 Shill.

MARGARET & ANDREW CROCKET, 44 acs. Augusta Co. on the W side of the Calf Pasture

Riv., adj. James Poag; 5 Sep 1749, p.370. 5 Shill.

SAMUEL HARRISON, 400 acs. Augusta Co. on the South Br. of Linwells Cr.; 5 Sep 1749, p.371. £2.

THOMAS LOCKHAR, 120 acs. Augusta Co. on the Drafts of Smith's Cr.; 5 Sep 1749, p.373. for the Imp. of 3 Pers. whose Names are *William Philips, James Mills & Thomas Miller.*

JAMES ARBUCKLE, 400 acs. Augusta Co. on the N side of James Riv. below the Island Ford, at the lower End of an Island; 5 Sep 1749, p.374. £2.

WILLIAM MACLIN, 404 acs. Lunenburgh Co. on the N side of Difficult Cr., adj. John Russell & Little; 5 Sep 1749, p.375. £2.

SAMUEL STEWART, 180 acs. Augusta Co. on the middle Br. of Linwells Cr., adj. Robert Patterson; 5 Sep 1749, p.377. £1.

VALENTINE SEVERE, 375 acs. Augusta Co. on a Br. of Shanando called the long Meadow, Beg. near the Head of a Spring in the Meadow Side; 5 Sep 1749. p.378. for the Imp. of 6 Pers. whose Names are *John Lightfoot, Samuel Merefield, Samuel Irvording /Iwording, Elizabeth Overington, Henry Upton & Mary Upton* as also for 10 Shill.

VALENTINE SEVERE, 184 acs. Augusta Co., bet. the Limestone

Ridge and Smith's Cr.; adj. Andrew Burd & Robert Milsap; 5 Sep 1749, p.379. £1.

THOMAS WILLIAMSON, 400 acs. Amelia Co. on Spring Cr.; adj. Jacob Williamson, Cunningham, Scott & Collins; 5 Sep 1749, p.381. £2.

WILLIAM SMITH, 295 acs. Amelia Co. on both sides of the North Fork of falling Cr., by a Spring; adj. Elam, Lockit, Mcbride, Martin & Williamson; 5 Sep 1749, p.382. £1.S10.

RICHARD GLASSCOCK, 100 acs. Pr. Geo. Co., bet the Brs. of Mawhipponock Cr. and Nammisseen, Beg. near a large Rock by the Side of John Bradshaws Path; 5 Sep 1749, p.384. 10 Shill.

DRURY OLIVER, 138 acs. Pr. Geo. Co., bet. Mawhipponock Cr. and Hatchers Run, adj. his own old Lines; 5 Sep 1749, p.385. 15 Shill.

ABRAHAM CROWDER, 350 acs. Pr. Geo. Co. on the Forks of the great Br. of Mawhipponock Cr., over the Road; adj. his own Line, his Father, Banister, Oliver, & Matthew Mayes; 5 Sep 1749, p.386. £1.S15.

THOMAS GODSEY, 324 acs. Henrico Co. crossing a Br. of Lirser Cr., on the Co. Line [N49½°E], crossing Carys Br., on the falling Grounds of Tomahauk; adj. Harrison, Shatteen & Cary; 5 Sep 1749, p.387. £1.S15.

FRANCIS FARLEY, 376 acs. Henrico Co. by Parish's Br., on the Piney Fork of Parishes Br.; adj. Henry Hudson, Lepraid, the sd Farley, & Peter Hudson; 5 Sep 1749, p.389. £2.

WILLIAM BACON, 254 acs. Henrico Co. on the Eastern Br.; adj. Smith, Lacy, the sd Bacon, & Watson; 5 Sep 1749, p.391. £1.S5.

JAMES WHITLER, 404 acs. Henrico Co. in a Piney Slash on Cornelaus's Cr.; adj. Parker, Bailey & Good; 5 Sep 1749, p.392. £2.

HENRY DOWNES, 150 acs. Louisa Co. on the W side of the little Mountains, crossing Turkey Run, adj. Colo. Nicholas Meriweather dec'd & James Coleman; 5 Sep 1749, p.393. for and in Consideration of the Imp. of 3 Pers. whose Names are *James Geddy, George Webb & Robert Stevenson.*

JAMES BLAIR, 352 acs. Pr. Anne Co., in Black Water, by a Run called Hagolo Run; 5 Sep 1749, p.395. for 2 lbs. of Tobacco for every Acre of sd L. Whereas by Inquisition Indented taken in sd Co. 16 June 1747 by Virtue of a Warrant directed to Samuel Boush Gent. Escheator for the sd Co. It appears that John Vaughan died seised of a certain Tract of L. which is found to Escheat to us from the sd John Vaughan And Whereas James Blair hath made humble Suit and obtained a G. for the same.

JOHN FARLEY, 17 acs. Henrico Co. down a Br. of Proctors Cr., adj. the sd Farley; 5 Sep 1749, p.396. 5 Shill.

RICHARD TALIAFERRO, 783 acs. Lunenburgh Co. on the N side of Meherrin Riv. on the S side of the Beaver Br., to a Corner marked ꝺ [for David Bray] on flatt Rock Cr., adj. Buller Herbert; 5 Sep 1749, p.398. £4. Whereas by Pat. 28 Sep 1728 gtd. unto David Bray Gent. [PB 14 p.79] one certain Tract or Parcel of L. in Brunswick Co. now Lunenburgh And Whereas Beverly Randolph in whom the Right & Title of the sd L. by divers Mense conveyances is since vested hath failed to pay Quit Rents and to make Cultiv. and improv. and Richard Taliaferro hath made humble Suit and obtained a G. for the same.

WILLIAM BEVERLY, Esquire, 393 acs. Caroline Co. on Pewmanzens; adj. the honourable John Carter Esq. dec'd, Lindsey, Dean, Clapham, Adam Lindsey, the Lands held by William & Richard Taliaferro [their Line], a Pat. gtd. Lawrence Taliaferro now dec'd, and the Lands of the Heirs of the aforesaid John Carter Esquire dec'd; 5 Sep 1749, p.399. for and in Consideration of the Imp. one Pers. whose Name is *Richard Pringle*. 320 acs. Part being Part of a Pat. for 814 acs. formerly gtd. Harry Beverley by Pat. 23 Oct 1719 [831 acs. Essex Co. on

Pewmansend Cr. in PB 10 p.452] and by him sold & conveyed unto the sd William Beverly and 70 acs. other Part also formerly gtd. to the sd William Beverley by Pat. 5 Mar 1745/46 and 3 acs. the Residue never bef gtd.

ASHLEY JOHNSON, 300 acs. Amelia Co. on the lower side of the little Saylors Cr. adj. John Crawford; 5 Sep 1749, p.401. £1.S10. Whereas by Pat. 30 Mar 1743 gtd. unto Michael Holland [PB 20 p.481] And Whereas John Holland Son and Heir of the sd Michael Holland dec'd in whom the Right of the sd L. is since become vested hath failed to make Cultiv. and improv. and Ashley Johnson hath made humble Suit and obtained a G. for the same.

WILLIAM HARRIS, 2½ acs. Goochland Co. one certain Island lying bet. the L. of the sd William Harris and Sabott Island in James Riv.; 5 Sep 1749, p.403. 5 Shill.

THOMAS CARTER, JUNIOR, 113 acs. Goochland Co. on the Brs. of Willis's Riv. on the S side of James Riv.; adj. Robert Carter, Philip Mayo & James Shelton; 5 Sep 1749, p.404. 15 Shill.

JOHN RICHEY, 400 acs. Amelia Co. on the Head of Plumbtree Br. of Harris's Cr.; adj. Watson, Holland & Venable; 5 Sep 1749, p.405. £2.

RICHARD PHILLIPS, 400 acs. Hanover Co. on both sides of Cross Sw., in the Head of a Glade, on the

South Fork and the main Fork of sd Sw.; adj. CoLo. Meriweather & Captain Clark; 5 Sep 1749, p.407. £2.

JOHN WEBB, 225 acs. Albemarle Co. on both sides of Raccoon Cr. of the Rivanna, adj. George Hilton; 5 Sep 1749, p.408. £1.S5.

JAMES LONDON, 250 acs. Albemarle Co. on a North Br. of Stoney Run of Buffaloe, near Mr Braxton; 5 Sep 1749, p.410. £1.S5.

ARTHUR MCDANIEL, 400 acs. Albemarle Co. on both sides of Ripleys Cr. of Slate Riv.; adj. Thomas, Dabbs & his own line of a former Survey; 5 Sep 1749, p.411. £2.

HENRY FITZ, 400 acs. Pr. Geo. Co. on the lower side of Namisseen Cr., adj. Bolling & FitzGerrald; 5 Sep 1749, p.413. £2.

GEORGE STELL, JUNIOR, 200 acs. Pr. Geo. Co. on the N side of Bear Sw.; adj. Cross, own old Line, Featherstone, Mayes & Tatum; 5 Sep 1749, p.414. £1.

JOSEPH FOWLER, 400 acs. Pr. Geo. Co. on both sides of the Road on the Head Brs. of Mawhipponock Cr., up the South Fork of sd Cr.; adj. Matthew Mayes, Drury Oliver, his own & Fords Line; 5 Sep 1749, p.415. £2.

JAMES MOORE, 100 acs. Pr. Geo. Co. on the S side of

Butterwood Sw., adj. his own old Line; 5 Sep 1749, p.417. 10 Shill.

CHARLES WETHERFORD, 390 acs. Lunenburgh Co. on the N side of Meherrin Riv., down Bears Element Cr., adj. John Booker; 12 Mar (sic) 1749, p.418. £2.

WILLIAM FORD, 104 acs. Pr. Geo. Co. bet. Mawhipponock Cr. and Hatchers Run; adj. Fowler, Mayes, Williams & Drury Oliver; 5 Sep 1749, p.420. 10 Shill.

JAFFRIS CRAWLEY, 400 acs. Lunenburgh Co. on both sides of the North Fork of Little Otter Riv.; 5 Sep 1749, p.421. £2.

GEORGE WAINRIGHT, 1,000 acs. Pr. Geo. Co. on the N side of Tommahitton Sw., up Beaver Pond Cr.; adj. Poythress, Whitmore, Cleaton, his own old Line & Peniston; 5 Sep 1749, p.423. £3. 399 acs. part formerly gtd. to the sd George Wainright by Pat. 15 Oct 1741 [PB 20 p.56] and 601 acs. the Residue never bef gtd.

MATTHEW FORD, 200 acs. Pr. Geo. Co. on the Head Brs. of Mawhipponock Cr.; adj. Matthew Mayes & Traylor; 5 Sep 1749, p.424. £1.

ISRAEL PICKENS, 300 acs. Lunenburgh Co. on both sides of Chesnut Cr., in the Lowgrounds, adj. William Caldwell; 5 Sep 1749, p.426. £1.S10.

ANDREW WADE, 400 acs. Lunenburgh Co. on the N side

Dann Riv.; adj. Henry Morris, Byrd & Mitchell; 5 Sep 1749, p.427. £2.

BENJAMIN ORRICK, 88 acs. Lunenburgh Co. on the S side of Otter Riv. including the Mouth of Thickety Cr.; 5 Sep 1749, p.429. 10 Shill.

RICHARD & WILLIAM HILL, 500 acs. Lunenburgh Co. on the Head of Maherrin; 5 Sep 1749, p.430. £2.S10.

JAMES STEWART, 400 acs. Lunenburgh Co. on the S side of Wards Fork; adj. Lidderdale & Richard Austin; 4 Sep 1749, p.432. £2.

JOSIAH SEAT, 290 acs. Lunenburgh Co. on the S side of Dann Riv., adj. Byrd; 5 Sep 1749, p.433. £1.S10.

RICHARD JONES, 400 acs. Lunenburgh Co. on the upper side of Little Roanoack and on both sides of Sycamore Br., adj. Brumfield; 5 Sep 1749, p.435. £2.

PHILIP MAYO, 400 acs. Albemarle Co. on the Brs. of Hardware Riv., adj. Captain Hudson; 5 Sep 1749, p.436. £2.

ROBERT LEE, 400 acs. Albemarle Co. on the S side of Slate Riv., by Joshua's Cr.; adj. a tract formerly gtd. to Henry Martin, & Gereon; 5 Sep 1749, p.438. £2.

WILLIAM NOWLAND, 400 acs. Albemarle Co. on both sides of

Arthurs Cr. a Br. of Slate Riv.; adj. a former Survey of the sd Nowlands, & William Chambers; 5 Sep 1749, p.439. £2.

JAMES WARREN, 400 acs. Albemarle Co. on both sides of stoney Run of Buffalo Riv.; 5 Sep 1749, p.441. £2.

RICHARD COCKE, 215 acs. Surry Co. on the S side of Nottoway Riv., adj. Timothy Ezell Junior; 5 Sep 1749, p.443. £1.S5.

WILLIAM LOFTIN, 115 acs. Surry Co. on the S side of Nottoway Riv., Beg. in the little Sw., in the prickley Ash Meadow & down the Run of that Br., adj. his own Lines; 5 Sep 1749, p.444. 15 Shill.

WILLIAM WINKFIELD, 450 acs. Surry Co. down by the great Br. and up South Wester Sw., adj. Wynne; 5 Sep 1749, p.446. 15 Shill. 300 acs. formerly gtd. unto the sd William Winkfield by Pat. 12 Sep 1733 [PB 15 p.120] and 150 acs. the Residue never bef gtd. [This apparently is an amended pat. of PB 27 p.227]

CHARLES MABERY, 119 acs. Surry Co. on the N side of the three Creeks, on the main Run & up the South Prong of little Ploughman Sw., adj. Martin Johnson & James Sammon; 5 Sep 1749, p.447. 15 Shill.

HENRY RICHARDSON, 171 acs. Surry Co. on the S side of Nottoway Riv.; adj. Henry

Manwaring, Benjamin Richardson & William Brown; 5 Sep 1749, p.449. £1.

WILLIAM WOMACK, 80 acs. Lunenburgh Co., in the Fork of Allens Cr., up the South Fork; 5 Sep 1749, p.450. 10 Shill.

ISAAC BENNING, 298 acs. Albemarle Co. on the N side of the North Fork of Slate Riv.; adj. Arthur McDaniel, William Perkins, James Webb, Richard Taylor, Faris & Thomas Turpin; 5 Sep 1749, p.452. £1.S10.

JAMES FREELAND, 394 acs. Albemarle Co. on both sides of Davids Cr. of the Fluvanna, crossing a Fork of sd Cr.; 5 Sep 1749, p.453. £2.

JAMES FREELAND, 400 acs. Albemarle Co. on both sides of Bent Cr. of the Fluvanna; 5 Sep 1749, p.455. £2.

MOSES RAY, 400 acs. Albemarle Co. on the S side of James Riv., adj. John Goodwin; 25 Dec 1749, p.457. £2.

MOSES RAY, 9 acs. Albemarle Co. one certain Island being the uppermost and largest of the Swift Islands in the Fluvanna bet. the Plantations of CoLo: William Mayo dec'd and William Cabell; 15 Dec 1749, p.458. 5 Shill.

MOSES RAY, 343 acs. Albemarle Co. on both sides of Gilberts Cr. of the Fluvanna, adj. CoLo: William

Mayo; 15 Dec 1749, p.459. £1.S15.

MOSES RAY, 400 acs. Albemarle Co. on both sides of Rock Island Cr. of the Fluvanna; 15 Dec 1749, p.461. £2.

JAMES ANDERSON, 50 acs. Augusta Co. over the long Glade, adj. George Cathey & James Anderson; 15 Dec 1749, p.462. 5 Shill.

WILLIAM ARMSTRONG, 85 acs. Augusta Co., down Smiths Cr., adj. Daniel Monahan; 15 Dec 1749, p.464. 10 Shill.

ROBERT EWING, 160 acs. Augusta Co. on a Br. of Roanoak called the Glade Cr., by the Mouth & to the head of a large Spring; 15 Dec 1749, p.465. £1.

JOSEPH LOVE, 137 acs. Augusta Co. on a Br. of Roanoak called Robinsons Br.; adj. Bryan Cuff, Stephen Rentfro & George Robinson; 15 Dec 1749, p.467. 15 Shill.

JOSEPH LOVE, 171 acs. Augusta Co. on a Br. of Goose Cr. called Rentfroes Br.; adj. Rentfroe & George Robinson; 15 Dec 1749, p.468. £1.

DAVID BRYAN, 166 acs. Augusta Co. on the Waters of Roanoak; 15 Dec 1749, p.470. £1.

JACOB BROWN, 91 acs. Augusta Co. on the S side of the North

Fork of Roanoak Riv.; 15 Dec 1749, p.471. 10 Shill.

JOHN MILLS, 100 acs. Augusta Co. on a Br. of Woods Riv. called the little Riv., Beg. against the Point of an Island; 15 Dec 1749, p.473. 10 Shill.

EPHRAIM VAUSE, 360 acs. Augusta Co. on both sides of Goose Cr., Beg. in an Island; 15 Dec 1749, p.474. £2.

BENJAMIN COPLAND, 400 acs. Augusta Co. on a Br. of the North Fork of Shanando called Buffalo Spring; 15 Dec 1749, p.475. £2.

EPHRAIM VAUSE, 320 acs. Augusta Co. on both sides of Goose Cr.; 15 Dec 1749, p.477. £1.S15.

JOHN HAYMES, 200 acs. Amelia Co. bet. the Burchen Sw. & Harricane Sw., Beg. by a Path in Richard Jones's Line; 15 Dec 1749, p.478. for the Imp. of one Pers. to dwell within this our Colony and Dominion of Virginia whose Name is *Richard Parr* and also for 15 Shill.

ROBERT RALSTON, 364 acs. Augusta Co. on a Br. of Catheys Riv. called Moffets Br., adj. John Smith; 15 Dec 1749, p.480. £2.

JOHN PATTERSON, 400 acs. Albemarle Co. on the Head Brs. of Appamatox, adj. his Lines & John Phelps; 15 Dec 1749, p.481. £2.

JAMES McNEAL, 395 acs. Albemarle Co. on the Brs. of Glovers Cr. and other Brs. of Slate Riv., near the Road on the S side thereof, adj. Robert Glover; 15 Dec 1749, p.483. £2.

ROBERT BUMPAS, 400 acs. Amelia Co. on the S side of little Nottoway Riv., adj. Evans & Ellis; 15 Dec 1749, p.485. £2.

THOMAS LEE, 243 acs. Amelia Co. on the N side of Vaughns Cr., adj. his own old Lines & Holland; 15 Dec 1749, p.486. £1.S5.

WILLIAM FAIN, 240 acs. Amelia Co. on the N side of Buffalo Riv.; adj. Wallace, Baldwin, Harvey & Nickson; 15 Dec 1749, p.488. £1.

TIRE HARRIS, 315 acs. Albemarle Co. on the S side of James Riv. on the Brs. of Willis's Cr.; adj. Gideon Patterson, Edmund Gray, William Gray & John Cook; 15 Dec 1749, p.489. £1.S15.

RICHARD MAYES, 120 acs. Amelia Co. bet the head of Bent Run and the Brs. of Flatt Cr.; adj. Hill, Gillington, Boston, Austin & Murfy; 15 Dec 1749, p.491. 15 Shill.

FRANCIS CLEMMENTS, 400 acs. Amelia Co. on the upper side of Flatt Cr., down Walnut Br.; adj. Craddock now Cocks, Hendrick & John Harris; 15 Dec 1749, p.492. £2.

GEORGE EWING, 400 acs. Amelia Co. on both sides of the Cedar Br. on the lower side of Vaughanes Cr., adj. Elam & Wingfield; 15 Dec 1749, p.494. £2.

JOHN HUGHES, 298 acs. Albemarle Co. under the E side of Willis's Mountain, adj. Abraham Childres; 15 Dec 1749, p.495. £1.S10

BENJAMIN BENNETT, 83 acs. Amelia Co. on the lower side of Sweathouse Cr.; adj. William Tucker, Bland, his own old Line & Hinton; 15 Dec 1749, p.497. 10 Shill.

CASTLETON HARPER, 84 acs. Albemarle Co. on the Brs. of Hardware Riv., adj. Thomas Sowel & the late Secretary Carter; 15 Dec 1749, p.498. 10 Shill.

JOHN PENN, 400 acs. Pr. Geo. Co. on the Head of Mawhiponock Cr., on a Br. of Bear Sw.; adj. Dickenson, Glascock & Bradshaw; 15 Dec 1749, p.500. £2.

WILLIAM MALONE, 100 acs. Brunswick Co. on both sides of Taylors Cr., adj. his own old Line & William Pennington; 15 Dec 1749, p.502. 10 Shill.

WILLIAM VAUGHAN, 441 acs. Brunswick Co. on the N side of the three Creeks, adj. Isaac Hows; 15 Dec 1749, p.503. £2.S5.

WILLIAM GILLIAM, 304 acs. Brunswick Co. on the Brs. of

Kettle Stick; adj. Theodorick Bland, Wallis & Micajah Perry; 15 Dec 1749, p.505. £1.S10.

JAMES BASS, 415 acs. Brunswick Co. on the Brs. of Avents Cr.; adj. John Duger, Winfield, Cole, Hix & Peterson; 15 Dec 1749, p.506. £1.S5.

HENRY FITZ, 204 acs. Pr. Geo. Co. on both sides of Mawhipponock Cr., adj. Edward Traylor; 15 Dec 1749, p.508. £1.

HENRY CLAY, 40 acs. Henrico Co. adj. Ellison Clerk & Cooke; 15 Dec 1749, p.510. 5 Shill.

THOMAS HURST, 400 acs. Brunswick Co. on the S side of the three Creeks; 15 Dec 1749, p.511. £2.

JAMES OVERBY, 36 acs. Pr. Geo. Co., in the Fork of George's Br. of Namiseen Cr., adj. John Eppes & William Vaughan; 15 Dec 1749, p.512. 5 Shill.

SAMUEL BUTLER, 270 acs. Henrico Co. crossing the Horspen Br., near the Head of a Bottom; adj. Roberts, John James Flournoy & the sd Butler's upper Survey; 15 Dec 1749, p.514. £1.S10.

SAMUEL BUTLER, 270 acs. Henrico Co. down a Br. of Horspen Br.; adj. the sd Butlers lower Survey, John James Flournoy, Mosley & Roberts; 15 Dec 1749, p.516. £1.S10.

ROBERT OWEN, 400 acs. Surry Co. on the S side of Nottoway Riv. and on both sides of the Raccoon Sw., adj. Silvanus Stokes; 15 Dec 1749, p.517. £2.

TERISHA TURNER, 200 acs. Goochland Co. on the S side of James Riv. on the Brs. of Snow Quarter, adj. William Faris & Nicholas Davies; 15 Dec 1749, p.519. £1.

JAMES MASON, 178 acs. Lunenburgh Co. on both sides of a lower Br. of Stoney Cr., on the Road, adj. Garratt & Barram; 15 Dec 1749, p.521.

JOHN GWIN, 400 acs. Lunenburg Co. in the County [sic] Line, along the Country Line [West]; 15 Dec 1749, p.522. £2.

JOHN COX, 302 acs. Lunenburgh Co. down crupper Run, adj. Henry Roberson; 15 Dec 1749, p.523. £1.S10.

ROBERT BRIGGS, 162 acs. Lunenburgh Co. on the lower side of Crooked Cr.; 15 Dec 1749, p.525. £1.

EDMUND CLARK, 154 acs. Lunenburgh Co. on the Brs. of Butchers Cr., adj. John Bolling; 15 Dec 1749, p.527. 15 Shill.

JAMES GEE, 230 acs. Lunenburgh Co. on the head Brs. of Bears Element, adj. Mason; 15 Dec 1749, p.528. £1.S5.

WILLIAM ALEXANDER, 260 acs. Goochland Co. on the Brs. of Muddy Cr. and Snow Quarter of the S side of James Riv.; adj. John Gill, Ashford Hughes, Thomas Joplin & Thomas Carter; 15 Dec 1749, p.530. £1.S10.

WILLIAM POPE, 160 acs. Is. of Wight Co. on the N side of Tarraro Cr.; adj. Robert Crocker, the sd Pope's old Line & William Rugless; 15 Dec 1749 *in the 23rd year of our Reign of George the Second, Thomas Lee Esqr. President of our Council and Commander in Chief*, p.532-533. £1.

March 25th. 1751
This Book Examined from the former Settlement & the Rights burnt John Blair D.Audr.

PATENT BOOK NO. 28

12 Jan 1746/47 to 5 Sep 1749 [12 Mar 1749/50]

JOHN SKELTON, 335 acs. Henrico Co. crossing 3 brs. of the middle Cr., crossing the middle creek Road alias Skin Quarter Road; adj. William Moseley, Clay & the sd Skelton; 12 Jan 1746/47 *in the 20th year of our Reign of George the Second, William Gooch Esqr. our Lieut. Governor and Commander in Chief*, p.1. £1.S15.

JOHN SKELTON, 150 acs. Henrico Co. crossing Brs. of middle Cr.; adj. Willm. Perdue, William Clay, the sd Skeltons upper Survey & Richard Belsher; 12 Jan 1746/47, p.3. 15 Shill.

VALENTINE WINFREY, 314 acs. Henrico Co. down Proctors Cr., up Crooked Br.; adj. Matthew Farlow, Daniel Worsham, William Hatcher, Stephen Beasley, Thomas Tanner, Robert Mosley & Charles Clay; 12 Jan 1746/47, p.4. £1.S15.

JOHN FITZGERRALD, 44½ acs. Henrico Co. on the S side of Swift Cr., adj. Capt. Field Jefferson & the sd FitzGerralds other Lands; 12 Jan 1746/47, p.5. 5 Shill.

PERRIN GILES, 156 acs. Henrico Co., Beg. at his Corner on a ridge;

adj. Mosley, Tullit's great Tract, John Welch, Flournoy & William Giles; 12 Jan 1746/47, p.6. £1.

SAMUEL JORDAN, 270 acs. Henrico Co., down a br. of Horspen Br.; adj. John James Flournoy, Mosley & Roberts; 12 Jan 1746/47, p.8. £1.S10.

JAMES RICHEE, 44 acs. Henrico Co. on the N side of Buckengame Road; adj. Wooldridge, John Bolling & Roberts; 12 Jan 1746/47, p.9. 5 Shill.

JOHN HARE, 37 acs. Nansemond Co. on W side of Sumerton Sw.; adj. Thomas Jones, John Ralls & George Keen; 12 Jan 1746/47, p.11. 5 Shill.

THOMAS PEIRCE, 236 acs. Nansemond Co., in a place called *the Gums*; adj. John Peirce, Edward & Aaron Moore, John King & his own Land; 12 Jan 1746/47, p.12. £1.S5.

THOMAS CORE, JUNR., 285 acs. Nansemond Co. in Wyanoak Neck on the N side of Summerton Cr., Beg. near the head of the Miery Br., down the Deep Br., up the

Short Sw.; adj. Thomas Core Senr. & William Baker; 12 Jan 1746/47, p.13. £1.S10.

JAMES GOODALL, 400 acs. Orange Co., to [& crossing] the County Line; adj. Edward Watts junr., Richard Derrit & Bartholomew Derrit; 12 Jan 1746/47, p.15. £2. [Part of this land was in Louisa Co., now Albemarle Co.]

WILLIAM COURSEY, JUNR., 350 acs. Louisa Co. near the foot of the Piney Mountain; adj. Thomas Ballard, Samuel Dalton & John Poindexter; 12 Jan 1746/47, p.17. £1.S15.

JOSEPH PHILLIPS, 277 acs. Louisa Co. adj. John Ennis; 12 Jan 1746/47, p.18. £1.S10.

SAMUEL DALTON, 404 acs. Louisa Co. on both sides of the North br. of the North fork of James Riv. beyond the Mountains, Beg. on Wolf Trap Br., on S side of Jacobs Run; 12 Jan 1746/47, p.19. £2.

WILLIAM BIGGER, 400 acs. Louisa Co. on both sides of Bunches Cr., adj. John Tait; 12 Jan 1746/47, p.21. £2.

JOHN EUBANK, 290 acs. Louisa Co. & Par. of Fredericksville on the Brs. of the South Fork of Rockey Cr. under the foot of the Ragged Mountain, on a Spur of a Mountain; adj. John Goodall, Mosias Jones, Henry Bunch & Capt

Joseph Martin; 12 Jan 1746/47, p.22. £1.S10.

SAMUEL GARLICK, 2,400 acs. Louisa Co. on both sides of Buck Mountain Cr., on a Spur of a Mountain & a Spur of Lick Mountain; adj. John Hackett, Mr Robertson, James Cox & Thomas Hackett; 12 Jan 1746/47, p.23. 1,200 acs. part formerly gtd. to Samuel Garlick by Pat. 25 July 1741 [Hanover Co., PB 19 p.1072 which included William Carr's 400 acs. in PB 19 p.707] and 1,200 acs. the residue also formerly gtd. unto Henry Blackgrave by Pat. 25 November 1743 [PB 21 p.643] and by him sold and conveyed unto the sd Samuel Garlick.

CHRISTOPHER HARRIS, 350 acs. Louisa Co., under the foot of the ragged Mountains and on both sides of a West fork of Rockey Cr., on the Goochland Co. Line [N65°W], on a ridge, adj. Mosias Jones & James Merideth; 12 Jan 1746/47, p.25. £1.S15.

ARMISTEAD BURWELL, 3,404 acs. Brunswick Co. on S side of Finney Wood and on both sides of the Brs. thereof, Beg. on Finney Wood Cr., down a Br. of Bouchers Cr., in the fork, on Maherrin Riv. by a small Island; 12 Jan 1746/47, p.27. £17.

JAMES BARNES, 400 acs. Brunswick Co. on the W side of Bluestone Cr., adj. Roberson; 12 Jan 1746/47, p.28. £2.

THOMAS BULL, 249 acs. Brunswick Co. on the N side of the Reedy Cr., up a Great Br., adj. Ralph Jackson; 12 Jan 1746/47, p.30. £1.S5.

JOHN HOWELL, 144 acs. Brunswick Co. on both sides of Stoney Cr. joining Parkers upper Line; 12 Jan 1746/47, p.31. 15 Shill.

THOMAS JONES, JUNIOR & CHARLES IRBY, 604 acs. Brunswick Co. on the S side of Crooked Run, adj. Jones; 12 Jan 1746/47, p.32. £3.

JOHN INGRAM, 364 acs. Brunswick Co. on both sides of Shining Cr., adj. Owen Strange & John Stith; 12 Jan 1746/47, p.34. £1.S5. 129 acs. part formerly gtd. William Nance by Pat. 1 June 1741 [PB 19 p.974] the Right & Title of which has since become vested in the sd John Ingram and 235 acs. the residue never before gtd.

CHARLES JONES, 400 acs. Brunswick Co. on the N side of Peahill Cr.; 12 Jan 1746/47, p.35. £2.

DANIEL CATO, 398 acs. Brunswick Co. on the S side of Fountains Cr., adj. John Cato; 12 Jan 1746/47, p.36. £2.

MARY HALLEY, 300 acs. Brunswick Co. on both sides of Fountains Cr.; adj. John Hill, Mary Deene & and her own Line; 12 Jan 1746/47, p.38. £1.S10.

WILLIAM LINDSEY, 400 acs. Brunswick Co. on both sides of Wild Catt Cr.; 12 Jan 1746/47, p.39. £2.

MATTHEW TALBOT, 600 acs. Brunswick Co., being an island in Stanton Riv. below the mouth of Seneca Cr., 12 Jan 1746/47, p.41. £3.

SIMON TURNER, 300 acs. Brunswick Co. on the S side of Meherrin Riv. adj. his own Land; 12 Jan 1746/47, p.42. £1.S10.

SIMON TURNER, 115 acs. Brunswick Co. on the S side of Meherrin Riv. adj. Michael Sulivant; 12 Jan 1746/47, p.43. 15 Shill.

SIMON TURNER, 250 acs. Brunswick Co. on the S side of Meherrin Riv.; 12 Jan 1746/47, p.44. £1.S5.

THEODORICK BLAND, 396 acs. Brunswick Co. on the W side of Nottoway Riv.; adj. Wilson, Tilman & John Cook; 12 Jan 1746/47, p.46. £2.

JOHN RACHEL, 330 acs. Brunswick Co. adj. Edloe; 12 Jan 1746/47, p.47. £1.S15.

WILLIAM READMOND, 400 acs. Brunswick Co. on the lower side of Little Roanoke Riv.; adj. Jacob Magee, John Hardin & Richard Randolph; 12 Jan 1746/47, p.48. £2.

HENRY ROBERSON, 354 acs. Brunswick Co. on the S side of the

Middle Fork of Maherrin Riv., Beg. on the Riv. below the bent, down Croper run [Crupper Run]; 12 Jan 1746/47, p.50. £1.S15.

RICHARD GREEN, 165 acs. Brunswick Co. on the N side of Dan Riv.; adj. William Stephens & James Parrish; 12 Jan 1746/47, p.51. £1.

WILLIAM HAGWOOD, 404 acs. Brunswick Co. on the E side of Stiths Cr.; 12 Jan 1746/47, p.53. £2.

JOHN COLE, 253 acs. Brunswick Co. on the N side of Roanoak Riv.; 12 Jan 1746/47, p.54. £1.S5.

THOMAS BOULDIN, 400 acs. Brunswick Co. on the ridge between the brs. of Twittys Cr. & the brs. of Little Roanoak; 12 Jan 1746/47, p.56. £2.

WILLIAM LIGON JUNR., 800 acs. Amelia Co. on both sides of Saylors Cr., adj. Benjamin Ruffin; 12 Jan 1746/47, p.57. £2. 400 acs. formerly gtd. Peter Jefferson by Pat. 25 May 1734 [Pr. Geo. Co., PB 15 p.222] the Right & Title of which is since become vested in the sd William Ligon Junr. and 400 acs. the residue never before gtd.

ROBERT GEE, 413 acs. Brunswick Co. on the S side of Sturgeon Run; adj. Lanier, Reed, Harwell & Lloyd; 12 Jan 1746/47, p.58. £2.S5.

CHARLES BINNS, 748 acs. Brunswick Co. on the N side of Roanoak Riv. and on the lower side of the Great Cr., down Cocke's Cr., adj. Munford & Jones; 12 Jan 1746/47, p.59. £3.S15.

HENRY HATCHER, 400 acs. Brunswick Co. on both sides of the middle fork of Maherrin Riv.; 12 Jan 1746/47, p.61. £2.

JOHN KELEY, 248 acs. Brunswick Co. on N side of the Great Cr. of the Maherrin Riv., by the Indian Line [East], adj. Henry Edloe; 12 Jan 1746/47, p.62. £1.S5. Whereas by Pat. under the Great Seal bearing date 28 Sep 1728 gtd. unto William Keley [PB 14 p.84] And whereas John Keley, Son and Heir of the sd William Keley dec'd, hath failed to pay Quitrents and to make Cultiv. & Improv. and James Petillo hath made humble Suit and hath obtained a G. for the same which he hath assigned unto the sd John Keley. [This land was North of the Sappone-Sioux Indian 6-mile square tract (23,040 acs.) at Fort Christanna]

JAMES SCOTT, 404 acs. Brunswick Co. on both sides of Allens Cr.; 12 Jan 1746/47, p.63. £2.

WILLIAM SAMFORD, 274 acs. Brunswick Co. on the N side of the Great Cr. bet. the Lines of Parish & Edmonds, in Spells Mill Pond; 12 Jan 1746/47, p.64. £1.S10.

WILLIAM TURNER THOMERSON, 314 acs. Brunswick Co. on both sides of Butchers Cr. adj. John New; 12 Jan 1746/47, p.65. £1.S15.

DRURY STITH, 334 acs. Brunswick Co. on the N side of Youngs Cr.; 12 Jan 1746/47, p.66. £1.S15. [This 334 acs. & Richard Kennon's 379 acs. in PB 24 p.263 included in sd Kennon's 4,453 acs. Lunenburgh Co. in PB 31 p.86]

RICHARD STONE, 400 acs. Brunswick Co. on the Heads of the Brs. of Fucking Cr., adj. William Pool & John Stone; 12 Jan 1746/47, p.66. £2.

RICHARD WITTON, 638 acs. Brunswick Co. on both sides of Rose's Cr., down the spring Br., up the Little Cr., near a Spring, down the Road; adj. Rose, Ravenscroft & Brown; 12 Jan 1746/47, p.67. £1.S15. 305 acs. part being part of a Pat. for 541 acs. formerly gtd. to John Humphreys 28 Sept 1728 [John Humphris, PB 13 p.391] the right & title of which sd 305 acs. is since become vested in the sd Richard Witton and 333 acs. the residue never before gtd. [See Amos Timms's 464 acs. in PB 25 p.232]

RICHARD WARD, 404 acs. Brunswick Co. on S side of Wards fork; 12 Jan 1746/47, p.68. £2.

THOMAS BIRCHFIELD, 134 acs. Brunswick Co. on N side of Banister Riv., adj. James Wood; 25 Jun 1747 *in the 21st year of our Reign of George the Second, Witness our Trusty and Welbeloved Sir William Gooch Bart. our Lieut. Governor and Commander in Chief of our sd Colony and Dominion at Williamsburgh*, p.69. 15 Shill. [Coronation Day for George the Second must have been in the last week of June]

ROBERT NOBBEL, 190 acs. Brunswick Co. on N side of Maherrin Riv. bet. the Mouth of Flat Rock Cr. and the Haw Br.; 25 Jun 1747, p.70. £1.

THOMAS HARMAN, 1,000 acs. Pr. Geo. Co. on both sides of Glancys Quarter Br., Beg. on the watercourse of the sd br. and on the N side thereof below his house; adj. George Smith, Williams & Petty Poole; 25 Jun 1747, p.71. £5.

WILLIAM EAVENS, 427 acs. Brunswick Co. on both sides of the South Fork of Maherrin Riv., on a Great Br.; 25 Jun 1747, p.72. £2.S5.

CHARLES GOLDSTON /GOLESTON, 250 acs. Brunswick Co. on the N side of Waqua Cr., down Possom Quarter Br., adj. John Dunkley; 25 Jun 1747, p.73. £1.S5.

STEPHEN EVANS, 804 acs. Brunswick Co. on the heads of the brs. of blue stone cr., adj. Munford; 25 Jun 1747, p.74. £4.

JOSEPH BLANKS, 421 acs. Brunswick Co. on the N side of Crooked Cr.; adj. Lidderdale, Kelley, Herbert & himself; 25 Jun 1747, p.75. £2.S5.

WILLIAM BUTTROM, 170 acs. Brunswick Co. on the S side of Banister Riv.; 25 Jun 1747, p.75. £1.

ROBERT BROOKS, 630 acs. Brunswick Co. on both sides of Maherrin Riv., adj. Scott & his own Line; 25 Jun 1747, p.76. £3.S5.

EDMOND FLOYD, 180 acs. Brunswick Co. on the N side of Dan Riv. joining William Hogans upper Line; 25 Jun 1747, p.77. £1.

RICHARD ECKHOLS, 221 acs. Lunenburgh Co. on the S side of Bannister Riv.; 25 Jun 1747, p.78. £1.S5.

DRURY ALLEN, 404 acs. Brunswick Co. on the heads of the brs. of Couches Cr. and Fucking Cr., adj. Brigs; 25 Jun 1747, p.79. £2.

JOHN STEWART, 179 acs. Brunswick Co. on N side of Dan Riv., down Sandy Riv. to the main Riv., 25 Jun 1747, p.80. £1.

HENRY MAY, 554 acs. Brunswick Co. on both sides of the first cr. of little Roanoake Riv., adj. John Martin; 25 Jun 1747, p.80. £2.S15.

ROBERT SCOTT, 400 acs. Brunswick Co. on both sides of Maherrin Riv., to an Elm in a small Island in sd Riv.; 25 Jun 1747, p.82. £2.

BATT PETERSON, 343 acs. Brunswick Co. adj. his own Line, Robert Ellis, Batts & Matthew Parham; 25 Jun 1747, p.82. £1.S15.

RICHARD COCKE, 503 acs. Brunswick Co. on the N side of Bears Element Cr.; 25 Jun 1747, p.83. 303 acs. formerly gtd. unto the sd Richard Cocke by Pat. 22 Sep 1739 [PB 18 p.365] and 200 acs. the residue being also formerly gtd. John Rachel by Pat. 15 Mar 1741/42 [PB 20 p.244] the Right & Title whereof is since become vested in the sd Richard Cocke.

WILLIAM MARRABLE, 425 acs. Lunenburgh Co. on the Ridge bet. Blue Stone and Meherin Riv., down a Fork of Bluestone Cr. & up the South Fork, adj. his own Line; 25 Jun 1747, p.84. £2.S5. [Included in sd Marrable's 1,870 acs. in PB 31 p.712]

WILLIAM MARRABLE, 425 acs. Lunenburgh Co. on the head brs. of Bluestone and Finney Wood, Beg. on the Meadow of Finney Wood; 25 Jun 1747, p.85. £2.S5. [Included in sd Marrable's 1,870 acs. in PB 31 p.712]

JOHN TWITTY, 292 acs. Brunswick Co. on the Ridge bet. Twitty's Cr. and licking hole, adj.

his own Line & Magehee; 25 Jun 1747, p.86. £1.S10.

ABRAHAM LITTLE, 154 acs. Brunswick Co. on the N side of Dan Riv., up Sandy Riv.; 25 Jun 1747, p.87. 15 Shill.

WILLIAM ROGERS, 350 acs. Brunswick Co. on both sides of Turnup Cr.; 25 Jun 1747, p.88. £1.S15.

JOHN YEATES, 204 acs. Brunswick Co. on the S side of Dan Riv.; 25 Jun 1747, p.89. £1.

RICHARD WITTON, 374 acs. Lunenburgh Co. on the W side of Blackston's Cr., down the Fork; 25 Jun 1747, p.90. £2.

ELIZABETH COLESHAW, 117 acs. Pr. Geo. Co. on upper side of Mawhipponock Cr., on a br. of the Miery Br.; adj. Spain, the sd Elizabeth Coleshaw, Jacob Summerwell & Ream; 25 Jun 1747, p.91. 15 Shill.

THOMAS PENNINGTON, 730 acs. Surry Co. on the S side of Nottoway Riv., on the Outermost Prong & the Innermost Prong of the double br., up the double br. & up the long br.; adj. his 1st & 2nd Surveys, Thomas Davis & a Line formerly Capt. Wm. Hamlins; 25 Jun 1747, p.92. £1. 250 acs. part formerly gtd. unto the sd Thomas Pennington by Pat. 31 Oct 1726 [PB 13 p.67] and 290 acs. other part also formerly gtd. unto the sd Thomas Pennington by Pat. 20 May 1742 [Thomas Pennenton, PB 20

p.267] and 190 acs. the residue never before gtd.

RICHARD TALLY, 250 acs. Amelia Co. on the lower side of Winticomaick Cr., Beg. near the Mouth of a small spring Br. above Robert Beavill; 25 Jun 1747, p.93. £1.S5. Whereas by Pat. 17 Aug 1725 Gtd. unto Charles Judkins then in Pr. Geo Co. [PB 12 p.272] now Amelia And Whereas the sd Charles Judkins hath failed to make Cultiv. and Improv. and Daniel Coleman hath made humble Suit and hath obtained a G. for the same which he hath assigned unto Richard Tally.

THOMAS GREEN, 390 acs. Amelia Co. on the N side of the long Br. of Winticomaick Cr., adj. Greens & Reames lines; 25 Jun 1747, p.94. £2. Whereas by Pat. 12 Mar 1739/40 gtd. unto Joseph Pattyson [Joseph Pattyson junr., PB 19 p.603] And Whereas the sd Joseph Pattyson hath failed to make cultivation and improvement & Thomas Green hath made humble Suit and hath obtained a G. for the same.

JOSHUA GLASS, 292 acs. Amelia Co. on the S side of the long Br. of Winticomaick Cr., Beg. at the Mouth of the Harricane Br., adj. Daniel Coleman; 25 Jun 1747, p.95. £1.S10. Whereas by Pat. gtd. 22 Sep 1739 unto Richard Newman [PB 18 p.378] And Whereas the sd Richard Newman hath failed to pay Quitrents and to make Cultiv. & Improv. and Daniel Coleman hath made humble Suit and obtained a g. for the same Which he hath assigned unto Joshua Glass.

WILLIAM WATSON, 1,300 acs. Amelia Co. on the heads of the Brs. of Snales Cr. and Sandy Riv., crossing a fork of Sandy Riv. to a Spring; adj. Dejarnat, Brown, Sil Johnson, his own old lines, Henry Johnson & Collicoate; 25 Jun 1747, p.97. £4. 500 acs. part being part of a Pat. for 1,600 acs. formerly gtd. sd Watson 30 Jul 1742 [PB 20 p.375] and 800 acs. the residue never before Gtd.

JOHN WHITE, 200 acs. Amelia Co. on the N side of Falling Cr.; adj. Ellit, Culwell, Hardin & Harris; 25 Jun 1747, p.98. £1.

JOHN BARTHOLOMEW DUPUY, 400 acs. Amelia Co. on both sides of Little Nottoway Riv.; adj. Yarbrough, Watson, Peter Jones & Batte Jones; 25 Jun 1747, p.99. £2.

SAMUEL CORNWELL, 100 acs. Surry Co. on the S side of Black Water Sw., down the Run of the Indian Br., near the edge of Seacock Sw.; adj. his Ptd. Land, William Handcock, his former Survey & William Bradley; 25 Jun 1747, p.100. 10 Shill.

GEORGE ROBINSON, 75 acs. Surry Co. on the N side of Nottoway Riv.; adj. James Matthews, Majr. Benjamin Harrison & Marmaduke Brown; 25 Jun 1747, p.101. 10 Shill.

JAMES FISHER, 200 acs. Pr. Geo. Co. on the S side of Butterwood Sw., adj. William Eaton & Poythress; 25 Jun 1747, p.102. £1.

WILLIAM STANLY, 167 acs. Pr. Geo. Co. on the N side of White Oak Sw.; adj. John Stell, Grigg's & his own old lines; 25 Jun 1747, p.103. £1.

JOHN MANSON, 346 acs. Pr. Geo. Co. on both sides the Main Road between Sappone Cr. and Rockey Run; adj. Richard White, Tabb, Charles Williamson & Blackstone; 25 Jun 1747, p.104. £1.S5.

THOMAS NANCE, 172 acs. Pr. Geo. Co. on the upper side of the Mealy Br. of Sappone Cr.; adj. John Tapley & Capt. Stark; 25 Jun 1747, p.105. £1.

JOHN CROW, 490 acs. Goochland Co. on the Brs. of Tuckahoe Cr., in a Valley; adj. Daniel Clayton, John Black, Thomas Harlop, Harlow, Charles Burrus, Rene Leaforce & John Watson; 25 Jun 1747, p.106. £1.S10. (200 acs. part being part of 400 acs. formerly gtd. to John Uttley by Pat. 24 Mar 1725/26 [John Utley, Henrico Co. in PB 12 p.409] the right and title of which sd 200 acs. by diverse mesne Conveyances is since become vested in the sd John Crow and 290 acs. the residue never before gtd.)

the Reverend WILLIAM STITH, Clerk, 2,470 acs. Albemarle Co.

on the N side of the Fluvanna on both sides Ballengers and Totier Creeks commonly known by the name of *Rock Field*, at the North Fork & the main Cr. of Ballengers Cr.; adj. his first Survey, John Lewis, Thomas Stone & Mr Stith; 25 Jun 1747, p.107. £2. (1,650 acs. part formerly gtd. to the sd William Stith by Pat. 10 Jun 1740 [Goochland Co., PB 19 p.652] and 420 other part acs. formerly gtd. unto the sd William Stith by Pat. dated 12 Feb 1742/43 [Goochland Co., PB 21 p.149] and 400 acs. the residue never before gtd.)

MACKERNESS GOODE, 1,030 acs. Brunswick Co. on both sides of Bluestone Cr., down a great Br. of sd Cr.; adj. Munford, Carrill & Barnes; 25 Jun 1747, p.109. £5.S5.

WILLIAM CRYER, 773 acs. Pr. Geo. Co. on the lower side of Butterwood Sw.; adj. Francis Coleman, Majr. Eppes old Line & Clayton; 25 Jun 1747, p.110. £4. (385 acs. part formerly gtd. Thomas Eppes & William Eppes by Pat. 24 Mar 1725/26 [Epes, PB 12 p.413] and 388 acs. the other part also formerly gtd. to sd Thomas Eppes & William Eppes by Pat. 24 Mar 1725/26 [Thomas & William Epes, PB 12 p.414] and for want of Cultiv. and Improv. and for non payment of our Quitrents the same became forfeited and vested again in Us as by a Judgment of the General Court of our sd Colony bearing date 22 Oct 1744 Relation being thereunto had may more fully and at large appear.)

JOSEPH MOTLEY, 1,383 acs. Amelia Co. on both sides of Flatt and Little Creeks; adj. Matthew May's, Royal, William Mays, the Land purchased of Tanner, Craddock now Cocks, John Ellis, Dupuy, William Watson & Clerk; 25 Jun 1747, p.111. 1,083 acs. part formerly gtd. sd Joseph Motley by Pat. 10 Jul 1745 [Joseph Motly's PB 22 p.275, which included 400 acs. to Mattox Mayes junior part of 1,200 acs. in PB 17 p.33 & PB 17 p.457] and 300 acs. other part formerly gtd. Thomas Tanner by Pat. 30 Jul 1742 [PB 20 p.372] the Right & Title whereof is since become Vested in the sd Joseph Motley.

CHRISTOPHER HINTON, 804 acs. Amelia Co. on the head of the Sweathouse Cr., in the Hunting Path; adj. Watson, his own old Lines, Thomas Jones, Munford, Bennitt & Bland; 25 Jun 1747, p.113. £2. (400 acs. part formerly gtd. sd Christopher Hinton by Pat. 2 Jan 1737/38 [PB 17 p.439] and 404 acs. the residue never before gtd.

EDWARD ALMAND, 360 acs. Is. of Wight Co. on S side of the main Black Water, up Tuckers Sw.; adj. William Boykins, Edward Britt & Joseph Turner; 25 Jun 1747, p.114. £1.S5. 135 acs. part formerly gtd. Thomas Sherrod by Pat. 24 Mar 1725/26 [Thomas Sherrer, PB 12 p.447] the right & title of which is since become vested in the sd Edward Almand and 225 acs. the residue never before gtd.)

THOMAS WILLIAMS, 2,600 acs. Brunswick Co. on the E side of Cubb Cr., Beg. at the mouth of a Br. on the Horsepen Fork, on the Ridge bet. Brunswick and Amelia; adj. Thomas Dugon, Daniel Terry, Thomas Alexander, Samuel Moore, John Marshal & Joseph Morton; 25 Jun 1747, p.115. £13.

Augt. 20. 1747 Settled for the Rights thus far & to pag. 84 in t'other Book [PB 26], John Blair D.Audr.

JACOB SEAY, 400 acs. Amelia Co. on both sides the road bet. the brs. of Saylors Cr. and Dawsons Cr.; adj. Osborn, Bromfeild /Bromfield, Meadows, Dawson, Henry Isbell & Holland; 20 Aug 1747, p.117. £2.

ELIJAH GRAVES, 400 acs. Louisa Co. on both sides of the lower Fork of the Beaverdam Fork of Mechunks Cr., crossing the Horsepen Br., adj. John Graves; 20 Aug 1747, p.118. £2.

JOHN IRBY, 340 acs. Surry Co. on the S side of Black Water Sw.; adj. John Scott, the Widow Gilbert & Mr Ruffin; 20 Aug 1747, p.119. £1.S15.

BENJAMIN MOSS, 232 acs. Surry Co. on the S side of Nottoway Riv.; adj. John Spain, John Wilborn & Thomas Wynne; 20 Aug 1747, p.120. £1.S5.

FRANCIS FLOURNOY, 391 acs. Henrico Co. on the S side of James Riv., crossing Horsepen Br.; 20 Aug 1747, p.122. £2.

THOMAS DENTON, 51 acs. Hanover Co. on the S side the South, on the River Bank; adj. Colo. David Meriwether, John Glen, Robert Clapton & George Matlock; 20 Aug 1747, p.123. 5 Shill.

THOMAS LANKFORD, 171 acs. Louisa Co. in the Fork of Buck Mountain Cr. under the foot of the Great Mountains, adj. John Whatley & Robert Thomson; 20 Aug 1747, p.124. £1.

WILLIAM GRAVES, 431 acs. Louisa Co. on both sides the Beverdam Fork of Mechunk Cr. and the brs. thereof, on the Goochland Co. Line [N60°W], crossing the North fork of Beverdam Fork, adj. John Graves & near Nathaniel Williams; 20 Aug 1747, p.125. £2.S5.

ELKANAH ANDERSON, 400 acs. Goochland Co. on both sides of Beverdam Cr. of Willis's Riv., adj. Peter Brooks; 20 Aug 1747, p.126. £2.

JAMES FLANEGEN, 250 acs. Louisa Co., crossing 3 small brs. of Bunches Cr., adj. the sd Flanegen & Silvanus Morris; 20 Aug 1747, p.127. £1.S5.

WILLIAM GRAVES, 400 acs. Louisa Co. on both sides of Goochland Road on some of the small brs. of the Beaverdam Fork of Mechunk Cr., on the Goochland

Co. Line [S60°E]; 20 Aug 1747, p.128. £2.

JOSEPH PARKS, 450 acs. Brunswick Co.; adj. his own old Line, Edward Machem [Meacham], Jefferies, Turner & Haley [her Line]; 20 Aug 1747, p.129. £2.S5.

JOHN MCDANIEL, 400 acs. Brunswick Co. on the N side of the South Fork of Mountain Cr.; 20 Aug 1747, p.130. £2.

CHARLES ANDERSON, 400 acs. Goochland Co. on both sides of Mallorys br. of Appomattox Riv., adj. Joseph Dabbs & Peter Brooks; 20 Aug 1747, p.131. £2.

FRANCIS ELLEDGE, 400 acs. Brunswick Co. on both sides of the North Fork of Allen's Cr.; 20 Aug 1747, p.132. £2.

THOMAS GADDEY, 200 acs. Brunswick Co. on the brs. of Otter Riv., adj. Randolph; 20 Aug 1747, p.133. £1.

WILLIAM CLEMENT JUNR., 74 acs. Amelia Co. on the head of the Bent Run; adj. George Haines, Gillington, Jacob Say & Clement; 20 Aug 1747, p.134. 10 Shill.

CHARLES EVANS, 120 acs. Brunswick Co. on Stiths Cr., at a Gut on the first Fork of Miles Cr., adj. Philip Morgan; 20 Aug 1747, p.135. 15 Shill.

THOMAS BALDWIN, 400 acs. Lunenburgh Co. on both sides of

Cubb Cr., on Rattle Snake Br.; 20 Aug 1747, p.135. £2.

FRANCIS EALIDGE, 331 acs. Lunenburgh Co. on both sides of the North fork of Allens Cr., adj. Francis Ealidge; 20 Aug 1747, p.136. £1.S15.

NICHOLAS CAIN, 100 acs. Augusta Co. on the North Riv. of Shanando within the Gap of the Mountain, adj. Bernard McHenry; 20 Aug 1747, p.137. 10 Shill.

GILBERT GIBSON, 200 acs. Albemarle Co. on both sides of Ballengers Cr.; 20 Aug 1747, p.138. £1.

THOMAS MOORE, 180 acs. Augusta Co. on the long Meadow Br., Beg. on the W side of the long Meadow, on the W side of the West Fork & the East Fork, adj. Thomas Rutherford; 20 Aug 1747, p.139. £1.

SAMUEL STEELE, 175 acs. Augusta Co., bet. the South Riv. and the Mountain, with the Line of *Beaverly Mannor*, at a Meadow; 20 Aug 1747, p.140. £1.

WILLIAM HUMPHREYS, JOHN HUMPHREYS, THOMAS HUMPHREYS & CHARLES HUMPHREYS, 366 acs. Brunswick Co. on both sides of Allen Cr., adj. Dunkley; 20 Aug 1747, p.141. £2.

SAMUEL SOUTHERLAND, 354 acs. Amelia Co. on both sides of Falling Cr. of Buffallo Riv.; adj.

Randolph, Nickson & Wallace; 20 Aug 1747, p.142. £1.S15.

JOHN GOODWIN, 350 acs. Albemarle Co. on the South br. of Rock Island Cr., Beg. on the S side of Slate River Road; 20 Aug 1747, p.144. £1.S15.

JOHN WADDILL, 188 acs. Amelia Co. on the upper side of Saylors Cr.; adj. Goodlow, Turpin, Morris & Richee; 20 Aug 1747, p.144. £1.

SAMUEL TUDOR, 100 acs. Surry Co. on Clays Br.; adj. him, Thomas Williams, John Tyus & Bartholomew Andrews; 20 Aug 1747, p.145. 10 Shill.

THOMAS PATERSON, 400 acs. Albemarle Co. on Ripleys Cr. a Br. of Slate Riv., adj. the sd Patterson; 20 Aug 1747, p.146. £2.

THOMAS BUTLER, 235 acs. Surry Co. on the N side of Nottoway Riv.; adj. Richard Pepper, John Davis, himself, John Davis Junr. & Nathaniel Chamblis; 20 Aug 1747, p.147. £1.S5.

JOHN RAVENSCROFT, 489 acs. Brunswick Co. on the Brs. of Roses Cr.; adj. John Rose, Timms, himself & Humphrey; 20 Aug 1747, p.148. 312 acs. formerly gtd. John Simmonds by Pat. 13 Oct 1727 [John Simmons Junr., PB 13 p.178] and 132 acs. other part also formerly gtd. Thomas Ravenscroft by Pat. 17 Sep 1731 [PB 14 p.347] and 45 acs. also formerly gtd. to the sd Thomas Ravenscroft by Pat. 10 Sep 1735 [PB 16 p.210] the Right & Title of which sd Tracts is since become vested in the sd John Ravenscroft.

JAMES FLANEGEN, 400 acs. Louisa Co. on both sides the North Fork of Hudsons Cr., adj. Stuart & Dansies; 20 Aug 1747, p.150. £2.

JACOB PENCE, 164 acs. Augusta Co. at the upper end of the peeked Mountain on a Br. of Cub Run, by a hollow, adj. John Lawrence; 20 Aug 1747, p.151. £1.

JOHN MAFFIT, 100 acs. Augusta Co. on N side the Middle Riv. of Shanando; 20 Aug 1747, p.152. 10 Shill.

JAMES WARREN JUNR., 217 acs. Albemarle Co. on the S side of the Rivanna on the Brs. of Moores Cr., at the North Fork of sd Cr., at long br., adj. David Lewis; 20 Aug 1747, p.153. £1.S5.

JOHN MASSENBURGH, 75 acs. Elizabeth City Co. on the side of house Dams, along the run of the Dams, adj. sd John Massenburgh & the heirs of Alexander Carver; 20 Aug 1747, p.154. 10 Shill.

STERLING CLACK, 286 acs. Brunswick Co., down the Reedy Cr.; adj. John Duke, Mumford & John Edwards; 20 Aug 1747, p.155. £1.S10.

THOMAS PETERSON, 1,570 acs. Albemarle Co. on the Brs. of Waltons Fork of Slate Riv., in Low

Ground on the S side of Ripleys Cr., adj. the old Lines of the former Survey; 20 Aug 1747, p.156. £8.

THOMAS GRANTHAM, 500 acs. Surry Co. on the S side of Nottoway Riv., on the N side of the double Br., adj. the old Line & John Weaver; 20 Aug 1747, p.157. £2. 100 acs. part formerly gtd. William Hamlin by Pat. 14 Jul 1718 [PB 10 p.405] and 400 acs. the residue never before gtd.

RICHARD JONES, 230 acs. Surry Co. on the N side of Black Water Sw.; adj. Robert Smith, the Orphan of John Jones, his own Line, Thomas Griffis, William Short, Margaret Stewart & Robert Smith; 20 Aug 1747, p.158. £1.S5.

ROBERT ROBERTS, 81 acs. York Co. on the S side the Horse Road to York Town, up Kings Cr. & up the Fork; 20 Aug 1747, p.159. for 2 lbs. of Tobacco for every Acre of sd L. Whereas by Inquisition Indented taken in sd Co. 24 Apr 1742 by Virtue of a Warrant directed to William Byrd Esqr. Escheator for the sd Co. It appears that Martha Dowling died seised of a certain tract of land containing 66 acs. more or less but by a Survey lately made by James Shields Surveyor of the sd Co. is found to contain 81 acs. which is found to Escheat to us from the sd Martha Dowsing And Whereas William Whitaker hath made humble Suit and hath obtained a g. for the same which he hath assigned to Robert Roberts.

HENRY ANDERSON, 1,202 acs. Amelia Co. bet. the brs. of Bush Riv. and the Brs. of Meherrin on both sides the Road, by a Spring; adj. his own now Watkins's, Randolph & Davis; 20 Aug 1747, p.160. £4.S5. 380 acs. part being part of a Pat. for 780 acs. formerly gtd. Joseph Farguson by Pat. 30 Jul 1742 [John Fargusson, PB 21 p.111] and 822 acs. the residue never before Gtd. [see PB 28 p.255 to Thomas Watkins Junr.]

DAVID WILLIAMS, 340 acs. Brunswick Co. on the S side of Roanoake Riv., Beg. on the W side Smiths Cr.; 20 Aug 1747, p.161. £1.S15. Whereas by Pat. 28 Sep 1728 gtd. John Rabourn since dec'd [PB 14 p.73] And Whereas John Fowler in whom the right of the sd L. is since become vested hath failed to pay Quitrents and to make Cultiv. and Improv. and James Petillo hath made humble Suit and obtained a G. for the same Which he hath assigned unto David Williams.

JOSEPH MAN, 187 acs. Essex Co., up the NE side of the main road; adj. the L. formerly Hilliards, & Baker; 20 Aug 1747, p.163. for 2 lbs. of Tobacco for every of the sd L. Whereas by inquisition indented taken in sd Co. on 19 May 1739 by Virtue of a Warrant directed to John Robinson Esqr. Escheator for the sd Co. It Appears that Edward Smart died siezed of 200 acs. more or less but by Survey lately made by Robert Brooke, Surveyor of sd Co. is found to contain only 187 acs.

which is found to Escheat to us from sd Edward Smart And Whereas John Wynel Sanders hath made humble suit and hath obtained a G. for the same Which he hath assigned unto Joseph Man.

ALEXANDER TRENT, 2,098 acs. Goochland Co. Beg. on the lower side of Willis's Cr.; crossing Willis's Riv., Hatchers Cr., Bear Cr. & Horn Quarter Br.; adj. Harvey, Moore, Thomas Tilman, Samuel Allen, Trents own Line, Thomas Hughes & Joseph Farrar; 20 Aug 1747, p.164.   £4.S5. 1,040 acs. part being part of a Pat. for 17,000 acs. formerly Gtd. Henry Cary by Pat. 20 July 1738 [PB 18 p.90 which included his 3,942 acs. in PB 13 p.423 at a place Called *Buckingham*] and 226 acs. other part being part of a Pat. for 400 acs. formerly gtd. Joseph Farrar by Pat. 13 Oct 1736 [PB 17 p.201] the Right & Title is since become vested in the sd Alexander Trent and 832 acs. the residue never before gtd.   [see Trent's PB 25 p.84]

HENRY ROBERTSON, 1,604 acs. Brunswick Co. on both sides of Blue Stone Cr., up Otter Cr.; 20 Aug 1747, p.165.   £8.

THOMAS LOCKITT JUNR., 1,531 acs. Amelia Co. on both sides of the North Fork of Falling Cr. and Harris's Cr., in a bottom; adj. Randolph, Venable, Harris, the 200 acre Tract, & White; 20 Aug 1747, p.167.   £5.   342 acs. part formerly gtd. to the sd Lockitt by Pat. 30 Jul 1742 [Thomas Lockett Junr., PB 21 p.95] and 200 acs. other part also formerly gtd. sd Lockitt by Pat. 30 Jun 1743 [Thomas Lockett, PB 21 p.370] and 989 acs. the Residue never before gtd.

ROBERT FERGUSON, 840 acs. Pr. Geo. Co. on the upper side of the Oldfeild Br. of Butterwood Sw., in a Valley; adj. Coleman, Wyatt, Woodleif, Mills, Robert West, Poytheross, FitzGerrald & Anne Andrews; 20 Aug 1747, p.168.   £2.S5.   400 acs. part formerly gtd. Ferguhard Grant by Pat. 15 Mar 1744/45 [Farquhard Grant, PB 23 p.825] and by him sold & conveyed unto the sd Robert Ferguson and 440 acs. the residue never before Gtd.   [Included in his 990 acs. in PB 28 p.704]

THOMAS FELTS, 1,070 acs. Surry Co. on the S side of Nottoway Riv., down & crossing the North Prong of the Poplar Sw. (called Calf Penn Sw.), down the South Prong of the Poplar Sw. to the Mouth of the Calf Pen or the Fork of the main Poplar Sw., down the long Br.; adj. his Brother Nathaniel Felts, William Woodland, John Richardson, David Rozar & Robert Berry; 20 Aug 1747, p.170.   £4.S10.   200 acs. part being part of 285 acs. formerly gtd. sd Thomas Felts by Pat. 28 Sep 1732 [PB 14 p.495] and 870 acs. the residue never before Gtd. [see Nathaniel Felts, PB 25 p.181]

ALEXANDER SPIERS, 1,700 acs. Amelia Co. on both sides of Saylor Cr.; adj. Ruffin, Osborn, Booker,

Brumfield, Holland, Crawford, Selby & Townes; 20 Aug 1747, p.171. £8.S10.

RICHARD BLUNT, 285 acs. Surry Co. on the S side of Black Water Sw.; adj. his own Lines, Samuel Maget & Bartholomew Figures; 20 Aug 1747, p.172. £1.S10.

SAMUEL GLOVER, 376 acs. Albemarle Co. on the S side of James Riv. & in the Fork of Slate Riv.; adj. Thomas Jones, Thomas Jerrald & Samuel Glover; 20 Aug 1747, p.173. £2.

JOHN NICHOLAS SENR., 233 acs. Norfolk Co. on Broad Cr., Beg. on sd Cr. near Nash's Landing and binding upon Hardins Pat., by the Road, to a Pohiccory [Tree]; 20 Aug 1747, p.174. for 2 lbs. of Tobacco for every Acre of sd L. Whereas by Inquisition Indented taken in sd Co. 13 Oct 1738 by Virtue of a Warrant directed to Samuel Boush Escheator for the sd Co. It Appears that Hugh Campbell died seised of 200 acs. more or less but by Survey lately made by James Nimmo, surveyor of the sd Co. is found to contain 233 acs. which is found to Escheat to us from the sd Hugh Campbell And Whereas John Nicholas Senr. hath made humble Suit and hath obtained a G. for the same.

JOHN MULLINS, 200 acs. Albemarle Co. on the Brs. of Moremans Riv., on the County Line [N65°W]; 20 Aug 1747, p.176. £1.

RICHARD ANDREWS JUNR., 400 acs. Surry Co. on the S side of Black Water, down Snake Br., adj. Mr William Gray; 20 Aug 1747, p.176. £2.

JOHN ELLIS, 180 acs. Surry Co. on S side of Nottoway Riv., adj. John Hill & Jeremiah Bullock; 20 Aug 1747, p.177. £1.

WILLIAM PERKINS, 400 acs. Albemarle Co. on a Br. of Taylors Cr. of Slate Riv., adj. Arthur McDaniel; 20 Aug 1747, p.178. £2.

WILLIAM PERKINS, 387 acs. Albemarle Co. on both sides of Slate Riv., adj. David Griffith; 20 Aug 1747, p.179. £2.

SAMUEL GLOVER, 375 acs. Albemarle Co. on the S side of James Riv. & on both sides of the Poplar Run of Slate Riv.; adj. Richard Taylor, John Farish & Samuel Glover Junr.; 20 Aug 1747, p.180. £2.

SAMUEL GLOVER, 400 acs. Albemarle Co. on the S side of James Riv. on N Brs. of Slate Riv., adj. Samuel Glover & Richard Taylor; 20 Aug 1747, p.181. £2.

JOHN PENNINGTON, 100 acs. Surry Co. on the S side of Nottoway Riv., adj. the Honble. Philip Lightfoot & Solomon Hawkins; 20 Aug 1747, p.182. 10 Shill.

ARTHUR McDANIEL, 400 acs. Albemarle Co. on the Ridge bet. Ripleys Cr. and a br. of Slate Riv., adj. William Perkins; 20 Aug 1747, p.183. £2.

ARTHUR McDANIEL, 400 acs. Albemarle Co. on the Brs. of Ripleys Cr. of Slate Riv., adj. his former survey; 20 Aug 1747, p.184. £2.

THOMAS EVANS, 246 acs. Albemarle Co. on the S side the Rivanna on the Brs. of Moors Cr. among the Ragged Mountains, on the E side of a Mountain, adj. Benjamin Wheeler & Evans; 20 Aug 1747, p.185. £1.S5.

JOHN CHILDERS, 300 acs. Albemarle Co. on the S side of James Riv. on a North Fork of Willis's Cr., adj. Gideon Patterson; 20 Aug 1747, p.186. £1.S10.

JOHN GLOVER, 400 acs. Albemarle Co. on the S side of James Riv. on both sides of a Cr. of Slate Riv. called Glovers Cr.; 210 Aug 1747, p.186. £2.

MARTIN DAWSON, 300 acs. Albemarle Co. on the S side the Rivanna on the Brs. of Buck Island Cr., adj. John Carter Esqr. dec'd; 20 Aug 1747, p.187. £1.S10.

JOSEPH THOMAS, 200 acs. Albemarle Co. on a head br. of Rock Island Cr.; 20 Aug 1747, p.188. £1.

PATRICK OBRIAN, 400 acs. Albemarle Co. on the S side of James Riv. & on the South fork of Slate Riv.; 20 Aug 1747, p.189. £2.

HENRY HAMILTON, 400 acs. Albemarle Co. on both sides of Slate Riv., adj. William Allen; 20 Aug 1747, p.190. £2.

WILLIAM WOOLDRIDGE, 400 acs. Albemarle Co. on the S side of James Riv. on a S br. of Slate Riv. called Jones's Cr.; 20 Aug 1747, p.191. £2.

WILLIAM NOLAND, 400 acs. Albemarle Co. on Arthurs Cr. of Slate Riv., crossing both brs.; 20 Aug 1747, p.192. £2.

JOHN MATTHEWS, 140 acs. Augusta Co. on a br. of Roanoak called back Cr. at a place called *Turkey Bottom*, on the side of a Steep Lorrell Hill; 20 Aug 1747, p.193. 15 Shill.

EDMUND SMITH, 400 acs. Brunswick Co. on both sides of Falling Riv., adj. Thomas Dugon; 20 Aug 1747, p.194. £2.

JOHN LAWRENCE, 400 acs. Augusta Co. on a Br. of Cub Run at the upper end of the Peeked Mountain, adj. Jacob Pence; 20 Aug 1747, p.194. £2.

RICHARD WOOD, 200 acs. Brunswick Co. on the N side of Teag cr., adj. the sd Richard Wood & Harrison; 20 Aug 1747, p.195. £1.

RICHARD PARKER, 171 acs. Brunswick Co. on the N side of Staunton Riv.; 20 Aug 1747, p.196. £1.

SAMUEL LOCKHART, 179 acs. Augusta Co. crossing the North Riv. of Shanando & crossing a Meadow, adj. Alexander Thompson; 20 Aug 1747, p.197. £1.

SAMUEL WYNNE, 100 acs. Brunswick Co. on both sides of Hounds Cr., above & below the falls of sd Cr.; 20 Aug 1747, p.198. 10 Shill.

GEORGE RENKIN, 328 acs. Augusta Co. on Catheys Riv. opposite to the Land of David Logan, Beg. on the N side of sd Riv. near the mouth of a Hollow; 20 Aug 1747, p.199. £1.S15.

GEORGE MCLAIN, 81 acs. Brunswick Co. on the N side of Staunton Riv., adj. William Westbrooke; 20 Aug 1747, p.200. 10 Shillings.

WILLIAM CUNNINGHAM, 293 acs. Lunenburg Co. on S side of Turnip Cr., Beg. at Bookers Foard, 20 Aug 1747, p.201. £1.S10.

HUBARD QUALLS, 132 acs. Brunswick Co. on the N side of red oak Run; adj. Edmonds, Joshua Fry, Stephen Cordle, Hugh Williams & his own Line; 20 Aug 1747, p.202. 15 Shill.

JOHN SPEED, 280 acs. Brunswick Co., in the fork of Miles Cr.,

down the Reedy Br.; 20 Aug 1747, p.202. £1.S10.

JAMES SPEED, 178 acs. Brunswick Co. on both sides of Wytches Br.; adj. William Kimball & Harrowson; 20 Aug 1747, p.203. £1.

HUBARD FARRILL, 230 acs. Brunswick Co. on the E side of Cocks Cr. adj. his own lower Line; 20 Aug 1747, p.204. £1.S5.

JOSEPH MORTON JUNR., 500 acs. Brunswick Co. on the W side of the North fork of Cubb Cr. adj. Thomas Dugon; 20 Aug 1747, p.205. £2.S10.

WILLIAM ECKHOLES, 1,091 acs. Amelia Co. on both sides of Little Saylors Cr.; adj. Nash, Wilcox, Norris, Crawford & Smith; 20 Aug 1747, p.206. £5.S10.

WILLIAM ELAM, 400 acs. Amelia Co. on the lower side of Vaughans Cr., adj. Cook, Lodwick Elam & Scott; 20 Aug 1747, p.207. £2.

GEORGE TUCKER, 275 acs. Amelia Co. on the upper side of Woody Cr.; adj. Roberts, Fletcher, Dandy, Joseph Gray & Thweat; 20 Aug 1747, p.207. £1.S10.

MARY HAWKINS & FRANCIS WYATT, 100 acs. Pr. Geo. Co. on the lower side of Cooks Br. of Butterwood, to the Falls of Cooks Br., adj. Woodleif; 20 Aug 1747, p.208. 10 Shill.

HENRY GOTHARD, 159 acs. Goochland Co. on the N side of James Riv. on the Brs. of the Little Byrd, at Straw Camp Br.; adj. John Kirby, Peter Massie, Pinchbeck & John Moss; 20 Aug 1747, p.209. £1.

WILLIAM EASLEY, 400 acs. Goochland Co. on both sides of Pidey Rock Run of Willis Riv., on a Br. of Tear Wallet; 20 Aug 1747, p.210. £2.

CHARLES MASSIE, 400 acs. Goochland Co. on the N side of James Riv. on the Brs. of the Byrd and Fork Creek on both sides the three Notched Road, by a Pond; adj. Humphrey Parish, Joseph Lewis, Thomas Eme'son [Emmerson] & John Moss; 20 Aug 1747, p.211. £2.

MARY HAWKINS & FRANCIS WYATT, 200 acs. Amelia Co. on N side of the Harricane Sw., down a fork of the Great Br., adj. Poythress; 20 Aug 1747, p.211. £1.

THOMAS WILLIAMSON, 400 acs. Amelia Co. on both sides of Harris's Cr., adj. Lockitt; 20 Aug 1747, p.212. £2.

FRANCIS COOLEY, 107 acs. Goochland Co. on the Brs. of Licking Hole and the Byrd on both sides of the three Notched Mountain Road; adj. John Walker, Michael Holland & James Howard; 20 Aug 1747, p.213. 15 Shill.

STEPHEN DEWEY, Gentleman, 400 acs. Brunswick Co. on the N side of the Reedy Cr., at the mouth of Cabbin Br., adj. Ralph Jackson & Thomas Bull; 1 Oct 1747, p.214. £2.

WILLIAM BEEN, 354 acs. Brunswick Co. on N side of Dan Riv., Beg. on the Riv. below the double Creeks; 1 Oct 1747, p.215. £1.S15.

JOHN BROWN, 304 acs. Brunswick Co. on the N side of the Middle Riv. of Maherrin; 1 Oct 1747, p.216. £1.S10.

SAMUEL ALLEN, 273 acs. Brunswick Co. on both sides of Cub Cr.; 1 Oct 1747, p.217. £1.S10.

THOMAS MUCKLEHONEY, 342 acs. Brunswick Co. on both sides of Bears Element Cr., adj. Matthews; 1 Oct 1747, p.218. £1.S15.

LEWIS PARHAM, 388 acs. Brunswick Co. on both sides of the middle Fork of Bluestone Cr.; 1 Oct 1747, p.218. £2.

SAMUEL MOORE, 405 acs. Brunswick Co. on both sides of a Fork of Cubb Cr., adj. Marshall; 1 Oct 1747, p.219. £2.

MATTHEW TALBOT, 143 acs. Brunswick Co. on the S side of Stanton Riv.; 1 Oct 1747, p.220. 15 Shill.

THOMAS JARRATT, 153 acs. Brunswick Co. on the W side of Stoney Cr. adj. his own Line, Wray & Mice; 1 Oct 1747, p.221. 15 Shill.

HUBERT FERRIL, 223 acs. Brunswick Co. on the S side of the upper fork of Miles's Cr., Beg. at the Mouth of a Br. below the Road; 1 Oct 1747, p.222. £1.S5.

WILLIAM WISE, 130 acs. Brunswick Co. on the head of Cattail Cr.; 1 Oct 1747, p.223. 15 Shill.

WILLIAM JORDAN, 104 acs. Brunswick Co. on the S side of Fountains Cr., Beg. at the Mouth of the Spring Sw., adj. William Turner & New; 1 Oct 1747, p.223. 10 Shill.

GEORGE VAUGHAN, 290 acs. Brunswick Co. in the Fork of Eagles Nest Cr., on the Road; 1 Oct 1747, p.224. £1.S10.

WILLIAM BOWEN, 326 acs. Brunswick Co. on the lower side of the Little Cr.; 1 Oct 1747, p.225. £1.S15.

JAMES GEE, 273 acs. Brunswick Co., up Kittle Stick Cr.; adj. Thomas Huckaby, William Gower & Shearing; 1 Oct 1747, p.226. £1.S10. Whereas by a Pat. 28 Sep 1728 Gtd. Richard Carter [PB 13 p.440] And Whereas the sd Richard Carter hath failed to pay Quit Rents and to make Cultiv. and Improv. and James Gee hath made humble

Suit and obtained a G. for the same.

THOMAS WILLIAMS, 186 acs. Lunenburgh Co. on the N side of Stanton Riv. above the mouth of Senaca Cr.; 1 Oct 1747, p.227. £1.

ALEXANDER FINNIE, 200 acs. Brunswick Co. on both sides of Waquigough Cr. on the S side of Nottaway Riv.; 1 Oct 1747, p.228. £1. Whereas by Pat. 16 June 1727 Gtd. Jarvis Winfield [PB 13 p.116] And Whereas Alexander Finnie in whom the Right of the sd L. is since become vested hath failed to pay Quit Rents and to make Cultiv. and Improv. and Richard Bland Gent. hath made humble Suit and obtained a G. for the same which he hath assigned unto the sd Alexander Finnie.

ABRAHAM COCKE, 448 acs. Brunswick Co. on both sides of the Reedy Cr., adj. Embry & his own Line; 1 Oct 1747, p.229. £2.S5.

JOHN LETT, 232 acs. Brunswick Co. on the N side of Miles Cr., by the Great Meadow, adj. Homes & Johnson; 1 Oct 1747, p.230. £1.S5.

DRURY STITH, HENRY MORRIS & MICHAEL CADIT YOUNG, 412 acs. Brunswick Co. on the Ridge bet. Little Bluestone and the Middle Fork, Beg. near a Pond; 1 Oct 1747, p.230. £2.S5.

JOHN GEORGE PENNINGTON, 235 acs. Brunswick Co. on the E

side of Taylors Cr., adj. William Pennington; 1 Oct 1747, p.231. £1.S5.

ANNE MASSEY, 350 acs. Brunswick Co. on both sides of the Cattail Cr., adj. Joseph Massey; 1 Oct 1747, p.232. £1.S15.

DRURY STITH, HENRY MORRIS & MICHAEL CADIT YOUNG, 637 acs. Brunswick Co. on both sides of bluestone Cr., just above the Middle Fork, adj. Byrd; 1 Oct 1747, p.233. £3.S5.

HENRY EMBRY, 388 acs. Brunswick Co., adj. his own Lines & Michael Mackey; 1 Oct 1747, p.234. £2.

NICHOLAS SHEPARD LANIER, 415 acs. Brunswick Co. on the upper side of Mitchells Cr.; 1 Oct 1747, p.235. £2.S5.

THOMAS MINOR, 263 acs. Spotsyl. Co., on a Level, on the N side a Valley, in Low Grounds; adj. Colo. John Lewis, John Hoard (since sold to Joseph Red), William McWilliams, Robert Farish & Thomas Minor; 1 Oct 1747, p.236. 5 Shill. 220 acs. part being part of a Pat. for 850 acs. formerly Gtd. William Johnston by Pat. 28 Sep 1728 [William Johnson, PB 13 p.305] and by him sold & conveyed unto the sd Thomas Minor and 43 acs. the residue never before gtd.

CHARLES STEWART, 300 acs. Surry Co. on the S side of Nottoway Riv., by the Co. Line [S10°W]; adj. Capt. Thomas

Avent, Nathaniel Hauthorn & his own Lines; 1 Oct 1747, p.237. £1.S10.

JOHN ANDERS, 192 acs. Henrico Co. on Stoney Cr., crossing Wolfpen Br.; adj. Benjamin Granger & Handy; 1 Oct 1747, p.238. £1.

BENJAMIN CLARKE, 90 acs. Henrico Co., up a small br. of Ufnam Brooke & up the Ufnam Brook, adj. William Gordon & Benjamin Clarke; 1 Oct 1747, p.239. 10 Shill.

OWEN EVAN OWEN, 427 acs. Henrico Co. on the W side of Sappony Cr., near Middle Creek Road; adj. John Rud, Richard Wood, John Reed/Read, William Harding & John Red; 1 Oct 1747, p.239. £2.S5.

THOMAS HAYES, 168 acs. Gloucester Co. on the E side of Eastermost Riv.; adj. James Callis, Matthew Gates, Alexander Cray, Henry Knight, Pool & Joseph Billups; 1 Oct 1747, p.240. £1.

JOHN DAVIS JUNR., 167 acs. Pr. Geo. Co. bet. Wallace's Cr. and the Long Br.; adj. his Uncle John Davis, Capt. Hamlin & John Jones; 1 Oct 1747, p.241. £1.

WILLIAM HAMLIN, Gent., 74 acs. Pr. Geo. Co. on the lower side of Nammisseen Cr. bet. his own & Richard Newmans Lines; 1 Oct 1747, p.242. 10 Shill.

JOSEPH LANE, 280 acs. Surry Co. on the S side of black Water Sw., up the Run of the Lightwood Sw.; adj. Mr George Briggs, Benjamin Kitchen, Patrick Gray & Joseph Hart; 1 Oct 1747, p.243. £1.S10.

JOSEPH LANE, 286 acs. Surry & Is. of Wight Counties on the S side of black Water Sw., crossing the Co. Line; adj. Mr George Briggs, Joshua Hays, Nicholas Jones, William Hix & Benjamin Kitchen; 1 Oct 1747, p.244. £1.S10.

ERASMUS OAKLEY, 340 acs. Henrico Co. on the N side of the South Br. of White Oak Sw., in a small Slash, on the W side of a Piney Slash near Daniels Path; adj. Nicholas Hobson, John Williams, Edmond Allen & Joseph Watson; 1 Oct 1747, p.245. £1.S15.

GEORGE BOOTH, 428 acs. Brunswick Co. on both sides of the Ridge Cr.; adj. William Tucker, Rayburn, Thomas Eldridge & Thomas Roberts; 1 Oct 1747, p.246. £2.S5.

JOHN BELL, 635 acs. Surry Co. on the S side of Nottoway Riv. & on both sides of the Great Spring Sw., down the run of the Great Br., up the Crooked Br., in the Meadowy Br.; adj. Thomas Weathers, Silvanus Stokes, Charles Judkins & Joseph Bell, by the Lines of the old Land; 1 Oct 1747, p.247. £2. 235 acs. part formerly Gtd. William Hamlin Gent. by Pat. 24 March 1725/26 [PB 12 p.462] the Right & Title whereof is since

become Vested in the sd John Bell and 400 acs. the residue never before Gtd.

WILLIAM HAMLIN, Gent., 718 acs. Pr. Geo. Co. on both sides of Wallaces Cr.; adj. the Lines of his 400 acs. purchased of Thomas Booth, John Davis, Thomas Moor, William Andrews Line from Overby, & the sd Hamlin; 1 Oct 1747, p.249. £1.S15. 400 acs. part formerly Gtd. Thomas Booth by Pat. 13 Oct 1727 [Wallice's Cr., PB 13 p.203] & by him sold & conveyed unto the sd William Hamlin and 318 acs. the residue never before Gtd.

MATTOX MAYS, 798 acs. Brunswick Co. on the N side of Staunton Riv., down Turnip Cr., in a Slash & by a great Pond; 1 Oct 1747, p.250. £2. 400 acs. part formerly gtd. to the sd Mattox Mays by Pat. 2 Aug 1736 [Mattocks Mayes, PB 17 p.139, on the North Fork of Roanoak Riv.] and 398 acs. the residue never before gtd.

DAVID WALKER, Gent., 3,015 acs. Pr. Geo. Co. on both sides of Buckskin Cr.; adj. Short, Richard Thomas, Abernathy, Miles Williams, Evans, Stark, Thomas Stunk, Davis, Bolling & John Roberson; 1 Oct 1747, p.251. £7.S15. 100 acs. part formerly Gtd. Edward Roberson by Pat. 31 Oct 1726 [PB 13 p.68] also 183 acs. other part formerly Gtd. Joseph Stroud by Pat. 28 Sept 1730 [PB 13 p.503] the Right & Title of which sd 2 Tracts or Parcels of L.

by diverse mesne Conveyances is since become vested in the sd David Walker and 1,217 acs. other part also formerly Gtd. unto the sd Walker by Pat. 16 June 1727 [PB 13 p.123] and 1,515 acs. the residue never before Gtd.

CHARLES LYNCH, 1,221 acs. Brunswick Co. on the N side of Staunton Riv. above the mouth of Otter Riv. joining his back Lines; 1 Oct 1747, p.252. £3.S10. 200 acs. part formerly Gtd. to the sd Charles Lynch by Pat. 25 July 1741 [PB 19 p.1037] & 341 acs. other part formerly gtd. the sd Charles Lynch by Pat. 20 Aug 1741 [PB 19 p.1130] & 680 acs. the residue never before Gtd.

ROBERT BRUMFEILD, 400 acs. Amelia Co. on the upper side of Flatt Cr.; adj. Hans Hendrick, Turner, William Farley, Craddock & Brumfield; 1 Oct 1747, p.253. £2.

THOMAS HINTON, 400 acs. Amelia Co. on both sides of the South Fork of Nottoway Riv., up the Stone House Br.; adj. Bumpas, Yarbrough, Dupuy, Jones & Dyer; 1 Oct 1747, p.254. £2.

THOMAS WATKINS JUNR., 1,200 acs. Amelia Co. on both sides of Bush Riv.; adj. Randolph & the L. purchased of Farguson; 1 Oct 1747, p.255. £2. 400 acs. part formerly Gtd. to the sd Thomas Watkins by Pat. 30 Aug 1743 [PB 21 p.550], 400 acs. other part being part of a Pat. for 780 acs. formerly gtd. John Farguson

by Pat. 30 Jul 1742 [PB 21 p.111] and by him sold & conveyed unto the sd Watkins and 400 acs. the residue never before gtd. [see Henry Anderson's 1,202 acs. in PB 28 p.160]

WILLIAM WATSON, 1,500 acs. Amelia Co. on both sides of Mallory's Cr.; adj. James Anderson, Leaden, Weatherford, Edward Jones, Dupuy & Peter Jones; 1 Oct 1747, p.257. £1.S15. 1,150 acs. part being part of a Pat. for 1,500 acs. formerly Gtd. the sd William Watson by Pat. 25 Nov 1743 [PB 21 p.268] and 350 acs. the residue never before Gtd.

JOHN HEARD, 275 acs. Albemarle Co. on both sides of Hardway South fork, at the Falls, adj. Mildred Meriwether; 1 Oct 1747, p.258. £1.S10.

GEORGE CLOPTON, 400 acs. Hanover Co. on the S side of the Southanna Riv.; adj. Broadhouse, Charles Hudson & Drummond; 1 Oct 1747, p.259. £2.

BENJAMIN BROWN, 37 acs. Louisa Co. on the Great Mountains, on the Albemarle Co. Line [N66°W]; 1 Oct 1747, p.260. 5 shill.

BENJAMIN BROWN, 190 acs. Louisa Co. on the Great Mountains, 1 Oct 1747, p.261. £1.

JOHN HARDYMAN, 127 acs. Goochland Co. on the S side of James Riv. and below Willis's Cr., on the S side of the Muster field

Br.; adj. Joseph Terry, Mr Cary & Philip Hudgins; 1 Oct 1747, p.261. 15 Shill.

JOHN MAY, 220 acs. Amelia Co. on the S side of Appamattox Riv., adj. Ray; 1 Oct 1747, p.262. £1.S5.

GEORGE STEWART, 167 acs. Amelia Co. on the upper side of Mountain Cr. on both sides the Road; adj. Nash, Ligon, Davison & Dejarnat; 1 Oct 1747, p.263. £1.

JAMES FARGUSON, 1,550 acs. Amelia Co. on the S side of the Harricane Sw., crossing the long br.; adj. Jones, Leveritt & Mitchell; 1 Oct 1747, p.264. for the Imp. of 7 Pers.: *John Norton, Patrick Stewart, Bryant [Critisley or Carlisley?], Lazarus Jessee, William Cammel, George Hankisson & John Bushel.* 1,200 acs. part formerly Gtd. to the sd Farguson by Pat. 12 March 1739/40 [PB 19 p.579] and 350 acs. the residue never before Gtd.

THOMAS ELLIS, 273 acs. Amelia Co. on the N side of Great Nottoway Riv., adj. Robert Evans & John Mitchell; 1 Oct 1747, p.265. £1.S10.

ALEXANDER BOLLING, 400 acs. Amelia Co. on the head brs. of Buffalo Cr. in the Fork of Nottoway Riv., adj. Bolling; 1 Oct 1747, p.266. £2.

THOMAS CHAPPLE/CHAPPEL, 202 acs. Amelia Co. on the Ridge bet. the brs. of Little Nottoway and

Deep Cr., adj. Isham Epes; 1 Oct 1747, p.267. £1.

JOHN RAY, 154 acs. Amelia Co. on both sides the road bet. the brs. of Sandy and Saylor Creeks; adj. Meadows, Jordan, Dawson & Harris; 1 Oct 1747, p.268. for the Imp. of 3 pers. whose Names are *William Selcock, Thomas Maxvell & Jannett Farley.*

WILLIAM WATSON, 400 acs. Amelia Co. on both sides of the Plumtree Br. of Harris's Cr.; adj. Stovall, Senter, Holland & Venable; 1 Oct 1747, p.269. £2.

BENJAMIN HENDRICK, 400 acs. Amelia Co. on both sides the Walnutt Br. of Flatt Cr.; adj. Craddock now Cocks, Tanner, Ellis & Crawford; 1 Oct 1747, p.269. £2.

RICHARD WILLIS, 262 acs. Amelia Co. on both sides of Buffalo Bed Cr. in the fork of Nottoway Riv; 1 Oct 1747, p.270. £1.S10.

JAMES ANDERSON JUNR., 104 acs. Amelia Co. on the N side of Little Nottoway Riv.; adj. Peter Wynn, Chappel, Cox, John Thomas & Eppes; 1 Oct 1747, p.271. 10 Shill.

JAMES BROWNE, 400 acs. Amelia Co. on the S side of Appamattox Riv.; adj. Thomas Baldwin, Callihan, Robert Peak & William Fain; 1 Oct 1747, p.272. £2.

RICHARD BLAND, 1,167 acs. Surry & Isle of Wight Countys on both sides of the three Creeks, along the edge of the Lowgrounds of the sd Creeks, by the Co. Line [N60°E], up the S or Main Run of sd Creeks, down the North Run of sd Creeks, up Odiums Br., down Lewis's Br., down the Gum Br.; adj. Samuel Alsobrook, John Nanney, Edward Lunday, Timothy Tharp, Capt. Avent, the L. the sd Bland bought of Richard Hayes, the L. the sd Bland bought of Lewis Solomon, Hamilton, William Soloman & Joseph Tharp; 1 Oct 1747, p.273. 10 Shill. 420 acs. part [PB 22 p.134] and 532 acs. other part [PB 22 p.131 which included William More's PB 10 p.277 & Richard Bland's PB 14 p.365] formerly Gtd. sd Richard Bland by Patents 13 Aug 1745 and 135 acs. another part also formerly Gtd. sd Richard Bland by Pat. 5 Mar 1745/46 [George Hamilton's PB 12 p.106 & sd Bland's PB 24 p.171] and 80 acs. the Residue never before gtd. [Included in David Mason's PB 34 p.781]

JOHN GRAY & ROBERT CUZZINS, 400 acs. Amelia Co. on the lower side of Woody Cr. of Deep Cr.; adj. Thweat, Bagley, Kennon, Short & West; 1 Oct 1747, p.275. £2.

WILLIAM TUCKER, 400 acs. Amelia Co. bet. the Sweathouse & Seller Creeks; adj. Charles Clay, Abraham Jones, Abraham Haukes, Jos. Haukes & Richard Jones; 1 Oct 1747, p.276. £2.

JOSEPH TERRY, 400 acs. Amelia Co. on the S side of Appamattox Riv. above Buffalo, adj. Woodson; 1 Oct 1747, p.277. £2.

HENRY VAUGHAN, 182 acs. Amelia Co. on the upper side of Flatt Cr.; adj. Edward Jones, Dupuy, Villan & Callicoat; 1 Oct 1747, p.278. £1.

SAMUEL MATTHEWS, 400 acs. Amelia Co. on both sides of the Mill Fork of Vaughans Cr.; adj. Hudson, Bartho. Zackory & Wingfield; 1 Oct 1747, p.279. £2.

SAMUEL MATTHEWS, 300 acs. Amelia Co. on both sides of Sawneys Cr.; 1 Oct 1747, p.280. £1.S10.

JOHN JACKSON, 260 acs. Amelia Co. on the S side of the Burchen Sw.; adj. Bryan Fannin, John Hughs, his own Line & Edward Lewis; 1 Oct 1747, p.281. £1.S10.

JOHN LIDDERDALE & ELIZABETH his Wife, 400 acs. Louisa Co. on both sides of Buck Mountain Cr., by the side of a Valley & on the side of Buck Mountain; 1 Oct 1747, p.282. £2.

JOHN LIDDERDALE & ELIZABETH his Wife, 400 acs. Louisa Co. on both sides Buck Mountain Cr., Beg. on a spur of Buck mountain; 1 Oct 1747, p.283. £2.

RICHARD STANLEY, 100 acs. Amelia Co. on the S side of Tommahitton Sw.; adj. Tabb &

Edward Lewis; 1 Oct 1747, p.284. 10 Shill.

JOHN DYER, 400 acs. Amelia Co. on the S side of the South Fork of Little Nottoway Riv., adj. Beasley & Bumpas; 1 Oct 1747, p.285. £2.

ROBERT KENT, 260 acs. Goochland Co. on both sides of Pidey Rock of Willis's Riv.; adj. Anthony Christian, Orlando Hughes, Ralph Flippin, William Mills, Miles & Levillian; 1 Oct 1747, p.286. £1.S10.

EDWARD HARPER, 330 acs. Amelia Co. on the upper side of Flatt Cr.; adj. Beasley, Watson, Weatherford, Jones, Dupuy & Keeling; 1 Oct 1747, p.287. for £1.S5 as also for and in Consideration of the Imp. of 2 Pers. to dwell within this our sd Colony and Dominion whose Names are *John Killison & Mary Killison.*

JASON MEADOR, 244 acs. Amelia Co. on the head of Sandy Cr. on both sides of the Road; adj. John Harris, his own Lines, Morris, Matthew Harris, Crawford & Dawson; 12 Jan 1747/48, p.287. for £1 also for the Imp. of one Pers. whose name is *Thomas Rothwell.*

THOMAS BARROW, 120 acs. Is. of Wight Co. on the N side of Meherrin Riv., up Cocks Sw.; adj. Richard Taylor, Joshua Claud & Thomas Wrenn; 12 Jan 1747/48, p.288. 15 Shill.

JAMES FENTRIS, 60 acs. of Swamp L. in Pr. Ann Co. known by the name of the Quack Sw.; adj. the sd Fentris, George Williamson & Moses Fentris Son of John Fentris, 12 Jan 1747/48, p.289. 10 Shill.

JOHN CARR, 290 acs. Louisa Co. on the S or W side of the North Fork of James Riv., on the Albemarle Co. Line [S65°E], adj. the sd Carr; 12 Jan 1747/48, p.290. £1.S10.

SIMON WHITEHURST & JAMES LOVET, 185¾ acs. of Swamp L. in Pr. Ann. Co. known by the name of the Negro Sw.; adj. Murden, Carraway & Lovet; 12 Jan 1747/48, p.291. £1.

WILLIAM KEATON, 331 acs. Louisa Co. on both sides of the South Fork of Rockey Cr., adj. Henry Bunch & Mosias Jones; 12 Jan 1747/48, p.292. £1.S15.

NATHANIEL BUTT, 103 acs. of Swamp L. in Norfolk Co. in the Green Sea, upon the Gallberry Sw., adj. the sd Butt; 12 Jan 1747/48, p.293. 10 Shill.

SAMUEL MANNIN, 290 acs. Is. of Wight Co. on the S side of the main black Water Sw., by the side of Tarrapin Sw., up the Meadow Br., adj. Thomas Joiner; 12 Jan 1747/48, p.294. £1.S10.

JONAH WILLIAMS, 450 acs. Is. of Wight Co. on the N side of Nottoway Riv., on the S side of Nottoway Sw., by the West Fork of sd Sw., crossing the Miery Br.; adj. Thomas Drake, George Williams, Arthur Williams, Nathaniel Jones, Bridgman Joiner & Thomas Gray; 12 Jan 1747/48, p.295. £2.S5.

MOSES PRISCOTT & JOHN HALSTEAD, 400 acs. of Swamp L. in Norfolk Co. adj. the sd Priscott; 12 Jan 1747/48, p.296. £2.

THOMAS PURCELL, 400 acs. Is. of Wight Co. on the W side of the Angelica Sw., Beg. on the N side of Purcells Br., up Ridleys Br., down the Fork Br.; adj. the sd Purcells own old Lines, John Turner & William Blake; 12 Jan 1747/48, p.297. £2.

BAXTER DAVIS, 1,218 acs. Pr. George Co. on both sides of Buckskin Cr.; adj. Jones Williams, Watkins, Stunks, Walker, his own old Lines, Bolling, Holloway & Wilson; 12 Jan 1747/48, p.298. £2.S5. 80 acs. part formerly Gtd. Robert Abernathy by pat. 14 Mar 1731/32 [PB 13 p.280], 270 other acs. part also formerly Gtd. William Davis by Pat. 22 June 1722 [PB 11 p.114 known by the name of *Rich Neck*], 204 acs. other part also Gtd. Ephraim Lisles by Pat. 20 Jun 1733 [PB 15 p.31] the Right & Title of which sd several Tracts or Parcels of L. by diverse Mesne Conveyances is become Vested in the sd Baxter Davis and 232 acs. other part also formerly Gtd. unto the sd Baxter Davis by Pat. 30 Jul 1742 [PB 21 p.51] and

432 acs. the Residue never before Gtd.

JOSEPH PARRISH, 404 acs. Brunswick Co. on both sides of Waqua Cr.; adj. Gilliam & Daniel; 12 Jan 1747/48, p.299. £2.

HENRY WALTHALL, 800 acs. Amelia Co. on the N side of Brier Riv.; adj. Nash, Thomas Franklin, Joseph Jackson, Mullins & Gross; 12 Jan 1747/48, p.300. £4.

WILLIAM THOMPSON, 1,316 acs. Pr. Geo. Co. on the S side of Stoney Cr.; adj. Joseph Turner, his own old line, Smith, William Turner, Robert Jones, Goodwin, Isaac Tucker & Edward Hawkins; 12 Jan 1747/48, p.302. £6. 150 acs. part of 300 acs. formerly Gtd. Edward Hawkins by Pat. 31 Oct 1726 [PB 13 p.58] and 1,166 acs. the Residue never before Gtd.

ARTHUR WHITEHEAD JUNR., 290 acs. Is. of Wight Co. on the S side of Nottoway Riv., down the Cypress Sw., down the Cabbin Br., by the Co. Line [S60°W]; adj. Arthur Whiteheads other L. & John Barrot; 12 Jan 1747/48, p.302. £1.S10.

LARKIN CHEW, 183 acs. Spotsyl. Co., beg. on flat Ground near a lick, on the N side the main Road, on a high Ivey Bank, on Levell Ground & on a Stoney Ridge bet. two old Plantations; adj. Richard Bayley dec'd, Philip Bush, David Bruce, Robert Andress & Mr James Garnet; 12 Jan 1747/48, p.303. £1. 183 acs. part of a Pat.

for 800 acs. formerly Gtd. John Bush by Pat. 30 Jun 1726 [PB 12 p.493 on Bare Sw. & Bare Run] and by Judgment of our General Court bearing date 21 Oct 1745 the sd 183 acs. for Non payment of our Quit Rents according to Law and the condition of the sd Pat. is adjudged to be forfeited and vested again in us.

THOMAS HAWKINS, 430 acs. Brunswick Co. on both sides of the Great Br., adj. William Thomoson; 12 Jan 1747/48, p.304. £2.S5.

HENRY RANDOLPH, 1,790 acs. Henrico Co. on the S side of Swift Cr., on a Hunting Path, to a Wolf Pit, on the W side of Youls Br., on Nottoway Run; adj. James Frankling Junr., Capt. Jefferson, Thomas Totty, John Gill, Mr John Archer & Colo. Francis Epes; 12 Jan 1747/48, p.305. £9. Whereas by Pat. 22 Jan 1718 gtd. Francis Eppes Gent. since dec'd [dated 22 Jan 1717/18 in PB 10 p.346 to Francis Epes]; And Whereas William Kennon & Ann his wife, James Thompson & Mary his wife, William Poythress & Sarah his wife, and Elizabeth Randolph Widow; to which sd Ann, Mary, Sarah and Elizabeth the same was devised by their Father the sd Francis Eppes dec'd, have failed to pay Quit Rents and to make Cultiv. and Improv. and Henry Randolph having Petitioned our Lieut. Governor and Commander in Chief hath obtained a G. for the same.

JOHN BRASSIL, 400 acs. Is. of Wight Co. on the N side of Meherrin Riv.; adj. Samuel Westbrook, Joshua Claud & Thomas Harris; 12 Jan 1747/48, p.307. £2.

THOMAS HARVEY, 400 acs. Goochland Co. on both sides of Tearwallet Run; adj. Robert Peak, William Kent, Adolphus Hendrick & William Daniel; 12 Jan 1747/48, p.308. £2.

JOHN SMITH, 400 acs. Albemarle Co. on the Middle fork of Cunningham Cr., adj. Martin Duncan; 12 Jan 1747/48, p.309. £2.

ARTHUR NEALE & ANDREW DUNN, 400 acs. Amelia Co. on both sides of Spring Cr.; adj. Scott, Doram, Martin, Lodwick Elam & William Elam; 12 Jan 1747/48, p.310. £2.

ELISHA EASTES, 400 acs. Amelia Co. on the S side of Bryer Riv., adj. Parson & Atwood; 12 Jan 1747/48, p.311. £2.

PEW PRICE, 400 acs. Amelia Co. on the upper side of Buffalo Riv., Beg. on the Riv. just above Baker, adj. Wallace & Terry; 12 Jan 1747/48, p.312. £4.

BURWELL BROWN, 652 acs. Brunswick Co. on the S side of Meherrin Riv.; adj. his own Line, Hix & John Mason; 12 Jan 1747/48, p.312. £3.S5. [This L. is now in SE Greensville County, old Is. of Wight Co., where the Saponie Indians once dwelt before moving to Fort Christanna]

JOHN PARKER, 276 acs. Brunswick Co. on both sides of the Little Cr., adj. James McDaniel & William Macklin; 12 Jan 1747/48, p.313. £1.S10. [This Little Cr. is now Aarons Cr.]

ANTHONY HAYNES, 791 acs. Amelia Co. on the N side of Tomahitton Sw., crossing Mingo's Horsepen Br., along the Co. Line [South] & up the Tommahitton Sw.; adj. Eatons now his own, & Cryer; 12 Jan 1747/48, p.314. £4. Whereas by Pat. 16 Sep 1740 gtd. Anthony Haynes [PB 19 p.768 which included William Eaton's 204 acs. Pr. Geo. Co. in PB 14 p.492] And Whereas the sd Anthony Haynes hath failed to make Cultiv. and Improv. and Robert Bolling Gent. hath made humble Suit and obtained a G. for same which he hath assigned to the sd Anthony Haynes.

JOSEPH JOHNSON & ISAAC JOHNSON, 400 acs. Brunswick Co. on both sides of the Middle fork of Meherrin Riv.; 12 Jan 1747/48, p.315.

CHARLES BAILEY, 180 acs. Albemarle Co. on both sides of Baileys Run of the Byrd on the N side James Riv., adj. Thomas Bailey; 12 Jan 1747/48, p.316. £1.

RICHARD HEWSON, 200 acs. Surry Co. on the E side of Sappony Cr., Beg. on the North Prong of the Reedy Br., by the Co. Line [S60°W], down the South Prong of the Reedy Br., adj. his own Line &

Mr Harper; 12 Jan 1747/48, p.317. £1.

RICHARD VICK, 280 acs. Is. of Wight on the S side of Nottoway Riv., up the Run of the Cyprus Sw.; adj. the sd Vicks other L. & Thomas Barns; 12 Jan 1747/48, p.318. £1.S10.

JOSHUA YARBROUGH, 400 acs. Amelia Co. on the head of Whetstone Cr. in the Fork of Nottoway; adj. Cabinis, Thomas Yarbrough Senr. & Thomas Yarbrough Junr.; 12 Jan 1747/48, p.319. £2.

JAMES GRIFFIN, 211 acs. Essex Co. on the N side of Hoskins's Cr., to an ancient marked Hiccory on a Hill, on a Point by the Cr., adj. Lieut. Colonel Thomas Goodrich; 12 Jan 1747/48, p.320. £1.S5.

DENNIS BIRCH, 167 acs. Amelia Co. on the N side of the Horsepen Cr. in the Fork of Nottoway; adj. John Thomas, Edward Thweat & Nance; 12 Jan 1747/48, p.321. £1.

ABRAHAM HAUKES, 284 acs. Amelia Co. on the lower side of the lower Fork of the Seller Cr., adj. Christopher Hinton & Joseph Haukes; 12 Jan 1747/48, p.322. £1.S10.

WILLIAM EZELL, 292 acs. Brunswick Co. on the N side of Fountains Cr., up the Road; adj. Wytche, Clark & Peter Wyche; 12 Jan 1747/48, p.322. £1.S10.

JOHN PENNENTON, 80 acs. Surry Co. on the S side of Nottoway Riv.; adj. Mr Thomas Eldridge, the sd John Pennington, Collo. Philip Lightfoot & Clement Hancock; 12 Jan 1747/48, p.323. 10 Shill.

HENRY WOODARD, 95 acs. of Swamp Land in Norfolk Co., by the Maple Br., Beg. in the Line of a former Survey made for Nathaniel Butt; 12 Jan 1747/48, p.324. 10 Shill.

JEREMIAH WALTHALL, 400 acs. Amelia Co. on both sides of Bryer Riv., adj. Richard Woodson & Baly; 12 Jan 1747/48, p.325. £2.

JOHN PLEASANT, 200 acs. Goochland Co., in the fork of Crooms Quarter Br. of Willis Riv., adj. William Bradley & Samuel Allen; 12 Jan 1747/48, p.326. £1.

JOHN WILLIFORD, 50 acs. Is. of Wight Co. on the S side the Main Blackwater Sw., up Tarrapin Sw.; adj. Josiah John Hollyman, Samuel Lancaster & the sd Willifords other L.; 12 Jan 1747/48, p.327. 5 Shill.

BYRD THOMAS LANIER, 374 acs. Brunswick Co. on the S side of Allens Cr.; 12 Jan 1747/48, p.328. £2.

JOSEPH GRAY, 150 acs. Is. of Wight Co. on N side of the Lightwood Sw., by the side of Harts Br.; adj. George Branch, John Washington, William Cobb &

Joseph Phillips; 12 Jan 1747/48, p.329. 15 Shill.

JAMES MACKGEHEE, 400 acs. Albemarle Co. on N side the River Rivanna on both sides little Mychunk Cr.; 12 Jan 1747/48, p.330. £2.

THOMAS FRANKLIN, 400 acs. Amelia Co. on the N side of Bryer Riv., adj. Baley/Baly & Jeremiah Walthall; 12 Jan 1747/48, p.331. £2.

RICHARD BUSH, 400 acs. Amelia Co. on the E or lower side of Buffalo Bed Cr. in the Fork of Nottoway; adj. Crenshaw, Austin Ellis, his own Line & Evans; 12 Jan 1747/48, p.331. £2.

ROBERT BRYANT, 400 acs. Is. of Wight Co. on the N side of Maherrin Riv., down the Mirey Br.; adj. Edward Barrot, Oliver Woodward & sd Robert Bryants own old Lines; 12 Jan 1747/48, p.332. £2.

JOHN WILKINS, 119 acs. of Swamp Land in Norfolk Co. in the *Point of Pines* in Black Water Sw.; adj. to the late Survey of Moses Priscod & John Halstead; 12 Jan 1747/48, p.333. 15 Shill.

BENJAMIN COOPER, 130 acs. Is. of Wight Co. on the S side of Nottoway Riv., down the Run of the Gum Sw.; adj. his own old Lines, John Myrick, Christopher Foster, Thomas Gold, Daniel Williams & Richard Lundy; 12 Jan 1747/48, p.334. 15 Shill.

BENJAMIN CROCKER, 115 acs. Is. of Wight Co. on the N side of Maherrin Riv., down the Run of the Little Sw., adj. Robert Bryant & John Rotchell; 12 Jan 1747/48, p.335. 15 Shill.

Colo. SAMUEL BUSH, Gent., 45 acs. of Low Sunken Land in Norfolk Co. being Coves of a Cr. called Tanners Cr. and adj. to the L. of the sd Samuel Bush, Beg. on a Point near a Br. of the sd Cr. that leads up to the dwelling Houses of the sd Samuel Boush, to a Point of Land near the Mouth of the sd Tanners Cr. intersecting several Beacons at sundry Stations; 12 Jan 1747/48, p.336. 5 Shill.

ERASMUS HAYNES, 58 acs. Pr. Anne Co. near to Matchepungo Landing, by the Procoson, upon the North Riv. & upon a Point making out of the sd Procoson; 12 Jan 1747/48, p.337. 10 Shill.

JOHN TOOK, 95 acs. Brunswick Co. on the N side of Fountains Cr., adj. James Parham; 12 Jan 1747/48, p.338. 10 Shill.

TIMOTHY REAVES, 140 acs. Brunswick Co. adj. his own old Lines; 12 Jan 1747/48, p.339. 15 Shill.

THOMAS HOLT, 140 acs. Surry & Is. of Wight Counties, Beg. on the E side of the North Prong of the Hornet Sw., by the Co. Line [N60°E], adj. Holliday Fort & Thomas Newsum; 12 Jan 1747/48, p.340. 15 Shill.

JAMES CARTER, 125 acs. Surry Co. on the S side of Nottoway Riv., Beg. at the mouth of a br. which runs out of the Raccoon Sw. and divides him from Edward Skelton, down the Run of the blew Marsh Meadow & up the Run of the Raccoon Sw.; 12 Jan 1747/48, p.341. 15 Shill.

THOMAS BREWER, 175 acs. Surry Co. on the S side of Nottoway Riv., Beg. on the South Fork of the Hunting Quarter Sw., on the side of Allens Road; adj. Thomas Grantham, Robert Tucker & John Weaver; 12 Jan 1747/48, p.341. £1.

JAMES SMITH, 238 acs. Brunswick Co. on both sides of Fountains Cr., adj. John Brown & John Smith; 12 Jan 1747/48, p.342. £1.S5.

RICHARD BLOW, 475 acs. Surry Co. on the S side of Seacock Sw.; adj. his own Lines, William Brittle & John Phillips; 12 Jan 1747/48, p.343. £2.S10.

GEORGE PAINE JUNR., 382 acs. Albemarle Co. on the Middle Fork of Cunningham, crossing the Cr., adj. Holland; 12 Jan 1747/48, p.344. £2.

JAMES HENDERSON, 132 acs. Albemarle Co. on S side of the Rivanna on the brs. of Meadow Cr.; adj. James Fidler, How & Cash, Joel Terrill & Michael Holland; 12 Jan 1747/48, p.345. 15 Shill.

JOHN SLEDGE, 371 acs. Brunswick Co. on the N side of Fountains Cr., adj. James Judkins; 12 Jan 1747/48, p.346. £2.

OBEDIAH SMITH, 427 acs. Lunenburgh Co. on the S side of Dan Riv., Beg. at the Mouth of Teawayhomany Cr.; 12 Jan 1747/48, p.347. £2.S5.

WILLIAM LUCAS JUNR., 77 acs. Louisa Co. on one of the Little Mountains; adj. Capt. George Hoom & the late Line of Colo. Nicholas Meriwether; 12 Jan 1747/48, p.348. 10 Shill.

JOHN SPAIN, 300 acs. Surry Co. on the S side of Nottoway Riv.; adj. William Spain, Nathaniel Hood & Richard Rives; 12 Jan 1747/48, p.349. £1.S10.

JOHN MITCHELL/MITCHEL, 83 acs. Amelia Co. on the S side of Whetstone Cr. in the Fork of Nottoway, on Polecatt Br., adj. Thomas Anderson; 12 Jan 1747/48, p.350. 10 Shill.

GEORGE BOOTH, JUNR., 1,854 acs. Pr. Geo. Co. on both sides of Turkey Egg Cr.; adj. William Tucker, Lacy Mathis, William Bird, Nicholas Maidlin, Williamson & his own old Lines; 12 Jan 1747/48, p.351. £2. 400 acs. part formerly Gtd. sd Booth by Pat. 20 Sep 1745 [PB 24 p.62] and 1,054 acs. other part formerly Gtd. unto his Father George Booth by Pat. 16 Jun 1727 [PB 13 p.124] and by him Given & Conveyed to the sd

George Booth Junr. And 400 acs. the Residue never before Gtd.

VALENTINE CAWLEY, 300 acs. Goochland Co. on the S side of Appamattox Riv. on the Brs. of Angola; adj. Edward Davison, William McCoy, Richard Witt & John Patterson; 12 Jan 1747/48, p.352. £1.S10.

WILKINSON HOULY [HONLY?], 460 acs. Amelia Co. on the Little Cr. of Flatt Cr., in the Low Grounds of the sd Cr.; adj. Mottley, Ellis, his own old Lines & Clarke; 12 Jan 1747/48, p.353. 10 Shill. 400 acs. part being part of a Pat. for 1,200 acs. formerly Gtd. Matthew Mayes by Pat. 2 Jan 1737/38 [Matthew Mayes Junr. in PB 17 p.457, which included his 400 acs. in PB 17 p.33] the right & title of which sd 400 acs. is since become vested in the sd Houly and 60 acs. the Residue never before Gtd.

ISAAC COLLIER, 755 acs. Brunswick Co. on the N side of the Otter Dams Cr. and on both sides of Jacks Br.; adj. John Brown, John Davis, Lawrence Hows, Whitington, Harrison & Bradford; 12 Jan 1747/48, p.354. 10 Shill. 440 acs. part formerly Gtd. William Smith by Pat. 22 Feb 1724/25 [Surry Co., PB 12 p.172], 220 acs. other part being part of Pat. for 645 acs. formerly Gtd. William Smith 30 Jun 1743 [PB 20 p.537] the Right & Title of which sd 660 acs. is since become vested in the sd Collier and 95 acs. the Residue never before Gtd.

WILLIAM HOWELL, 410 acs. Surry and Is. of Wight Counties, Beg. by the side of the Piney Br., up the Snake Br., down Tarrarar Br.; adj. Majr. Joseph Gray (in Is. of Wight), his own Survey (which lies in Surry) & his new & old Surveys, John Blow, Henry Blow & William Brittle; 12 Jan 1747/48, p.355. £2.S5.

LAWRENCE TALIAFERRO, 162 acs. & 69 Perches in Caroline Co. on the S side of Long Br.; adj. Francis & Anthony Thornton, Buckner, Peter Lanton [Lauton?] & Deval; 12 Jan 1747/48, p.357. £1. Whereas by Pat. 20 June 1733 Gtd. unto William Bell [PB 15 p.50] And Whereas the sd William Bell hath failed to pay Quit Rents and to make Cultiv. & Improv. and Richard Long hath made humble Suit and hath obtained a G. for the same which he hath assigned unto Lawrence Taliaferro.

JAMES HALL, 436 acs. Pr. Geo. Co. on lower side of White Oak Sw.; adj. Jordan, the sd Halls old L. & Dewey; 12 Jan 1747/48, p.358. 15 Shill. 286 acs. part formerly Gtd. Justance Hall dec'd by Pat. 22 Jun 1722 [Justant Hall, PB 11 p.133] and devised to his Son the sd James and 150 acs. the Residue never before Gtd.

JOSEPH MORTON, 2,800 acs. Amelia Co. on both sides of Bryer Riv. and on the Brs. of Buffalo; adj. Martin, William Brown, the L. purchased of Obediah Woodson, Bibb, Cole now Nicksons, & his own old Lines; 12 Jan 1747/48,

p.359. £2. 1,600 acs. part formerly gtd. Joseph Morton by Pat. 20 Aug 1745 [PB 22 p.449] and 800 acs. other part also formerly Gtd. Obediah Woodson by Pat. 25 Sep 1746 [PB 22 p.579 duplicated in Joseph Morton's PB 24 p.460] The Right & Title whereof is since become vested in the sd Joseph Morton and 400 acs. the Residue never before Gtd.

JOHN CHEW & FRANCIS TALIAFERRO, Church Wardens of the Parish of St. George for them and their Successors for a Glebe; 577 acs. Spotsyl. Co. on the S side of the Riv. Po; on the S side Johnstons Race Ground, on the S side a path, by the Glebe old Field in the head of a Br.; adj. Roger Cason, William Johnston, formerly Edward Piggs L., & Harry Beverley [His New Land Tract Line]; 20 Sep 1748 in the 22nd year of our Reign of George the Second, p.360. 512 acs. being part of a Pat. Gtd. Larkin Chew, Gent. 26 Apr 1712 [2,143 acs. K. & Q. Co. in PB 10 p.57] and 32 acs. the Residue being part of a Pat. gtd. Harry Beverley, Gent. 23 Mar 1715/16 [1,250 acs. in PB 10 p.281, no Co. given] and by diverse mesne Conveyeances is since become vested in the aforesd Church Wardens in right of the Parish.

JOSEPH HOOPER, 175 acs. Albemarle Co. adj. to Appamattox Riv. near Appamattox Mountain; 20 Sep 1748, p.362. £1.

RICHARD WARD, 500 acs. Amelia Co. on the S side of Little Saylor Cr., in the old Line by a Br. of the North Fork of Flatt Cr., by the Hunting Path; 20 Sep 1748, p.363. £2.S10. the sd 500 acs. being part of a Pat. for 3,146 acs. formerly Gtd. John Crawford by Pat. 5 Jun 1736 [PB 17 p.100] and upon the Petition of the sd Richard Ward to our General Court the sd L. for want of Cultiv. and Improv. according to Law and the Condition of the sd Pat. was by our sd Court 21 Apr 1742 adjudged to be forfeited and vested again in us.

JOHN ERWIN, 180 acs. Augusta Co. on a Br. of the North Riv. of Shanando called the Long Glead Cr., by a hallow, on a Ridge, adj. Andrew Erwin; 20 Sep 1748, p.364. £1.

ANDREW ERWIN, 150 acs. Augusta Co. on the long Glade; 20 Sep 1748, p.365. 15 Shill.

RICHARD BURTON, 400 acs. Augusta Co. on the Brs. of Buffalo Cr., adj. Benjamin Borden & Richard Wood; 20 Sep 1748, p.366. £2.

DAVID CLOYD, 400 acs. Augusta Co. on the head of a North Br. of James Riv. joining on William Mills; 20 Sep 1748, p.367. £2.

DAVID CLOYD, 400 acs. Augusta Co. on a South Br. of Cedar Cr.; 20 Sep 1748, p.368. £2.

ISAAC WHITE, 243 acs. Augusta Co. on the W side the Blue Ridge, Beg. on the South Riv. of Shanando & on the E side thereof; 20 Sep 1748, p.368. £1.S5.

JOHN HERBERT, 2,270 acs. Pr. Geo. Co. on S side of Moccosonock Cr., Beg. at the old Line of the Fox Br. Tract at the dividing Br., in Rive's old field, in the Fork of the Fox Br. & crossing the upper Fork of sd Br., along the Line of the L. formerly belonging to John Stroud, to the old Line formerly of Henry King dec'd in a Meadow, down the Line dividing Stroud and Pettypoole dec'd; 20 Sep 1748, p.369. £6.S5. 280 acs. part being part of a Pat. for 400 acs. formerly gtd. Henry King 24 Oct 1701 [PB 9 p.382, Charles City Co.] and 300 acs. other part being part of a Pat. for 405 acs. formerly gtd. John Anderson & Robert Mumford 1 May 1706 [PB 9 p.715], 46 acs. other part formerly gtd. John Stroud by Pat. 15 July 1717 [PB 10 p.355], 400 acs. other part formerly gtd. Richard Herbert by Pat. 28 Sep 1728 [PB 14 p.18] the Right and Title whereof by divers mesne Conveyances is since become vested in the sd John Herbert and 1,244 acs. the other part never before gtd.

DAVID CLOYD, 262 acs. Augusta Co. on a Br. of James Riv. called Possimon Run on the N side of the same joining a Tract of Land belonging to David Mitchel and a Tract of L. belonging to William Mills; 20 Sep 1748, p.371. £1.S10.

STEPHEN HUGHES & BOOTH NAPIER, 400 acs. Albemarle Co. on the N side of Pedlar Riv., at a Br. of Horseleys Cr.; 20 Sep 1748, p.372. £2.

JOSEPH ROBINSON, 190 acs. Augusta Co. joining the L. of George Robinson and the L. of James Cole on the Water of Roanoak, on the S side of Buffalo Cr.; 20 Sep 1748, p.373. £1.

WILLIAM PIRKINS, 150 acs. Augusta Co., Beg. on a Timber Ridge (in a line of the Pat. L. of Joist Hyte, Robert McCay & Robert Green lying on Linwells Cr.), on the W side of a Draft; 20 Sep 1748, p.374. 15 Shill.

METHUSELAH GRIFFITHS, 400 acs. Augusta Co. on the W side of Masons Cr.; 20 Sep 1748, p.375. £2.

METHUSELAH GRIFFITHS, 400 acs. Augusta Co., Beg. in a Valley on the E side of Peters Run, crossing the sd Run; 20 Sep 1748, p.376. £2.

JAMES BURK, 400 acs. Augusta Co. on the W side the blue Ridge, down Goose Cr.; 20 Sep 1748, p.376. £2.

JAMES BURK, 100 acs. Augusta Co. on the S side of Goose Cr., adj. William Campbell; 20 Sep 1748, p.377. 10 Shill.

THOMAS LOOKER, 300 acs. Augusta Co. on a Br. of the North Riv. of Shanando called Smiths Cr,

Beg. in a Hollow on the E side of sd Cr.; 20 Sep 1748, p.378. £1.S10.

CORNELIUS COOK, 350 acs. Augusta Co. on the Brs. of Brocks Cr., on the N side of a Ridge; 20 Sep 1748, p.379. £1.S15.

HUGH CAMPBELL, 333 acs. Augusta Co. on the North Br. of Shanando, Beg. on the SW side of sd Riv., on the N side of Browns Br., cross a Meadow, adj. Robert Fowler; 20 Sep 1748, p.380. £1.S15.

JOHN MILLS, 400 acs. Augusta Co. on the E side of Woods Riv., adj. Francis Reiley; 20 Sep 1748, p.381. £2.

DANIEL McNARE, 27 acs. Augusta Co., down the Middle Riv. of Shanando; adj. the sd McNares old Line & William Brody; 20 Sep 1748, p.381. 5 shill.

DANIEL McNARE, 23 acs. Augusta Co., up & crossing the middle Riv. of Shanando; 20 Sep 1748, p.382. 5 Shill.

JOHN PETER SALLING, 170 acs. Augusta Co. on the E side of the North Br. of James Riv., at the foot of the Mountain; 20 Sep 1748, p.383. £1.

JOHN STEVENSON, 300 acs. Augusta Co. on a Br. of Naked Cr.; 20 Sep 1748, p.384. £1.S10.

JOSEPH SNORGRASS, 364 acs. Augusta Co. on the Waters of Ronoak, adj. James Coates L.; 20 Sep 1748, p.385. £2.

TASKER TOSH, 220 acs. Augusta Co., crossing Goose Cr.; 20 Sep 1748, p.386. £1.S5.

THOMAS BRYAN, 200 acs. Augusta Co. on a Draft on the SE side of Linwels Cr.; adj. the Pat. L. of Joist Hyte, Robert McCay & Robert Green; 20 Sep 1748, p.387. £1.

STERLING CLACK, 492 acs. Brunswick Co. on the S side of the Reedy Cr., adj. Christopher Tatum & James Vaughan; 20 Sep 1748, p.388. £2.S10. Whereas by Pat. 13 Oct 1736 gtd. Peter Overby [PB 17 p.192] And Whereas the sd Peter Overby hath failed to make Cultiv. and Improv. And Whereas Sterling Clack hath made humble Suit and obtained a G. for the same.

TIMOTHY REEVES, 100 acs. Brunswick Co. on the N side of the Great Sw., up Foxes Br.; adj. Thomas Carter, William Doglass & Reives; 20 Sep 1748, p.389. 10 Shill.

JAMES McCARRELL, 130 acs. Augusta Co. on Cub Run bet. the sd Run and the Peeked Mountain, adj. Crosswait; 20 Sep 1748, p.389. 15 Shill.

THEODORICK CARTER, 975 acs. Amelia Co., bet. Bush and Brier Rivers; adj. Richard

Woodson, Walthall & Randolph; 20 Sep 1748, p.390. £5.

RICHARD JONES, JUNIOR, 631 acs. Amelia Co. on both sides of the South Fork of Deep Cr., down a small Branch & Winninghams Cr.; adj. Hall Hudson, Philemon Crane, Ambrose Crane, Tanner, Moody, Jefferson & Brown; 20 Sep 1748, p.391. £3.S5.

WILLIAM HILL, 400 acs. Amelia Co. on both sides the Cedar Br. on the lower side of Vaughans Cr., adj. Jennings & Wingfield; 20 Sep 1748, p.392. £2.

SAMUEL JORDAN, 286 acs. Amelia Co. on lower side of Snales Cr.; adj. Bagly, Ellington, Hudson, Ellis, Shelton & Presnall/Presuall; 20 Sep 1748, p.393. £1.S10.

PHILEMON HALCOMB, 718 acs. Amelia Co. on E or lower side of Bryer Riv.; adj. Flournoy, Atwood, Parson & Martin; 20 Sep 1748, p.394. £3.S15.

JOHN NASH, 242 acs. Amelia Co. on the S side of Appamattox Riv., adj. Randolph & his own old Lines; 20 Sep 1748, p.395. £1.S5.

WILLIAM IRBY, 371 acs. Lunenburgh Co. on the N side of Dann Riv., adj. Bird & William Ghent; 20 Sep 1748, p.396. £2.

SAMUEL JORDAN, 400 acs. Amelia Co. on the S side of Harricane Sw., in the head of the Long Br.; adj. Martin, Peter Wynn

& Farguson; 20 Sep 1748, p.397. £2.

WILLIAM COLE, 63 acs. Amelia Co. on the S side of Appamattox Riv. and on both sides of Rough Cr.; 20 Sep 1748, p.398. 10 Shill.

WILLIAM CHISOLM, 400 acs. Amelia Co., bet. the Middle and Lower Seller Forks of Deep Cr.; adj. Dennis, Leath, & Bolling [her Line]; 20 Sep 1748, p.399. £2.

DUNCOM BLEW, 228 acs. Amelia Co. on the lower side of Sandy Riv. on both sides the Road, in the Head of a br.; adj. Daniel Brown, Lester, Searcey, King & Childrey; 20 Sep 1748, p.401. for the Importation of 5 Persons to dwell within this our Colony and Dominion of Virginia who Names are *Duncom Blew, Ann Blew, Elianor Blew, Mary Blew & Catherine Blew.*

PETER COFFEE, 220 acs. Amelia Co. on both sides of the Mill Fork of Vaughans Cr.; adj. Matthews, Wingfield & Jennings; 20 Sep 1748, p.402. £1.S5.

JOHN ROBERTS, 400 acs. Amelia Co. on the Brs. of Camp Cr. of Bush Riv., adj. Randolph & Nash; 20 Sep 1748, p.403. £2.

ROBERT ROWLAND, 400 acs. Amelia Co. on the Head Brs. of Sandy Riv.; adj. Penick, Watson & Dejarnat; 20 Sep 1748, p.405. £2.

GEORGE LUMKIN, 400 acs. Amelia Co on the S side of Appamattox Riv. adj. Randolph; 20 Sep 1748, p.406. £2.

ALEXANDER FRASOR, 177 acs. Amelia Co. on the Lower side of Mountain Cr.; adj. Atkins, Randolph, Rutlidge, his own Line & Womack; 20 Sep 1748, p.408. £1.

GODFREY PILES, 152 acs. Amelia Co. on Upper side of Mountain Cr., adj. Ligon & Nash; 20 Sep 1748, p.409. 15 Shill.

HENRY LESTER, 200 acs. Amelia Co on both sides of the Road on the Lower side of Sandy Riv.; adj. Womack, Villan & Brown; 20 Sep 1748, p.410. £1.

BARNABY WELLS, 153 acs. Amelia Co on the N side of Mallory's Cr.; adj. Leadon, Anderson, Roberson, Bruce & Wilson; 20 Sep 1748, p.412. 15 Shill.

JOHN JOHNS, 404 acs. Brunswick Co. on the South Fork of Crooked Run, adj. Rivers; 20 Sep 1748, p.414. £2.

JAMES FERGUSON, 150 acs. Lunenburgh Co. on the Lowes Sides of the Nap of Reeds Cr.; 20 Sep 1748, p.415. 15 Shill.

WILLIAM SALLY, 350 acs. Goochland Co. joining to the French Line on the back of the Manacan Town; 20 Sep 1748, p.416. £1.S15. Whereas by Pat. 13 Oct 1727 gtd. unto George Marchbanks [PB 13 p.218] formerly in the Co. of Henrico now Goochland And Whereas the Right & Title of the sd L. by divers mesne Conveyances became vested in William Gray & Elizabeth his Wife Executrix of the last Will & Testament of William Chamberlayne dec'd, who have failed to make Cultiv. & Improv., and William Sally hath made humble Suit and obtained a G. for the same.

JOHN WARREN, 376 acs. Albemarle Co. on the Meadows on the N side of Buffalo Ridge; adj. James Warren & Capt. John Harvie; 20 Sep 1748, p.418. £2.

JOY ASQUE, 440 acs. King & Queen Co.; adj. Mr James Taylor, Majr. Temple, Berryman & Boyd; 20 Sep 1748, p.419. 15 Shill. 300 acs. Part being Part of a Pat. for 1,000 acs. formerly gtd. George Chapman 8 Aug 1658 [N of Mattapany Riv. in New Kent Co., PB 4 p.186 (274)] the Right & Title of which sd 300 acs. is since become vested in the sd Joy Asque and 140 acs. the Residue found to be Surplus Land within the Bounds aforesd.

THOMAS WILLIAMSON, 420 acs. Is. of Wight Co. on the S side of the main Blackwater Sw., up Jackson's Br., up the Run of Warreak Br.; adj. his own old Lines, Josiah John Hollyman & Joseph Allen; 20 Sep 1748, p.420. £2.S5.

PETER HAY, 130 acs. Is. of Wight Co. on the S side of

Nottoway Riv., down the Run of the three Creeks & down the Great Sw.; adj. his own old Lines, Edward Morgan & Adam Heath; 20 Sep 1748, p.422. 15 Shill.

JAMES BAKER, 190 acs. Is. of Wight Co. on the S side of the first Sw. of the Main Black Water, up the Run of the Mile Br., in the Great Pocoson; adj. his own old Lines, Joseph Mangum, Thomas Humphrey, William Goodrich, Benjamin Goodrich & Benjamin Hodges; 20 Sep 1748, p.423. £1.

JOHN NASH, 3,100 acs. Amelia Co. on Mountain Cr. and the Brs. of Camp Cr., in the head of a Br. of Maherrin, down the East or Lower Fork of Mountain Cr.; adj. Ligon, Bagby, Randolph & Harden; 20 Sep 1748, p.425. £7.S15. 1,570 acs. part formerly gtd. sd John Nash by Pat. 20 Aug 1745 [PB 22 p.411] and 1,530 acs. the Residue never before gtd.

JOHN NASH, 1,334 acs. Amelia Co. on both sides of Bryer Riv., near the Road; adj. Spencer, Brown, the L. Purchased of Morton, Halcomb, Atwood, Cobb & Watson; 20 Sep 1748, p.427. £4.S15. 400 acs. part formerly gtd. sd John Nash by Pat. 5 Jun 1746 [PB 25 p.82] and 934 acs. the Residue never before gtd.

JOHN WOODSON, 1,498 acs. Amelia Co. on both sides of Buffillo Riv.; adj. Randolph, George Lumkins & Callihan; 20 Sep 1748, p.429. £7.S10.

PETER COFFEE, 192 acs. Amelia Co., bet. the heads of Vaughans Spring and Cubb Creeks, Beg. at the head of the Mill Fork of Vaughans Cr., near a Spring of Cubb Cr.; adj. Jennings & Williams; 20 Sep 1748, p.431. £1.

RICHARD WOODSON, 1,152 acs. Amelia Co. on both sides of Bryer Riv.; adj. Walthall, Gauling, Joseph Mortons now his own Line; 20 Sep 1748, p.432. £4. 364 acs. part formerly gtd. the sd Richard Woodson by Pat. 30 Jun 1743 [PB 20 p.526] and 788 acs. the Residue never before gtd.

WILLIAM WATSON, 619 acs. Amelia Co. on the lower side of Winticomaick Cr. and on both sides the Road, Beg. on Tucker's Br. of Nammisseen, by a Spring, above the Bridge; adj. Bolling, Tucker, Crawley & Bland; 20 Sep 1748, p.434. 5 Shill. 577 acs. part formerly gtd. the sd William Watson by Pat. 10 Jul 1745 [PB 22 p.257] and 42 acs. the residue never before gtd.

SAMUEL WALLACE, 2,017 acs. Amelia Co. on both sides of Fort & Falling Creeks; adj. Briswate, Baldwin & Harden; 20 Sep 1748, p.435. £10.S5. [Column note: *Rites received by T.D.*]

MATTHEW CABINIS, 612 acs. Amelia Co. on both sides the Lazaritta Cr., down the North Fork of sd Cr.; adj. Bruce, his own old Lines, Brown & Jefferson, Robertson & Watson; 20 Sep 1748, p.437. £1.S5. 400 acs. part

formerly gtd. the sd Matthew Cabinis by Pat. 30 Jun 1743 [PB 21 p.348] and 212 acs. the Residue never before gtd.

WILLIAM RODGERS, 150 acs. Lunenburgh Co. on both sides of Turnip Cr.; 20 Sep 1748, p.438. 15 Shill. [Column note: *Rites received by T.D.*]

THOMAS RODGERS, 204 acs. Lunenburgh Co. on both sides of Turnip Cr., adj. his Line & Bartholomew Austin; 20 Sep 1748, p.440. £1.

JAMES PATTON, 183 acs. Augusta Co. on the North Fork of Roanoak, crossing the Riv.; 20 Sep 1748, p.441. £1.

MARK EVANS, 400 acs. Augusta Co. on the Waters of Ronoak called Cedar Spring at a place called *naked Farm*, Beg. on a Hill above the big Spring, crossing the big Spring Run; 20 Sep 1748, p.442. £2.

JOHN DAWSON, 85 acs. Is. of Wight Co. on both sides of Black Cr. on the S side of the Main Black Water Sw.; adj. James Hasty & sd John Dawson's own old Line; 20 Sep 1748, p.444. 10 Shill.

SIMON TURNER, JUNIOR, 245 acs. Is. of Wight Co. on the S side of Nottaway Riv., on the N side of Townsend's Br.; adj. Edward Drew, Abraham Saul & Henry Townsend; 20 Sep 1748, p.445. £1.S5.

ANSELM BAILEY JUNR., 190 acs. Is. of Wight Co. on the S side of the Main Black Water, up the Cabbin Br.; adj. John Hallyman & Micajah Edward's Line; 20 Sep 1748, p.446. £1.

MARK EVANS, 400 acs. Augusta Co. on the waters of Roanoak at a Place called the *Naked Farm*, Beg. on the NW side of a Br. of Caravies Cr., in clear Land or Barrens; 20 Sep 1748, p.448. £2.

MARK EVANS, 87 acs. Augusta Co. on the S side of Roanoak bet. Charles Hungat and a Tract of L. belonging to sd Evans, down the sd Riv.; 20 Sep 1748, p.449. 10 Shill.

MARK EVANS, 400 acs. Augusta Co. on a Br. of Roanoak called Cedar Spring at a place called the *Naked Farm*, Beg. on the SE side of the Head of the Great Spring by sd Mark Evans's House, crossing Spring Br.; 20 Sep 1748, p.450. £2.

JAMES PATTON, 150 acs. Augusta Co. on the Brs. of James Riv. on the W side of the Blue Ridge, on a Stoney Point, standing on the sd Riv. at Luny's Ford; 20 Sep 1748, p.452. 15 Shill.

JOHN ERVIN, 300 acs. Augusta Co. on the Long Glade, adj. the Widow Patterson; 20 Sep 1748, p.453. £1.S10.

EDWARD ERVIN, 141 acs. Augusta Co. adj. another Pat. of the sd Edward Ervin's; 20 Sep 1748, p.454. 15 shill.

JOSIAS RANDLE, 504 acs. Lunenburg Co. on the E of a Br. of Butchers Cr., adj. John Mitchel; 20 Sep 1748, p.455. £2.S10.

WALTER CAMPBELL, 265 acs. Lunenburgh Co. on both sides of Tusling Quarter Br., adj. Thomas Loyd & Henry Simmons; 20 Sep 1748, p.457. £1.S10.

JOHN EZARD [EZELL], 620 acs. Lunenburg Co. on the upper side of Feneywood Cr., adj. Munford; 20 Sep 1748, p.458. £3.S5. [Included in William Marrable's 1,870 acs. in PB 31 p.712]

JOHN BOLLING, Gentleman, 5,000 acs. Lunenburg Co. on the Heads of the Brs. of Falling Riv. Joyning the Ridge bet. Rack Island Cr. and the Brs. of the sd Falling Riv., on the Ridge bet. the Counties of Brunswick and Albemarle, adj. Thomas Dugons & Adam Beard; 10 Jan 1748/49, p.459. £25.

JOHN WRIGHT, 224 acs. Lunenburgh Co. on the upper side of Flatt Cr., adj. Thomas Roberts & Edward Morgan; 10 Jan 1748/49, p.462. £1.S5.

JOHN WRIGHT, 386 acs. Lunenburg Co. on upper side of Flatt Cr., down the Rocky Br.; 10 Jan 1748/49, p.463. £2.

LEWIS DELONY, JUNR., 300 acs. Lunenburgh Co. on the E side

of Cocks Cr., up the School Br., on Cock's Cr. aforesd just below Delony's Mill; adj. Delony, Haward, Hayward & Harwell; 10 Jan 1748/49, p.465. £1.S10.

JAMES DANIEL, 400 acs. Lunenburgh Co. on both sides of Crupper Run; 10 Jan 1748/49, p.466. £2.

PAUL CHILES, 400 acs. Lunenburgh Co. including some of the head Brs. of Falling Riv., adj. Henry Chiles & John Beard; 10 Jan 1748/49, p.467. £2.

WILLIAM WILLIAMS, 1,550 acs. Lunenburgh Co. on the Brs. of Stoney Cr., down the Great Br., adj. John Parker & Howell; 10 Jan 1748/49, p.469. £7.S15.

WILLIAM RIVERS, 435 acs. Lunenburgh Co. on both sides of Crooked Run; 10 Jan 1748/49, p.470. 15 Shill. 311 acs. Part formerly gtd. Robert Rivers by Pat. 2 Jan 1737/38 [on Green Cr. in Brunswick Co., PB 17 p.437], the Right & Title of which is since become vested in the sd William Rivers and 124 acs. the Residue never before gtd.

HUGH MILLER, 1,254 acs. Lunenburg Co. on both sides of the South Fork of Meherrin Riv., adj. John Cox; 10 Jan 1748/49, p.472. £6.S5.

JOHN BEARD, 364 acs. Lunenburgh Co. including the Head of Cub Cr. and some of the head

Brs. of Falling Run, adj. Chiles; 10 Jan 1748/49, p.474. £2.

PETER OVERBY, 182 acs. Lunenburg Co. on both sides of Tewahomony Cr. on the S side of Dan Riv., adj. Griffin; 10 Jan 1748/49, p.476. £1.

JOHN BEARD, 350 acs. Lunenburgh Co. on the upper side of Falling Riv. including both sides of Reedy Cr., adj. Bolling; 10 Jan 1748/49, p.477. £1.S15.

JOHN BEARD, 200 acs. Lunenburgh Co. on both sides Falling Riv., adj. Jones & Manley; 10 Jan 1748/49, p.478. £1.

SUSANNA CHILES, 50 acs. Lunenburg Co. on the S side of Staunton Riv., adj. Henry Chiles; 10 Jan 1748/49, p.480. 5 Shill.

ELIZABETH CHILES, 130 acs. Lunenburgh Co. on the S side of Stanton Riv., to a Deer's Eye Tree on the Riv., adj. Henry Chiles; 10 Jan 1748/49, p.481. 15 Shill.

DANIEL HAY, 245 acs. Lunenburgh Co. on both sides of Maherrin Riv., down the South Fork of sd Riv.; 10 Jan 1748/49, p.482. 25 Shill.

AMOS TIMMS SHELLY, 400 acs. Lunenburgh Co. on the lower side of Flatt Cr., up Parham's Cr.; adj. his own Line, Mirick & Humphrey Huey; 10 Jan 1748/49, p.484. £2.

FRANCIS RANN, 250 acs. Lunenburgh Co. on the Lower side

of Keeths Br.; 10 Jan 1748/49, p.485. £1.S5.

RICHARD PARSONS, 180 acs. Lunenburgh Co. on both sides of Banister Riv., Beg. at the Mouth of the Rocky Br., adj. Nowell Burton; 10 Jan 1748/49, p.487. £1.

RICHARD PARSONS, 204 acs. Lunenburgh Co. on both sides of Great Cherry stone Cr.; 10 Jan 1748/49, p.488. £1.

ROBERT MITCHEL, 40 acs. Lunenburgh Co. on the N side of Roanoak Riv., along his own Line; 10 Jan 1748/49, p.490. 5 Shill.

RICHARD DUDGEON, 404 acs. Lunenburgh Co. joyning Kennon's line; 10 Jan 1748/49, p.491. £2.

MALCOLM McNEAL, 167 acs. Lunenburgh Co. on the upper side of Grassey Cr., adj. Munford; 10 Jan 1748/49, p.492. £1.

JOHN COX, 404 acs. Lunenburgh Co. on both sides of the South Fork of Maherrin Riv., down Finnywood Cr., adj. Mitchell; 10 Jan 1748/49, p.494. £2.

WELCOM WILLIAM HODGES, 254 acs. Lunenburgh Co. on both sides of Childres Cr.; 10 Jan 1748/49, p.495. £1.S5.

JOHN STEWART, 22 acs. Lunenburgh Co. on the N side of Staunton Riv., adj. Roger Neal; 10 Jan 1748/49, p.496. 5 Shill.

WILLIAM STROUD, 304 acs. Lunenburgh Co. on both sides of a great Br. of Allen's Cr.; 10 Jan 1748/49, p.498. £1.S10.

THOMAS SMITH, 400 acs. Lunenburgh Co. on the S side of Otter Riv.; 10 Jan 1748/49, p.499. £2.

EDWARD MOBBERLY, 330 acs. Lunenburgh Co. on the N side of Otter Riv., Beg. on the Riv. Bank (above the Mouth of the Oak Mountain Br.); 10 Jan 1748/49, p.501. £1.S15.

OWEN DAY, 400 acs. Lunenburgh Co. on both sides of Medway Riv.; 10 Jan 1748/49, p.502. £2.

BENJAMIN MOSBY, 400 acs. Lunenburgh Co. on both sides of White Oak Cr., adj. his own Line; 10 Jan 1748/49, p.504. £2.

CHRISTOPHER HUDSON, 337 acs. Lunenburgh Co. on the S side of Allen's Cr.; adj. his own old Line, Simmon's, Stith's & Edward's; 10 Jan 1748/49, p.505. £1.S15.

ANTHONY HAYNES, 424 acs. Lunenburgh Co. on the Ridge bet. Butcher's Cr. and Allen's Cr., up the Tusling Quarter Br., adj. John Mitchell; 10 Jan 1748/49, p.507. £2.S5.

JAMES MURRAY, 395 acs. Lunenburgh Co. on the Heads of the Brs. of Allen's Cr., adj. Peter Jones; 10 Jan 1748/49, p.508. £2.

JAMES COCKE, JUNIOR, 1,022 acs. Lunenburgh Co. on the S side of Stanton Riv., up the Great Br., adj. King; 10 Jan 1748/49, p.510. £3. 418 acs. part formerly gtd. John Russell by Pat. 1 Feb 1738/39 [281 acs. & 137 acs. Brunswick Co. in PB 18 p.185 & p.202] the Right & Title of which by divers mesne Conveyances is since become vested in the sd James Cocke and 604 acs. the Residue never before gtd.

RICHARD DAVIS, 307 acs. Lunenburg Co. on the S side of Childres Cr., in a Meadow, adj. Mattox Maye's Line; 10 Jan 1748/49, p.511. £1.S10.

WILLIAM LIDDERDALE, 288 acs. Lunenburg Co. on both sides of Little Fork of Blue Stone Cr., up Little Bluestone Fork; adj. Stith & Company and Bird; 10 Jan 1748/49, p.513. £1.S10.

JOHN STEWART, 318 acs. Lunenburgh Co. on both sides of Buffalo Cr., adj. Lanceford & Talbot; 10 Jan 1748/49, p.514. £1.S15.

JOHN PHELPS, 325 acs. Lunenburg Co. including some South Brs. of Little Otter Riv., crossing Merry Camp Br., adj. Thomas Smith; 10 Jan 1748/49, p.516. £1.S15.

THEOPHILUS FIELD, 1,304 acs. Lunenburgh Co. on the Lower side of Parham's Cr.; 10 Jan 1748/49, p.517. £6.S10.

JAMES LANGLEY, 750 acs. Norfolk Co. near the NorthWest Riv. known by the name of Black Water Sw., adj. John Priscod; 10 Jan 1748/49, p.518. £3.S15.

DAVID DORCH, 160 acs. Lunenburg Co. on the N side of Miles Cr., adj. Coller; 10 Jan 1748/49, p.520. £1.

WILLIAM MACKONICO, 400 acs. Lunenburg Co. on the S side of Nottoway Riv. including both sides of a Br. of Dry Cr., adj. Nicholas Christopher; 10 Jan 1748/49, p.521. £2

JOHN PHELPS, 350 acs. Lunenburg Co. on both sides of Otter Riv., up Troublesome Cr.; 10 Jan 1748/49, p.522. 15 Shill. 226 acs. part formerly gtd. unto the sd John Phelps by Pat. 30 Jul 1742 [Brunswick Co., PB 20 p.381] and 124 acs. the Residue never before gtd.

BENJAMIN MOSBY, 337 acs. Lunenburgh Co. on the Brs. of White Oak Cr., adj. Nowel Burton; 10 Jan 1748/49, p.524. £1.S15.

ROBERT MITCHEL, 286 acs. Lunenburgh Co. on the S side of Roanoak Riv.; 10 Jan 1748/49, p.525. £1.S10.

ROBERT MITCHEL, 135 acs. Lunenburgh Co. on both sides of Island Cr., along Country Line [East]; 10 Jan 1748/49, p.527. 15 shill.

THOMAS WILLINGHAM & DANIEL MELONE, 200 acs. Lunenburgh Co. on the upper side of Ledbetter's Cr.; 10 Jan 1748/49, p.528. £1.

EDWARD BOYAKIN, 100 acs. Lunenburgh Co. [sic] on the S side of Fountain's Cr., along the Country Line [E2½°S], adj. Sugar; 10 Jan 1748/49, p.529. 10 Shill. [This L. is now in Greensville County, then Brunswick Co.]

JAMES PATTON, 337 acs. Augusta Co. on James Riv. on the W side the Blue Ridge, Beg. on the N side of the sd James Riv. and under the foot of a Mountain, up the sd Mountain, by the Head of a Spring; 1 Apr 1749, p.530. £1.S15.

JAMES PATTON, 400 acs. Augusta Co. on the Brs. of James Riv. on the W side the Blue Ridge, down the N side of James Riv.; 1 Apr 1749, p.532. £2.

JAMES PATTON, 60 acs. Augusta Co. on the Brs. of James Riv. on the W side the Blue Ridge, Beg. on the S side of the South Br. of James Riv. at Lunies Ford, on a Stoney Point, adj. Daniel Monahan & Robert Luney; 1 Apr 1749, p.533. 10 Shill.

JAMES PATTON, 238 acs. Augusta Co. on the Brs. of James Riv. on the W side the Blue Ridge, Beg. on the E side the sd Riv., up the side of a Mountain; 1 Apr 1749, p.534. £1.S5.

ROBERT DAVIS, 400 acs. Goochland Co. on the Brs. of Pedlar Riv., adj. his own Line & William Floyed; 1 Apr 1749, p.535. £2.

ROBERT DAVIS, 400 acs. Goochland Co. on the N side the Fluvanna; 1 Apr 1749, p.536. £2.

ROBERT DAVIS, 200 acs. Goochland Co. up & across Pedlar Riv., into the Woods, adj. his own Line; 1 Apr 1749, p.538. £1.

WILLIAM MILLS, 400 acs. Goochland Co. on both sides of Pedlar Riv., into the Woods, crossing two Brs. and Dancing Cr., by the side of a Valley; 1 Apr 1749, p.539. £2.

WILLIAM WALKER, 130 acs. Goochland Co. on the N side of Appamattox Riv.; adj. his own Land formerly Robert Hencock's, John Patterson, Edward Davidson & John Nelson; 1 Apr 1749, p.540. 15 Shill.

JOSEPH GLOVER, 200 acs. Surry Co. on the S side of Nottoway Riv. and in the Fork of the Poplar Sw., Beg. on the South Prong of the sd Sw. at a C. between him and Thomas Felts, down the long Br.; 1 Apr 1749, p.541. £1.

EDWARD NIX, 204 acs. Lunenburgh Co. on the S side of Staunton Riv.; 1 Apr 1749, p.542. £1.

ANNE BROOKS, 150 acs. Is. of Wight Co. on the N side of

Maherrin Riv., by the side of Brooks's Br., up the Little Sw., adj. James Brooks & Arthur Taylor; 1 Apr 1749, p.543. 15 Shill.

LEWIS FRANKLIN, 850 acs. Lunenburg Co. including some of the Head Brs. of Falling Riv., adj. Edward Nix & Chiles; 1 Apr 1749, p.545. £4.S5.

JOHN EDWARDS, 285 acs. Is. of Wight Co. on the N side of Maherrin Riv., Beg. by the side of the Cabbin Sw., in the Wolf Pitt Br., by the Country Line [West], adj. Edward Chitty Junr.; 1 Apr 1749, p.546. £1.S10.

JOSEPH PHILLIPS/PHILIPS, 294 acs. Louisa Co. in the Parish of Fredericks Ville; adj. Richard Meadows, Captain Joseph Martin & Henry Bunch; 1 Apr 1749, p.547. £1.S10.

STEPHEN EVANS, 88 acs. Lunenburg Co. on the N side of the North Fork of Fucking Cr., adj. David Stokes & Hunt; 1 Apr 1749, p.549. 10 Shill.

JAMES EASTER, 360 acs. Lunenburg Co. on the E side of Little Roanoak Riv., adj. Thomas Jones; 1 Apr 1749, p.550. £2.

RICHARD HAYS, 300 acs. Amelia Co. on the upper side of the Main Deep Cr. and on both sides of Motes Path; 1 Apr 1749, p.521. £1.S10.

JAMES CROWDER, 104 acs. Amelia Co. on both sides of the long Br. of the Harricane Sw.; adj. Burges, Leverit, Bridgeforth & Ledbiter Jones; 1 Apr 1749, p.552. 10 Shill.

JOSEPH PHILLIPS/PHILIPS, 300 acs. Louisa Co.; adj. Richard Meadows, William Owen, Henry Bunch & the sd Phillips/Philips; 1 Apr 1749, p.553. £1.S10.

JOHN OWEN, 800 acs. Amelia Co. on the main Fork of Sandy Riv.; adj. Hudson's old Survey, John Garrat, Cobb, Jones & Brown; 1 Apr 1749, p.555. £4.

JOHN ORNSBY, Clk., 6,920 acs. Lunenburgh Co. on the N side of Staunton Riv. including some of the Head Brs. of Senaca Cr. and the Head of Bryery Cr. and the Head of the South Fork of falling Riv.; 1 Apr 1749, p.556.

JOHN ORNSBY, Clerk, 145 acs. Lunenburgh Co. on the lower side of Otter Riv.; 1 Apr 1749, p.559. 15 Shill.

JOHN ORNSBY, Clerk, 370 acs. Amelia Co. on the Head of Harricane Sw., by the Road; adj. Wallis, his own Lines, Tomlinson, Gamlin & Martin; 1 Apr 1749, p.560. £2.

JOHN OWEN, 400 acs. Amelia Co. on the upper side of Sandy Riv.; adj. his own old Line, Blake, Smith, Womack & Rutlidge; 1 Apr 1749, p.561. £2.

THOMAS DUGGINS, 275 acs. Lunenburgh Co. including the three Forks of Cub Cr., Beg. on the Middle Fork, on Rattle Snake Cr., on the Main Cr., adj. Samuel Allein; 1 Apr 1749, p.562. £1.S10.

THOMAS DUGGINS, 875 acs. Lunenburg Co. on both sides of Emry Br.; 1 Apr 1749, p.563. £4.S10.

HENRY HATCHER JUNR., 300 acs. Henrico Co., in a Bottom; adj. Garron's Survey, James Farlow, James Hill, the sd Hatcher, John Welch, & the Line formerly Tullit's now Cary's; 1 Apr 1749, p.565. £1.S10.

JOHN ALLEN, 358 acs. Spotsyl. Co. on the Brs. of Pamunkey Riv., in a Pond; adj. the Land of the Honorable Sir William Gooch Bart., a Pat. gtd. to Roger Tandy, Mr Baylor, White, Michael Guinny dec'd, Corbin & Garnet; 1 Apr 1749, p.567. for the Imp. of 8 Pers.: *Mary Whitehouse, John Callahan, Andrew Savage, Nathaniel Snape, James Willson, George Atkinson, Peter Maguire & Catherine Maguire.*

WILLIAM CHAMBERS, 190 acs. Albemarle Co. on a cr. of Slate Riv. called and known by the Name of Arthur's Cr., adj. William Nowland; 1 Apr 1749, p.568. £1.

JAMES WOODS, 200 acs. Albemarle Co. on both sides Stockton's Br. of Mechams Riv., adj. William Whiteside & Ambrose

Joshua Smith; 1 Apr 1749, p.569. £1.

JAMES SHASTOOD, 150 acs. Albemarle Co. on the Head Brs. of Huff's Cr. on the side of the Tobacco Row Mountain, adj. Benjamin Stennet; 1 Apr 1749, p.571. 15 Shill.

HUGH GREEN, 212 acs. Albemarle Co. on the S side of Slate Riv. on both sides of Green's Cr., adj. Hugh Green (a former Survey) & William Lawhorn; 1 Apr 1749, p.572. £1.S5.

JOHN THOMAS, 100 acs. Albemarle Co. on the S side of the Fluvanna joining Majr. Allen Howard's back Line; 1 Apr 1749, p.573. 10 Shill.

BISHOP TONEY, 150 acs. Albemarle Co. joining the S side of the Fluvanna, Beg. at a Cotton Tree at the Mouth of a Drain; 1 Apr 1749, p.575. 15 Shill.

BISHOP TONEY, 99 acs. Albemarle Co. on the S side of the Fluvanna, up the Grassy Patch Cr., adj. Benjamin Mims; 1 Apr 1749, p.576. 10 Shill.

ZACHARIAH BURNLEY, 394 acs. Albemarle Co. on the Brs. of Woodson's Cr. of Hardware Riv., crossing sd Cr., adj. Harden Burnley; 1 Apr 1749, p.577. £2.

WILLIAM PHELPS, 350 acs. Albemarle Co., in a Glade; adj. William Phelps, Doctor Nicholas,

Hugh Morris & Hugh Rice Morris; 1 Apr 1749, p.579. £1.S15.

HARDEN BURNLEY, 400 acs. Albemarle Co. on both sides of Woodson's Cr. of Hardware Riv., adj. John Dameron; 1 Apr 1749, p.580. £2.

WILLIAM PHELPS, 400 acs. Albemarle Co. on the Brs. of Totier Cr.; adj. Mr Stith, Doctor Nicholas, John Lewis, William Harris & Hugh Rice Morris; 1 Apr 1749, p.581. £2.

FREDERICK JONES, 219 acs. Pr. Geo. Co. on the N side of Hatcher's Run; adj. John Davis, Thomas Moore, John Banister Esq. & William Mayes; 20 Jun 1749 *in the 23rd Year of our Reign of George the second*, p.583. £1.S15. Whereas by Pat. 29 June 1739 gtd. Samuel Rather [PB 18 p.307] And Whereas Peter Jones, Son and Heir of Abraham Jones dec'd, in whom the Right & Title is since vested hath failed to pay Quit Rents and to make Cultiv. & Improv. and Frederick Jones hath made humble Suit and obtained a G. for the Same.

FREDERICK JONES, 200 acs. Pr. Geo. Co. on both sides of the Picture Br., adj. John Davis; 20 Jun 1749, p.584. £1. Whereas by Pat. 16 Jun 1727 gtd. Thomas Moore [PB 13 p.125] And Whereas Peter Jones (Son and Heir of Abraham Jones dec'd) in whom the Right & Title is since vested hath failed to pay Quitrents and to make Cultiv. & Improv. and Frederick

Jones hath made humble Suit and hath obtained a G. for the same.

FREDERICK JONES, 300 acs. Pr. Geo. Co. on both sides of Leadbiters Cr., by the Poplar Br.; 20 Jun 1749, p.586. £1.S10. Whereas by Pat. 13 Oct 1727 gtd. Laughlan Flynn [PB 13 p.278] And Whereas Peter Jones, Son and Heir of Abraham Jones dec'd, in whom the Right & Title is vested hath failed to pay Quitrents and to make Cultiv. & Improv. and Frederick Jones hath made humble Suit and hath obtained a G. for the same.

FREDERICK JONES, 425 acs. Brunswick Co. on the S side of Meherrin Riv., crossing Geneto Cr.; adj. Robert Hix Junr., George Hix & Daniel Hix; 20 Jun 1749, p.587. £2.S5. Whereas by Pat. 28 Sep 1728 gtd. Henry Bedingfield Junior [PB 14 p.88] And Whereas Peter Jones, Son and Heir of Abraham Jones dec'd, in whom the Right & Title is vested hath failed to pay Quit Rents and to make Cultiv. & Improv. and Frederick Jones hath made humble Suit and obtained a G. for the same.

WILLIAM HANDCOCK, 250 acs. Surry Co. on the S side of Blackwater Sw, up the Run of the Indian Br., on the Edge of the Low Grounds of Ford's Br.; adj. William Bradley, Joseph Handcock, Robert Nicholson, his own Lines & Samuel Cornwell; 20 Jun 1749, p.589. £1.S5.

JOHN RICHARDSON, 280 acs. Surry Co. on the S side of

Nottoway Riv. and on the W side of the Calfpen Br., up the Run of the Calfpen Sw., adj. William Woodland; 20 Jun 1749, p.590. £1.S10.

RALPH SHELTON, 400 acs. Lunenburgh Co. on the Lower side of Ledbetters Cr.; adj. John Ingram, Jonathan Davis, Johnson & Samuel Ingram; 20 Jun 1749, p.592. £2.

CALEB ELLIS, 163 acs. Surry Co. on the N side of Blackwater Sw., Beg. at a Paupau Gum on the main Run of sd Sw.; 20 Jun 1749, p.593. £1.

GEORGE DELK, 75 acs. Surry Co. on the N side of Blackwater Sw., over Roast Pork Meadow on a Line of the Glebe Land; adj. Thomas King, Robert Gray & William Crew; 20 Jun 1749, p.594. 10 Shill.

ELIZABETH LILES, 200 acs. Lunenburgh Co. on the N side of Meherrin Riv. including the Bent, Beg. on the Riv. at the Mouth of a Gut; 20 Jun 1749, p.595. £1.

NICHOLAS MEALER, 300 acs. Henrico Co. crossing a Br. of Cornelius's Cr., in a Slash; adj. Bailey, Whitlow, Burton & Mayo; 20 Jun 1749, p.596. £1.S10.

ROBERT YOUNG, 112 acs. Augusta Co. on the W side the Blue Ridge in the Fork of James Riv., adj. the sd Young, & Benjamin Borden; 20 Jun 1749, p.597. 15 Shill.

PATRICK FRAZIER, 140 acs. Augusta Co. on the SE side of Shanando Riv.; Beg. at a Lynn on the Riv. Side opposite to Henry Downes's Mill, to an Elm & Bunch of Lynns on the Riv. opposite to the L. of Robert Scott; 20 Jun 1749, p.599. 15 Shill.

ADAM MILLER, 350 acs. Augusta Co. bet. Shanando Riv. and the South Mountain, crossing a Meadow and Elk Run, adj. the L. the sd Miller now lives on; 20 Jun 1749, p.600. £1.S15.

ROBERT POAGE, 150 acs. Augusta Co. on a Br. of Roanoak called back Cr. at a place called *the Forks*, Beg. on the S side of sd cr. above a Fall at the Point of a Hill, in a Hollow; 20 Jun 1749, p.601. 15 Shill.

ADAM RIDER, 200 acs. Augusta Co. at a place called *the Sinking Spring*, Beg. on a Ridge, in a Draft at a Sink Hole, adj. the L. the sd Rider lives on; 20 Jun 1749, p.602. £1.

ADAM RIDER, 100 acs. Augusta Co. on the W side of the L. the sd Rider lives on, Beg. on the E side of a Draft, crossing the Run; 20 Jun 1749, p.603. 10 Shill.

JAMES CARR, 235 acs. Augusta Co. on a Br. of Buffalo Cr. called Broad Cr., on a Ridge; 20 Jun 1749, p.604. £1.S5.

JOHN ARCHER, 400 acs. Augusta Co. on Moffets Cr.; 20 Jun 1749, p.605. for the Imp. of 4 Pers.:

Francis McCowin & Mary his Wife,
Madrhim McCowen & Elizabeth
McCowen as also for £1.

THOMAS WEST, 176 acs.
Augusta Co., at a Place called the
Hair Lick on the Head of Benjamin
Allen's Riv., Beg. in a Fork of the
sd Riv. above a Gap in the
Mountain, crossing the North Fork
along the Foot of the Mountain,
down the South Fork of the Riv.;
20 Jun 1749, p.606. £1.

JOHN POAG, 214 acs. Augusta
Co. on the West Br. of Cedar Cr.
a Br. of James Riv. at a Place
called *Poag's Farm*, Beg. on a
Ridge, in a Hollow, adj. Robert
Renick; 20 Jun 1749, p.607.
£1.S5.

JOHN HOGSHEAD SENR., 108
acs. Augusta Co. on Anderson's
Br., in a Meadow; adj. the L. the
sd John Hogshead now lives on, &
John Finley; 20 Jun 1749, p.608.
15 Shill.

ALEXANDER BROWN LEE, 400
acs. Augusta Co. on the N side of
the Southernmost Br. of the North
Riv. of Shanando, on the side of a
Gully Ridge; 20 Jun 1749, p.609.
£2.

THOMAS WILLIAMS, 400 acs.
Augusta Co. on a Br. in the Fork
of James Riv., adj. a Survey of
Erwin Pattersons; 20 Jun 1749,
p.610. £2.

ROBERT RENICK, 300 acs.
Augusta Co. on a head Br. of
Cedar Cr. a Br. of James Riv. at a

place called the *Timber Plain*, on a
Ridge, adj. John Poack;
20 Jun 1749, p.611. £1.S10.

ANDREW McNAB, 138 acs.
Augusta Co. on a br. of Fees Cr.
called back Cr., adj. *Borden's
great Tract*, 20 Jun 1749, p.612.
15 Shill.

ANDREW GAHAGAN, 400 acs.
Augusta Co. on the W side of the
Blue Ridge and on the main Br. of
James Riv., Beg. on the side of a
Hollow, down the Stream to
include the Island then crossing the
Riv.; 20 Jun 1749, p.613. £2.

TIMOTHY MURRILL, 52 acs.
Amelia Co. on the N side of deep
Cr., in the Sw. or the Beverpond
of the sd Cr.; adj. Wilson &
Higdon Roberson; 20 Jun 1749,
p.613. 5 Shill.

PHILIP TURPIN JUNR., 188 acs.
Henrico Co.; adj. Thomas Farmer,
William Hatcher, the sd Turpin,
Robert Ealom & Collo. Bird;
20 Jun 1749, p.614. £1.

WILLIAM WATSON, 5,077 acs.
Amelia Co. on both sides of Flatt
Cr. and on the head Brs. of Deep
Cr., in the hunting Path Br., up
little Cr., on the Great Fork of
Flatt Cr., down the sd [Flatt] Cr.
to just above the Mill Dam; adj.
Dupuy, Barnaby Wall, Tunstall,
Moore, Hudson, the L. purchased
of Coleman, Foster, Harper, the sd
Watson's old L., & Beasley; 20
Jun 1749, p.615. £1.S5. (4,423
acs. Part of a Pat. for 4,623 acs.
formerly gtd. the sd William

Watson by Pat. 5 Jun 1745 [5 Jun 1746, PB 25 p.47], 200 acs. other Part formerly gtd. Barnaby Wells by Pat. 10 Jul 1745 [PB 23 p.888], 2 acs. other Part being Part of a Pat. for 390 acs. formerly gtd. John Dyer by Pat. 5 Jun 1746 [PB 25 p.53], 225 acs. other Part formerly gtd. Daniel Coleman by Pat. 1 Aug 1745 [PB 22 p.383] and 227 acs. the Residue never before gtd.)

BENJAMIN HARRISON, Gent., 730 acs. Surry Co. on the W side of the Cypress Sw., up Tyus's Br., down Clay's Br., to the main run of sd Sw.; adj. Doctor Kenneth Mackenzie & James Davis; 20 Jun 1749, p.617. for 2 lbs. of Tobacco for every Acre of sd L. Whereas by Inquisition indented taken in sd Co. 17 Feb 1736/37 by Virtue of a Warrant directed to John Allen Gent. Escheator for sd Co. It Appears that Robert Randall died seised of 750 acs. more or less but upon a Survey thereof lately made by Richard Cocke Surveyor of the sd Co. is found to contain but 730 acs. which is found to Escheat to us for the sd Robert Randall. And Whereas Benjamin Harrison Gent. hath made Humble Suit and hath obtained a G. for the same. [for the history of this L., see Jno. Fludd's 2,100 acs. James City Co. in PB 1 p.548 dated 12 May 1638, Capt. John Flood's 1,100 acs. James City Co. in PB 2 p.227 dated 7 Jun 1750, Ralph Creed's 750 acs. Surry Co. in PB 6 p.44 dated 14 May 1666, John Cary's 230 acs. in PB p.269 dated 27 Dec 1669 and William Edwards's 750 acs. in PB 8 p.213 dated 20 Oct 1691]

WILLIAM CARRELL/CARREL, 325 acs. Surry Co. on the S side of Black Water Sw., down Wall's Br.; adj. Richard Wall, Henry Vaughan & Manwaring; 20 Jun 1749, p.618. £1. (125 acs. Part formerly gtd. Henry Manwaring by Pat. 26 Jul 1735 [PB 16 p.71] the Right & Title of which sd L. is since become vested in the sd William Carrell and 200 acs. the Residue never before gtd.)

PHILIP MOODY, 192 acs. Louisa Co. on the Top of one of the great Mountains near one of the Brs. of Buckmountain Cr., Beg. on an Arm of the Ledge, in a Bottom; 20 Jun 1749, p.619. £1.

JAMES KNIGHT, 247 acs. Nansemond Co. on the N side Oropeak Sw.; adj. the sd James Knight, Thomas Ellis dec'd, the L. of William Trevethan, the L. of John Riddick & Thomas Boid, & Edward Arnold; 20 Jun 1749, p.620. £1.S5.

BENJAMIN TUCKER, 635 acs. Is. of Wight Co. on the S side of Tarrarro Cr., by the Country Line [West], down the Quarter Br.; adj. John Edwards, Thomas Pitman, James Allen, Henry Dawson & Robert Bryant; 20 Jun 1749, p.621. £3.S5.

JOHN PAYNE, 320 acs. Albemarle Co., in the Fork of James Riv. on both sides of Bremo

Cr., adj. Noble Ladd; 20 Jun 1749, p.622. £1.S15.

RICHARD RICKS, 300 acs. Is. of Wight Co. on the N side of Nottoway Riv., down the Run of the Flaggy Sw., adj. Richard Washington; 20 Jun 1749, p.623. £1.S10.

JAMES WIMBISH, 1,020 acs. Amelia Co. on the S side of the South Fork of Buffalo Riv., in a Br. of Codees Cr.; adj. Bigger's, Anderson, George Davis, Archtacon, Arbuckle & Thackston; 20 Jun 1749, p.624. £5.S5.

BENJAMIN CROCKER, 295 acs. Is. of Wight Co. on the S side of Nottoway Riv., by the side of Brown's Br.; adj. his own old Lines, Simon Turner, William Rugless, Thomas Bryant & John Rotchell; 20 Jun 1749, p.625. £1.S10.

WILLIAM THURMAN, 296 acs. Amelia Co. on both sides of the South Fork of Appamattox Riv., Beg. on the N side of the sd Fork just above James Matthews; 20 Jun 1749, p.626. £1.S10.

JAMES OLIVER, 25 acs. Amelia Co. on both sides of deep Cr., Beg. on the Edge of the Sw. or bever Pond of the sd Cr.; adj. Samuel Jones, Worsham, Higdon Roberson, Booker & Bruce; 20 Jun 1749, p.627. 5 Shill.

JAMES BEARD, 369 acs. Augusta Co. on the N side the North River of Shanando, adj. Robert Scott &

Samuel Scott; 20 Jun 1749 *in the 23rd Year of our Reign of George the second, In Witness our Trusty and Welbeloved Sir William Gooch Baronet our Lieutenant Governor and Commander in Chief of our sd Colony and Dominion at Williamsburgh*, p.628. £2.

Exd. Feb. 8. 1749. Settled & burnt the Rights thus far. John Blair.

JOHN HUGHES, 285 acs. Albemarle Co. on the N Brs. of Willis's Cr., adj. Thomas Harvie; 5 Sep 1749 *in the 23rd year of our Reign of George the second, In Witness our Trusty and welbeloved Thomas Lee Esqr. President of our Council and Commander in Chief of our sd Colony and Dominion at Williamsburgh*, p.629. £1.S10.

JOHN HARVIE, 400 acs. Albemarle Co. on the Head of the North Br. of Harris's Cr., on a Ridge, adj. his own Line; 5 Sep 1749, p.630. £2.

GEORGE HOMES GWINN, 400 acs. Albemarle Co. on S side of James Riv. on a Br. of Willis's Cr. called Bolling's Cr.; adj. Sachevrel Whitebread, Collo. John Bolling & Thomas Potter; 5 Sep 1749, p.631. £2.

ALEXANDER HENDERSON, 280 acs. Albemarle Co. on both sides of Rock fish Riv., on the Spurr of a Mountain, adj. Clapham; 5 Sep 1749, p.632. £1.S10.

JOHN HARVIE, 400 acs. Albemarle Co. on the N side of the

Buffalo Ridge, Beg. near the Meadow; 5 Sep 1749, p.633. £2.

GEORGE BRIGGS, 197 acs. Surry Co. on the S side of Blackwater Sw., in Tuscarora Br., adj. Henry Sorry; 5 Sep 1749, p.634. £1.

RICHARD FELTS, 90 acs. Surry Co. on the S side of Nottoway Riv.; adj. his own Lines, Thomas Dunn, James Hearn & William Felts; 5 Sep 1749, p.635. 10 Shill.

WILLIAM BATTLE, 133 acs. Surry Co. on the S side of Nottoway Riv., down little Ploughman Sw.; adj. William Barlow, Gilbert Prince & Samuel Carlisle; 5 Sep 1749, p.636. 15 Shill.

ISAAC ROBINSON, 115 acs. Surry Co. on the W side of Sappony Cr., up Gillion's Br., in the Edge of the Sw.; adj. William Harper, his own Lines and Harper's Home Land; 5 Sep 1749, p.637. 15 Shill.

WILLIAM BROWN, 400 acs. Surry Co. on the S side of Blackwater Sw., down the Winding Br., adj. Joseph Richardson & John Brittle; 5 Sep 1749, p.638. £2.

JOSEPH HARWOOD, 188 acs. Surry Co. on the N side of the Poplar Sw., up the Run of the Hornet Sw., by the Co. Line which divides Surry from Is. of Wight [N60°E]; adj. Robert Bullock, his own old Lines, his Corn field & George Cornet; 5 Sep 1749, p.639. £1.

GEORGE BRIGGS, 236 acs. Surry Co. on the S side black Water Sw., adj. his own Lines; 5 Sep 1749, p.640. £1.S5.

AUGUSTINE HARGROVE, 225 acs. Surry Co. on the S side of black Water Sw., down Grigory's Br.; adj. Thomas Lisle, Thomas Wren & his own Line; 5 Sep 1749, p.641. £1.S5.

ALLEN WARREN, 250 acs. Surry Co. on the N side of black Water Sw., by the side of a Pond; adj. Henry Atkins, Thomas Avery, John Brown, John Bradley & Thomas Edwards; 5 Sep 1749, p.643. £1.S5.

JOHN WHITMORE, 400 acs. Pr. Geo. Co. on the lower side of bever Pond Cr.; adj. Garrald, William Elder & Clayton; 5 Sep 1749, p.644. £2.

THOMAS ALLEN, 50 acs. Is. of Wight Co. on the N side of Nottoway Sw., by the side of the South Prong of the Reedy Br.; adj. Thomas Oberry, John Drake & the sd Allen's own old Lines; 5 Sep 1749, p.645. 5 Shill.

THOMAS ALLEN, 50 acs. Is. of Wight Co. on the N side of Nottoway Riv.; adj. John Drake, his own old Lines, Thomas Drake & Richard Drake; 5 Sep 1749, p.646. 5 Shill.

CHRISTOPHER FOSTER, JUNIOR, 120 acs. Is. of Wight Co. on the S side of Nottoway Riv., adj. Charles Barham & Christopher

Foster Senior; 5 Sep 1749, p.647. 15 Shillings.

JOHN ADAMS, 150 acs. Is. of Wight Co. on the N side of Meherin Riv., by the side of the Gum Sw., down the Flat Sw.; adj. Henry Ivy, Henry Adams & Samuel Harrison; 5 Sep 1749, p.648. 15 Shill.

THOMAS DELOACH, 200 acs. Is. of Wight Co. in the Fork of the Horse Pen Br. on N side of Nottoway Riv., down the W side of the North Prong of the sd Br.; 5 Sep 1749, p.649. £1.

ROBERT HANCOCK, 400 acs. Lunenburgh Co. on both sides of Strait Stone Cr., on the S side of the North Fork of the sd Cr., adj. John Steen; 5 Sep 1749, p.650. £2.

JOSEPH COLLINS, 250 acs. Lunenburgh Co. on both sides the North Fork of Panther Cr., crossing the Cr. just below the Falls, adj. Richard Kennon; 5 Sep 1749, p.651. £1.S5.

WILLIAM BREWER, 400 acs. Lunenburgh Co. on the S side of Meherrin Riv.; 5 Sep 1749, p.653. £2.

WILLIAM BRUMFIELD, 404 acs. Lunenburgh Co. on the upper side of Little Roanoak, on Sycamore Br., adj. Read; 5 Sep 1749, p.654. £2.

WILLIAM CALDWELL, 400 acs. Lunenburg Co. on both sides of Snow Cr., adj. David Caldwell; 5 Sep 1749, p.655. £2.

WILLIAM CALDWELL, 250 acs. Lunenburg Co. on both sides of Chestnut Cr.; 5 Sep 1749, p.656. £1.S5.

JAMES TILLY, 145 acs. Lunenburgh Co. on the N side of Otter Riv.; 5 Sep 1749, p.657. 15 Shill.

THOMAS BASSETT, 791 acs. Lunenburgh Co. on both sides of Ward's Fork; 5 Sep 1749, p.658. £4.

WILLIAM ATKINSON, 400 acs. Lunenburgh Co. on both sides Pig Riv. on S side of the Riv., crossing Ruddy's Cr.; 5 Sep 1749, p.659. £2.

ISRAEL PETERSON, 170 acs. Lunenburgh Co. on the N side of Staunton Riv. on the Lower side of Goose Cr.; adj. Verdeman; 5 Sep 1749, p.660. £1.

CHARLES TALBOT, 315 acs. Lunenburgh Co. on both sides of a Br. of Ward's Fork, adj. David Lee; 5 Sep 1749, p.661. £1.S15.

DAVID STOKES, 400 acs. Lunenburgh Co. on one of the Brs. of Grassey Cr.; 5 Sep 1749, p.662. £2.

THOMAS GILL, 275 acs. Lunenburgh Co. on both sides of Gill's Cr. a Br. of Black Water Riv., crossing Pounding Mill Run; 5 Sep 1749, p.663. £1.S10.

RANDALL BRACEY, 273 acs. Brunswick Co. on a Br. of Cocke's Cr., adj. William Tucker & John Naper; 5 Sep 1749, p.665. £1.S10.

WILLIAM MACLIN, 326 acs. Brunswick Co. adj. Sissum & Johnson; 5 Sep 1749, p.666. £1.S15.

JOSEPH MORTON JUNR., 1,437 acs. Lunenburg Co. on both sides of Licking Hole Cr., adj. Joseph Morton Senr.; 5 Sep 1749, p.667. £4.S5. 600 acs. Part formerly gtd. sd Joseph Morton by Pat. 12 Jan 1746/47 [Brunswick Co., PB 25 p.585 & PB 21 p.92] and 837 acs. the Residue never before gtd.

NICHOLAS LANIER, 420 acs. Brunswick Co. on the S side of Meherrin Riv., on Cold Water Run, adj. William Edward's & Adam Sim's; 5 Sep 1749, p.669. £2. Whereas by Pat. 28 Sep 1728 gtd. Alexander Bruce [PB 14 p.89] And Whereas the sd Alexander Bruce hath failed to pay Quitrents and to make cultiv. and improv. and Nicholas Lanier hath made humble Suit and obtained a G. for the same.

JOHN HUNT, 104 acs. Brunswick Co., adj. James Watson; 5 Sep 1749, p.670. 10 Shill.

JOHN HARWELL, 229 acs. Brunswick Co. on the S side of the three Creeks, adj his own old Line; 5 Sep 1749, p.671. £1.S5.

SAMUEL ALLEN, JUNIOR, 640 acs. Goochland Co. on the N side Bear Cr. a Br. of Willis's Riv.; adj. William Holiday, Henry Cary, Alexander Trent & William Hudgins; 5 Sep 1749, p.672. £1.S5. 400 acs. Part formerly gtd. unto the sd Samuel Allen by Pat. 6 Jul 1741 [PB 19 p.1028] and 230 acs. the Residue never before gtd.

BENJAMIN MOSBY, 400 acs. Goochland Co. on S side of James Riv. on the Brs. of Little Muddy Cr. and Willis's [Cr.]; adj. James Blevins, James Knot's, the sd Benjamin Mosby, & Sylvanus Witt; 5 Sep 1749, p.674. £2.

WILLIAM AMOS, 400 acs. Goochland Co. on the Little Byrd, adj. Captain Thomas Massie; 5 Sep 1749, p.675. £2.

EDWARD CREWS, 233 acs. Brunswick Co., up Pee Hill Cr., along the Country Line [East], adj. William Gray; 5 Sep 1749, p.676. £1.S5.

EDWARD WINFIELD, 410 acs. Brunswick Co. on the Brs. of Avents Cr., on a Road; adj. John Brown, Cole & Dugger; 5 Sep 1749, p.678. £2.S5.

JOHN FENNILL, 186 acs. Brunswick Co. on both sides the Spring Sw., along the Country Line [W 2 ½ ° N]; adj. Turner, Southerland & Jordan; 5 Sep 1749, p.679. £1. [this Greensville Co. Pat. is a duplicate of John New's 186 acs. in PB 18 p.412]

ROBERT SANDIFORD, 380 acs. Surry Co. on the N side of the three Creeks, up the Run of the Little Ploughman Sw., down the Run of the Cow Br.; 5 Sep 1749, p.680. £2.

HENRY STURDIVANT, 330 acs. Surry Co. on the S side of Nottoway Riv., up the Run of the Deep Br., down the long Br., up the Run of the Middle Br.; adj. Edward Acolls, Charles Partin, his own Lines, Sloman Wynne & Hollum Sturdivant; 5 Sep 1749, p.682. £1.S15.

WILLIAM SMITH, 104 acs. Surry Co. on the N side of Nottoway Riv.; adj. his own Line, Lawrence Gibbons & Richard Pepper; 5 Sep 1749, p.683. 10 Shill.

GEORGE ROBERTSON, 22 acs. Surry Co. on the N side of Nottoway Riv.; adj. the sd Robertson, Colo. Benjamin Harrison & James Oliver; 5 Sep 1749, p.684. £5.

HENRY JOHNSON, 60 acs. Surry Co.; adj. Mr Newsum, John Tyus & Thomas Williams; 5 Sep 1749, p.686. 10 Shill.

JOSEPH ROWLAND, 275 acs. Surry Co. on the S side of Nottoway Riv. on the S side of the Spring Sw., Beg. on the S side of the Great Spring Sw.; adj. Richard Rose, John Bell Junr. & John Bell Senr.; 5 Sep 1749, p.687. £1.S10.

BENJAMIN LITTLE, 140 acs. Surry Co. on the N side of black

Water Sw., adj. Allen Warren & John Brown; 5 Sep 1749, p.688. 15 Shill.

CHARLES LYNCH, 233 acs. Albemarle Co. on a br. of black Water Cr. known by the name of Rock Castle Br., in the Fork & crossing sd Br.; 5 Sep 1749, p.690. £1.S5.

JOHN HARVIE, 329 acs. Albemarle Co. on both sides of the Road on the N side of the Buffalo Ridge, adj. Fry; 5 Sep 1749, p.691. £1.S15.

BENJAMIN GRAY, 320 acs. Surry Co. on the S side of black Water Sw., Beg. in Gregory's Br.; adj. William Atkins, Henry Hart, David Andrew's, Robert Atkins, Thomas Lisles & Augustine Hargrove; 5 Sep 1749, p.692. £1.S15.

WILLIAM KING, 354 acs. Amelia Co. on the lower side of Sandy Riv., down the Great Br.; adj. Morton, Hamblin, Searcey, Brown & Joseph Ligon; 5 Sep 1749, p.694. £1.S15.

MATTHEW WHITTALL, 400 acs. Albemarle Co. under Buffalo Ridge on the Brs. of Rocky Cr. and Christian's Path to Moses Higginbotham's Mill, near a Ridge over a Br. of Rockey Cr., in a Slash, adj. John Warren; 5 Sep 1749, p.695. £2.

JOHN HODNETT, 425 acs. Albemarle Co. on both sides of the lower Fishpond Cr. of Appamattox

Riv., crossing the Cr. to naked Land, adj. the other Land of the sd Hodnett, & Obediah Woodson; 5 Sep 1749, p.697. £2.S5.

JOSEPH WALTON, 192 acs. Albemarle Co. on both sides of Bremore Cr. of the Fluvanna, adj. John Payne; 5 Sep 1749, p.698. £1.

JOSEPH HIGGINBOTHAM, 150 acs. Albemarle Co. on both sides of Buffalo Riv., adj. Benjamin Higgenbotham; 5 Sep 1749, p.699. 15 Shill.

JOHN HENRY, 2,284 acs. Albemarle Co. on the E side of Tye Riv. under the three ridged Mountain, adj. Chew & Company; 5 Sep 1749, p. 701. £6.S5. 1,050 acs. Part being Part of a Pat. for 1,500 acs. formerly gtd. James Churchill 1 Feb 1738/39 [PB 18 p.205] the Right & Title of which sd 1,050 acs. is since become vested in the sd John Henry and 1,234 acs. the residue never before gtd.

WILLIAM MACLIN & JOHN WALL, 4,174 acs. Lunenburg Co. on both sides of Difficult Cr., adj. John Jones; 5 Sep 1749, p.703. £21.

ROBERT FERGUSON, 990 acs. Pr. Geo. Co. on the N side of Butterwood Sw., down the Old Field Br., in a Valley; adj. Coleman, Woodleif, Mills, Robert Nash, Poythress, Fitzgerrald & Ann Andrew's; 5 Sep 1749, p.704. 840 acs. part formerly gtd. unto the

sd Robert Ferguson by Pat. 20 Aug 1747 [PB 28 p.168], 150 acs. the Residue formerly gtd. Peter Wynn by Pat. 10 Jan 1735/36 [Peter Wynne, PB 16 p.424] the Right & Title if of which sd 150 acs. by divers mesne Conveyenaces is since become vested in the sd Robert Ferguson.

WILLIAM ROBINSON, 11 acs. of Swamp Land in Pr. Ann Co.; adj. William Hancock & Mrs McClenahan; 5 Sep 1749, p.706. 5 Shill.

THOMAS RIDDLE, 400 acs. Goochland Co. among the N Brs. of little Guinea Cr., adj. L. surveyed for Charles Anderson; 5 Sep 1749, p.707. £2.

JOHN LIGHTFOOT, 2,050 acs. Lunenburgh Co. on both sides of Buckhorn Cr., Beg. on a Br. of Pine Cr., on the Holly Br., down the North Fork of Buckhorn Cr.; adj. Tally, Booker, Johnson, Cock, Weatherford & Russell; 12 Mar 1749/50, p.708. £10.S5.

WILLIAM RICE, 440 acs. Goochland Co. on the Brs. of Great Buffalo Cr.; adj. Susanna Carnor, Grizel Coleman, George Holmes, Benjamin Strange & Richard Gwin; 5 Sep 1749, p.710. £2.S5.

JAMES FORGUSON, 417 acs. Goochland Co. adj. to the E side of Licking Hole Cr. on the N side of James Riv., Beg. on the W side of sd Cr.; adj. John Smith dec'd, David Parish, Humphrey Parish &

Welcom William Hodges; 5 Sep 1749, p.711. £2.S5.

HENRY CROWDER, 123 acs. Pr. Geo. Co. on the Forks of the Great Br. of Mawhipponock Cr., crossing the Rockey Br., adj. Abraham Crowder & Matthew Mayes; 5 Sep 1749, p.713. 15 Shill.

JOHN MALLARY, 290 acs. Orange Co. on a Br. of Pamunkey Riv., down the Mountain Road; adj. the sd Mallary & Theodosius Stage; 5 Sep 1749, p.714. for the Imp. of 6 Pers.: *William Wyatt, John Adam Corn, John Colthard, Thomas Dickson, George Holden & Samuel Pennell.*

NATHANIEL HARRIS, 200 acs. Amelia Co. on the upper side of Vaughan's Cr., adj. Benjamin Harris; 5 Sep 1749, p.715. £1.

FRANCIS HISTILY, 400 acs. Amelia Co. on the head of Snales Cr.; adj. Collins, Griffin, Johnson & Jones; 5 Sep 1749, p.717. £2.

BARNABY WELLS, 125 acs. Amelia Co. on the upper Side of Flatt Cr.; adj. Garrat, Beasley, Dupuy & Childrey; 5 Sep 1749, p.718. 15 Shill.

GRIFFIN EVANS, 400 acs. Amelia Co. on the upper side of Buffalo Riv.; adj. Woodson, Baldwin, Nickson & Marr; 5 Sep 1749, p.719. £2.

ROBERT BICKERS, 220 acs. Orange Co. on the Brs. of Pamunkey Riv., up Berry's Run, on a Ridge; adj. a Pat. gtd. Isaac Waters, another Pat. of the sd Bickers's, & Jeremiah Dear; 5 Sep 1749, p.721. for the Imp. of 4 Pers.: *William Cooper, Robert Thomson, Elianor Cross, Sarah Thurston* as also for 5 Shill.

NATHANIEL BRIGGS, 9 acs. of low sunken Land in Surry Co., on the E side of Assamuseck Sw. & joining upon the Plantation whereon he now lives, down the Run of a Br. which divides him from Stephen Hamlin & down the Main Run of sd Sw., adj. Simon Murfey; 5 Sep 1749, p.722. 5 Shill.

JOHN MACLEMORE, 100 acs. Surry Co. on S side of the Poplar Sw., in the South & North Prongs of the Reedy Br.; 5 Sep 1749, p.723. 10 Shill.

JOHN BRYAND, 351 acs. Lunenburgh Co. on the S side of Hounds Cr.; adj. Michaux, Cocke & John Mitchell; 5 Sep 1749, p.725. £1.S15.

LAVETER JOHNSON, 193 acs. Surry Co. on the N side of Black Water Sw., Beg. on the side of the Meadow Br., up the Mirey Slash, adj. Colo. Willis; 5 Sep 1749, p.726. £1.

JOSEPH THARP, 46 acs. Surry Co. on the N side of the three creeks, up Locust/Lucust Br., adj. Colo. Richard Bland & Captain Avent; 5 Sep 1749, p.727. 5 Shill.

JOSEPH THARP, 272 acs. Surry Co. on both sides of the three

creeks, down the Great Br., on the
Side of a Meadow; adj. Samuel
Alsobrook & William Solomon, &
his [Tharp's] ptd. L.; 5 Sep 1749,
p.728-730. 10 Shill. 175 acs. Part
formerly gtd. sd Joseph Tharp by
Pat. 23 Mar 1733/34 [Joseph
Thorp, PB 15 p.189] and 97 acs.
the Residue never before gtd.

*Examined March 25th. 1751. This
Book Examined from the former
Settlement and the Rights due
thereon were burnt,   John Blair
D.Audr.*

A NOTE TO THE USER

Personal Names: The user of this index should be as imaginative in his pursuit of a surname as a colonial clerk might have been in his spelling. Virtually all variant spellings of personal names in the abstracts are unchanged in the index. The indexer has not presumed to decide, for example, whether *Thomas Bailey* is the same person as *Thomas Bayley*. Nor have "see also's" been included since it would be impossible to suggest all of the possibilities. When the subentry Mr or other title is listed without a given name, no given name appears in the abstract (or in the patent book). The underline (_____) is used in place of given names or surnames if information was missing or illegible in the patent.

Place-Names: Variant spellings of place-names and variant abbreviations of geographical term have been retained in the index. The user should remember that colonial clerks were recording many names for which there were no standard English spellings. No attempt is made to indicate the best or most frequent spellings of place-names used during the colonial period.

Patentees: The given names of all patentees appear in capital letters.

Subject Headings: Researchers will find entries for these major subject categories under the following headings that appear in the index in capital letters:

Barns	Inlets
Bays	Islands
Boroughs	Joiners
Branches	Landings
Bridges	Marshes
Brooks	Meadows
Churches	Mills
Cities	Mountains
Clerks	Necks
Counties	Parishes
County Lines	Plantations
Courthouses	Paths
Courts	Pocosons
Coves	Points
Creeks	Ponds
Dams	Prongs
Drafts	Quarters
Escheators	Ridges
Falls	Rivers
Fences	Roads
Ferries	Runs
Fields	Seas
Fords	Slashes
Forks	Sink Holes
Forts	Springs
Gaps	Surveyors
Gardens	Swamps
Glebes	Towns
Guts	Tracts
Houses	Valleys
Indians	Wharfs
Indian Towns	

Please see " A Note to the User" on the preceding page.

INDEX

Eelbank
  Daniel, Capt. 11
Eelbeck
  JOSEPH 34, 50
Eely
  Eely 75
Eglestone 199
Egleton
  THOMAS 76, 219
Elam 131, 160, 184, 295, 301
  Gilbert 277
  John 82, 198, 248
  Lodwick 319, 329
  LODWICK 160
  William 329
  WILLIAM 319
Elder 293
  JOHN 292
  Thomas 292
  William 203, 353
  WILLIAM 175
  WILLIAM, Junr. 208
Eldridge 145, 213
  Thomas 12, 100, 135, 323, 331
  THOMAS 121
Eliste
  CALEB 115
Elkins
  Ralph 253
Elledge
  FRANCIS 120, 313
Ellet
  John 9
Ellett
  John 153
Ellington 211, 337
  David 74
  DAVID 184
  JOHN, Junr. 219
Ellis 34, 66, 91, 96, 102, 105, 118,
    157, 159, 192, 260, 261, 300,
    325, 333, 337
  Austin 331
  Benjamin 79
  CALEB 349
  Edward 223
  EDWARD 53
  Jeremiah 19
  John 2, 62, 85, 91, 102, 156,
    161, 172, 200, 256, 311
  JOHN 57, 137, 194, 317
  John, Junr. 151
  Robert 308

Thomas 106, 184, 351
THOMAS 325
WILLIAM 9
Ellit 310
Elmore
  William 106
Embre
  JOHN 279
Embrey
  Col. 270
Embry 34, 187, 238, 321
  Henry 255
  HENRY 254, 322
Eme'son
  Thomas 320
Emeson
  Thomas 240
Emmerson
  Thomas 320
Emmery
  JOHN 160
English
  MARY 289
Ennis
  John 304
  JOHN 100
  Raman 75
Enon
  Robert 204
Epes
  Francis, Col. 329
  Isham 325
  ISHAM 267
  Thomas 311
  William 311
  WILLIAM 267
Eppes 17, 60, 61, 95, 102, 104, 156,
    185, 205, 257, 276, 325
  Col. 202
  Francis 58, 83, 131, 192, 195,
    260, 329
  Francis, Capt. 58, 83, 138
  Francis, Col. 196
  Isham 41, 83, 86, 95, 114, 120,
    131, 161, 260
  ISHAM 83, 118, 192, 196
  John 257, 301
  JOHN, Junr. 120
  Maj. 311
  Thomas 311
  William 114, 311
  WILLIAM 220
Epps 71

Hayward 342
FRANCIS 230
William 213
Hayworth
Absalom 216
Head
George 207
Healey
John 282
WILLIAM 279
Heard
CHARLES 80
JOHN 134, 324
Stephen 57
Hearn
James 353
JAMES 265
Heart
John 264
Heath 62
Adam 339
Benjamin 74
John 49
William 114, 186
WILLIAM 28
Heathcock
JOSEPH 245
Heirs
Francis 181
Heming
William 241
Hencock
Robert 345
Henderson
Alexander 169
ALEXANDER 352
JAMES 332
Richard 55, 194
RICHARD 56
Thomas 291
THOMAS 139
Hendrick 300
Adolphus 164, 266, 329
BENJAMIN 325
Hans 166, 201, 324
HANS, Junr. 200
HANS, Senr. 201
James 49, 133
Hendricks 237, 241
William 132
Henley
LEONARD 81, 102, 104
Henry

John 262
JOHN 74, 191, 357
John, Maj. 56, 214
Maj. 54, 187, 240
Major 62, 110, 123, 261
Henslee
Benj. 203
Henson 23
John 270
Herbert 42, 85, 87, 120, 132, 133,
247, 267, 308
Buller 49, 296
JOHN 335
Matthew 76
Richard 335
Hern
William 201
Herndon
Edward 127
EDWARD 32
Edward, Jr. 127
Hernton
Edward 127
Hester
Robert 100
ROBERT, Junr. 136
Hewlet
FRANCIS 3
Hewson
Richard 223
RICHARD 330
Hickman 3, 172, 226
Edwin 49, 133
JOSHUA 251
Richard 261
William 179
Hicks
Robert 21
Higgenbotham
Aaron 292
Benjamin 357
BENJAMIN 292
Higginbotham
JOSEPH 357
Moses 356
High 267
John 2, 257
JOHN, Junr. 258
John's father 258
High Round Rounds 14
Hightower
AUSTIN 166

Rochester 179
Rock Field 311
Rocky Ridge 84, 217
Rode
    JOHN 80, 81
Rodgers
    THOMAS 340
    WILLIAM 340
Roe
    John 289
Rogers
    Adduston 289
    GEORGE 261
    Giles 115
    John 54, 83, 261
    JOHN 261, 262
    JOHN, Junr. 180
    Joseph 138
    Joseph Jr. 134
    William 42, 284
    WILLIAM 61, 164, 309
Roper
    JOHN 89
Rose 307
    Henry 199
    HENRY 279
    John 314
    Richard 163, 222, 356
    Robert 109, 115
    ROBERT 78
    Thomas 48
    THOMAS 48
    William 48
Ross 177
    Andrew 138
    CHARLES 151
Rosser
    John 18, 47, 218
    Michael 47, 218
    MICHAEL 17
    PETER 90
    Thomas 218
Rotchell
    John 332, 352
Rothwell
    Thomas 327
Rottenberry
    John 290
Round Gut 14
Rouse
    Edward 23, 94
Row
    John 170

Michael McDearma 156
MICHAEL McDERMOT 286
Rowel
    Thomas 283
Rowell
    RICHARD 60
Rowland 193, 199, 290, 293
    Christopher 197
    JOHN 176
    JOSEPH 356
    JOSHUA 28
    ROBERT 131, 185, 209, 338
    Thomas 106
Rowler
    Peter 207
Rowlet
    Peter 28
Rowlett
    P. 271
    William 61
Rowlins
    ROBERT 164
Rowlitt 170
Royal 104, 311
    Henry 109
Royall 128, 156
    JOHN 61
    JOSEPH 269
    RICHARD 29, 116
Royley
    Miles 143, 144
Royston
    John 79
Rozar
    David 316
Rucker
    John 79
    PETER 108
Rud 260
    JAMES 58
    John 83, 322
    John Senr. 33
    John Sr. 195
    JOHN, Junr. 33
    JOHN, Junr. 169
Ruffin 83, 86, 96, 106, 250, 312, 316
    Benjamin 96, 306
    BENJAMIN 114
    Edmund 114, 223
    JOHN, Capt. 15, 16
    JOHN 11
Rugless
    William 302, 352

Sellars
  WILLIAM 21
Seller Survey 83
Sellers
  William 30, 35
Semore 74
Senaca
  NATHANIEL 79
Sentall 118
Senter 184, 325
Sertain
  John 127
Serus?
  Joseph 281
Sevear
  VALENTINE 216
Severe
  VALENTINE 294
Sevier
  Valentine 236
Seward
  BENJAMIN 96
  Joseph 199
  William 21
Sews
  Joseph 281
Sexton
  James 17
  JAMES 134
  LISWELL 196
Shands
  William 279
Sharp
  Francis 15, 51
  John 30
  JOHN 94
  Robert 27
  Thomas 179
  William 30, 190
Sharpe
  FRANCIS 121
  WILLIAM 70
Sharroon
  Anthony 224
Shastood
  JAMES 347
Shatteen 295
Shaw
  Jane 241
  William 169
  WILLIAM 172
Shearing 321
Shehorn

WILLSON 196
Shelley
  AMOS TIMMS 169
Shelly
  AMOS TIMMS 342
Shelton 240, 337
  EDWARD 170
  James 296
  JOSEPH 168
  RALPH 106, 349
  Thomas 45, 135
Shepard
  James 77
Shephard
  JACOB 55
  JAMES 53
Shepherd
  James 177
Shepperd
  John 128
Shereron
  Anthony 84, 166
Sheroon
  Anthony 258
Sherrer
  Thomas 311
Sherrod
  Thomas 311
Sherroon
  Anthony 86, 224, 284
Sherwin 116, 132
Shields
  James 181, 238, 315
Shildrake
  Robert 98
Ship Rock 215
Shirkey
  PATRICK 216
Shoemaker 104
  Evan 203
  John 9
  JOHN 104
SHOPS
  Enix's 218
Short 97, 98, 199, 323, 326
  William 290, 315
Sicks
  THOMAS 1
Sim
  Adam 355
  William 114
Simes 131
Simkins